Understanding, Assessing, and Teaching Reading

A Diagnostic Approach

Eighth Edition

Understanding, Assessing, and Teaching Reading

A Diagnostic Approach

James A. Erekson
University of Northern Colorado

Michael F. Opitz
Professor Emeritus, University of Northern Colorado

Roland K. Schendel
Metropolitan State University of Denver

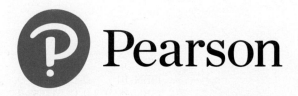 Pearson

Director and Publisher: Kevin Davis
Portfolio Manager: Drew Bennett
Managing Content Producer: Megan Moffo
Content Producer: Yagnesh Jani
Portfolio Management Assistant: Maria Feliberty
Managing Digital Producer: Autumn Benson
Digital Studio Producer: Lauren Carlson
Digital Development Editor: Kim Norbuta
Executive Product Marketing Manager: Krista Clark
Procurement Specialist: Deidra Headlee
Cover Design: Pearson CSC, Jerilyn Bockorick
Cover Art: MirageC/Moment/Getty Images
Full Service Vendor: Pearson CSC
Full Service Project Management: Pearson CSC, Padmarekha Madhukannan
Editorial Project Manager: Pearson CSC, Mirasol Dante
Printer-Binder: LSC Communications
Cover Printer: Phoenix Color/Hagerstown
Text Font: PalatinoLTPro-Roman

Credits and acknowledgments borrowed from other sources and reproduced, with permission, in this textbook appear on the appropriate page within text.

Library of Congress Cataloging-in-Publication Data

Names: Opitz, Michael F., author. | Erekson, James A., author. | Schendel, Roland K., author.
Title: Understanding, assessing, and teaching reading : a diagnostic approach / Michael F. Opitz, Professor Emeritus, University of Northern Colorado, James A. Erekson, University of Northern Colorado, Roland K. Schendel, Metropolitan State University of Denver.
Description: 8th edition. | Hoboken : Pearson, [2018]
Identifiers: LCCN 2018049151 | ISBN 9780135175552 | ISBN 0135175550
Subjects: LCSH: Reading. | Reading--Ability testing. | Reading--Remedial teaching.
Classification: LCC LB1050.42 .O65 2018 | DDC 372.4--dc23 LC record available at https://lccn.loc.gov/2018049151

1   19

ISBN-10:   0-13-517555-0
ISBN-13: 978-0-13-517555-2

To Dorothy Rubin
For conceiving the original and allowing us to continue her legacy.

M.F.O., J.A.E., and R.K.S.

Brief Contents

Contents

About the Authors

JAMES A. EREKSON has been teaching and researching in literacy for over twenty years, with experience in elementary and secondary grades. His work emphasizes the vital role of engagement and motivation in literacy achievement. He is the author of practical texts for educators including *Engaging Minds in Social Studies Classrooms: The Surprising Power of Joy*, ASCD, 2014, and co-author of *Accessible Assessment: How 9 Sensible Techniques Can Power Data-driven Reading Instruction*, Heinemann, 2011.

MICHAEL F. OPITZ is professor emeritus of reading education from the University of Northern Colorado and has investigated reading assessment and other literacy topics for over two decades. He is the author of numerous books, articles, and reading programs.

ROLAND K. SCHENDEL is a former elementary classroom teacher. With twenty years of experience in elementary and secondary education and educational research, he has committed his career to understanding and meeting the learning needs of striving readers and providing professional development to their teachers. He is co-author of *25 Essential Language Arts Strategies to Help Striving Readers Succeed*, Scholastic, 2011.

Preface

About the Authors

Understanding, Assessing, and Teaching Reading: A Diagnostic Approach, Eighth Edition, is based on the premise that a diagnostic approach to assessment and instruction involves asking and answering questions about each child's reading. Our goal is to provide key knowledge about the teaching of reading, to model how to ask and answer assessment questions based on this knowledge, and then to provide teaching strategies that fit best with common answers to assessment questions. To achieve this goal we have combined theory, knowledge, and skills with practical application.

The demand is greater than ever for teachers who understand why they do what they do in reading assessment. We emphasize the importance of teachers and explain the roles they play for young readers. Good teachers must understand factors that affect reading and also assessment techniques they can use to better understand how these factors affect individual readers. Good teachers ask questions about each student to help teachers select, administer, and interpret the most appropriate assessments. When information is gathered to answer questions about students, assessment is a powerful process. When teachers administer assessments based only on mandates and requirements, the validity of assessment is compromised. With the right information, teachers can make much better decisions about how to help readers. To this end, we present many reading skills, strategies, and teaching techniques that are appropriate follow-ups to appropriate assessments. We make no assumption that any one strategy or teaching technique will meet the needs of all students, so we encourage teachers to look for students' strengths first and then to find teaching strategies and techniques that build on these strengths.

We know the term *diagnostic assessment* can be intimidating. In Chapter 1 we set the stage by describing our beliefs about the diagnostic approach clearly and in student-centered ways. We hope this introduction will help teachers demystify and humanize reading diagnosis.

In Chapters 2 through 5 we present information on specific aspects of assessment each teacher must be able to apply with understanding. They have been written in a specific order to prioritize techniques that provide immediately useful information about each child as a reader. These chapters are oriented to three guiding questions that help teachers choose the most appropriate assessment techniques: *What do I want to know? Why do I want to know it? How can I best discover this information?*

In Chapters 6 through 13 we focus on assessment and teaching of specific aspects of reading and writing. Each of these chapters follows a standard format and is written to stand alone, to be read and used in any order. We have provided titles for many children's literature texts that could be used with young readers to give teachers a head start on carrying out as much assessment and instruction as they can with authentic texts.

In Chapter 14 we provide suggestions on partnering with parents, other teachers, and the broader community to help readers grow.

A full Informal Reading Inventory is provided in the Appendix to enable full implementation of the IRI as presented in Chapter 4 without requiring the purchase of supplemental books. We have streamlined the IRI process of scoring and interpretation to match our diagnostic approach.

New to This Edition

Understanding, Assessing, and Teaching Reading: A Diagnostic Approach is a teacher-friendly book designed to boost teachers' confidence in helping young readers. We have kept this goal in mind in making the following substantial revisions to the current edition:

- A dedicated chapter on writing. Writing is fundamental to literacy growth, and many students' strengths and needs in writing can be related to their growth as readers.

- Bridge exercises have been added between the subsections of the chapters to show readers how teachers would make decisions from understanding reading to assessing readers, and from assessing readers to teaching them, and how teaching leads to further understanding. These exercises can help instructors improve student interaction with text. The bridges are found in 2–3 locations in each chapter, to mark transition between subheadings: Understanding, Assessing, and Teaching.

- Each content chapter (Chapters 8–13) features video examples newly selected to demonstrate best practices described in the book. By linking to visual media, readers will be able to see and hear what is being taught in the book.

- Application Exercises have been added to each chapter, offering students opportunities to apply what they are learning to realistic classroom situations. The specific challenges of assessing and teaching English learners are featured strongly in each set of exercises. These exercises are found throughout each chapter near the "bridge" sections.

- Updated children's literature references are inserted throughout the book. More recent books will match better what teachers will find in public and school libraries. A special focus on updated children's literature is given in Chapter 7.

- The updated research base and references include review of 110 research articles and chapters published since the last edition, with dozens of references added or changed to refresh the book's identification with current research. The text connects readers to the most up-to-date information on diagnostic assessment, reading engagement, teaching with texts, factors that affect reading achievement, comprehension, vocabulary, phonics, reading fluency, and the role of teachers. These new references can be found in each chapter's endnotes.

- Printable sample assessment forms are included. Readers can see what assessment record keeping looks like, with both blank masters and copies filled in with teacher coding. These documents are linked within Chapters 8–13.

Video-Enhanced Pearson eText

Understanding, Assessing, and Teaching Reading: A Diagnostic Approach is available for the first time as a Pearson eText. The affordable, convenient, interactive version of this text includes tools to help navigate and understand important, current content. The Pearson eText is available with a black-and-white, loose-leaf printed version of the text.

Features of the Pearson eText include:

- Tools to take and share notes, highlight and bookmark chapter concepts, and search by keyword

- Accessible from your computer, iPad, or Android tablet with the Pearson eText app
- More affordable than a traditional textbook
- Extended-access upgrade is available.
- Glossary key terms are linked to the eText glossary, offering students an opportunity to clarify any term while they are reading, without skipping concepts they do not understand.
- Videos are an interactive eText feature in every chapter. These videos offer a glimpse at the real world of teaching. View interviews of experts and footage of teachers and administrators discussing and applying chapter concepts.

Enjoy the advantages of an eText, plus the benefits of print, all for less than the price of a traditional book! To learn more about the enhanced Pearson eText, go to www.pearsonhighered.com/.

Support Materials for Instructors

The following resources are available for instructors to download on pearsonhighered.com/educator. Click the "Support for Educators" link, then click Download Supplements and enter the author or title of this book, select this particular edition of the book to log in, and download textbook supplements.

Test Bank (0135178576)

The Test Bank includes a robust collection of test items. Some items (lower-level questions) simply ask students to identify or explain concepts and principles they have learned. But many others (higher-level questions) ask students to apply those same concepts and principles to specific classroom situations—that is, to actual student behaviors and teaching strategies.

PowerPoint Slides

These lecture slides (0135465974) highlight key concepts and summarize key content from each chapter of the text.

Acknowledgments

We appreciate the editing work of Mirasol Dante and Padma Rekha Madhukannan, who improved the book with their careful review of the manuscript and all the resources in the new edition. We would like to thank the reviewers of this edition: Cynthia Walters, University of Central Florida; Nance Wilson, SUNY Cortland; Patricia Ann Jenkins, Albany State University.

Chapter 1
Understanding a Diagnostic Approach to Assessing and Teaching Reading

Igorstevanovic/Shutterstock

 ## Chapter Outline

English Learners in a Diagnostic Approach to Assessing and Teaching Reading

Ages and Stages of Literacy Development to Consider in a Diagnostic Approach to Assessing and Teaching Reading

 # Learning Outcomes

After reading this chapter, you should be able to . . .

1.1 Discuss the attributes of a diagnostic approach to assessing and teaching reading and the beliefs on which it is based.

1.2 Describe the basic ideas that form the foundation of Response to Intervention and how they connect to a diagnostic approach.

1.3 Explain how reading can be defined and how defining reading influences a diagnostic approach.

1.4 Compare and contrast proficient and less proficient reading behaviors.

1.5 Define English Learners and explain the levels of language proficiency through which they progress.

1.6 Construct a timeline that shows how readers change over time.

Scenario

Assessing and Teaching Reading: A Diagnostic Approach in Action

When you walk into Ms. Prazzo's third-grade classroom, you realize that something special is taking place; you can sense the excitement of learning. Often no one notices your arrival because they are so engrossed in what they are doing; they are both motivated and engaged.

Ms. Prazzo's classroom hums with learning noise. It's a room in which children and teacher alike are involved in a dynamic and interactive teaching and learning program driven by ongoing assessment. Ms. Prazzo is constantly asking her students questions, and answering theirs. These questions range from those about how readers feel and what they believe about reading to questions about how they think before, during, and after reading to questions about how they use structures such as words, letters, sounds, and grammar. She returns constantly to three powerful questions when choosing assessment tools: What do I want to know? Why do I want to know that? How can I best discover this information? She also asks a fourth question: How can I use what I discover? Because she answers these questions for each student she works with, she can design targeted, purposeful instruction and groupings to help her advance the growth of all readers.

Throughout the day, you can observe Ms. Prazzo "zooming in" to focus on individuals and then "zooming out" to apply what she knows to groups or the whole class. This requires flexible, dynamic grouping tailored to children's strengths and needs. Children flow from one group to another, depending on the purpose of the group. Groups are formed and dissolved based on specific goals and purposes, not as ongoing ability groups. It's not unusual at any given moment to see her class split into a variety of group types: small groups, pairs, and individuals.

Conferencing is at the heart of Ms. Prazzo's *zoom in, zoom out* approach. She meets with each of her students at least once every week to review progress and to establish new goals. She keeps copious notes from these conferences and uses them to inform her future instruction.

Ms. Prazzo is always probing, questioning, and keeping a sharp eye out for what her students do well and for that they are showing her they need to learn. But she also continually reflects to evaluate herself as a teacher, the materials she uses when teaching, and the classroom context. For example, she constantly adds to the classroom library as a result of what she learns from talking with students about reading interests. She fully understands that interest and attitudes significantly influence reading and wants to make sure that the classroom environment supports her students' interests and promotes a positive association with reading. To that end, she has learned from her students that many different types of text count as reading, and she has included them as a part of the classroom library and explicit reading instruction. These include magazines, brochures, newspapers, comics, and electronic texts. She also regularly shares with students what she is reading and explains why she reads.

Ms. Prazzo is passionate about assessing, learning, and teaching reading, and her passion plays out every day in her classroom. She continually strives to be the best possible teacher. A diagnostic approach is central to her ongoing growth as a teacher and her students' learning and development.

Defining a Diagnostic Approach

A diagnostic approach to assessing and teaching reading is a comprehensive way of using data that is gathered by examining three primary components of effective reading instruction: learner, instruction, and context. This examination is ongoing and multi-faceted in that it requires teachers to use a variety of assessment techniques, including student self-assessment, teacher self-assessment, and assessment of instructional materials and contexts to provide the best possible instruction for all learners. It is based on the following beliefs:

1. *Problem-solving for any complicated system requires diagnostic tools.* Systems are made of components that in turn have their own moving parts. Components interact with each other in a system to make something larger happen. Monitoring the inner workings of a system helps people notice when something goes wrong, to keep it in good working order and figure out how to improve the system. Moreover, diagnostics can help people avoid tinkering with components that need no help.

   Reading is one such complex system. When people read, different sets of "moving parts" interact among the texts they read, the contexts in which they read, and themselves as readers. To help all learners achieve strong reading potential, educators use a diagnostic approach to examine all three areas and identify learner strengths and needs.

2. *Reading diagnosis is about knowing readers.* Although the word *diagnosis* is frowned on by many educators for one reason or another, we maintain that when the original Greek meaning, "to come to know," is emphasized, it is a useful term to discuss how to identify children's reading strengths and needs. We subscribe to the definition of *diagnosis* offered in *The Literacy Dictionary*:

   > The act, process, or result of identifying the nature of a disorder or disability through observation and examination. As the term is used in education, it often includes the planning of instruction and an assessment of the strengths and weaknesses (i.e., needs) of the student.[1]

When analyzing this definition, two points that relate to a diagnostic approach to assessing and teaching reading become evident:

- Using observation and other assessment techniques throughout the school day is necessary to figure out students' strengths and needs.
- Using what is discovered from the observations and assessment techniques is essential for planning appropriate instruction.

The necessity of looking for both strengths and needs cannot be overstated. Knowledge of what a child *can* do is always helpful in providing insight into their needs. Just as important is to recognize that many factors affect reading performance (the topic of Chapter 2).

Our rationale for using the word *diagnosis* leads us to use a computer coder as a positive metaphor for diagnostics. Consider the tasks of computer coders. They use diagnostic tools that will help them to identify strengths and potential in the code they write and any possible errors or bugs. Coders who apply diagnostic tools can improve and find new uses for good code as well as use the same tools to repair faults.

Therefore, it is the diagnostic approach to assessing and teaching reading that we promote in this text. Teachers first search for strengths and use those strengths to build up to what students need to learn. This search for strengths extends beyond the learner and includes instruction, texts, and contexts—all of which influence reading development.

Our view of diagnosis is supported by the 10 principles set forth by the position statement *Excellent Reading Teachers*, from the Board of Directors of the International Reading Association (IRA):

- Diagnosis underlies prevention.
- Early diagnosis is essential in order to ameliorate reading problems from the start.
- Diagnosis is continuous.
- Diagnosis and instruction are interwoven.
- Diagnosis is a *means* to improvement; it is not an end in itself.
- Teacher-made as well as published reading assessment instruments are used in diagnosis.
- Noneducational as well as educational factors are considered.
- Diagnosis identifies strengths as well as needs.
- Diagnosis is an individual process; that is, in diagnosis, the teacher focuses on an individual child. (Diagnostic information can be obtained from various contexts: working in a one-on-one relationship with a child, observing a child in a group, or observing a child doing seatwork.)
- The teacher works to establish rapport and treats each student as an individual worthy of respect.[2]

3. *Identifying readers' strengths is a good first step in accelerating readers' growth.* Children are always showing what they know and need to know. For example, a child who is reading every word correctly yet cannot discuss what has been read shows that the reader knows how to identify words. What needs attention is comprehension. Using the strength to teach to the need, a teacher might begin by using a previewing technique, such as identifying key words in a text that support discussion on what the book will be about. Strong word identification makes this comprehension strategy more viable.

As you can see, beginning with strengths is anything but pretending that students know everything and just need to be encouraged. Instead, teachers who look for strengths first see the child as the one who can bring something to the new learning to begin from a position of strength. We are under no false assumptions about reader factors that might need to be addressed to help the reader achieve. But we also acknowledge that many readers have not had sufficient opportunities to develop strengths before they are labeled with a term such as *at risk, deficient,* or *below grade level.* Until each child has had *many engaged opportunities* to develop and apply her strengths to texts and contexts (over weeks and months of time), we should not be too hasty in assuming that all reading difficulties emanate from the reader. In fact, this is one of the premises behind intervention models such as those that are often used under the auspices of Response to Intervention: teachers should first assume the need is for a different instructional approach.

4. *Identifying needs is an important part of a diagnostic approach.* As stated above, learners are always showing what they know and need to know. Part of helping children to move forward is to carefully document their needs and to design appropriate instruction to address those needs. Our diagnostic approach to assessing and teaching reading suggests a clear priority of first looking for strengths in all three dimensions of reading. That is, a teacher will want information from the affective domain (i.e., interests, attitudes, and identity), cognitive domain (i.e., metacognition and comprehension), and perceptual domain (i.e., word knowledge and phonics).

5. *Zooming in and out is essential.* Another key aspect of our model is what we call "zooming in and zooming out." *Zooming in* means spending time getting to know just one learner very well and learning to teach based on this knowledge. *Zooming out* means figuring out how to scale the management of information and planning for groups and whole classes. As Ms. Prazzo illustrates in our opening scenario, when teachers *zoom in*, they get to know one student in depth. Doing so can help teachers to develop dispositions, knowledge, and skills necessary for working with young learners. When teachers *zoom out*, they learn to apply this same disposition, knowledge, and skill when teaching small groups or a whole class. They generalize their understandings to the wider audiences.

Scenario

Sarah Zooms In and Zooms Out

"I don't know how you handle all that chaos!" says Audra, observing free-choice reading in Sarah's second-grade class. Crates of books on a central table look like a feeding frenzy as students move back and forth, picking out and replacing books. Before the observation, Audra learned that all the books were selected based on an interest inventory. "How do you help them find the right level?" she asks.

"I look at text levels in a broad way," Sarah answers. "The research is pretty clear that books within the K–1 range are more or less the same. The same is true for the discrete levels in second grade. By third grade, the range of texts is broader. The librarian and I keep the crates in a range that matches grades K–3. But if books the kids ask for come from higher levels, we put them in the crate anyway. I want to help each kid find an emotional match—a kind of text, a topic, a genre, or whatever can hook them. I have learned that there is more than one way to match readers and texts and that this emotional (affective) matching is powerful. When the emotional match is good, the words and sentences seem much easier to read for some readers."

"Yeah, but it looks like most of the kids aren't really staying with any one text. What if they never get focused and get down to reading?"

"Oh, I'm totally with you there. I never would have been able to handle the constant shift of interests if I hadn't learned the importance of zooming in closely on one student for an entire trimester before thinking about "zooming out" to my whole class. Raul couldn't stay focused on one topic week to week in our tutoring sessions, but I finally learned that it was all part of the search. When he learned that I was really going to follow through on bringing him what he was interested in, he was *always* engaged in what I brought and 'tried it on for size.' Gradually, he became more willing to tell me what he wanted next. It took us a few weeks, but we soon had a pile of texts he was interested in browsing through, and before long, we found one he got totally hooked on—his touchstone text. He helped me learn that it's natural for kids to need a lot of time to get to know a lot of texts before they settle on those they can get addicted to. It took a crate of books just for him! So then I figured if it was really important, I should zoom out and scale it for the whole class. Let me show you how I organize it."

Audra and Sarah walk over to a file cabinet, and Sarah pulls out a student folder. Opening it, she comments, "Each student's interest—what they're looking for now and what they've liked in the past—is all in the sticky notes on the interest section of the reader profile. All the students know they're on the hunt for what will get them hooked. That's what we talk about in our individual conferences each week. When their interests change, I write about it on a sticky note and add it to the profile. For example, when I look over and see Mandy sifting through the pile, I know she's already got her crocodile books and she's looking for something else! I'm comfortable with the whole class looking like chaos because I know that it really is not; on the personal level, each student is pursuing a goal to find reading that will engage them."

"I don't know if I could do this all at once like you're doing," Audra says.

"I don't think you should," Sarah replies. "I would suggest zooming in on one student for six to eight weeks as a tryout. The power you experience with one student will help you get a feel for how it works and the confidence you need to start scaling it for your whole class—to zoom out."

> **Enhanced eText** **Application Exercise 1.1:** Developing Questions in a Diagnostic Approach

Response to Intervention and its Connection to a Diagnostic Approach to Assessing and Teaching Reading

Our diagnostic approach to assessing and teaching reading aligns with intervention models that fall under the recent *Response to Intervention* initiative.

The 2004 update of the Individuals with Disabilities Education Improvement Act (IDEIA) specifies that it is no longer necessary to identify all learning problems (e.g., learning to read) as severe enough to be classified as learning disabilities. This policy is called *Response to Intervention*. See the Appendix for the International Literacy Association's Guiding Principles on RtI. The ILA commission on RtI summarizes the actual laws and provides clear principles for how to put the intent of the laws into action.

The three-step process entails providing children who appear to be struggling with the best possible instruction in the regular classroom and taking a look at how they perform. If the child makes little or no progress, the second step involves providing supplementary instruction, either individually or in a small group. The classroom

Bridge: From Understanding to Assessment

When teachers understand that _____,	then teachers will _____.
Diagnostic assessment depends on asking questions about individual readers,	Select and design assessment tools best fit to answer questions they have about individual readers.
	Not rely solely on information from required tests, because these tools are not usually selected with questions about individuals in mind.
Good questions arise from listening to and observing readers,	Take notes on reading behaviors.
	Make time to talk with readers about the invisible cognitive and affective processes during reading.
	Review their own understanding of important components of reading, such as texts, motivation, comprehension, vocabulary, or phonics, so they can make sense of observations.
Outside factors can impact reading,	Investigate the impact of outside factors before assuming anything about individual readers.
Meaningful data are those that answer specific questions about readers,	Use assessment tools that offer convincing and usable data about reading behaviors and about readers' cognitive and affective reading processes.
Strengths should be used to plan for needs,	Systematically gather and document strengths for each student that can be used to plan instructional situations.
Answers to questions about individuals can be "zoomed out" to find diagnostic patterns that apply to groups or a whole class,	Chart assessment data for whole classes to look for patterns.
	Rebuild groups regularly to fit known student strengths and needs, avoiding static ability groups.
	Be able to avoid the labels for readers that tend to come with ability grouping rather than diagnostic groupings.

teacher or another professional provides this instruction. If the child still makes little progress, additional tests are administered to determine whether there is a specific learning disability. If there is an identifiable disability, the child is assigned special education support and given more intensive intervention.

Intervention is a key word here. Just as with a *diagnostic approach*, RtI insists that identifying a problem early on and doing something to improve reading ensures that students will continue to progress in reading. The point of intervening is to avoid building patterns of frustration and failure so hard for young people and their teachers to overcome. And, as discussed in nearly every chapter in this book, there are important reading assessment techniques teachers can use to identify student strengths and needs beginning in preschool and kindergarten. Each technique is accompanied by teaching suggestions to assist teachers with planning appropriate instruction.

However, policies of intervention can come at a cost. Readers are acutely aware when instructional interventions turn into social groups. Stratifying classrooms into an economy of "haves and have-nots" is not the intent of Response to Intervention. It is well known that grouping already-strong readers together means that other groups get organized based on progressive identification of weaknesses—not strengths. Teachers must be prepared to group students based on strengths and flexible needs rather than contributing to the problem of tracking students in the early years of schooling. Teachers can be part of the solution by doing all they can to dismantle language that labels students, such as calling them "my high kids" or "my low kids."[3]

The climate of assessment in the United States pushes teachers to perceive children who have not yet learned to read by the end of grade one as deficient, and implies that these deficiencies are cognitive and must be corrected by teaching, and that difficulties with learning to read are unusual. A diagnostic approach should enable teachers to overcome these pressures: to focus on young people who are still learning to read as part of a normal spectrum of learning, and to understand that many of these readers' difficulties are social and affective rather than cognitive, and that reading is difficult for many normal people to master.[4] All assessment and teaching strategies must be about ensuring learners receive the instruction that builds on strengths first. When teachers are asked to look at children's progress or lack thereof, looking beyond learners to the instruction they have or have not received is essential to ensure that they did indeed receive a fair chance to learn to read for their age.

What are Models of the Reading Process?

Definitions of reading are usually classified into one of three models. In fact, the field of reading is replete with theories, and different catchphrases are sometimes assigned to the same general theories, further confusing those who try to understand the various theories. Controversy has centered on whether the reading process is a holistic one (emphasis on meaning)—that is, a **top-down model**; a subskill process (code emphasis)—that is, a **bottom-up model**; or, more recently, an **interactive model**. The interactive model is somewhat but not entirely a combination of the top-down and bottom-up models in that both processes can take place simultaneously, depending on the difficulty of the material for the individual reader. (See Figure 1.1.)

There is widespread agreement that reading is a complex process orchestrating multiple areas of learning and development, not a single skill. Simply learning how to decode words with phonics does not result in reading if this is not paired with listening comprehension to result in reading comprehension. Listening comprehension is related to knowledge of word meanings (in speaking and listening vocabulary). Both of these aspects of spoken language can impact both word reading and reading comprehension.[5] Further, those who read with a sense of purpose and meaning make more appropriate strategic decisions when reading, as compared with readers who merely decode words accurately. Readers who are motivated and will engage in wide reading, and are more likely to apply skills than those who prefer not to read. Motivation and engagement go beyond the behavioral and cognitive and into the affective areas of human thinking. Teachers who teach with a diagnostic mindset work simultaneously across these areas, embracing reading as a complex process for any person, let alone the young people who are expected to master it!

Classroom practices are based on the theories that teachers embrace. Those who believe in a bottom-up model may emphasize decoding to the exclusion of meaning; those who believe primarily in a top-down model might emphasize meaning at the expense of word knowledge. Those who believe in an interactive model will probably use a combination of both.

Figure 1.1 Models of Reading

Interactive Model of the Process of Learning Reading. Learning to read is neither a bottom-up model only nor a top-down model only. In an interactive model, readers move back and forth between larger meaning and less meaningful pieces and parts of words. Learning about sounds and letters is informed by knowing that reading is about making meaning with texts. Likewise, purposeful meaning-making with texts motivates learners to master the less meaningful pieces and parts we use to make words, sentences, and texts.

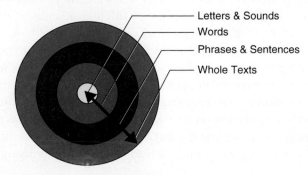

Reading theorists sometimes tend to be exclusive; they promote their own theory and neglect others. The classroom teacher, however, need not accept any either–or dichotomy, but rather should seek a synthesis of all elements that have proven workable; that is, a classroom teacher can take elements from any research-based theories to best fit the individual strengths and needs of students. Good teachers realize readers are complex and that there are no one-size-fits-all answers.

Extreme perspectives prejudice teachers' diagnostic decisions, making it difficult for them to examine all aspects of reading. Each reader is different, and some readers' minds lean toward a top-down model, which needs to be nurtured as a strength while being balanced with attention to meaning. Likewise, some readers lean toward sense-making and pay less attention to phonics cues. This is a strength that becomes more powerful when balanced with usable phonics knowledge. In the interest of each individual student, the interactive version of the diagram shown in Figure 1.1 is designed to enable teachers to move back and forth between work with meaningful wholes, such as phrases, sentences, paragraphs, chapters, and articles, and discrete parts, such as words, sounds, syllables, and letters. The interactive model of reading is more flexible than any model that assumes one direction of teaching works best for all learners.[6]

Defining Reading for a Diagnostic Approach to Assessing and Teaching Reading

Reading is a dynamic, complex act that involves bringing meaning to the printed page, and taking meaning from the printed page. Too often, educators view reading only as passive reception of an author's meaning. Cognitive research has demonstrated that strong readers bring their backgrounds, experiences, and emotions into play as they read. This research further implies that students who are upset or physically ill will bring these feelings to their reading, influencing their performance. Yet another implication is that a person with existing background knowledge from home, movies and games, or other books will gain more from reading the material than someone who is less knowledgeable. For example, a student who is a good critical thinker will gain more from a critical passage than one who is not. A student who has strong dislikes will come away with a different understanding and feelings than a student with strong likes related to a given text.

As this explanation suggests, the definition we choose influences the assessment and teaching of reading. This particular definition, for example, suggests that one would be interested in addressing students' backgrounds relative to a given text or topic, their feelings (or affect), and their overall wellness.

Our Definition

As noted above, we see reading as a balance between three domains. In Fitzgerald's review,[7] she characterized these as follows:

1. Affective: how readers feel and what they believe about reading. A clear body of research exists on readers' attitudes, identity, and interests. This research has been applied to both assessment and teaching.

2. Global: how readers think and process meaning when they read (comprehension) and when they think about their reading (metacognition)—cognitive and metacognitive processes.

3. Local: how readers use the structural parts of language to help them think. This includes how readers decode, apply vocabulary knowledge, and use their sense of syntax.

To teach these domains of reading well, teachers must ask and answer questions about all three aspects of reading for each student. This is foundational for diagnostic assessment. The affective domain has a governing effect on the global and local processes. That is, when students experience high interest, positive attitudes, and a strong identity with reading, these pave the way for progress in learning global and local skills such as comprehending sentences and paragraphs or identifying new words. Conversely, when readers experience unengaging material, develop negative attitudes, and believe reading is more for other people than for them, then teaching of global and local skills falls on stony ground—the seeds of teaching will not grow there! A comprehensive, diagnostic approach to assessment and teaching begins with the affective mind, and keeps its governing role front and center while asking questions about other aspects of reading.

Our diagnostic model puts teachers in a position of asking questions about these three domains constantly throughout teaching and learning. This is evident in the assessment tools we provide in this text.

Good Reader Characteristics

Teachers need to be mindful of what makes someone a good reader, because these characteristics help to set "big picture" goals for readers in a diagnostic approach to assessing and teaching reading. Regardless of how theorists frame the reading process and regardless of the definitions teachers adopt for reading, some reader characteristics remain constant and cut across all definitions.

Proficient readers have a large repertoire of strategies at their disposal, which they use to help them better comprehend the text at hand. (See Table 1.1.) The strategies they employ will shift, depending on their background for the text and the manner in which the text is written. If they have read and heard stories, for instance, they most likely have an understanding of story structure (i.e., the pattern used to write stories). This text structure poses few, if any, difficulties, so they are able to read with greater ease.

In essence, then, good readers are active, purposeful, evaluative, thoughtful, strategic, persistent, and productive.[8] We explain attributes of a good reader in Table 1.2. But what do we do with children who do not carry this label? Can we teach them the "good reader" characteristics? Thanks to the work of researchers who have designed metacognition learning programs to explore this question, we know that the answer is "yes." But the characteristics must be explicitly taught; for whatever reason, less proficient readers do not acquire them with as little explicit instruction as do many good readers.

Regardless of a child's level of proficiency, helping all children to maximize their full potential as readers is more important than assigning a label, a view that is supported by the Council for Exceptional Children.[9] Remember that the goal is to discover children's strengths and needs and to design appropriate instruction to address these. Put another way, children are always ready to learn something and our job as teachers is to figure out what that something is. Learning is what we're after. The success of education depends on adapting teaching to the individual differences among learners. The fact that children vary is natural; what is unnatural is to assume that all children are the same.[10]

English Learners in a Diagnostic Approach to Assessing and Teaching Reading

What we have said about the diagnostic approach in this chapter (and continue to espouse in the chapters that follow) applies to all learners, because we insist that individualization is central to successful reading instruction. English learners are children

Table 1.1 Summary of Proficient and Less Proficient Reading Behaviors

Proficient Reading Behaviors	Less Proficient Reading Behaviors
Attempt to make what is read sound like language and make sense.	Attempt to identify all of the words correctly.
Monitor what is read for sense and coherence.	Monitor what is read for correct letter/sound and word identification.
Build meaning using the text, the reader's purpose, and the reader's background.	Build meaning by attempting to identify the letters and words correctly.
Use a variety of strategies when a reader gets stuck on a word or phrase, and is losing both fluency and meaning: reread, rethink, read on and return if necessary, substitute, skip it, sound it out, seek assistance, use text aids (pictures, graphs, charts), ignore it, or stop reading.	Use a limited range of strategies when meaning breaks down: Sound it out or skip it.
Selectively sample the print; use a mixture of visual (print) and nonvisual (background) information.	Use most of the visual (print) information.
Use and integrate a variety of language systems to create meaning.	Rely heavily on graphemes, graphophonemics, and morphemes.
Vary the manner in which texts are read based on purpose.	Read all texts in a similar manner regardless of purpose.
Correct one in three miscues, on average.	Correct one in 20 miscues, on average.
Attempt to correct miscues that affect meaning.	Attempt to correct miscues that fail to resemble the word.
"Chunk" what is read.	Process letter by letter, which results in tunnel vision.

Source: Copyright © 2005 From Dimensions of Literacy: A Conceptual Base for Teaching Reading and Writing in School Settings by Kucer, S. Reproduced by permission of Taylor and Francis Group, LLC, a division of Informa plc.

Table 1.2 Explanations of Good Reader Attributes

Good Reader Attributes	Explanation
Active	Readers bring their own experiences to reading the text and to constructing meaning. They make predictions and make decisions such as what to read and reread, and when to slow down or speed up.
Purposeful	Readers often have a purpose in mind when they read a text. For example, they might choose to read for enjoyment or entertainment. At other times, they might read to discover specific details.
Evaluative	Readers evaluate what they are reading, asking themselves whether the text is meeting their initial purposes for reading it. They also evaluate the quality of the text and whether it is of value. They react to the text both emotionally and intellectually. Readers also evaluate their interaction with others in different instructional groupings as well as their ability to function as both leaders and followers in the group.
Thoughtful	Readers think about the text selection before, during, and after reading. *Before reading*, they think about what they might already know. *During reading*, they think about how the current text relates to what they already know. *After reading*, they think about what the text offered and formulate their interpretations of it.
Strategic	Readers use specific strategies such as predicting, monitoring, and visualizing to ensure that they are comprehending the text.
Persistent	Readers keep reading a text even when it might be rather difficult if they feel that the text is helping them to accomplish a set purpose.
Productive	Readers are productive in more than one way. For instance, they bring their own experiences to the text at hand to construct or *produce* their understanding of it. Because they are engaged with reading, they are more productive in terms of the amount of reading they do.

Source: Based on Duke, N. K., and Pearson, P. D., "Effective Practices for Developing Reading Comprehension," in A. E. Farstrup and S. J. Samuels, eds., What Research Has to Say about Reading Instruction, 3rd ed. Newark, DE: International Reading Association, 2002, pp. 205–242.

who collectively bring a vast array of languages other than English to school. Because teachers may not know English learners' home language(s), the diagnostic approach to assessing, learning, and teaching might seem impossible. But this need not be the case.

Let's begin by understanding who English language learners (ELLs) are and how they become proficient English speakers.

Researchers have identified different levels of language proficiency through which language learners progress.[11] Figure 1.2 draws on these initial delineations of levels as well as others' adaptations of them.[12] Through it, we show the levels as delineated in the TESOL standards,[13] and provide a brief description of each. Keep in mind that when learning a new language, most people progress through these levels, regardless of age or grade in school.

Also, as Freeman and Freeman[14] make clear, language learning is not one single process. Rather, there are several lines of proficiency that develop, depending on social situations. When using language in less formal settings, such as when having conversations with friends, ELLs may demonstrate that they have acquired Basic Interpersonal Communicative Skills (BICS) and be functioning at level 5 (bridging), an advanced level of language acquisition. However, these same learners can have difficulty using language in more formal settings, such as school, where they may demonstrate that they are functioning at level 3 (developing), the middle level of language proficiency. They need assistance in acquiring academic language. In other words, children who appear to be functioning at one given level are instead functioning at different levels, depending on how they are called on to use language.

Teachers should first learn all they can about existing literacy skills in home languages. Research clearly agrees that reading and writing practices in a home language can be used to the advantage of English learners, helping them develop reading processes and practices that can be generalized to English literacy.

Moreover, schools must survey the languages represented among students and provide contrastive analyses of home languages compared with English.[15] In particular, literacy teachers need to know major differences among phonemes and grammatical words. For example, many world languages have far fewer vowel sounds than English—the short-i and short-e phonemes do not exist in Spanish. The opaque and often illogical spellings of English vowels may be hard to master when some learners cannot yet hear these new phonemes perfectly. Many world languages do not have articles like *the* or *a*, instead having other ways to specify things about nouns. Such linguistic facts about home languages clearly have an impact on teaching reading and should be gathered and compiled for teachers to use in planning and administering assessments and instruction.

Figure 1.2 Levels of Language Proficiency, Descriptions, and Implications

Levels of Language Proficiency	*Description*
Level 1: Starting	Students have a limited understanding of English. They may respond using nonverbal cues in an attempt to communicate basic needs. They begin to imitate others and use some single words or simple phrases.
Level 2: Emerging	Students are beginning to understand some phrases and simple sentences. They respond using memorized words and phrases.
Level 3: Developing	Students' listening comprehension improves, and they can understand written English. Students are fairly comfortable engaging in social conversations using simple sentences, but they are just beginning to develop their academic language proficiency.
Level 4: Expanding	Students understand and frequently use conversational English with relatively high accuracy. They are able to communicate their ideas in both oral and written contexts. They are also showing the ability to use academic vocabulary.
Level 5: Bridging	Students comprehend and engage in conversational and academic English with proficiency. They perform at or near grade level in reading, writing, and other content areas.

Ages and Stages of Literacy Development

Reading ability continues to develop throughout life. For that matter, so do writing, speaking, listening, and viewing abilities. In fact, we might say that reading ability grows with active involvement in using oral language, print, and other media. In general, children at given ages share common characteristics in terms of reading and writing abilities. Different reading researchers and educators cast these characteristics into stages of growth to help teachers determine who is displaying age-appropriate reading behaviors.[16] Knowing some of these behaviors can also be extremely helpful in trying to determine who might need further assistance with learning to speak, listen, read, or write.

Table 1.3 shows the stages of literacy growth and some of their descriptors. Keep in mind that stages can overlap and that students rarely display every characteristic of one stage before they move into another. Many of the characteristics stay the same from

Table 1.3 Stages and Descriptors of Literacy Growth

Stage	Brief Description	Sample Benchmarks
Early Emergent.	Viewed as a foundation on which children develop oral language and a curiosity about print.	Attends to read-alouds.
Typically before kindergarten.		Uses oral language for different purposes. Likes playing with movable or magnetic letters. Knows several nursery rhymes. Uses paper and writing utensils to attempt writing.
Emergent Literacy.	Children show more interest in all aspects of literacy.	Retains oral directions. Enjoys tongue twisters.
Typically kindergarten; may overlap into the beginning of first grade.		Knows some concepts about print such as book parts, word boundaries, and how to handle a book. Recognizes and names most letters. Shows evidence of being phonemically aware. Can write own name. Uses some punctuation.
Beginning Reading and Writing.	Oral language facility expands. Children develop word analysis skills, and start to show fluency in reading and increased understanding of many words. Their writing begins to follow print conventions.	Uses increased oral vocabulary. Participates in discussions.
Typically first grade; continues into second and third grade for some readers.		Recognizes and names all letters in any order. Identifies many sight words. Uses phonics to determine word pronunciation. Uses a variety of comprehension strategies. Reads and retells stories. Enjoys writing. Uses a computer to write.
Almost Proficient Reading and Writing.	Children grow in their understanding of literacy. Oral language shows increased vocabulary, writing is more frequent, and silent reading increases.	Grows in use of standard English. Uses new oral vocabulary. Uses context to determine word meaning.
Typically begins at end of second grade and continues into fourth or fifth grade.		Self-corrects. Reads independently. Reads for many purposes. Begins learning research skills. Writes for many purposes. Shows growth in writing conventions. Chooses to write in free time.
Proficient Reading and Writing.	Children use reading and writing for a variety of purposes. The majority of skills are acquired and used as appropriate.	Listens to presentations with understanding. Uses oral language for a variety of purposes. Seldom needs help with word recognition.
Typically begins in fourth grade and continues through life.		Uses several comprehension strategies. Enjoys reading. Writes for many purposes. Edits own writing. Experiments with different writing forms.

Source: Based on Cooper, J. D., and Kiger, N. D. (2005). Literacy assessment: Helping teachers plan instruction. Boston, MA: Houghton Mifflin.

stage to stage, but they become more sophisticated. Also, as when anyone is learning something new, there can be plateaus. So, although the table shows a neat linear process that happens in a smooth tempo, in reality, the tempo of progress is marked more by stops and starts, or slowing down and then speeding up.

All of these stages are based on the assumption that children receive a tremendous amount of support and reading experiences on their way to becoming proficient readers. Gladwell has noted that expertise is usually linked to thousands of hours of experience.[17] Jim Loehr echoes and extends Gladwell by emphasizing that it is not only hours, but also intense cycles of engagement and rest that turn regular people into experts.[18] The key word here is *engagement*, and using our diagnostic approach to assessing, learning, and teaching reading capitalizes on it. That is, we are far more interested in helping teachers understand how to spend time with their students being engaged in reading—reading they will *want to* spend time on. When we talk to lifelong readers, we usually find that their reading history is punctuated by intense binges of reading followed by periods of less reading and/or lighter content. And this is exactly our goal for all readers. We want to enable them to find their way to this kind of investment in time and engagement.

Enhanced eText **Application Exercise 1.2:** Developing Questions in a Diagnostic Approach

---

Bridge: From Understanding to Assessment

When teachers understand that _____ ,	then teachers will assess _____ .
Learning English involves not one but many proficiencies,	Students' knowledge of bookish or academic language in speaking and listening.
Response to Intervention means learning what will work best for each student,	Each student individually, and plan to design instruction to build on strengths first and needs second.
Each reader starts every school year at a different developmental level of reading and progresses at his own rate during the school year,	Interests, to learn what kinds of texts are likely to meet students halfway with existing vocabulary knowledge and motivation. Actual development, to learn what reading proficiencies students already have and to determine the reasonable range of just-right text levels.
Good readers orient many problem-solving strategies to comprehending texts,	Whether students approach texts purposefully, instead of out of compliance with school requirements.
The interactive model better explains learning to read for most learners than does a top-down or bottom-up model alone,	Whether students approach reading with balance between their orientation to meaning (comprehension) and their orientation to word parts (phonics).
Affective, motivational processes govern attention and persistence in reading tasks,	Interests, attitudes, and identity, systematically learning about strengths that can work to students' advantage and about motivational needs that block the effectiveness of comprehension and word instruction.
Global comprehension processes govern and guide the need for phonics knowledge,	Listening comprehension, retelling, and summarization.
Successes with learning words and word parts (local knowledge) affect both comprehension and motivation,	Knowledge of phonemes and phonics elements.

Revisiting the Opening Scenario

Now that you have had time to learn about the beliefs and components of the diagnostic approach to assessing and teaching reading that frames this book, reread the opening scenario. Which ideas does Ms. Prazzo best exemplify?

Authors' Summary

Before reading our summary statements for each outcome, we suggest you read each outcome and summarize it in your own words.

Once finished, cross-check your response with our brief summary to determine how well you recalled the major points.

1.1 Discuss the attributes of a diagnostic approach to assessing and teaching reading and the beliefs on which it is based.

- Teachers with a diagnostic approach use problem-solving tools to know each complex aspect of their students as readers. They prioritize discovery of student strengths, and plan learning and teaching activity to build on what readers already know and can do. As readers build on strengths, teachers help them to discover and achieve what they need to learn for ongoing growth. The diagnostic process is highly individualized, but excellent teachers learn how to manage and orchestrate it for groups and for whole classes of readers by zooming in and zooming out between individuals and groups.

1.2 Describe the basic ideas that form the foundation of Response to Intervention and how they connect to a diagnostic approach.

- The diagnostic process helps teachers continually adjust teaching based on student strengths and needs. This kind of ongoing adjustment by teachers in the interest of student growth is the heart of Response to Intervention.

1.3 Explain how reading can be defined and how doing so influences a diagnostic approach.

- Definitions of reading in research and curriculum programs determine whether they address the affective, global, and local aspects of reading. A diagnostic approach requires attention to all three, and teachers must learn to recognize when definitions of reading might prevent them from addressing all three. Many existing programs for assessment and teaching either ignore or address indirectly the affective aspect of reading. Because of its governing role, strong teachers learn to address this aspect as the top priority despite its exclusion from many programs.

1.4 Compare and contrast proficient and less proficient reading behaviors.

- Paying close attention to what good readers do helps teachers set and achieve goals for all readers. Knowing what less proficient readers do helps teachers attend to the potential buildup of frustration that comes from these behaviors. Often, these less proficient behaviors come from beliefs, attitudes, or feelings about reading or from misconceptions about what good readers do.

1.5 Define English learners and explain the levels of language proficiency through which they progress.

- English learners may speak more than one world language at home, but they are expected to use primarily English at school. The levels of proficiency from starting to bridging represent typical progress. Teachers who grew up using primarily English in many contexts must recognize that there is nothing wrong with students who are in typical stages of progress, and that these stages may progress unevenly for different social and academic uses of English (e.g., a learner may progress rapidly in English for friendship, but a bit slower for learning math and at a different rate for learning in social studies).

1.6 Construct a timeline that shows how readers change over time.

- This timeline helps adults recognize that their view of proficient reading develops over years and that there is nothing wrong with students who are in a recognized stage. It is important to remember the basic order of progress and to be able to diagram it.

Think About It!

1. You have been assigned to a special committee to develop a diagnostic approach to assess and teach reading. Discuss what factors you would consider in developing such a plan.

2. Ask a number of teachers how they define reading. Observe their classes and try to discern whether their reading program reflects their stated definition of reading. Discuss whether your observations show top-down, bottom-up, or interactive models of reading.

3. Observe teachers to determine how they assess, learn, and teach reading. Which combinations of elements seem to be most evident? How do you know?

4. Use Table 1.1, "Summary of Proficient and Less Proficient Reading Behaviors," to observe a reader. Highlight the characteristics you notice and provide an example of what you see.

Websites

- http://www.readwritethink.org
  A partnership between the International Literacy Association and the National Council of Teachers of English (NCTE), this site provides professional resources.

- http://www.sedl.org/reading/framework/
  Providing a cognitive framework for reading comprehension, this site offers information on cognitive elements of reading, a glossary of reading terms, instructional resources, research, and other resources.

Endnotes

1. Harris, T. L., & Hodges, R. E. (Eds.). (1995). *The literacy dictionary*. Newark, DE: International Reading Association, p. 50.

2. International Reading Association Board of Directors. (2000). *Excellent reading teachers: A position statement of the international reading association*. Newark, DE: International Reading Association.

3. Johnston, P. H. (2004). *Choice words: How our language affects children's learning*. Stenhouse.

4. Miller, S., et al. (2016). It only looks the same from a distance: How US, Finnish, and Irish schools support struggling readers. *Reading Psychology, 37.8*, 1212–1239.

5. Cain, K. (2015). Learning to read: Should we keep things simple? *Reading Research Quarterly, 50.2*, 151–169.

6. Rumelhart, D. E. (1994). Toward an interactive model of reading. In R. B. Ruddell, M. R. Ruddell, & H. Singer (Eds.), Theoretical models and processes of reading (pp. 864–894). Newark, DE, US: International Reading Association.

7. Fitzgerald, J. (1999). What is this thing called "balance?" *The Reading Teacher, 53*(2), 100–107.

8. Duke, N. K., & Pearson, P. D. (2002). Effective practices for developing reading comprehension. In A. E. Farstrup & S. J. Samuels (Eds.), *What research has to say about reading instruction*, 3rd ed. (205–242). Newark, DE: International Reading Association.

9. Council for Exceptional Children. (2003). *What every special educator must know: Ethics, standards, and guidelines for special educators*, 5th ed. Upper Saddle River, NJ: Pearson/Merrill/Prentice-Hall.

10. Flurkey, A. (2006). What's 'normal' about real reading? In K. Goodman (Ed.), *The truth about DIBELS: What it is and what it does* (pp. 40–49). Portsmouth, NH: Heinemann.

11. Krashen, S., & Terrell, T. (1983). *The natural approach: Language acquisition in the classroom*. Oxford: Pergamon.

12. Freeman, D. E., & Freeman, Y. S. (2000). *Teaching reading in multilingual classrooms*. Portsmouth, NH: Heinemann. See also Kendal, J., & Khuon, O. (2005). *Making sense: Small group comprehension lessons for English language learners*. Portland, ME: Stenhouse.

13. TESOL. (2006). *Pre-K-12 English language proficiency standards*. Alexandria, VA: Teachers of English to Speakers of Other Languages.

14. Freeman, D. E., & Freeman, Y. S. (2007). *English language learners: The essential guide*. New York, NY: Scholastic.

15. Swan, M. & Smith, B. (1987). Learner English: A teacher's guide to interference and other problems. Cambridge, UK: Cambridge University Press.

16. Chall, J. (1983). *Stages of reading development*. New York, NY: McGraw-Hill; International Reading Association and the National Association for the Education of Young Children. (1998). Learning to read and write: Developmentally appropriate practices for young children. *The Reading Teacher, 52*, 193–216; Cooper, J. D., & Kiger, N. (2005). *Literacy assessment: Helping teachers plan instruction*, 2nd ed. Boston, MA: Houghton Mifflin.

17. Gladwell, M. (2008). *Outliers*. New York, NY: Little Brown.

18. Loehr, J. (2012). *The only way to win*. New York, NY: Hyperion.

Chapter 2
Factors That Affect Reading Performance

Pathdoc/Shutterstock

 ## Chapter Outline

Scenario: Cheyenne and Sara—a Study in Contrast

Differentiating Between In-School and Out-of-School Factors

Educational Factors

Out-of-School Factors

 ## Learning Outcomes

After reading this chapter, you should be able to . . .

2.1 Differentiate between in-school and out-of-school factors that affect reading performance.

2.2 List and describe educational factors that can impact reading growth.

2.3 List and explain out-of-school factors that can impact reading growth.

Scenario

Cheyenne and Sara—A Study in Contrast

Mr. Ley knows the nationwide research showing that family income is powerfully related to reading successes and failures. He has students from homes with a wide variety of economic backgrounds. He wonders what actual factors are impacting each of these individual students. He decides to zoom in on two students, Cheyenne and Sara, to ask and answer questions.

Having met all of his students' families at back-to-school events, he knows Cheyenne's family lives in a middle-income neighborhood. Cheyenne's mom is a software engineer who travels regularly. Because Cheyenne is an only child, she often gets to travel with her mom. Mr. Ley reflects on the family's engagement with school and reading. Cheyenne completes all tasks he sends home, and brings her own books from home to read. Mr. Ley has used a "books in the home" survey with his class, and learned that Cheyenne has more than 100 books.

Sara lives in an apartment building with her grandmother, dad, and three siblings. Sara's family has a sandwich shop, which her dad owns and manages. Since her grandmother sometimes needs to work at the shop, Sara is often responsible for her younger siblings in the back room of the shop. After school she is often reading to her brothers and sister, helping them with their homework, or playing with them. Moreover, she has become good at a number of jobs around the shop. On the "books in the home" survey, Sara selected "more than 10."

Mr. Ley knows only a little about each child's home life. But he knows enough to create and manage authentic reading expectations for Cheyenne and Sara individually. He realizes that a great list of home circumstances creates challenges for him. He is likely to think he cannot help Sara and that he doesn't need to help Cheyenne. But both readers need and deserve instruction designed to help them move forward as readers, building on home literacy strengths.

Outside the classroom, he chooses to focus on Cheyenne's travel and Sara's life with family at the shop as ways to deepen and widen what counts as reading for school. Mr. Ley realizes both students can benefit from his focus on factors outside school, knowing each student's strengths may come from home, family, and community.

As Cheyenne and Sara's profiles help to illustrate, there are many factors associated with learning to read. Researchers have learned that for children who have difficulty learning to read across years of school, finding a path forward involves alignment of factors that cross the individual, the home, and the school.[1] In this chapter, we present a number of factors that cross these boundaries and explain how they affect reading performance. Although there may be some factors over which educators have little control (e.g., low income, little or no reading material in the home, and family structure), there are factors over which they have more influence. Understanding these factors puts teachers in better positions to set their students up for success.

Differentiating Between In-School and Out-of-School Factors

There are many ways to classify factors that affect children's reading performance. For the purposes of this text, we classify the different factors as either *in-school* or *out-of-school* factors. In Table 2.1, we provide an overview of these categories, a definition of each category, and a list of the specific factors we discuss in this chapter. When people talk about **in-school factors**, they generally are referring to factors that influence learning which come under the domain or control of the educational system. In this category, we would include the teacher, school materials, the instructional time, and the school environment. Under **out-of-school factors**, we would include family structure, home environment, physical health (general), vision, hearing, personality, and gender. Out-of-school factors are those that the educational system does not influence directly. Although the two categories appear distinct at first glance, a second look shows that many factors overlap. For instance, although gender cannot be influenced by the schools, gender-based social roles and cultural biases can be understood and addressed in school. A case can even be made for general physical health being influenced by educational practices. For example, children who are doing poorly in school may wish to avoid school to such an extent that they become physically ill every morning. Their emotional health influences their physical health so that they actually get a stomachache or headache, or throw up. Their emotional state may so affect them that they cannot eat or sleep. The physical symptoms are real, even though the cause may not be a virus or bacterium.

Rather than spending time debating which factors belong in one category or the other, the important idea is the interrelatedness among factors that affect reading performance. A child who has difficulty learning to read may have accompanying emotional and social problems. Clearly, when using a reading diagnosis and improvement program, many factors need to be considered in order to help all children advance in their ability to read.

In-School Factors

In-school factors are decisions made within the educational system. Examples are content (what is taught) and pedagogy (how these things are taught). Instructional materials, time, personnel, and facilities are also in the domain of the education system. If a child is experiencing difficulty in reading, it is generally a good idea to check her school record to see if there is any information that might shed light on the problem. From

Table 2.1 Factors Affecting Reading Performance

Category	Definition	Factors
In-school	Those factors that come under the domain or control of the educational system and influence learning	• Teaching methods • Instructional materials • The teacher • Instructional time • School environment • Diagnosed disability
Out-of-school	Those factors that do not come under the domain or control of the educational system and cannot be influenced by it	• Home environment • Dialect and language differences • Gender • Physical: illness and nutrition • Perceptual: visual and auditory • Emotional: self-concept, learned helplessness, motivation, and attitude

Source: Pearson/Hope Madden.

records, teachers may be able to learn more about methods and materials the child has been exposed to in previous years. For example, a third-grade student might appear to have difficulty with decoding. Yet examination of school records might reveal that this child has been in systematic phonics programs since kindergarten. Rather than reteaching systematic phonics from the beginning, another approach (e.g., literature-based phonics, chunking strategies, whole word, or language experience) would be warranted. The National Reading Panel's review of research on phonics has shown that the effectiveness of systematic, sequential phonics instruction decreases each year after first grade.[2] In this case, the *reading model* could be a major contributing factor to the problem.

Content

Schools are obliged to provide reading material that supports extensive reading. This means high-interest material for free reading and material chosen to support content areas such as literature, science, social studies, visual and performing arts, and physical education. One of the first assessments any teacher should make in a new job is an assessment of the classroom and school library resources. During the nationwide financial downturn starting in 2008, many schools cut resources for school librarians and the school library collections. Lack of funding for teachers' individual classroom libraries is a fundamental problem in many schools throughout the United States. Many teachers purchase classroom library books and magazines out of pocket. For this expense to be recognized, they have to wait each year to declare the loss on their tax return. Year in and year out, teachers purchase the books their students need as if this basic equipment for teaching reading were somehow unexpected by the school. Thus, availability of appropriate materials is far from standard from classroom to classroom.

One simple appraisal of support is to ask the school or district to provide the previous year's expenditures for school library and classroom library materials, and to ask to see receipts for commercial reading programs. These expenditures should be in a reasonable balance. The content and instructional routines in a commercial reading program have nowhere to go when a school or classroom has too few books for students to apply the skills and strategies they learn about in a commercial reading program.

Widespread differences in reading achievement are repeatedly explained by differences in oral language. However, schools often attribute all oral language proficiency to the home and fail to give students a full and rich curriculum in speaking and listening. The content of oral language is well known. The range of oral language genres includes conversation, oral storytelling, singing, reciting rhymes and poems, jokes and riddles, drama, topical discussions, and informational presentations—all genres with which people are familiar. Yet these speech genres must be included purposefully in the curriculum—they do not take care of themselves outside of school. Although oral language teaching is an investment that pays dividends in literacy success (for those whose home language is English, as well as for English learners), a well-articulated oral language curriculum is a rarity in today's schools. Teachers who see a widespread trend of low achievement in reading should not be surprised when they discover no curriculum for storytelling or conversation. Teaching speech genres during school has clear impact on students' awareness of how to use words and grammatical phrases in context.

Pedagogy

Pedagogy is how content is taught. Researchers and educators have studied best practices in pedagogy for more than 100 years. Questions about effectiveness are often at the forefront of this research, and teachers can lean on a number of high-quality books that gather and summarize what researchers have found about teaching and learning reading. Gambrell and Morrow's *Best Practices in Reading Instruction* offers

16 summaries of research on high-value topics from motivation to comprehension, from phonics to fluency, and from intervention to English learners. The multiple volumes of the *Handbook of Reading Research* have done likewise, answering many key questions about what we have actually learned about topics such as how motivation affects skills and strategies, how metacognition affects comprehension and word identification, or how phonics processes actually work cognitively.[3] The *National Reading Panel Report* presented a meta-analysis of many statistical studies with an experimental design, to identify pedagogical techniques shown to be effective across multiple research studies. These results are worth searching partly because of the vibrant and thoughtful rebuttals that challenged the report's biases and findings.[4] Finally, some of the best answers to teachers' questions about learning to read were made available decades ago in the First Grade Studies, a series of research reports by many researchers who worked to answer teachers' most pressing questions about learning and teaching reading.[5] Over the decades, these studies have proven robust, because learning to read English print still involves the same processes it did many years ago. Today, recent and forthcoming researchers are still investigating pedagogy, including how digital literacy and multi-modal literacy are changing the landscape of reading and writing.

Instructional Materials

A former third-grade student of mine (MO) helped me to understand the importance of instructional materials—in this case the use of hardcover books instead of softcover books. We were provided multiple copies of the same text, some hardcover and others softcover. In the distribution, he was given a softcover text. Seeing this, he broke into loud sobs, saying that he couldn't read the book. In my effort to calm him, I assured him that of course he could read the book, and I pointed out the similarities of the versions. It didn't work. He kept crying, telling me I didn't understand. He was correct; I didn't understand, so I asked him to explain. He pointed out that in the softcover book, there wasn't as much space around the sides of the page and the lines were all squished together. Taking another look at the books, I saw what he was explaining and once again, I had to admit that he was correct. The hardcover book appeared much easier to read because of the extra space devoted to the margins and the line spacing. The problem was resolved by letting him read from a hardcover version—which he did with ease. The point here is that instructional materials matter more than we might think. The materials not only should be in alignment with the teaching approach, but also should entice children to read.

When a student resists reading, we need to take a look at what we are putting in front of the child to better understand whether this resistance is a problem with the child or a problem with the instructional materials. We then need to make any necessary changes to keep the child reading.

The Teacher

In the words of Albert Harris and Edward Sipay, "Teacher effectiveness has a strong influence on how well children learn to read."[6] Like other scholars, we could not agree more.[7] This is one reason we've devoted Chapter 6 to the teacher's role in reading diagnosis and improvement programs. Following are some teaching practices reading educators have seen contribute to reading problems:

1. Failing to ensure that students are prepared to learn a skill or strategy
2. Using reading materials that are too difficult
3. Pacing instruction either too fast or too slow

4. Ignoring unsatisfactory reading behaviors until they become habits

5. Rarely expecting a certain child to perform the same tasks required of others

6. Asking questions and then answering them without giving students time to respond

7. Failing to acknowledge student efforts when they try

8. Expressing disapproval or sarcasm when a mistake is made

9. Allowing other children to disparage a child's efforts

10. Expecting a child to perform a task in front of others that is difficult to do well

11. Expecting a child to do well or poorly because older brothers and sisters did so in previous years

Instructional Time

Sometimes research proves what common sense would tell us. A case in point is instructional time. As a result of Rosenshine's findings related to academic engaged time (i.e., the time students spend on academically relevant activities at the right level of difficulty), we now have proof that the more time students spend on a task, the higher their academic achievement will be.[8] And, as other researchers have reported, students spend more time on task when they are engaged with the teacher and the content. Let us always remember teacher enthusiasm! It can go a long way toward keeping students focused.[9] When students are not receiving instruction, individual work still needs to be meaningful and engaging. Independent activities need to extend and refine their reading abilities. It is well understood that reading extensively in just-right text is one of the best ways to grow in reading.[10] Instead of simply assigning free reading time, it is now well understood that teachers are central supports, instructing students in how to monitor their own independence and engagement with texts, and how to select texts that are likely to encourage persistence and effort. For too long, educators have assumed every reader already knows how to select and engage in just-right texts, because the successful readers do these things invisibly and automatically. It is often the job of teachers to make the invisible processes of successful readers concrete and knowable to students who need these processes.

School Environment

Context matters. When children feel safe, they are more likely to take the necessary risks and efforts on their way to becoming proficient readers.

Beyond safety, however the actual physical environment of the classroom has a great influence on learning. To become readers, children need to be exposed to much of print in many forms. A classroom full of print, such as children's literature, magazines, brochures, cookbooks, catalogs, comic books, and board games, sends a powerful message to students. A classroom littered with print on shelves, in bins, and on the classroom walls helps demonstrate that there are many reasons to read (and write). Moreover, readers need places to read where they feel comfortable and able to pay attention. A variety of locations designed for readers to engage in texts quietly and without distraction are also essential equipment for a successful reading classroom.

Diagnosed Learning Disability

Diversity in the classroom encompasses students with learning disabilities. Fortunately, there are by law professionals within each school whose job it is to understand disabilities and to help teachers plan appropriate instruction. We have put this factor last in the list of in-school factors on purpose. We echo veteran literacy educator Vivian Paley, who found that when children were struggling she was able to teach them when she first looked within school for the source of the problem, not within the child. This is wise, because their own teaching is the arena in which teachers make decisions, and where assessment can be used to recommend changes. Often, learning problems have much to do with institutional structures and policies that affect literacy learning.

Specific learning disorders for reading frequently manifest in early childhood in phonological awareness.[11] Some estimates suggest between 10% and 20% of all people have difficulty perceiving spoken words in phonological pieces and parts such as syllables and phonemes.[12] Readers who perceive words mostly as a whole are common, and teachers should expect to see readers like this each year. Researchers have demonstrated repeatedly that readers can learn to perceive phonological parts of words with instruction, practice, and application to authentic reading. Because of this, assessments of phonological and phonemic awareness are part of the usual landscape of reading assessment. Early identification is important, because accommodations in primary-grades phonics instruction may be needed for students to experience successes in early reading.

Out-of-School Factors
Home Environment

Socioeconomic class, parents' education, and the neighborhood in which children live are some of the factors that shape children's **home environments.** Researchers have concluded that the higher the socioeconomic status of a family, the better the verbal ability of the children[13] and the better children usually achieve in school.[14]

Enhanced eText **Application Exercise 2.1:** Forming Questions About Educational Factors that Affect Reading

---

Bridge: From Understanding to Assessment

When teachers understand that _____,	then teachers will assess _____.
How they teach is as important as what they teach,	Their own access to high-quality summaries of research on reading. Knowledge of best practice will help teachers form good questions about learners.
The depth of the literate environment determines whether students will be able to apply reading instruction,	The classroom library and school library to learn whether the collection of reading materials is broad enough to support each individual.
Learners read successfully when processes of meaning and decoding work together in an interactive model,	The policies and programs of the school to learn whether a single-direction model is favored at the expense of the other (top down versus bottom up).
Oral language proficiency has a great impact on success with reading books,	Students' knowledge of speech genres such as conversation, storytelling, drama, or information presentations. The curriculum to learn whether it invites or ignores daily speaking and listening.
Individual teachers are known to have the greatest effects on student achievement,	Their own pedagogy to learn which best practices can be put in place, and which poor practices can be eliminated.
Instructional time on reading is vital to success,	The schedule of the school day and week, to find many areas where reading will help students succeed (e.g., science, social studies, art, music, or physical education).
Public performances of reading can be among the most damaging to readers' attitudes and identities,	The schedule, to learn where large-group public performances might be replaced with safer pedagogy, such as reading partners or book clubs.
Learning disabilities are often compounded by difficulties with reading,	The curriculum, to learn whether individualized reading pedagogies have been applied well to each student.

Children who have adult language models and who are spoken to and encouraged to speak will have an advantage in the development of language and intelligence. Similarly, children who come from homes where there are many opportunities to read, where there are many different types of text, and where they discuss what they read with their parents will likely make reading achievement gains earlier than children without these advantages.[15] Some researchers have found that socio-economic status makes a difference in families' knowing what to do to boost their children's education at home. One group of researchers found that in homes where the mother had a high school education, the contributions of both mothers and fathers added up to early successes for their children in reading. However, in homes where the mother had a college bachelor's degree, the mother's educational activities alone were enough to result in the same successes. Fathers still contributed, but the mothers' influence alone was measured as enough to explain success for these homes. This is the kind of situation where a "Matthew Effect" can quickly appear for households with low income or high school education only—the rich get richer and the poor get poorer. Households with college-educated mothers need only the influence of a mother thinking about her child's reading, whereas households with no more than a high school education need a wider network of people doing their part.[16]

The reader's home environment also has an impact. Teachers want to be attentive to whether a child is comfortable or in stress at home. Stress might include traumatic experiences, changes in who is present and not present at home, perception of safety at home, or the availability of places to do school work. Interestingly, whether parents were good readers or not does not appear to be a determining factor in reading successes or failures. What appears to be a more important factor is the number of books in the home.[17] This is heartening, because parents cannot change their own past but the literate environment of the home is something families, schools, and communities can address together. Another group of researchers found the interesting result that reading attitudes were affected less by home reading activities, and more by the simple frequency of parent–child interactions, and by parental expectations about reading.[18] Caregivers accomplish much simply by being with their children and making reading into a declared value of the family.

Language Differences

We live in a pluralistic society.[19] In a diagnostic approach to assessing and teaching reading, teachers must recognize that school classes will be a composite of children who speak many different languages. For example, one student might grow up with two non-English languages spoken at home (such as Spanish and Quechua), and another student in the same class may have grown up with both English and another heritage language spoken at home (such as in Navajo or Hindi families). Still others come from homes where only one language is spoken. English learners from various backgrounds face unique problems in phonology, orthography, grammar, usage, and pragmatics.[20]

The challenge teachers face is one of helping all students to value and develop their home language(s) while at the same time learning English as a new language.[21] Spanish is an important and widespread language in the United States. And yet we do ourselves and our students a disservice when we prepare only for Spanish–English diversity. Imagine a school where 65% of parents identify their children as coming from Spanish-speaking homes, and 34% from English-speaking homes. That leaves 1% of students who are not from either group. Good teachers learn how to design reading instruction for the 1% as well as for those speaking the dominant languages of the school population. They also understand that good teachers do not confuse variability with disability.[22]

In the United States, regional dialects differ very little from each other, perhaps almost exclusively in pronunciation. We would be more likely to speak of a regional "accent" than a "dialect."[23] Children who speak a variation or dialect of English or another language are not inferior, nor is their heritage language inferior. Research by linguists has shown that many variations of English, including African American vernacular, that of Creoles from Caribbean islands, and Indian English, are highly structured systems and not accumulations of errors deviating from standard American English. Labov states that "it is most important for the teacher to understand the *relation* between standard and nonstandard and to recognize that *nonstandard English is a system* of rules, different from the standard but not necessarily inferior as a means of communication."[24]

To help children participate in the dominant cultures of power, we want them to become flexible language users—that is, we want to help them develop the understanding that every social situation may have its own rules for language. To successfully communicate with members of any given group of people, one needs to be able to switch registers as needed.

Gender

Preferences for texts are a key factor that distinguishes gender. One problem is that male students report a shortage of texts in classrooms and school libraries that hold their interest. Both male and female students need exposure to many different types of texts that will help each person to develop an identity as a reader.[25] Students who identify as transgender may have difficulty identifying with gendered book characters. Many authors of children's books avoid gendering their main characters at all to avoid problems with identification. Teachers need to be aware of how books represent gender and evaluate the classroom library collection accordingly.

Physical Health

Illness   A child who is ill is not able to do well in school. This statement is obvious; however, it may not be obvious when a child is ill. A teacher needs to be alert for symptoms that may suggest a child is not well or is not getting enough sleep. For example, a child who is listless, whose eyes are glazed, who seems sleepy, and who actually does fall asleep in class may need a physical checkup.

The reason a child who is ill does not usually do well in school is always frequent absence from school. Children who have recurrent illnesses are generally absent from school many days of each school year. This lack of attendance can contribute to reading problems because it causes the child to miss important reading instruction and hours of in-school reading opportunities. In fact, such long absences, especially in first and second grade, are often a main reason children struggle with reading.[26]

Nutrition   The effects of nutrition, and particularly malnutrition, on learning have been evident for a long time.[27] It should come as no surprise that children who are hungry and malnourished have difficulty learning. They cannot concentrate on the task at hand; they also lack drive. They simply lack the energy to perform at their best. For several decades, some researchers have suggested that severe malnutrition in infancy may lower children's IQ scores.[28] Other researchers have found that the lack of protein in an infant's diet may adversely affect the child's ability to learn.[29] Still others have found that the effects of certain food additives may be a deterrent to learning for some children.[30]

Childhood obesity is in the media spotlight; some even call it an epidemic and point to possible reasons why children are becoming obese in increasing numbers. Not surprisingly, nutrition is a major factor, as are the types of food that children consume. Is it any wonder that many children have trouble performing in school when they eat processed foods that contain a lot of sugar?[31]

Perceptual Factors

Vision and hearing are two key areas of perception in reading. Ruling out visual and auditory issues as factors that contribute to reading problems is important. For example,

Figure 2.1 Symptoms of Vision Problems

Child's Name: _____

Date of Observation: _____

Symptoms
The child . . .   **Yes**   **No**

1. Complains of constant headaches

2. Eyes show some of the following: red rims, swollen lids, crusted lids, redness, frequent sties, watering

3. Squints while reading

4. Asks to sit closer to the board

5. Can't seem to sit still while doing close-up tasks

6. Holds reading material very close to face when reading

7. Skips many words and/or sentences when reading

8. Makes many reversals when reading

9. Confuses letters

10. Avoids reading

11. Mouths words or lip-reads

12. Confuses similar words

13. Makes many repetitions while reading

14. Skips lines while reading

15. Has difficulty remembering what was read silently

a struggling reader who also has astigmatism is at a heightened disadvantage. The same holds true for readers with auditory perception problems.

Visual Perception   Sometimes children have difficulty reading because they need glasses. Yet visual problems are not always obvious and, as a result, are not always detected. (See Figure 2.1.) Most schools have some kind of visual screening. The most common screening is for **myopia,** or nearsightedness. The Snellen chart test is usually done by the school nurse. In this familiar test, a child must identify letters of various sizes with each eye. A score of 20/20 is considered normal. A score of 20/40 or 20/60 means that a child has defective vision because the child with normal vision can see the letters at a distance of forty or sixty feet, whereas the child with defective vision can only see these letters at a distance of twenty feet. Other tests are used to identify farsightedness (**hypermetropia**) and **astigmatism.**[32] Nearsightedness is more likely to impact reading in whole group instruction, when reading a screen or board from across the room. Farsightedness, although less common, is more likely to have a negative impact on individual reading of books.

Auditory Perception   Sometimes children have difficulty reading because of hearing problems. Most schools have some sort of audiology screening that is administered in primary grades. These tests check for hearing acuity and hearing loss. School audiologists have the ability to follow up with tests on phonological processing, binaurality, and masking.

The acquisition of speech sounds for any given language is learned very early in life and is usually established before the child starts school. For children who speak languages other than English at home, distinguishing among English phonemes may be difficult, especially at the beginning of English language learning.

Emotional Well-Being

Self-concept, learned helplessness, motivation, and attitude are four aspects related to emotional health. Each needs to be considered when thinking about a child's emotional well-being and how it can affect reading performance.

Self-Concept   Self-concept is the way an individual feels about herself. Although the verdict is still out on specific origins of self-concept, our lives are a testament to the fact that it exists and that it can change depending on the task at hand. For example, if we feel adequate, confident, and self-reliant about reading, we are more apt to be good readers. We would say that we have a positive self-concept as it relates to reading. However, if we are feeling less than adequate, have little confidence, and are not self-reliant about reading, we are more likely to be poor at reading. One factor to consider, then, is how children feel about themselves as readers. This can be discovered with a student reading perceptions and attitudes interview, such as Gambrell's Motivational Reading Profile.[33] Moreover, Harter's surveys assess students' self-perceptions of competence, and this survey can provide useful information about students' general sense of belonging with respect to school tasks.[34]

Learned Helplessness   Related to self-concept is learned helplessness. When learners repeatedly experience failure at a task regardless of how hard they try, they are apt to develop the idea that they simply cannot perform the task; this is called *learned helplessness*. As a result, any time they are expected to perform the task, they become passive and wait for help. Children who feel that they simply cannot perform well at reading are likely to show avoidance behaviors. The important point to keep in mind is that learned helplessness is the child's viewpoint. Giving students many success opportunities over weeks and months of time will help change this viewpoint to one of competence and confidence.

Motivation   Like Paris and Carpenter, we believe there are several components that facilitate *motivation* to read. These include how readers perceive their ability to read, the text, the reason for reading, and the surrounding environment.[35] Take, for example, children who attend an optional sleepover at school and are told to bring their favorite book for reading and sharing with others. Children who elect to attend the event are more likely to be motivated to read. After all, they get to choose the text with the purpose in mind. Self-selection means that they are likely to pick out a text they feel they can read with ease. They need not be embarrassed when they share a part of it aloud with another person. Likewise, because everyone will be reading, the environment encourages all children to do the same.

Attitude   If we simply take a look at ourselves and our relationship to reading, we can fully understand what researchers have concluded over the years: *Attitude* is a major factor that affects reading performance.[36] In fact, a positive attitude can override missing skills,[37] enabling a reader to perform far better than expected based on past reading performances. A former student of mine (MO) helped me to understand this. She selected a book that presented many challenges for her—too many, from my perspective. As much as I tried to persuade her to read other, easier texts, she kept returning to "her" book and simply would not give it up. For whatever reason, she wanted to read the book, and after continual assistance, she read it with ease. What seemed like a miracle was a positive attitude in action. Deep down, she wanted to read the book and felt that she could get it, and so she did. Excited about her newfound reading ability, I wondered whether she could read other texts at a similar level of complexity. My subsequent observations revealed that she could not. In fact, she often chose to read much easier books after she did a repeated reading of her favorite, but more difficult book.

Enhanced eText **Application Exercise 2.2:** Forming Questions about Non-Educational Factors that Affect Reading

---

Bridge: From Understanding to Assessment

When teachers understand that _____,	then teachers will assess _____.
Opportunities for speaking and listening vary widely across U.S. homes,	Student proficiency in oral language genres such as conversation and storytelling.
The home language of English learners is a strength on which to build,	Their knowledge of best practices for teaching English learners.
Chronic reading disabilities are diagnosed disproportionately among boys compared with among girls,	The classroom library to learn whether a wide variety of texts is available that either represents students' actual gender identities or favors no gender.
A variety of physical and perceptual processes can impact learning to read,	Students' access to physical activity and adequate nutrition during the school day. What is known about students' vision and hearing.
Emotional well-being can impact learning to read,	Students' self-perceptions as learners, their interests and attitudes toward reading outside school, and what motivates and engages them outside school.
Reading with adults who over-prompt and control reading can lead to a pattern of learned helplessness,	How frequently students turn to an adult or peer for prompts and other help during reading tasks. Themselves for knowledge of pedagogical techniques that encourage independence in problem solving during reading.

Revisiting the Opening Scenario

Having read about several factors that can affect reading, return to the scenario at the beginning of the chapter. Which of the factors discussed might be affecting each of these girls? Which factors are in-school and which are out-of-school?

Authors' Summary

Before reading our summary statements for each outcome, we suggest you read each outcome and summarize it in your own words.

Once finished, cross-check your response with our brief summary to determine how well you recalled the major points.

2.1 Differentiate between in-school and out-of-school factors that affect reading performance.

- There are many different factors that can impact children's reading performance. One way of thinking about these factors is to put them into two categories: *in-school* and *out-of-school*. *In-school*

factors are those that come under the domain or control of the educational system. *Out-of-school* factors do not come under the domain or control of the educational system and often cannot be influenced by it.

- Regardless of how one chooses to classify the factors, the most important point to consider is that there are many interrelated factors that impact reading growth, and that any combination of them can exist. Looking at a variety of factors rather than one single factor is central to the diagnostic approach and critical to advance the growth of readers.

2.2 **List and describe in-school factors that can impact reading growth.**

- *In-school factors* in learning are those that come under the domain or control of the education system. These factors include teaching methods, instructional materials, the teacher, instructional time, and the school environment.

- When reading growth seems to be thwarted, there can be a tendency to see the lack as child-centered, when in fact educational factors can be major contributors to this lack of growth. For example, if children learn best in a more holistic manner yet are taught in a piecemeal fashion, they may not be able to make sense of the instruction. Therefore, they can fail to learn the content. In yet another example, if the classroom context is such that children feel threatened or unsafe, they are less likely to take the necessary risks to become competent readers. Although it takes courage, teachers must look at in-school factors to discover and address the direct or indirect influence these factors have on reading growth.

2.3 **List and explain out-of-school factors that can impact reading growth.**

- *Out-of-school factors* in learning are those that do not come under the domain or control of the educational system and often cannot be influenced by it. These factors include home environment, dialect and language differences, intelligence, gender, physical health, perceptual factors, and emotional well-being.

- Teachers can do little about out-of-school factors such as home environment, family makeup, or languages and dialects. However, becoming aware of the environments in which their students live enables teachers to provide experiences at school that either enhance or enrich their students' learning experiences and contribute to their reading growth. For some out-of-school factors, schools take an active part. For example, being mindful of nutrition and emotional well-being is essential because both are basic needs of all learners. Children who are well-nourished, have a high sense of self-efficacy, are motivated, and have positive attitudes about reading and themselves as readers stand a much better chance of becoming proficient readers. Schools take an active part when they provide breakfast and lunch programs, summer programming, and clearly defined opportunities for physical activity.

Think About It!

1. You have been asked to give a talk to your colleagues about why there are more reading disabilities among boys than among girls in the United States. What will you say?

2. How could the community be considered an educational factor that could affect children's reading positively?

3. Imagine a child who has multiple out-of-school factors impeding her reading success. How would you determine all the contributing factors?

4. A colleague is throwing up her hands in despair over her class's reading problems. Many of her students have multiple out-of-school factors that impact their reading. Explain how she can balance out out-of-school factors by strengthening educational factors.

5. There are many in-school and out-of-school factors that could affect reading success. Think of others that go beyond those already listed, and describe how they would affect reading.

Websites

- http://bookadventure.com/
   Although primarily devoted to children, this site also provides information for parents and teachers. For children, this site offers book lists, quizzes, and prizes, addressing external motivational factors. For teachers, the site presents activities and resources for engaging young readers.

- http://www.readingrockets.org/helping/target/
   The site provides information about the five components of reading and the difficulties occurring in each area. Within each section, the component is defined and described as to what the problem looks like from students', parents', and teachers' perspectives.

- http://www.readingrockets.org/helping/target/otherissues

  This page includes information on out-of-school factors affecting reading, including processing (auditory processing, phonological processing, and language processing), memory, attention, and English language learning.

- https://www.kidsreads.com/features/great-books-for-boys

  This site provides an extensive list of books for boys. Included are series titles and stand-alone fiction that cover a variety of genres: fantasies, mysteries, thrillers, action/adventure novels, and historical fiction. Although many of these selections also will appeal to girls, they are especially geared toward capturing the attention of boys, who are often much more reluctant readers.

Endnotes

1. Northrop, L. (2017). Breaking the cycle: Cumulative disadvantage in literacy. *Reading Research Quarterly*, 52(4), 391–396.

2. National Institute of Child Health and Human Development. (2000). *Report of the National Reading Panel: Teaching children to read: An evidence-based assessment of the scientific research literature on reading and its implications for reading instruction*. Washington, DC: U.S. Government Printing Office.

3. Pearson, P. D., Barr, R., Kamil, M. L., & Mosenthal, P. (Eds.). (2003). *Handbook of reading research (Vol. I)*. New York, NY: Routledge.

4. Garan, E. M. (2001). Beyond the smoke and mirrors: A critique of the National Reading Panel Report on Phonics. *Phi Delta Kappa 82*(7), 500–506; Allington, R. (2002). *Big Brother and the national reading curriculum: How ideology trumped evidence*. Portsmouth, NH: Heinemann.

5. Pearson, P. D. (1997). The First Grade Studies: A personal reflection. *Reading Research Quarterly 34*, 428–432.

6. Harris, A. J., & Sipay, E. R. (1990). *How to increase reading ability: A guide to developmental and remedial methods*, 9th ed. New York, NY: Longman, p. 355.

7. Allington, R. L. & Shake, M. C. (1986). Remedial reading: Achieving curricular congruence in classroom and clinic. *The Reading Teacher 39*(7), 648–654; Wharton-McDonald, R., Pressley, M., & Hampston, J. (1998). Literacy instruction in nine first-grade classrooms: Teacher characteristics and student achievements. *The Elementary School Journal*, 99, 101–128; International Reading Association Board of Directors. (2009, October). *Excellent reading teachers: Position statement*. Retrieved from International Reading Association. (2000). *Excellent reading teachers: A position statement of the International Reading Association*. Newark, DE: Author.

8. Rosenshine, B. V. (1978). Academic engaged time, content covered, and direct instruction. *Journal of Education, 60*, 38–66.

9. Bettencourt, E. M., et al. (1983). Effect of teacher enthusiasm on student on-task behavior and achievement. *American Educational Research Journal 20*, 435–450.

10. Allington & Shake, 1986.

11. DSM-V

12. IDLA

13. Loban, W. D. (1976). *Language development: Kindergarten through grade twelve*. Urbana, IL: National Council of Teachers of English, Research Report 18.

14. Statement of Emerson J. Elliot, Commissioner of Education Statistics, at the Release of *National Assessment of Educational Progress 1994 Reading Assessment: A First Look*. April 27, 1995, p. 2; Heath, S. B. (1983). *Ways with words: Language, life, and work in communities and classrooms*. New York, NY: Cambridge University Press; Purcell-Gates, V. (1995). *Other people's words: The cycle of low literacy*. Cambridge, MA: Harvard University Press; Edwards, P. A., Pleasants, H. M., & Franklin, S. H. (1999). *A path to follow: Learning to listen to parents*. Portsmouth, NH: Heinemann.

15. National Center for Education Statistics. (2013). *The nation's report card: Trends in academic progress 2012* (NCES 2013-456). Washington, DC: U.S. Department of Education, Institute of Education Sciences. Retrieved from https://nces.ed.gov/nationsreportcard/subject/publications/main2012/pdf/2013456.pdf

16. Foster, T. D., et al. (2016). Fathers' and mothers' home learning environments and children's early academic outcomes. *Reading and Writing 29*(9), 1845–1863.

17. Bergen, E., et al. (2017). Why are home literacy environment and children's reading skills associated? What parental skills reveal. *Reading Research Quarterly 52*(2), 147–160.

18. Ozturk, G., Hill, S., & Yates, G. (2016). Family context and five-year-old children's attitudes toward literacy when they are learning to read. *Reading Psychology 37*(3), 487–509.

19. Office of English Language Acquisition (OELA). (2007). *The Growing number of limited English proficient students 1995–96, 2005–06*. Washington, DC: Office of English Language Acquisition.

20. Swan, M., & Smith, B. (2001). *Learner English: A teacher's guide to interference and other problems*. London: Cambridge University Press.

21. Escamilla, E. (2007, October 8). Considerations for literacy coaches in classrooms with English language learners. Literacy Coaching Clearinghouse. Retrieved from https://eric.ed.gov/?id=ED530358

22. Roller, C. (1996). *Variability not disability*. Newark, DE: International Reading Association.

23. Hughes, J. P. (1962). *The Science of language*. New York, NY: Random House, p. 26.

24. Labov, W. (1970). *The Study of nonstandard English*. Urbana, IL: National Council of Teachers of English, p. 14.

25. Cole, N. S. (1997). *The ETS Gender Study: How females and males perform in educational settings (executive summary)*. Princeton, NJ: Educational Testing Service, p. 26; Zambo, D., & Brozo, W. G. (2009). *Bright beginnings for boys: Engaging young boys in active literacy*. Newark, DE: International Reading Association.

26. Harris & Sipay, 1990.

27. Florence, M. D., Asbridge, M., & Veugelers, P. J. (2008). Diet quality and academic performance. *Journal of School Health, 78,* 209–215; Satcher, D. (2008). School Wellness and the Imperative of Leadership. In *Progress or promises? What's working for and against healthy schools: An Action for Healthy Kids report*. Skokie, IL: Action for Healthy Kids, pp. 8–10.

28. Medina, J. (2009). *Brain rules*. New York, NY: Pear Press.

29. Scrimshaw, N. S. (1968, March 16). Infant malnutrition and adult learning. *Saturday Review*, pp. 64–66, 84.

30. Chernick, E. (1980, November). Effect of the Feingold Diet on reading achievement and classroom behavior. *The Reading Teacher, 34,* 171–173.

31. Opitz, M. F. (2010). *Literacy lessons to get kids fit and healthy*. New York, NY: Scholastic.

32. Harris & Sipay, 1990, p. 347.

33. Gambrell, L., Palmer, B., Codling, R., & Mazzoni, S. (1996). Assessing Motivation to Read. *The Reading Teacher, 49*(7), 518–533.

34. Harter, S. (1982). The perceived competence scale for children. *Child development 53*(1), 87–97.

35. Paris, S. G., & Carpenter, R. D. (2004). Children's motivation to read. In J. V. Hoffman & D. L. Schallert (Eds.), *The texts in elementary classrooms*. Mahwah, NJ: Erlbaum, pp. 61–85.

36. Lipson, M. Y., & Wixson, K. K. (2003). *Assessment and instruction of reading and writing difficulty: An interactive approach*, 3rd ed. Boston, MA: Allyn and Bacon.

37. Paris, S. G., Olson, G., & Stevenson, H. (Eds.). (1983). *Learning and motivation in the classroom*. Hillsdale, NJ: Erlbaum.

Chapter 3
Classroom Assessments

Pressmaster/Shutterstock

 ## Chapter Outline

∨ Learning Outcomes

After reading this chapter, you should be able to . . .

3.1 Describe a "big picture" view of assessment, putting measurement and evaluation in the proper place.

3.2 State the three guiding questions teachers can use to select the appropriate informal assessment tool, and provide one example.

3.3 Discuss the pros and cons of using performance-based assessment.

3.4 Explain how to use portfolios as a part of a diagnostic reading approach.

3.5 Discuss how a teacher using a diagnostic approach can use observation.

3.6 Explain what anecdotal records are and how they can be made objective.

3.7 Describe some of the various kinds of checklists and explain how a rating scale can be used with a checklist.

3.8 Explain what a teacher using a diagnostic approach can learn by using interviews, interest inventories, and attitude surveys.

Scenario

Teachers Talking

Read the following conversation overheard in the faculty lounge:

MS. ANDERSON: I don't know what to do with Hunter. His behavior is driving me crazy.

MR. DALE: Why? What does he do?

MS. ANDERSON: What doesn't he do? He's forever getting up from his seat. He can't seem to sit still for a moment. He's always disturbing someone. If there is any commotion in the room, you can be sure Hunter is there.

MR. DALE: Have you spoken to his parents?

MS. ANDERSON: Yes, but they say they don't see the same kind of behavior at home. So they feel that it's something related to school. I've just about had it.

MR. DALE: I know that I had another student who acted just like Hunter, and the behavior was making my life miserable. In my master's course at college, we discussed observation techniques to learn about student behavior. I decided to try it, and I was surprised how observation made me aware of how broad my judgments about Susan were. Would you like to see what data I collected?

What kind of data do you think Mr. Dale showed Ms. Anderson?

Assessment: The Big Picture

Assessment

Assessment is a term with powerful potential. In everyday language, it means simply figuring out what is going on. For example, when we walk into a room full of people, we assess the situation. When we are looking at buying a home, we might assess its condition or location. When someone bumps our car fender, we get out and assess the damage. Assessment in school must preserve some of this everyday meaning. Assessment helps teachers figure out what students know, what skills they have, what they can do, and whether they are learning anything. Because knowing someone else's mind can be tricky, instruments of measurement and evaluation exist to help teachers gain confidence in what they know about readers' cognitive and affective processes.

The terms *assessment*, *measurement*, *evaluation*, and *test* are often treated as synonyms. But they are not. This chapter is a chance for teachers reclaim the assessment process and make it work to the advantage of readers and teachers alike. We show these four terms as a hierarchy, with assessment as the primary category, measurement and evaluation underneath, and testing connecting to both measurement and evaluation. (See Figure 3.1.) We intend for Figure 3.1 to show that having knowledgeable questions about readers is the starting point for good assessments. These questions lead to measurement, or collection of evidence. Tests are common measurement instruments. Teachers must then evaluate the evidence, interpret the evaluation, and then check their interpretation against their original assessment questions.

Measurement

Measurement is how educators obtain evidence. It is parallel to evaluation in the hierarchy because without measurement, there would be no evidence to evaluate and interpret. The educational community leans heavily on metaphors of scales and rulers. These are literally instruments of measurement. Once we have the evidence from putting something on a scale or laying down a tape measure, then we can begin to evaluate what its weight or length means. Usually when we are measuring something, we have a desired "fit" in mind, a plan or purpose—that is, we don't usually just walk around weighing and measuring things for no apparent reason. It should be so with educational

Figure 3.1 Attitude Survey

Statement	Rating				
	Strongly Agree	**Agree**	**Unsure**	**Disagree**	**Strongly Disagree**
My friends think I am a good reader					
I read well compared to my friends					
When I read a difficult part in a book I usually figure it out					
When I read by myself, I usually understand what I read					
I am a good reader					
I worry about what other people think about my reading					
When a teacher asks me a question about what I am reading I can usually answer					
Reading does not frustrate me					
Reading is easy for me					
When people talk about stories, I like to talk about my ideas					
I sometimes read things that are for older readers					
When I read out loud I am not usually nervous					
TOTAL NUMBER OF MARKS IN EACH COLUMN					

assessment. First, we must decide *what* we want to learn about each reader; second, we must consider *why* those questions are important; and third, we must decide *how* to answer those questions. Any tool used in answering questions about readers' behaviors, cognition, and affects is part of measurement. Measurement instruments are the answer to the question of the "how" of assessment. In tests—one type of measurement instrument—the emphasis is often on readers using a question/answer sequence to demonstrate what they know. We find this narrow emphasis unfortunate. There are other important values in assessment which we discuss throughout this chapter.

The positive values of measurement outweigh the negative connotations often associated with tests alone. Measurement is useful for diagnostic, review, and predictive purposes. For example, a cloze test can be used to determine how much students use vocabulary knowledge to help them decode unfamiliar words; a response journal can be used to review engagement and motivation; and a listening comprehension test can be used to predict potential for reading comprehension. Measurement can be used as a motivating technique for students to help them self-monitor their own progress, and measurement also provides a basis for discussing achievement with families, teachers, administrators, and other community members. Through ongoing measurement, teachers are also able to reevaluate the strengths and weaknesses in their own pedagogy, their repertoire of teaching methods.

Diagnostic measurement means we puzzle out what data are needed and then figure out how to gather these data. When planning to teach an individual student, tests are only a part of the assessment picture because they may not provide the kind of evidence we want or need. For example, if we want to know whether a past traumatic experience affects a child's reading performance, we might use test data, but we would also use our own observations and reports from counseling and family conferences, and listen to students in regular conferences. All of these latter techniques are less easy to evaluate in a numeric score, but are more likely to provide answers to the actual questions we value about a specific reader. Evaluation in this case simply means working to achieving a satisfactory answer to the valued question about the reader.

For measurement to be an effective part of the evaluative process, teachers must know varied instruments and be able to select them, administer them, and interpret the results. Such instruments include standardized tests and teacher-made tests, as well as direct observations of student behavior. Further, student self-reports are also necessary in order to collect data for valid evaluations.

Evaluation

Evaluation is the interpretation of evidence gathered through measurement. When we have gathered evidence with measurement instruments, we return to the assessment question "What do we want to know?" and see whether the evidence provides a reasonable answer. The scores on a test are one type of evidence, but they mean nothing in and of themselves. They have to be interpreted with respect to *why* we used the test as a measurement in the first place and *what* we hoped to learn about our students. When we write our own tests, we can track student responses back to individual items and also look for trends across items. By contrast, standardized test authors usually keep both test items and student responses private, providing general results within a category of items. Teachers must rely on the testing company to score the test and evaluate the results. The main benefits and risks of standardized tests will be discussed in Chapter 5. Classroom assessment is discussed first because classroom assessments are the main means for answering questions about individual readers throughout the school year. In particular, diagnostic assessment depends on using a variety of classroom-based tools designed to answer typical questions teachers and readers have about learning to read. Classroom assessments give teachers the opportunity to own the processes of measurement and evaluation when they select the appropriate tool for the job.

Evaluation, one of the roles of a good teacher, is to interpret evidence gathered through assessment. Basic principles of assessment design are supposed to give teachers confidence when interpreting evidence. The *teacher* is the one who makes the diagnosis; no single test asks and answers the specific questions teachers have about individual readers. Once again, the knowledgeable professional is at the core of decisions that will lead to reading improvement.

Tests

A **test** is one way to provide evidence for evaluation. We use tests when other classroom instruments do not give us confidence in what we know about our students. For example, we might have rich classroom discussions about a book but still worry that only some students comprehend. A test is a way to give each individual a chance to provide evidence of knowledge. If previously silent students respond well on written tests, confidence in their knowledge increases.

We might need the confidence of evaluation when trying a new method or program, when our school is compared with other schools, or when our country is compared with other countries. We might have doubts when we compare one student's skill with other students' skills or with what is typical for an age grade. A variety of assessment methods, including tests, can inspire confidence in our evaluation of students' knowledge, abilities, and performance. One of the best reasons for using tests is that good test design provides confidence that responses represent students' thinking. The best reason to go beyond tests is to increase confidence that we understand how students apply knowledge in authentic reading and writing situations. Teachers taking a diagnostic approach will ask what they want to know, why they want to know that, and how they can best learn this. The next section provides a guide for understanding these situations.

Diagnostic Questions

Teachers using a diagnostic approach need to ask and answer three diagnostic questions related to reading assessment: What do I want to know? Why do I want to know that? How can I best discover this information? In this chapter, we focus on asking and answering these questions using various classroom-based assessment tools. These tools are more open to bias than standardized measurement tools presented in Chapter 5. But in many cases, subjective understanding gained by someone close to a student is exactly what is needed to find the best path forward for each student. Classroom-based assessment tools provide a foundation for interpreting and better understanding test data; they help explain why and how students performed as they did on a test. Your specific purpose (the *what* and *why* questions) guides your selection of the assessment tools you actually use (the *how* question). In Table 3.1, we provide an overview of classroom-based assessment techniques reviewed in this chapter. Chapters 4–13 will feature a wide range of classroom-based assessment tools appropriate for answering diagnostic questions.

Authentic Assessment

The assessment techniques outlined in this chapter all rely on authentic reading experiences and situations. Whereas test situations are contrived and separated from real-world experience, we can learn much about readers through "direct, 'authentic' assessment of student performance."[1]

In a reading diagnosis and improvement program, looking at both the cognitive and affective characteristics of students is important. Attitudes and interests will affect what readers learn and whether they learn because these affective characteristics of readers determine effort and persistence. Unfortunately, many students are not choosing to read. The reasons for this lack of interest in reading are varied. Understanding students' attitudes and interests enables teachers to teach for motivation and to help

Table 3.1 Authentic and Performance-Based Assessment Techniques

What Do I Want to Know?	Why Do I Want to Know?	How Can I Best Discover?
Do the children use what they know about reading regardless of what they read?	To show competence in reading, children need to show that they can use what they have learned. I need to see if they can do this, and if they cannot, I need to determine why.	Performance Assessment Project
Do children show growth over time?	Children continue to grow as readers, and I need to provide evidence of that growth. I want to be able to show the kind of progress the children are making.	Portfolio
How do children perform in a variety of contexts?	Watching children as they perform a variety of reading-related tasks is an excellent way for me to see firsthand what they are able to do. I can also develop intuitions about what they do well and what might need additional work. I can use these observations as a way of selecting additional reading assessments that will help me to better understand the children.	Direct Observation
How can I remember everything I see when observing?	Watching children can help me to learn more about them, but I simply cannot remember everything. I also need a way to document what I have actually observed as a way of showing others that I have detected a pattern of behavior that sheds light on a student's performance.	Anecdotal Record
What specific behaviors do the children show when they complete reading tasks?	There are a variety of behaviors that children need to exhibit on their way to becoming accomplished readers. I need to determine which they show and which they need to learn, and to be able to document this in a quick and clean way. I can then use the results to plan appropriate instruction.	Checklists
How do the children view reading?	Faulty perceptions of what it means to read can inhibit reading growth. Uncovering the children's views can help me to see which are correct and which need to be added to or altered.	Informal Student Interview
What reading strategies do children think they use when they are reading?	Good readers use a variety of strategies to assist them as they try to comprehend a text. Relying on one or two strategies to the exclusion of others can prevent growth. I need to know which strategies readers do and do not use so that I can help all the children to develop a full array of strategies.	Informal Student Interview
What do children like to read?	We are more prone to read if we are interested in the reading material. Identifying the children's interests can help me to select texts for instruction and inclusion in the classroom library. I can also use interests to group children in different ways, making it possible for them to work with a variety of peers.	Interest Inventories
How do children feel about themselves as readers?	Feelings of self-efficacy play a big part in reading success. I need to know how students feel about themselves as readers. Then I can identify children who view themselves as failures and work to help them gain confidence as competent readers.	Projective Strategies Reading Autobiography
What kinds of attitudes do the children have about reading?	Attitude has a big impact on reading. Identifying attitudes will help me to see if I need to help a child develop a more positive outlook, which will make reading a more enjoyable experience. Children with a positive attitude are more likely to attempt reading.	Primary Reading Survey Reading Attitude Survey for Grades 3 and Up

students shape their attitudes toward reading. In one recent study, researchers reported that comprehension was impacted more by intrinsic motivation to read than by the amount students read.[2] Affective concerns impacted valued outcomes even more than practice with reading did. Students can provide valid information about their own learning that cannot be gleaned from other sources.

Student Interviews

The easiest way to learn about students' likes or dislikes is to ask them. Teachers should set up special times during the school day to meet with students for conferences, which can include an **informal interview.** Doing so helps teachers build rapport with students, as well as yielding important information about them.

Another purpose for interviewing students who are having difficulty with reading is to gain insight into how they perceive reading.[3] Because perception determines behavior, a change in behavior follows rather than precedes perceptions. To change reading behaviors, the students' perceptions of reading must also change. Thus, gaining an insight into students' existing perceptions assists the teacher in better understanding why students function as they do. Researchers recently found that many students are not largely aware of their self-perceptions of reading. This may mean the stigma of reading poorly does not impact overall self-perception of competence for all students the way adults might predict for them. But it also may mean that many students are not given direct opportunities to self-assess their own growth, proficiency, strengths, and weaknesses in reading.[4]

A third purpose for interviewing students is to enable them to explore their own reading behaviors—to help them understand themselves. In talking about their reading, students become more aware of how they perceive and approach it. Self-awareness is essential because it is the first step toward change. Thus, becoming aware of their perceptions about reading can help students realize whether these perceptions are accurate and, if not, which additional aspects need to be incorporated into their understanding of the reading process. For example, the first three questions in Figure 3.2 are designed to elicit students' perceptions of their purposes for reading. A student who responds "I'm trying to understand the story" or "Get the words right so I'll understand the book" is showing a perception that emphasizes comprehension.

In addition, becoming more conscious of the strategies that they presently use in reading may, with teacher guidance, lead students to see there are additional strategies

Figure 3.2 Student Interview Protocol

Name: _____

Student Interview

1. What is the most important thing about reading?

   _____

   _____

2. When you are reading, what are you trying to do?

   _____

   _____

3. What is reading?

   _____

   _____

4. When you come to a word you don't know, what do you do?

   _____

   _____

5. Do you think it's important to read every word correctly? Why? Why not?

   _____

   _____

6. What makes a person a good reader?

   _____

   _____

7. Do you think good readers ever come to a word they don't know? If yes, what do you think they do?

   _____

   _____

they may need to learn. Once aware of these options, students can decide which strategies to use and when to use them to ensure comprehension. In other words, they can exercise control over their cognitive actions.

Figure 3.2 is an example of a protocol that can reveal both perceptions of reading and strategies used in reading. The first three questions focus on perceptions of reading, whereas the last four are designed to elicit strategies used in reading.

The following are some suggestions for managing interviews:

1. Count on spending about 10 minutes for each interview.

2. Because the interviews require one-to-one attention, plan independent activities for the other children to minimize interruptions.

3. Interview children more than once. You might consider interviewing students at the beginning, middle, and end of the year, making note of shifts in their perceptions of reading and the repertoire of strategies they use on the form shown in Figure 3.3.

Figure 3.3 Student Interview Summary

Name: _____   Interviewer: _____

Grade: _____ Age: _____ School: _____

Beginning of School Year   ***Date:*** _____

Perceptions of Reading   Strategies Used

Middle of School Year   ***Date:*** _____

Perceptions of Reading   Strategies Used

End of School Year   ***Date:*** _____

Perceptions of Reading   Strategies Used

4. Interpret the responses. Do students primarily focus on reading as a meaning-seeking activity? Do the responses primarily focus on reading as being an act of pronouncing words with no attention to their meanings? Do the responses focus on something other than understanding of words? Do the responses show that the reader has a limited set of strategies?

5. Make a list of the strategies students mention for identifying difficult words. Some strategies they might mention are: Sound it out, ask, use other words, break it into parts, skip it, use a dictionary, spell it, wait for the teacher, and stop reading.

The following are some suggestions for using information revealed from the interviews:

1. Use what you discover to plan appropriate instruction. For example, if students comment that the purpose of reading is to say the words, prepare and teach lessons that emphasize the meaning aspect. Such a lesson might begin like this: "Today, I want to teach you another way of figuring out words. When you come to a word you cannot pronounce, say 'blank' and keep reading until the end of the sentence. When you get to the end of the sentence, go back to the word that caused you some problems and ask yourself what word might make sense that looks like the word that is actually printed."

2. Consider using a whole-class brainstorming session to create a chart showing what to do to gain pronunciation of a word and what to do to gain the meaning of a word when reading.

3. If the interviews as a whole seem to indicate that students lack understanding about what good readers do when they read, create a list and post it in the classroom.

Interest Inventories

The purpose of an **interest inventory** is to help teachers learn about their students' likes and dislikes. In this book, we are particularly invested in finding out about students' likes or dislikes so that we can use this information to help stimulate them to read.

Interest inventories usually employ statements, questions, or both to obtain information. The statement or questionnaire method enables the teacher to gain a great amount of information in a relatively short period of time. Teachers who have good rapport with their students will be able to gain the trust of their students and can often get them to speak more candidly. Before administering the inventory, teachers can discuss its purpose and ask students to speak frankly.

Teachers can use a checklist type of questionnaire, where they read the question aloud and the children mark the appropriate space. Figure 3.4 shows an example. As with other instruments, teachers use an interest inventory to answer basic assessment questions: "What do I want to know?" and "Why do I want to know it?" When the inventory is finished, it should be treated like other data or information and used to make instructional plans. Using the results is essential. In the case of interest inventories, the results should first be used to gather reading material that matches students' declared interests. Then these books should be matched to readers to see how well they engage with the books. Do not be worried if the earliest books are not a perfect match. Many students need time, teaching and much exposure to a wide variety of books before they find multiple books with which they can engage as readers. Remember that readers are people! They like to be asked what they want, and they thrive on having someone listen to them. Readers will refine what they say about their interests in follow-up conferences once they learn you are on the hunt with them for engaging books!

Enhanced eText
Video Example 3.1. Reader Attitude Survey.

In this video, a teacher administers a survey on reading attitudes, with the student filling in the results. Consider which questions are likely to yield useful information, and which questions are leading, or which have a socially appropriate answer different from actual attitudes. https://www.youtube.com/watch?v=HENQoNZlQv0

Enhanced eText
Teacher Resource:

Primary Attitude Survey What Kinds of Books do you Like?

Figure 3.4 Interest Inventory

Name _____ Date _____

Please ✔ all that apply!

1. Do you like to read?

   _____ yes   _____ sometimes   _____ no

2. What kinds of texts do you like to read? (✔ all that apply.)

   _____ animals   _____ science   _____ true stories   _____ series books

   _____ make-believe   _____ biographies   _____ science fiction   _____ game manuals

   _____ mysteries   _____ poetry   _____ humor   _____ how to

   _____ myths   _____ folktales   _____ plays   _____ scary stories

   _____ riddles/jokes _____ picture books _____ chapter books   _____ other

3. Which do you prefer?

   _____ hard copy text   _____ electronic text

4. Who is your favorite author?

5. What is your favorite book?

6. What book would you like to read?

7. What magazines do you like to read?

8. Which do you like best?

   _____ hardcover books   _____ softcover books

   Why?

9. What helps you to choose a book or other text to read?

Enhanced eText
Teacher Resource:
Interest Inventory

Enhanced eText
Video Example 3.2. Reading Interest Inventories.

In this video, a kindergarten teacher works with a small group to apply the results of interest inventory assessment. https://www.youtube.com/watch?v=wiWHKKk3RO0

Reading Attitude Surveys

Attitude has a significant impact on reading. This should come as no surprise if we take a minute to think about ourselves as readers. When we have a positive outlook on our ability to read, we are more likely to read because we enjoy it, and more likely to be successful. We are also more likely to comprehend any given text when we have a positive attitude about it. The inverse is true for negative attitudes.

Teachers can uncover student attitudes by using an attitude survey. Figure 3.5 is a reading attitude survey intended for primary grades, and Figure 3.6 is for intermediate grades.

Figure 3.5 Primary Reading Survey

Name: _____

How do you feel when:

	😊	😐	🙁
1. your teacher reads a story to you?			
2. your class has reading time?			
3. you can read with a friend?			
4. you read out loud to your teacher?			
5. you read out loud to someone at home?			
6. someone reads to you at home?			
7. someone gives you a book as a present?			
8. you read a book to yourself at home?			

How do you think:

9. your teacher feels when you read out loud?			
10. your family feels when you read out loud?			

How do you feel about how well you can read?

Make this face look the way you feel.

Figure 3.6 Reading Attitude Survey for Grades 3 and Up

Name: _____

Directions: The 20 statements that follow will be read to you. After each statement is read, circle the letter that best describes how you feel about that statement. Your answers will not be graded because there are no right or wrong answers. Your feeling about each statement is what's important.

SA = Strongly Agree   A = Agree   U = Undecided
D = Disagree   SD = Strongly Disagree

SA A U D SD   1. Reading is for learning but not for enjoyment.

SA A U D SD   2. Money spent on books is well spent.

SA A U D SD   3. There is nothing to be gained from reading books.

SA A U D SD   4. Books are a bore.

SA A U D SD   5. Reading is a good way to spend spare time.

SA A U D SD   6. Sharing books in class is a waste of time.

SA A U D SD   7. Reading turns me on.

SA A U D SD   8. Reading is only for students seeking good grades.

SA A U D SD   9. Books aren't usually good enough to finish.

SA A U D SD   10. Reading is rewarding to me.

SA A U D SD   11. Reading becomes boring after about an hour.

SA A U D SD   12. Most books are too long and dull.

SA A U D SD   13. Free reading doesn't teach anything.

SA A U D SD   14. There should be more time for free reading during the school day.

SA A U D SD   15. There are many books that I hope to read.

SA A U D SD   16. Books should not be read except for class requirements.

SA A U D SD   17. Reading is something I can do without.

SA A U D SD   18. A certain amount of summer vacation should be set aside for reading.

SA A U D SD   19. Books make good presents.

SA A U D SD   20. Reading is dull.

Source: Based on Johns, J. L., & Lenski, S. D.(2014) Improving reading: Strategies and resources, 3rd ed. Kendall Hunt Publishing Company.

Observation

Direct observation is an essential part of any reading program, and it is especially helpful in diagnosing reading strengths and needs. Observation is also useful for evaluation because it helps teachers become aware of students' attitudes and interests. It is one thing for students to say that they enjoy reading, but quite another for them to actually read. Through observation, teachers can observe many reading-related behaviors, such as whether students are voluntarily choosing to read in their free time and how they approach silent reading, oral reading, selecting texts, completing assignments, and writing in response to reading. Most often, the best method for determining whether students have learned something is to observe whether they are actually using what they have been taught. Moreover, watching children in a variety of contexts reveals additional information not provided by tests, surveys, and questionnaires.[5]

For observations to be of value, teachers must be as objective as possible and avoid making premature generalizations about a student's behavior. For example, by observing that Sharon on one or two occasions is reading mystery stories, Sharon's teacher might conclude that Sharon likes mysteries. This may be so, but it may be that she is just trying them out. Sharon may actually like only a few mystery writers, and she may read only one or two mysteries before moving on to something else. Here are some suggestions on how to make observations as objective and useful as possible:

1. Use anecdotal records (observed behavior without interpretations) and checklists to record observations. (See the next two sections.)

2. Observe the student over an extended period of time before making any inferences about the student's behavior.

3. Avoid projecting feelings or attitudes onto the student's behavior.

4. Use observations in conjunction with other measurement techniques, including those that allow students to report about themselves.

5. Allow someone else to observe.

6. Make sure that only observed behavior is recorded and record it immediately, or as soon as possible.

7. Look for a pattern of behavior before making any inferences about behavior.

8. Remember that anecdotal records and checklists do not reveal causes of the observed behaviors; they only help to identify patterns of behavior from which a teacher can try to deduce the existence of possible strengths and needs.

9. Note the date and time on all observations.

As valuable and powerful as observation is, for some teachers, it can seem overwhelming. There are so many skills that teachers need to observe accurately that they hardly know where to begin. For example, oral reading can help a teacher to observe much about a child's reading ability. Questions such as the following can guide the observation:

- Does the child read for meaning?
- What does the child do when meaning is not maintained?
- How well can the child retell what was read?
- Does the child read with a sense of meaning, expression, and fluency?

Focusing on all the possible questions through observation at one time can seem daunting. When teachers consider the unique needs of English language learners, the task may appear even more complex.

Our suggestion is this: Less is more. That is, rather than trying to use all questions at once, choose one question that best fits your purpose. What is it that you want to know most about this student? Once you have determined this, you can record your observations on a form such as the one shown in Figure 3.7.

Another way to lessen any anxiety related to observation is to use **anecdotal records**, a record of *observed behavior* that is as objective as possible. When recording observed behavior, make every attempt to put down exactly what has taken place *as soon as possible.* Record the date and time of the event, as well as an interpretation of the observed behavior; however, the teacher's interpretation should be put in brackets or set off in some way to avoid confusion with the actual observed behavior. Recording and observing the student over an extended period of time is best. Look for a pattern of

Figure 3.7 Observation Guide

Class Observation Form	
Focal Question: _____	
Date: _____	
Name of Student	**Notes**

behavior, rather than making conclusions based on one observation. Figure 3.8 shows one example of an anecdotal record.

What information should be recorded? This is a difficult question to answer, and can be overwhelming for any teacher. Because teachers using this method record everything that happens, anecdotal records sometimes capture unusual behavior. For example, you might observe a student taking a break from reading and staring into space. Making a note that the student was staring and then overinterpreting the staring could lead to a false assumption about the learner. However, recording common behaviors *over an extended period of time* can be very helpful. Consider the following scenario.

Scenario

Mr. Jackson Checks and Writes

Mr. Jackson has a reading checklist for each student, and after each reading lesson and at other appropriate times, he checks off what he has observed. To supplement his checklist, Mr. Jackson also employs anecdotal information. Whenever he notices anything unusual, he records the observed behavior. For example, yesterday Joshua started a fight with his best friend, and then for the rest of the day, he refused to do any work. Mr. Jackson made note of this.

Figure 3.8 Rachael's Anecdotal Record

Strategies Implemented	Result
Spelling	
3/11 Start a list of trouble words and tape to desk. These become no excuse words.	3/11 She refers to list and keeps it out. Because of CSAP we didn't do any writing.
3/17 Go through published pieces and find words she wants to use as spelling words. (Find 5)	3/17 She said in a conference "I was writing and noticed I spelled **her** and it didn't look right. I meant it to be **here.** The list helped and I know that her is **her** not **here.**"
3/19 Do **look, say, cover, write,** and **check** practice.	3/17 We added 3 words to her list (their, there, and white).
3/23 Had her look through writing and check to see all no excuse words were spelled correctly.	3/19 She was able to do the list she has on her desk. She is also working on definitions.
	3/23 No words misspelled from her list.
Sentence Starters	
3/17 Conference with her about past writings and discuss how authors start sentences in different ways. Ask her to try to vary her sentences as she writes today.	3/17 I showed her examples of her writing, and we went over strengths and weaknesses. I had her read a past piece where she repeated the beginning. I had her identify and highlight what was repeating. We took 1 paragraph and rewrote to change the sentences.
3/22 We focused on one sentence beginner and changed old sentences from past writing into new ones (used Writer's Express).	3/22 Sample two shows how she was working on using introductory phrases.
	3/23 Shared with me that she noticed an old piece was too repetitive. She changed the sentence beginnings as she typed.

Mr. Jackson also observed and noted that Joshua rested his head on his desk during reading.

1/9 Joshua puts head on desk—reading period

1/13 Joshua puts head on desk—reading period

1/16 Joshua puts head on desk—reading period

1/20 Joshua puts head on desk—reading period

1/23 Joshua puts head on desk—reading period

1/27 Joshua puts head on desk—reading period

Joshua's behavior of putting his head on the desk has become such a normal occurrence that Mr. Jackson could have overlooked it. Only by recording when Joshua put his head on the desk could Mr. Jackson see that it was always during a reading period. By recording the dates, Mr. Jackson could check to see what kinds of reading lessons were involved. It may be that Joshua was tired or sleepy, but that is most unlikely. It is more probable that by checking further, Mr. Jackson will find that Joshua is bored because the work is too easy for him or that he is frustrated because the work is too hard for him. It may be that Joshua cannot do sustained silent reading because of an eye problem. Joshua's resting behavior may be related to any number of factors. The point is that Mr. Jackson would not be aware of these problems had he not recorded what appeared to be "common" behavior.

Although there are no specific guidelines about what should or should not be recorded, teachers should record a variety of types of behavior, including physical, verbal, and social. As with any other assessment, the focus of observation should be "What do I want to know?" and "Why do I want to know it?" However, alert teachers who are aware of individual differences among students in their classes will recognize situations that warrant recording.

Here are some examples:

1. Bela always seems to want to go to the restroom. Recording when and how often she goes may point to a physiological problem or an emotional problem, or it may be that she wants to "escape" from a certain classroom situation.

2. Michael is always causing disruptions in class. Recording when Michael acts up will help to determine whether there is a pattern. Are there any immediate antecedents to his acting up? It may be that causing disruptions is Michael's way of avoiding reading. What is he avoiding? Is he bored or is he frustrated?

Remember that observations and the resultant anecdotal record do not explain causes of behavior. Observation is a technique for gathering data; it helps teachers learn more about the behavior of students. When used with other assessment techniques discussed in this chapter, as well as test data (see Chapter 5), anecdotal records can help teachers hypothesize about causes.

Performance Assessment

Performance assessment is often used as a synonym for authentic assessment because it calls on learners to show understanding by completing tasks like those "required in the instructional environment."[6] These demonstrations are sometimes documented in a *portfolio* (i.e., a selection of the student's work that is meant to show learning progress over time) or by having students complete a project. For both portfolios and projects, a scoring system (i.e., rubric) is used to help teachers determine how well students have achieved specified standards. The *rubric* is a set of criteria that assigns value to students' performance in certain areas. Students are usually given these rubrics—or invited to help construct one—in advance of the performance task so they can see how they will be evaluated. They can use this rubric as a guide when preparing for performance. Figure 3.9 shows a sample rubric. As you can see, certain criteria are established, but the teacher must still evaluate how well students have met the criteria. In other words, rubrics can help to reduce subjectivity, but they cannot completely do away with it. In fact, we would say that rubrics have "objective subjectivity" because the rubric creates an objective standard, but humans must still use subjective judgments when scoring and giving feedback on the rubric.

Although performance assessments are time-intensive, they are an excellent way to learn about students' reading behaviors, and they must be used in the type of reading diagnosis and improvement program we describe and explain in this text. As a result of watching students complete a task, we can note strengths and needs, and design tomorrow's instruction accordingly. Authentic, performance-based assessment is based on a set of assumptions, which include

1. Authentic reading contexts are appropriate for answering assessment questions about individual learners.

2. Learners are active participants who should be made aware of their growth and taught to value it.

3. Teachers decide what to teach as they evaluate and interpret assessment results.

4. Both the end product and the means of arriving there (i.e., the process) are important.

5. A body of evidence from many sources needs to be collected, interpreted, and used over time.

Figure 3.9 Rubric for Writing to Learn

Criteria / Quality	3	2	1
Ideas & Content	Clear and focused. Provides several relevant examples from the text and own experiences. Shows own thinking about the topic.	Beginning to develop the paper. Some examples. Own thinking is starting to become evident but full explanation is lacking.	No real focus. Few examples are cited and original thinking is not evident.
Organization	Paper written with an introduction, body, and conclusion. Written in format as explained in class.	Paper has two of the three: introduction, body, conclusion. Written in the format as explained in class.	Paper has one of the three: introduction, body, conclusion. The format explained in class is not used.
Voice	Speaks to the reader; shows attention to audience.	Beginning to speak to the reader but still rather general; not always aware of audience.	Passive; writing appears distant; lack of attention to audience.
Print Conventions	Makes use of all print conventions: spelling, grammar, punctuation.	Most print conventions are used but occasional misspellings and incorrect grammar and/or punctuation are evident.	Little attention to print conventions as evidenced by misspelled words, incorrect grammar, and/or misuse of punctuation.
Legibility	Neat—easy to read. One side of paper is used and there are no crossouts.	Semilegible—can be read but takes some effort. One side of paper is used; occasional crossouts	Sloppy—hard to read. Both sides of the paper are used and there are several crossouts.
Totals	_____	_____	_____

_____ ÷5 = _____ Average score for this assignment

6. Planned instruction should focus first on identifying and using students' strengths to their advantage, especially when addressing identified weaknesses.

7. The teacher is not the only contributor to the body of evidence. Others, including the students themselves, can provide valid input.

Portfolio Assessment

Many educators have promoted portfolios as a way to enhance students' reading and writing, and today portfolios are used for a variety of purposes. However, confusion sometimes exists between the general concept of portfolios and that of portfolio assessment.

Portfolios are primarily a storage system that represents samples of students' reading and writing over a period of time. **Portfolio assessment** deals with some form of evaluation. Portfolio assessment takes place when what has been stored in the portfolio is deemed ready for evaluation in some way. This evaluation is often initiated by the student and usually includes not only self-evaluation but also teacher and peer evaluation. For the evaluation to be effective, the students and teachers must be aware of the criteria used for the assessment.

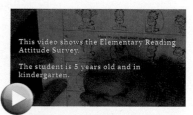

This video shows the Elementary Reading Attitude Survey.

The student is 5 years old and in kindergarten.

Enhanced eText
Video Example 3.3

In this **video clip** the teacher uses portfolios to review past work with his students. Student portfolios help students participate in their own learning, monitor their progress, and gain confidence.

Portfolios can be a powerful tool for a diagnostic approach because they provide teachers with an ongoing record of their students' reading and writing behavior; however, there are several questions that need to be asked and answered in order to get the most from using portfolios. (See Figure 3.10.)

Figure 3.10 Portfolio Checklist

The following questions are those you may wish to pose to yourself as you go about implementing portfolios. Remember that more than one item may be "checked" to answer each question. Also note that your ideas are also important! These are **suggestions!**

How will the portfolio be used?
_____ for student self-reflection
_____ as part of regular school evaluation/report card
_____ at parent conferences
_____ in IEP meetings
_____ in communicating to next year's teacher(s)
_____ in curricular planning
_____ in acknowledging students' accomplishments

How will the portfolio be organized?
_____ for finished pieces only from several subject areas
_____ to show progress from first idea to final copy
_____ to show samples of a week/month/year's work
_____ "best" work only
_____ group work included

How will the items in the portfolio be arranged?
_____ chronologically
_____ by student: from worst to best (reasons stated for each)
_____ by teacher: from worst to best (reasons stated for each)
_____ from beginning of idea to final product
_____ by subject area

What procedures will be used to place items in the portfolio?
_____ select specific times for pulling student work
_____ show students how to select items
_____ pull items that meet established criteria
_____ random

What will the portfolio look like?
_____ two pieces of posterboard stapled or taped together
_____ box or other container (e.g., milk crate with a hanging file for each student)
_____ scrapbook
_____ manila folder or some other large envelope
_____ CD-ROM or DVD

Who will do the evaluating?
_____ teacher
_____ several teachers
_____ student self-evaluation
_____ peer evaluation
_____ parent evaluation

How will the portfolio be evaluated?
_____ number of entries
_____ use of benchmarks or standards
_____ degree of self-reflection
_____ demonstrated improvement from past performances
_____ achievement of preset goals (student, teacher, and/or school)
_____ combination of products, perceptions, reflections

Source: Based on Tom Armstrong. Multiple Intelligence in the Classroom. Alexandria, VA: Association for the Supervision of Curriculum Development (ASCD), 1994.

Portfolios do not give students the skills they need to become good readers and writers. They help teachers gain an idea of the kinds of skills students have and the kinds they need. A close examination can help teachers to design appropriate instruction that will increase student learning.

The use of portfolios can give students more decision-making power. In this sense, they can give more "ownership" to students. They can also be a good way for students, teachers, and parents to see the progression of the students' learning over a period of time.

Checklists

Checklists usually consist of lists of important and typical behaviors that the observer marks as being present or absent. Checklists are a means of systematically and quickly recording a student's behavior. The formats vary. Some are used for a whole class or small group, some are used for individual children, and some use rating scales. Your purpose for using the checklist will determine the one you choose.

Group checklists can be used to follow up on hunches or to find general trends among a whole class of learners. At a glance, a teacher can see who might need help in a specific area and who obviously does not. A group checklist can be helpful in planning instruction for the group as well as for the individual, whereas an individual checklist is useful in assessing the strengths and weaknesses of an individual student only.

For example, to ascertain students' reading interests, I (MO) administer a reading interest inventory to each student. I then compile the results on a class profile, which is shown in Figure 3.11. At a glance, I can see who has common interests. I can use the results to group students when I have them do investigations. I can also use the list to make sure the classroom library reflects the interests of the class.

A teacher who wishes to see a complete profile of a child may prefer the individual checklist. A teacher who wishes to see a profile of the strengths and needs of an entire class for instructional planning will prefer a group checklist. For example, when listening to a student read, I (JE) record miscues on a photocopy of the passage the student is reading. Once all students in the class have read, I note the scores on a class profile. Figure 3.12 shows an individual's performance and Figure 3.13 shows the group's performance.

Regardless of whether a group or individual checklist is used, it should contain an itemized list of behaviors in a domain of reading, a space for dates, and a space for special notes. An example of an individual diagnostic checklist for comprehension in oral and silent reading is shown in Figure 3.14.

Rating Scales

A checklist that uses a **rating scale** is similar to a rubric. A rating scale is used by the teacher to quantify a student's progress. These numbers can also be used to make students aware of their progress in a specific reading domain. Although children may not completely understand reading theory and terms, progress from a 2 to a 3 is easy for them to grasp.

Rating criteria need to be set up beforehand to help teachers give a valid rating to a particular student. For example, during a retelling of a passage, the established expectation for a rating of 3 is that students can identify setting and character traits. Therefore, a student whose retell includes clear statements about story setting and character traits will receive a rating of 3.

Contrastive Analysis Checklists

For English learners, teachers can expect greater variety in home languages as each year passes. In many areas of the United States, multilingual classrooms have been a reality for decades. Refugee and migrant families come to every state and settle in towns and

Figure 3.11 Reading Interest Inventory

Names \ Interests	animals	true stories	science fiction	fantasy	mysteries	stories about people	poetry	funny books	science topics	series books	magazines (sports)	magazines (computers)
Hank	✔									✔	✔	
Meredith			✔		✔							✔
Brenda	✔	✔					✔	✔				
Jay	✔		✔	✔		✔				✔		
Corey		✔				✔						
Kamal			✔						✔			
Jason	✔											
Joel					✔			✔				✔
Holly	✔		✔				✔		✔			
Marni	✔					✔					✔	
Sarah				✔			✔	✔				✔
Derrick		✔	✔	✔					✔			
Ryan												
John		✔			✔					✔		
Sandi										✔		
Robyn	✔									✔		
Annie		✔								✔		
Kurt				✔						✔		
Jeff												✔
Tina			✔	✔								
Hailey	✔								✔			
Bo				✔				✔			✔	
Jake			✔					✔			✔	
Shari								✔			✔	
Jessie	✔							✔		✔		

cities where they can find sponsors, work, and housing. Planning only for bilingual education involving English and Spanish is only a fraction of the answer most teachers will need to teach readers with a diagnostic approach. They must find ways to learn more about each student's home language. A contrastive analysis checklist is a technique for comparing English with any other language in terms of which components of the languages are the same and which are different.

Figure 3.12 Individual Performance Checklist

Name: *Brenda*

Pettranella

Long ago in a country far away lived a little girl named Pettranella. She lived with her father and mother in the upstairs of her grandmother's tall, narrow house.

Other houses just like it lined the street on both sides, and at the end of the street was the mill. All day and all night smoke rose from its great smokestacks and lay like a grey

blanket over the city. It hid the sun and choked the trees, and it ~~withered~~ the flowers that   ll

tried to grow in the window boxes.
     street hand   *un*

One dark winter night when the wind blew cold from the east, Pettranella's father
                               ow

came home with a letter. The family gathered around the table in the warm yellow circle of   l
                             are

the lamp to read it; even the grandmother came from her room downstairs to listen.
             goose   *through*

"It's from Uncle ~~Cris~~ in America," began her father. "He has his homestead ~~there~~ now,   ll
        claring   *cropes*

and is already clearing his land. Someday it will be a large farm growing many ~~crops~~ of   ll
gran

~~grain.~~" And then he read the letter aloud.   l

When he had finished, Pettranella said, "I wish we could go there, too, and live on a homestead."
   Here

Her parents looked at each other, their eyes twinkling with a secret. "We *are* going,"
                              sheep

said her mother. "We are sailing on the very next ship."   l

1.
    couldn't remember anything for
2.
    sure - even w/ prodding
3.

4.

Source: Opitz, M. F. (1998). Flexible grouping in reading: Practical ways to help all students become better readers. New York, NY:Scholastic.Reprinted by permission.

Swan and Smith published a book titled *Learner English* providing contrastive analysis for educators on 22 languages or language groups.[7] Teachers who can expect to serve households with any of these languages should use the lists and descriptions in the book to create checklists to be used across the school. Because not all languages or language groups are presented in the book, creating a contrastive analysis checklist is an important exercise. Many languages spoken by incoming immigrants or refugee populations will not have a pre-made contrastive analysis. Fortunately, the main structural aspects of language can be found easily for all world languages, including reliable online articles in Wikipedia and on linguistics sites such as Omniglot or the Center for Applied Linguistics. We recommend this kind of analysis be done in a meeting with a community/family partner who speaks the home language, and that the results be distributed to the entire school or presented in professional development meetings. This is an excellent opportunity for home–school collaboration, and will help teachers learn the differences between English and home languages and to perceive students' home languages as strengths and assets rather than as deficits and weaknesses.

Phonology checklist. The basic equipment for a phonology checklist starts with a chart of English phonemes. We provide a phoneme chart in International Phonetic Alphabet style (a worldwide alphabet for writing sounds for every world language), with color-coded examples of English words for each phoneme (sound). To do a

> **Enhanced eText**
> **Teacher Resource:**
> IPA 2005 English-Tigrinya Checklist

Figure 3.13 Group Performance Checklist

Level 1 — Pettranella				
Name	**W. Rec. 0–12**	**Comp 3–4**	**P/F**	**Comments**
Hank	10	+2	F	because of comp.
Meredith	4	+4	P	very fluent
Brenda	9	+0	F	looks like comp. needs work but could be expressive voc.
Jay	3	+3	P	fairly fluent; could retell a bit
Corey	3	+4	P	fluent
Kamal	1	+4	P	very fluent
Jason	26	+3	F	applies knowledge of phonics
Jack	4	+0	F	looks like comp. but most likely expression is what needs work
Holly	7	+2	F	very fluent; comp. appears weak
Marni	3	+4	P	very fluent
Sarah	3	+4	P	
Derrick	3	+4	P	
Ryan	1	+3	P	fluent
John	13	+2 1/2	P	—marginal
Sandi	0	+4	P	
Robyn	7	+4	P	fairly fluent
Annie	0	+4	P	
Kristy	1	+4	P	very fluent; good intonation
John	4	+4	P	very fluent
Jeff	0	+4	P	
Zack	21	+2 1/2	F	will need curr. adap. to read this text successfully
Jeff	11	+3	P	fairly fluent
Sara	0	+4	P	
Haitley	0	+3	P	
Tina	0	+4	P	
Kyle	1	+4	P	

Source: From Flexible Grouping in Reading by Michael Opitz. Pub-lished by Scholastic Teaching Resources/Scholastic, Inc. Copyright © 1998, by Michael Opitz. Reprinted by permission.

contrastive analysis of a home language for their students, teachers would need to look up that language's phonemes and use the English chart to check similarities and differences. Tigrinya is a language spoken in Eritrea, Ethiopia, Djibouti, and Somalia. Tens of thousands of refugee and immigrant families from these countries have children in U.S. schools. A phonemes checklist was made using the phonology section of the Wikipedia article on Tigrinya. This work takes time, but is essential for knowing students from many cultures! Information on world languages is widely available on the Internet.

Many difficulties with reading and writing can be assessed when teachers know basics about each reader's home language. For example, Tigrinya does not have either

Figure 3.14 Comprehension Observation Checklist

	Date	Text	Comments
Can put an easy sentence or passage in own words _____			
Makes simple inferences putting in own words _____			
Can explain what just happened _____			
Can do blow-by-blow repetition of a story _____			
Can retell a story in a different context _____			
Self-monitors when lost in a story: with help _____ without help _____			
Asks questions when self-monitoring: with help _____ without help _____			
"Gets" stories that demand "big picture" inferences: with help _____ without help _____			
Looks back at details to "get" stories that demand "big picture" inferences: with help _____ without help _____			
Uses relevant prior knowledge to "get" stories that demand "big picture" inferences: with help _____ without help _____			
Can explain where information to "get" stories came from: with help _____ without help _____			
Anticipates what will happen later in story _____			
Explains reasons for anticipation: with help _____ without help _____			
Makes relevant connections between book and personal experience: with help _____ without help _____			
Can distinguish between relevant and irrelevant personal experience connections: with help _____ without help _____			
Projects self into situations in book: with help _____ without help _____			
Extracts important information from book: with help _____ without help _____			
Can organize information from a book: with help _____ without help _____			
True summary: with help _____ without help _____			

Source: Based on James Erekson and Eliot A. Singer, Observational Checklist for Reading, 1996.

the short-e vowel (as in *bed*) or the short-i vowel (as in *fit*). For Tigrinya students, and for speakers of many other world languages, these two vowels sound almost identical and are hard to tell apart. Students who speak such languages will perform differently on tests of phonics, phonology, and phonemic awareness and may have difficulty perceiving the phonemic differences between words like "bit" and "bet," or "hid" and "head."

Syntax checklist. A checklist of syntax (or grammar) elements also begins with an English checklist. Checklisting the syntactic differences among world languages might revolve around elements of grammar known to be different across many world languages: articles (e.g., *a*, and *the*), pronouns, prepositions, gender, plurals, and possessives.

Syntax element (or grammar)	English	Tigrinya
Articles	a (adjective that describes *any* example of the noun: *a girl*)	No comparable adjective to English "a" to describe *any* example of a noun. 'eta
	the (adjective that describes *a specific* example of the noun: *the girl*)	An adjective like English "the" or "that," describing a specific example of the noun
Gender	English is gendered only in the singular pronouns: e.g., *he, she,* or *it.*	Tigrinya has gendered nouns and adjectives. Inanimate objects are usually neutral (as in English *it).*
Plural	English has two ways of showing plurals, an internal phoneme change (mouse → mice) or a suffix (book → books).	Tigrinya also has these two ways of showing plurals.
Possessive	English shows possession by the use of endings (the horse's mane), and by possessive pronouns (my horse, their horse).	Tigrinya adds word endings to show possession as in the English -s suffix (the horse → the horse's owner). But Tigrinya adds its endings even where English would use a possessive pronoun. (*My horse, their horse,* and *our horse* all have an ending that shows who it belongs to.)

There are many other syntax (grammar) elements one could compare. The point of a contrastive analysis is to use this tool to learn how errors in grammar that impact reading and writing may not be errors at all in the home language. Specific instruction should demonstrate how learners can come to understand English-only structures, or how to compare the ways shared structures are used between English and another home language.

Enhanced eText Application Exercise 3.1: Making Decisions about Assessment

---

Bridge: From Understanding to Assessment

When teachers understand that _____,	then teachers will assess _____.
They must ask and answer questions about each student's reading,	Their own practical knowledge of learning processes vital to reading success. Their own practical knowledge of assessment instruments appropriate for each learning process involved in learning to read.
Tests are contrived and often feel inauthentic to students,	Reading using authentic materials and situations whenever possible.
Tests measure performance at one point in time, whether or not that time is best for the student to demonstrate knowledge.	Students in ongoing ways throughout the school day, inside regular routines of teaching and learning reading.
They can learn much about readers by watching and listening to them read authentic material,	Using rubrics and checklists to match classroom observations of readers to what researchers have learned and published about reading processes and behaviors.
Assessments should gather information on student affects and perceptions,	Using techniques that go beyond cognitive skills and strategies, to include data on attitudes, self-perception, interests, and how students identify with reading.

Revisiting the Opening Scenario

Now that you have had a chance to read about many different instruments for informal assessment, take a look back at the opening scenario in this chapter. Take on the role of Mr. Dale and think about what you would say to Ms. Anderson about how to use different informal assessment techniques to inform her instruction.

Authors' Summary

Before reading our summary statements for each outcome, we suggest you read each outcome and summarize it in your own words.

Once finished, cross-check your response with our brief summary to determine how well you recalled the major points.

3.1 Describe a "big picture" view of assessment, putting measurement and evaluation in the proper place.

- Assessment is the entire process of getting information related to a goal or objective. Measurement involves specific techniques educators use to try to assess—to figure out what students know, what they feel or believe, and what they can do. Evaluation is the process of interpreting what one might learn in assessment and measurement. Consider how these common terms map onto the three guiding questions.

3.2 State the three guiding questions teachers can use to select the appropriate informal assessment tool and provide one example.

- There are numerous assessment techniques to choose from when using a diagnostic approach to assessing, learning, and teaching reading. Asking and answering three guiding questions can help ensure proper selection: What do I want to know? Why do I want to know it? How can I discover this information? Remember that purpose is what determines which tool you will use.

- One example of asking and answering the three questions related to detecting students' attitudes about reading is this:

What kinds of attitudes do children have about reading?	Attitudes impact reading. Identifying those attitudes will help me see whether I need to help a child develop a more positive outlook, which will make reading a more enjoyable and lasting experience.	I can use a reading attitude survey to learn about students' attitudes.

3.3 Discuss the pros and cons of using performance-based assessment.

- Pros for using performance-based assessment include that it requires learners to show understanding of skills by using them in natural contexts. Because rubrics are used to gauge student performance and students see them before they begin to work on their performance, students can use them as a guide and take more ownership for their level of performance.

- Cons for using performance-based assessment include that it can be time-consuming because it is individualized and often requires teacher analysis that extends beyond class time. A second con is that some students have difficulty performing to show their understanding. Last, all students need to be able to work independently when the teacher is assessing individual performances.

3.4 Explain how to use portfolios as a part of a diagnostic reading approach.

- The artifacts that are used to form the contents of portfolios can show teachers the skills students have and those they need to learn. Examining the contents can help teachers design appropriate instruction that capitalizes on the strengths to teach the needs.

- Portfolios can give learners more ownership in their learning if students are permitted to make some decisions about what goes into their portfolio and justify those decisions.

3.5 Discuss how a teacher using a diagnostic approach can use observation.

- Teachers can use observation to observe reading-related behaviors such as how students engage with reading during independent reading time, how they select texts, how they complete assignments, and whether they are using their newly acquired skills across different learning experiences.

- Teachers using a diagnostic approach need to be mindful of making observations as objective as possible. Using checklists and using written notes to document what has been observed are two ways that observation can be made more objective.

3.6 **Explain what anecdotal records are and how they can be made objective.**

- Closely related to observation, anecdotal records are notes of students' observed behaviors. To get the most from them and to keep them objective, teachers need to record specific information, including the date and time of the observation, the observed behavior, and the interpretation of the observed behavior. Another way to best use anecdotal records is by observing students and using anecdotal records to record the observations over time in an effort to look for a pattern of behavior rather than basing an instructional decision on one observed event.

3.7 **Describe some of the various kinds of checklists and explain how a rating scale can be used with a checklist.**

- A checklist is a way to systematically record student behavior. Consequently, there are many different kinds of checklists, each focused on different reading behaviors. Examples include the types of texts students like to read, the strategies students use when reading, and the word analysis skills students use.

- Checklists can reflect both individuals and groups of students. Many times, teachers will collapse information they learn about individual students onto a class matrix to show how the class is functioning as a whole.

- A rating scale is sometimes used as a part of a checklist. The rating scale is used to quantify student performance. Many times, it takes the form of a 1–5 scale, with 1 representing little learning and 5 representing much of it. Scales such as these are easy for students to understand.

- Rating criteria for the rating scales need to be established before the scales are used with students, so that all students will be rated in an objective manner. For example, if the rating of 3 is established to indicate that a student was able to complete a retelling with clear statements related to story setting and character traits, all students who could perform such a retelling would be rated 3.

3.8 **Explain what a teacher using a diagnostic approach can learn by using interviews, interest inventories, and attitude surveys.**

- Talking with students and listening to what they say is an excellent way to learn about students. Interviews, interest inventories, and surveys are all vehicles that can be used to initiate these discussions and leave a record about what students stated. Interviewing students about their perceptions of reading and the strategies they use when reading, for example, can help reveal whether students have misconceptions about what readers really do when they read. Teachers can also learn which strategies students have in their reading repertoires and can broaden them to include others as necessary.

- Interest inventories are tools that enable teachers to learn about what interests students. The information that students share can be used in many different ways. Three ways to use student interests are grouping students by interests for small-group reading, pulling in texts that correspond to their interests for forming a classroom library, and choosing a whole-class topic to investigate.

- Attitude surveys shed light on students' reading attitudes—the degree to which they might like reading and their outlook on it. Once this is understood, teachers can work to help change students who have negative attitudes about reading. They can also make note of the positive associations students have with reading and reinforce them during the school day.

Think About It!

1. Construct a checklist for a specific reading skill to use for instruction; create a rating scale for the checklist; expand it to include other reading behaviors.

2. Use one of the checklists in this chapter to learn more about the behavior of a particular child.

3. Observe a child at various times in class. Record her behavior by using a checklist or anecdotal record.

4. Discuss portfolios with a teacher who uses them.

5. Develop a plan to use portfolios in your class. Discuss how the portfolios would help you diagnose your students' reading strengths and needs.

Websites

- http://rubistar.4teachers.org/index.php

    This site provides the space for teachers to create and store their own rubrics using numerous templates and topics. It also enables users to search a vast store of rubrics by topic, author, or author e-mail.

- http://www.teachervision.fen.com/classroom-management/curriculum-planning/6281.html?detoured=1

    With an entire section on assessment tools, this site provides information on portfolio evaluation, alternative assessments, group evaluations, rubrics, and much more. Limited free access.

- https://www.air.org/resource/connecting-formative-assessment-research-practice-introductory-guide-educators/

    This site provides a collection of alternative assessments designed by the North Central Regional Educational Laboratory (NCREL). Topics explored include equity in assessments, formative assessment, what research has to say about assessment, and much more.

- http://www.teach-nology.com/currenttrends/alternative_assessment/

    Technology offers numerous sources for teaching, including various alternative assessment information, research literature, knowledge mapping, performance-based assessment, portfolios, and rubrics. This source also provides information and/or tools on authentic assessment, assessment and accountability programs, and more.

Endnotes

1. Barrentine, S. J., & Stokes, S. M. (Eds.). (2005). *Reading assessment: Principles and practices for elementary teachers*, 2nd ed. Newark, DE: International Reading Association; Bratcher, S., & Ryan, L. (2004). *Evaluating children's writing: A handbook of grading choices for classroom teachers*, 2nd ed. Mahwah, NJ: Erlbaum.

2. Schiefele, U., & Löweke, S. (2017). The nature, development, and effects of elementary students' reading motivation profiles. *Reading Research Quarterly*. DOI: 10.1002/rrq.201

3. Groff, C. (2014). Making their voices count: Using students' perspectives to inform literacy instruction for striving middle grade readers with academic difficulties. *Reading Horizons (Online)* 53(1), 1.

4. Lindeblad, E., Svensson, I., & Gustafson, S. (2016). Self-concepts and psychological well-being assessed by Beck Youth Inventory among pupils with reading difficulties. *Reading Psychology* 37(3), 449–469.

5. Choate, J., & Miller, L. (1987). Curricular assessment and programming. In J. Choate, J. Bennett, B. Enright, L. Miller, J. Poteet, & T. Raledy (Eds.), *Assessing and programming basic curriculum skills*. Boston: Allyn and Bacon, pp. 35–50.

6. Easley, S., & Mitchell, K. (2003). *Portfolios matter: What, where, when, why and how to use them*. Portland, ME: Stenhouse.

7. Swan, M., & Smith, B. (2001). *Learner English: A teacher's guide to interference and other problems*. London: Cambridge University Press.

Chapter 4
Oral Reading Assessments

Ollyy/Shutterstock

 Chapter Outline

Learning Outcomes

After reading this chapter, you should be able to . . .

4.1 State the three guiding questions teachers can use to select the appropriate oral reading assessment tool and provide one example.

4.2 Describe the components of an Informal Reading Inventory and state the purposes of each.

4.3 Explain the basic procedure for administering an informal reading inventory.

4.4 Define *modified miscue analysis* and state the purpose for using it.

4.5 Explain the basic procedure for scoring and interpreting a modified miscue analysis.

4.6 Compare and contrast the running record and the informal reading inventory.

4.7 Explain the basic procedure for scoring and interpreting a running record.

Scenario

Using Oral Reading to Learn More About Tori

Tori is a new student in Ms. Janis's fifth-grade class. She and her family just moved into the school district, and Ms. Janis is making every effort to make Tori feel a part of the classroom community. She knows how difficult it can be on readers when they move into a new school midyear, because they have to leave all of their familiar surroundings and friends only to come to a new neighborhood and school where they do not know anyone.

One way that Ms. Janis tries to make Tori feel a part of the community is by talking with her informally during recess and other times of the day to get to know her. During their conversations, Ms. Janis learns about Tori's reading interests and the types of texts she likes to read. Fortunately, there are texts in the classroom library that match up with Tori's interests.

She wants to find out how Tori processes text from the fifth-grade basal reader when she reads and how well she comprehends it. She selects one that aligns with Tori's interests and prepares a passage from it for Tori's oral reading. She tells Tori that she wants her to read the passage aloud and that when she's finished, she will retell the story and answer questions about it. Ms. Janis provides her with some background about the story before Tori begins reading aloud.

While Tori is reading, Ms. Janis takes notes of Tori's reading on a copy of the passage that she has made for herself. Ms. Janis makes notes about how Tori processes the text, what she does when she comes to unknown words, and what she does if meaning is lost. She notices that Tori reads in single word units and uses one primary strategy when she comes to unknown words, sounding them out. She also notices that Tori goes back to correct herself when she miscalls a word.

When Tori is finished reading, Ms. Janis asks her to tell her the story like she was telling it to someone who had never heard it. And that's exactly what Tori does, recalling every detail. Ms. Janis then asks Tori some inferential questions to determine how well Tori can think beyond the text. Tori is unable to answer any of these questions.

Based on this brief informal reading assessment, Ms. Janis begins to form a couple of hunches about Tori, which she will continue to verify over the coming weeks as she continues to have Tori read in a variety of contexts. For now, she sees that Tori is excellent at using one reading strategy to decode unknown words but suspects that Tori needs some explicit instruction to learn other ways to decode unknown words. She also suspects that Tori understands that reading has to make sense and that this is why she self-corrected—and the retelling confirmed that she was making sense. Ms. Janis will make sure she emphasizes the strength of self-correction as one of several reading strategies she will teach Tori. Tori's retelling and performance on answering inferential questions have led Ms. Janis to form a hunch that Tori is able to comprehend at the literal level and that she needs some help in understanding the purpose of inferences and how to think inferentially while reading.

Three Guiding Questions for a Diagnostic Approach

Listening to students read aloud is a rich source of information about reading behaviors, cognitive processes, and even affective processes. Learning how to use oral reading to assess readers is a vital ingredient in diagnostic approach. Oral reading can help teachers find insight into both what students do well and what they need to learn. As with the other assessments in this book, teachers using oral reading assessment will ask and answer three guiding questions—What do I want to know? Why do I want to know that? How can I best discover this information? In Table 4.1, you will find an overview of three oral reading assessment techniques we provide in this chapter: the informal reading inventory, the modified miscue analysis, and the running record.

Understanding the Informal Reading Inventory

What Is an Informal Reading Inventory?

The **Informal Reading Inventory (IRI)** originated from the work of Emmett A. Betts and his doctoral student Patsy A. Kilgallon, and is used to determine three reading levels and a listening capacity level[1]. An IRI is administered one-on-one and usually consists of oral and silent reading passages selected from basal readers from pre-K to eighth-grade levels. (Some exist up to the 12th grade.) Factual, inferential, and word meaning questions accompany each passage. Many authors have published IRI packages that include student materials, administration and scoring guides, and reproducible score

Table 4.1 What, Why, and How of Oral Reading Assessment

What Do I Want to Know?	Why Do I Want to Know?	How Can I Best Discover It?
What are the students' functional reading levels?	All readers have three reading levels: independent, instructional, and frustrational. I want to help readers read books of varying difficulty to become strong readers.	Informal Reading Inventory (Appendix); Running Record
What strategies do students use when reading?	Using a variety of reading strategies rather than relying on one or two is a hallmark of a good reader. I need to discover which strategies students are using to determine other strategies that I should explicitly teach.	Modified Miscue Analysis; Running Record; IRI (Appendix)
How well do readers comprehend?	Comprehension is the essence of reading. I need to make sure that readers are comprehending, and explicitly teach those readers who are having difficulty.	IRI (Appendix); Retelling
Are students able to identify words when reading connected text?	Word identification is one part of successful reading. I need to determine if students have a large store of words to draw on when reading.	IRI (Appendix); Modified Miscue Analysis; Running Record

Table 4.2 Code for Marking Errors

Type of Miscue	Coding Marks
Omission Leaves out words or word parts	Early in April ~~of~~ 1872
Substitution Changes one word for another	counted the Davidsons' ~~covered~~ wagon
Insertion Adds words not in the text	out rolled ⋀ onto their 160-acre
Prompts 4+ seconds pause, teacher reads word	P land claim in eastern Nebraska.
Reversals Word order changed	waiting | for | them.
Repetitions Word or phrase repeated	there was no shelter
Self-Corrected Error Without prompting, student rereads	sitters SC Like ~~settlers~~ on the Great Plains

sheets. We have included a full IRI package in the Appendix to this text for convenience in applying what you learn with this book.

Teachers use graded word lists to decide the grade levels of passages to begin with. Students begin by reading a word list two levels below their present grade level. The highest grade level at which students make few errors on the graded word list is the grade level at which they begin reading the oral passage. Students then read the oral passage aloud, and the teacher records omissions, substitutions, insertions, prompts, reversals, repetitions, and self-corrections. (See Table 4.2.) When a student reads the oral passage at the independent or instructional level, the teacher asks comprehension questions; the student then reads the silent passage at the same grade level and the teacher asks comprehension questions about the silent passage. Students continue to read increasingly difficult passages until they reach frustrational level. When students make enough miscues in oral reading to approach frustrational level, the teacher stops them and reads the rest of the passage aloud and finishes with listening comprehension questions. This continues with the next passage, and so on, until the student's listening comprehension reaches frustrational level. This is called a listening capacity test.[2]

What Are the Purposes of an Informal Reading Inventory?

An essential function of an IRI is to help the teacher determine the reader's functional reading levels: independent, instructional, and frustrational. Because the passages are constructed and inauthentic, this test is best used when you know very little about students, such as the beginning of the school year or when a new student moves in. Because the passages are normed within a grade level, success with an IRI passage is one way to narrow down a range of readable authentic texts for each student. Administering an IRI at the beginning of a summer tutoring program has been found to be an effective start when working to prevent summer achievement loss (summer slide).[3] Teachers also use the IRI to get an estimate of a student's listening capacity. Used judiciously and as starting points, an IRI can help match readers with appropriate texts.

Another important reason for administering and interpreting an IRI is to learn about reading strengths and needs so the teacher can design appropriate individualized instruction. For example, if while giving a reader an IRI the teacher notes difficulty answering inference comprehension questions, the teacher can develop lessons to help build skill in this area. From listening to a student reading aloud, the teacher can discover whether the student has word identification problems that may interfere with comprehension when the reader is reading silently. If a teacher pairs the IRI with marking techniques from another assessment, such as the modified miscue analysis, the teacher can add further insight into how the reader uses language cues to process text.

The IRI can be an excellent instrument for estimating reading levels and for helping teachers and readers to diagnose strengths and needs. But the IRI is only as useful as the interpretation of its results. Halladay's reported findings[4] serve as reminders that when we teachers think too narrowly about levels, teachers can actually block readers' progress rather than helping them advance. When looking at second-grade readers' independent-versus frustrational-level texts to assess their comprehension, Halladay discovered 25% had comprehension scores equal to or better than their IRI score for independent level would have predicted, even when reading texts that were categorized as frustrational. Teachers need to stay focused on the purposes for using the IRI and use their own expertise and experience to best interpret the results. Levels are often misused in schools and libraries to push students away from books educators think will be too challenging. It is best to just let readers try reading what they choose and assess their performance with this authentic text. Teachers can help students learn to self-monitor how challenging a text is for them as readers.

Getting a grade-level norm is supposed to give teachers clues about how to start *narrowing down the search* for engaging and independent books for free-choice reading. Levels are not intended to be used to prevent or prescribe books. Programs for leveling books tend to become less reliable as predictors of individual success when they attempt to specify months within a school year. An IRI provides a broad grade-level range to be used as an estimate of independent reading.

Determining Reading and Listening Capacity Levels

The criteria for reading levels on the IRI were originally determined by Betts, and many commercial informal reading inventories still use the same levels or modifications of them. The research on how to determine reading levels today is not conclusive.[5]

In designating these levels, Betts gave not only percentage determinants but also other criteria teachers should look for at each level.[6] The levels (as Betts determined) and his percentages designating the levels follow:

Betts Reading Levels

Independent Level*	Readers read on their own without any difficulty.	Word recognition—99% or above; comprehension—90% or above
Instructional Level	Teaching level	Word recognition—95% or above; comprehension—75% or above
Frustrational Level	This level is to be avoided. It is the lowest level of readability.	Word recognition—90% or below; comprehension—50% or below
Listening Capacity Level*	Highest level at which a listener can comprehend when someone reads to him	Comprehension—75% or above

*Betts also called the *independent level* the *basal level*, and the *listening capacity level* the *capacity level*.

Independent Level   The **independent reading level** "is the highest level at which an individual can read and satisfy all the criteria for desirable reading behavior in silent- and oral-reading situations."[7] At the independent level, a reader can read words without any assistance and comprehend the text. When the student is reading orally or silently at this level, a minimum comprehension score on literal and interpretive questions of at least 90% should be achieved.

Instructional Level   The **instructional reading level** is the one at which explicit teaching is done. This level must not be so challenging that it frustrates the student or so easy that the student needs no assistance. It leaves room for the reader to problem-solve with coaching from the teacher. This level is sometimes referred to as the "zone of proximal development," or ZPD.[8] At this level, there should be a minimum comprehension score of at least 75% for both oral and silent reading on literal and interpretive questions, and in the oral reading there should be accurate pronunciation of at least 95% of the text.

Readers can have an instructional level that spans more than one grade level. When this happens, the instructional level is reported as a range. A student may read passages beyond an identified grade level for a number of reasons, including interest, background information, and content.

Frustrational Level   The **frustrational reading level** is when the balance of effort outweighs the value of the return. At this functional level, the student reads with many comprehension errors and miscues; this may appear observably frustrating to the reader or the reader may dutifully work through the reading. It is helpful for teachers to know what this level is so that they can determine a student's reading range. A teacher would have to spend so much time in instruction and scaffolding for this type of passage that the return would not warrant the amount of time and energy spent by both teacher and reader. A teacher can often tell that a reader has reached frustrational level with a comprehension score of 50% or less on literal and interpretive questions for oral and silent reading, and with accurate word reading lower than 90%.

Listening Capacity Level   The **listening capacity level,** as first determined by Betts, is the highest level passage where "the learner can comprehend when the material is read to him."[9] Betts also established the minimum comprehension score of at least 75%, based on both factual and inferential questions for listening capacity. He noted that the term "*level* refers to the grade level at which the material was prepared for use; for example, preprimer, primer, first reader, second reader, and so on."[10] The listening capacity level is often called a *listening comprehension level.*

The Buffer Zone of the IRI   The **buffer zone** of the IRI is the area that falls between the instructional and frustrational levels. For word recognition, it is 94% to 91%, and for comprehension it is 74% to 51% (Betts's criteria). When a reader's score falls in the buffer zone, the teacher must decide whether to continue testing reading or move on to listening comprehension. If the reader appears interested in continuing, then continue. If the reader exhibits symptoms of frustration or disengagement, testing should be stopped. Even though the decision of whether to continue testing is made subjectively, there are some factors that the teacher can take into consideration; for example, the types of miscues the reader has made, the reader's personality, the reader's prior reading record, the reader's health, and whether the reader speaks another language at home. Also, it may be more important that the teacher has already made an estimate of the border between independent level and instructional level, which offers good information for choosing many texts for independent reading and for teaching.

Readers who stay in the buffer zone for more than one passage level but do not exhibit signs of frustration may have proficiencies and strategies that work well across texts. Conversely, readers who score at frustrational level immediately after reaching the instructional level may not have a wide repertoire of word strategies. Staying in the buffer zone shows that the student has enough skills to be able to continue.

Teacher judgment plays an important role in determining whether to continue testing. For example, it is possible to stop testing even when a reader has not reached a frustrating passage, when the reader appears nervous or upset. Again, the most useful information for teaching is gained by identifying each reader's independent and instructional ranges. Also, even though minimum criteria are usually given for estimating the various reading levels of IRIs, these are general standards. Remember, the teacher and the reader are the final judges of what levels of texts to seek out, not a mechanical calculation or application of scores.

Reporting and Using Students' Reading Levels

From a diagnostic approach, the intent of an IRI is to provide an estimate for selecting a wide range of authentic texts for students to read. It is vital that teachers and students move quickly from the IRI to the classroom library and school library to discover what else can be learned by listening to students read text selected for motivation and engagement. The passages in an IRI are usually not very interesting, and usually do not have engaging illustrations. They are not intended to be used for more than a quick estimate of ability. For example, if a third-grade student reading IRI passages finds instructional level for miscues at third-grade passages and for comprehension with second-grade passages, instead of spending more time with IRI passages, a teacher might immediately go to the classroom library to help the reader select several high-interest topics across second- and third-grade levels. Interest and background knowledge can affect word reading and comprehension positively. However, if those same grade level scores were reached by a fifth-grade student on an IRI, the teacher may need to work with a librarian to find high-interest text that does not feel like reading for "little kids." Publishers are making great strides in creating authentic and interesting books with a variety of small passages to read: captions, diagrams, fact boxes, and small side stories are common features even in complicated texts. Magazines provide many of these same features. This kind of differentiated informational text can be just what older readers need—short passages about interesting things—when it might be embarrassing for them to read books written for second- and third-graders.

The independent level is reported as one level only: the highest level at which the reader can read and satisfy the criteria for the independent level. If a reader reads independently from passages at level 1 (first grade), 2^1 (first semester of second grade), 2^2 (second semester of second grade), and 3^1 (first semester of third grade), the reader's independent level will be reported as the highest level—in this case reader level 3^1. The score means that the reader should be able to read many books at or below that level.

The frustrational level is also reported as one level only. The first passage at which the reader reaches frustration is reported as the frustrational reading level. The teacher does not continue to have the student read passages after reaching the frustrational reading level. Most books at or above that level would be frustrational (unless readers have deep interest and background knowledge to help them read words and maintain focus and persistence).

The instructional reading level is often reported as more than one level, because it includes all levels between the independent and frustrational. A reader's instructional reading level can span several grade levels and is reported as a range instead of a single number. For example, if a student reads at the instructional level at passage levels 4, 5, and 6 before going into the buffer zone or reaching the frustrational level, the reader's instructional reading level is reported as a 4–6 range.

To determine a reader's independent and instructional reading levels, the criteria for both word identification and comprehension should be met. For the independent level, the student should meet the criteria of 99% accuracy in word recognition and 90% in comprehension. For instructional level, the student should meet the criteria of 95% to 98% for word recognition and 75% to 89% in comprehension. For the frustrational level, however, only one of the criteria has to be met—that is, 50% or less in comprehension or 90% or less in word recognition. Both loss of understanding and excessive effort to decode words are common signs of frustration.

Keep in mind, however, that collapsing the two IRI measures—comprehension and word identification—to determine one overall level can be problematic. Doing so can cause teachers to lose sight of which aspect of reading might be posing the most difficulty for a student. It is more important for teachers to interpret the relationship between the two measures than it is to simplify the score for reporting. For example, some students might continue to meet the established criteria for word recognition at the independent, instructional, and buffer zone areas yet fail to meet the established criteria for comprehension—a case common among English language learners. The converse can also be true. That is, some students have difficulty with word recognition, but are nonetheless able to meet the comprehension criteria for independent, instructional, and buffer zones. A teacher using a diagnostic approach to assess and teach reading understands that these students need very different kinds of reading instruction. Our suggestion is that teachers continue with the passages until the reader shows a pattern of behavior. That is, if the student reads the first two or three passages with perfect word identification yet little comprehension at either the literal or inferential level, the pattern would indicate that the reader is strong in word recognition and that comprehension needs attention. The strength in word identification would be used to design instruction in comprehension. Likewise, if the reader shows ability to comprehend yet struggles with word recognition over a couple of passages, the pattern would indicate that comprehension is a strength and that word recognition needs work. The strength in comprehension would be used to design instruction in word identification.

Teachers should be mindful that answering comprehension questions requires students to rely heavily on short-term memory, so those who have difficulties in this area will probably not do well when answering literal-level comprehension questions. One way to alleviate this reliance on short-term memory and to more accurately assess comprehension is to allow readers to refer back to the text when answering questions. A second way is to have readers retell the story, using their sense of the narrative plot as a mnemonic. Narrative structures are often part of the process of moving information from short- to long-term memory.

Code for Marking Oral Reading Miscues on the IRI

Becoming proficient in marking oral reading miscues is beneficial so that you can focus on what each student is doing when reading. The code is a shorthand method for recording information quickly. It is only an aid, not a rigid system. It can be adapted to describe reading behaviors the way you see them. (See Table 4.2.) The code is also shown in the upper-right corner of the IRI examiner booklet shown in the Appendix.

Scoring Oral Reading Miscues on the IRI

The scoring scale is based on the philosophy that good readers make miscues when they read, and that miscues usually demonstrate strengths that led to that specific miscue. Miscues are not called mistakes, because they are intended to point you toward what each reader is doing well, rather than focusing on what readers cannot do. In the scoring scale, multiple miscues on the same word will only count as one miscue; substitutions or pronunciations due to dialect differences or regional pronunciation will not count as miscues; substitutions of difficult proper nouns will not count as miscues; repetitions and self-corrections will not count as miscues. Even though all these miscues should be marked on the sheet, they are not tallied in the score. All other miscues, such as omissions, substitutions, insertions, mispronunciations, and word reversals, count against the total number of words in the passage.

Counting miscues is the first step in beginning to understand how readers process text. But the count does little to inform our thinking about why readers made the miscues. Analyzing the miscues using the modified miscue analysis is what will help you actually design instruction. When teachers keep a record of miscues, they can determine what kinds of strategies readers are using to figure out words, whether a pattern exists among miscues, and whether readers rely more on graphic, semantic, or syntactic cues. We cannot overstate the importance of using the score to figure out what the reader *can* do well, instead of dwelling on what the reader *cannot* do.

Sample Markings of Oral IRI Passages

Sample 1

P polet
"What is mak(ing the lake ~~polluted~~?" asked Jill.

S
"It could be a lot ^ of things," said Mr. Brown.

"Let's go down to the lake and look at it."

big
Mr. Brown and the students went to the ^ lake.

They looked into the water. It wasn't clean. They

about   was
walked ~~around~~ the lake. Then they ~~saw~~ why it wasn't clean.

Total Error Count = 6 (*Polluted* counts for one miscue even though the student made two different errors.)

Sample 2

Fritz and Anna live(d) on a farm. It was a small farm. It was (also) very dry, and things did not grow well. So Fritz and his wife, Anna, were poor.
     One day there was a tap, tap, (tap) on the door. A woman had come to the farm. She had been walking most of the day, and she was hungry. She asked Fritz and Anna to give her something to eat. Fritz and Anna had a pot of soup. They let the woman come in to eat.

Total Miscue Count = 3 (The repetitions on *hungry* and *something* do not count miscues.)

Administering, Scoring, and Interpreting the IRI

There are many published IRIs, such as *The Critical Reading Inventory, The Flynt-Cooter, The Basic Reading Inventory,* and *The Qualitative Inventory.* We have included a complete IRI in the Appendix of this book for readers to use. Regardless of which inventory is used, all have five common steps, shown in Figure 4.1 along with their rationales. Scoring and interpretation procedures are embedded in each step and are ongoing when reading any given published IRI. These steps also match the IRI in the Appendix.

     Remember: The IRI is a tool to enhance a teacher's ability to listen to readers read and to an estimated range of levels for authentic reading, to learn what readers do when processing text, and how they think about what they have read. In the end, it's not about the forms or scoring procedures but rather about the ability to truly listen to how readers read and to interpret what is heard. Because it is not a standardized measure, it is more important to pay attention to the broader purposes for each step than it is to follow a strict script.

     Counting the number correct to determine the independent, instructional, and frustrational levels does little to inform teachers' thinking about how deeply a reader

Figure 4.1 Common Administration, Scoring, and Interpretation Procedures

Step	Purpose
1. Establish Rapport	To make the reader feel more at ease with the reading that is to ensue
2. Word Lists/Sentence Reading	To determine where to begin having students read the graded passages so that their initial encounter is highly successful. If the examiner already has a good hunch about where the students can start and meet with a high degree of success, this step is often omitted.
3. Oral and Silent Reading of Graded Passages	To listen to students read increasingly difficult passages, taking note of word recognition strategies and comprehension abilities. Some IRIs rely on oral reading and see silent reading as a supplemental assessment. They also offer options for ways to assess comprehension and scoring analyses.
4. Listening Capacity	To determine how well students comprehend through listening. This test is often started when the student frustrates out on reading orally and silently.
5. Consolidate Results	To provide an overview of the reader's performance, all scores are written on a summary form.

Enhanced eText
Video Example 4.1

In this video, Ms. Carpenter administers an Informal Reading Inventory with a third-grade reader. Cue the video to 0:00 until 3:26 to see the Word Recognition Inventory used to decide on the starting level of the first passage. Cue the video to 3:27 until 8:30 to see assessment with reading passages. Cue the video from 8:33 until the end to see assessment of listening comprehension. https://www.youtube.com/watch?v=HQkXWc4oydk

comprehends. By taking a look at the reader's performance across passages and analyzing how well each reader addresses different comprehension questions, a teacher can better pinpoint where the reader is showing strengths or areas in which more educating is needed. For example, if a reader shows strength in comprehension, is it more in the literal or inferential mode of thinking? Or, are word meanings getting in the student's way?

Likewise, counting substitutions, omissions, insertions, and self-corrections is a first step in beginning to understand how readers process text. But the score leaves teachers with little understanding about why readers do what they do. For example, which language cues did the reader use when making a miscue? Or, when looking across the passages, does a pattern of behavior emerge that suggests the reader relies on a limiting set of language cues? Using a modified miscue analysis will help answer these important questions.

Enhanced eText **Application Exercise 4.1:** Understanding the Informal Reading Inventory (IRI)

Bridge: From Understanding to Assessment with the IRI

When teachers understand that _____,	then teachers will assess _____.
An IRI yields a broad estimate of reading level,	Students with an IRI to determine appropriate texts for everyday reading.
The word recognition inventory is only intended to be used for selecting the easiest passage most likely to be at an independent level,	Word identification instead by looking closely at miscues in the IRI passage, or by using a phonics test (see Chapter 11) or vocabulary text. (See Chapter 10.)
Students often find constructed reading passages in tests boring, including those in informal reading inventories (IRI),	With an IRI, mainly to get a quick estimate of proficiencies and levels, when first getting to know readers.
Comprehension and word identification processes affect each reader in different ways,	Students in ways that yield data on each of these processes, and analyze these scores separately for diagnostic purposes (instead of compiling them into an overall score).

Understanding Modified Miscue Analysis

Forty years ago, Kenneth Goodman shifted the way educators thought about readers' oral reading by referring to any unexpected responses to print as miscues rather than errors. He deliberately used the term *miscue* rather than *error* because he felt that nothing a reader does in reading is accidental and that the term *error* implied randomness.[11] In everyday language, *error* suggests that the reader has done something wrong, or has a deficiency, which Goodman also hoped to avoid. When we approach readers as people who are still trying to learn a complex task, instead of comparing them negatively with other readers who may have caught on to reading without much help, we avoid contributing to the stigma that so often accompanies slower reading growth.

Goodman developed a process to help explain how miscues could signal what readers were doing right with language cues in order to comprehend text. He called this process **miscue analysis.** He noted that it enabled educators listening to readers to go beyond the "superficial behavior of readers" to a deeper understanding about what readers do when their purpose is to comprehend.[12] The assumption behind miscue analysis is that when teachers understand how **miscues,** which are unexpected responses to print, relate to the expected responses (the actual text), they will better understand how readers use existing language knowledge to interact with printed text in order to comprehend.

To analyze readers' miscues, Goodman developed an analytic taxonomy that considers the relationship between the expected response (ER) and the observed response (OR). Teachers who use this taxonomy can analyze the causes of a reader's miscues from a number of angles. However, the original taxonomy is extremely time-consuming for classroom teachers. It contains 19 questions, and each miscue is analyzed in terms of these 19 questions. Recognizing that teachers would be more inclined to use miscue analysis if it were made more classroom/teacher–friendly, Yetta Goodman designed a more streamlined version, the Reading Miscue Inventory (RMI). She condensed the 19 questions, which involved 4–15 possible responses for each, to 9 questions with 3 choices each.

Miscue analysis, with its emphasis on reading as a meaning-making process, has greatly influenced how we assess student reading. It has heightened the consciousness of those using the IRI. Many teachers are now concerned not only with the number of miscues but also with the positive information those errors reveal about their students, information that can be used immediately in teaching. Most would agree that constructing meaning is more important than absolute accuracy of word pronunciation.[13] Stephen Kucer recently checked this hypothesis by asking fourth-graders to read demanding literary and scientific text. He found that readers who made meaning-preserving miscues (such as substituting the word *hard* where the book says *difficult*) scored better on comprehension than did readers who made no miscues. This research suggests that when readers are focused on understanding what they read, they frequently insert meaningful substitutions. However, readers who are focused only on reading the words accurately, demonstrating competent phonics and word identification, were less likely to understand what they read.[14]

Even less complex than the RMI is the modified miscue analysis (MMA) procedure shown following, which is easily applied in the classroom and can be used with nearly any text from any content area. One of our former students was an eighth-grade science teacher. She used passages from her science textbook when applying the MMA. She also expedited the process—and saved paper—by slipping an acetate sleeve over the text to note miscues with a dry-erase marker. She had one piece of acetate for each student, but had to make only one copy of the text.

Administering, Scoring, and Interpreting a Modified Miscue Analysis

Preparing for the Modified Miscue Analysis[15]

1. Choose an appropriate text. A passage of 150 words is acceptable for this assessment. The passage should be long enough to help you see if and how the reader uses reading strategies. You might want to use a passage from a book the student is reading. You can also use passages students have read at the independent, instructional, and buffer levels of the IRI.

2. Make a copy of the passage for the reader as well as for yourself. You can write on your copy while the student reads from his.

3. Make enough copies of the Modified Miscue Analysis forms shown in Figure 4.2A and Figure 4.2B.

Administering the Modified Miscue Analysis

1. As with administering the IRI, you want to establish rapport with the student who will be reading.

2. Explain the procedure, saying something like "I would like to listen to you read so that I can hear what you do when you read. I will take notes."

3. Ask the student to begin reading from his copy.

4. Watch the reader. Does his body language or facial expressions note comfort or anxiety? Does the reader hold the book too close or too far away?

5. As the student reads, make notes on your copy of the passage using the same notations as stated for coding the IRI. (See Table 4.2).

6. After the reading, ask the student to retell what he remembers from the reading and record performance on the form shown in Figure 4.2B.

Scoring and Interpreting the Modified Miscue Analysis

Remember that the premise behind miscue analysis is that there is a logical reason for what the student is doing when reading. The purpose of the analysis is to get a glimpse of this logic and to see which specific language cues the student uses when reading. The procedures listed here can help in this analysis.

1. Using the Modified Miscue Analysis form in Figure 4.2A, write every word the reader miscued and the actual word as it appears in the text. If using graded passages from an IRI, use miscues from those passages where the student read independent, instructional, and buffer-zone levels. Remember that self-corrections and repetitions are not counted as miscues.

2. As you attempt to figure out which cues the reader used to miscue, you will need to look at the passage in which you recorded the student's reading behaviors.

3. Ask yourself the three questions shown on the form *for every miscue*. If the answer is "yes," circle the appropriate letter(s): M, S, and/or V.

4. For each self-correction, ask yourself what made the reader do so. Ask:

   - Was meaning disrupted, and the self-corrected word an attempt to fix it? If so, circle the M.

   - Did the text sound odd—structure out of sync—and the self-correct was an attempt to fix it? If so, circle S.

   - Did the miscued word look unlike the word the author used, and the self-correct was an attempt to fix it? If so, circle V.

Enhanced eText

Figure 4.2A Modified Miscue Analysis Form

Figure 4.2B Modified Miscue Analysis: Summary of Observations

5. Answer all questions and record any other observations, including retelling performance, on the Summary of Observations form shown in Figure 4.2B.

6. Based on your analysis, make a decision about what you think the reader knows and what he needs to learn, and design instruction accordingly. Readers who score many "M" marks are trying to make the text make sense, even when they do not recognize all the words—reading for *comprehension*. This is a strength. Readers who score many "S" marks are monitoring syntax, or grammatical *structure*. The miscues they make are words that would still be an appropriate part of speech for the sentence (a verb where a verb should go, an adjective where an adjective should go). This is also a strength. Finally, readers who score many "V" marks are using visual cues, reading words with letters similar to those in the actual word. Readers who do this are using *phonics* knowledge, which is also a strength.

To get a visual showing the degree to which a reader used each cue, consider using the spider chart method developed by Karen Wohlend. Go to http://e339blog.blogspot.com/2012/01/visualizing-reading-processes-with.html to access this interactive tool.

> **Enhanced eText** **Application Exercise 4.2:** Understanding the Modified Miscue Analysis (MMA)

Bridge: From Understanding to Assessment with MMA

When teachers understand that _____,	then teachers will assess _____.
Miscues are not random mistakes, but rather purposeful uses of existing knowledge,	Oral reading to determine which strengths readers lean on when they make miscues (meaning, structure, and visual).
Miscues provide clues about what readers already know,	The exact qualities of miscues students make, looking for patterns in the knowledge readers apply to oral reading.

Understanding the Running Record

What is a Running Record?

A **running record** is a documentation of a student's reading. Like the IRI and MMA, it is a systematic way of observing and chronicling a student's oral reading behavior. Introduced in the United States by Marie Clay, the running record was originally designed so that teachers could observe the behaviors readers use as they read text in a naturally occurring context. With a blank piece of paper, a teacher could sit down next to a reader and use a specific coding system to note what the reader did when reading aloud to the teacher. Teachers could take these records "on the run" as they moved from student to student. The notes could then be further analyzed to assess what specific readers were doing when reading.[16]

What Are the Purposes of a Running Record?

Clay lists and explains several reasons for running records. The one that most teachers are concerned with focuses on using results of running records to inform instruction.[17] Teachers interpret readers' performances to evaluate text difficulty, to group readers, to adjust instruction, to show progress with reading behaviors, and to identify readers' specific strengths and difficulties.

How Do Running Records, Modified Miscue Analysis, and IRIs Compare?

Running records, Modified Miscue Analysis, and IRI assessments share several common aspects. Three of the most important are listed in the following paragraphs.

Enhanced eText
Video Example 4.2

In this **video clip**, marking conventions for running records are explained.

First, they are based on similar beliefs about the value of having students read aloud as a way of showing what they are able to do as readers. All three require students to read orally so that the teacher can get a glimpse of how students are reading, the strategies they use in reading, and whether they self-correct any miscues. All three help the teacher to determine readers' functional reading levels (i.e., independent, instructional, and frustrational) so that appropriate texts can be provided for both independent and instructional reading experiences.

Second, running records, MMA, and IRIs each use similar coding systems to mark miscues readers make. Consistency within a school is important so that teachers can better interpret and share their markings when analyzing reading behaviors.

Third, each of these assessments uses connected text rather than isolated words when assessing word reading. That is, all are based on the philosophical premise that having readers reading "real" text is reflective of what they actually do when reading. Therefore, connected text must be used to assess reading if we want to see what strategies readers apply when they approach texts with meaningful sentences as opposed to lists of single words.

How Are Running Records, MMA and IRIs Different?

Although running records, MMA, and IRIs have much in common, they also have some differences. The most notable difference is that, as originally conceived, running records had no comprehension measure, because more attention was paid to word accuracy. Self-corrections were viewed as evidence of comprehension. However, most teachers and reading specialists who use running records also recognize the importance of a separate comprehension measure, and they have readers do some sort of retelling or answering of questions after a running record, which is an adjustment that makes it more comparable to an IRI.

The greatest difference between an IRI on the one hand and the MMA and running record on the other is that a running record and MMA can be completed with any text, whereas an IRI uses a set of grade-normed passages. Teachers who want to use the running record to get information on levels of independence should use a leveled set of books or benchmark books during running records, and chart readers' progress relative to each book's level. This adjustment makes running records more comparable to the IRI. Text levels are available to teachers from a variety of sources. Authentic texts tend to use natural language patterns, and are written for the purpose of sparking interest and engagement, and thus many teachers find the running record and MMA give them more trustworthy data than the contrived passages of the IRI. We recommend using the IRI as a quick and convenient estimate when starting work with new readers and using authentic text measures such as the running record and MMA as diagnostic assessment tools throughout the school year.

Although most IRI authors provide first-grade passages, this measure often tells teachers less about the youngest readers. Most often, the passages are too difficult, especially at the beginning of the year. The running record resolves this issue because teachers can select leveled texts young readers are interested in reading. The *Developmental Reading Assessment* (DRA)[18] is often used by primary-grade teachers because it offers leveled texts and accompanying materials that are easy to use for narrowing down the strengths of beginning readers.

Another major difference is that IRI scores are used for estimating achievement. This is not the case with running records or MMA. Running records and MMA information are gathered to fine-tune decisions about instruction, and many teachers administer them frequently to inform readers' ongoing selection of books and other texts. Running records and MMA should be used much more frequently than IRIs, whereas IRIs should be used to achieve an initial working estimate of text level, comprehension skill, and word identification strategies.

> **Enhanced eText** Application Exercise 4.3: Understanding Running Records

Administering a Running Record

Although running record administration and scoring procedures are similar to those used for IRIs, there are a few differences. You might want to take a look at the completed examples in Figures 4.6 and 4.7 before reading the following administration and scoring procedures.

1. Choose a text.
2. Make copies of both the Running Record form (Figure 4.3) and the Running Record Summary (Figure 4.5). You might want to use the Running Record form as is, or you might want to write the words from the text you will be using on each line, as shown in the example in Figure 4.6.
3. Assess readers individually and begin by saying something like this: "I would like to listen to you read this book. While you are reading, I am going to take some notes so that I can remember how well you read." Sit next to the reader so that you can watch her behavior rather than in the reverse!

> **Enhanced eText**
> **Figure 4.3** Running Record
> **Figure 4.4** Retelling
> **Figure 4.5** Running Record Summary

Figure 4.6 A Running Record of Your Reading

Page	The reading performance	Miscues M S V	Self-Corrects M S V
1	✓ ✓ ✓ spring I like the ~~summer~~.	(M)(S) V	
1	✓ ✓ woke ✓ ✓ The birds ~~wake~~ me up.	(M)(S)(V)	
2	✓✓ ✓ ✓ ✓ ✓ ✓ I like wearing shorts and a T-shirt.		
3	✓ ✓ to wear ✓ ✓ ✓ I like ~~wearing~~ sandals without socks.	(M)(S) V (M)(S)(V)	
4	✓✓ ✓ ✓ ✓ ✓ ✓ I like playing outside in the sun.		
5	✓have sc ⌐R ✓ ✓ ✓ ✓ I ~~like~~ helping Mom in the garden		(M)(S)(V)
6	✓✓ ✓ ✓ ✓ I like climbing the (apple) tree.	(M)(S)(V)	
7	✓✓ ✓ ✓ ✓ ✓ I like eating in the backyard.		
8	✓ ✓ ✓ ✓ ✓ ✓ ✓ (when sc ✓ ✓ But, I don't like going to bed ~~before~~ it's dark!		M S (V)
	Totals (Types of language cues used)	M S V 5 5 2	M S V 1 1 2
	Totals	5	2

4. Have the reader read the book while you record the reading on the Running Record form. If you are using a form with no text, use the following notations:

- Make a check for each word read as shown in the book.
- Write and circle any word that is omitted.
- Add a caret for any word that the reader inserts and write the word.
- Write and draw a line through any word that is substituted and write what the reader said in its place.
- If the reader repeats, draw an arrow to indicate where the reader went back to reread.
- Write *SC* when the reader self-corrects.
- If the reader stops for more than 5 seconds, tell the student the word. Put a "T" for the stated word.
- If the reader loses her place or begins reading something that is far different from the text, stop the reader, point to where you want the reader to start reading again, and say something like "Try reading this again." Put brackets to indicate the problem section and write *TTA* inside the brackets.

If you are using a form that includes the text the student is reading, use the following notations:

- Place a check above each word read as shown in the book.
- Circle any word that is omitted.
- If a reader inserts a word, add a caret where it occurs and write the word.
- If the reader substitutes a word, draw a line through the word, and write the word the reader stated above it.
- If the reader repeats, draw an arrow to indicate where the reader went back to reread.
- Write *SC* on or above the word when the reader self-corrects.
- If the reader stops for more than 5 seconds, tell the student the word. Put a "T" for the stated word on or above the word.
- If the reader loses her place or begins reading something that is far different from the text, stop the reader, point to where you want the reader to start reading again, and say something like "Try reading this again." Put brackets around the problem section and write *TTA* above the section.

5. To check comprehension, have the reader do a retelling, and note the degree to which the reader was able to retell using the rating scale shown in Figure 4.4.

Enhanced eText
Video Example 4.3. Running Record Assessment.

In this video, a teacher administers this assessment with one reader. https://www.youtube.com/watch?v=dQtLFZHWP88&t=5s

Scoring a Running Record

The following are counted as miscues:

- Omissions
- Insertions
- Substitutions
- Student is given words or told to try reading a passage again.

Special Note
All repeated miscues are recorded. For example, if the reader substitutes the word "a" for "the" two times, this substitution would count as a miscue both times. Clay comments, "It is only when you go to the trouble of analyzing *all the errors* [miscues] that you get quality information about the way the reader is working on print."[19]

As with modified miscue analysis, the running record can shed some light on the language cues the reader may have used to read the text as he did. To get the most out of the running record, we need to go beyond simply counting the number of miscues the reader makes and look at why the reader might have performed the way he did. In the short term, this analysis can help teachers to see which language cues the reader uses as well as those that may need additional work. In the long term, the analysis of miscues over time can yield a pattern of behavior. Here are some suggestions for going beyond accuracy to look more closely at what the reader did when reading:

1. Write *M*, *S*, and/or *V* for each miscue and self-correction. Remember that a self-correction is not counted as miscue, nor is a repetition.

2. Read the sentence where each miscue occurred and ask yourself these questions:
   - Does the sentence make sense? If so, circle the M. This indicates that the reader was attending to meaning when reading.
   - Does it sound like language? If so, circle the S. This indicates that the reader was attending to the grammatical structure.
   - Does it look like the actual word in the text? If so, circle the V. This indicates that the reader was attending to the printed text.

3. For each self-correction, ask yourself what made the reader go back to self-correct. Ask yourself these questions:
   - Did the reader self-correct because meaning was disrupted? If so, circle the M.
   - Did the reader self-correct because it didn't sound right? If so, circle the S.
   - Did the reader self-correct because the word didn't look like the one shown in the text? If so, circle the V.

4. Calculate the accuracy rate and the self-correction rate using the formula shown on the Running Record Summary form in Figure 4.5.

5. Record additional observations on the Running Record Summary form (Figure 4.5).

6. Take a look at the comprehension retelling to determine how well the reader appeared to comprehend the selection.

7. Use the results to design appropriate instruction.

To get an overall visual that shows the degree to which the reader used each cue, consider using the spider chart method developed by Karen Wohlend. Go to http://e339blog.blogspot.com/2012/01/visualizing-reading-processes-with.html to access this interactive tool.

Interpreting a Running Record

Taking a look at the summary (Figure 4.7), we are now in a position to interpret Jesse's reading behavior and make some inferences about what we need to do next. Let's first take a look at what Jesse appears to be doing well (his strengths). We'll then consider what he might need to learn (his needs) to advance as a reader.

Strengths

- Monitors self, as evidenced by his self-corrections.
- Uses all three language cues: letter/sound knowledge, syntax, and meaning.
- Attempts a word more than once when he senses that there is a problem.
- Uses all three language cues to self-correct.

In terms of comprehension, Jesse was able to retell the story with ease and also talked about what he likes to do in the spring. Neither literal nor inferential comprehension appeared to pose any problems with this particular text.

Figure 4.7 Running Record Summary

Title of Book: *Summertime* _____ Author: _____

Summary of Reading Performance

Total # of Words _58_ Total # of Miscues _5_ % of accuracy _91%_

Reading Level (Circle the one that matches the % of accuracy.)

95% – 100% = Independent (90% – 94% = Instructional) 89% or lower = Frustrational

Total # of Self-Corrections _2_ Self-Correction Rate 1: _3.5_

Note: Self-correction rates of 1:3, 1:4, or 1:5 are good. Each ratio shows that the reader is attending to discrepancies when reading.

Summary of Observations

1. What did the reader do when unknown words were encountered? (✔ all that apply)

_____ asked for help   _____ looked at pictures

_✓_ used letter/sound knowledge   _✓_ used meaning

_✓_ used structure (syntax)   _✓_ tried again

_____ skipped it and continued reading _____ looked at another source

2. How often did the reader attempt to self-correct when meaning was not maintained?

(Circle one)   always   frequently   (sometimes)   seldom   never

3. When the reader did self-correct, which cues were used? (✔ all that apply)

_✓_ letter/sound knowledge (visual)   _✓_ meaning   _✓_ syntax (structure)

Calculating Accuracy Rate

1. Subtract the total # of miscues from the total # of words in the text to determine the number of words that were correctly read.

2. Divide the number of words correctly read by the number of words in the passage to determine % of accuracy.

Example: 58 total words – 12 miscues = 46 words read correctly
46 words read correctly ÷ 58 total words = 79% accuracy

Calculating Self-Correction Rate

Use this formula: $\dfrac{\text{self-corrections + miscues}}{\text{self-corrections}}$ = 1: _____

Retelling (Circle the number that best characterizes the retelling.)

1. Little understanding: few details; limited talking about text.

2. Some understanding: recalls several details; talks about different parts.

3. Much understanding: recalls nearly all; sometimes shows thinking beyond the text.

Fotolia/© Monkey Business

Needs

- Expand strategies to include cross-checking with pictures or looking back to see where he has seen a word before as ways of figuring out unknown words.

- Increase sight word vocabulary. This might enable him to advance to a more sophisticated instructional level.

Give additional attention to visual cues. Jesse uses all three language cues; however, according to the results of this running record, he relies most heavily on meaning and syntax.

Bridge: From Understanding to Assessment with Running Records

When teachers understand that _____,	then teachers will assess _____.
Children often feel nervous about their performance with timed tests and tests where teachers only make marks for errors,	Using the running record, because it uses authentic reading material (not scripted test passages), it is not timed, where teachers only make marks when students make an error.
A large set of miscues is needed to learn what cognitive processes readers are applying well, which processes they are over-using, and which processes they are not applying,	Using the running record over time to gather sets of miscued words to analyze.

Revisiting the Opening Scenario

Based on Ms. Janis's analysis of Tori's reading performance on the IRI, how can she use Tori's strengths as a reader to inform instruction focused on her needs? Develop a plan to present to Ms. Janis.

Authors' Summary

Before reading our summary statements for each outcome, we suggest you read each outcome and summarize it in your own words.

Once finished, cross-check your response with our brief summary to determine how well you recalled the major points.

4.1 State the three guiding questions teachers can use to select the appropriate oral reading assessment tool and provide one example.

- These questions are in order of priority. *What do I want to know?* comes first because it sets the purpose for any and all assessments used. *Why do I want to know this information?* comes second because it pushes teachers to connect their questions to the larger picture of the whole student as well as what is known about literacy research. *How can I best discover this information?* guides the teacher to be the one who actively selects assessments that match the questions that need to be answered about students.

4.2 Describe the components of an informal reading inventory and state the purposes of each.

- The Word Recognition in Isolation (WRI) is a brief survey for an unknown reader, which gives the teacher an estimate of which passage to begin with. The WRI is not used for any kind of scoring.

- The Oral and Silent Reading passages are sets of grade-leveled texts used to gather information about both word knowledge and comprehension. For an unknown reader, the IRI's Oral and Silent Reading passage's should be a quick way to find an estimated range of levels for authentic reading.

4.3 Explain the basic procedure for administering an informal reading inventory.

- Build rapport to ensure that the student is interested and involved in providing the information you are seeking and that the student understands that the information will be used to help both of you find authentic text.

- Administer the WRI to conserve time in selecting a "just right" passage to start with.

- Administer the Oral and Silent Reading passages using the options that make the most sense for answering questions about this student.

- Score the Word Recognition and Comprehension sections and interpret the relationship between the two.

- Administer the Listening Capacity only to answer additional or unanswered questions about comprehension.

4.4 Define *modified miscue analysis* and state the purpose for using it.

- The MMA is an assessment system based on oral reading of passages from authentic text. In the MMA, a teacher codes specific types of miscues as clues about how students think during reading. This information helps teachers see whether a student's conception of reading draws on a narrow or wide range of information and strategies during reading.

4.5 Explain the basic procedure for scoring and interpreting a modified miscue analysis.

- Record all miscues that the reader made when reading. Then use three questions to determine which, if any, language cues the student used to make the miscue: meaning (Does the miscue make sense?), structure (Does the sentence sound right?), and visual (Does the miscue resemble the printed word?) Circle each letter to indicate answers to your questions. Regardless of the score, the process for interpreting an MMA is to look for evidence of the student's thinking and purpose for reading. Look for deep structure information, which is invisible, as opposed to accepting the first hint of surface structure issues. For example, a high number of meaning-based miscues may mean the student was reading for meaning and skimming words that did not make much difference to content, or the same score may mean that the student does not know when and how to apply phonics knowledge. A high number of visual-based miscues may mean the words and grammar are too hard for the student, or it may mean the student was nervous about reading in front of an adult audience. Based on your analysis, make a decision about what the reader knows and needs to learn, and design appropriate instruction.

4.6 Compare and contrast the running record and the informal reading inventory.

- The running record is based on authentic text and provides more information about student thinking during this kind of reading. The IRI, by contrast, uses preselected passages to gain an estimated range of text levels that will help teachers and students select authentic texts.

4.7 Explain the basic procedure for scoring and interpreting a running record.

- Teachers make tally marks for each correct word a student reads and make miscue codes for all others. Teachers also make marks showing whether students appear to use meaning cues, structure cues, and/or visual cues during reading. They then use this information to discover strengths first and needs when and if they are apparent.

Think About It!

1. Administer an IRI, a modified miscue analysis, or a running record to a reader who has a reading problem.

2. Practice coding miscues on an oral reading passage by listening to a tape of a student reading a passage.

3. Practice analyzing miscues using a student's taped reading and the forms shown in Figure 4.2A and Figure 4.2B.

4. Explain when you might choose to do a running record instead of an IRI.

Websites

- http://e339blog.blogspot.com/2012/01/visualizing-reading-processes-with.html

This site provides an online tool for creating miscue analysis spider charts.

Endnotes

1. Kilgallon, P. A. (1942). A study of relationships among certain pupil adjustments in language situations (Doctoral dissertation). Pennsylvania State University, University Park, PA.

2. A listening capacity test may also be referred to as a listening comprehension test.

3. McDaniel, S. C., et al. (2017). Supplemental summer literacy instruction: Implications for preventing summer reading loss. *Reading Psychology, 38*(7), 673–686.

4. Halladay, J. L. Reconsidering frustrational level texts: Second graders' experiences with difficult texts. (Paper presented at the National Reading Conference, Orlando, FL, December 3–5, 2008); Halladay J. L. (2012). Revisiting key assumptions of the reading level framework. *The Reading Teacher, 66*(1) 53–62.

5. Johnson, M. S., Kress, R. A., & Pikulski, J. (1987). *Informal Reading Inventories,* 2nd ed. Newark, DE: International Reading Association, p. 13; Glasswell, K., &

Ford, M. (2011). Let's start leveling about leveling, *Language Arts, 88*(3), 208–216; Peterson, B. (1991). Selecting books for beginning readers. In D. De Ford, C. Lyons, & G. Pinell (Eds.), *Bridges to Literacy*. Portsmouth, NH: Heinemann.

6. Adapted from Emmett A. Betts, Foundation of Reading Instruction (New York: American Book Company, 1946), p.445

7. Ibid., p. 445.

8. Vygotsky, L. S. (1978). *Mind in society.* Cambridge, MA: Harvard University Press.

9. Betts (1946), p. 452.

10. Ibid., p. 439.

11. The National Assessment of Educational Progress in its Reading Report Cards uses *deviation from text* in place of the term *error.*

12. Goodman, K. S. (1973). Miscues: Windows on the reading process. In K. S. Goodman (Ed.), *Miscue analysis.* Urbana, IL: National Council of Teachers of English, p. 5.

13. Kucer, S. B. (2009). *Dimensions of literacy,* 3rd ed. New York: Taylor & Francis; Johnson, P. (2008). *Assessment in reading.* Newark, DE: International Reading Association.

14. Kucer, S. B. (2016). Accuracy, miscues, and the comprehension of complex literary and scientific texts. *Reading Psychology, 37*(7), 1076–1095.

15. Opitz & Rasinski (2008).

16. Clay, M. (1995). *The early detection of reading difficulties.* Portsmouth, NH: Heinemann.

17. Ibid.

18. Beaver, J. (2001). *The developmental reading assessment.* New York, NY: Scott Foresman.

19. Clay (1995).

Chapter 5
Commercial Tests

Lisa F. Young/Shutterstock

 ## Chapter Outline

Scenario: Ms. Holz—A Teacher Who Knows the Purpose of Tests

Understanding the Purposes of Tests

Criteria for Good Tests

Standardized Tests

Norm-Referenced Tests

Criterion-Referenced Tests

Indicator Tests

 ## Learning Outcomes

After reading this chapter, you should be able to . . .

5.1 Describe how test scores are best used in a diagnostic approach.

5.2 Apply principles of test selection based on quality of design.

5.3 Recognize standardized tests. Know how to find a test's purposes and the contexts for which it was designed. Define and apply test score terminology.

5.4 Describe the uses and misuses of norm-referenced tests. Define this type of test as compared with others.

5.5 Describe the uses and misuses of criterion-referenced tests. Define this type of test as compared with others.

5.6 Describe the uses and misuses of indicator tests. Define this kind of test as compared with others.

Scenario

Ms. Holz—A Teacher who Knows the Purpose of Tests

Ms. Holz, a sixth-grade teacher, is handed a file with last year's test scores for all the students in her incoming class. She sits at her desk for a long time, staring at the folder. She has been told she should use these data in planning instruction for the coming year. But she remembers that last year, when looking at these scores, they gave her false impressions of several students. She also did not like the way the scores almost forced her to label students as low, medium, and high. She just heard on the news that harmful ability-grouping has surged over the past 15 years, even though there is a strong, historical research base that refutes this practice. After a few more moments, she opens her drawer and puts the folder inside. Right then, Ms. Olmsted from the classroom next door comes in.

"You're going to wait to look, huh?"

"Do you do that, too?" she asks.

"Yes, I like to wait until I match learners with high-interest texts and get to listen to them read. I also have a couple of classroom-based assessments I use before I look. All this helps me not to use the test scores the wrong way."

"Is there a right way?" she asks.

"I think so," Ms. Olmsted replies. "I look at the scores to see how they agree and disagree with what I get from my classroom assessments—to help me follow up hunches I've come up with about each student. Sometimes I find useful information, and sometimes I don't. I think this is the spirit of what the principal means when she asks us to 'use the data.'"

Understanding the Purposes of Tests

A test is one way to gather information to interpret when teachers have specific questions about students. Teachers use information from tests when classroom assessment techniques do not give them confidence that they know all they need to about a student. Teachers also use information from tests to check what they have already learned—how the scores either match or contradict what they know from classroom assessment. In a diagnostic approach, test scores become useful information after rich classroom-based assessments have already been selected, administered, and interpreted.

Anne Anastasi wrote, "[T]he most effective tests are likely to be those developed for clearly defined purposes and for use within specified contexts."[1] We agree wholeheartedly. In a diagnostic approach, this means the designed purpose of the test must be a clear match with the first assessment questions: What do I want to know? and Why do I want to know? Over the past 20 years, test abuse has developed into a national epidemic.[2] We believe much of this test abuse comes from interpreting test results outside their defined purposes and contexts.

The three assessment questions we use to frame the diagnostic approach to assessing and teaching reading apply to tests as well. When teachers are already asking and answering questions that help them apply classroom assessments, they can then look for ways test scores might answer some of their existing questions. The use of classroom assessments helps teachers first to ensure that their questions are not vague and general: "I just want to know how well he is reading." Instead, they are specific: "I want to know how I can use his interest in airplanes to help him identify words." Asking specific questions helps teachers investigate test scores for usable information: "I see that the scores on his vocabulary test show a need, just like what I discovered when I administered the informal word test. So I may be right to build on his prior knowledge of airplane vocabulary."

Criteria for Good Tests

In today's education climate, many teachers feel that they first need permission to make decisions without consulting test scores. (You have our permission!) In the diagnostic approach we advocate in this book, tests and scores must match the specific questions that led to their use in the first place. We hear too frequently from teachers today that the school decision-making process is dominated by calls to analyze the data in an effort to be "scientific"—often because large sums of money are spent on the tests. But this practice is far removed from how scientists actually work.

Scientists gather data to test hypotheses—questions they want to investigate. They design the data-collection process to match their questions. They use existing techniques only where this helps them answer their specific questions. The same process applies to our diagnostic approach to assessing and teaching reading. The "science" aspect of teaching children to read lies in learning to ask good questions and then matching information-gathering techniques to those questions. When a test is chosen, there are four criteria all good tests should meet.

1. *Suitability:* In selecting or preparing a test, the teacher must determine not only whether it will yield the type of data desired, but also whether the test is suitable for the age and type of students and for the locality in which they reside.

2. *Validity:* Educators often talk about the validity of a test, and generally define validity as the degree to which a test measures what we hope for it to measure. We can question a test's validity (i.e., whether the items relate well to the purposes we are measuring). But we can also question the validity of inferences people make from the test. Individual student factors can affect the validity of evaluation, or the inferences educators make from tests. For example, consider the four students described below, who each got 4/20 correct on a true/false test. How confident are we that the score measures the students' knowledge of content?

   Student A: English language learner. For this student, the true/false format is new and confusing. The test may have measured her comfort with the format rather than her content knowledge.

   Student B: Stress at home. This student's father is frequently away from home for extended periods. This affective challenge may affect a student's performance on a test, and thus the test may not be measuring the content knowledge it purports to measure in its objectives statement. Instead, for this student, it may have simply measured stress.

   Student C: Does not care about the test. This student has already taken dozens of tests this year and is questioning their value. She chooses true/false items randomly. When a student's effort and engagement in the test are low, the score has not measured content but rather may have provided evidence about motivation.

Student D: Does not understand what the test is asking for. This student is genuinely confused by the test items themselves. He thinks they are worded strangely and gets confused by words that might mean more than one thing. Item for item, we are really not sure what we have measured for this student. It may be we have measured nothing. We wonder whether other low-scoring students had similar problems with the wording of the items. The randomness of responses for this type of student makes us question validity, but as noted below, this example also prompts us to question reliability.

Validity is among the main concerns diagnostic teachers have when the balance of assessment tips toward standardized testing. First, the standardized testing company has almost 100 percent of the responsibility for ensuring the validity of the structure of the test and the individual items on the test. Teachers usually cannot examine the actual tests and items at any length. This is a great problem, because tests sometimes have structural problems with validity. For example, researchers have demonstrated what many people know from experience, that readers can answer many reading comprehension test questions without even reading the passage the questions are about![3] Second, teachers seem to have few opportunities to explain or provide a rationale for individual student scores. Larger trends in score manipulation have revealed these frustrations. In the past, school administrators were known to purposefully exclude English learners and students with diagnosed disabilities from standardized testing. They knew the standardized system would not allow them to explain the special circumstances of these individuals, so they met this frustration by taking those students out of the scoring pool.

According to the *Standards for Educational and Psychological Testing*, "Validity is the most important consideration in test evaluation. The concept refers to the appropriateness, meaningfulness, and usefulness of the specific inferences made from test scores. Test validation is the process of accumulating evidence to support such inferences."[4] If a test or test items are not valid, then one of two things has happened: (a) We measured something else, or (b) nothing really got measured.

3. *Objectivity:* The ways of giving an answer are controlled (such as true/false, multiple-choice, multiple-response, and matching questions). The range of answers is limited, usually to one acceptable response. The same score must result regardless of who grades the test. Since essay questions allow for a variety of ways to express an answer in language, each scorer is likely to interpret essay responses differently. Developers of less-controlled tests should give specific training for scorers and should make the essay questions as explicit and as plain as possible.

Objective testing puts strict limits on student responses. This constrains our ability to learn what they might know. So why would we want an objective test? The key reason we administer objective tests is to eliminate our own biases. Many of our biases are hidden to us. For example, many teachers are surprised the first time they observe themselves on video and learn that they tend to favor one side of their classroom when calling on students. Similar biases are likely to influence our scoring (measurement) and the inferences we make from scores (evaluation). For example, sometimes teachers change their pattern of scoring essays from the beginning of a pile of papers to the end. Reading the early essays can affect the teacher's interpretation of those that follow. The scorer might also just be more tired at the end. Objectivity is an important principle to help us rule out biases in assessing student knowledge.

4. *Reliability:* Reliability is about consistency. It is highly related to objectivity because reliable instruments help us control the influence of outside factors on the score. When educators design and administer a reliable test, they can be more confident that factors in the test items, instructions, and administration do not create variation in answers. In testing reading, we want to ensure that the differences in individual scores actually come from students' reading skills and not from how they received the instructions. What if one of our students showed radical growth from test to test, but later we found out that our way of reading the instructions the second time gave students inadvertent clues? To control this kind of bias, standardized tests often come with extremely rigid scripts for delivery. If teachers want reliability in a teacher-made test, they need to follow this same principle and write a script for delivery. These scripts should ensure that they do not have one way of giving the instructions on one day and another way the next. When a test is rewritten in a foreign language, its reliability must be rechecked to ensure that translation (differences in how the items are actually expressed) does not affect the way students answer items.

Another way of defining reliability is that we want to ensure that the *same thing* happened to all the students. Otherwise, what we are really testing may be the difference in how the test is presented.

Why is reliability important? If we use an objective test and the items on it get unpredictable responses, it is not a worthwhile part of our assessment program. For example, on a teacher-made multiple-choice test, we might see the following analysis of items:

Test item 25: 85% of students mark response B, which is the correct response. When given to two different groups of students, the results come back roughly similar: 82% correct and 88% correct. I am therefore reasonably confident that when most students see this item, they have a good chance of getting it correct. I do further investigation into the 15% (or so) who responded incorrectly and see that they also scored poorly on classroom assignments correlated with item 25. I am confident that students who have learned this material will answer the question correctly, and that those who do not know it will answer it incorrectly.

Test item 18: 25% of students mark C, the correct response. 27% mark B. 23% mark D. 25% mark A. When I reinstruct students on the principle involved and retest the item, the results are different: 40% mark C, 27% mark B, 25% mark D, and 11% mark A. And it looks like many of those who originally answered the question correctly are now answering it incorrectly. I am therefore not very confident that this item will get me reliable results. When I administer it the next semester, I get 55% marking C, 30% marking B, 10% marking D, and 5% marking A. I am now pretty suspicious about this item, because the percentages do not look similar at all. I don't know why students are getting the item right or wrong. With item 25, I was pretty sure about why students were giving the responses they did. I take item 18 out of the test and try to write another one that gets me more predictable results for my purposes across students and across time.

When a student takes a test, teachers hope the score will remain consistent, even if the conditions under which the test are taken change slightly, even if different scorers are used, or even if similar but not identical test items are used.

Standardized Tests

Standardized tests are commercially published tests most often constructed by experts in the field. They are developed in a very precise fashion and have specific instructions for both administration and scoring. These instructions are supposed to be followed exactly by everyone who administers the tests. This eliminates the bias each of us might introduce, with tendencies to prompt students, or to overestimate and underestimate student achievement.

Confusion may exist concerning the definition of standardized tests. In the past, the term *standardized* referred mainly to *norm-referenced* tests; however, a **standardized test** may or may not be norm-referenced. We consider a test to be standardized if it is a published test with mandatory instructions for administration and scoring.[5, 6] There are many kinds of tests with these kinds of objective instructions.

Standardized tests are often referred to as *high-stakes tests*. The term *high-stakes* implies undesirable consequences for those who fail. Performance benchmarks for these tests are usually determined by policy, not by students' needs. Although evaluation and interpretation are out of the hands of teachers, the results are often used to reward or penalize students, teachers, and schools. Without a doubt, the political use of high-stakes testing data affects the lives of students and teachers.

Selecting a Standardized Test

Like it or not, teachers are often left out of the loop when it comes to selecting a standardized test. Generally, administrators select these tests and teachers are told rather than asked to administer them. This means that test data are frequently gathered without any diagnostic questions asked about individual readers to warrant the use of the test.

There are times, however, when teachers are in a position to select a test with the three questions posed earlier at the forefront of their minds: What do I want to know? Why do I want to know? Will a test best help me to discover this information? Some teachers might feel a bit lost when it comes to answering the last question, but fortunately, there are references that provide much assistance.

The *Mental Measurements Yearbooks* are excellent resources for teachers selecting standardized reading tests that best suit their purposes. The books help acquaint teachers with most tests in the field. Critical evaluations of tests are written by authorities in the field. Test users are also warned about the dangers of standardized tests and are told of their values. An essential contribution that the books make is to "impress test users with the desirability of suspecting all standardized tests—even though prepared by well-known authorities—unaccompanied by detailed data on their construction, validity, uses, and limitations."[7]

The *Twentieth Mental Measurements Yearbook*, published in 2017, continues in the tradition of the others by providing valuable information about tests. Other sources of test information that teachers would find helpful are *Tests in Print; Tests: A Comprehensive Reference for Assessments in Psychology, Education, and Business*; and *Test Critiques*, as well as journals such as *The Reading Teacher* and the *Journal of Adolescent & Adult Literacy* (formerly the *Journal of Reading*) that periodically review various tests.

Enhanced eText
Video Example 5.1. What Testing Has Done to Schools.
Former testing advocate Diane Ravitch discusses problems created for schools by improper use of standardized tests.
https://www.youtube.com/watch?v=Vx_2n4t6SjE

Enhanced eText Application Exercise 5.1: Understanding Standardized Tests

Test Score Terminology

There are many potentially confusing terms test makers use in discussing standardized achievement tests. Following is a guide to some of the terms teachers will probably encounter at one time or another.[8]

Raw Score The **raw score** is the number of items a student answers correctly on a test. (The number of test items, as well as the difficulty of the items, may vary from one section of a test to another; therefore, the weighting of the test items should vary.) The raw score is usually not reported, because it does not convey meaningful information. Test makers use the raw scores to derive their scale scores.

Standard Scores   **Standard scores** are used to compare test takers' assessment scores. They are presented in terms of standard deviations (measures that define a range of scores around the mean—that is, "how widely the scores vary from the mean"[9]). If the standard deviation is large, it means that the scores are more scattered in relation to the mean. Conversely, if the standard deviation is small, the scores are more clustered around the mean.[10]

Standard Deviation   Measurement experts like to work with **standard deviations** because they feel that they produce more accurate appraisals of a student's scores in relation to others', and they are exceptionally helpful in understanding test results. For example, on one test, the standard deviation is 10, and the **mean** or average of all the scores is 100. On another test, the standard deviation is 5, and the mean or average of all the scores is 100. Two students take the two different tests. Student A scores 110 on one test and Student B scores 105 on the other test. Even though the students have different scores, they both have scored one standard deviation above the mean. The 110 score is therefore equivalent to the 105 score. The same logic would apply to tests with different means.

Normal Curve   Many teachers are familiar with the bell-shaped symmetrical curve (**normal curve**), in which the majority of scores fall near the mean (average) of the distribution, and the minority of scores fall farther away from or below the mean. In Figure 5.1 we show a sample of a bell-shaped symmetrical curve.

Grade Equivalent   A **grade equivalent** is a description of the year and month of school for which a given student's level of performance is typical. A grade equivalent of 6.2 on the *TerraNova California Achievement Test (CAT)* is interpreted as the score that is typical of a group of students in the third month of the sixth grade. (September is designated as month .0, October as .1, November as .2, December as .3, and so on up to June, which is .9.) These scores are useful in the elementary grades because fairly regular gains are expected in basic skill development at each grade level.

Extreme grade equivalents, those that are more than two years above or below grade level, must be interpreted with great caution because they are based on "extrapolations" rather than actual student performance. A very low or very high score just means that the student scored far below or far above the national average. A grade equivalent score of 6.6 by a third-grader does not mean the third-grader is able to do

Figure 5.1 A Bell-Shaped Symmetrical Curve

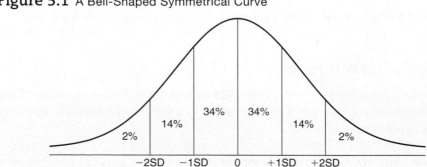

sixth-grade work or should be in the sixth grade. It does mean that this student is scoring well above the average for third-grade students.

Percentile   A **percentile** is a point on the distribution below which a certain percentage of the scores fall. A test score equivalent to the 98th percentile means that the student's score is higher than those of 98% of others who took the test.

Remember that the 50th-percentile score is the middle score, or the median; it is the point above and below which half of the students scored. Likewise, remember that percentile and percent correct are not the same. A percentile score of 75 on an achievement test by a fifth-grader means that the fifth-grader obtained a score higher than 75 out of every 100 students in a representative sample of fifth-graders in the nation who took the test. A student might get 60 percent of the test items correct and still be in the 75th percentile.

Norm-Referenced Tests

Norms are average scores for a given group of students, which allow comparisons to be made among different students or groups of individuals. The norms are derived from a random sampling of a cross-section of a large population of individuals.

Enhanced eText
Video Example 5.2
In this video, limitations of norm-referenced measures are discussed.

Norm-referenced tests are used to help teachers learn where their own students stand in relation to others who have taken the test. Although a child may be doing average work in a particular class, the child may be above average when compared to norms on a test. Similarly, it is possible for a child to be doing above-average work in their own third-grade class but get a test score below average compared with all third-graders in the nation.

Also keep in mind that norm-referenced tests have limitations. Identified by Wayne Otto and paraphrased by us, these limitations are listed in the following section.

Limitations of Norm-Referenced Measures

1. The measure may be inappropriate for use with some groups or individuals. It might be too hard for some and not challenging enough for others.

2. Allocated time limits may be unrealistic, which means that the scores of students who work slowly but with precision are most likely not accurate.

3. Items may sample breadth of reading rather than depth, which results in a superficial view of the students' reading behaviors.

4. Administering the test in a group setting might invalidate the results in that children who fail to understand the directions may be unable to answer any of the items they actually know.

5. The test format limits the kinds of items used. Multiple-choice formats are often used, and these do not measure some reading behaviors appropriately.

6. Norm-referenced tests generally provide an overestimate of the students' appropriate instructional reading level.[11]

Teachers must be cautious when they use these tests. In addition to the limitations mentioned above, teachers must ask the three assessment questions to determine whether a test is appropriate for their students: What do I want to know? Why do I want to know? How can I best discover this information?

Another important factor concerns the students themselves. Students who feel comfortable, alert, well-fed, rested, and highly motivated are better prepared to perform at their best. Such factors do affect test performance. Teachers want to administer tests under the best possible circumstances. Good teachers remind students and parents before a test that students need to sleep well, eat breakfast, pay attention, and expect to do well on a test.

Enhanced eText **Application Exercise 5.2:** Understanding Norm-Referenced Tests

---

Criterion-Referenced Tests

Criterion-referenced reading tests are based on an extensive inventory of reading objectives. These tests are designed to help teachers learn about students' specific strengths and needs. Teachers use them to gain more information about students' various skill levels. The information they get from the tests is used in conjunction with other valid assessment data to plan appropriate instruction.

Criterion-referenced tests can be administered individually or to a group, and they can be teacher-made or standardized. They are considered standardized if they are published tests that have been prepared by experts in the field and have precise instructions for administration and scoring. Criterion-referenced tests are concerned primarily with mastery of predetermined **objectives**, which are based on content material. On criterion-referenced tests, an individual is supposed to compete only with herself. While there may be very little difference in appearance between a norm-referenced test and a criterion-referenced test, differences do exist in the objectives of the tests.

For a criterion-referenced test to be valid, a **content domain** must be specified, and the test items must be representative of the content domain. Test makers identify various content area domains and write measurable objectives within each domain; then they develop detailed item specifications to ensure detailed measurement of the skills stated in the objectives. Usually, there are several items written for each objective.

Criterion-referenced tests are not norm-based; however, as odd as it may sound, "criterion-referenced tests and norm-referenced tests are no longer seen as a strict dichotomy."[12] When a criterion-referenced test has equated norms, it means that "the scores on one test have been statistically matched to the scores on a normed test."[13]

Some test makers are including a "cutoff or passing score" with criterion-referenced tests, perhaps because the term *criterion* implies a benchmark for performance. With a criterion-referenced interpretation of scores, the focus is on what students can do and the comparison should be with a content domain, not with other students.

Teachers can write their own criterion-referenced tests, such as the example shown following. The test item is correlated to the objective for a specific skill. The important factor is whether we can infer that the test item does indeed measure what it is supposed to—in this case, the ability of the child to draw inferences. In other words, is the test item a valid representation of its content domain? Let's take a look.

- **Content domain:** Reading comprehension
  Skill: Drawing inferences
  Objective: The student will draw inferences about the personality of the main character based on the content of reading material.

- **Administration Procedure:** The child is asked to read a short story carefully. After finishing the reading, the child is asked to answer questions based on the story.
- **Question:** What can you infer about the personality of Dennis?

The child is then asked to choose the best answer from the given statements. In criterion-referenced testing, *every* test item is related to a corresponding objective.

Limitations of Criterion-Referenced Tests

1. Some qualities, such as appreciation or attitudes about reading, are difficult to assess using content objectives.
2. Stated objectives are sometimes considered mastered if the student can perform them one time. Retention and transfer of what the student has learned may not be considered important.
3. Determining specific instructional objectives to be taught and tested can be difficult.
4. Establishing the mastery standard can be difficult. Performance standards may need to fluctuate depending on the objective being assessed.

Indicator Tests

One of the test types seen commonly in schools is indicator tests. These tests focus on highly specific elements of reading, known to have predictive power. For example, knowledge of correct alphabet letter names is known to predict success and failure with early reading instruction. Focusing on predictive elements helps point (or indicate) teachers in directions where classroom assessment should investigate further. A reader who does not know all alphabet letters may also not yet have learned other key functions about print, such as directionality of words and pages, or spacing between separate words.

Indicator test elements for K–1:

- Alphabet letter naming
- Phonemic segmenting and blending
- Nonsense word fluency (phonics)
- Oral reading fluency passages
- Retelling of oral reading fluency passages

Because indicator tests focus only on elements with high predictive power, they have limited usefulness in a diagnostic approach. This is because these tests ignore other aspects of learning to read, such as the relationship between oral language vocabulary and reading vocabulary, or between background knowledge and comprehension, or between interest and effort.[14] These tests also appear to emphasize and promote a bottom-up model of reading rather than an interactive model, where meaning and intent inform word skills and vice versa.

The purpose of indicator tests is to raise a question: Is this indicator actually pointing directly to a need, or indirectly to some other need, or to no need at all? Indicator test results should always be followed up by classroom assessments and authentic tasks to determine validity and to discover how students actually perform outside the test. Predictors of reading success can be perceived as being like gateways. For example, phonics instruction depends on readers quickly understanding what teachers mean

Enhanced eText
Video Example 5.3
In these videos, a variety of assessment methods are discussed in Part 1 and Part 2.

when they talk about letters. Students who score low on alphabet letter naming both in tests and in authentic classroom tasks are likely to misunderstand much systematic sequential instruction in how letters match to sounds.

Oral reading fluency is known to predict comprehension. Indicator test authors have developed norm-referenced oral reading passages, where they use timed words per minute as an estimate of oral reading fluency (ORF). The advantage of these timed tests is that they are quick to administer for an estimate of fluency, which is an estimate of comprehension. They would be an appropriate way to quickly get ideas about readers at the beginning of a school year or when new students come to the school. Unfortunately, many school administrators have become focused on increasing scores on the indicator test, which are estimates of an estimate, rather than on using indicator tests for their intended purpose—to raise questions that can and should be cross-checked with classroom assessments. Moreover, many states and districts have mistakenly approved indicator tests as overall achievement tests or as diagnostic tests, and mandate that teachers misapply tests this way. Teachers can appropriately insist that indicator tests be cross-checked with other known measurement tools to discover more about learners.

Another unfortunate use of indicator tests has been for progress monitoring. Test authors often recommend that students with low indicator scores be retested as frequently as every three weeks. Again, indicator tests of oral reading fluency do not monitor overall growth in all essential areas of reading development, only in one carefully selected gateway predictor. There is no guarantee that children making gains in applying instruction on comprehension or fluency will demonstrate these in one-minute timed passage-based tests. As students become acculturated to timed tests that measure words per minute (WPM), teachers and students alike come to believe that the key to reading proficiency lies in increasing rates to match national norms. Kucer and others have found it is far more important for readers to focus on reading for meaning than to maintain ongoing focus on testing how many words one can read accurately per minute.[15] The oral reading tools discussed in Chapter 4 and the Classroom Assessments discussed in Chapter 3 are designed to provide diagnostic information on the processes readers are developing as they learn to read.

Enhanced eText **Application Exercise 5.3:** Understanding Tests and Teacher Accountability

---

Bridge: From Understanding to Assessment

When teachers understand that _____,	then teachers will assess _____.
Individual teachers may underestimate or overestimate achievement,	Using a standardized instrument, always administered the same way.
Reporting about achievement to families and administrators requires a well-designed scale,	Using norm-referenced or criterion-referenced tests, where scores have clear points of reference (such as national age norms or research-based criteria).
Standardized tests have best explanatory power for high scores, but cannot explain why readers miss items,	Students with low scores using an IRI or a classroom-based assessment to confirm or disconfirm the low score.
Long-term ability grouping based on test scores is not what tests were designed for,	With standardized tests to get an objective viewpoint and a widely comparable estimate of achievement, but not to establish reading groups.
Indicator tests were designed to provide directional guidance based on predictors of success,	With indicator tests only to gain questions to look into with classroom assessments.

Revisiting the Opening Scenario

At the beginning of October, Ms. Holz takes the test scores out of her desk drawer. She has three students whose reading still confuses her after the first month of classroom assessment and instruction. For Raul, she sees the test score is way higher than she might have thought based on observations. This prompts her to think more about whether she has listened to Raul read from the right material. For Mesuna, whose family is from Ethiopia, she notices the test has confirmed Ms. Holz's observation that word reading and phonics elements are strengths, but that comprehension is lagging behind. For Ashley, she notices that the test score isn't even close to how she actually reads. She reads like an old pro from high-interest texts Ms. Holz has helped her find. She will help Ashley out how to apply the strengths she is gaining when the next test comes around.

Now that you have read this chapter, what do you think of Ms. Holz's practice of waiting to look at test scores?

Authors' Summary

Before reading our summary statements for each outcome, we suggest you read each outcome and summarize it in your own words.

Once finished, cross-check your response with our brief summary to determine how well you recalled the major points.

5.1 Describe how test scores are best used in a diagnostic approach.

- Test scores are best used in a diagnostic approach to triangulate—to confirm or disconfirm ideas we get from observation and classroom-based assessments. Tests are highly inauthentic situations for reading, and the scores give little useful information about how students read with authentic text or for other school purposes. For the best use, it is helpful to have a standardized test that can be broken out into specific aspects of reading such as comprehension, vocabulary knowledge, or phonics knowledge.

5.2 Apply principles of test selection based on quality of design.

- The main principle of design to watch for is the usefulness of the scores in helping discuss specific aspects of reading. A "general reading" score tells a student and teacher little about specific strengths and needs that will help a student grow. To be specific, look for tests that have specific sub-scores dedicated to various aspects of reading.

5.3 Recognize standardized tests. Know how to find a test's purposes and the contexts for which it was designed. Define and apply test score terminology.

- Standardized tests have specific rules for administration to ensure that the results are due to student performance and not to different ways teachers might administer the test. Norm-referenced tests are constantly readjusted with new items to ensure that nationwide, the test is likely to have just as many people score in the top 50% as in the lower 50%. Criterion-referenced tests are indexed to specific skills or knowledge expected at a certain grade level—it is inappropriate to compare percentages or norms for this kind of test.

5.4 Describe the uses and misuses of norm-referenced tests. Define this type of test as compared with others.

- Norm-referenced tests are used to give teachers an idea of how a class, a school, a district, or a state compares with the average of the nation as a whole. It is inappropriate to judge an individual student as "behind." There are many positive reasons why an individual student would be behind the norm: For example, the student started to learn to read later than others, but will soon catch up. Among the worst misuses of norm-referenced tests is to create ability groups and to assign students to specific instruction based on these test scores.

5.5 Describe the uses and misuses of criterion-referenced tests. Define this type of test as compared with others.

- Criterion-referenced tests are indexed to specific knowledge or skills. As with norm-referenced tests, there is a tendency to use these tests to create ability groups. Because these tests should give specific information about a category of skills and knowledge, they should be used to confirm and disconfirm classroom-based assessment. When the scores cannot be broken down into the specific grade-level criteria, they are not useful for planning instruction. Many state tests break scores down only into broad categories and are not useful for planning instruction.

5.6 Describe the uses and misuses of standardized and indicator tests. Define this type of test as compared with others.

- Indicator tests are used to give teachers a quick idea of areas to explore with classroom-based assessments. They are often misused and even abused in school settings, where their purpose to raise a question is set aside. Instead, many schools misuse the tests to diagnose reading problems and to prescribe instruction. Such uses of indicator tests provide invalid data and often lead to inappropriate instructional decisions.

Think About It!

1. Your school is interested in using criterion-referenced tests. You have been appointed to explain the differences between criterion-referenced and norm-referenced tests. What will you say?

2. Choose a reading content domain that is not likely to be represented on a current published test—for example, text messaging. Create a criterion-referenced measure to assess students' understanding of this domain.

3. Discuss some of the important criteria that good tests must have.

Websites

- https://www.teachervision.com/assessment-vs-evaluation

    This site contains limited free articles (i.e., three free). This particular article discusses the difference between assessment and evaluation. Also included are criteria for teachers to consider in their own classrooms. Teachers can sign up for a 7-day free trial for access to over 20,000 resources for Pre-K–12, downloadables, and over 180 printable books.

- http://nces.ed.gov/nationsreportcard/

    Known as the Nation's Report Card, the National Assessment of Educational Progress (NAEP) is one of the primary assessments referenced when looking at our nation's educational progress. Navigating this site will prove informative and keep teachers up-to-date regarding the educational state of affairs.

Endnotes

1. Anastasi, A. (1985). Mental measurements: Some emerging trends. *The Ninth Mental Measurements Yearbook.* Lincoln, NE: Buros Institute of Mental Measurements, University of Nebraska, p. xxix.

2. Ediger, M. (2017). Excessive testing and pupils in the public schools. *Reading Improvement, 54*(2), 67–71.

3. Roy-Charland, A., et al. (2017). Passage independence within standardized reading comprehension tests. *Reading and Writing, 30*(7), 1431–1446.

4. The Committee to Develop Standards for Educational and Psychological Testing of the American Educational Research Association, the American Psychological Association, and the National Council on Measurement in Education. (1985). *Standards for educational and psychological testing.* Washington, DC: American Psychological Association, p. 9.

5. Teacher's Guide, *California Diagnostic Reading Tests Levels A and B.* Monterey, CA: CTB/McGraw-Hill, 1989, p. 7.

6. Zieky, M. (2001). Executive Director, Officers Division, Educational Testing Service (ETS), Princeton, NJ.

7. Buros, O. (Ed.). (1968). *Reading: Tests and reviews.* Highland Park, NJ: Gryphon Press, p. xvi.

8. *Test interpretation guidelines, comprehensive tests of basic skills,* 4th ed. Monterey, CA: CTB/McGraw-Hill, 1988.

9. Woolfolk, A. E. (2007). *Educational psychology,* 10th ed. Boston: Allyn and Bacon, p. 527.

10. Ibid.

11. Otto, W. (1973). Evaluating instruments for assessing needs and growth in reading. In W. MacGinitie (Ed.), *Assessment problems in reading.* Newark, DE: International Reading Association, pp. 14–20.

12. Ibid.

13. Zieky.

14. Goodman, K. S. (2006). *The truth about DIBELS: What it is, what it does.* Portsmouth, NH: Heinemann Educational Books.

15. Kucer, S. B. (2016). Accuracy, miscues, and the comprehension of complex literary and scientific texts. *Reading Psychology, 37*(7) 1076–1095.

Chapter 6
Becoming the Teacher with a Diagnostic Mindset

Vladimir Gjorgiev/Shutterstock

 Chapter Outline

Scenario: Mr. Lane Teaches Reading

The Diagnostic Mindset of Good Teachers

Characteristics and Practices of Good Reading Teachers

Four Teacher Roles for a Diagnostic Approach to Assessing, Learning, and Teaching Reading

Moving from Assessment to Instruction

 Learning Outcomes

After reading this chapter, you should be able to . . .

6.1 Describe attributes that define good teachers.

6.2 Explain characteristics and practices of good reading teachers.

6.3 Discuss how teacher expectations influence children's learning.

6.4 Explain the four roles of a teacher who embraces a diagnostic approach to assessing, learning, and teaching reading.

6.5 Use self-assessment data to plan subsequent instruction.

Scenario

Mr. Lane Teaches Reading

Mr. Lane's students find their way to where an old overstuffed chair anchors the reading corner. Mr. Lane opens the day by asking all his students to stand up. He quickly flashes cards with names on them. Students sit down as soon as they see their name go by, and all discover quickly that Daisy and Damon are absent today. He hands their cards to the attendance taker, who fills out the attendance slip and posts it outside the room. He holds the poetry book *Lunch Money and Other Poems about School* (Shields, 1995) and reads a new poem aloud. They ask him to read it again as well as a few more old favorites from this same book. When the reading is finished, he leaves the poem books out and invites the students to try reading them on their own during independent reading time.

The students complete their routine morning tasks to get ready for the day, and soon it is time for their reading block. During most of the block, Mr. Lane will teach small groups of children who have been grouped according to a comprehension strategy they all need to learn. During the last 15 minutes of the reading block the entire class, including Mr. Lane, participates in independent reading. While all are engaged in reading, Mr. Lane glances around the room and notices that Sheryl is reading from the required reading anthology. He jots a note in his daily lesson planner to ask Sheryl if she chose that book because of the stories in the section about mysteries. Sheryl had been excited about the mysteries that Mr. Lane had introduced them to the week before.

To bring the reading block to a close, Mr. Lane invites students to pair-share their responses to what they have been reading. Mr. Lane is pleased with what has occurred in reading today and will use the notes he has taken throughout the reading block to inform tomorrow's instruction.

The Diagnostic Mindset of Good Teachers

Researchers recently found that putting teachers as decision makers at the center of reading intervention programs yielded positive results for students.[1] Teachers who know how to make decisions for students are more valuable than any program or scripted process. A positive expectation of good reading teachers is that all children can read age-appropriate texts if they are provided with the support they need for those texts. The more teachers know about their students, the better able they are to plan for them. Teachers influence students' learning through their expectations about students' abilities.[2] Teachers must be mindful that the assumptions they project on children, and the labels they use to describe them (e.g., "my low kids," or "my high kids") can become self-fulfilling prophecies. Test results often force teachers to adopt biases about young readers. Unfortunately, children then develop self-perceptions to match what teachers believe.[3] Over time, these kinds of hidden assumptions define a child's reading identity and school career. Leigh Hall[4] found that children's identities as readers can actually override reading ability when they are working on authentic reading. Also, "the social consequences of failing to learn to read in the early grades are severe. Longitudinal studies find that disadvantaged third-graders who have failed one or more grades and are reading below grade level are extremely unlikely to complete high school."[5] Rather than shape a child's identity by assuming that past scores or performance on curriculum materials defines a competent reader, a good reading teacher will start with a positive mindset that all students are capable; they are half-full rather than half-empty.

Although a school may have the best equipment, the most advanced school facility, a superior curriculum, and children who want to learn, "good teachers"—those with positive expectations for all students—are crucial for learning to take place. With today's emphasis on accountability, the spotlight is even more sharply focused on the teacher. Although there is no definitive agreement on how to evaluate teachers, researchers and educators agree that teachers influence students' behavior and learning. We agree with Allington, who summed it up best when he commented that much research on teaching reading can be boiled down to five words: Kids differ and teachers matter.[6]

Researchers have long known that it is difficult to compare different methods or sets of materials and that students seem to learn to read from a variety of materials and methods.[7] More importantly, researchers consistently point to the teacher as the key to improving reading instruction. For example, the authors of *Becoming a Nation of Readers* state that "studies indicate that about 15 percent of the variation among children in reading achievement at the end of the school year is attributable to factors that relate to the skill and effectiveness of the teacher."[8] By contrast, "the largest study ever done comparing approaches to beginning reading found that about 3 percent of the variation in reading achievement at the end of the first grade was attributable to the overall approach of the program."[9] The remaining factors are largely external, meaning that of those within schools' control, the teacher is the key to improving reading instruction:

> The main lesson, it seems to me, is that the teacher is of tremendous importance in preventing and treating children's reading and learning disabilities . . . good teaching is probably the best way to help children.[10]

Although the precise factors may vary according to grade level and individual students, effective teachers share some general qualities.[11]

For example, researchers on teacher dispositions have found that effective teachers tend to

- Perceive others as competent and able to solve their own problems
- Perceive themselves as identified with their students, sharing in success and failure
- Have a broad sense of purpose that goes beyond immediate events or requirements
- Keep a frame of reference on people and their overall well-being as opposed to orienting themselves to content objectives, tasks, and requirements.

Colvin further explains the importance of the teacher on any learner's performance when discussing deliberate practice: "Decades or centuries of study have produced a body of knowledge about how performance is developed and improved, and full-time teachers generally possess that knowledge. At least in the early going, therefore, and sometimes long after, it's almost always necessary for a teacher to design the activity best suited to improve an individual's performance . . . anyone who thinks they've outgrown the benefits of a teacher's help should at least question that view."[12]

In line with Colvin's comments, the National Center for Research on Teacher Learning (NCRTL) identified three basic abilities successful schools expect of their best teachers:[13]

- Good teachers know how to identify and work on changing assumptions and beliefs they hold about teaching and learning.
- Good teachers work to improve their knowledge of content and their knowledge of how to teach diverse learners.
- Good teachers learn to reason and reflect on their work while they are doing it.

Notice how some of these general characteristics appear more specifically in the next section, which describes research on good *reading* teachers.

Good teaching requires self-knowledge: It is a secret hidden in plain sight (Palmer 1998, pg. 3). The abilities described above by the NCRTL may not be as simple as they sound for some teachers to acquire. However, each can be achieved through retrospective analysis of our own beliefs and behaviors. Whether our challenges to improve as teachers are technical or adaptive (Powell, W., & Kusuma-Powell, O.), we can work towards changing our assumptions and consequently improving our content knowledge and instructional practices. Then can we truly embrace a growth mindset for our own professional growth. Our own positive adaptive transformation as teachers allows us to be more deliberate about content, instruction, and individual students' strengths and needs in our daily instruction.

Characteristics and Practices of Good Reading Teachers

Reading researchers have identified the practices and beliefs of teachers whose students demonstrated the highest reading achievement. For example, among first-grade teachers, eight characteristics have emerged:

1. Coherent and thorough integration of skills with high-quality reading and writing experiences

2. A high density of instruction (i.e., integration of multiple goals in a single lesson)

3. Extensive use of scaffolding (i.e., support)

4. Encouragement of student self-regulation (i.e., solving their own problems)

5. A thorough integration of reading and writing activities

6. High expectations for all students

7. Masterful classroom management

8. An awareness of their practices and the goals underlying them[14]

In research among fourth-grade teachers, the following eight characteristics of exemplary teachers emerged:

1. Extensive reading

2. Diverse grouping patterns

3. Attention to skills and strategies

4. Background development

5. Writing instruction

6. Diverse assessments

7. Content integration

8. Attention to motivation[15]

Although these lists look rather different on the surface, what they have in common is that teachers who are deliberate about content, instruction, and individual students' strengths and needs are likely to use effective practices to maximize students' reading potential.[16] As Willingham notes, there are many attributes that teachers have in common, yet there are two qualities that matter most. Effective teachers can "connect personally with their students, and they organize the material in a way that makes it interesting and easy to understand."[17]

Enhanced eText Application Exercise 6.1: Understanding Teacher Self-Assessment

Bridge: From Understanding to Self-Assessment

When teachers understand that _____,	then teachers will assess _____.
They are the key to meeting student learning needs,	Their role as a school leader and classroom teacher to make plans for greater impact.
Good teachers know how to identify and work on changing assumptions and beliefs they hold about teaching and learning,	Their own views of each student and juxtapose those views with the perceptions of their students to explicitly teach with a growth mindset.
Good teachers work to improve their knowledge of content and their knowledge of how to teach diverse learners,	Their own knowledge needs as they relate to diverse learners, and organize professional development plans and manage using high-leverage classroom practices that meet the needs of diverse learners.
Good teachers learn to reason and reflect on their work while they are doing it,	Their own self-evaluation practices and set goals for narrowing in on what they can do to meet individual student literacy needs.

Four Teacher Roles in a Diagnostic Approach to Assessing, Learning, and Teaching Reading

Teaching is a complex behavior that requires teachers to perform different but related roles. We see the teacher as planner, explicit reading teacher, organizer, manager, and self-evaluator. (See Figure 6.1.) In the following sections, we explain each role.

Role 1: Planner

> "I read the word problem but I still don't know if I am supposed to add or subtract," says John, a second-grade student in Bill's class.
> "Read it to me," Bill responds. As John reads, Bill notes that John reads the problem so quickly that he pays little attention to understanding the words that signal which mathematical operation to use. In fact, he miscues on a

Figure 6.1 Teacher Roles

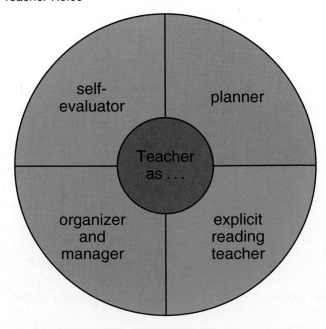

key word, saying "today" for the printed word "together." Once John is finished reading, Bill comments, "I think I see why you might not know what you are supposed to do to solve this problem, John. Try reading it to me again, but this time, I want you to read it like you are talking to me to help me understand the problem. Please read it more slowly so that I can better understand."

John begins rereading the text following Bill's advice and before he is finished, he smiles.

"Why the smile, John?" Bill asks.

"I know I am supposed to add because I see the words 'and' and 'all together,'" John responds.

"So you figured out the problem by slowing down and paying attention to understanding what you are reading. It's not enough to read quickly, is it? What's most important is understanding what you read, and this means that sometimes you need to read more slowly."[18]

Teachers like Bill realize that content reading often demands that students think deeply while they are reading. This means teachers need to help students adjust the speed of reading by monitoring their sense of purpose. He plans to teach his whole class how to use elements of fluency to help them comprehend content reading.

Teachers who use a diagnostic approach must also be good planners. Planning helps guide teachers in making choices about instruction; clarifying their thinking about objectives; discerning their students' needs, interests, and developmental levels; determining what motivating techniques to use; developing a positive classroom culture; and nurturing a propensity for attending to teachable moments and immediate needs revealed by learners.

The teacher using a diagnostic approach bases instruction on continuous analysis of students' strengths and needs. The teacher is flexible and always alert to student feedback to determine whether to proceed with instruction, slow down instruction, or stop to correct or clarify some misconception. In other words, the teacher uses **diagnostic teaching**, "the practice of systematic trial and evaluation of a variety of instructional strategies (including materials, methods of presentation, and methods of feedback) with individual students as part of their everyday educational program."[19] Teachers use a number of assessment instruments and techniques in such teaching, and they make modifications based on feedback from their students.

The teacher in a reading diagnosis and improvement program must wisely plan time blocks for reading. And as Durkin[20] noted decades ago, there are different ways to do just that. Sometimes the instruction will be *planned and intentional.* This is the type of instruction in which the teacher has designed a lesson that focuses on a specific reading skill or strategy. The lesson includes a specific objective, teaching procedures that will enable students to attain the objective, and an individual assessment that will help the teacher to determine how well the students learned the objective of the lesson.

Unplanned, intentional instruction is another way to plan time. This type of planning requires teachers to be responsive to what students are doing and to think on their feet. For example, sometimes students might show a misunderstanding of a topic through their spoken responses. As a result, the teacher may decide to clear up any misunderstandings; this requires on-the-spot thinking of intentional ways to teach students. At other times, something might happen that will encourage the teacher to seize the moment to teach students. Take, for example, an experience I (MO) encountered when the lights unexpectedly went out during one school day. The students lost all focus on the lesson I was conducting, so I decided to abandon it altogether. Instead, I used the occasion to teach something about electricity. I first had students talk about everyday objects that use electricity. I recorded their words on a semantic map using "electricity fuels objects" as the defined center, and we read the chart together. I then read them a book about electricity and had them compare our chart with what was mentioned in the book.

I had just read an article shortly before this happened that reminded me there are multiple paths to comprehension, and that teachers must be willing to be flexible in the interest of helping students achieve it. In this case, too many students were fully distracted by immediate circumstances to focus on the text I had chosen to teach semantic mapping. A return to the planned task would have been difficult for all, myself included. Instead, I redirected the comprehension strategy in my lesson through the distraction itself. I might not have done this had I not been seeking ongoing professional knowledge. The article I read helped me understand that flexibility with the unplanned is actually part of strong planning.

Role 2: Explicit Reading Teacher

A teacher and five students in a fourth-grade class are engaged in a reading comprehension lesson. They are reading a trade book about the Civil War. They have been studying the Civil War, and this is a short novel depicting the lives of two different families during that period. Mr. Rojas, the teacher, prepares his students for the book by showing them a picture of President Lincoln reading the Gettysburg Address and using this as a stimulus to discuss what they have learned about the Civil War. He then presents some key vocabulary words that he feels students may need to read the chapter. Next, he tells them that they will be acting as investigative reporters. Even though they had previously discussed what investigative reporters do, he wants to review it with them because he wants them to read as if they are investigative reporters.

Today, he will help them become better investigative reporters. He tells the students that before they return to their seats to read the first chapter silently, he wants to make sure they know how to collect information, especially if the information is not directly stated. Mr. Rojas hands out a short selection to each of the students and asks them to read it to try to determine how many soldiers had started out on the mission and in what direction they were headed. (None of the information is directly stated.) After the students finish reading the short selection, Mr. Rojas says that he will tell them how he figures out the answers. He tells them that he will "think out loud" to show them his thought process.

Mr. Rojas says that as he reads the selection to answer the first question, he notices some key information—namely, that the remaining one-third of the soldiers were exhausted. It also says that the nine remaining ones could not last much longer. From this information, he can determine that two-thirds have died or are missing. If nine equals one-third of the original number, then there were 27 soldiers at the beginning of the special mission. The selection also states that the soldiers were walking toward the mountain range, and in another sentence it states that the sun was setting behind the mountain range. He says that he knows the sun rises in the east and sets in the west. Since the soldiers are walking toward the mountain range and the sun is setting behind the mountain range, they are heading west.

Mr. Rojas has students read another selection and has them answer questions based on information that is not directly stated. He asks for volunteers to explain how they went about answering the questions.

He then tells them that he wants them to go back to their seats and read silently the first chapter in their books. While they are reading, he wants them to collect evidence from this chapter to make some predictions about the two main characters introduced in the chapter and to record their predictions. He also lets them know that tomorrow they will discuss their predictions, and as they read the book, they will check to see on what kind of thinking their predictions were based.

Mr. Rojas understands that most students need help in acquiring reading skills and strategies; they do not gain these simply by being in class or being around strong readers. The kind of instruction teachers use to teach reading explicitly will affect how well their students learn to read.

To help students become good readers, teachers must have metacognitive ability, so they know when to do what and how. In other words, they must know multiple teaching strategies for each aspect of reading, and consistently monitor their teaching to decide which teaching makes the best sense for their students.

Good teachers recognize that good readers interact with the text and bring their background of experiences to the act of reading. Good teachers also become part of this interactive process by using explicit instruction.

What Is Explicit Instruction?   **Explicit instruction** is guided by a teacher, who uses different kinds of strategies to help students gain understanding of what they are reading. More often than not, it is planned and intentional. There are many instructional strategies that teachers can use to teach reading explicitly, and the strategies teachers use are not tied down to the kinds of materials they use. For example, in one class, a teacher may use a published reading program, whereas in another, a teacher might use trade books—that is, library books. In yet another class, a teacher might use a combination of different printed matter, including newspapers. All these teachers can still employ similar instructional strategies to help students achieve despite the different materials in use.

Explicit instruction requires the following:

1. Objectives are well stated and activities are designed to accomplish these objectives.
2. Students know the objectives.
3. Students are given clear opportunities to learn.
4. Teachers assess and give prompt feedback.
5. Teachers arrange ways to assess and adjust to successes and failures at reaching objectives; they provide appropriate interventions.

Role 3: Organizer and Manager

One teacher and six children are engaged in reading at a round table. The rest of the class is involved in a variety of activities: A number of children are working individually at their seats or at learning centers; one child, sitting in a rocking chair, is reading; two children are working together; and a group of children are working together in the back of the room.

The teacher says to his group at the round table, "We've talked about what *inference* means, and we've given examples of it. Who can tell us what we mean by *inference*?" A few children raise their hands. Mr. Mills calls on one, who gives an explanation of inference. "Good," says Mr. Mills. "Now, I'd like you to read the paragraph about Mr. Brown and then tell us what inferences you can make about Mr. Brown. Be prepared to support your inferences with evidence from the paragraph."

Mr. Mills looks at each of the children as they are reading. He then glances around the room. He says, "Judy, may I see you for a moment?" Judy comes to Mr. Mills. The teacher asks Judy in a very quiet tone if he can help her. He says, "Judy, you look confused. What's wrong?" Judy says that she is having trouble figuring out the answer to a question. Mr. Mills tells Judy to work on something else for about 10 minutes, and then he will help her. As Judy goes back to her seat, Mr. Mills again quickly glances around the room. As his eyes meet those of some of the children, he smiles at them. Mr. Mills then looks at the children in his group. He sees that they are ready and asks them what inferences they can make about Mr. Brown. All raise their hands. Mr. Mills calls on one student, who makes an inference about Mr. Brown. Mr. Mills asks the rest of the group if they agree with the inference. Two students say that they do not agree. Mr. Mills asks everyone to skim the paragraph to find clues that would support their position. Mr. Mills again looks around the room. A child approaches and asks him a question. He answers the question and then goes back to the group. After a while, Mr. Mills and the group discuss whether they have accomplished what they were supposed to. They then discuss, for a moment, what they will be doing next time. They all go back to their seats. Before Mr. Mills calls another group, he checks off in his plan book the objectives that the group has accomplished. He also makes some remarks in his record book about the individual children in the group. Mr. Mills puts down his book and walks around the room to check on what the students are doing. He smiles at a number of the students, helps Judy with her problem, and listens in on the group that has been working together on a special project. Mr. Mills asks the group members how they are doing and how much more time they will need before they will be ready to report their progress to him and the class. Mr. Mills then goes back to the reading table and teaches another group.

Experienced reading teachers like Mr. Mills are good organizers and managers. They know how to work with large groups, small groups, the whole class, and individual students. As Table 6.1 shows, each type of grouping has advantages and disadvantages. When thinking about grouping students, teachers need to think through what they are using as a basis for grouping. Usually the basis for placement in reading groups is the student's achievement level. During the first few weeks of the term, teachers collect data concerning the achievement levels of each of the students in their classes through observation, teacher-made tests, and standardized tests. After evaluating the collected data, the teacher organizes tentative groups. The number of groups in a skill area depends on the amount of variability within the class. For some areas, there may be three or four groups; for some, there may only be two groups; for some, the teacher may decide to work with the whole class as a unit; and for some areas, the teacher may have a number of children working individually. The grouping pattern is flexible, and the groups themselves are recognized as flexible units; children can easily flow from one group to another. When the purpose for the group has been met, the group dissolves.

The teacher as a good manager is able to deal with more than one situation at a time. A teacher working with a group should be aware of what is going on not only in that group but also with the other children in the class. A teacher cannot "dismiss" the rest of the class because she is working with a particular group. Even though the children have been given challenging work based on their individual needs, the teacher must be alert to what is happening to ensure safety for all children and to keep children on task. The alert teacher is able to prevent problems. The scenario above presents an example of a good manager. Notice especially how Mr. Mills is able to manage a number of ongoing activities at the same time. Notice how he is always aware of what is going on in his class, and notice how he prevents problems from arising.

Enhanced eText
Video Example 6.1
Flexible Classrooms.

In this video, one school district demonstrates its organizational and management techniques for flexible learning. https://www.youtube.com/watch?v=4cscJcRKYxA

Table 6.1 Group Size for Guided Reading Experiences

Group Size	Description	Advantages	Disadvantages	When It Works
Whole Class	Teacher works with the whole class and everyone participates in similar activities. In one way or another, the same text is often read by all students.	• Builds a community of learners. • Provides a common knowledge base for all.	• Differentiating instruction is more difficult. • Some students can get frustrated or bored, depending on the level of instruction. • Students may not interact as planned.	• Different learners are considered when planning instruction. • All members of the class are provided with a similar experience.
Small Group	Groups of 2–5 students work together to accomplish a given task.	• Provides for focused instruction. • Engages more learners. • Students learn to work with one another.	• Students may not interact. • Creates a higher noise level. • Students might be grouped together for too long. • Student perceptions of the group can be negative.	• Group membership changes on a regular basis. • Students are taught how to respond to one another.
Partners	Students are paired up with one another to read text in one or more ways.	• Students stay focused. • Enables relationships to develop. • Encourages independent learning so the teacher can help those who need it.	• One of the two students may become too dependent on the other. • One of the two may dominate.	• Partners are switched on a regular basis. • Procedures are clearly understood by both.
Individual	Students work by themselves, and each often reads a different text.	• Allows students to read at a comfortable level and to develop their own understanding. • Enables teacher to evaluate individual progress to determine what students know and need to know.	• Can be hard to organize. • Students may become distracted and/or lose focus. • Little sense of community	• Reading is at the appropriate level. • Students understand procedures. • An effort is made to bring students back together in either small or large groups to discuss what they've learned.

Role 4: Self-Evaluator

Sarah decides to administer a word test to learn whether students have a store of words that they can identify instantaneously (i.e., sight words). When analyzing the results of the test, she discovers that according to this measure, several students appear to have a limited store of words. She decides to form a special needs group, placing all students who need to acquire more words into the group. Sarah then designs a lesson to teach the words she wants them to know. Several of the students have difficulty with the lesson, as indicated by their inability to identify the words at the conclusion of the lesson, and Sarah finds this troubling. Without a doubt, the lesson should have set students up for success, and by the conclusion of it, all of the students should have been able to show that they accomplished the objective. Why didn't they? Sarah is confused because the lesson was designed based on specific data she collected from her students for a specific reason—this kind of targeted instruction is supposed to work! Because Sarah talks with her students frequently about herself as a reader, she realizes that in her own reading, she sometimes omits or substitutes some of these connecting words. She also has difficulty finding definitions for these words out of context. Because she stopped to try to understand reading and readers, she decides to revisit her lesson. She takes a close look at her lesson to see if there is anything she might have done differently to help her students. Her examination helps her to see that the words she was trying to teach needed context because they are very abstract: *is, the, of, was.* Yet another look at the lesson helps her to see that students may have little or no understanding of how these words relate to reading whole texts. She had not provided them with time to read books that could have been selected with these words in mind. As a result of her analysis, Sarah realizes that she needs to redesign the lesson. She will use books to emphasize how these words appear in meaningful phrases and sentences. Her self-assessment plays a role in helping students to succeed.

Although the major goal of this text is to provide you with an understanding of the many ways to assess and evaluate children's reading growth, teacher self-assessment plays an important part in the diagnosis cycle. As a matter of fact, an insightful look at our mission, identity, and beliefs might lead to enhancement of our capabilities and instructional behaviors. Also, taking time to reflect on lessons and how students perform can help you to measure the effectiveness of the lesson. Did all students attain the lesson objective? If not, why not? Asking questions such as these can illustrate that sometimes problems with learning are about the design of the teaching.

There are many ways to self-evaluate. Videotaping and reviewing lessons using specific criteria is one. Evaluating student performance is another. In addition, a checklist can be designed to help evaluate the entire diagnostic reading and improvement program in general. Another checklist can be constructed to reflect on reading lessons. In Figure 6.2, we provide a self-evaluation rubric for the four roles effective teachers bring to their work. Another method is to write notes on the lesson itself, either during the lesson or afterward. The underlying assumption is that there is a written plan for the lesson, which indicates that the teacher has thought through the lesson and the many associated considerations, such as the students who will be receiving the lesson, the materials, and teaching strategies.

Figure 6.3 is an example of a survey that can be used to look at the diagnostic reading program in general. Figure 6.4 shows a sample self-assessment teachers can use to reflect on reading lessons. After reading each question, teachers using this checklist can rate themselves on a scale, with 1 being poor and 5 being excellent, and then write out any thoughts and/or ideas related to each question.

Figure 6.2 Sample Teacher Self-Assessment

Question	Yes/No	Reflection	Plan
Teacher as Planner			
1. Did I use student data to plan the lesson?	Y	Based on individual reading conference data collected this week during silent reading	Determine additional groups during one-to-one conferences.
2. Did I set a goal for my instruction and follow a plan for reaching that goal during the lesson?	Y	My goal: Only include students in the group who have proven the need for the lesson.	Form subsequent groups based on other shared needs.
Explicit Reading Teacher			
3. Did I use specific strategies that were purposefully aligned with the objectives for the lesson based on student need?	Y	Objective: Student identifies evidence in text to support claims/draw conclusions. Guided reading group (GRG) Objective written and read for students Teacher modeling Guided student practice individually	Continue using this structure.
4. Did students have meaningful opportunities to practice and show their abilities?	Y	Student practice after teacher modeling Whisper reading or silent reading with teacher questioning	Give students a chance to practice their strategy use with a peer in the next GRG.
Teacher as Organizer and Manager			
5. Did each of the students included in the lesson need the lesson?	Y/N	Jasmine used the strategy consistently throughout the guided group.	Monitor Jasmine's strategy use during future conferences. Introduce inferring strategy.
6. Did I strategically engage all learners during the lesson?	N	Trevor uninterested in text	Have Trevor bring self-selected text to next guided reading group.
Self-Evaluator			
7. Did I achieve my instructional goal from above (question #2)?	Y	Each student proved to need the explicit instruction. Jasmine caught on right away and can move on.	Monitor goal New goal: encourage student selected texts
8. Do I have an instructional goal and plan for my next lesson?	Y	Trevor, Sean, and Carmen seem to need modeling and guided practice for this strategy.	GRG tomorrow with three students and Aaron (new student) Option to bring self-selected text

Figure 6.3 All Children Survey

> **"All children can learn in a system that respects their abilities."**
> —C. Roller

Statement	Yes	No
1. All children are provided the same amount of time to read authentic books and /or stories throughout the day.		
2. All children spend the same amount of time on skill/drill work.		
3. All children are permitted to read without interruptions.		
4. All children are expected to solve problems when reading.		
5. All children are provided time to solve problems when reading.		
6. All children are provided the same amount of time to read books during guided reading instruction.		
7. All children are provided many "just right" books.		
8. All children are engaged with high-level questions.		
9. All children preread silently before reading orally in front of a group.		
10. All children appear to enjoy reading.		
11. All children have the opportunity to self-select books.		
12. All children are provided time to read independently.		

Source: From *Flexible Grouping in Reading* by Michael Opitz. Published by Scholastic Teaching Resources/Scholastic, Inc. Copyright © 1998 by Michael Opitz. Reprinted by permission.

Enhanced eText **Application Exercise 6.2:** Understanding Teacher Self-Assessment

---

Bridge: From Understanding to Assessment

When teachers understand that _____,	then they will assess _____.
Student successes depend on teachers' growth as planners,	Themselves and their own practice, using self-assessments, video of their teaching, and peer observations.
Student successes depend on teachers' growth in delivering explicit instruction,	The effectiveness of instruction by collecting data and reflecting on student growth following explicit instruction.
Students create their identities as readers in the social situations teachers develop for teaching and learning reading,	The variety of strategies they have for flexible grouping; how long reading groups stay together; and how frequently reading groups mix people of different abilities.
Managing the growth of 20–30 young readers is one of the most difficult things about teaching in grades K–12,	How well their organization systems work for keeping track of the growth of all readers to use in a. conferring with students, b. reporting to stakeholders, and c. reflecting on teacher effectiveness.
Accountability rules within states and districts rarely provide the best tools for reflection and self-evaluation,	Their grade level's and school's use of professional development structures to encourage ongoing reflection and self-evaluation (Consider the teacher self-assessment in Figure 6.1.).

Figure 6.4 Teacher Self-Assessment of a Reading Lesson

Reading Lesson: _____ Date: _____		
Question	**Rating Scale**	**Thoughts / Ideas**
1. Did I capitalize on students' interests?	1 2 3 4 5	
2. Was I enthusiastic about the lesson?	1 2 3 4 5	
3. Was I clear in presenting the lesson objective?	1 2 3 4 5	
4. Did all activities relate to the objective and did they progress from concrete to abstract?	1 2 3 4 5	
5. Did I provide for individual differences?	1 2 3 4 5	
6. Did my assessment of students align with the objective for the lesson?	1 2 3 4 5	
7. Did I allow enough time for students to complete the activities under my guidance?	1 2 3 4 5	
8. Did I use positive reinforcement?	1 2 3 4 5	
9. Did I give specific feedback so that students knew how well they were progressing?	1 2 3 4 5	
10. Did I alter the lesson as needed?	1 2 3 4 5	

Revisiting the Opening Scenarios

Now that you have had some time to learn about the importance of the teacher in a diagnostic approach to assessing, learning, and teaching reading, take another look at what Mr. Lane was doing in his classroom. Which characteristics does he seem to exemplify?

Authors' Summary

Before reading our summary statements for each outcome, we suggest you read each outcome and summarize it in your own words.

Once finished, cross-check your response with our brief summary to determine how well you recalled the major points.

6.1 Describe attributes that define good teachers.

- Although schools might have the newest technologies, instructional materials, and other equipment, knowledgeable teachers are the most important ingredient for learning to occur.

- Different entities have identified specific attributes that are used to define good teachers. These include competence with the subject matter and the necessary pedagogical procedures to teach that subject matter, purposeful instruction, care for students and their learning, and the ability to reflect on their craft, which they use to perfect their instruction.

6.2   Explain characteristics and practices of good reading teachers.

- Regardless of grade level, there are common practices that teachers who maximize student potential use. Motivating students is but one of these factors.

- Good teachers appear to be most effective when they connect personally with their students and organize information in interesting, meaningful ways that lead students to understand the desired learning.

6.3   Discuss how teacher expectations influence children's learning.

- Because children will live up—or down—to teacher expectations, teachers need to be aware of a self-fulfilling prophecy where assumptions about children become true because of teacher attitudes and the schoolwide structure.

- Having a positive mindset about all learners, one that assumes that learners are half-full rather than half-empty, better ensures that all students will receive equal opportunities to learn.

6.4   Explain the four roles of a teacher who embraces a diagnostic approach to assessing, learning, and teaching reading.

- Teaching is a complex behavior that calls on teachers to function in many different roles. Four of these roles that we elucidate in this chapter are planner, explicit reading teacher, organizer and manager, and self-evaluator.

- Effective teachers continually strive to teach to their best abilities by refining these four roles. They also identify themselves as readers and convey that identity to their students.

6.5   Use self-assessment data to plan subsequent instruction.

- Teaching is downright challenging. We can make our lives easier by gathering data that reveal directions for where we spend our instructional time and energy next. Our self-assessment and student data provide a roadmap to instruction. The data take the guesswork out of our efforts.

- Good teachers use data to make decisions and back up their actions with that data.

Think About It!

1. Think of one of the best teachers you have ever had. Discuss the characteristics of the teacher you remember best. Compare and contrast this teacher with other teachers you remember as being less effective.

2. Use the information in this chapter to create an observational checklist. Observe a teacher during a reading lesson, or videotape yourself teaching one. Check off all the characteristics you observe. What do you notice?

3. You have been assigned to a special committee that is concerned with teacher professional development.

Based on your understanding of teacher characteristics and roles, what suggestions would you have for the committee?

4. Use the information from your self-assessment to determine and write goals for your instruction. Start by setting one goal for each lesson. Be sure to share your goal with your students as an effort to make yourself accountable and to model and guide the students through goal-setting practices associated with each lesson.

Websites

- https://www.cultofpedagogy.com/goal-setting-for-teachers/

    This site provides guidance for the goal-oriented teacher.

- https://www.teachingchannel.org/video/student-goal-setting

    This site showcases strategies that can be used to guide student learning, like goal setting. Each strategy may also be used by the teacher as a model or use of best practice for their own learning.

- http://www.readingrockets.org/article/differentiated-instruction-reading

    This site contains a definition of differentiated instruction pertaining to reading as well as articles geared toward defining this concept. The site includes an extensive annotated list of articles on the importance of differentiated instruction and various other relevant topics. The articles are geared toward teachers and parents. Each article also provides links to strategies and articles on related topics.

- http://eduscapes.com/tap/topic43.htm

    This site explores three different types of instructional approaches: project-based learning, problem-based learning, and inquiry-based learning. The authors provide various resources in each section, enabling teachers to choose which approach, or which combination thereof, might work in their specific classrooms.

- http://www.readwritethink.org/classroom-resources/lesson-plans/

    Providing a wealth of lesson plans centered on literacy, learning language, learning about language, and learning through language, this site enables teachers to search for lessons targeting specific grades (K–12) and literacy topics. The site also offers various student materials designed to enhance literacy learning and engagement.

- https://www.teachervision.com/lesson-planning-forms-resources

    In addition to having an entire section on teaching methods, this site provides sections on standards for good teaching, adapting lessons for all students, multiple intelligences overview, and much more. The site offers limited free access.

Endnotes

1. Liebfreund, M., & Amendum, S. (2017). Teachers' experiences providing one-on-one instruction to struggling readers. *Reading Horizons, 56*(4), 5.

2. Rosenthal, R., & Jacobson, L. (1968). *Pygmalion in the classroom*. New York: Holt, Rinehart and Winston.; Pidgeon, D. (1970). *Expectation and pupil performance*. London: National Foundation for Educational Research, England and Wales.

3. Johnston, P. (2003). *Choice words*. Portland, ME: Stenhouse.

4. Hall, L. (2009). *Improving middle school students' ability to understand, apply, and talk about comprehension strategies*. Poster session presented at the International Reading Association Convention, Phoenix, AZ.

5. Slavin, R., Karweit, N., & Wasik, B. (1992, February). Preventing early school failure: What works. *Educational Leadership, 50*(4), 10–18.

6. Allington, R. (2005). *What really matters for struggling readers: Designing research-based programs (2nd ed.). New York: Allyn & Bacon.*

7. Bond, G., & Dykstra, R. (1967, Summer). The cooperative research program in first-grade reading instruction. Reading Research Quarterly 2, 1–142.; Harris, A., & Morrison, C. (1969, January). The CRAFT project: A final report. The Reading Teacher, 22, 335–340.

8. Anderson, R., Hiebert, E., Scott, J., & Wilkinson, I. (1985). *Becoming a nation of readers* (p. 85). Washington, DC: National Institute of Education.

9. Ibid.

10. Chall, J. (1978). A decade of research on reading and learning disabilities. *What Research Has to Say about Reading Instruction* (pp. 39, 40). Newark, DE: International Reading Association.

11. Waczisko, M. (2007). The perceptual approach to teacher dispositions: The effective teacher as an effective person. In M. Diez & J. Raths (Eds.), *Dispositions in Teacher Education* (pp. 53–89). Charlotte, NC: Information Age Publishing.

12. Colvin, G. (2008). *Talent is overrated* (p. 67). New York: Penguin.

13. National Center for Research on Teacher Learning (NCRTL), About the NCRTL, Retrieved November 19, 2018, from https://education.msu.edu/NCRTL/PDFs/NCRTL/SpecialReports/sr691.pdf
     Powell, W., & Kusuma-Powell, O. (2015). Overcoming resistance to new ideas. *Phi Delta Kappan, 96*(8), 66–69.

14. Wharton-McDonald, R., Pressley, M., & Hampston, J. (1998). Literacy instruction in nine first-grade classrooms: Teacher characteristics and student achievements. *The Elementary School Journal, 99*, 101–128.

15. Schechter, R., Kazakoff, E., Bundschuh, K., Prescott, J., & Macaruso, P. (2017). Exploring the impact of engaged teachers on implementation fidelity and reading skill gains in a blended learning reading program. *Reading Psychology* 38, 553–579.; Dilts, R. (1994). Effective presentation skills. Capitola, CA: Meta Publications.

16. Allington, R., & Johnson, P., eds. (2002). *Reading to learn: Lessons from exemplary classrooms*. New York: Guilford.

17. Willingham, D. (2009). *Why don't students like school? (p. 65)*. San Francisco, CA: Jossey-Bass.

18. Adapted from Opitz, M. (2007). *Don't speed. READ! 12 steps to smart and sensible fluency instruction*. New York: Scholastic.

19. Salvia, J., & Ysseldyke, J. (1988). *Assessment in special and remedial education (4th ed., p. 525)*. Boston: Houghton Mifflin.

20. Durking, D. (1993). *Teaching them to read*. Boston: Allyn and Bacon.

Chapter 7
Teaching with Texts

David Pereiras/Shutterstock

 Chapter Outline

Scenario: Mr. Hall's Text-Packed Classroom

Understanding the Importance of Reading Texts

Understanding the Importance of Teaching with Texts

Understanding and Teaching Text Types

 Learning Outcomes

After reading this chapter, you should be able to . . .

7.1 Discuss the importance of providing students with time to read texts in school.

7.2 Provide a rationale for teaching with a variety of texts in a diagnostic reading program.

7.3 Describe different types of texts, provide an example of a text, and explain how it can be used to teach reading in a diagnostic reading program.

Scenario

Mr. Hall's Text-Packed Classroom

When parents walk into Mr. Hall's room, they are immediately impressed with the huge variety of text. They see shelves, crates, tubs, cabinets, bulletin boards, and walls all filled or covered with different kinds of texts. They are also surprised to see children out of their seats and going to different places in the room, instead of reading quietly at their desks. Some are reading from *Sports Illustrated* magazine in a small group with Mr. Hall. Others are across the room looking at weather report charts from that day's newspaper. In yet another area, students are reading self-selected books independently. At another station, students are looking at a website about whaling in Greenland. During the next break, parents ask why Mr. Hall has students reading so many different kinds of texts. How might he respond?

Understanding the Importance of Reading Texts

Reading helps reading! Not only is the amount of time spent reading essential for success in reading, but also the amount of actual reading accomplished is vital to reading achievement.[1, 2] Researchers have found that children who excel in reading read significantly more text than those who find reading difficult. This is true both in and out of the classroom. Historically, children who need the most practice reading connected text have instead spent their classroom time learning isolated skills. They spend little or no time actually reading. In particular, struggling readers have few opportunities to practice silent reading behaviors.[3]

In the Nation's Report Cards, reported findings consistently show a positive relationship between achievement and exposure to intensive reading experiences.[4] In other words, those students who stated they read more frequently for fun on their own time, on the average, achieved better scores in reading than those who reported reading less frequently. Students who were involved in frequent discussions about their studies with friends or family had higher average reading proficiency than students who reported little or no discussion.[5]

As readers finish elementary school, some have internalized the misconception that only novels and textbooks count as "reading." Clearly, this is unfortunate, and it may happen for a variety of reasons. First, students may have been exposed primarily to these types of books at school, whereas other forms of text such as magazines, electronic texts, and comic books were not accessible or acceptable during the school day. So although students may have read these kinds of texts outside of school, they may have developed the idea that they do not count as reading during school. A second reason, which connects to the first, is that students perceive that "good" readers only read chapter books because that's what they see strong readers reading at school.

One way to guard against students' developing a limited view of what counts as reading is to make a variety of texts both accessible and acceptable throughout the school day. For example, when sharing information with students, the teacher might decide to read from a newspaper or a magazine. At other times, the teacher might decide to use electronic text and display it on an interactive whiteboard for all to see and manipulate. At still other times, the teacher might have students choose articles from a magazine to read during a small-group reading lesson. Using such different texts sends a message to students that these are valuable and should be encountered during the school day.

Bridge: From Understanding to the Importance of Teaching with Texts

When teachers understand that _____,	then teachers may want to _____.
Reading growth requires an abundance of meaningful reading practice,	Create a daily classroom routine that includes extended periods of reading time for all students.
More time reading is only the beginning of supporting the growth of readers, striving readers included,	Incorporate guided reading groups, decentralized text discussions,[6] and one-to-one conferencing in authentic and connected ways.
Student reading perceptions may hinder reading achievement,	Make a variety of texts available to students in the classroom and promote their value in supporting reading growth.

Understanding the Importance of Teaching with Texts

In everyday life, we read many different types of texts. What we read depends on factors including interest[7] and purpose. Using a variety of texts, then, is necessary to help students learn what it means to be a reader. Remember that we are teaching children to be readers rather than merely teaching them to read. Right from the start, children need to be reading books and other works written and illustrated by a variety of authors and illustrators. Here are seven reasons for using many different kinds of authentic texts:

1. *To motivate all children to be readers.* When students read from a wide variety of texts, they are likely to connect print in the classroom to the "real-world" print they encounter outside of school. Teachers who use a variety of text types honor the fact that what students see and do outside the classroom has value for school learning, too.[8] We want students to value reading.

2. *To capitalize on student interest.* Some students may prefer reading online rather than reading printed text.[9] Others would rather read information texts than stories. They like learning about specific details related to given topics. Providing children with texts they enjoy motivates them to read.[10]

3. *To address reading attitudes.* Attitudes have a directive and dynamic influence on all our lives, and once they are set, they are difficult to change. Concomitant learnings such as reading attitudes often remain with students more than the subject matter itself. Therefore, using many different texts can help children develop a love of reading.

4. *To help students understand that different texts are written in different ways.* Stories are written using a story grammar that includes setting, characters, problem, attempts to solve the problem, and resolution. Expository text (i.e., text written to inform) may encompass sequence of events or compare/contrast, or use other text structures. Knowing about these different formats or structures that are used to write texts helps students better comprehend them.[11, 12]

5. *To expose children to content-specific vocabulary and new concepts.* As a result of reading a variety of texts, students acquire larger vocabularies. For example, when reading an informational article about spiders, students learn words associated with spiders. An increase in knowledge ensures that better reading comprehension will occur.[13]

6. *To serve as a scaffold.* Because stories are generally easier for students to read than nonfiction, fiction and nonfiction can be paired so that when students are finished reading one book, they have a better understanding of the content.[14] For example,

as a way of helping children understand something about apples, a teacher could first have them take a look at *Dappled Apples* (Carr, 2001) or *The Apple Pie Tree* (Hall, 1996) before they look at *Apples* (Robbins, 2002), which is a nonfiction selection. Having acquired an understanding of the material presented in these texts, the reader is more likely to comprehend information presented in other books such as textbooks. Having students read texts that relate to a specific topic is a way to provide this scaffolding.

7. *To broaden students' knowledge base.* Good comprehension is dependent on knowledge. If we know something about the topic we are reading, we are more apt to understand what we have read and to remember it longer. The converse is also true. Exposing children to different ideas presented in different texts is a way of broadening a student's knowledge base.[15]

Enhanced eText **Application Exercise 7.2:** Understanding the Importance of Teaching with Texts

---

Bridge: From Importance of Teaching with Texts to Teaching Text Types

When teachers understand that _____,	then teachers may want to _____.
They are teaching children to be readers rather than merely teaching them to read,	Make reading experiences authentic, engaging, and interesting using a wide variety of texts.
Teaching with a variety of texts can motivate all children to be readers,	Provide high-interest texts that connect the "real-world" experiences of students to classroom learning to instill a value of reading.
Teaching with a variety of texts can support student understanding of various formats and structures of text,	Showcase and teach various text structures to promote student reading comprehension.
Exposing students to content-specific vocabulary and concepts is important for building background knowledge and scaffolding to more difficult texts,	Pair fiction and nonfiction texts on a particular topic.

Understanding and Teaching Text Types

There are many ways to use texts to help children grow as readers. Because there are so many different types of texts, we have divided them into three broad categories to better explain and describe them: commercial, trade, and other. *Commercial books* are texts that have been written for a given program. Three types of commercial books exist: little books, basal readers, and textbooks. *Little books* are small books that can be easily held by young children. The books are usually the same size, have a paperback cover, and have few pages. *Basal readers* are grade-level anthologies accompanied by additional materials such as teacher guides, workbooks, and commercially created tests. *Textbooks* are written for specific content areas and are used primarily for instructional purposes. Most often, these commercial texts have to be ordered directly from the publisher; they are not available in bookstores or public libraries.

Trade books can be found in bookstores and libraries. They are sometimes called *authentic literature* because they are written primarily to communicate a message to the reader. They are not created for a specific reading instruction program. Authors who write these books are most interested in conveying their ideas, and they do so using a variety of words and illustrations. For the purposes of this book, *children's literature*, *authentic literature*, and *trade books* have the same meaning.

Texts that don't fit neatly into either of the first two categories, such as magazines, Magazines, newspapers, real-life texts, and electronic texts will be treated as another category in this chapter.

Enhanced eText
Video Example 7.1

In this **video clip**, a teacher guides students in noting text features that are a part of a new reading assignment.

We also want to make clear that our list of texts is anything but exhaustive. There are additional types of texts, such as graphic novels, that captivate readers. Children's literature reviews (e.g., *Horn Book Guide*, or *Kirkus Reviews*) and the annual teacher's and children's choices published by the International Literacy Association are excellent resources to consult for lists of books with high reviews.

Two points of confusion can surface when we talk about using different texts to teach children. One involves the way trade books are used in other programs. Sometimes trade books are selected for grade-level anthologies which, when put together, compose a reading program (i.e., a basal reader). Another point of confusion involves the idea of "leveled" books. Basically, these are collections of books from two categories—commercial *and* trade—that are leveled according to difficulty.[16] As Figure 7.1 shows, specific features are used to determine the book's level of difficulty.

Table 7.1 illustrates the different texts that can be used for independent or whole or small-group reading instruction and shows the most appropriate grade levels in which the

Figure 7.1 Text Features

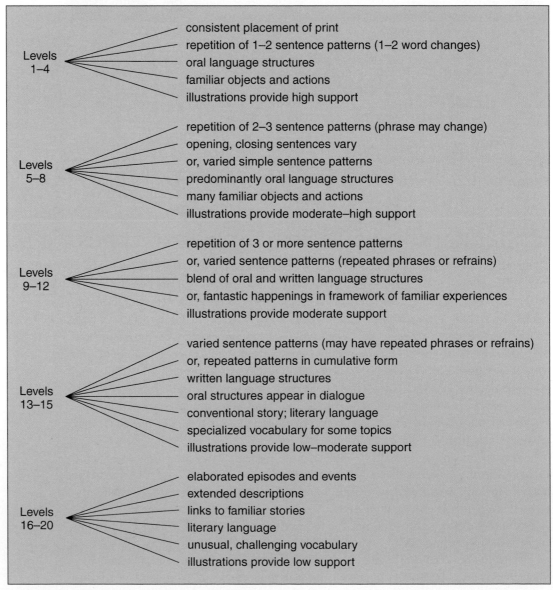

Source: Barbara Peterson. (1998). Characteristics of Text That Support Beginning Readers. Columbus, OH: The Ohio State University. Used with permission.

Table 7.1 Texts for Independent, Whole-Group, and Small-Group Reading Instruction

Text Type/Grade Level	K	1	2	3	4	5	6
Commercial books							
Little books	•	•					
Basal readers	•	•	•	•	•	•	•
Textbooks	•	•	•	•	•	•	•
Children's literature							
Predictable books	•	•	•				
Information (nonfiction)	•	•	•	•	•	•	•
Multilevel literature	•	•	•	•	•	•	•
Series books		•	•	•	•	•	•
Poetry	•	•	•	•	•	•	•
Chapter books			•	•	•	•	•
Multicultural literature	•	•	•	•	•	•	•
Other							
Magazines	•	•	•	•	•	•	•
Newspapers	•	•	•	•	•	•	•
Real-life texts	•	•	•	•	•	•	•
Electronic texts	•	•	•	•	•	•	•

texts are used. Additional information for each type of text—including a description, examples, reasons for using the text, and teaching suggestions—appears on the pages that follow.

Commercial Books

Little Books

Description   Little books are small books that are easily held by young children. They usually are packaged as sets of books that are the same size, have a paperback cover, and contain just a few pages. Many times, these books are written by different authors, yet all titles are leveled by the company that produces them. They are then assembled to create sets of readers that can be used for small-group reading instruction.

Examples   Sets of little books are available from a number of publishers, including the following:

- Pair-It Extreme (Houghton Mifflin Harcourt, 2013)
- Literacy by Design (Harcourt Archive, 2013)

Why Use Them?   Little books are especially designed for use with beginning readers, starting in kindergarten and continuing through first grade. They are sometimes used with children in second grade as well. As leveled texts are packaged in multiple sets, the books can be used for demonstrations and interventions with young readers in small-group settings. Likewise, the increasingly challenging texts facilitate the scaffolded instruction discussed earlier. They have the look and feel of real books, and their use more closely parallels reading experiences in which children's literature is used. They have a strong appeal to young readers because they convey a sense of reading whole books. Generally inexpensive, they can be used to create a classroom library of accessible books for use during independent reading time as well as guided reading.

Teaching with Little Books

- Select an appropriate title for a group of children who are reading at a similar general achievement level. After providing an introduction to the text, invite children to read it to themselves. After they have read the book, engage the children in one or more ways. They may first discuss the text and read aloud a part they liked the best. If you are focusing on teaching different ways to figure out unknown words, select a word from the text that posed difficulty, write it and the sentence in which it appears on the board, and ask children how they can go about figuring out this unknown word.

- Using some common element such as story setting, select texts at different levels to represent the readers in the group. After children have had time to read their assigned books, teach them about story setting. Allow students time to share details about where their stories took place.

Basal Readers

Description   Basal readers are the central components of commercially developed reading programs. They are often structured as anthologies of grade-leveled texts with additional supportive materials such as teacher guides and student workbooks available. Basal readers are most often selected and purchased to provide a cohesive, consistent, continuous reading curriculum across and between grade levels throughout a school district or within individual schools. In most classrooms, each child is provided a copy of the anthology (i.e., reader) to use during guided reading.

Examples

- Journeys (Houghton Mifflin Reading, 2013)
- Reading Street (Scott Foresman, 2013)

Why Use Them?   The use of basal readers is strongly encouraged and expected in many school districts. In fact, after these materials are purchased, little if any money is left over to purchase other materials that can be used to teach reading. One reason for using basal readers, then, has to do with district administrators' level of expectation. Another has to do with access. All students are provided with reading materials, and teachers are provided with ample materials for instructional support. The selections are somewhat organized by increasingly sophisticated vocabulary, concepts, and text structures so that the selections within the anthologies can be used to scaffold instruction in much the same way as the "little books" discussed above.

Teaching with Basal Readers

- Choose individual selections within the basal anthology to use for a demonstration or intervention lesson.
- Newer basal reading anthologies have the added advantage of having selections organized by theme. Using these themed stories for common and shared-response activities with small groups of students is a natural. Assign all students within a group the same selection within a theme and then ask them to share something of interest. Another way to capitalize on the use of these themed stories is to have different students read different stories within the theme. Once finished, students can compare and contrast their stories and tell how their stories relate to the overall theme.

Textbooks

Description   Besides the materials purchased for and used in the classroom reading/language arts program, a number of other commercially prepared texts are written for specific content areas, such as science, social studies, and mathematics. Often, one series is selected for a school or school district. A series is most often composed of a set of core texts, each containing grade-level-appropriate presentations of increasingly sophisticated subject area content. Each student is provided a copy of the grade-level text.

Examples of Companies That Publish Textbook Series

- Scholastic
- Prentice-Hall
- Pearson

Why Use Them? As is the case with basal readers, both teachers and students usually have easy access to textbooks. They are often selected, purchased, and distributed by school district personnel as a foundation for content area curricula. As with basal readers, the use of textbooks is often strongly encouraged because significant resources have been used to purchase them. Therefore, one reason to use textbooks is to meet externally mandated expectations. Another, perhaps more essential reason for using textbooks centers around student success. As we all know, students will encounter textbook-based instruction in specific content areas. Students' success depends on their ability to handle the reading demands of these texts. The goal is to improve students' ability to negotiate their way through these texts with maximum comprehension.[17]

Enhanced eText
Video Example 7.2
Watch as a fifth-grade teacher guides her class through nonfiction reading intervention strategies by providing guided instruction when using the text features of a content textbook.

Teaching with Textbooks

- Choose a specific section of the textbook to show students how to do a preview as a warm-up for successful reading. After students have previewed the section, allow time for them to read the text to themselves. Once they have finished reading, have students relate information that they discovered.

- Most textbook chapters are divided by subheadings. Either assign a section or invite students to choose the section they would like to read; then, ask them to look for three specific ideas they can share with others in the group. Once they have finished reading, have students in the group create a note-taking guide to record information about the other sections of the chapter that they did not read.

Children's Literature

Predictable Books

Description Predictable books are written with specific features that enable children to read with ease. They share the following characteristics:[18]

- *Pictures that support the text.* These pictures illustrate what the text says, so children can use them to help read the text.

- *Repeated sentence or phrase.* The same sentence or phrase is repeated on nearly every page. The repetition helps young readers use memory to read the sentence or phrase.

- *Rhyme and rhythm.* The use of both rhyme and rhythm cues readers with oral language features that facilitate reading.

- *Cumulative pattern.* As the story progresses, new lines are added, but previous lines are repeated, thus providing readers with practice.

- *Familiar sequence.* Days of the week and counting are two examples of this feature. Students use what they know about both to successfully read the text at hand.

Examples

- *The Napping House* (Wood, 2009)
- *Everywhere the Cow Says Moo* (Weinstein, 2008)
- *Hug* (Alborough, 2009)
- *The Deep Blue Sea: A Book of Colors* (Wood, 2005)
- *Good Morning, Digger* (Rockwell, 2005)

- *Mommies Say Shhh!* (Polacco, 2005)
- *Why Not?* (Wormell, 2000)
- *One Red Dot* (Carter, 2005)

Why Use Them? Predictable books are advantageous for several reasons.[19] First, these books employ the language features listed above, which enable children to read with greater ease. Second, they enable children to read authentic literature from the very beginning, thus helping children to see that they can read "real" books. Third, although they are most often used with beginning readers, predictable books provide a tremendous amount of support and success for English language learners and for older children who struggle with reading. Fourth, many predictable books are published as "big books"—oversized versions of a book. They lend themselves to interactive sessions with a large group, which helps all students to see that they are a part of the classroom community.

Teaching with Predictable Books

- Select an appropriate title for a group of children who are reading at a similar general achievement level. Introduce the text and then invite children to read it to themselves. After they have read the book, engage the children in one or more ways. They may first discuss the text and read aloud a part they liked the best. If you are focusing on teaching different ways to figure out unknown words, select a word from the text that posed difficulty, write it and the sentence in which it appears on the board, and ask children how they can go about figuring out this unknown word.

- Using some common element such as story setting, select texts at different levels to represent the readers in the group. After children have had time to read their assigned books, teach them about story setting. Allow students time to share details about where their stories took place.

- When using a big book that contains a repetitive passage, think about pausing during the reading as you come to the passage each time, to give children an opportunity to chime in. To help children develop a speech-to-print match, point to the words as they are read.

Information Books (Nonfiction)

Description Nonfiction books present factual information about a given topic. They are usually accompanied by photographs and illustrations to help students better understand the content.

Examples

- *Faces of the Moon* (Crelin, 2009)
- *Bird, Butterfly, Eel* (Prosek, 2009)
- *River of Dreams: Story of the Hudson River* (Talbott, 2009)
- *Panda Kindergarten* (Ryder, 2009)
- *Baby Sea Otter* (Tatham, 2005)
- *Into the Ice: The Story of Arctic Exploration* (Curlee, 1998)
- *Liberty Rising: The Story of the Statue of Liberty* (Shea, 2005)
- *On Earth* (Karas, 2005)
- *Show Off: How to Do Absolutely Everything One Step at a Time* (Stephens & Mann, 2009)
- *In 1776* (Marzollo, 1994)
- *Moon: Science, History, and Mystery* (Ross, 2009)

Enhanced eText
Video Example 7.3
A read-aloud with teacher attention to picture clues to support student comprehension
https://www.youtube.com/watch?v=DmuVsnK0lWQ

Why Use Them?   There are two sound reasons for using information texts. First, they present facts about the world around us. Because many children are curious about their surroundings, these texts provide motivating and interesting reading material. Second, the text structures used to write information texts differ from those used to write fiction. Students need to learn how to navigate all of these different types of texts in order to become competent readers. Informational text structures include compare/contrast, cause and effect, description, sequence, and problem/solution.

Teaching with Information Books

- Select a text with specific features that you want to teach students. For example, you might want to show them how to read a diagram and the way it relates to the written text. After providing instruction, have children read the text and follow up with a discussion in which children talk about how the diagram helped them read the text.

- Use a specific nonfiction selection to show students how to process the information presented: picture captions, subheadings, bold print, and other features. After providing this introduction, have students read the text. They can then report one or two ideas they learned from the text.

Multilevel Books

Description   Multilevel books are written with multiple story lines. Books that have simple story lines and contain more information about specific features in the text at the end of the book are also considered multilevel. Although some of these books are fiction, the majority are nonfiction (informational). Still others combine fiction and nonfiction.

Examples

- *Beaks!* (Collard, 2002) is a nonfiction selection that contains two story lines.

- *Heart of Texas* (Melmed, 2009) is a nonfiction alphabet text that celebrates Texas with three levels of reading on each page.

- *A Subway for New York* (Weitzman, 2005) is a nonfiction selection containing two story lines. *Elephants Can Paint Too!* (Arnold, 2005) is another example.

- *This Rocket* (Collicutt, 2005) is a nonfiction text that has a simple story line with accompanying information in the front and back of the text that gives a brief history of rockets (front) and tells about the Apollo 11 mission (back).

- *Sharks: And Other Dangers of the Deep* (Mugford, 2005) is an example that contains three story lines.

- *Wise Guy: The Life and Philosophy of Socrates* (Usher, 2005) is an example that contains two story lines and information at the end of the text.

- *Lucille Lost:* A True Adventure (George and Murphy, 2006) is an example that has a story line about a turtle's adventure and then corresponding nonfiction facts about turtles at the bottom of each page.

Why Use Them?   Regardless of reading level or background, all children can read all or some portions of these texts. Using these texts, then, is one way of showing students that they can all read a similar text and get something out of the experience, that they are part of one community of learners.

The books are also rich in content; they contain much information about objects or situations that interest children. These texts also provide a scaffold for meaningful repeated reading. That is, once children hear other parts of the story from either the teacher or classmates, they are more likely to be able to read the text themselves. Finally, in terms of resources, schools can get a great deal of use out of these books with fewer dollars spent.

Enhanced eText
Video Example 7.4
A rap that showcases the five informational text structures https://www.youtube.com/watch?v=7kWGQ-_ipBY

Enhanced eText
Video Example 7.5
A narrated PowerPoint overviews the five structures of informational text and how to identify them. Key words associated with each text structure are highlighted. https://www.youtube.com/watch?v=zVU8xoXRHys

Teaching with Multilevel Books

- If students are grouped by similar level or background, different groups can read different parts of the text. For example, those who are just getting a handle on how print functions and those who have little background about the topic at hand could be invited to follow along as the teacher reads part of text. Next, the teacher may have students choral-read their part while the teacher reads the additional text shown on the page, thus building children's background and knowledge base.

- After each group member has read through the parts of the text most appropriate for the given group, children can be grouped by twos (if the book has two story lines or parts) or threes (if the book has three story lines or parts). In turn, each person can read his part of the text while others listen. To emphasize listening comprehension, each group could be given one text that is passed from one person to the next as each part is read.

- In pair work, if the focus is on helping the less experienced reader attain a larger reading vocabulary and hear an example of fluent reading, each child could be provided a copy of the text and the less experienced reader could follow along as the partner reads aloud. This particular way of reading provides a scaffold to the less experienced reader or the child with a limited background, enabling him to read a good portion of the text at a later time.

Series Books

Description   Series books share common elements such as characters, author's style, words, and format. Children can often follow the development of story characters and share in their adventures in each succeeding book in the series.

Examples

- Mills, Claudia, *Gus and Grandpa* (grades 1–2)
- Willems, Mo, *Elephant and Piggie* (grades 1–2)
- Reilly-Giff, Patricia, *Polk Street Kids* (grades 2–3)
- Adler, David, *Cam Jansen* (grades 2–3)
- West, Tracey, *Planet Earth* (grades 2–4)
- Greenburg, Dan, *Zack Files* (grades 2–5)
- Kinney, Jeff, *Diary of a Wimpy Kid* (grades 2–4)
- Erickson, John, *Hank, the Cowdog* (grades 3–4)
- Stilton, Geronimo, *Geronimo Stilton* (grades 3–4)
- Hirschmann, Kris, *Planet Earth* (grades 4–6)
- Rowling, J. K., *Harry Potter* (grades 4–6)
- Lupica, Mike, *Comeback Kids* (grades 4–6)

Why Use Them?   Series books can be very effective as a source of reading material for three reasons. First, they provide meaningful reading practice. Once children get hooked on a series, they have a desire to read additional books in the series. Because characters, plot structure, and words are common to all books in the series, students get a lot of meaningful practice. In other words, the natural redundancy of these features provides support for even the most novice readers, enabling many children to read the texts and to gain confidence.

Second, series books provide opportunities for children to discuss and interpret events in the series. Students reading different titles in the series will make their own interpretations based on their own backgrounds. Talking with others broadens understanding.

Third, series books provide children with opportunities to make inferences. When reading the books out of order, especially, children must infer what has come before and how their book fits into the series. In effect, they get to solve a reading puzzle as they read different books in the series. Solving this puzzle can be very engaging for children and is even more challenging when the books in the series are numbered, but read out of order.

Teaching with Series Books

- Group students according to who is reading the same series. Children can then discuss their books with teacher guidance. Several different teaching points could emerge, such as what all of the books have in common, or how reading series books can increase comprehension.

- To help children experience being a part of a larger community of readers, provide each child in the class with a different book in the series. Children can then be grouped in a variety of ways for small-group reading instruction. For example, those children who need to learn how to better use words to create visual images can be grouped together to learn this task. Those children who need to learn how to pay attention to meaning as well as visual cues can be grouped together. After they have been taught the given strategy, they can then practice it using their series book as the teacher provides guidance.

Poetry

Description   Poetry is writing in which rhythm, sound, and language are used to create images, thoughts, and emotional responses. Usually concise, poetry takes on many forms, such as *narrative poetry*, which tells a story; *lyric poetry*, in which much rhythm is used; *humorous poetry*, in which everyday objects or events are portrayed in absurd ways; and *nonsense poetry*, which uses meaningless words and much exaggeration.[20]

Examples

- *Flying Eagle* (Bardhan-Quallen, 2009)
- *Sky Magic* (Hopkins, 2009)
- *The Scarecrow's Dance* (Yolen, 2009)
- *Dinothesaurus* (Florian, 2009)
- *A Foot in the Mouth: Poems to Speak, Sing, and Shout* (Janeczco, 2009)
- *In the Swim* (Florian, 1997)
- *School Supplies: A Book of Poems* (Hopkins, 1996)
- *Block City* (Stevenson, 2005)
- *Down to the Sea in Ships* (Sturges, 2005)
- *When I Heard the Learn'd Astronomer* (Whitman, 2004)

Why Use It?   Poetry uses different forms than other kinds of writing. Exposing children to poetry opens up this style of writing to them, increasing their comprehension of it. Because many poems are succinct and use words that convey images, poems are excellent selections to help children learn to visualize. And because they are short, poems tend to be less intimidating for even the most novice reader. Finally, poetry helps students develop numerous reading skills, such as phrasing, fluency, and comprehension.

Teaching with Poetry

- Select a poem to help students learn how to use words to create visual images. After modeling the process, provide students with another poem, giving them time to read it. Once they have read the poem, ask students to discuss specific lines and the images they saw when they read them.

Enhanced eText Application Exercise 7.3: Teaching with Poetry

- To model fluency and reading poetry for enjoyment, select a poem and read it to the students. Point out how the phrases helped you know how to read the poem. Next, provide students with several poetry books. Invite them to choose and read a poem. Once they have rehearsed reading it to themselves, provide time for students to read their poems aloud to the group.

- Students can also create materials to use during guided reading experiences once they become familiar with common core poems introduced during shared reading. Lines or stanzas from the poems can be printed on one side of a blank page. During independent work time, students can add illustrations to these pages, bind the pages, and create their own copy of a text. Then the teacher can invite students to bring their books to the guided reading table to use in demonstration and intervention lessons.

Chapter Books

Description   Chapter books are divided into different segments or chapters. They range in sophistication, beginning with the very easiest in first grade and increasing in difficulty throughout the grades.

Examples

- Chapter books for novice readers

  Henry and Mudge series (Cynthia Rylant)

  Frog and Toad series (Arnold Lobel)

  Little Bear series (Else Minarik)

- Chapter books for older readers

  Newbery Medal and Honor books

  The Graveyard Book (Gaiman, 2008)

  Holes (Sachar, 2008)

  Bud, Not Buddy (Curtis, 2004)

  Missing May (Rylant, 2003)

  The Giver (Lowry, 2002)

  Walk Two Moons (Creech, 1996)

  Shiloh (Naylor, 2000)

Why Use Them?   Chapter books afford children with an opportunity to extend themselves into books that they will be reading in their everyday lives. Chapter books help students learn how a story is connected by individual sections. Reading these books is also a signal to children that they are becoming more competent readers. Chapter books also provide logical stopping points for instructional purposes.

Teaching with Chapter Books

- Provide all students in the group with the same chapter book and give a structure for reading the book.

- Use chapter books to engage children in an author study. Different groups of children can read different chapter books by the same author. Author style across texts can become a focal point for instruction. Certain authors, such as Cynthia Rylant,

Patricia Reilly Giff, Gary Paulsen, and William Steig, have written at all levels— picture books, simple chapter books, complex young adult novels, and adult fiction and nonfiction. Studies of these authors allow teachers who work with a wide range of readers to match appropriate texts to their students' levels, while still engaging all students in a cohesive classroom conversation about the author.

Multicultural Books

Description   Multicultural literature refers to all genres that portray the likenesses and differences among social, cultural, and ethnic groups. They are written to reflect our diverse society.

Examples

- *Hansel and Gretel* (Isadora, 2009)
- *Babu's Song* (Stuve-Bodeen, 2003)
- *Rent Party Jazz* (Miller, 2001)
- *Most Loved in All the World* (Hegamin, 2009)
- *Erika-San* (Say, 2009)
- *Muktar and the Camels* (Graber and Mack, 2009)
- *The Beckoning Cat* (Nishizuka, 2009)
- *Celia Cruz, Queen of Salsa* (Chambers, 2005)
- *Rosa* (Giovanni, 2005)
- *My Nana and Me* (Smalls, 2005)
- *Meow: Cat Stories from Around the World* (Yolen, 2005)
- *Beyond the Great Mountains: A Visual Poem About China* (Young, 2005)

Why Use Them?   All children need books that represent their cultural heritage. Reading multicultural books gives all children characters with whom they can identify. Multicultural literature also provides children with opportunities to learn about similarities and differences among people and to consider different points of view.

As Diakiw states, "Young children find it easier to assimilate new information when this information is presented within the structure of a story."[21] The story acts as a bridge to help children "link their growing understanding of other cultures to their personal experience and background knowledge."[22]

The characteristics of "good" books are operative for all children regardless of background. Any book they read must help them to feel good about themselves. It must help them to view themselves in a positive light, to achieve a better self-concept, and to gain a feeling of worth.

When selecting books for a class library, teachers should try to put themselves in the position of their students and ask these questions: How would I feel if I read this book? Would this book make me come back for another one? Will this book interest me? Are these books written on many readability levels? Does the book portray the black child or any other minority child as an individual? Are the adults portrayed in a nonchildlike manner? Are the characters supplied with traits and personalities that are positive? Would all children want to read the book?

The importance of providing children with books that convey hope, and with which children can identify because the books mirror their lives, cannot be overemphasized. Another factor, which is as important, concerns the images that children obtain when they read a book about people with different racial or ethnic backgrounds. Since children are greatly influenced by what they read, the way that people are portrayed in books will have a profound effect on children's perceptions of them.

The Notable Books for a Global Society Committee, a subgroup of the Children's Literature and Reading Special Interest Group of the International Literacy Association, publishes an annual list of multicultural books that meet specific criteria. The list is available at www.literacyworldwide.org.

Teaching with Multicultural Books

- Select a topic or theme that will encourage students to select multicultural books during reading instruction. For example, if the focus is on the effects of prejudice and discrimination, students can explore nonfiction and fiction titles at many different levels. Some might be reading picture books, such as Robert Coles's *The Story of Ruby Bridges*, and others might be reading novellas, such as Mildred Taylor's *The Gold Cadillac*. The teacher brings small groups of students together to discuss the issues and ideas in their books related to the topic.

- Encourage literacy by selecting certain texts and then guiding students to look at those texts from perspectives other than their own. A teacher working on a frontier/pioneer theme may have small groups of students reading different trade books, such as Laura Ingalls Wilder's *Little House in the Big Woods* and Carol Ryrie Brink's *Caddie Woodlawn*. Discussions can be structured by the teacher to encourage students to respond to what was written by assuming various roles (Native Americans, pioneer children, modern women, etc.) to show how taking different perspectives helps readers to critically analyze texts. Introducing contrasting texts such as Michael Dorris's *Sees Behind Trees*, which focuses on a Native American perspective, allows the teacher to guide students through additional comparisons and contrasts as they look critically at historical events and the sources of the texts written about them.[23]

Other Texts

Magazines

Description Magazines are compilations of articles and stories designed to inform readers about many different topics. Columns of text, pictures with captions, short tidbits about different topics, diagrams, and advertisements are often used to create a magazine. Most magazines focus on a specific audience and feature articles that would appeal to this audience.

Examples

- *Sesame Street Magazine* (ages 0–6)
- *Ladybug Magazine* (ages 2–6)
- *Zoobooks* (ages 6–14)
- *American Girl* (ages 8–12)
- *Cricket Magazine* (ages 8–14)
- *Faces Magazine* (ages 8–14)
- *National Geographic Kids* (ages 8–14)
- *Sports Illustrated Kids* (ages 8–14)

Why Use Them? Reading a magazine requires the reader to be "magazine-literate." According to Stoll, being magazine-literate means that the reader knows how the publication works—how it is organized, where to locate specific information, and how to maximize the magazine's potential.[24] Using magazines for guided reading, then, is an excellent way to help students become magazine-literate. Time can be devoted to teaching children how to read magazines and to explaining that magazines reflect many different personalities. Because some magazines include articles written by children and contain high-interest articles, they provide very motivating reading material. They can also serve as a catalyst for meaningful writing experiences; students can be encouraged to write their own articles to submit for publication and to write letters to the editor. Finally, because columns of text, pictures with short captions, short blurbs about given topics, and diagrams are used in magazines, they provide a wide range of information that can be accessed by all readers.

Teaching with Magazines

- Choose a specific magazine and devise a guided reading experience designed to show students the features of the magazine: how it is organized, the table of contents, the variety of articles, and so on. Students can then choose an article to read and share what they discovered with the rest of the group.

- Some magazines, such as *Zoobooks*, devote an entire issue to a given topic, such as elephants. Provide a copy of the magazine for each student in the group. Show them how to skim the text, looking for facts about elephants. Then have students do the same, searching for three facts about elephants that they want to share with others in the group. As they report their findings, make a chart that shows their ideas.

Newspapers

Description Newspapers are collections of articles, advertisements, comic strips, and features that are written to inform the public about current events. Newspapers are usually published daily or weekly.

Examples

- *Weekly Reader* (preschool–grade 6)
- *Scholastic News* (grades 1–6)
- Kids page or mini-page from local newspaper (grades 1–3)
- Local newspaper (grades 3–6)

Why Use Them? Newspapers provide a wealth of reading material relevant to everyday life. They supply information about current events at several levels. Like other reading materials, they are written with a specific format. Readers must learn how a newspaper is written so that they can find the information they need and successfully negotiate their way through it without feeling overwhelmed. Small-group reading instruction is a perfect fit for this. Specific newspapers and articles can be used to show students the variety of texts that is found in newspapers and how to read each one. Students can also learn how to read articles looking for the questions that most articles address: who, what, when, where, why, and how. Reading newspapers also helps students increase their world knowledge of given topics—thus enhancing their reading comprehension of these same topics when they are encountered in other texts. Finally, using newspapers helps students to see themselves as "real-life" readers. They see others reading newspapers outside of school and begin to recognize that they can too.

Teaching with Newspapers

- Use the mini-page of the local newspaper to show students how it is organized. If the purpose of using the newspaper is to show students that articles focus on specific questions (who, what, when, where, why, and how), list these key words on the board and then direct students to read a specific article to search for answers to these questions.

Enhanced eText
Video Example 7.6
How and why to use Scholastic News in the classroom. https://www.youtube.com/watch?v=1W-Es1_GoTQ

- As with other texts, news stories can present some challenging words for students to decipher. You may want to show students how to use context clues to determine the meaning of an unknown word. Once you have modeled this, have students apply the strategy to an article they choose to read or one that you have chosen for them.

- Once students are familiar with the various parts of the paper, use it to teach critical thinking skills. For example, bring in different newspapers and have students read the same story as presented in the different papers. Students can discuss the headlines for the story and make up their own headlines using different voices—neutral, positive, or negative. You can also talk about how the tone of the headline influences readers.

- Discuss with students the differences between editorials and regular news stories. Then have them compare different editorials with news stories on the same topic. Next, invite students to discuss whether the news was adequately explained and whether the editor expressed her views. Finally, have students write their own editorials about a story they have been following for a number of days.

- Encourage children to be reporters and to cover school or community events. They can write about the events as both news stories and editorials.

Real-Life Texts

Description   There are texts all around us in real life.[25] These include all print that children find in the world around them: packaging, advertising, corporate logos, notices, and other types of text. While all the types of text in previous sections of this chapter are certainly found in the real world, teachers should also make sure their rooms are well-stocked with all types of print students find around them in the world. These types of materials are not intentionally designed for classroom purposes, but they can certainly be used for instruction nonetheless. We classify real-life texts into the following categories: labels, games and entertainment, music, advertisements, signs, financial transactions, manuals, official documents, books (beyond those already discussed), correspondence, tables, schedules, calendars, maps, diagrams, charts, and lists.

Examples[26]

Labels
1. Product name
2. Ingredients
3. Safety cautions
4. Directions for use
5. Company information
6. Approvals
7. Nutritional information
8. Medicine information

Entertainment
9. Board games and card games (traditional)
10. Instructions (see Rules and Procedures in manuals)
11. Trading-card games (e.g., *Pokémon*, *Yu-Gi-Oh!*, and *Magic*)
12. Sports cards
13. Restaurant menus

Music
14. Lyrics from songs
15. CD inserts
16. List of song titles (from CDs, etc.)
17. Sheet music, with and without lyrics

Advertisements
18. Magazine and newspaper advertisements
19. Want ads
20. Billboards
21. Pull-out ad sections in newspapers and magazines
22. Catalogs
23. Brochures
24. Dot com websites (commercial ads)
25. Web banners
26. Posters
27. Flyers
28. Announcements/invitations
29. Bumper stickers
30. Logos
31. Slogans
32. Banners
33. Buttons
34. T-shirts, sweatshirts, and hats
35. Balloons

Signs

36. Words only
37. Picture plus words
38. Picture only

Financial Transactions

39. Receipts
40. Checks
41. Bills
42. Charge card slips
43. Online receipts
44. Shipping-and-handling charts
45. Coupons

Manuals

46. How-to books or sheets
    a. Assemble or install
    b. Diagnostics or schematics
    c. Repair and maintenance
    d. Make something work
47. Rules and procedures
48. Recipes
49. Handbooks (e.g., for cars, stereos, cameras, appliances, and video games)

Official Documents

50. Legal documents
51. Property documents (e.g., titles, deeds, and permits)
52. Certificates of birth, death, and marriage
53. Church records (such as baptisms and marriages)
54. Application forms
55. Gravestones

Books

56. Comic books
57. Comic strip collections
58. Photojournalism
59. Coffee table books

Correspondence

60. Informal personal letters
61. Formal business letters
62. Postcards
63. E-mail
64. Text messages/instant messages
65. Informal notes
66. Formal notes and messages
67. Directions

Tables, Schedules, and Calendars

68. Date books and planners (daily, weekly, monthly, and yearly formats)
69. Schedules of events
70. Regular schedules (such as air, train, and bus)
71. Score sheets
72. Tally sheets
73. Weather reports
74. Stock tables

Visuals

75. Maps (e.g., distribution, topographical, and globes)
76. Diagrams (e.g., flow charts, mind webs, and labeled parts)
77. Charts (e.g., raw data, bar graph, and scatter plot)
78. Lists (e.g., grocery lists and to-do lists)

Why Use Them?   Real-life texts are helpful for reaching students who need a motivation boost. Many readers have developed attitudes about typical classroom types of texts that create a wall, blocking their success. Certain real-life texts will enable readers to break down this wall and enable them to make better use of their subject knowledge, background experiences, and technical vocabulary, leading to greater success with reading. Because they may not view these texts as "reading," past negative associations with reading may not surface. Since these types of texts are well outside the realm of textbooks, tests, and text leveling systems, when students read real-life texts, they are likely to perceive the reading as authentic and more enjoyable. Also, each type of text above is written with a different structure and format. This helps students apply skills and strategies in flexible ways, encouraging transfer of school knowledge to the world outside the classroom. Using these types of text during the school day helps children expand their definition of what it means to be a reader, and makes these types of texts both acceptable and accessible.

Teaching with Real-Life Texts[27]

1. Add real-life texts to existing literacy centers. For example, adding catalogs and ads to a math corner, or applications and forms to a writing center, often leads to additional reading and writing opportunities.

2. Entire portable learning stations can be developed around real-life materials. Collections can be placed in tubs that students can take back to their desks to engage in explorations. Using one tub, students might sort and plan a shopping trip using coupons and grocery store ads. Using another, students might plan out a vacation using travel brochures and other travel information.

Electronic Texts

Description Electronic texts are any texts that exist in environments. These texts are primarily accessible through computers and available on the Internet. Kamil, Kim, and Lane[28] classify electronic text in two primary categories. First is any text found on the screen (e.g., e-mail messages, help screens, or instructions). They point out that this text exists digitally and can be transmitted from one computer to another. Except for navigational differences, readers often approach this text in much the same way as they do print formats. The second category is any electronic text augmented by hyperlinks, hypertext, or hypermedia. These more complicated, augmented texts are most often found on the Internet.

Examples In addition to the resources cited at the end of this chapter, we recommend the following three sites that are primarily designed for children:

> Children's Reading Room, http://www.unmuseum.org/crr/index.htm, provides a selection of stories that children can download and print. Stories vary in length.

> PBS Kids, http://pbskids.org/. *Arthur*, *Barney & Friends*, and *Clifford the Big Red Dog* are but a few of the PBS Kids shows this site features. *Martha Speaks*, *Word-World*, and *Between the Lions* are programs tightly focused on reading and writing. Children can access stories, games, music, video, and even coloring forms related to different story characters.

> Children's Storybooks Online, http://www.magickeys.com/books, offers free storybooks for young and older children. Many of the books are illustrated. The site also features riddles, puzzles, and information about how to publish a book.

Why Use Them? As with the other types of texts we showcase in this chapter, there are several reasons for using electronic texts with all readers, but especially with those who find reading challenging and therefore uninteresting. First, electronic texts are often perceived as something totally removed from the school reading materials (e.g., textbooks, novels, and anthologies) with which these children have not had much success. Electronic texts are seen as attractive, as something new and different. Second, electronic texts have features that can make reading easier.[29] Text is easily searchable—the computer will scan and skim more effectively than a reader can. It is easily modified. Software exists to reformat cybertexts into more viewer-friendly texts for different purposes.[30]

Electronic texts with hypermedia links can actually provide support for comprehension.[31] Imagine not understanding a word, concept, or idea you are reading about and then being able to click on the screen. The photo or video that comes up will provide the clarification you need to better understand the passage. Audio recordings found in many electronic texts allow children who rely on their auditory processes to receive this support. One site that provides several texts for students to read with auditory and visual support is https://www.starfall.com.

Third, electronic texts exist on an endless number of topics.[32] Teachers can easily find more than one topic they can use to entice their most difficult-to-reach readers.

Teaching with Electronic Texts

1. Students can independently (or with a partner) locate information related to a specific topic, with the expectation that they will then share their findings with others.

2. Students can visit preapproved websites of their choosing and read about topics of interest. With an instructional focus, cybertexts can be the resources independently

consulted as students work on research and inquiry projects. The Internet Work-shop is a fitting example.[33] Leu offers these four procedures:

a. Locate an appropriate site and set a bookmark for the location.

b. Design the activity, making sure students need to use the site in order to complete it.

c. Provide students with time to complete the activity.

d. Provide time for students to share their discoveries.

Leu notes that once students are familiar with this format, they can then conduct their own inquiry projects.

> **Enhanced eText Application Exercise 7.4:** Understanding and Teaching Text Types

---

Bridge: From Teaching Text Types to Understanding

When teachers understand that _____,	then teachers may want to _____.
Any text can be used to teach and assess readers,	Challenge students to identify texts that they encounter or appreciate and bring them into the classroom to be used for meaningful learning experiences.
Each type of text offers purposeful and powerful opportunities for teaching and assessing readers,	Practice exploring a variety of texts with colleagues on a regular basis in order to identify their teaching and assessment value.
It is not necessary to have a classroom set of each type of text,	Acquire a text or two of various types when navigating everyday activities like shopping, visiting a museum, or reading a magazine online (e.g., recipes, grocery lists, brochures, articles, and advertisements).

Revisiting the Opening Scenario

Now that you have read the chapter, how would you respond to parents about why Mr. Hall has students read from so many different kinds of texts? What are they learning from reading a variety of texts that they might not get from reading just a single type?

Authors' Summary

Before reading our summary statements for each outcome, we suggest you read each outcome and summarize it in your own words.

Once finished, cross-check your response with our brief summary to determine how well you recalled the major points.

7.1 Discuss the importance of providing students with time to read texts in school.

- Researchers frequently report that students with difficulty in language and reading often get far less time to read during school because they are in special programs. Spending time on engaging text is the foundational curriculum for students who need growth.

7.2 Provide a rationale for using a variety of texts in a diagnostic reading program.

- When teachers accept the curriculum of helping students find a variety of types of engaging text, these texts provide the most likely setting for reading progress. When students' views of text are limited, either by their school or by their own experience, teachers need to watch and listen to these students to figure out how to expand their view of what counts as reading.

7.3 Describe different types of texts, provide an example of one, and explain how it can be used to teach reading in a diagnostic reading program.

- There are everyday environmental texts, such as signs, menus, and bumper stickers. There are non-book publications such as newspapers, blogs, and magazines. There are almost too many types to list. One that is gaining ground in schools is the graphic novel. Up until the 1990s, this type of text, the "comic book," was frowned on in most school settings. But because words in graphic novels are mostly dialog, readers can use their knowledge of spoken language as a bridge to reading with these texts. Because they may be able to read dialog more fluently, this strength might be transferred to reading dramas or readers' theater. All of these would be ideal situations for addressing needs, such as practicing reading multiple-syllable words or making inferences.

Think About It!

1. You are thinking about the open house that is about to take place at your school, and want to make sure that your students' parents fully understand the importance of reading, both in and out of school. To help get this point across, you have decided to provide parents with some suggested children's literature titles that they can use at home. Construct the list.

2. Your principal just discovered that you are a believer in using many different texts to help children read. Although the idea makes sense to her, she doesn't fully understand how first-graders can read informational texts because she thinks they are way too hard for them. Besides, she thinks that children in first grade "learn to read" and that it is only after doing so that they can "read to learn." What will you say to her?

3. Construct a text set based on one topic you will be teaching. Include five or more different types of text. Keep your students in mind as you construct this text set. Which students will read which texts? How will the texts be assigned? Will you allow for student choice?

Websites

- http://www.readingrockets.org/article/educators-guide-making-textbooks-accessible-and-usable-students-learning-disabilities

   This link goes directly to an article addressing how teachers can make textbooks accessible and usable for students with learning disabilities. Perfect for new teachers and parents who are new to the disability arena or those searching for valuable resources, this article describes available software, e-text websites and a critique of these sources, school system resources, the National Instructional Materials Accessibility Standard (NIMAS), and the IEP process.

Children's Literature Cited

Adler, David. *Cam Jansen: The Catnapping Mystery*. New York, NY: Putnam, 2005.

Alborough, Jez. *Hug*. Somerville, MA: Candlewick, 2009.

Arnold, Katya. *Elephants Can Paint Too!* New York, NY: Simon & Schuster, 2005.

Bardhan-Quallen, Sudipta. *Flying Eagle*. Watertown, MA: Charlesbridge, 2009.

Carr, Jan. *Dappled Apples*. New York, NY: Holiday House, 2001.

Carter, David. *One Red Dot*. New York, NY: Simon & Schuster, 2005.

Chambers, Veronica. *Celia Cruz, Queen of Salsa*. New York, NY: Penguin, 2005.

Coles, Robert. *The Story of Ruby Bridges*. New York, NY: Scholastic, 1995.

Collard, Sneed. *Beaks!* Watertown, MA: Charlesbridge, 2002.

Collicutt, Paul. *This Rocket*. New York, NY: Farrar, Straus, & Giroux, 2005.

Creech, Sharon. *Walk Two Moons*. New York, NY: HarperCollins, 1996.

Crelin, Bob. *Faces of the Moon*. Watertown, MA: Charlesbridge, 2009.

Curlee, Lynn. *Into the Ice: The Story of Arctic Exploration*. Boston, MA: Houghton Mifflin, 1998.

Curtis, Christopher Paul. *Bud, Not Buddy*. New York, NY: Random House, 2004.

Erickson, John. *Hank, the Cowdog: The Secret Laundry Monster Files.* New York, NY: Viking, 2002.

Florian, Douglas. *Dinothesaurus.* New York, NY: Atheneum, 2009.

Florian, Douglas. *In the Swim.* San Diego, CA: Harcourt, 1997.

Gaiman, Neil. *The Graveyard Book.* New York, NY: HarperCollins, 2008.

George, Margaret, and Murphy, Christopher. *Lucille Lost: A True Adventure* New York, NY, Viking, 2006.

Giovanni, Nikki. *Rosa.* New York, NY: Henry Holt, 2005.

Graber, Janet. *Muktar and the Camels.* New York, NY: Henry Holt, 2009.

Greenburg, Dan. *The Boy Who Cried Bigfoot! (Zack Files).* New York, NY: Grosset & Dunlap, 2000.

Hall, Zoe. *The Apple Pie Tree.* New York, NY: Scholastic, 1996.

Hegamin, Cozbi. *Most Loved in All the World.* Boston, MA: Houghton Mifflin, 2009.

Hirschmann, Kris. *Big World, Small World (Planet Earth series).* New York, NY: Scholastic, 2009.

Hopkins, Lee Bennett. *School Supplies: A Book of Poems.* New York, NY: Simon & Schuster, 1996.

Hopkins, Lee Bennett. *Sky Magic.* New York, NY: Penguin, 2009.

Isadora, Rachel. *Hansel and Gretel.* New York: G. P. Putnam's Sons, 2009.

Janeczco, Paul. *A Foot in the Mouth: Poems to Speak, Sing, and Shout.* Somerville, MA: Candlewick, 2009.

Karas, G. Brian. *On Earth.* New York, NY: Putnam, 2005.

Kinney, Jeff. *The Last Straw (Diary of a Wimpy Kid series).* New York, NY: Abrams, 2009.

Lobel, Arnold. *Days with Frog and Toad.* New York, NY: HarperCollins, 1984.

Lowry, Lois. *The Giver.* New York, NY: Random House, 2002.

Lupica, Mike. *Two-Minute Drill (Comeback Kids series).* New York, NY: Puffin, 2007.

Marzollo, Jean. *In 1776.* New York, NY: Scholastic, 1994.

Melmed, Laura. *Heart of Texas.* New York, NY: HarperCollins, 2009.

Miller, William. *Rent Party Jazz.* New York, NY: Lee & Low, 2001.

Mills, Claudia. *Gus and Grandpa.* New York, NY: Farrar, Straus, & Giroux, 1997.

Minarak, Else. *Little Bear.* New York, NY: HarperCollins, 1957.

Mugford, Simon. *Sharks: And Other Dangers of the Deep.* New York, NY: St. Martin's Press, 2005.

Naylor, Phyllis. *Shiloh.* New York, NY: Aladdin, 2000.

Nishizuka, Koko. *The Beckoning Cat.* New York, NY: Holiday House, 2009.

Polacco, Patricia. *Mommies Say Shhh!* New York, NY: Philomel, 2005.

Prosek, James. *Bird, Butterfly, Eel.* New York, NY: Simon & Schuster, 2009.

Reilly-Giff, Patricia. Meet the Kids of the Polk Street School. New York, NY: Doubleday, 1988.

Robbins, Ken. *Apples.* New York, NY: Simon & Schuster, 2002.

Rockwell, Anne. *Good Morning, Digger.* New York, NY: Viking, 2005.

Ross, Stewart. *Moon: Science, History, and Mystery.* New York, NY: Scholastic, 2009.

Rowling, J. K. *Harry Potter and the Sorcerer's Stone.* New York, NY: Scholastic, 1996.

Ryder, Joanne. *Panda Kindergarten.* New York, NY: HarperCollins, 2009.

Rylant, Cynthia. *Henry and Mudge (series).* New York, NY: Aladdin, 1996.

Rylant, Cynthia. *Missing May.* New York, NY: Yearling, 2003.

Sachar, Louis. *Holes.* New York, NY: Farrar, Straus, & Giroux, 2008.

Say, Allen. *Erika-San.* Boston: Houghton Mifflin Harcourt, 2009.

Shea, Pegi Deitz. *Liberty Rising: The Story of the Statue of Liberty.* New York, NY: Henry Holt, 2005.

Smalls, Irene. *My Nana and Me.* New York, NY: Little, Brown, 2005.

Stephens, Sarah Hines, and Mann, Bethany. *Show Off: How to Do Absolutely Everything One Step at a Time.* San Francisco, CA: Candlewick, 2009.

Stevenson, Robert Louis. *Block City.* New York, NY: Simon & Schuster, 2005.

Stilton, Geronimo. *Geronimo Stilton.* New York, NY: Scholastic, 2004.

Sturges, Philemon. *Down to the Sea in Ships.* New York, NY: Putnam, 2005.

Stuve-Bodeen, Stephanie. *Babu's Song.* New York, NY: Lee & Low, 2003.

Talbott, Hudson. *River of Dreams: Story of the Hudson River.* New York, NY: G. P. Putnam's Sons, 2009.

Tatham, Betty. *Baby Sea Otter.* New York, NY: Henry Holt, 2005.

Taylor, Mildred. *The Gold Cadillac.* London, UK: Puffin Books, 1998.

Usher, M. D. *Wise Guy: The Life and Philosophy of Socrates.* New York, NY: Farrar, Straus, & Giroux, 2005.

Weinstein, Ellen. *Everywhere the Cow Says "Moo!"* Honesdale, PA: Boyds Mills, 2008.

Weitzman, David. *A Subway for New York.* New York, NY: Farrar, Straus, & Giroux, 2005.

West, Tracey. *Incredible Reptiles (Planet Earth series).* New York, NY: Scholastic, 2009.

Whitman, Walt. *When I Heard the Learn'd Astronomer.* New York, NY: Simon & Schuster, 2004.

Willems, Mo. *There Is a Bird on Your Head (Elephant & Piggie series).* New York, NY: Hyperion, 2007.

Wood, Audrey. *The Deep Blue Sea: A Book of Colors.* New York, NY: Scholastic, 2005.

Wood, Audrey. *The Napping House.* Boston, MA: Houghton Mifflin Harcourt, 2009.

Wormell, Mary. *Why Not?* New York, NY: Farrar, Straus, & Giroux, 2000.

Yolen, Jane. *Meow: Cat Stories from Around the World.* New York, NY: HarperCollins, 2005.

Yolen, Jane. *The Scarecrow's Dance.* New York, NY: Simon & Schuster, 2009.

Young, Ed. *Beyond the Great Mountains: A Visual Poem About China.* San Francisco, CA: Chronicle, 2005.

Endnotes

1. Allington, R., & McGill-Frances, A. (2012). *Summer reading: Closing the rich/poor achievement gap.* New York, NY: Teachers College Press.

2. Allington, R. (2005). *What really matters for struggling readers* (2nd ed.). Boston, MA: Allyn & Bacon.

3. Allington, R. (1980, November/December). Poor readers don't get to tread much in reading groups. *Language Arts, 57,* 874.

4. The Nation's Report Card: *Reading 2011.* Retrieved April 25, 2013, from https://www.nationsreportcard.gov/

5. Ibid.

6. Patterson, K. (2016). Making meaning with friends: Exploring the function, direction and tone of small group discussions of literature in elementary school classrooms. *Reading Horizons, 55,* 29–61.

7. Allington, R., et al. (2010). Addressing summer reading setback among economically disadvantaged elementary students. *Reading Psychology, 31,* 411–427.

8. Opitz, M., & Ford, M. (2006). *Books and beyond: New ways to reach readers.* Portsmouth, NH: Heinemann; Guthrie, J. (2011). Best practices in motivating students to read. In L. Morrow, L. Gambrell, J. De Nero, & N. Duke (Eds.), *Best Practices in Literacy Instruction* (4th ed., pp. 177–198). New York, NY: Guilford.

9. Ciampa, K. (2016). Motivating grade 1 children to read: Exploring the role of choice, curiosity, and challenge in mobile ebooks. *Reading Psychology, 37,* 665–705.

10. Reed, J., & Schallert, D. (1993). The nature of involvement in academic discourse. *Journal of Educational Psychology, 85,* 253-266; Crow, S. (2011). Exploring the experiences of upper elementary school children who are intrinsically motivated to seek information. *School Library Research Journal, 14,* 1–38.

11. Muth, K. (Ed.). (1989). *Children's comprehension of text.* Newark, DE: International Reading Association; Meek, M. (2011). *How texts teach what readers learn.* Katonah, NY, R.C. Owen.

12. Kletzien, S., & Dreher, M. (2017). What experiences do expository books on recommended book lists offer to K-2 students? *Reading Psychology, 38,* 71–96.

13. Willingham, D. (2010). *Why don't students like school?* New York, NY: Jossey-Bass; Alexander, P. (1996). The past, present, and future of knowledge research: A reexamination of the role of knowledge in learning and instructing. *Educational Psychologist, 31,* 89–92.

14. Camp, D. (2000). It takes two: Teaching with twin texts of fact and fiction. *The Reading Teacher, 53,* 400–408.

15. Alexander. (1996). See also Yopp, R., & Yopp, H. (2000). Sharing informational text with young children. *The Reading Teacher, 53,* 410–423; Willingham, D. (2010). *Why don't students like school?* New York, NY: Jossey-Bass.

16. Peterson, B. (1998). *Characteristics of text that support beginning readers.* Columbus, OH: The Ohio State University.

17. Barber, A., Buehl, M., Kidd, J., Sturtevant, E., Nuland, L., & Beck, J. (2015). Reading engagement in social studies: Exploring the role of a social studies literacy intervention on reading comprehension, reading self-efficacy, and engagement in middle school students with different language backgrounds. *Reading Psychology, 36,* 31–85.

18. Opitz, M. (1995, 2013). *Getting the most from predictable books.* New York, NY: Scholastic.

19. Thogmartin, M. (1998). *Teach a child to read with children's books* (2nd ed.). Bloomington, IN: Educational Resource Center; Cunningham, P. (2008). *Phonics they use* (5th ed.). New York, NY: Allyn & Bacon.

20. Goforth, F. (1998). *Literature and the learner.* Belmont, CA: Wadsworth; Norton, D. (2010). *Through the eyes of a child* (8th ed.). New York, NY: Allyn & Bacon.

21. Diakiw, J. (1990, January). Children's literature and global education: Understanding the developing world. *The Reading Teacher, 43,* 297.

22. Ibid.

23. Scharrer, L., & Salmerón, L. (2016). Sourcing in the reading process: Introduction to the special issue. *Reading and Writing,* 1539–1548.

24. Stoll, D. (Ed.). (1997). *Magazines for kids and teens,* (Rev. ed.). Glassboro, NJ: Educational Press of America: Newark, DE: International Reading Association.

25. Opitz, M., & Ford, M. (2006). *Books and beyond: New ways to reach readers.* Portsmouth, NH: Heinemann; Erekson, J. (2009). *What counts as reading?* (Unpublished document).

26. Erekson, J. (2009). *What counts as reading?* Unpublished document.

27. Opitz, M., & Ford, M. (2006). *Books and beyond: New ways to reach readers.* Portsmouth, NH: Heimemann.

28. Kamil, M., Kim, H., & Lane, D. (2004). Electronic text in the classroom. In J. Hoffman & D. Schallert (Eds.), *The Texts in Elementary Classrooms* (pp. 157–193). Mahwah, NJ: Lawrence Erlbaum Associates.

29. Ortlieb, E., Sargent, S., & Moreland, M. (2014). Evaluating the efficacy of using a digital reading environment to improve reading comprehension within a reading clinic. *Reading Psychology, 35,* 397–421.

30. Leu, D., Kinzer, C., Coiro, J., & Cammack, D. (2004). Toward a theory of new literacies emerging from the internet and other information and communication technology. In R. Rudell & N. Unrau (Eds.), *Theoretical models and processes of reading* (5th ed.). Newark, DE: International Reading Association; McKenna, M., Labbo, L., & Reinking, D. (2003). Effective use of technology in literacy instruction. In L. Morrow, L. Gambrell, & M. Pressley (Eds.), *Best Practices in Literacy Instruction* (2nd ed., pp. 307–331). New York, NY: Guilford.

31. Coiro, J. (2003). Reading comprehension on the internet: Expanding our understanding of reading comprehension to encompass new literacies. *The Reading Teacher, 56,* 458–464.

32. Leu, D., Jr. (2002). Internet workshop: Making time for literacy. *Reading Online.* Retrieved February 17, 2006 from www.literacyworldwide.org

33. Ibid.

Chapter 8
Early Literacy

Freeograph/Shutterstock

Learning Outcomes

After reading this chapter, you should be able to . . .

8.1 Discuss the differences among the terms *emergent literacy*, *reading readiness*, and *early literacy*. List and describe the essential components of early literacy.

8.2 Provide an example of one assessment tool and explain what it is designed to reveal.

8.3 Explain concepts, one way to assess them, and ways to teach them.

8.4 Define phonological awareness, one way to assess it, and ways to teach it.

8.5 Define letter identification, one way to assess it, and one way to teach it.

8.6 Explain story sense, one way to assess it, and one way to teach it.

8.7 Discuss early intervention, provide an example of an early intervention program, and explain three different ways to determine who is most in need of early intervention.

Scenario

Helping Children Advance as Language Learners

Ms. Berger is a highly qualified early childhood teacher who believes that literacy is an ongoing, dynamic process and that children are often at different places in their literacy acquisition. Rather than waiting for children to show that they are ready for literacy instruction, she uses what she knows about her students to plan developmentally appropriate instruction. She wholeheartedly believes that assessment drives instruction, but she recognizes that she must use a variety of assessment measures, each designed to evaluate different aspects of early literacy. She can then interpret the results to plan lessons and to determine which children might need additional instructional time so that they can learn essential literacy skills.

As is often the case, Ms. Berger's students come from a variety of backgrounds. Some come from high-poverty areas, whereas others come from middle-class neighborhoods. When she looks at the results of the many different assessment measures she uses, she recognizes that some children perform poorly when compared with their peers. That is, some are lagging in oral vocabulary, print concepts, letter identification, and phonological awareness. She knows that she will be able to offer some children additional instruction in each of these areas, whereas others will be better served by teachers who are specially trained in early intervention. She fully understands that children who don't do well on the assessments need more rather than less help. Their progress must be accelerated in order for them to function at the same level as their peers.

Ms. Berger recognizes that there are noneducational factors such as parental support, socioeconomic status, and nutrition that affect school performance. She also knows that there are several educational factors such as teacher experience, curriculum rigor, and time on task that affect how children fare in school. Although all factors are important, she focuses on what she can control—the educational factors—and strives to teach children to the best of her ability.

Recent government mandates have Ms. Berger quite concerned. Even though she is an advocate of accountability, she also understands that the results of early literacy tests are not supposed to be used to label and sort children into various groups. Nor should these results be used to judge overall success of schools. Yet this is what she sees happening. She is concerned that too much time is being spent on labeling children and not enough time is being spent on helping them advance as language learners.

Building an Understanding of Early Literacy

Many terms are used to describe what is currently called *early literacy*. One of the most common is **emergent literacy,** defined by Harris and Hodges as "the development of the association of print with meaning that begins early in a child's life and continues until the child reaches the stage of conventional reading and writing."[1] This definition suggests that children's involvement with language begins long before they come to school and that it continues to emerge over time. For example, what appears to be a young child's scribbling is really more than scribbling; it is the child's attempt at using written language. In the past, behaviors such as these were often thought of in terms of **reading readiness**—that is, children were showing that they were ready for reading instruction.

Although some may argue that emergent literacy and reading readiness are basically synonymous, they are not at all. Emergent literacy connotes an ongoing process that is developmental in nature. Reading readiness seems to connote a "waiting period." In literacy development, the notion of waiting violates the spirit and essence of literacy as a developmental process.

Some make the distinction between emergent literacy and *beginning reading* by noting that once children show a certain amount of understanding about how print functions, they are no longer emergent but actually beginning to read in the formal sense. Therefore, they are beginning readers. But exactly how much do children have to know to move from being emergent to beginner? At what age does this shift happen?

Although kindergarten is usually considered to be the bridge between emergent literacy and beginning reading, using kindergarten as a yardstick can be problematic for a couple of reasons. First, not all children attend kindergarten, because it is not required in several states. Therefore, lack of exposure to a language-rich environment could mean that the children will not exhibit several emergent literacy behaviors until first grade.

Second, there are still differences of opinion about the purpose and curriculum of kindergarten. Those who believe that children will grow or mature into reading provide children with many opportunities to learn all areas of literacy (speaking, listening, reading, viewing, and writing), yet do very little explicit teaching. Others believe that children are continually developing and that they need some help as they develop. Consequently, like their counterparts, they provide children with a language-rich environment, but they also believe in offering children explicit instruction based on what they have discovered as a result of using several different assessment techniques and interpreting what they reveal.

We base our view on the latter opinion, for which the International Literacy Association is using the broader term *early literacy*. We believe that children are always showing us what they know and what they need to learn. Children change over time in the way they think about literacy and the strategies they employ as they attempt to comprehend and/or produce text. Like Teale, we believe that children are always trying to make sense of their world and that there is a logic behind what they do that drives their attempts to solve the literacy mystery. Once we understand this logic, we are in a better position to plan instruction that will foster children's development toward conventional language use.[2]

One of the best ways to take a look at children's attempts at using language in meaningful ways is to create a language-rich environment and observe what the children do. Such an environment needs to employ authentic language experiences and much support. We apply the thinking of educators such as Brian Cambourne when working to design an ideal environment. (See Figure 8.1.)

Enhanced eText
Video Example 8.1

The examples presented in this **video clip**, from displaying children's work to labeling shelves, demonstrate some ways in which the classroom can be print-enriched.

Figure 8.1 How do educators create favorable conditions for learning? Engagement and motivation to learn are not mysteries. Good teachers organize their classrooms, lessons, and learning experiences to meet the conditions on the left of this chart, with the goal of creating noticeable engagement for each student in every class.

Exposure of learners to a classroom environment filled with a variety of real-world texts	
Modeling by others at all levels of competence, of how texts are used to make meaning	
Social Expectations are modeled in a community that values reading and writing and shares this value with others.	**Engagement** • Learners believe they are in a safe place to make efforts.
Decisions about what to learn and how to learn it are often given to the learners instead of made by others, such as teachers.	• Learners know the purposes for what they are learning. • Learners see themselves as
Applications of learning in realistic situations needs to be supported by time and opportunities in the schedule.	potentially competent at what they see others do.
Mistakes are appropriate and expected as learners try out their new learning.	
Feedback should be accepting and should respond to the decisions learners have actually made about what to learn.	

Source: Based on Cambourne, B. (1995). Towards an educationally relevant theory of literacy learning: Twenty years of inquiry. The Reading Teacher, 49(3), 182–202.

Areas of Early Literacy

In Chapter 1, we provided sample benchmarks that show some specific behaviors that we would expect to see from children. Whereas a number of the behaviors overlap and continue through different stages, many manifest themselves early on. In a broader sense, there are specific areas of emergent literacy that are viewed as the foundation for future reading and writing success. In Table 8.1, we provide an overview of these components.

Assessing Early Literacy

Pre-Reading Assessment

Before the label *emergent literacy* surfaced and replaced *reading readiness*, most school systems administered whole-group reading readiness tests to their students, usually at the end of kindergarten, to determine whether the children were "ready for reading."

Table 8.1 Early Literacy Components and Their Definitions

Early Literacy Component	Brief Definition
Oral-language concepts	Understanding concepts that are used in spoken language
Print concepts	Understanding written language related to books and some of the terms associated with it
Phonological awareness	Awareness that spoken language is made up of words, syllables, and phonemes
Letter identification	Understanding of the symbols used to form the alphabet
Alphabetic principle	Understanding that there is a systematic relationship among letters and sounds, and that this code can be used to communicate with others
Story sense	Awareness of the structure used to create narrative stories; understanding that stories have to make sense and that books contain stories

Source: Based on Snow, C., S. M. Burns, and P. Griffin, eds. Preventing Reading Difficulties in Young Children. Washington, DC: National Academy Press, 1998.

These tests were usually the first types of standardized tests that the children encountered in their lives at school.

Group-administered standardized tests are still being used. Most major standardized achievement assessment batteries still have some types of **pre-reading** tests that are usually administered to children at some point in preschool or kindergarten. Some school district personnel use these tests to predict reading success, as well as to determine those children who will be "at risk" in school. One example is the *Gates-MacGinitie Reading Tests*, 4th edition (MacGinitie et al., 2000). These tests are group-administered standardized reading tests. There is a pre-reading test (PR), which contains four subtests: literacy concepts, oral-language concepts, letters and letter/sound correspondences, and listening comprehension. According to the authors, the purpose of the test is to determine "a student's background for reading instruction."[3] The authors also note that the test is designed to help teachers learn "what each student already knows about important background concepts on which beginning reading skills are built and which concepts students may need additional help with as they begin to receive reading instruction."[4] A close examination of the testing manual provides the authors' rationale for the subtests and other important information. A separate volume entitled *Linking Testing to Teaching: A Classroom Resource for Reading Assessment and Instruction* provides teachers with some ideas about interpreting test scores as well as teaching suggestions related to each subtest.

Unfortunately, there are some dangers attached to pre-reading tests if they are misused. One danger is a self-fulfilling prophecy. If a child does poorly on such a test, the teacher may feel that the child cannot benefit from reading instruction; the child is not expected to be able to learn to read, and as a result, the teacher defers instruction in reading. Eventually, the teacher's feelings concerning the child's inability to read become part of the child's own self-concept. (See "The Diagnostic Mindset of Good Teachers" in Chapter 6.)

Uses of Group-Administered Standardized Pre-Reading Assessments

Researchers' reported findings have suggested that the predictive validity of pre-reading tests is not very high, that they could not predict with accuracy how well young children would learn to read, and that teachers' ratings were just as accurate in predicting reading success.[5] On the other hand, there is a great amount of evidence available to support the relationship between young children's letter naming and their later reading achievement, as well as school achievements.[6] This is also true of phonological awareness. Investigators' findings have shown that the alphabet subtest of the *Metropolitan Readiness Tests* "has consistently been the best predictor of scholastic achievement."[7]

According to Hillerich, "a great saving in testing time could well stem from using only the letters and numbers subtests or, perhaps, by not testing readiness at all. In either case, the sacrifice in information would be minimal."[8] Such statements continue, and educators still decry the misuses of pre-reading tests.[9] Despite many expressions of concern, test makers continue to produce such tests, and many teachers are required to use them.

Pre-reading tests, like other assessment measures, have their problems. Here are three that come to mind:

1. As any teacher who has ever tried to get a group of 20 kindergarten students all focused on the same item on the same page knows, actually administering the test can be extremely time-consuming. When test developers estimate how long it will take to administer the test, they do not take classroom management into account.

2. More often than not, there are too many prompts from the teacher. Therefore, a child's performance score may be inflated. Take, for example, a subtest that is designed to determine whether students can identify words. There is a sentence with one word missing, and four choices are given below the sentences. The examiner's manual directs the test administrator to read the sentence *and* the words under the sentence. Students are then supposed to choose the word to complete the sentence so that the sentence will make sense. The problem? Although the test is designed to shed light on how well students can identify words, it does not do this at all because the teacher does all of the reading. All the students have to do is *recognize* a word, which is much easier than identifying it. The only conclusion that can be drawn about students who successfully complete a subtest such as this is that they appear to be able to recognize some words. But can they read them independently, as their performance on this test is supposed to indicate? We cannot say.

3. Yet another problem is the lack of congruence between *emergent literacy* and one single way to assess it. Because children are constantly emerging and changing, it can be extremely difficult to obtain valid and reliable scores indicative of their development and learning from a one-time, group-administered standardized test.

Suggestions for Choosing and Using Required Pre-Reading Tests

Here are some suggestions on how to choose and use pre-reading tests if they are required in your school system:

1. Use a test that can provide you with information on a child's present level of literacy development.

2. Check the subtests to determine how directly the tasks required are related to reading. For example, some tests require children to match pictures and geometric figures rather than letters. Those children who do well in matching pictures and geometric figures may not do well in matching letters. Check to see if the subtests are similar to the activities presented in the beginning reading program.

3. Check the administration time of the test. Make sure that it is suited to the attention span of your students.

4. Make sure children comprehend the terminology used on the test and understand the directions.

5. Use the results of the test and your interpretation of them to gain information about each child's present level of development so that you can provide the best possible program for her.

6. Use the pre-reading test as one measure; also use classroom assessments and your judgment to make decisions concerning the child's literacy development. (See Chapter 1.)

Current Ways to Assess Early Literacy

One of the recommended policies set forth by the authors of the joint position statement of the International Literacy Association (ILA) and the National Association for the Education of Young Children (NAEYC) calls for "appropriate assessment strategies that promote children's learning and development."

Does this mean that there is no place for standardized tests in assessing and teaching early literacy? Not necessarily. Standardization doesn't automatically make a test evil. Many times it is the *content* of these standardized tests, in conjunction with a teaching philosophy and a district or state policy, that causes problems. For example, one test that appears to be sweeping the nation is the *Dynamic Indicators of Basic Early Literacy Skills (DIBELS)* and its updated version, DIBELS Next.[10] This battery of tests was created by researchers at the University of Oregon. (For more information, visit the website at dibels.uoregon.edu; https://dibels.org/dibelsnext.html.) The tests begin in kindergarten and continue through sixth grade. Early literacy skills are typically identified for children in kindergarten through second grade. One problem is that the creators of this test use the word *fluency* where they actually mean *proficiency*. Thus, the letter recognition subtest is called "fluency of letter recognition" (LRF). Students are given one minute to say the displayed letters. Their performance is then interpreted as a reading level. The problems we see with this battery of tests in general, and the letter recognition test in particular, stem from their lack of congruence with our view of what it means to be a reader. (See Chapter 1.) First, when we are assessing fluency, students need time to rehearse; a "cold" read tells teachers little about how fluently a child reads. Second, what does it help a teacher to know *how quickly* a child can say letters of the alphabet? What teachers want to know is which letters the child knows and which still need to be learned. Third, good readers adjust their rate of reading to their purpose for reading. But will students learn to adjust their reading rate, slowing down when needed and speeding up when appropriate, if they are constantly timed on all subtests? Not likely. Instead, tests such as these can potentially distort what reading means to a child, leaving children with misconceptions that speed is one of the most important aspects of reading. In reality, the one-minute time standard on DIBELS is a standardized way of keeping the test simple and quick to administer. Yet interpreting the results as "fluency" creates a misconception of what fluency is about. The misconceptions surrounding protocols and labeling on this test can prevent children from becoming willing and able readers.[11]

We all want to be efficient with our use of time. But speed is not what matters, especially for early reading. Instead, what matters in a diagnostic approach is asking and answering the assessment questions we first posed in Chapter 1 and continue to pose throughout this text: What do I want to know? Why do I want to know it? How can I best learn this information? When making decisions about selecting assessment strategies, staying focused on the purpose of the assessment and how the results will be used to inform instruction is essential. With standardized measures, teachers need to find and understand the statements of purpose usually provided by test authors in training materials.

And let's remember that most often, teachers are told rather than asked about using standardized measures. Fortunately, there are several standardized measures that can be used to meaningfully and appropriately assess different aspects of early literacy. For example, the *Yopp-Singer Test of Phonemic Segmentation*[12] is a useful standardized tool to help ascertain how well children can segment phonemes in spoken words. *Concepts About Print*[13] is another useful tool that is designed to tap students' understanding of books and terminology related to them. Rathvon[14] lists additional standardized measures.

The majority of these measures are individually administered and can be given several times so that the teacher can note progress over time. When contrasted with group-administered tests, these individual assessment measures can also yield much more information, because the examiner can watch what the child does on given tasks. For example, after reading a passage, a child might stop and talk about something that happened to him that is similar to what happened in the story. This type of response indicates that the child is making some self-to-text connections, that he is comprehending.

To standardize or not to standardize is not the question. Instead, the pertinent question is "What are the children showing they know and what do they need to know to advance as language users?" Addressing these strengths and needs at the onset is about ensuring that children get a fair start, rather than needing to catch up later on. Just as regular maintenance can prevent costly car repairs, so, too, early intervention saves resources, human as well as monetary.

Table 8.2 What, Why, How of Early Literacy Assessment Techniques

What Do I Want to Know?	Why Do I Want to Know?	How Can I Best Discover It?
Do children have an understanding of basic language concepts?	Knowing the language concepts children understand and those they need to learn will better help me to explain instruction.	Informal Inventory of Concepts
Do children have an understanding of how print functions?	Understanding how print functions and knowing the terminology associated with reading are essential for effective reading.	Print Concepts
Do children display phonological awareness?	Phonological awareness can assist reading success.	Phonological Awareness Test
Can children identify letters of the alphabet?	Knowing letters appears to be associated with competent reading.	Letter Identification
To what degree do students write?	Understanding about the alphabetic principle and using other print conventions are essential for writing success.	Writing Vocabulary Message Writing
Do children understand how stories are structured, and do they show listening comprehension?	Understanding how stories are structured will facilitate future reading success. Showing listening comprehension indicates that students realize that understanding is essential for reading.	Wordless Picture Story

Because there are different components of early literacy, we need to use a variety of measures to assess them. However, variety can be a bit overwhelming if we aren't sure what it is we're looking for. This leads us once again to ask three important questions: What do I want to know? Why do I want to know? How can I best discover it? Table 8.2 provides some help in answering these questions. The answers to these three questions lead to a fourth: How can I use what I discover to design data-driven, purposeful instructions?

Understanding, Assessing, and Teaching Concepts

Concept Development, Language, and Reading

Concept development is closely related to language development. Much language use depends on knowing the relational meanings of words rather than just labeling concrete experiences. A person can experience "green" in a concrete way and use the word *green* to describe what she sees, but "color" is a conceptual word—a category header under which specific concrete experiences can be organized. When a green light changes to yellow and then red, a child thinking concretely would simply name the changes. A child with a broader concept might say, "It changes color." When children develop concepts and learn the vocabulary words that go with these concepts, they are emerging toward the kind of abstract thinking that underpins reading and writing. Children who are more advanced in concept development tend to be more advanced in their use of abstract language, and vice versa. Children with deeper concept knowledge tend to be better readers.

What Is a Concept?

A **concept** is a group of stimuli with common characteristics. These stimuli may be objects, events, or persons. Concepts are usually designated by their names, such as *book, war, man, woman, animal,* or *teacher*. All these concepts refer to classes (or categories)

of stimuli. Some stimuli do not refer to concepts; Ms. Jones, the lawyer, Hemingway's *The Killers*, World War II, and the Empire State Building are examples. These are specific (and not classes of) people, stimuli, or happenings.

Concepts are needed to reduce the complexity of the world. When children learn that their shaggy pets are called *dogs*, for a while they may label all other similar four-footed animals as "dogs." Very young children often overgeneralize categories. When children grow in experience, they discern differences and similarities and begin to form more typical categories, concepts, or schemata.

A main step in acquiring concepts involves oral vocabulary, because concept meanings are associated with specific words: Vocabulary is a key toolkit for sharing and trying out concept development in the social world. Another step is gathering data—that is, specific information about the concept to be learned. In doing this, students use their strategies for processing information—they select data that are relevant, ignore irrelevant data, and categorize items that belong together. Concepts are formed when data are organized into categories.

How Do Concepts Develop?

Concept development is closely related to cognitive (thinking) development. Jean Piaget, a renowned Swiss psychologist, has written on children's cognitive development in terms of their ability to organize (which requires conceptualization), classify, and adapt to their environments.

According to Piaget, the mind is capable of intellectual exercise because of its ability to categorize incoming stimuli adequately. **Schemata** (structured designs) are the cognitive arrangements by which this categorization takes place. As children develop and take in more and more information, it becomes necessary for them to have some way to categorize all the new information. At the same time, their ability to categorize by means of schemata grows, too. That is, children should be able to differentiate, to become less dependent on sensory stimuli, and to gain more and more complex schemata. Children should be able to categorize a cat as distinct from a mouse or a rabbit. They also should be able to group cat, dog, and cow together as animals. Piaget calls the processes that bring about these changes in children's thinking **assimilation** and **accommodation**.[15]

Assimilation does not change a concept, but allows it to grow. It is a continuous process that helps the individual to integrate new, incoming stimuli into existing schemata or concepts. For example, when a child sees an unusual piece of kitchenware like a gravy boat, does she add this new item to the existing category for dishes? Comparing new experiences to existing categories helps us make sense of new things in the world.

If the child encounters stimuli that cannot be made to fit into the existing schema, then the alternative is either to construct a new category or to change the existing one. Accommodation occurs when a new schema or concept is developed, or when an existing schema is changed.

Although both assimilation and accommodation are important processes that the child must attain in order to develop adequate cognition, a balance between the two processes is necessary. If children over-assimilate, they will have categories that are too general to be useful; similarly, if they over-accommodate, they will have too many categories. Piaget calls the balance between the two **equilibrium.** A person having equilibrium would be able to see similarities between stimuli and thus properly assimilate them, and would also be able to determine when new schemata are needed for adequate accommodation of a surplus of categories.

As children develop cognitively, they proceed from more global (generalized) schemata to more particular ones. For the child, there are usually no right or wrong placements, but only better or more effective ones. That is what good education is all about.

How Does Concept Development Relate to Language and Reading?

Unless children attain the necessary concepts, they will be limited in reading as well as in all other aspects of the language arts (listening, speaking, writing, and viewing).

Knowledge of what concepts are and how children attain them is essential in a diagnostic approach. Teachers using this approach must recognize early when readers are developing concepts, and then help them along.

The quality of language development depends on the interrelationships of psychological and social factors in a child's life. The factors that influence language development also influence concept development. As a result, children who are more advanced in language development are also usually more advanced in concept development, and these children tend to be better readers.[16]

How Can Oral-Language Concepts Be Assessed?

Concepts are necessary to help students acquire increasing amounts of knowledge. For example, as students proceed through the grades in school, their learning becomes more abstract and is expressed in words, using verbal stimuli as labels for concepts. Many teachers take for granted that those spoken concept labels are understood by their students, but this is not always so. Young children's literal interpretation of oral and written discourse and their limited knowledge of the world around them affect their comprehension and ability to form correct concepts. If not enough information is given, concepts are often learned either incompletely or incorrectly.

When children enter school, the teacher must assess their concept development level, and then help them to add the attributes that are necessary and relevant for the development of particular concepts. At the same time, the teacher must help students to delete all those concepts that are faulty or irrelevant.

One way to assess language concepts is to use an informal inventory test of concepts, such as the one shown in Figure 8.2. It can be given orally to individual students.

Another method to determine whether children have a concept such as opposites is to ask each child to give some opposites for words such as these:

no	good	fat
boy	mommy	go
happy	early	fast

A third way to determine whether the children understand language concepts is to play games. For example, to see if children understand the concepts of left and right, play the game "Simon Says" with the children and use directions with the words *left* and *right*.

A fourth way to observe whether children understand specific language concepts is to use these concepts as part of classroom routines. For example, the concepts of *first* and *last* can be assessed by asking children to name who is first or who is last in line.

A fifth, more formalized way of assessing oral-language concepts is to use a standardized, norm-referenced test such as the *Boehm Test of Basic Concepts*, 3rd edition (2000), which is published in both English and Spanish. The test is designed to help teachers determine which of the 50 most frequently occurring concepts children know and which they need to learn.[17]

Enhanced eText
Video Example 8.2
Two college students demonstrate administering the Boehm Test of Language Concepts.
https://www.youtube.com/watch?v=u9yjHrxL0JM

Enhanced eText **Application Exercise 8.1:** Ms. Berger's Understanding of Concept Development

Figure 8.2 Informal Concept Inventory for Early Primary-Grade Students

This test gives a brief indicator of connections between vocabulary and concept knowledge. Students who mark items correctly likely have both concept and vocabulary knowledge. Students who mark items incorrectly may do so because of vocabulary and/or concept knowledge. Since the test is brief, questions should be followed up with more thorough concept assessments.

Directions: Teacher will read the script on the right and ask students to mark pictures on the left. The teacher should avoid prompting or demonstrating the italicized concept vocabulary words.

	Position concept: Above. "Mark the circle that has a line *above* it." (Teacher may make a sample line to show students what is meant by "line.")
	Position concept: Under. "Mark the circle that has a line *under* it."
	Shape concept. "Mark the shape that is *square*."
	Shape concept. "Mark the picture that is a *triangle*."
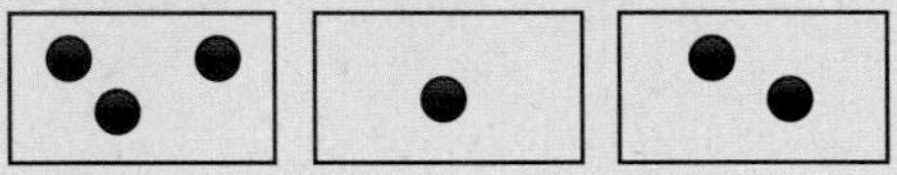	Quantity concept. "Mark the box that has the *most* circles in it."
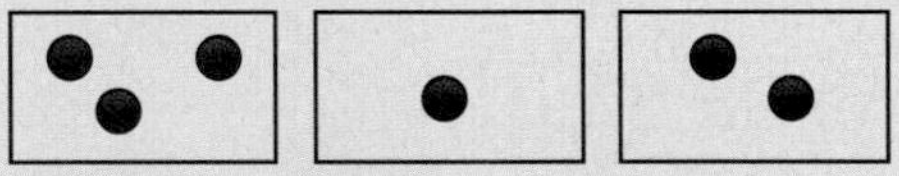	Quantity concept. "Mark the box that has the *fewest* circles in it."
	Size concept. "Mark the circle that is *smallest*."
	Size concept. "Mark the circle that is *largest*."
	Opposite concept. "Mark the *opposite* of *big animal*."
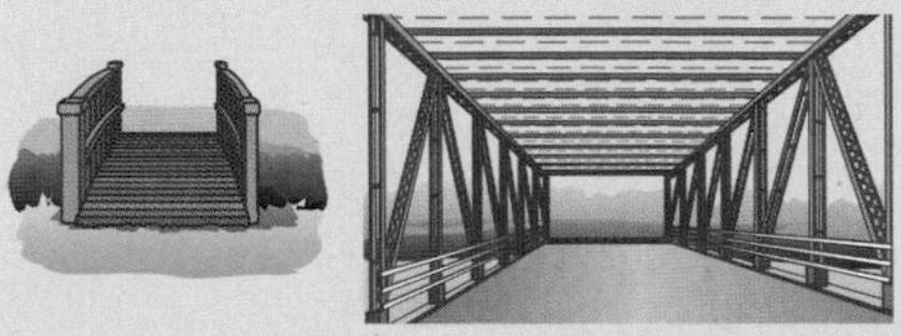	Opposite concept. "Mark the *opposite* of *wide bridge*."

Bridge: From Understanding to Assessment

When teachers understand that _____,	then teachers will assess _____.
Print concepts are not gained automatically,	What students already know about identifying books as language, and how printed materials work, by giving them reading material to handle and then observing.
Conceptual development of meanings and words in spoken language is foundational for reading comprehension,	Students' spoken language to learn in which kinds of meanings they already have strengths, and which meanings they may need to learn to be more successful readers.

Assessing Print Concepts

There are several print concepts that children need to know in order to read. Children's understanding of these concepts is important to their early reading success. These concepts include: Print carries a message, left-to-right progression, return line sweep, and linguistic terms such as *word, letter, beginning,* and *ending*.

One way to assess for these print concepts is to use the *Print Concepts Test* shown in Figure 8.3. It is a modification of the original *Concepts About Print* test developed by Marie Clay.[18] The main difference between this version and Clay's is that this one is not standardized. It also permits the examiner to use just about any children's literature selection.

Print Concepts Administration Procedures

1. Choose a book that is relatively short. *The Hungry Monster* by Phyllis Root (Candlewick, 1997) an example of an appropriate text.[19]

2. Make a copy of the *Print Concepts* form for each child (Figure 8.3).

3. Read through the form to become familiar with what you will be asking and to make sure that the book you will be using has the appropriate examples as noted on the form.

4. Individually administer the *Print Concepts* assessment using the prompts shown on the *Print Concepts* form.

Scoring Procedures

1. Look at the responses the child provides.

2. Record your observations on the *Summary of Print Concepts* form shown in Figure 8.4.

3. Use the results to plan instruction.

As noted in Chapter 3, compiling the results of individual assessment measures on a class matrix can be helpful in seeing the class at a glance. The *Concepts About Print: Class Profile* form shown in Figure 8.5 can be used for this purpose. The form is also helpful in that it shows which items are related to directionality, terminology, and punctuation.

Those who need to use a norm-referenced standardized test will want to use Clay's *Concepts About Print* test. Standard prompts are used, and the literature selections used to assess the print concepts are specified.

Bridge: From Assessment to Teaching

When teachers learn from assessments that _____,	then teachers will teach _____.
Many students enter school still developing print concepts,	These concepts through repeated meaningful demonstrations over weeks and months of time, such as structured read-alouds and discussions.
Children respond to books, magazines, and other materials in different ways,	About different kinds of printed material and how these are meaningful in everyday life.

Figure 8.3 Print Concepts

Name: _____

Directions: Using the book that you have selected, give the following prompts to encourage the child to interact with it. Read the story aloud as you proceed. Place a ✔ next to each item answered correctly.

Prompt	Response (✔ = correct)	Print Concept
1. Hand the child the book upside down, spine first, saying something like: "Show me the front of this book." Then read the title to the child.		layout of book
2. Say: "I would like to begin reading the story, but I need your help. Please open the book and point to the exact spot where I should begin reading."		print conveys message
3. Stay on the same page and say: "Point to where I need to start reading."		directionality: where to begin
4. Say: "Point to where I should go after I start reading."		directionality: left-to-right progression
5. Say: "Point to where I go next." Read the pair of pages.		directionality: return sweep
6. Turn the page and say: "Point to where I should begin reading on this page. Now point to where I should end." Read the page.		terminology: beginning and end
7. Turn the page and say: "Point to the bottom of this page. Point to the top of it. Now point to the middle of it." Read the page.		terminology: top, bottom, middle
8. Using the same page, say: "Point to one letter."		terminology: letter
9. Again using the same page, say: "Point to one word."		terminology: word
10. Turn the page. Make sure that this page contains words that have corresponding upper and lowercase letters. Read the page. Then point to a capital letter and say: "Point to a little letter that is like this one."		matching lower to uppercase letters
11. Turn the page and say: "Let's read these pages together. I'll read and you point." Read the pages.		speech-to-print match
12. Finish reading the book. Then turn back to a page that has the punctuation marks you want to assess. Point to the punctuation mark and say: "What is this?" "What is it for?"		punctuation: period, question mark, quotation marks

Source: From *Flexible Grouping in Reading*, by Michael Opitz. Published by Scholastic Teaching Resources/Scholastic, Inc. Copyright © 1995 by Michael Opitz. Reprinted by permission.

Teaching Oral-Language and Print Concepts

A rich oral-language program is a necessary first step to prevent reading failure because it helps prepare children for reading. The closer the children's language is to the written symbols encountered in reading, the greater their chance of success. Hearing English in the context of something meaningful with which they can identify helps children gain "facility in listening, attention span, narrative sense, recall of stretches of verbalization and the recognition of new words as they appear in other contexts."[20]

Figure 8.4 Summary of Print Concepts

Title of Book: _____

Directions: Use this form to summarize your observations of print concepts.

Observations

The child demonstrates knowledge of the following print concepts (✔ the appropriate spaces)

_____ layout of books (item 1)

_____ print conveys written message (item 2)

_____ directionality (items 3, 4, 5)

_____ terminology associated with reading (items 6, 7, 8, 9)

_____ uppercase letters (item 10)

_____ lowercase letters (item 10)

_____ speech-to-print match (item 11)

_____ punctuation (item 12)

Comments/Notes

_____
_____
_____
_____
_____
_____
_____
_____
_____
_____
_____
_____
_____
_____
_____
_____
_____
_____

Source: From *Flexible Grouping in Reading,* by Michael Opitz. Published by Scholastic Teaching Resources/Scholastic, Inc. Copyright © 1995 by Michael Opitz. Reprinted by permission.

Teachers using a reading diagnosis and improvement program understand that one main reason for assessing students is to determine what students know and what they need to learn. Teachers can then use the results to plan appropriate instruction. There are several ways to teach language and print concepts.

Read Aloud to Children   Numerous researchers investigating the power of the read-aloud have arrived at the same findings: Reading aloud increases children's listening vocabularies.[21] Other researchers have discovered that children who speak nonstandard

Figure 8.5 Concepts about Print: Class Profile

Name	1 layout of books	2 print conveys message	3 where to begin	4 left-to-right progression	5 return sweep	6 beginning, end	7 top, bottom, middle	8 letter	9 word	10 upper- and lower-case matching	11 speech-to-print match	12 period, question mark, quotation marks
	Directionality					Terminology						Punctuation

Source: From *Flexible Grouping in Reading*, by Michael Opitz. Published by Scholastic Teaching Resources/Scholastic, Inc. Copyright © 1995 by Michael Opitz. Reprinted by permission.

English make significant gains toward standard English when they are involved in a rich oral program, one that stresses reading stories aloud and actively involving children in related activities. In terms of language and print concepts, there is much a teacher can do:

- Before reading, the teacher can emphasize "front" by saying something like "The title of our book is on the front cover."

- The teacher can also point to the words while reading, which helps children to see that print carries the message and that there is a match between what is said and the print on the page (i.e., speech-to-print match).

- Upon completion of the story, the teacher can emphasize language concepts such as "first" and "last" by using the terms as he asks the children to tell the class what happened first and last.
- Concepts (such as "pair") can be emphasized, such as by telling students to pair up. Each pair can then be invited to chime in during a rereading of the story at their designated time.

As you can see, there are many ways language concepts can be reinforced through read-alouds. Children's literature titles often focus on language concepts. *A Pair of Protoceratops* by Bernard Most (Harcourt, 1998), *Parts* by Shelley Rotner (Walker, 2001), *Over, Under, Through* by Tana Hoban (Macmillan, 1973), and *What's Opposite?* by Stephen Swinburne (Boyds Mills, 2000) are a few of the many available titles.

Reading a story to children can be a rewarding, interactive learning experience if it is done properly. Here are some suggestions to ensure your success when reading aloud to children.

Preparing for the Story

1. Choose a short storybook that is at the attention, interest, and concept development levels of the children and that has large pictures that can be easily seen.
2. Have the children sit comfortably and in a position that allows them to see the pictures easily.
3. Make sure to limit distractions in the room.
4. State the title and show the book to the children. Ask them if they can figure out what the story will be about from the title.
5. Tell them to listen carefully for certain things. (Of course, this will be based on the story being read.)

Reading the Story

1. Read the story aloud to the children.
2. Stop at key points and ask students to discuss what is happening, or have them say aloud the repeated refrain, if the story contains one.
3. Ask more questions for them to think about while they are listening to the story.
4. If children interject comments during the story, you should acknowledge these by saying "Good thinking" if it shows they are thinking, and then continue reading.

After the Story

When the story is finished, have the children answer some of the unanswered questions and do some of the following based on their attention and interest levels:

1. Tell what the story is about.
2. Retell the story in sequence.
3. Discuss whether the story is based on fantasy or reality.
4. Act out the story.
5. Make up another ending for the story.

Engage Children in Language Play.   Learning language can and should be fun. Fun allows for a positive association with learning language. Games such as "Simon Says" are perfect for developing further understanding of specific language concepts. And playing the "Hokey Pokey" is a perfect way to help children to better understand specific language concepts. A rich oral-language classroom should involve singing songs, reciting poems and verse, oral storytelling, and dramatizations (including reader's theater, student-authored plays, and puppet shows). All oral-language play can be

Table 8.3 Halliday's Functions of Language and Sample Instructional Activities

Function of Language	Use	Sample Instructional Activities
Instrumental ("I want")	To satisfy needs or desires	Check out library books. Sign in for attendance. Provide directions for others.
Regulatory ("Do as I tell you!")	To control behavior of others	Establish guidelines for taking care of classroom equipment. Play follow-the-leader–type games.
Interactional ("Me and you")	To establish and maintain relationships	Write messages to one another. Have children share work areas and/or materials. Have children work together to plan a project.
Personal ("Here I come!")	To express one's personal feelings or thoughts	Provide time for students to talk with one another. Read stories and ask students to share their thoughts about the stories.
Heuristic ("Tell me why.")	To discover and find out why something happens	Create problems for students to solve. Conduct simple experiments.
Imaginative ("Let's pretend.")	To create an imaginative world of one's own	Use puppets. Have a dress-up center.
Informative ("I have something to tell you.")	To provide information to others	Provide time for students share announcements. Provide time for students to tell current events.

Source: Based on Halliday, M., Exploration in the Functions of Language, 1975.

accompanied by print in some form to help children make the connection between their playfulness and printed text.

Do Some Focused, Explicit Teaching.   You might decide that in addition to focused story reading, you want to design some lessons that teach specific language concepts. Looking at the class matrix described earlier can help you to see who needs some extra instruction in certain areas so you can teach them the needed concepts.

Use Language in a Variety of Ways.   Several years ago, Halliday identified seven distinct functions that children often use for language. However, some children appear to be limited language users. Knowing about these functions can help teachers to create classroom situations in which children need to use all seven functions, which will help them become flexible language users.[22] In Table 8.3, we show these functions and provide sample classroom activities.

Understanding, Assessing, and Teaching Phonological Awareness

What Is Phonological Awareness?

Although the terms *phonological awareness* and *phonemic awareness* are sometimes used interchangeably, this is incorrect. **Phonological awareness** refers to awareness of three aspects of spoken language: words, syllables within words, and sounds or phonemes within syllables and words. **Phonemic awareness** is one aspect of the larger category of phonological awareness: the awareness that words are made up of individual sounds in sequence. One way to remember the difference between the terms is to visualize a brick house. Awareness of all pieces and parts such as windows, doors, walls, and bricks are like phonological awareness. By contrast a focus on the smallest building blocks— bricks, boards, panes of glass—is like phonological awareness. Both terms, however,

Enhanced eText
Video Example 8.3
Teaching Phonemic
Awareness (video 1927).

This **video** shows an example of phonemic awareness instruction.

Table 8.4 Stages of Phonological Awareness

Phonological Awareness Level	Sample Activity
Recognizing that words represent a sound unit—word awareness	Provide children with some sort of counter. After reading a story, select one sentence and say it aloud. Repeat the sentence slowly and instruct students to drop a counter into a cup every time they hear a word.
Detecting that words are made up of different parts—syllable awareness	After reading a story, select some words that have single and multiple syllables. Invite students to clap out the parts as words are read.
Recognizing that words are made up of individual sounds—phoneme awareness	State a given word from a story and ask students how many sounds they hear in the word.

Source: From Rhymes and Reasons: Literature and Language Play for Phonological Awareness, by Michael Opitz. Copyright © 2000. Published by Heinemann, Portsmouth, NH. Reprinted by permission.

refer to spoken language. A child who is phonologically and phonemically aware is not necessarily able to connect the sound units with written symbols.

Phonological awareness develops in stages. Learners first become aware that their spoken language is composed of single words in sequence. They then progress to the stage in which they become aware that words are constructed of syllables. The last stage is the one in which learners become aware that words and syllables are made up of individual sounds (i.e., phonemes). Children who end up being proficient readers usually have developed a strong sense of phonology, all the way down to phonemic awareness, whereas children who end up struggling with reading and writing often have needs in this area during early literacy.[23] Table 8.4 shows the different stages of phonological awareness and sample tasks associated with each.

Phonemic Awareness Tasks.   There are many tasks associated with phonemic awareness; some are more difficult than others. When children can perform all of these tasks, they are considered to have phonemic awareness. Identifying and producing rhyme appear to be the least difficult of these tasks. Another phonemic awareness task is *phoneme matching*, which calls for the learner to identify words that have a given sound or to generate a word that has a given sound. When children are expected to listen to a sentence and then state the sound that they hear at the beginning of a word, or to state some words that begin like a given word, they are performing phoneme matching.

In a *phoneme blending* task, students are expected to put sounds together to form a given word. For example, the teacher might say, "I'm thinking of a word that names something we have at lunch. It's /m/ ilk. What's the word?" Children must blend the first sound with the rest of the sounds to state the word *milk*.

In a *phoneme segmentation* task, children are given a word and asked to tell how many sounds they hear in it. They are also often expected to produce the actual sounds. For example, the teacher might say, "Tell me the sounds you hear in the word *mom*." Learners might be asked to drop a counter into a cup to represent each sound they hear in a word.

Phoneme manipulation entails manipulating sounds within a given word in different ways. Sometimes, children are expected to substitute one sound for another, as in "What word do we have if we change the /m/ in *man* to /p/?" Other times, children are asked to add sounds to a given word, as in "Add /s/ to *nail*. What's the new word?" Another task requires children to delete a sound within a word, such as when the teacher says, "Take away the first sound in *gate*. What's the new word?"

Enhanced eText
Video Example 8.4 Phoneme Blending.

In this video, a teacher introduces her class to blending phonemes into whole words. https://www.youtube.com/watch?v=vsqEGq7VSF4&t=40s

Enhanced eText
Video Example 8.5 Phoneme Segmenting.

In this video, a teacher works with a small group of readers on segmenting whole words into phonemes. https://www.youtube.com/watch?v=TMnmtvlM-ag

Enhanced eText Application Exercise 8.2: Ms. Berger's Understanding of Phonological Awareness

Bridge: From Understanding to Assessment

When teachers understand that _____,	then teachers will assess _____.
Phonological and phonemic awareness predict success with reading,	Students' ability to perceive and produce language in parts, including individual words, syllables, and phonemes.
Phonological awareness is about spoken words, and not necessarily printed words,	Using manipulatives that help readers demonstrate speech sounds with concrete tools (such as tiles or cards).

How Can Phonological Awareness Be Assessed?

Phonological awareness in general and phonemic awareness in particular appear to be important for reading success. Recently, the National Reading Panel performed a meta-analysis of several studies and concluded that phonemic awareness is an important reading skill and that some children needed explicit instruction.[24] Likewise, the Board of Directors of the International Literacy Association (called the International Reading Association at the time) published a position statement on phonemic awareness and the teaching of reading.[25] By posing several questions and answers in the statement, the group explained the intricacies of phonemic awareness.

There are both informal and formal ways of assessing the different levels of phonological awareness. The one shown in Figure 8.6 has been adapted from the one that MO created for *Summer Success Reading*.[26]

Administering the Phonological Awareness Test

1. Make copies of the scoring form, one for each student.

2. Using the wording shown on the scoring form, administer the test to individual students.

Scoring the Phonological Awareness Test

1. Write the number correct for each part of the overall test in the Summary section.

2. Write any other observational notes as necessary.

A second way to assess phonological awareness is to use a norm-referenced measure such as the *Test of Phonological Awareness,* Second edition, or TOPA-2,[27] which is a group-administered test.

Enhanced eText
Video Example 8.6 Testing Phonological Awareness.
In this video, a teacher demonstrates a test of phonological awareness with one child. https://www.youtube.com/watch?v=uY8XlgL6d-g&t=18s

Bridge: From Assessment to Teaching

When teachers understand that _____,	then teachers will teach _____.
Not all children demonstrate phonological awareness automatically,	Phonology with a variety of authentic texts, including those that feature singing, rhymes, and alliteration.
Phonemic awareness involves fine-grained analysis of a word,	With one technique at a time (such as segmenting words) to avoid confusing readers with different activities that have different rules and procedures.

Teaching Phonological Awareness

For many children, phonological awareness is more caught than taught. Children who come to kindergarten or first grade with this awareness have been raised in a rich language environment where they were exposed to read-alouds, songs, nursery rhymes, poems, and other forms of language play. The reverse is true for those children who are lacking in phonological awareness. More than likely, they have not been afforded a rich language environment that facilitates an understanding of spoken language.

Here are six specific suggestions drawn from the work of researchers who have shed light on how best to help children acquire phonological awareness.[28] Keep in mind that while much unintentional instruction occurs throughout a school day, planned

Figure 8.6 PRETEST: Part A: Phonological Awareness Score Sheet

Name: _____ Date _____

For each item, put a + next to every correct response. Leave blank if incorrect. Award one point for each +.

1. Word Level: Counting Words in Sentences

Directions: "I am going to say a sentence to you. I want you to clap every time you hear a word. Let's try one: 'I am here.'" (Pause for child to clap or repeat the sentence and clap.) "Good! You clapped three times! Now do the same for these sentences."

Sentence	*Response*	
I can run (3)	—	
Winter is cold. (3)	—	
The boy reads and writes. (5)	—	
Can you read? (3)	—	
Jim likes his dog. (4)	—	Score _____

2. Syllable Level: Counting Syllables in Words

Directions: "I am going to say some words to you, and I want you to clap for each word part. For example, dog (clap once), father (clap twice). Try some with me: fig, better, funny. This is fun! Let's do some more!"

Word	*Response*	
Mom (1)	—	
bunny (2)	—	
festival (3)	—	
cat (1)	—	
waterfall (2)	—	Score _____

3. Phoneme Level: Rhyming

Directions: "I am going to say two words. If they rhyme, nod your head yes. If they don't, nod your head no. Let's try some: bat/cat, mom/bet, Let's try some more."

Word Pairs	*Response*	
fit/bit (*yes*)	—	
say/dog (*no*)	—	
sat/mat (*yes*)	—	
sun/fun (*yes*)	—	
ten/no (*no*)	—	Score _____

deliberate instruction in phonemic awareness is most effective when it is kept within short time frames. The National Reading Panel suggests effectiveness maxes out at about 200 minutes per school year, or about 7 minutes per day.

1. *Embed phonological awareness into everyday reading and writing experiences.* Doing so helps children understand how this awareness of sounds relates to reading and writing. Table 8.5 provides a list of typical reading and writing experiences, a sample activity for each, and an explanation of how the experience promotes phonological awareness.

Figure 8.6 (*Continued*)

4. Phoneme Level: Matching

Directions: "Now let's think of words that begin with the same sound. For example, van, vote, vase begin with /v/." NOTE: Remember to say the sound rather than name the letter!. "Let's try one. I'll say a sound and you tell me a word that begins with that sound: /z/. Remember to accept ANY word that begins with /z/." You have the idea! Let's do some more of these.

Sound	Response
/m/	—
/n/	—
/s/	—
/r/	—
/f/	—

Score _____

Summary

1. Word Level: Counting Words in Sentences   _____

2. Syllable Level: Counting Syllables in Words   _____

3. Phoneme Level: Rhyming   _____

4. Phoneme Level: Matching   _____

Total _____ /20

Table 8.5 Reading and Writing Experiences That Foster Phonological Awareness

Typical Reading/Writing Experiences	Sample Activity	Phonological Awareness
Read-aloud	Reading books that emphasize language features such as rhyme and alliteration	Words are made up of sound elements that sometimes sound alike.
Shared reading	Reading a big book and asking children to clap every time they hear a word	Words are separate units in the speech stream. They can be used to create stories and sentences.
Guided reading	Providing children with a text to read and directing them to point to each word as they read	Stories are made up of words. Spaces show where a word starts and ends.
Independent reading	Providing time for children to read their own books	Stories are a written form of language. There are units of sound in the speech stream— including words, syllables, and sounds—that are used to write these stories.
Modeled writing	Inviting children to watch as words are written on a chart or on the board, saying each word slowly to stretch it out—either by syllable or by sound	Several word parts/sounds can be used to create a word. These need to be put in a specific sequence.
Interactive writing	Encouraging children to participate in creating a message by stating their ideas	Speech can be written. It is written in chunks.
Independent writing	Providing time for children to write	Sounds are used to create words to communicate an idea to others.

2. *Provide children with time to write using invented spelling.* Although it is true that phonological awareness is focused on sounds of language rather than on its printed form, there is a wealth of research that points to the value of having children write to develop phonological awareness. As children write, they learn to represent spoken language with written symbols and to hone their skills at segmenting phonemes.

3. *Read aloud books that use specific language features.* These kinds of texts draw the learners' attention to given language features such as rhyme, alliteration, phoneme substitution, and phoneme segmentation. As a result of being exposed to books such as these, children learn to make distinctions among sounds and may develop phonological awareness in general and phonemic awareness in particular in meaningful contexts. Fortunately, several such titles are written every year. *Clickety Clack* (Spence & Spence, 1999) is a rhyming story about what happens when many different kinds and numbers of animals decide they want to ride a train. Much initial consonant substitution is used to create the rhymes, making this an excellent book not only for exposing children to rhyme but also for providing some meaningful practice with phoneme substitution. *Pignic* (Miranda, 1996) is an example of alliterative text in which each member of the pig family brings to the pignic something that begins with the same sound that begins their name. Children can join in the fun by going on their own imaginary picnic and bringing along some item that begins with the same sound as their name. *Things That Are Most in the World* (Barrett, 2001) is a repetitive text that tells about some of the silliest, heaviest, and smelliest things in the world! Once they have finished reading the book, children can learn more about phoneme deletion by playing the take-away game. Using words from the text, children might be asked to "Take *-est* away from wiggliest. What's the new word?" *Earthsong* (Rogers, 1998) is a poetry text that includes a rhythmic, rhyming pattern in the dialogues between parents and their offspring. It is an excellent book to help children further understand rhyme.

   Songs can also be used to further children's understanding of phonological awareness. Song picture books have been created to illustrate specific songs. For example, *Hush Little Baby* (Frazee, 1999) is true to the original song, but uses updated illustrations. Once children have sung the song, each word can be framed on a second reading to help children understand word boundaries.

   Finally, texts that use language in humorous ways, such as those written by Dr. Seuss, help children to see that we often play with the sounds in our language. Along with this learning comes a heightened sense of phonological awareness. For example, in *Altoona Baboona* (Bynum, 1999), the author inserts a sound at the end of several words, making this a perfect book to help children further understand sound deletion and sound addition. Children can be directed to take the last sound off the word and say the remaining word (i.e., phoneme deletion), or to add a sound to the end of their names (i.e., phoneme addition). Additional books that invite language play are listed in Table 8.6.

4. *Involve children in fun oral-language activities.* Some children may need more explicit instruction to develop all levels of phonological awareness. These children need to be engaged with the three points listed above as well as with activities that will stimulate their curiosity about and understanding of their spoken language. If children need to understand the concept that words represent a sound unit, they can be provided with some sort of counter. Once a story has been read, students can be directed to pick up a counter for each word they hear. If children need to better understand that words are constructed of syllables, they can be invited to clap out the parts as words are read aloud. If students need additional practice with recognizing that words are made up of individual sounds (i.e., phonemes), they can be asked what sounds they hear in given words from the story.

Table 8.6 Additional Books That Invite Language Play

Rhyme

Arnold, T. 2003. *Dirty Gert.* Holiday House.
Aylesworth, J. 2012. *Cock-a-doodle-doo, Creak, Pop-pop, Moo.* Holiday House.
Baker, K. 2011. *No Two Alike.* Beach Lane Books.
Bonwill, A. 2013. *The Frazzle Family Finds a Way.* Holiday House.
Bunting, E. 2011. *Hey Diddle Diddle.* Boyds Mills.
Burleigh, R. 2009. *Clang! Clang! Beep! Beep! Listen to the City.* Simon & Schuster.
Chaconas, D. 2010. *Don't Slam the Door.* Candlewick.
Dewdney, A. 2010. *Roly Poly Pangolin.* Viking.
Donaldson, J. 2010. *A Gold Star for ZOG.* Scholastic.
Downey, L. 2000. *The Flea's Sneeze.* Holt.
Ginkel, A. 2013. *I've Got an Elephant.* Peachtree Publisher.
Griffith, H. V. 2012. *Moonlight.* Greenwillow.
Hall, M. 2012. *Cat Tale.* Greenwillow.
Marshak, S. 1999. *The Absentminded Fellow.* Farrar, Straus, & Giroux.
Martin, B. 1999. *A Beasty Story.* Harcourt.
Meadows, M. 2010. *Hibernation Station.* Simon & Schuster.
Morrow, B. 2009. *Mr. Mosquito Put on His Tuxedo.* Holiday House.
Spence, R. & Spence, A. (1999). Clickety Clack. Viking Juvenile.
Thomas, J. 2009. *Rhyming Dust Bunnies.* Beach Lane Books.
Wood, A & D. 2010. *Piggy Pie Po.* Harcourt.

Alliteration

Barron, R. 2000. *Fed Up! A Feast of Frazzled Foods.* Putnam.
Duncan, P. 1999. *The Wacky Wedding: A Book of Alphabet Antics.* Hyperion.
Edwards, P. D. 2010. *Princess Pigtoria and the Pea.* Orchard Books.
Fotakis, N. 2011. *Eating Ketchup from a Tub.* CreateSpace.
Kroll, V. 2011. *Mosquito.* Pelican Publishing.
Miranda, A. (1996). Pignic. Boyds Mills Press.
Pavey, P. 2009. *One Dragon's Dream.* Candlewick.
Shapiro, Z. 2009. *We're All in the SAME BOAT.* G.P. Putnam's Sons.

Repetition

Barrett, J. (2001). Things that are Most in the World. Atheneum.
Bauer, M. 2002. *Sleep, Little One, Sleep.* Aladdin.
Collicut, P. 1999. *This Train.* Farrar, Straus, & Giroux.
Fleming, C. 2012. *Oh, No!* Random House/Schwartz & Wade.
Fleming, D. 2010. *Sleepy, Oh So Sleepy.* Henry Holt.
Hamilton, K. 2009. *Police Officers on Patrol.* Viking.
Haughton, C. 2010. *Little Owl Lost.* Candlewick.
Himmelman, J. 2010. *Pigs to the Rescue.* Henry Holt.
Litwin, E. 2010. *Pete the Cat: I Love My White Shoes.* HarperCollins.
Stead, P. 2010. *A Sick Day for Amos McGee.* Roaring Brook Press.
Stein, P. 2010. *Cars Galore.* Candlewick.
Underwood, D. 2010. *The Quiet Book.* Houghton Mifflin.
Weinstein, E. 2008. *Everywhere the Cow Says "Moo!"* Boyds Mills.

Poetry

Hoberman, M. 2012. *Forget-Me-Nots: Poems to Learn by Heart.* Little, Brown Books for Young Readers.
Lewis, J. P. 2012. *National Geographic Book of Animal Poetry: 200 Poems with Photographs That Squeak, Soar, and Roar!* National Geographic Children's Books.
Lobel, A. 2009. *The Frogs and Toads All Sang.* HarperCollins.
Raczka, B. 2010. *GUYKU: A Year of Haiku for Boys.* Houghton Mifflin.
Rogers, S. (1998). Earthsong. Dutton Children's Books.
Rylant, C. 1998. *Bless Us All: A Child's Yearbook of Blessings.* Simon & Schuster.
Schertle, A. 2009. *Button Up!* Houghton Mifflin Harcourt.
Singer, M. 2010. *Mirror Mirror: A Book of Reversible Verse.* Dutton.
Stevenson, R. 1999. *My Shadow.* Harcourt.

Song

Catrow, D. 2012. *Monster Mash.* Orchard.
Colandro, L. 2012. *There Was an Old Lady Who Swallowed a Rose!* Scholastic.
Dean, J. 2012. *Pete the Cat and His Four Groovy Buttons.* HarperCollins.
Emberley, R. 2009. *There Was an Old Monster!* Orchard.
Fleming, D. 2012. *The First Day of Winter.* Henry Holt.
Frazee, M. (2007). Hush, Little Baby. HMH Books for Young Readers.
Hoberman, M. 2000. *The Eensy-Weensy Spider.* Little, Brown.
Norworth, J. 1999. *Take Me Out to the Ballgame.* Aladdin.
Raspo, J. 2013 *Sing.* Holt.
Scieszka, J. 2009. *Truckery Rhymes.* Simon & Schuster.
Tobin, J. 2009. *Sue MacDonald Had a Book.* Henry Holt.

(continued)

Table 8.6 (*Continued*)

Goofy
Banks, K. 2011. *Max's Castle.* Farrar, Straus, & Giroux.
Bynum, J. (1999). Altoona Baboona. Harcourt Children's Books.
Cleary, B. 2011. *Six Sheep Sip Thick Shakes: And Other Tricky Tongue Twisters.* Milbrook Press/Lerner.
Feldman, E. 2009. *Billy & Milly Short & Silly.* G.P. Putnam's Sons.
Lichtenhel, T., & Fields-Meyer, E. 2011. *E-mergency!* Chronicle.
London, J. 2001. *Crunch Munch.* Harcourt.
Marsalis, W. 2012. *Squeak, Rumble, WHOMP! WHOMP! WHOMP!* Candlewick.
Palatini, M. 2009. *Boo-Hoo Moo.* HarperCollins.
Stevens, J., & Stevens Crummel, S. 2012. *Find a Cow NOW!* Holiday House.

5. *Assess to see where children need the most help.* This can be accomplished through observing children as they participate in literacy-related activities such as writing. Observations during writing could reveal those children whose writing shows spaces between words or words that have representative symbols for sounds. These would indicate that the child has developed a sense of all levels of phonological awareness. And the results of assessments such as those shown and mentioned above can be used to detect which children might need some additional help.

6. *Get families involved!* One way to accomplish this is to provide a book and a brief explanation of how to complete an accompanying activity. For example, if the book that is being sent home contains much alliteration, the letter can explain how to point out to the child that all of the words on a given page begin with a certain sound. The child can then be asked to listen for the sound and to state it after a page has been read. The parent can then be instructed to have the child think of other words that begin with the same sound. The letter must focus on exactly what the parent needs to do when working on the book with the child.

Understanding, Assessing, and Teaching Letter Identification

What Is Letter Identification?

Letter identification is just that—identifying the letters of the alphabet. Although common sense would tell us that being able to identify and name the letters of the alphabet is important for reading and writing tasks, there is also ample evidence that being able to name letters is a predictor of end-of-year achievement for kindergarten students.[29]

Letter identification also helps students learn letter–sound associations (i.e., alphabetic principle). This should come as no surprise, because it would be pretty difficult to make any kind of association if one part of the equation were unknown! And, as Rathvon notes, "Only when children have developed the insight that written word forms are related to the sounds rather than the meaning of language can they learn the specific correspondences between letters and phonemes."[30]

Many games teachers are likely to play with words depend on children's being able to identify letters from their names. Therefore, children will have much more fun and be more likely to participate well in such games when they can identify letters early on.

Enhanced eText
Video Example 8.7
The teacher in this **video clip** has designed a classroom activity for 4-year-olds aimed at exposing children to the letters of the alphabet using their first names.

Enhanced eText **Application Exercise 8.3:** Ms. Berger's Understanding of Letter Identification

Bridge: From Understanding to Assessment

When teachers understand that _____,	then teachers will assess _____.
Letter names are fundamental for communicating about letters when learning to read and write,	Letter names not only with tests, where the letters are often isolated, but also within words already in students' speaking vocabularies.

Figure 8.7 PRETEST: Part A: Letter Identification, Student Copy

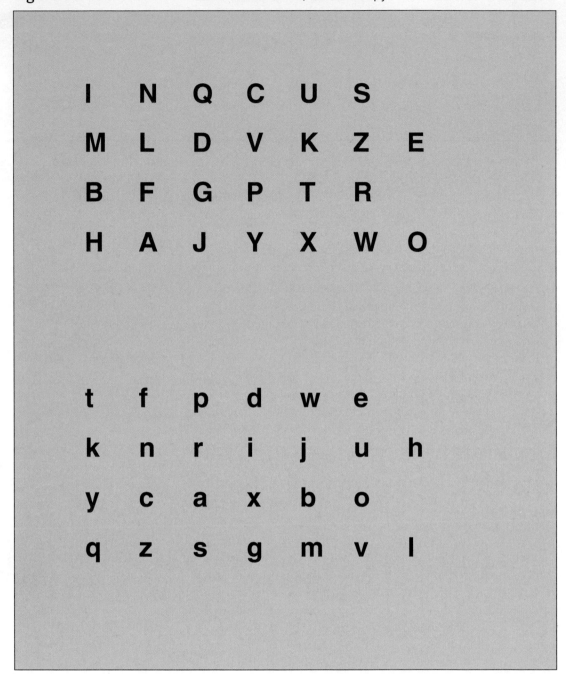

How Can Letter Identification Be Assessed?

Any kindergarten or first-grade teacher will tell you that a good way to assess letter identification ability is to individually ask children to name the letters in random order. Both uppercase and lowercase letters are assessed because knowing one form of the letter doesn't necessarily mean that a child knows the other form.

The protocol in Figure 8.7 and Figure 8.8 shows one informal way of assessing letter identification.

Administering the Letter Identification Test

1. Place the letter identification page in front of the child. Say something like "Here are some letters. Take a look at each one and tell me what it is. You may say 'pass' if you cannot remember the name of the letter."

Figure 8.8 PRETEST: Part A: Letter Identification, Score Sheet

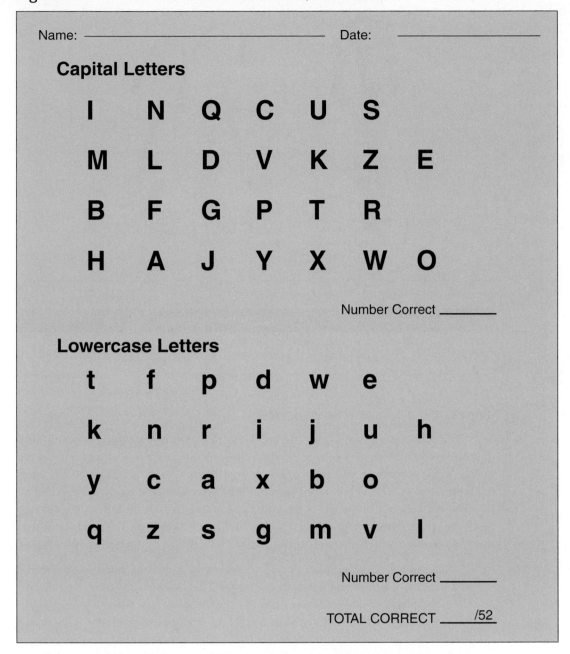

Name: ————————————————   Date: ————————————

Capital Letters

I   N   Q   C   U   S

M   L   D   V   K   Z   E

B   F   G   P   T   R

H   A   J   Y   X   W   O

Number Correct ————————

Lowercase Letters

t   f   p   d   w   e

k   n   r   i   j   u   h

y   c   a   x   b   o

q   z   s   g   m   v   l

Number Correct ————————

TOTAL CORRECT ——— /52

2. Use index cards to cover everything but the lines being read. If necessary, point to each letter shown in Figure 8.8 with your finger (or have the child point).

3. As the child responds, use your copy of the assessment to note correct responses and incorrect responses. When responses are incorrect, record the actual response, or "DK" (doesn't know) if the child doesn't know the specific letter. If the child self-corrects, write OK. Remember that self-corrections can be made at any time and should not be counted as errors.

Scoring the Letter Identification Test

1. Count the number of correct responses for the uppercase letters and lowercase letters.

2. Note the scores in the box on the scoring form in Figure 8.8.

Marie Clay's *Observation Survey* (Heinemann, 1985) provides a formal, norm-referenced, standardized way of assessing letter identification. The assessment is similar to the one described above, and it is individually administered. However, norms are provided, as are some additional assessment procedures.

Figure 8.9 Melissa, who is 4, knows "M" is for "Mom."

Source: Used with permission of Sharon Johnson, Student artwork.

Bridge: From Assessment to Teaching

When teachers understand that _____,	then teachers will teach _____.
Letter naming is a concept, and must develop over time,	Letter names using a variety of authentic and engaging experiences, including people's names, alphabet books, writing, and household objects.

Teaching Letter Identification

Many children come to school already knowing the letters of the alphabet, so the suggestions given here simply enhance their understanding. We catch others right in the middle of the process. However, there are some children who are just beginning to learn to identify letters. This is not to say that these children haven't already noticed letters. Few can escape environmental print, and most understand at an intuitive level that certain marks are used to record their names and other meanings. They simply cannot put a label to the sign. Here are a few suggestions for helping children to identify letters:

1. *Use their names!* Meaningful association is necessary for any of us to learn anything, and this is also true of children learning letters. That is why many kindergarten and first-grade teachers use children's names and family names when thinking about which letters to teach first (see Figure 8.9). In other words, the fact that children can identify their names is no guarantee that they know every letter in the name. Because names are meaningful, teachers often begin by having children learn these letters.

2. *Use alphabet books.* One sure way to help children see the connection between letters and reading is to share alphabet books with them. Different letters can be pointed out along the way. There are numerous alphabet books that would appeal to just about any interest. *ABC Disney,* by Robert Sabuda (Hyperion, 1998) is a pop-up book that features different characters from Disney movies. Others include *The Accidental Zucchini,* by Mary Grover (Harcourt, 1997); *Flora McDonnell's A B C,* by Flora McDonnell (Candlewick, 1997); and *ABC Kids,* by Laura Ellen Williams (Philomel, 2000).

3. *Create an alphabet book.* Staple enough pages together for each letter of the alphabet. You might print one letter on each page in alphabetical order, or you may decide to have the children write the letters in the order they learn them. In either case, the letter can be written at the top of the page and children can find pictures associated with the letter. These pictures can be labeled and children can trace over the letter shown at the top of the page.

4. *Be newspaper detectives.* Tear pages of the local newspaper into four parts and give each child a part. Have them search out letters that match the ones they are learning. They can use a yellow marker to highlight the letters.

5. *Use objects.* Have children bring in toys or other objects whose names begin with letters they are learning. These could be put in a big tub and could be used for sorting into different pockets, each labeled with a different letter. Likewise, labels from cans and other food products can be brought into the classroom and students can identify the letters shown on the various labels.

Understanding, Assessing, and Teaching Story Sense

What Is Story Sense?

Story sense is the understanding that there is a structure used to tell stories and that stories are written to be understood. In other words, not only does it involve understanding a simple story line, it also includes comprehension.

Enhanced eText **Application Exercise 8.4:** Ms. Berger's Understanding of Story Sense

---

Bridge: From Understanding to Assessment

When teachers understand that _____,	then teachers will assess _____.
Story sense involves comprehending the unique combination of story elements: the events, problems, and resolutions in a story,	Students' story sense using authentic text, such as asking them to narrate wordless picture books or to discuss story elements from read-alouds.

How Can Story Sense Be Assessed?

An excellent way to assess story sense and story comprehension in early reading is to use wordless picture books such as *Good Dog, Carl,* by Alexandra Day (Green Tiger, 1985). Asking students to narrate as the book pages turn, teachers can note whether the students are able to maintain the sense of problems and resolutions that structure a story from page to page. Checklists and rubrics can be used to keep track of data on readers' story sense.

Bridge: From Assessment to Teaching

When teachers understand that _____,	then teachers will teach _____.
Students do not always know the difference between stories and other forms of discourse (such as conversation, explanation, or personal talk),	Children to recognize elements of story (narrative).

Teaching Story Sense and Story Comprehension

Telling oral stories is among the best ways to help young readers develop a sense of story. Reading aloud to them from storybooks also provides key experiences in story structure and purposes for sharing stories. Likewise, giving readers time to share their thoughts about a story after the verbal storytelling or a read-aloud can be a good way to check their comprehension.

What we're really doing in these instances is building a foundation of listening comprehension. Students who tell and listen to stories are engaging with texts without decoding words, and receiving valuable input from the world around them.

In teaching writing, teachers may become familiar with the most rudimentary skills of narrative, asking students to write a beginning, middle, and end to a story. But in reading, stories are usually structured with a more complicated middle than what young children would write.

Yet, the middle part of the story is every bit as important as the beginning and ending. Teachers need to teach students how to attend and comprehend the middle section.

For example, the story of Goldilocks does not end when she eats the baby bear's porridge—the middle of this basic fairy tale is far more complicated than its beginning and ending. Based on research into how story elements are put together, we know that many stories cycle back and forth between *what people want, what problems they encounter, what they do about them, and what happens next.*[31] Teachers have translated this "story grammar" for students by teaching them to recognize and discuss four elements: a. Somebody tried to (starting event), b. But (problem), c. So (attempted solution), and d. Then (consequence). Stories might combine these elements in many ways, and cycle through several rounds of the elements before ending.

To help children understand the middle elements of a story, managing a focused discussion is essential. Using the *Directed Listening–Thinking Activity* shown in Table 8.7 is an excellent way to teach students how to listen and to work on story sense and comprehension simultaneously. This activity structure can be applied to stories and informational presentations, because it is designed to facilitate discussion.

The Directed Listening–Thinking Approach The **directed listening–thinking approach** requires teachers to ask questions before, during, and after a talk. The steps in this approach are as follows:

Step 1: Preparation for talk, lecture, audiotape, or film. The teacher relates to students' past experiences, gives an overview of the presentation (or story), and presents special vocabulary and questions students should try to answer while listening. These questions can be framed around the story elements so students can identify events, problems, solutions, and consequences.

Step 2: Students listen to the presentation (or story). During the presentation, the teacher stops, asks students to answer some of the previously given questions, and interjects some more thought-provoking questions to guide students.

Step 3: After the presentation (or story). Children answer unanswered questions and are presented with some more challenging questions. In addition, the teacher asks the children to identify the central idea of the talk, as well as to give a short summary.

Step 4: After the discussion. The teacher asks students to devise some good questions.

Table 8.7 Directed Listening/Thinking Approach (DLTA) Chart

What Teachers Do	What Children Do	What Teachers Need to Observe
Relate talk to children's past experiences.	Listen carefully; relate to past experiences.	Students' attentiveness and their interest level based on the kinds of questions that students ask
Present motivating technique and vocabulary necessary to understand talk.		
Present questions as a guide before, during, and after talk.	Answer and ask questions.	Students' responses to questions

Putting It All Together: Who Is in Most Need of Early Intervention?

Enhanced eText
Video Example 8.8 Directed Listening/Thinking Approach.
In this video, a teacher guides students through processes in the DLTA. https://www.youtube.com/watch?v=MIUnhbH_gpU

What Is Early Intervention?

Early intervention is just what the term suggests: helping children to become successful as early as possible. Once their strengths and needs are identified, children receive specialized instruction that focuses on their strengths and addresses their needs. Accelerating foundational knowledge through rich early literacy experiences sets students up for success in attaining proficient reading. Teachers using a diagnostic approach will often provide this instruction themselves, but they may also call on others to help them.

Extra reading help sometimes comes in the form of an early intervention program such as *Reading Recovery*.[32] The purpose of this program is to identify those children who are experiencing difficulty in their first year of reading instruction. In this short-term curriculum, children who are the lowest-achieving readers in a given first-grade class receive daily individualized, 30-minute lessons from a specially trained *Reading Recovery* teacher in addition to the regular classroom reading instruction. Every individualized lesson is tailored to engage children in authentic reading and writing activities that will help them catch up with their peers.

> **Enhanced eText** **Application Exercise 8.5:** Ms. Berger's Understanding of Early Intervention

Who Is in Most Need of Early Intervention?

But how do we determine which children could benefit from additional instruction and assessment? The most obvious way is to make a class composite of each of the subtests shown in this chapter. The class composite will show how children performed, and can signal which children need the most help with a given aspect of early literacy.

A second way is to follow a process similar to the one used by *Reading Recovery* teachers. Children complete each test of Clay's *Diagnostic Survey*: letter identification, word test, concepts about print, writing vocabulary, dictation, and text reading. The examiner then adds the scores together to get an overall score. However, combining scores in this way is useful only for identifying a student with needs. To design appropriate instruction, the teacher will need to take a look at the child's performance on each subtest. Doing so will help to reveal where the child needs some additional instruction.

As it relates to the measures we show in this chapter, teachers can use the form shown in Figure 8.10 to note scores for each test. As with the *Diagnostic Survey* noted above, the scores can be added together and the students with the lowest overall scores can then receive individualized additional reading instruction designed to address their reading needs.

A third way to identify those children who need the most help is to use a rating tool such as the *Teacher Rating of Oral Language and Literacy (TROLL)*,[33] which was created to guide observations of children's literacy skills in all areas of the language arts (speaking, listening, reading, and writing). This instrument provides a way for teachers to record what they see. The authors note that the TROLL also does something that a direct assessment cannot—it enables the teacher to observe children's interests in a variety of oral-language and written-language activities.

Another advantage of the TROLL is that teachers can use the results to inform instruction (e.g., to identify children who are showing evidence of oral-language delay, those who may need further testing to explore learning needs, and those who

Figure 8.10 Summary of Early Literacy Test Results

Child's Name	Oral Language Concepts (9 possible)	Print Concepts (12 possible)	Phonological Awareness (20 possible)	Letter Identification (52 possible)	Story Sense (17 possible)	Total (110 possible)

are functioning above average and need additional stimulating activities). For further explanation about TROLL and its development, see the article by Dickinson, McCabe, and Sprague. The authors include the entire instrument, along with an explanation about what the scores mean.

Bridge: From Teaching to Understanding

When students _____,	then teachers will understand _____.
Show strengths in some but not all areas of early literacy,	That many early literacy concepts must be developed over weeks and months of experience with text, including explicit teaching.
Know some of the letters of the alphabet,	That these letters are strengths that can be built on to learn other letters.
Have difficulty identifying phonemes, or segmenting words into phonemes,	That not all children have equal experiences in their past, and that some children may be more naturally disposed to recognizing individual sounds.
Do not look at or point at each word on the page,	That word awareness develops over time, and that many other concepts of print may need to be developed before tracking words can be expected.

Revisiting the Opening Scenario

Now that you have read the chapter, describe the various assessments that Ms. Berger uses to figure out how best to advance her students in oral language and early literacy. How can she simultaneously demonstrate accountability to those concerned with meeting government mandates?

Authors' Summary

Before reading our summary statements for each outcome, we suggest you read each outcome and summarize it in your own words.

Once finished, cross-check your response with our brief summary to determine how well you recalled the major points.

8.1 Discuss the differences among the terms *emergent literacy, reading readiness,* **and** *early literacy.* **List and describe the essential components of early literacy.**

- The term *emergent literacy* suggests that children's involvement with print begins before school and continues to evolve over time. Behaviors such as scribbling are seen as children's emerging attempts to show their understanding of writing. The term *reading readiness* suggests that there is a waiting period before children are ready to learn about literacy. *Emergent literacy* connotes an ongoing developmental process, whereas *reading readiness* connotes a fixed single point in time.

- *Early literacy* is the term endorsed by the International Literacy Association, and suggests that children are continually developing in their understanding of literacy and that they need some help

from teachers to continue to evolve. These teachers provide children with a language-rich environment and also offer children explicit instruction based on what they see children showing that they know and that they need to know. They often frame their teaching using Cambourne's conditions of learning.

- Early literacy encompasses six areas: oral-language concepts, print concepts, phonological awareness, letter identification, alphabetic principle, and story sense.

8.2 Provide an example of one assessment tool and explain what it is designed to reveal.

- The *Concepts About Print* assessment tool is useful for helping to reveal students' understanding of books and the terminology related to them. Terminology includes word; letter; front, middle, and back of the book; top and bottom; and sentence.

8.3 Explain concepts, one way to assess them, and ways to teach them.

- A concept is a group of stimuli that have common characteristics. They are usually designated by their names, such as *book, man, woman,* or *animal.*

Concepts are ways to help us reduce the complexity of our world. They help us categorize into meaningful chunks. As might be inferred, they develop over time as we continue to acquire new information.

- Concepts can be oral or written. One way to assess oral-language concepts is to use an informal inventory of concepts provided in this chapter. Using a *Print Concepts Test* is one way to assess print concepts.

- There are many ways to teach both oral and written concepts. Reading aloud to children following specific guidelines before, during, and after the read-aloud is one sure way to teach many different concepts. Engaging children in language play, planning lessons focused on explicitly teaching concepts, and using language in a variety of ways are all methods of helping children to develop concepts.

8.4 Define phonological awareness, one way to assess it, and ways to teach it.

- Phonological awareness refers to awareness of the three aspects of spoken language: words, syllables within words, and sounds (phonemes) within syllables and words.

- Using an informal *Phonological Awareness Test* designed to assess all three of these aspects is one way to assess phonological awareness. Children's performance on it can help teachers design purposeful instruction.

- Using writing, reading aloud books that use specific language features such as rhyme, and including oral-language activities—such as substituting sounds in words and singing songs that emphasize specific spoken-word features—are some ways to teach children phonological awareness.

8.5 Define letter identification, one way to assess it, and one way to teach it.

- Letter identification is the ability to identify letters of the alphabet. One way to assess it is to administer a letter identification test in which the child looks at each letter and states what it is. The teacher records what the child says. Assessing multiple fonts and both uppercase and lowercase letters is critical because knowing one form of a letter is no guarantee that other forms are known. A sample test is shown in this chapter.

- Ideas for teaching letter identification include using students' names, using alphabet books such as *ABC Disney*, creating alphabet books with children, using the newspaper, and using objects such as toys and classroom supplies that begin with a given letter.

8.6 Explain story sense, one way to assess it, and one way to teach it.

- Story sense is the understanding that narrative structures are used to organize meaning; it is a form of comprehension.

- One way to assess story sense is to use a wordless picture book, asking students to tell the story and noting whether they are able to tell it with any kind of logical order connecting one page to the next.

- The *Directed Listening/Thinking Approach* is one way to teach students about story structure. It calls on teachers to ask questions before, during, and after reading or talking, and includes four main steps: preparation before the reading, having students listen and stopping along the way to ask them predetermined questions, asking questions that remain unanswered after the experience, and having children devise some questions that reflect the discussion once the discussion has concluded.

8.7 Discuss early intervention, provide an example of an early intervention program, and explain three different ways to determine who is most in need of early intervention.

- Early intervention is helping children to become literate as early as possible and watching for signs that typically lead young children to become frustrated as readers. Teachers are constantly looking for what children know and need to know, and intervening by developing lessons that will help children develop strengths that are necessary and positive literacy behaviors. Often these lessons are designed and taught by classroom teachers. At other times, children take part in early intervention programs, such as *Reading Recovery*. Programs such as these are designed to accelerate children's growth and are provided in addition to the instruction that the children are already receiving.

- Identifying children who are most in need of additional help with acquiring literacy happens in one of three ways. The first entails making a class composite that shows how well children performed on a given task relative to one another. A second is to provide children with a variety of tests, one for each area of early literacy explained in this chapter; those who score consistently low across this variety of measures are at a different starting point. A third way is to use a published early-literacy rating tool.

Think About It!

1. Observe a kindergarten classroom, making note of the classroom environment. How do you see Cambourne's conditions of learning exemplified?

2. Create a list of alphabet books that could be used to help children learn more about the alphabet, and identify different features that each book brings to students.

3. Using the guidelines, develop a list of books that can be used to teach children about the different aspects of phonological awareness.

4. During your interview for a teaching position, the committee members ask you to explain how you would determine kindergarten students' strengths and needs. Construct your response.

Websites

- http://www.starfall.com/

  This colorful site provides information and activities for teachers, parents, and children. Geared toward emergent literacy, the site includes printable books, downloadables for teachers and parents, and information and activities on phonemic awareness, systematic phonics, vocabulary, and so on. Also contains a scope and sequence page lining up texts with objectives.

- https://readingrecovery.org/reading-recovery/teaching-children/basic-facts/

  In this portion of the Reading Recovery Council of North America site, teachers have access to basic information regarding Reading Recovery. Other links in the site offer access to lessons, professional development resources, and information on a comprehensive literacy plan.

- http://ericae.net/edo/ed272922.htm

  Defining invented spelling and its development, this site covers the developmental stages of spelling and the implications for teachers and their instructional planning. The site provides useful background research for teachers interested in developing students' strategies for learning Standard English spelling as opposed to memorization as the key to mastery.

Children's Literature Cited

Barrett, J. (2001). *Things that are Most in the World.* Atheneum.

Bynum, J. (1999). *Altoona Baboona.* Harcourt Children's Books.

Frazee, M. (2007). *Hush, Little Baby.* HMH Books for Young Readers.

Grover, M. (1997). *The Accidental Zucchini.* Harcourt.

Hoban, T. (1973). *Over, Under, Through.* Macmillan.

McDonnell, F. (1997). *Flora McDonnell's ABC.* Candlewick.

Miranda, A. (1996). *Pignic.* Boyds Mills Press.

Most, B. (1998). *A Pair of Protoceratops.* Harcourt.

Rogers, S. (1998). *Earthsong.* Dutton Children's Books.

Root, P. (1997). *The Hungry Monster.* Candlewick.

Rotner, S. (2001). *Parts.* Walker.

Sabuda, R. (1998). *ABC Disney.* Hyperion.

Spence, R. & Spence, A. (1999). *Clickety Clack.* Viking Juvenile.

Swinburne, S. (2000). *What's Opposite?* Boyds Mills Press.

Williams, L. (2000). *ABC Kids.* Philomel.

Endnotes

1. Harris, T., & Hodges, R. (1995). *The literacy dictionary.* Newark, DE: International Reading Association.

2. Teale, W. (1995). Emergent literacy. In T. Harris & R. Hodges (Eds.), *The literacy dictionary* (pp. 71–72). Newark, DE: International Reading Association.

3. MacGinitie, W., MacGinitie, R., Maria, K., Dreyer, L., & Hughes, K. (2000). *Gates-MacGinitie Reading tests* (4th ed.). Itasca, IL: Riverside Publishing.

4. Ibid.

5. Coltheart, M. (1979). What can children learn to read --and when should they be taught? in T. Waller & G. MacKinnon (Eds.), *Reading research: Advances in theory and practice* (Vol. 1, p. 15). New York: Academic Press.

6. Walsh, D., Price, G., & Gillingham, M. (1988, Winter). The critical but transitory importance of letter naming. *Reading Research Quarterly*, 23, 110; Stahl, S., Osborn, J., & Lehr, F. (1990). *Beginning to read: Thinking and learning about print by M. Adams: A Summary* (p. 10). Urbana, IL: Center for the Study of Reading.

7. Ibid., p. 110.

8. Hillerich, R. (1977). *Reading fundamentals for preschool and primary children* (p. 25). Columbus, OH: Merrill.

9. (1988, March). See NAEYC position statement on standardized testing of young children 3–8 years of age. *Young Children*, 43, 42–47; Bredekamp, S., & Shepard, L. (1989, March). How best to protect children from inappropriate school expectations, practices, and policies. *Young Children*, 44, 14–24; Kamii, C. (Ed.) (1990). *Achievement testing in the early grades*. Washington, DC: National Association for the Education of Young Children.

10. (2001). *Dynamic indicators of basic early literacy skills. (2000, DIBELS). DIBELS NEXT* Eugene, OR: University of Oregon.

11. Goodman, K. (2006). *The truth about DIBELS: What it is—what it does*. Portsmouth, NH: Heinemann.

12. Yopp, H. (1995). A test for assessing phonemic awareness in young children. *The Reading Teacher*, 49(1), 20–29.

13. Clay, M. (1995). *The early detection of reading difficulties* (3rd ed.). Portsmouth, NH: Heinemann.

14. Rathvon, N. (2004). *Early reading assessment: A practitioner's handbook*. New York: Guilford.

15. Piaget, J. (1952). *The origins of intelligence in children*. New York: International Universities Press.

16. Loban, W. (1976). *Language development: Kindergarten through grade twelve* (Research Report #18). Urbana, IL: National Council of Teachers of English.

17. Boehm, A. (2000). Boehm Test of Basic Concepts (3rd. ed.). New York: Pearson.

18. Clay (1985).

19. Boehm, A. (2000). Boehm Test of Basic Concepts (3rd. ed.). New York: Pearson.

20. Cohen, D. (1968, February). The effect of language on vocabulary and reading achievement. *Elementary English*, 45, 217; See also Yaden, D., Jr., Rowe, D., & MacGillivray L. (2000). Emergent literacy. *Handbook of Reading Research* (Vol. III, pg. 429). Mahwah, NJ: Lawrence Erlbaum Associates, Inc.

21. Elley, W. (1989, Spring). Vocabulary acquisition from listening. *Reading Research Quarterly*, 24, 174–187.

22. Halliday, M. (1975). *Explorations in the functions of language*. London: Arnold.

23. Ehri, L., et al. (2001). Phonemic awareness instruction helps children learn to read: Evidence from the national reading panel's meta-analysis. *Reading Research Quarterly*, 36(3), 250–287.

24. National Institute of Child Health and Human Development. (2000). *Report of the national reading panel: Teaching children to read*. NIH Publication 00–4654. Washington, DC: Government Printing Office.

25. Board of Directors of the International Reading Association. (1998). *Phonemic awareness and the teaching of reading* [Position Statement]. Newark, DE: International Reading Association.

26. Opitz, M. (2001). *Summer success reading*. Boston, MA: Great Source Education Group.

27. Torgesen, J., & Bryant, B. (2004). *Test of Phonological Awareness* (2nd ed.). PLUS (TOPA-2$^+$0) Western Psychological Services.

28. Opitz, M. (2000). *Rhymes and reasons: Literature and language play for phonological awareness*. Portsmouth, NH: Heinemann.

29. Bond, G., & Dykstra, R. (1967). The cooperative research program in first-grade reading instruction. *Reading Research Quarterly*, 2, 5–142.

30. Rathvon, N. (2004). *Early reading assessment: A practitioner's handbook*. New York: Guilford.

31. Stein, N. (1982). What's in a story: Interpreting the interpretations of story grammars. *Discourse Process*, 5(319), 319–335.

32. Clay (1995).

33. Dickinson, D., McCabe, A., & Sprgue, K. (2003). Teacher rating of oral language and literacy (TROLL): Individualizing early literacy instruction with a standards-based rating tool. *The Reading Teacher*, 56(6), 554–564.

Chapter 9
Comprehension

John Wollwerth/Shutterstock

 ## Chapter Outline

Scenario: Alan's Comprehension

Understanding Comprehension

Assessing Comprehension

Teaching Comprehension

Teaching Specific Comprehension Skills

Teaching Specific Comprehension Strategies

 ## Learning Outcomes

After reading this chapter, you should be able to . . .

9.1 Discuss how listening comprehension relates to reading comprehension.

9.2 Discuss different ways to assess comprehension.

9.3 Explain one comprehension teaching strategy.

9.4 Explain what comprehension skills are, one way to assess them, and one way to teach them.

9.5 Define comprehension strategies, one way to assess them, and one way to teach them.

Scenario

Alan's Comprehension

Alan is a fifth-grader who scored at a 4.2 level on the reading comprehension subtest of the *California Achievement Tests* in the fall of this school year. Observing Alan when he is reading many different kinds of texts in many different contexts, Ms. Maddox sees that Alan appears able to comprehend and recall information that is mentioned in the texts. She also notices that he appears to need help with higher-level comprehension skills such as making inferences. She decides to review the specific items on the reading comprehension subtest to see if Alan's comprehension performance coincides with her observations and discovers that it does. Her analysis shows that Alan answered all literal-level questions accurately but answered higher-level comprehension questions incorrectly. Using the results of her observations and test item analysis, Ms. Maddox concludes that literal-level comprehension is Alan's strength. What he needs is help in learning how to use higher-order thinking skills such as inferring to comprehend beyond the literal level.

Understanding Comprehension

Comprehension

Comprehension happens in a reader's mind, which means it cannot be observed or measured directly. We can only infer from overt behavior that someone "understands." *Webster's Third New International Dictionary* defines *comprehension* as "the act or action of grasping (as an act or process) with the intellect," and *intellect* is defined as "the capacity for rational or intelligent thought especially when highly developed." The more intelligent an individual is, the more able she is to comprehend. What may not be so obvious is that people who have difficulty understanding may have this difficulty because they have not had experiences that required a variety of levels of thinking; thus, they may not have learned how to comprehend.

Listening Comprehension

To be able to recognize expressions in print, students must have heard these phrases in the past; they must be in the students' listening vocabulary. Reading comprehension depends on comprehension of spoken language. Students who are sensitive to the arrangement of words in oral language are more sensitive to the same in written language. Strong listening comprehension also involves speaking, since children figure oral language out by testing out their ideas in speech situations.[1] Through listening and speaking, children learn many expressions they will eventually see in print. Listening and speaking take place all the time. Teachers orally explain word meanings and discuss what the text says. Students listen to other children read orally, talk about books, and explain their contents. Participation in any language-rich activities, such as conversation or viewing media with dialog, will enhance children's listening comprehension.

Many students prefer to listen to read-alouds rather than to read independently. These children gain more comprehension and retention from listening because of the important added cues they receive from the speaker, such as stress given to words or phrases, and facial expressions.[2] Other children prefer to read independently because they can set their own rate of reading for maximum comprehension and retention. Both listening and reading are important, and the teacher's goal should be to get students to feel comfortable in both situations.

Sometimes, a student can understand a passage when it is read orally, but cannot understand it when reading it alone. This indicates that the words are in the student's *listening vocabulary* but that the student may not have gained the skills necessary for understanding their written forms.

A person who does not do well in listening comprehension skills will usually not do well in reading comprehension skills. Help in one area usually enhances the other because both listening and reading contain some important, similar skills,[3] as researchers going as far back as the 1930s have noted. For example, an investigation made in 1936 found that children who did poorly in comprehension through listening also did poorly in reading comprehension.[4] Research in 1955 on the relationship between reading and listening found that practice in listening for detail will produce a significant gain in reading for the same purpose.[5] Others have also found that teaching and learning listening comprehension skills will produce significant gains in reading comprehension,[6] and that reading and listening involve similar thinking skills.[7]

Findings from a number of other studies strongly support the link between reading and listening comprehension. In one such study, a researcher sought to learn whether the reason some good decoders in reading were poor comprehenders was an overemphasis on word accuracy when decoding or whether it was because of a lack of listening comprehension; that is, the decoders were "word callers" who do not have the words in their listening vocabulary. The results of the study suggested that the students' "listening vocabulary was not better than their reading comprehension. So, decoding does not seem to distract or otherwise interfere with comprehension among children whose decoding skills are well developed. [Instead, according to the investigator] once a child has become a good decoder, differences in reading ability will reflect differences in listening ability."[8]

Although there are many common factors involved in the decoding of reading and listening—which would account for the relationship between the two areas—listening and reading are, nonetheless, separated by unique factors. The most obvious is that listening calls for *hearing,* whereas reading calls for *seeing.* As previously stated, in the area of listening, the speakers are doing much of the interpretation for the listeners through their expressions, inflections, stresses, and pauses. Similarly, the listeners do not have to make the proper *grapheme (letter)–phoneme (sound) correspondences* because these have already been done for them by the speakers. It is possible for students to achieve excellent listening comprehension but not to do as well in reading comprehension.

Readers must identify words and organize them into phrases and sentences to build basic meaning. Readers must also be able to build a larger meaning for a whole text, to determine the shades of meaning implied by the words, to recognize any special figures of speech, and to synthesize the ideas expressed in a text.

In Table 9.1, we show some of the similarities between listening comprehension skills and reading comprehension skills. We also show the different levels of listening and offer a brief definition of each level.

Reading Comprehension

Reading comprehension is a complex intellectual process involving a number of abilities. The two major abilities involve knowing word meanings and using verbal

Table 9.1 Comparison of Listening Comprehension and Reading Comprehension

Listening Levels and Brief Definitions	Listening Comprehension Skills	Reading Comprehension Skills
Discriminative Listening: knowing which sounds to attend to and which to ignore; distinguishing verbal and nonverbal cues		
• Phonological awareness	X	
• Vocal expression	X	
• Onomatopoeia	X	
Precise Listening: paying attention and ascertaining details		
• Associating words with meanings	X	X
• Deducing meanings of words from context	X	X
• Recalling details and sequences	X	X
• Following directions	X	X
• Recognizing multiple characters	X	X
Strategic Listening: listening to gain understanding of the intended meaning of the message		
• Connecting prior knowledge	X	X
• Summarizing	X	X
• Predicting	X	X
• Asking questions	X	X
• Making inferences	X	X
• Identifying main ideas	X	X
Critical Listening: analyzing the message and evaluating it		
• Recognizing emotive language	X	X
• Recognizing bias	X	X
• Distinguishing between fact and opinion	X	X
• Evaluating sources	X	X
• Detecting propaganda devices	X	X
Appreciative Listening: listening to appreciate oral style		
• Recognizing the power of language	X	X
• Appreciating oral interpretations	X	
• Understanding the power of imagination	X	X

Source: Based on Opitz, M., and M. Zbaracki. Listen Hear! 25 Effective Listening Comprehension Strategies. Portsmouth, NH: Heinemann, 2004.

reasoning. Without word meanings and verbal reasoning, there would be no reading comprehension, and without reading comprehension, there is no reading. Most people would agree with these statements; however, disagreement surfaces when we ask, "How does an individual achieve comprehension while reading?" In 1917, Edward Thorndike put forth his statement that "reading is a very elaborate procedure, involving a weighing of each of many elements in a sentence, their organization in the proper relations to one another, and the cooperation of many forces to determine final response."[9] He stated further that even the act of answering simple questions includes all the features characteristic of typical reasoning. Today investigators are still exploring reading comprehension in attempts to understand it better, and through the years many have expounded and expanded on Thorndike's theories.[10]

For more than half a century, research into the process of understanding has been influenced by the fields of psycholinguistics and cognitive psychology. As a result, terms such as *surface structure, deep structure, microstructure, macrostructure, semantic networks, schemata, story grammar, story structure,* and *metacognition* are used by authors who provide explanations about comprehension.

Although it is difficult to state definitively how people achieve comprehension while reading, researchers report that good comprehenders appear to have certain characteristics.[11, 12] Good comprehenders are skilled at inferential reasoning; they can state the main or central ideas of information; they can assimilate, categorize, compare, see relationships, analyze, synthesize, and evaluate information. They engage in meaningful learning by assimilating new material into concepts already existing in their cognitive structures;[13] that is, good comprehenders relate their new learning to what they already know. Also, good comprehenders are able to think beyond the information given; they are able to come up with new or alternate solutions. In addition, they seem to know what information to attend to and what to ignore. Clearly, people who have good strategies for processing information are able to bring more to and gain more from what they are reading or listening to than those who do not have these strategies. Good comprehenders are active, purposeful, evaluative, thoughtful, strategic, persistent, and productive.

Schema theory deals with the relations between prior knowledge and comprehension. "According to schema theory, the reader's background knowledge serves as scaffolding to aid in encoding information from the text."[14] A person with more background knowledge for a given text will comprehend better than one with less background. Preparing readers for what they will be reading "by actively building topic knowledge prior to reading will facilitate learning from text."[15]

Reading Comprehension Taxonomies

A number of **reading comprehension taxonomies** exist, and many appear similar to one another. This similarity is not surprising. Usually, the individuals who develop a new taxonomy do so because they are unhappy with an existing one for some reason and want to improve on it. As a result, they may change category headings, but keep similar descriptions of the categories, or they may change the order of the hierarchy. Most of the existing taxonomies are adaptations in one way or another of Bloom's taxonomy of educational objectives in the cognitive domain, which is concerned with the thinking that students should achieve in any discipline. Bloom's taxonomy is based on an ordered set of objectives ranging from simpler skills to more complex ones. Bloom's objectives are cumulative in that each one includes the one preceding it.[16] And most taxonomies that have evolved since are also cumulative.

In this text, we use an adaptation of Nila Banton Smith's model.[17] In her original model, she presented literal-level reading skills as requiring no thinking. We believe that literal-type questions do require thinking, even though it is a low-level type of thinking. In our model, we divide the comprehension skills into four categories. Each category is cumulative in building on the others. The four comprehension categories are (1) literal comprehension, (2) interpretation, (3) critical reading, and (4) creative reading.

Two cautions are in order here. Grade level and age have little to do with the taxonomy. That is, children of all ages can engage at all levels of the taxonomy. Second, we need to guard against a strict linear type of thinking. Our own teaching experiences have shown us that there are some children who are able to answer higher-level comprehension questions, yet have difficulty answering literal questions. We offer the taxonomy as a way of helping you to think about the variety of questions that need to be used to better ensure thoughtful learners.

Literal Comprehension. **Literal comprehension** represents the ability to obtain a low-level type of understanding by using only explicitly stated information. This category requires a lower level of thinking skills than the other three categories. Answers to literal questions simply demand that the student recall from memory what the book says.

Although the ability to answer literal-type questions is considered a low-level type of thinking, it should *not* be construed that reading for details to gain facts that are explicitly stated is unimportant. A fund of knowledge is important and necessary in order to read texts in many different content areas. It is also the foundation for high-level thinking. If we want students to graduate to higher levels of thinking, we need to make sure that we ask more than just literal questions.

Interpretation. **Interpretation** is the next step in the hierarchy. This category demands a higher level of thinking because the questions require answers that are suggested or implied by the text, but are not directly stated. To answer questions at the interpretive level, readers must have problem-solving ability and be able to work at various levels of abstraction. Obviously, children with learning difficulties will have trouble working at this level, as well as in the next two categories.

The interpretive level is the one for which the most confusion exists when it comes to categorizing skills. The confusion concerns the term *inference*. *Inference* can be defined as something derived by reasoning; something that is not directly stated but suggested in the statement; a logical conclusion that is drawn from statements; a deduction; or an induction. From the definitions, we can see that inference is a broad reasoning skill and that there are many different kinds of inferences. All the reading skills in interpretation rely on the reader's ability to "infer" the answer in one way or another. However, grouping all the interpretive reading skills under *inference* meant "Some of the most distinctive and desirable skills would become smothered and obscured."[18]

Some of the reading skills that are usually grouped under interpretation are as follows:

- Determining word meanings from context
- Finding main ideas
- "Reading between the lines" or drawing inferences[19]
- Drawing conclusions
- Making generalizations
- Recognizing cause-and-effect reasoning
- Recognizing analogies

Critical Reading. **Critical reading** is at a higher level than the first two categories because it involves evaluation—making a personal judgment on the accuracy, value, and truthfulness of what is read. To be able to make judgments, a reader must be able to collect, interpret, apply, analyze, and synthesize the information. Critical reading involves skills such as the abilities to differentiate between fact and opinion and between fantasy and reality, as well as to discern propaganda techniques. Critical reading is related to critical listening because they both require critical thinking.

Creative Reading. **Creative reading** uses divergent thinking skills to go beyond the literal comprehension, interpretation, and critical reading levels. In creative reading, the reader tries to come up with new or alternate solutions to those presented by the writer.

Enhanced eText Application Exercise 9.1: Ms. Maddox's Understanding of Comprehension

Bridge: From Understanding to Assessment

When teachers understand that _____,	then teachers may want to _____.
Listening comprehension is strongly related to reading comprehension,	Assess student listening comprehension by having students retell, pose and answer questions, and discuss the text during and after read-alouds.
Reading comprehension is enhanced when a student can access background knowledge of the topic,	Determine a student's background knowledge on a particular topic and pre-teach content-specific vocabulary to give the student word knowledge that promotes listening and reading comprehension.
A taxonomy of comprehension skills can be used to ask a variety of questions to ensure thoughtful reading and thinking,	Ask a purposeful variety of questions to assess students' literal, interpretive, critical, and creative comprehension.

Assessing Comprehension

As we emphasize throughout this text, assessment drives instruction. This is true for comprehension instruction as well as any other aspect of reading. The three questions cited in previous chapters also apply when we think about comprehension assessment: What do I want to know? Why do I want to know? How can I best discover it? (See Table 9.2.) There are four ways we can answer these questions.

First, some of the assessment techniques mentioned in earlier chapters are excellent tools for answering the questions. These include retelling, asking questions representative of the different comprehension levels (such as those used in the informal reading inventory), and observation.

Second, teachers can use teacher-created informal assessments, such as those shown throughout this chapter, and then use students' performance on these assessments to determine whether they need additional explicit comprehension instruction.

Third, teachers can look at how students perform on comprehension-related tasks in content reading. That is, we want students to see that teachers expect them to use comprehension skills and strategies any time they read. For example, if teachers expect students to summarize, they can provide a summarizing activity during social studies reading and note whether students use what they know about summarizing in this context.

Fourth, teachers can use cloze or maze procedures, which require teachers to prepare the text in special ways.

Observation

Authentic texts chosen by students provide an ideal setting for observing comprehension. Students' reading comprehension will be best when they have interest, background

Table 9.2   Selecting Appropriate Comprehension Measures

What Do I Want to Know?	Why Do I Want to Know?	How Can I Best Discover It?
Are students acquiring and applying specific comprehension skills and strategies when reading?	Good readers have many skills and strategies at their disposal, and they use those they find most appropriate when reading given texts. I want to make sure that all students are acquiring and applying both comprehension skills and strategies, because both will help them become able readers.	• Observation (pages 191–194) • Performance on daily skills and strategies comprehension tasks (pages 194–196) • Cloze (pages 196–200) • Maze (page 200)
Are students able to comprehend at different levels?	Many different levels of comprehension are necessary for excellent comprehension. I want to make sure that students are using higher-level comprehension as well as literal comprehension.	• Retelling • Comprehension questions from IRI Examiner Booklet (Appendix) • Talking with students • Questioning (pages 194–196) • Comprehension Response Analysis (Figure 9.5, pages 196–197)
Are students aware of the strategies they use to comprehend text?	Metacognition is an important part of comprehension. If students are aware of the strategies they use in reading, they are more likely to use them. I can also help students to expand their repertoire of strategies, if necessary.	• Student interview • Student self-assessment (page 194) • Meta-Comprehension Strategy Index (page 200)

knowledge, and a purpose for reading. Keep in mind that teacher-selected passages and IRI passages will have the feel of an assignment to many students, which is less ideal for ascertaining comprehension. Information gathered using assigned passages must be compared with observations of authentic reading to create a more valid overall picture of a reader. We cannot overstate the importance of using many different reading experiences and looking for a pattern of behavior when assessing students to determine their strengths and needs.

The checklist in Figure 9.1 offers a menu of choices. To get the most from the menu, we suggest using one choice for any one observation of one or more students. If

Figure 9.1 Diagnostic Checklist for Selected Reading Comprehension Skills

Student's Name: _____

Grade: _____

Teacher: _____

	Yes	No
1. The student is able to state the meaning of a word in context.		
2. The student is able to give the meaning of a phrase or a clause in a sentence.		
3. The student is able to give variations of meanings for homographs (words spelled the same but with more than one meaning, for example, *train, mean, saw, sole,* and so on).		
4. The student is able to give the meaning of a sentence in a paragraph.		
5. The student is able to recall information that is explicitly stated in the passage (literal questions).		
6. The student is able to state the main idea of a paragraph.		
7. The student is able to state details to support the main idea of a paragraph.		
8. The student is able to summarize a paragraph.		
9. The student is able to answer a question that requires reading between the lines.		
10. The student is able to draw a conclusion from what is read.		
11. The student can hypothesize the author's purpose for writing the selection.		
12. The student can differentiate between fact and opinion.		
13. The student can differentiate between fantasy and reality.		
14. The student can detect bias in a story.		
15. The student can detect various propaganda tactics that are used in a story.		
16. The student can go beyond the text to come up with alternate solutions or ways to end a story or solve a problem in the selection.		
17. The student shows that he or she enjoys reading by voluntarily choosing to read.		
18. The student shows the ability to use a variety of comprehension strategies when reading (e.g., visualizing, predicting, monitoring, asking questions).		

Figure 9.2 Classroom Observation Form

Date: _____	Focus Skill: _____
Name of Student	Notes

zooming in on one student, consider making a copy of the checklist and putting a date next to a specific item to mark when it was observed, and noting whether the student was able to show evidence of using the specific skill.

To zoom out to the whole class, consider using a whole-class matrix such as the one in Figure 9.2. Write the date and the focus skill to be observed. Then write students' names in the spaces provided and make notes about how different students showed evidence of using the specific skill, or evidence of needing to focus on it. This one skill could form the focus on your observation over a couple of days—or even a week—and could be used across content areas. Rather than trying to focus on all students within one day, you could easily divide your class into fifths and observe that many learners each day of the week.

If students are assessing themselves on a specific skill, consider giving them an index card and directing them to write their name and the skill being addressed at the top. At given points in the day, have them reflect on the skill, making a note on the card when they used it with an accompanying example. Students could also use a self-evaluation form such as the one shown in Figure 9.3 to analyze their reading comprehension.

Keep in mind that observations of comprehension are always indirect (teachers cannot actually see mental, covert processes); each of the items on the checklist is a performance that helps teachers infer comprehension. Another important point is that each authentic text has its own unique comprehension demands. For example, one passage may support distinction between fact and opinion (such as in a political speech), but the next might require a more literal memory of steps or procedures (such as a magazine article on how to make a craft). In the earliest observations, a teacher may help a student by matching checklist items to the comprehension demanded by the text. But the checklist should soon become the student's responsibility, and a menu for deciding what matches best.

Figure 9.3 Analyzing My Reading

Name: _____ Date: _____

What I read: _____

Here's what I did and how well I think I did it:

	Little	*Some*	*Much*
1. I formed questions before reading.			
2. I tried to make pictures using the author's words.			
3. I made some connections with other books.			
4. I knew when I was having a problem and I did something to fix the problem so that I could continue reading with understanding.			
5. I was able to comprehend this text.			

In many of the same ways, the listening comprehension checklist in Figure 9.4 can be used as a menu from which teachers or students can select after a read-aloud or as a follow-up to an audiobook. Each of the four categories focuses on questions designed to address a different form of active listening.

Questioning as a Diagnostic Technique

Asking questions is not only an important part of teaching and learning, but also very useful in a diagnostic approach to assessing and teaching reading. Teachers' questions, which can stimulate students to use literal or higher-level thinking, yield insight into students' comprehension. Student responses can help a teacher to see whether students are organizing information for memory, whether they are able to see relationships and make comparisons, and whether the materials the students are reading or listening to are too difficult or too easy.

Student-generated questions are an important part of their learning, and they are essential diagnostic aids in giving teachers feedback on students' ability to understand. To ask good questions, students must know their material. As a result, those students who ask the best questions are usually those who know the material best. When students ask confusing questions, it is a signal that the teacher needs to slow down or reteach certain material. The same is true when students' responses to posed questions do not make sense.

Teachers can use questioning as a diagnostic technique to learn about their students' thinking ability. Here are some examples.

The teacher has the children read a short story. The story is about a boy who wants to go to school, but he can't because he is too young. The teacher tells the children that she is going to make up some questions about the story, and the children have to tell her whether the questions that she makes up can actually be answered based on information from the story. If a question can be answered, the student should answer it; if a question cannot be answered, the student must tell why. The teacher makes up the following questions:

1. What are the names of Ben's sister and brother who go to school?

2. Why does Ben want to go to school?

Figure 9.4 Diagnostic Checklist for Listening Comprehension

Student's Name: _____

Grade: _____

Teacher: _____

	Yes	No
1. Precise listening. The child, after listening to a passage, can answer questions that relate to information explicitly stated in the passage.		
2. Strategic listening. The child, after listening to a passage, can answer questions dealing with		
a. finding the main idea.		
b. generalization.		
c. "reading between the lines."		
d. conclusions.		
e. cause–effect relationships.		
f. multiple meanings.		
3. Critical listening. The child, after listening to a passage, can answer questions dealing with		
a. propaganda.		
b. fact or opinion.		
c. bias.		
d. emotive language.		
4. Appreciative listening. The child voluntarily chooses to listen to various recordings.		

*The length and difficulty of the selection used are determined by the grade level and the developmental level of the individual child. Also, this is not an inclusive list of listening comprehension skills.

3. Can you make up an adventure for Ben?

4. Why can't Ben go to school?

5. What are the names of the bus driver's children?

6. What does Ben do in the summer?

This technique can help the teacher learn which children are able to concentrate, as well as which children are able to do different kinds of thinking. Questions 1 and 4 are literal questions; question 2 is an inferential question; question 3 is a creative question; and questions 5 and 6 are not able to be answered because no such information was given in the story, either directly or indirectly.

A more difficult questioning technique that the teacher could use with children is to have them make up questions for a selection that they have read.

After students have read a selection, the teacher can ask them to make up three different questions. The first question should be one for which the answer is directly stated in the passage. The second question should be one for which the answer is not directly stated in the passage. The third question should require an answer that goes beyond the text.

In early primary grades, the teacher can use pictures as the stimuli for questions, or the teacher can relate a short story to the children and have them devise questions for it.

Here are some questions that a group of fourth-grade children made up after reading a story about Melissa and her friend Fred, who were always getting into trouble:

1. Who is Melissa's best friend? (literal)

2. What is the main idea of the story? (inferential)

3. From the story, what can we say about the main character's personality? (inferential)

4. Can you relate an event where you think Melissa could get into some trouble? (creative)

The children who made up the questions challenged their classmates to answer them and then they were responsible for determining whether their classmates had answered them correctly.

Comprehension Response Analysis

The IRI passages in this book (see Appendix C) have been pre-analyzed to help teachers gather information about different kinds and levels of comprehension, such as literal (lower-level), inferential, main idea, and vocabulary knowledge (higher-level). The Comprehension Response Analysis scoring sheet in Figure 9.5 can help teachers compile this information.

For example, a student may score well for inferential questions but not literal ones. This may mean the reader pays attention to the big picture of a text without paying attention to details. Another student might answer literal questions but not identify the main idea. For both examples, the IRI Comprehension Response Analysis scores give the teacher an idea on which to follow up when the student reads authentic text. Interpreting comprehension is complex, so the IRI must be used to form ideas that can be checked with ongoing assessment in authentic reading. (See the section Observation on page 191 and Figure 9.1 and Figure 9.4.)

Cloze Procedure

Can you supply the _____ that fits this sentence? When you came to the missing word in that sentence, did you try to gain closure by supplying a term such as *word* to complete it? If you did, you were engaged in the process of *closure,* which involves the ability of the reader to use context clues to determine the needed word.

The **cloze procedure** was primarily developed by Wilson Taylor in 1953 as a measure of readability—that is, to test the difficulty of instructional materials and to evaluate their suitability for students. It has since been used for a number of other purposes, especially as a measure of a student's comprehension.

Cloze procedure is not a comprehension skill; it is a technique that helps teachers gain information about a variety of language facility and comprehension skills. A **cloze test** or exercise is one in which the reader must supply words that have been systematically deleted from a text at a particular grade level.

There is no set procedure for determining the length of the passage or the number of deletions that a passage should have. However, if you wish to apply the criteria for reading levels that have been used in research with the traditional cloze procedure, you should follow these rules. First, only words must be deleted, and the replacement for each word must be the *exact* word, not a synonym. Second, the words must be deleted in a systematic manner. The researchers who have developed the criteria for scoring cloze tests state that "any departure from these rules leaves the teacher with uninterpretable results."[20]

The traditional cloze procedure consists of deleting every fifth word of a passage that is representative of the material being tested. The passage that is chosen should be able to stand alone. Usually the first and last sentences of the passage remain intact. Then, beginning with either the first, second, third, fourth, or fifth word of the second sentence, every fifth word of a 250–260-word passage should be deleted.

Figure 9.5 Comprehension Response Analysis

Scoring Directions:

1. Remember to use only those passages in which students score in the independent, instructional, and buffer zone.
2. For each of these passages, record the number correct for each type of comprehension question.
3. Add each column to determine the number correct out of the number possible.
4. To get an overall view of how a student performed on lower-level versus higher-level comprehension, consolidate the scores from the different columns and put the totals in the corresponding blanks in Part II: Analysis by Level of Comprehension.
5. Look for patterns of behavior and make any pertinent notes in Part III: Comments/Observations.

Student's name: _____   Examiner's name: _____

Part I: Analysis by Type of Question

Grade	Literal Oral	Silent	Inference Oral	Silent	Word Meaning Oral	Silent	Main Idea Oral	Silent
P	___/6	___/6	___/2	___/2	___/0	___/0	___/0	___/0
1	___/5	___/8	___/4	___/2	___/1	___/0	___/0	___/0
2(1)	___/5	___/8	___/4	___/1	___/1	___/1	___/0	___/0
2(2)	___/7	___/4	___/2	___/4	___/1	___/2	___/0	___/0
3(1)	___/6	___/6	___/2	___/2	___/1	___/1	___/1	___/1
3(2)	___/5	___/5	___/2	___/3	___/2	___/1	___/1	___/1
4	___/5	___/5	___/3	___/4	___/1	___/0	___/1	___/1
5	___/4	___/5	___/4	___/3	___/1	___/1	___/1	___/1
6	___/5	___/5	___/3	___/3	___/1	___/1	___/1	___/1
7	___/4	___/5	___/4	___/3	___/1	___/1	___/1	___/1
8	___/5	___/4	___/4	___/5	___/0	___/0	___/1	___/1
Number Correct/Number Possible	___/___	___/___	___/___	___/___	___/___	___/___	___/___	___/___

Part II: Analysis by Level of Comprehension

	Lower-Level (Literal questions only) Oral	Silent	Higher-Level (Inference, Word Meaning, and Main Idea questions) Oral	Silent
Total Number Correct/Total Number Possible	___/___	___/___	___/___	___/___

Part III: Comments/Observations

Source: Based on Opitz, M. and J. Erekson. 2014. Understanding, Assessing, and Teaching Reading: A Diagnostic Approach, 7th ed. New York: Allyn & Bacon.

At the intermediate-grade levels and higher, the passage is usually 250 words, and every fifth word is deleted. For maximum reliability, a passage should have at least fifty deletions. At the primary-grade level, the passage is usually shorter, and every eighth or tenth word is deleted. A cloze technique would not yield as reliable a score for the primary-grade level as for the intermediate-grade level, because passages for the former are shorter and have fewer deletions.

Teachers can use cloze exercises for diagnosis, review, instruction, and testing. In constructing the exercise, the main point to remember is its *purpose.* If the purpose is to test a student's retention of some concepts in a specific area, the exact term is usually necessary; however, if the purpose is to gain information about a student's language facility, ability to use context clues, vocabulary development, or comprehension, the exact term is not as important, because often many words will make sense in a passage.

Scoring the Cloze Test.   If you have deleted 50 words, the procedure for scoring the cloze test is fairly easy. Multiply the number of correct insertions by two and add a percentage symbol. For example, 25 correct insertions would be equal to 50 percent. If you have not deleted exactly 50 words, use the formula illustrated by the following calculation, in which the number of correct insertions is divided by the number of blanks and multiplied by 100 percent.

$$\frac{40}{60} \times 100\% = (40 \div 60) \times 100\%$$
$$= 67\% \text{ (rounded to nearest digit)}$$

For a traditional cloze test, in which only exact words are counted as correct and every fifth word has been deleted, a score below 44 percent would indicate a frustration level. A score between 44 percent and 57 percent would indicate the instructional level, and scores above 57 percent would indicate the independent level. It is important to note that these criteria should be used only if the exact words are used and if every fifth word has been deleted from the passage. These levels are indicative of the text that was used to design the test. In other words, they tell how the student matches up to the text to be used for instruction.

Reading Levels Scale for Cloze Procedure

Independent level	58 percent and above
Instructional level	44 percent through 57 percent
Frustration level	43 percent and below

Variations of the Traditional Cloze Procedure: An Emphasis on Diagnosis.   Variations of the cloze technique are sometimes used. For example, rather than deleting every fifth or tenth word, every noun or verb is deleted, or every function or structure word (definite and indefinite articles, conjunctions, prepositions, and so on) is deleted. This technique is used when the teacher wishes to gain information about a student's sentence sense. For example:

Jane threw _____ ball _____ Mary. (the; to)

Another variation of the cloze technique is to delete key words in the passage. This technique is useful for determining whether students have retained certain information. For example:

A technique in which the reader must supply words is called the _____ procedure. (cloze)

Cloze technique can also be adapted for other uses. Students can be presented with a passage in which they must complete the incomplete words. For example:

Dick r _____ his bike every day. (rides)

Another adaptation is to present students with a passage in which every *nth* word is deleted. (Choose the number for *n* beforehand.) They must then choose words from a given word list that *best* fit the blanks.

Here is an example of an exercise using the cloze technique for an upper primary grade. Notice how explicitly the instructions are stated for the students, and also notice that the first and last sentences of the passage are given intact.

In addition, note that the deletion pattern is not the same throughout the passage.

Directions: Read the first and last sentences, which have no missing words in them, to get a clue as to what the story is about. Then read very carefully each sentence that has a missing word or words in it. Using context clues, figure out a word that would make sense in the story and put it in the blank.

In the forest live a kind old man and woman. (1) _____ have been living in (2) _____ forest for almost ten (3) _____ . They had decided to (4) _____ to the forest because they (5) _____ nature.

The kind old (6) _____ and woman make their (7) _____ by baking breads and cakes and (8) _____ them to the people who (9) _____ the forest. Everyone who (10) _____ the forest usually buys (11) _____ bread or cake from the old (12) _____ . The kind old man and woman are happy in the forest.

Answers: 1. They; 2. the; 3. years; 4. move; 5. love; like; 6. man; 7. living; 8. selling; 9. visit; 10. visits; 11. some; 12. couple.

Here is an example of an exercise using cloze technique for an intermediate grade.

Directions: Read the first and last sentences of the story to get a clue as to what the story is about. Then read each sentence that has a missing word or words very carefully. Using context clues, insert a word in each blank so that the story makes sense.

Everyone was looking forward to Friday night because that was the night of the big basketball game. This (1) _____ would determine the championship (2) _____ Deerville High and Yorktown (3) _____ . For years Deerville High and (4) _____ High have been rivals. This (5) _____ was very (6) _____ because so far (7) _____ school had won (8) _____ equal number of games. (9) _____ game on Friday night would break the (10) _____ .

Friday night finally arrived. The game (11) _____ the championship title (12) _____ being played in the Deerville High (13) _____ because the game (14) _____ year had been played (15) _____ the Yorktown High gym. (16) _____ gym was so (17) _____ that many spectators were without (18) _____ . When the two teams (19) _____ the gym from the dressing areas, (20) _____ were thunderous (21) _____ and whistles from the (22) _____ . Each team went through (23) _____ warm-up drills of (24) _____ baskets and passing. Then the buzzer (25) _____ . The game would begin (26) _____ a moment. Just as the referee (27) _____ the ball in the (28) _____ for the starting jump ball, the lights (29) _____ the gym went (30) _____ . There was complete darkness. Everyone (31) _____ taken by surprise. Almost immediately a (32) _____ on the loudspeaker (33) _____ that the game would have (34) _____ be postponed because of a (35) _____ failure. The game would take (36) _____ next Friday. All were (37) _____ to remain where they (38) _____ until someone with a flashlight came to help them. Everyone was disappointed that the game had to be cancelled.

Answers: (1) game; (2) between; (3) High; (4) Yorktown; (5) game; (6) important; (7) each; (8) an; (9) The; (10) tie; (11) for; (12) was; (13) gym; (14) last; (15) in;

(16) The; (17) crowded; (18) seats; (19) entered; (20) there; (21) cheers; (22) specta-tors. audience, *or* crowd; (23) its; (24) shooting; (25) sounded *or* rang; (26) in; (27) threw; (28) air; (29) in; (30) out; (31) was; (32) voice; (33) announced; (34) to; (35) power; (36) place; (37) told; (38) were.

Maze Procedure

Some teachers prefer to use a maze instead of a cloze procedure because they find it easier for students to use. Because words are added rather than deleted every fifth word, these teachers believe that it gives students more support. To compensate for this ease, the scoring is a little different. Students have to achieve at higher levels to reach independent, instructional, and frustrational levels.

Basically, the **maze** is the same as the cloze with the exceptions of adding words and establishing cut-off scores. The Venn diagram shown in Figure 9.6 shows how the two are alike and different.

Meta-Comprehension Strategy Index

The *Meta-Comprehension Strategy Index* is another meaningful way to assess students' awareness of the strategies they use in understanding what they read. Complete informa-tion—including the test, administration and scoring procedures, and suggested instruc-tional techniques—can be found in *The Reading Teacher* (Schmitt, March, 1990): 454–461.

Figure 9.6 Comparison of Cloze and Maze Testing Procedures

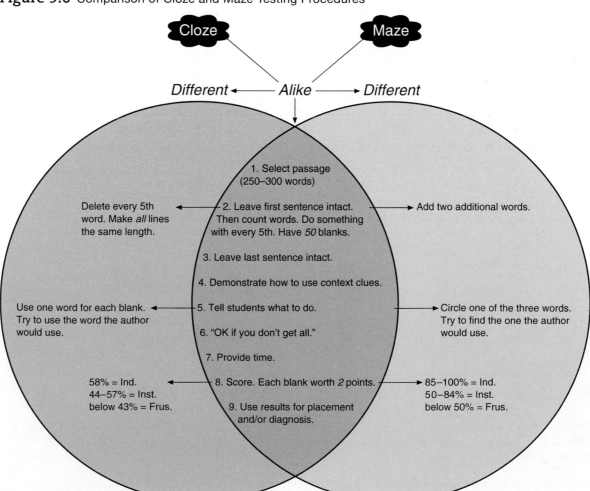

Cloze | Maze

Different ← Alike → Different

1. Select passage (250–300 words)

Delete every 5th word. Make *all* lines the same length. ← 2. Leave first sentence intact. Then count words. Do something with every 5th. Have *50* blanks. → Add two additional words.

3. Leave last sentence intact.

4. Demonstrate how to use context clues.

Use one word for each blank. Try to use the word the author would use. ← 5. Tell students what to do. → Circle one of the three words. Try to find the one the author would use.

6. "OK if you don't get all."

7. Provide time.

58% = Ind. 44–57% = Inst. below 43% = Frus. ← 8. Score. Each blank worth *2* points. → 85–100% = Ind. 50–84% = Inst. below 50% = Frus.

9. Use results for placement and/or diagnosis.

Enhanced eText **Application Exercise 9.2:** Ms. Maddox Assesses Comprehension

Bridge: From Assessment to Teaching

When teachers learn from assessment that _____,	then teachers may want to teach _____.
Assessment and instruction are essential to one another,	Each student comprehension skills based on individual needs identified from assessment data.
Readers sometimes get stuck not understanding, and don't know what to do,	Students a wider variety of strategies for comprehending different kinds of texts.
Readers become so used to literal questions and quizzes that they may learn to rely only on literal comprehension,	Strategies and skills that build a relationship between literal- and higher-level comprehension.
Readers often don't realize when their comprehension is breaking down, and just keep reading words,	Students to be aware of comprehension as the main point of almost all reading, and aware of strategies they use to comprehend. Consider using checklists, student self-assessments, or the Meta-Comprehension Strategy Index.

Teaching Comprehension

Time spent in reading seems to be an important variable for success in reading, whether it is direct instructional time or time spent reading independently. However, we cannot count on students reading outside school, because of the many other competing enjoyable activities and responsibilities that compete for their time and attention. Therefore, we must plan for students to have time to read in school, as well as time for explicit instruction in reading comprehension.

There are various teaching strategies that can be used with explicit instruction; some are less structured than others. Explicit instruction requires teachers to present strategies to help their students comprehend the material being read; this is done in addition to asking children questions before, during, and after they read. "Direct [explicit] instruction in comprehension means explaining the steps in a thought process that gives birth to comprehension."[21] The instructional pattern that teachers use to help students gain comprehension will vary based on the concept being learned, the composition of the class, and the ability of the teacher.

Providing supportive instruction throughout a reading activity is critical. Before reading, prepare the students for the reading activity by doing some of the following: previewing the reading selection, going over new vocabulary or difficult words, teaching any strategies that students will need to read the material, and actively building topic knowledge.

During reading, give students a number of questions to think about as they read, or encourage students to ask questions about the text material. Challenge students to act as investigative reporters while they are reading.

After reading, students can answer their own questions or the teacher's questions, state the main idea of the selection, summarize it, discuss their feelings toward the material, or tell how they used a specific comprehension strategy, such as visualizing. There are numerous comprehension teaching strategies that can be used as a part of an explicit reading lesson.

When teaching comprehension, focus first on *listening comprehension* so the students can learn the strategy or skill without the demands of word identification. Then teach the same skill, but have students do the reading, which places emphasis on reading comprehension (transfer of learning).

Purpose is what guides the selection of the specific teaching strategy chosen for any given lesson. The following sections provide nine suggestions for teaching strategies.

The Directed Reading–Thinking Activity

The **Directed Reading–Thinking Activity (DR–TA)** can be an especially effective approach in the hands of good teachers, whether they use a basal reader series or trade books.

DRTA requires that students be active participants. "The reading–thinking process must begin in the mind of the reader. He must raise the questions and to him belongs the challenge and the responsibility of a judgment. The teacher keeps the process active and changes the amount of data to be processed."[22] Here is an outline of the process:[23]

I. Student actions

    A. Predict (set purposes)

    B. Read (process ideas)

    C. Prove (test answers)

II. Teacher actions

    A. What do you think? (activate thought)

    B. Why do you think so? (agitate thought)

    C. Prove it. (require evidence)

To use DRTA effectively, teachers must know how to encourage students to ask questions that stimulate higher-level thinking; teachers must be well-versed in facilitating the inquiry process.

Think Aloud

Many good teachers probably have used this approach but not been aware of it. Often when a teacher has students who have difficulty understanding something that is being explained, the teacher may "model" the skill for them. That is, the teacher "thinks aloud" or verbalizes thoughts to give students insight into the process. The teacher literally states out loud exactly the steps that she goes through to solve the problem or gain an understanding of a concept. Many reading program authors are including modeling as part of their instructional plans.

Here are some suggested teaching procedures:[24]

1. Choose a passage to read aloud. The passage should have some areas that will pose some difficulties, such as unknown words. It could also contain an excellent description that would be perfect for teaching students about visualizing.

2. Begin reading the passage orally while students follow. When you come to a trouble spot, stop and think through it aloud while students listen to what you say.

3. When you have finished reading, invite students to add any thoughts to yours.

4. Partner the students up and have them practice.

5. Remind students to use the strategy when they are reading silently. A self-evaluation form such as the one shown in Figure 9.3 might help students evaluate how well they read.

Repeated Reading

Repeated reading is a technique that has gained favor among a number of teachers to help students who have poor oral reading skills to achieve fluency in reading. Repeated readings also offer students chances for deeper comprehension. A suggested procedure for repeated readings follows:[25]

    Passage length: short; about 50–100 words

    Types of passages: any reading materials that will be of interest to the child

Enhanced eText
Video Example 9.1

In this **video clip**, Ms. Sanchez explains and models the think-aloud strategy with her fourth-graders. Listen carefully to her explanation of the steps of the process and her purpose for instruction.

Readability level of passage: Start at independent level; proceed to more difficult passages as the child gains confidence in oral reading; controlled vocabulary is not imperative.

Assisted reading: Use the read-along approach (assisted reading with a model or tape) to help with phrasing and speed; use when speed is below 45 words per minute (WPM), even though the child makes few errors.

Unassisted reading: Use when the child reaches 60 WPM.

Reciprocal Reading Instruction

Reciprocal reading instruction, which is used in a group setting to help students gain comprehension skills,[26] is a teacher-directed technique because it requires the teacher to first model the four steps for students before having them perform the task. Also, like all techniques, reciprocal reading instruction is only as good as the teacher presenting it.

The four steps involved in this technique are summarizing, questioning, clarifying, and predicting. When the students in the group have all read a specified passage, the teacher models the four steps for them. After the teacher has modeled the passage using all four steps, he has the students do the same. The amount of help given and the number of times that the teacher will model the procedure for the children will vary depending on the individual needs of the children.

Literature Webbing

Success breeds success! If children have good experiences in reading at an early age, these experiences will help instill good attitudes about reading in them. Predictable books appear to be one way to provide these experiences.[27] **Literature webbing** is a story map or graphic illustration that teachers can use as one approach to guide them in using predictable trade books with their students.

The literature webbing strategy lesson (LWSL), which is an adaptation by Reutzel and Fawson of Watson and Crowley's Story Schema Lessons to "provide support for early readers,"[28] includes a six-step process. The preliminary preparation includes the teacher's reading of the text and excerpting a number of samples from it that are large enough that children can make predictions about them. (The excerpts can be accompanied by enlarged illustrations if this procedure is used early in the year.) After the excerpts are chosen, the title of the book is written in the center of the board, with various web strands projecting from the title. (There are three more strands than needed for the number of excerpts. These strands, which are used for discussion purposes, are *personal responses to the book, other books we've read like this one,* and *language extension activities.*) Then the children follow these six steps:[29]

1. Sample the book by reading the randomly ordered illustrations and text excerpts that are placed on the chalk tray below the literature web.

2. Predict the pattern or order of the book by placing the excerpts in clockwise order around the literature web.

3. Read the predictable book straight through. (It may be a big book or a number of copies of the normal-sized text.)

4. Confirm or correct the students' predictions.

5. Discuss the remaining three strands that are on the board. (See above.)

6. Participate in independent or supported reading activities.

Questioning Strategies

Some children need help in developing higher-level reading comprehension skills. Asking many types of questions that demand higher-level skills will better ensure that students become thoughtful and insightful readers.

The kinds of questions the teacher asks will determine the kinds of answers he receives. In addition to asking a question that calls for a literal response, use questions that call for higher levels of thinking. This process can begin as early as kindergarten or first grade. For example, suppose the children are looking at a picture in which a few children are dressed in hats, snow pants, jackets, and scarves. After asking the children what kind of clothes the children in the picture are wearing, try to elicit from students the answers to the following questions: "What kind of day do you think it is?" "What do you think the children are going to do?"

This type of inference question is very simple because it is geared to the cognitive development level of the children. As the children progress to higher levels of thinking, they should be confronted with more complex interpretation or inference problems. Work with children according to their individual levels. Expect all the children to be able to perform, but avoid putting students in situations that frustrate rather than stimulate them.

Critical reading skills are essential for good readers. Use primary-graders' love of folktales to begin to develop some critical reading skills. For example, after the children have read *The Little Red Hen*, ask questions such as the following:

1. Should the Little Red Hen have shared the bread with the other animals? Explain.
2. Would you have shared the bread with the other animals? Explain.
3. Do you think animals can talk? Explain.
4. Do you feel sorry for the other animals? Explain.
5. Do you think this story is true? Explain.

Creative reading questions are probably the most ignored. To help children in this area, learn how to ask questions that require divergent rather than convergent answers. Some questions that should stimulate **divergent thinking** on the part of the reader would be the following:

1. After reading *The Little Red Hen*, try to come up with another ending for the story.
2. Try to add another animal to the story of *The Little Red Hen*.
3. Try to add another part to the story of *The Little Red Hen*.

Divergent answers require more time than convergent answers. Also, there is no one correct answer.

Following are a short reading selection and examples of four different types of comprehension questions. Read both as practice in recognizing the different types of questions at the four levels.

> One day in the summer, some of my friends and I decided to go on an overnight hiking trip. We all started out fresh and full of energy. About halfway to our destination, when the sun was almost directly overhead, one-third of my friends decided to return home. The remaining four of us, however, continued on our hike. Our plan was to reach our destination by sunset. About six hours later, as the four of us—exhausted and famished—were slowly edging ourselves in the direction of the setting sun, we saw a sight that astonished us. There, at the camping site, were our friends who had claimed that they were returning home. It seems that they did indeed go home, but only to pick up a car and drive out to the campsite.

The following are the four different types of comprehension questions:

Literal comprehension: What season of the year was it in the story? What kind of trip were the people going on?

Interpretation: About what time of day was it when some of the people decided to return home? How many people were there when they first started out on the trip?

In what direction were the hikers heading when they saw a sight that astonished them? At about what time did the sun set?

Critical reading: How do you think the hikers felt when they reached their destination? Do you feel that the people who went home did the right thing by driving back to the site rather than hiking? Explain.

Creative reading: What do you think the exhausted hikers did and said when they saw the two who had supposedly gone home?

Question–Answer Relationships (QARs)

The more children understand what they do when they are in the act of answering questions, the better they can be as question solvers. Raphael has designed an instructional strategy, **Question–Answer Relationships (QARs)**, that teachers can use to help their students gain insights into how they go about reading text and answering questions. It helps students "realize the need to consider both information in the text and information from their own knowledge background."[30]

In the QAR technique, students learn to distinguish between information that "they have in their heads" and information that is in the text. The following steps can help children gain facility in QAR. Note that the amount of time children spend at each step is determined by the individual differences of the students.

Step 1. Students gain help in understanding differences between what is in their heads and what is in the text. Ask children to read a passage, and then present questions that guide them to gain the needed understandings. Here is a short sample:

> Mike and his father went to the ball game.
> They were lucky to get tickets for the game.
> They saw many people they knew.
> At the game, Mike and his father ate hot dogs.
> They also drank soda.

Ask the students the following questions:

- Where did Mike and his father go? (to the ball game)
- Where did they see the people? (at the ball game)

Enhanced eText
Video Example 9.2 QAR Review.
Attend to the responses of students as the teacher guides them through each aspect of the Question–Answer Relationship technique.

Point out to the children that the first answer is directly stated, whereas the second is not; it is "in their heads."

Step 2. The "In the Book" category is divided into two parts. The first deals with information that is directly stated in a single sentence in the passage, and the second deals with piecing together the answer from different parts of the passage. (Raphael calls this step "Think and Search," or "Putting It Together.")[31] Give the children practice in doing this.

Step 3. This is similar to Step 2 except that now the "In My Head" category is divided into two parts: "Author and Me" and "On My Own."[32] Help students recognize whether the question is text-dependent or independent. For example, answering the first question below would require the student to read the text, even though the answer would come from the student's background of experiences. However, the student can answer the second without reading the passage.

- How else do you think the cat could have escaped?
- How would you feel if you were lost?

The QAR approach can be very useful in introducing children to inferential reasoning; it helps them to better understand what information is directly stated and what is implied. Teachers can modify the QAR approach to suit their students' needs.

Enhanced eText Application Exercise 9.3 (video):
Discussing Question–Answer Relationships (QARs)

Re-Quest

Re-Quest is short for *reciprocal questioning*. It is different from reciprocal teaching, and was developed to increase students' comprehension.[33] But it is also tied to engagement and motivation. Students get used to being "quizzed" about things they have read. This is not authentic communication, and they know it. In Re-Quest, students get a turn to think of questions and get answers from someone else. This reverses the typical power structure of questioning in the classroom. When paired with Question–Answer Relationships, Re-Quest becomes a tool for higher-level thinking. Coach students to ask questions that can be answered in two ways: (1) by looking at or remembering what was in the text, or (2) by problem solving, putting clues together, or using outside knowledge and opinion.

Decide with the students on a length of passage to read before stopping. In the original method, Manzo and Manzo stopped after every sentence for students who were losing comprehension at that level. You may stop after paragraphs, pages, or even chapters. Decide on an appropriate turn-taking strategy that involves both the teacher and the students reading. Decide whether you will read silently or orally. If reading orally, take turns reading and listening.

- Teacher reads.
- Stop at the determined place.
- Students ask questions for teacher (or other students) to answer.
- Student reads.
- Teacher gets to ask questions for students to answer.
- Continue taking turns.
- Use QAR procedure to reinforce higher-order thinking in questions.

Questioning the Author

Having a questioning mind, one that actively seeks to construct meaning from a text by using the author's words and one's own background relative to the text at hand, is a hallmark of good readers. Questioning the Author (QtA) is a comprehension strategy that guides readers in developing this questioning mind.[34] Through questioning, teachers lead students to evaluate an author's intent for writing the text and why the author included—or omitted—information. It includes the following teaching procedures:

1. Select a text that presents opportunities to consider an author's overall purpose, the author's choice of words, ideas supporting the author's purpose for writing the text , or patterns found within the text, such as *Don't Talk to Me About the War* (Adler, 2008).

2. Read the text carefully, placing sticky notes to indicate places in the text that will elicit discussion of the following:

   - What the author is trying to say?—in other words, the overall purpose
   - What the choice of words does to help the purpose
   - What the author has left out and why

Enhanced eText
Video Example 9.3 Reciprocal Questioning (Re-Quest).

This video is a whole-class demonstration of reciprocal questioning. Notice what student engagement and comprehension are like when students ask each other questions rather than answering only teacher-generated questions.
https://www.youtube.com/watch?v=fsrthW08ZCw

- Whether the author is clear in her presentation of ideas
- How the author encourages the reader to connect to the text and make inferences

3. Introduce the general topic of the lesson—in this case, war—connecting it to prior learning whenever possible.

4. Guide students through an interactive read-aloud, stopping at the places in the text that you previously identified. Elicit responses from students using techniques such as *think–pair–share*, *partner nominations* (i.e., choosing a partner's response for sharing with others), and *gestured response* (e.g., thumbs up, thumbs down).

5. As a class, determine the author's overall message, and ask students to think about how it applies in their own lives.

> **Enhanced eText** Application Exercise 9.4: Ms. Maddox Teaches Comprehension

Bridge: From Assessment to Teaching Specific Comprehension Skills

When teachers learn from assessment that _____,	then teachers may want to teach _____.
Readers need a wider repertoire of skills beyond literal understanding for a variety of texts,	Readers to identify the big picture in the texts they read—including main idea—and to make reasonable inferences given the information in the text.
Readers do not realize when they are misunderstanding, or do not realize there is more to be understood in a text,	Readers to be self-aware of the strategies they use to comprehend, using checklists, student self-assessment, and the Meta-Comprehension Strategy Index (pg. 200).

Teaching Specific Comprehension Skills

The comprehension taxonomy presented on pages 189–190 contains several comprehension skills for each level. Identifying the main idea of a paragraph, identifying the central idea of a passage, using visuals, and making inferences are just four skills. All of these are interpretive-level reading skills, and we present them here for both primary- and intermediate-grade children as examples of how skills can be assessed and taught.

Main Idea of a Paragraph

The main idea is probably the skill on which teachers and students spend the most time; this is good, because it seems to pose difficulty for some students. Students have more difficulty coming up with the main idea themselves than they do choosing one from a given list. In fact, identifying the main idea is much more difficult for many students, even if it is directly stated.[35]

Because of the difficulty of the main idea construction (identification) task, sufficient time must be allotted to provide the needed "think time." In addition, researchers have reported "that if readers' prior knowledge for the text topic is not sufficient, the difficulty of main idea construction is compounded."[36] Also, if the paragraph is not well constructed and cohesive, it becomes more difficult to discern its main idea.

Confusion in finding the main idea may exist because the very concept of a "main idea" seems to mean different things to different people. One researcher investigating the literature found that "educators have increasingly given attention to main idea comprehension, but with no concomitant increase in the clarity of what is meant by main or important ideas. The exact nature of main ideas and the teaching practices intended to help students grasp main ideas vary considerably."[37]

Even though the concept of main idea is nebulous to some researchers, and the "notion that different readers can (and should) construct identical main ideas for the same text has been questioned,"[38] finding the main idea in a text is a very important skill for reading, writing, and studying that can and should be taught. It is possible that the skepticism concerning the ability to teach main idea comprehension may result from "the failure to teach students to transfer their main idea skills to texts other than those found in their readers."[39] Some studies have found that "students who have been taught to identify main ideas using only contrived texts such as those found in basal reader skills lessons will have difficulty transferring their main idea skills to naturally occurring texts."[40] (The majority of reading programs in the recent past and present time have been literature-based, using whole pieces of literature rather than "contrived texts," which should counter the former criticism.)

In reading and writing, finding the main idea is very useful. In reading, the main idea helps readers to remember and understand what they have read. In writing, the main idea gives unity and order to a paragraph.

The **main idea** of a paragraph is the central thought of the paragraph. It is what the paragraph is about. Without a main idea, the paragraph would just be a confusion of sentences. All the sentences in the paragraph should develop the main idea.

Finding the Main Idea of a Paragraph.   To find the main idea of a paragraph, readers must find what common element the sentences share. Some textbook writers place the main idea at the beginning of a paragraph and may actually put the topic of the paragraph in bold print in order to emphasize it. However, in literature, this is not a common practice. In some paragraphs the main idea is indirectly stated, or implied, and you have to find it from the clues given by the author.

Although there is no foolproof method for finding the main idea, there is a widely used procedure that has proved to be helpful. To use this procedure, you should know that a paragraph is always written about something or someone. The something or someone is the topic of the paragraph. The writer is interested in telling her readers something about the topic of the paragraph. To find the main idea of a paragraph, you must determine what the topic of the paragraph is and what the author is trying to say about the topic that is special or unique. Once you have found these two things, you should have the main idea. This procedure is useful in finding the main idea of various types of paragraphs.

Reread the preceding paragraph and state its main idea. *Answer:* A procedure helpful in finding the main idea of a paragraph is described.

Now read the following paragraph. After you have read the passage, choose the statement that *best* states the main idea.

> Frank Yano looked like an old man, but he was only 30. Born to parents who were alcoholics, Frank himself started drinking when he was only 8. He actually had tasted alcohol earlier, but it wasn't until he was 8 or 9 that he became a habitual drinker. His whole life since then had been dedicated to seeking the bottle.

1. Frank Yano looks old, but he's not.
2. Frank Yano enjoys being an alcoholic.
3. Frank Yano was a child alcoholic.
4. Frank Yano has been an alcoholic since childhood.
5. Frank Yano would like to change his life of drinking, but he can't.
6. Frank Yano's parents helped him become an alcoholic.

   Answer: #4

Numbers 1 and 3 are too specific, because they each relate to only one detail in the paragraph. Numbers 2 and 5 are not found in the paragraph; that is, no clues are given about Frank Yano's wanting to change his life or about his enjoying his life as an alcoholic. Number 6 is also too specific to be the main idea, because it relates to only one detail. Number 4 is the answer because what is unique about Frank Yano is that he has been an alcoholic since early childhood. All the details in the paragraph support this main idea.

The main idea of a paragraph is a general statement of the content of a paragraph. You must be careful, however, that your main idea statement is not so general that it suggests information that is not given in the paragraph.

Textbook authors usually see to it that their paragraphs have clear-cut main ideas. The main ideas of paragraphs in other books may be less obvious. The literary author is usually more concerned with writing expressively than with explicitly stating the main ideas. The main idea may be indirectly given. If this is the case, the steps presented earlier are especially helpful. Let's look again at the steps involved in finding the main idea.

1. Find the topic of the paragraph.

2. Find what is special about the topic. To do this, gather clues from the paragraph, find out what all the clues have in common, and make a general statement about the clues.

Guidelines on Topic Sentences and Main Ideas

1. The topic sentence is usually the first sentence in a paragraph, and it states what the paragraph will be about by naming the topic. From the topic sentence, you can usually anticipate certain events. You can usually determine that the following sentences will supply **supporting details** as examples, contrasts, similarities, sequence of events, cause-and-effect situations, and so on to support the main idea.

2. The main idea can be developed in many different ways. Whatever technique is used to develop the main idea, it must support and add meaning to the main idea.

3. A topic sentence may or may not contain the main idea.

4. It is possible for any sentence in the paragraph to be the topic sentence.

5. Some paragraphs may not have a topic sentence.

6. Do not confuse the topic sentence with the main idea. The topic sentence usually anticipates both the main idea and the development of the main idea.

7. Even though the topic sentence is stated explicitly (fully and clearly) in a paragraph, the main idea may not be stated explicitly.

Some students may already know how to identify main ideas and others may not. In Figure 9.7, we provide a sample informal assessment for teachers to use to determine who can and cannot identify main ideas.

Instructional Suggestions for Primary Grades.   Here are some instructional techniques and materials to use with your students who need some additional explicit instruction.

1. Present the following paragraph to your students:

> Sharon was sad. She felt like crying. She still couldn't believe it. Her best friend, Jane, had moved away. Her best friend had left her. What would she do?

Ask your students what the topic of the paragraph is, or about whom or what the paragraph is written.

Answer: Sharon

Ask your students what the writer is saying that is special about Sharon.

Answer: Sharon is sad because her best friend moved away.

Tell your students that to find the main idea of the story, they need to figure out who or what the story is about and what is special about the who or what of the story.

Figure 9.7 Informal Assessment of Main Idea

PRIMARY-GRADE LEVEL

ASSESSING FOR MAIN IDEA

Objective 1: The students will choose a statement that best states the main idea of a short one-paragraph story.

Objective 2: The students will state a title for a story that gives an idea of what the story is about.

Directions: Read the short story. Then read the statements that follow the story. Choose the one that *best* states the main idea of the story. Also, state a title for the story.

Tom and Jim are not feeling very happy. They have just had their first fight. Tom and Jim have never had a fight before. Tom thought about the fight. Jim thought about the fight. They both felt sad.

1. Tom and Jim are sad.
2. Tom and Jim have never fought before.
3. Tom and Jim's first fight makes them feel sad.
4. Tom and Jim fight.
5. Tom and Jim feel ill.

Answers: Number 3. *Sample title:* Tom and Jim's First Fight
Tell students the results.

2. Present your students with exercises such as the following. Ask your students to read the short story below. Also ask them to read the statements that follow the short story, and to choose the one that best states the main idea of the story. Then ask your students to write a title for the story that gives readers an idea of what the story is about.

> Tom and Jim live on the moon. They spend a lot of time in their house. They have to, because it is very hot when the sun is out. It is also very cold when the sun is not out. On the moon, daylight lasts for 14 Earth days. Darkness or nighttime lasts for 14 Earth days, too.

1. It's cold on the moon.

2. Tom and Jim stay in their house a lot.

3. The moon's weather

4. Tom and Jim's house

5. The moon's weather forces Tom and Jim to stay in their house.

6. Tom and Jim like to stay in their house.

Answer: #5. *Sample title:* The Moon's Weather.

3. Discuss with your students the difference between the title and the main idea. Help them to see that the title and the main idea are not necessarily the same, and that the main idea is usually more fully stated than the title.

4. Another way of teaching main ideas is to use your hand. Trace a figure of your hand on an overhead transparency. Provide children with a statement (the main idea), which you write in the palm of the hand. For example, write the sentence "We are having fun at school today." Next, ask children to volunteer some ideas that prove they are having fun at school. As they volunteer their ideas, write each one in a finger. These are actually the supporting details, but students do not need to know this at this point in the lesson. Now invite the class to read the entire "hand" with you. Once

Figure 9.8 Main Idea/Supporting Details Hand

<u>Being in Mrs. Carter's class is</u>

<u>fun. We pick out of a prize box for</u>

<u>most stars. You can do math. She helps</u>

<u>people when they need help. She lets</u>

<u>us play on the computer.</u>

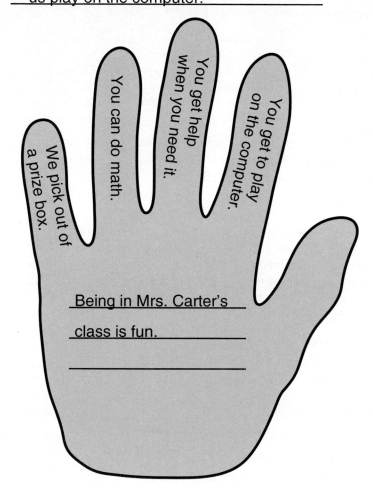

finished, tell students that they have just learned about main idea and supporting details. Just like the palm of your hand holds your fingers together, the main idea holds the details together. You may also want to show them how to rewrite the statements on the hand into paragraph form. See Figure 9.8 for a sample completed hand.

As with primary students, some intermediate students may already know how to identify the main idea and others may not. In Figure 9.9, we provide a sample informal assessment for the intermediate-grade level.

Instructional Suggestions for Intermediate Grades. Here are some instructional techniques and materials that you can use with your students who need additional explicit instruction:

1. Have your students read the following two paragraphs. After they read them, try to elicit from them which is the better paragraph and why. You should tell them that the first one makes sense because it is well organized. Readers can tell what the author is trying to say because there is only one main idea and all the sentences

Figure 9.9 Informal Assessment of Main Idea

INTERMEDIATE-GRADE LEVEL

SKILL: MAIN IDEA OF A PARAGRAPH

Objective: The students will state the main idea of a paragraph.

Directions: Read the paragraph carefully. Write the main idea of it in the space below.

Jim and his friends planned to go on a camping trip. For weeks, he and his friends talked about nothing else. They planned every detail of the trip. They studied maps and read books on camping. Everything was set. Everything, that is, except for asking their parents to let them go. Jim and his friends had planned everything. They had not planned on their parents not letting them go. However, that is what happened. Jim's and his friends' parents did not allow them to go.

Answer: Jim and his friends' plans to go camping are blocked by their parents.
Tell students the results.

in the paragraph expand on the main idea. Point out how disorganized the second paragraph is and how difficult it is to discover what the main idea is, because each sentence seems to be about a different topic.

Organized Paragraph

All through school, John's one goal was athletic success so that he could be in the Olympics. John's goal to be in the Olympics became such an obsession that he could not do anything that did not directly or indirectly relate to achieving his goal. He practiced for hours every day. He exercised, ate well, and slept at least eight hours every night. Throughout school, John allowed nothing and no one to deter him from his goal.

Disorganized Paragraph

All through school, John's one goal was to be the best, so that he could be in the Olympics. He practiced for hours every day. John's family was unhappy about John's obsession to be in the Olympics. John's social life was more like a monk's than that of a star athlete. John's coach was a difficult man to please.

2. Have your students reread the organized paragraph. After they read the paragraph, have them choose the word or words that *best* answer the two questions that follow.

   a. What is the topic of the paragraph?

      1. Exercise and practice

      2. Work

      3. Olympics

      4. John's goal

      5. Athletic success

      6. Attempts

      Answer: #4

   b. What is the author saying about John's goal to be in the Olympics (the topic) that is special and that helps tie the details together?

      1. That it needed time and patience

      2. That it was a good one

      3. That it was not a reasonable one

      4. That it was the most important thing in John's life

5. That it required good health

6. That it was too much for John

Answer: #4

Tell your students that if they put the two answers together, they should have the main idea of the paragraph. Main idea: The goal, being in the Olympics, was the most important thing in John's life.

3. Choose a number of paragraphs from the students' social studies or science books. First have them find the topic of each paragraph, and then have them state the main idea of each paragraph. Go over the procedure for finding the main idea with them.

Finding the Central Idea of a Group of Paragraphs

We generally use the term **central idea** rather than *main idea* when we refer to a *group* of paragraphs, a story, or an article. However, the procedures for finding the main idea and for finding the central idea are the same.

The central idea of a story is the central thought of the story. All the paragraphs of the story should develop the central idea. To find the central idea of a story, students must find what common element the paragraphs in the story share. The introductory paragraph is usually helpful because it either contains or anticipates what the central idea is and how it will be developed. The procedure for finding the central idea of a story is similar to that for finding the main idea of a paragraph.

You may wish to use the informal assessment for central idea that we show in Figure 9.10 to determine which students might need some instruction. The informal assessment in Figure 9.11 is intended for intermediate-grade students.

Figure 9.10 Informal Assessment: Central Idea

UPPER PRIMARY-GRADE LEVEL

SKILL: CENTRAL IDEA OF A SHORT STORY

Objective 1: The students will state the central idea of a short story.

Objective 2: The students will state a title for a story.

Directions: Read the story. Write the central idea of the story. Then write a title for the story that gives readers an idea of what the story is about.

Once upon a time in the deep green jungle of Africa, there lived a cruel lion. This lion frightened all the animals in the jungle. No animal was safe from this lion. One day the animals met and came up with a plan. The plan was not a very good one, but it was the best they could think of. Each day one animal would go to the lion to be eaten by him. That way the other animals would know that they were safe for a little while. The lion agreed to the plan and that is how they lived for a time.

One day it was the sly fox's turn to be eaten by the lion. Mr. Fox, however, had other plans. Mr. Fox went to the lion's cave an hour late. The lion was very angry. "Why are you so late? I am hungry," he said. Mr. Fox answered, "Oh, I am so sorry to be late, but another very, very big lion tried to catch me. I ran away from him so that you could eat me." When the lion heard about the other lion, he became more angry. "Another lion?" he asked. "I want to see him." The fox told the lion that he would take him to see the other lion. The fox led the lion through the jungle. When they came to a well, the fox stopped. "Look in there," said the fox. "The other lion is in there." The lion looked in the well, and he did indeed see a lion. He got so angry that he jumped in the well to fight the lion. That was, of course, the end of the lion.

Answers: *Central idea:* A clever fox outsmarts a cruel lion.

Sample title: The Clever Fox and the Cruel Lion or A Fox Outsmarts a Lion.

Tell students the results.

Figure 9.11 Informal Assessment: Central Idea

INTERMEDIATE-GRADE LEVEL

SKILL: CENTRAL IDEA OF A SHORT STORY

Objective 1: The students will state the central idea of a short story.

Objective 2: The students will be able to state a title for a story.

Directions: Read carefully the following short story to determine the central idea of the story. After you have found the central idea of the story, choose a title for the story that gives readers an idea of what the story is about.

A man and his son went to the market one morning. They took along a donkey to bring back whatever they would buy.

As they walked down the road, they met a woman who looked at them with a sour face.

"Are you not ashamed," she called to the father, "to let your little boy walk in the hot sun, when he should be riding on the donkey?"

The father stopped and lifted his boy to the donkey's back. So they went on.

After a little while they met an old man. He began at once to scold the boy. "You ungrateful son!" he shouted. "You let your poor old father walk while you sit there on the donkey like a lazy good-for-nothing!"

When the old man had passed, the father took his frightened son from the donkey and got onto the animal himself.

Further on they met another man who looked at them angrily. " How can you let your child walk in the dusty road?" he asked. "And you sit up there by yourself!"

The father was troubled, but he reached down and lifted his son up where he could sit on the donkey in front of him.

A little later they met a man and his wife, each of them riding a donkey. The husband called out, "You cruel man! How can you let the poor donkey carry such a heavy load? Get off at once! You are big enough and strong enough to carry the little animal instead of making it carry two of you."

The poor man was now really perplexed. He got off the donkey and took his son off, too.

Then he cut down a young tree for a pole and trimmed it. He tied the donkey's four feet to the pole. Then he and his son lifted the pole. They trudged along, carrying the donkey between them.

As they were crossing a bridge over a stream, they met with a crowd of young men. Seeing the donkey being carried on a pole, they started to laugh and shout. Their noise startled the poor donkey who started to kick violently and broke the ropes holding his feet. As he frisked about, he tumbled off the bridge and was drowned.

The man looked sadly into the stream and shook his head.

"My son," he said to the boy, "you cannot please everybody."

Answers: *Central idea:* A man and his son learn that you cannot please everyone.

Sample title: You Can't Please Everyone

Tell students the results.

Instructional Suggestions for Upper Primary Grades. Here are some instructional techniques you can use with your students who need additional explicit instruction.

1. Choose a short story the children know and enjoy reading. Have them state what the topic of the story is. Then have them go over the story and try to state the most important thing about the topic. Have them put the two together.

2. Have the children write their own short stories. Have them state the central idea of their short stories. Have them go over each of their paragraphs to see if each one helps develop their central idea. Have them write a title for their stories.

Instructional Suggestions for Intermediate Grades. Here are some instructional techniques you can use with your students who need additional explicit instruction.

1. Choose a story the students have read. Ask them to state the topic of the story. Then have them reread the story to state the most important thing about the topic. Ask

them to put these together. Then have them review the story to determine whether everything in the story is related to their central idea.

2. Ask students to write their own stories. Have them state the central idea and write a title for their stories.

3. Choose some short stories and follow the same procedure for finding the central idea. Present the short stories without the titles. Ask the students to make up a title for each short story. Discuss the fact that the title and the central idea are not necessarily the same, and explore what the differences are.

Visual Representations and Main Idea.   It is difficult to read a textbook, magazine, or newspaper without finding a variety of visual representations in the form of graphs, diagrams, and charts. Visuals provide relief from print, and a graphic representation is often worth a thousand words. Graphs, diagrams, and charts grab readers' attention, and pack a great amount of information into a small space. *USA Today* uses pictorial representations every day in each section of the newspaper for these reasons.

Writers use graphs, diagrams, and charts to convey information, and each one—like a paragraph—has a main idea. To understand charts, diagrams, and graphs, you must be able to get the main idea of them. Not surprisingly, the technique readers use to do this is similar to that for finding the main idea of a paragraph.

Figure 9.12 is a graph from *Health Behaviors* by Rosalind Reed and Thomas A. Lang (1988).[41] Let's go through the various steps to get the main idea of it. Remember, to find the main idea, we must first find the topic of the chart, diagram, or graph and then note what is special or unique about it. All the details should develop the main idea. (Note that writers also usually give clues to the topic of their graphs, diagrams, and charts.) Here are the steps readers would go through:

1. Look carefully at the graph to determine its topic. Notice that it deals with smokers and nonsmokers, and their mortality rates for selected diseases. Therefore, the topic is:

> The mortality rates of smokers and nonsmokers for selected diseases.

Figure 9.12 Mortality Rates for Smokers and Nonsmokers for Selected Diseases

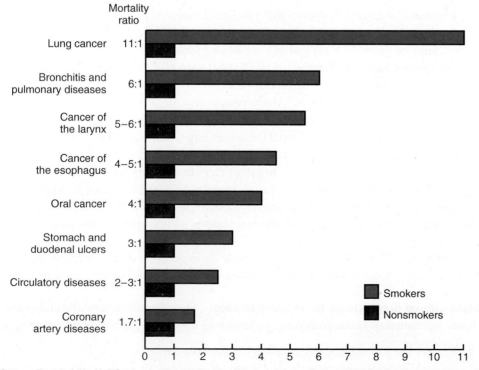

Source: Based on *Health Behaviors* by Rosalind Reed and Thomas A. Lang. St. Paul, MN: West Publication, 1988, p. 328.

2. Next, find what is special about the topic. In looking at the graph again, note that the writer is obviously making a comparison between smokers and nonsmokers. The comparison is about various types of diseases. In addition—and what is most crucial—is that the smokers have consistently higher mortality rates for all presented diseases. Therefore, the main idea must be:

> The mortality rates for smokers are consistently higher than for nonsmokers for all selected diseases.

Drawing Inferences

Enhanced eText
Video Example 9.4

In this video clip, a first-grade teacher works with a small group of students in a guided reading group to start a new story about hermit crabs. Watch for several components of guided reading being implemented in this clip.

Many times writers do not directly state what they mean, but present ideas in a more indirect, roundabout way. That is why inference is called the ability to "read between the lines." **Inference** is defined as *understanding that is not derived from a direct statement but from an indirect suggestion in what is stated.* Readers draw inferences from writings; authors make implications or imply meanings.

The ability to draw inferences is especially important in reading fiction, but it is necessary for nonfiction, also. Authors rely on inferences to make their stories more interesting and enjoyable. Mystery writers find inference essential to maintaining suspense. For example, *Sherlock Holmes* and *Encyclopedia Brown* mysteries are based on the sleuth's ability to uncover evidence in the form of clues that are not obvious to others around them until the author explains their significance.

Inference is an important process on which authors rely. Good readers must be alert to the various ways that authors encourage inference.

Implied Statements.   As noted, writers count on inference to make their writing more interesting and enjoyable. Rather than directly stating something, they present it indirectly. To understand the writing, the reader must be alert and be able to detect the clues that the author gives. For example, in the sentence *Things are always popping and alive when the twins Herb and Jack are around,* you are given some clues to Herb and Jack's personalities, even though the author has not directly said anything about them. From the statement, you could make the inference that the twins are lively and lots of fun to be around.

You must be careful, however, that you *do not read more* into some statements than is intended. For example, read the following statements and put a circle around the correct answer. *Example:* Mary got out of bed and looked out of the window. She saw that the ground had something white on it. What season of the year was it? (a) Winter, (b) summer, (c) spring, (d) fall, or (e) can't tell.

The answer is "(e) can't tell." Many people choose "(a) winter" for the answer. However, the answer is (e) because the "something white" could be anything; there isn't enough evidence to choose (a). Even if the something white was snow, in some parts of the world, including the United States, it can snow in the spring or fall.

Good readers, while reading, try to gather clues to draw inferences about what they read. Although effective readers do this, they are not usually aware of it. As Sherlock Holmes says in *A Study in Scarlet*, "From long habit the train of thought ran so swiftly through my mind that I arrived at the conclusions without being conscious of intermediate steps."

In Figure 9.13 and Figure 9.14, we provide an informal assessment procedure that you can use to assess inference at the primary-grade and intermediate-grade levels.

Instructional Suggestions for Primary Grades.   Here are some instructional procedures and materials to use with your students who need additional explicit instruction.

1. Present the following short selection to your students:

> Sharon and Carol are going out to play. They are dressed very warmly.

Figure 9.13 Informal Assessment: Inference

PRIMARY-GRADE LEVEL

SKILL: INFERENCE OR "READING BETWEEN THE LINES"

Objective: The students will read a short story and answer inference questions about it.

Directions: Read the short story. Then answer the questions.

Cleo and Scabbers are a cat and rat. They are good friends. They live on the moon. Cleo and Scabbers love to ride in space. Their school goes on a space trip every month. Cleo and Scabbers must wear their space clothes and their air masks in the spaceship. All the other moon cats and rats must wear them, too. Cleo and Scabbers want to be spaceship pilots. This is the same spaceship that brought Cleo and Scabbers to the moon. The spaceship has its own landing place. It is well taken care of. Special cats and rats take care of the spaceship. Cleo and Scabbers are happy that they can ride in the spaceship.

1. Is there air in the spaceship? Explain.

2. Were Cleo and Scabbers born on the moon? Explain.

3. Is the spaceship important to the moon cats and rats? Explain.

4. Is travel an important part of school learning? Explain.

5. Do Cleo and Scabbers know what they want to do when they grow up? Explain.

Answers:
1. No. Cleo and Scabbers wear their space clothes and their air masks in the spaceship.
2. No. It is stated that the spaceship is the same one that brought Cleo and Scabbers to the moon.
3. Yes. It is their means of travel. It is stated that there are special cats and rats who take care of the spaceship and that the spaceship is well taken care of.
4. Yes. Every month the school goes on a space trip.
5. Yes. It is stated that they want to be spaceship pilots.

Tell students the results.

Ask your students what they can say about the weather outside. They should say that it must be cold outside because the children are dressed very warmly. Even though the writer didn't say that it was cold outside, there was enough evidence to make this inference.

Now ask the children to tell you what season of the year it is. They should say that they can't tell because there is not enough evidence. It could be cold in the fall and spring. Some children might be able to state that they can't tell because different parts of the country and the world have different climates.

Figure 9.14 Informal Assessment: Inference

INTERMEDIATE-GRADE LEVEL

SKILL: INFERENCE OR "READING BETWEEN THE LINES"

Objective: The students will make inferences about short selections if enough evidence exists for the inferences.

Directions: Read the following selection *very carefully*. Without looking back at the selection, try to answer the questions.

The two men looked at each other. They would have to make the decision that might cost many lives. They kept rubbing their hands together to keep warm. Although they were dressed in furs and every part of them was covered except for their faces, they could still feel the cold. The fire that had been made for them from pine trees was subsiding. It was getting light. They had promised their men a decision at dawn. Should they go forward or should they retreat? So many lives had already been lost.

a. Did this take place at the North Pole or South Pole? _____

How do you know? _____

_____

_____

_____

b. Circle the word that best fits the two men. The two men were: (1) trappers (2) officers (3) soldiers (4) guides. Explain why you made your choice.

Explain: _____

_____

_____

c. What inference can you draw from this short passage? Circle the answer.
   (1) The men were on a hunting trip.
   (2) The men were at war with a foreign nation.
   (3) The decision that the two men had to make concerned whether to take an offensive or defensive position in some kind of battle.
   (4) The men were on a hunting trip, but they got caught in a bad storm.

Explain: _____

_____

_____

Answers:

(a) No. There are no pine trees at the North or South Pole. (b) Officers. Guides would not talk about *their* men. Guides usually act as advisers. They do not make decisions. Trappers trap animals for fur. Also, it is stated that the fire had been made for them. Officers do not usually prepare the camp. (c) The term *retreat* would be a commander's term. Nothing was stated about a storm nor was anything stated or suggested about a foreign nation. Hunters would not usually hunt under such adverse conditions. It was too cold to hunt big game, and hunters would very rarely lose so many lives.

Tell students the results.

2. Give your students a number of opportunities to make inferences from stories they are reading if enough evidence exists.

Instructional Suggestions for Intermediate Grades. Here are some instructional procedures and materials that you can use with your students who need additional explicit instruction.

1. Present your students with the following statements:

Jack looks out of the train window. All he sees are miles and miles of leafless trees.

Ask students whether Jack just began to look out of the window. Students may answer yes, no, or don't know. Direct them to read back the words and then discuss how they arrived at their answer.

Ask students whether Jack is traveling through a densely or sparsely populated area. Some may choose dense, others sparse, and still others may not know. Direct them back to the words in the text to learn whether their answer comes from their own inferences or from the words.

2. Have students read a number of stories and see what inferences they can draw from them. Help them to recognize that enough evidence should exist to make an inference. Tell them that many times people "jump to conclusions" before they have enough evidence. This can cause problems. Taking an educated guess is helpful in scientific activities and in searching for the answers to difficult questions. Students should be encouraged to make educated guesses, but they need to recognize when they do not have enough evidence to do so.

Enhanced eText Application Exercise 9.5: Ms. Maddox Teaches Specific Comprehension Skills

---

Bridge: From Assessment to Teaching Specific Comprehension Strategies

When teachers learn from assessment that _____,	then teachers may want to teach _____.
Readers' main purpose in comprehension is to answer teacher-initiated questions or to complete assignments,	Students to set authentic purposes for understanding what they are reading, beyond completion of assignments.
Students' answers to questions are mainly literal, 'in the book' answers,	Students to monitor what levels of thinking they are using when they read, and to expand the kinds of connections they make to self and the world.

Teaching Specific Comprehension Strategies

In addition to specific comprehension skills, there are comprehension strategies (i.e., mental processes) that may require some explicit instruction. As with the skills noted above, remember that students need plenty of time to read in order to actually apply these skills and strategies. The six strategies—making connections, making predictions, monitoring understanding, visualizing, questioning, and retelling/summarizing—are all research-based. A brief overview of each of these strategies is provided in the sections below along with some teaching suggestions and ideas for guiding students' practice. Table 9.3 provides a helpful list of children's literature selections that may be used to teach each strategy, though there are many others.

Our goal with strategic thinking is that students learn to use it as a problem-solving strategy when text is difficult. As students become more proficient with various types of text, we expect that the thinking they use for comprehension will become more automatic—that is, strategies will become skills.[42]

Comprehension Strategy: Making Connections

Making connections is a reading comprehension strategy in which readers achieve three goals:

- Connect their knowledge to a selection.
- Connect other texts to a selection.
- Connect their responses to a selection.

Table 9.3 Titles for Comprehension Strategy Development

Comprehension Strategy	Possible Titles to Use
Making Connections	Dewdney, Anna. *Llama Llama Mad at Mama.* New York: Penguin, 2007. Hall, Donald. *Ox-Cart Man.* New York: Puffin, 1983. Viorst, Judith. *Alexander and the Terrible, Horrible, No Good, Very Bad Day.* New York: Aladdin, 1987.
Making Predictions	George, Lindsay Barrett. *In the Garden: Who's Been Here?* New York: HarperCollins, 2006. Lewis, J. Patrick. *Spot the Plot: A Riddle Book of Book Riddles.* San Francisco, CA: Chronicle, 2009. Macdonald, Suse. *Shape by Shape.* New York: Simon & Schuster, 2009. Parish, Herman. *Amelia Bedelia's First Day of School.* New York: HarperCollins, 2009. Schaefer, Lola M. *An Island Grows.* New York: HarperCollins, 2006.
Monitoring Understanding	Adler, David. *Don't Talk to Me About the War.* New York: Penguin, 2008. Parry, Florence. *The Day of Ahmed's Secret.* New York: HarperCollins, 2005. Snicket, Lemony. *The Composer Is Dead.* New York: HarperCollins, 2009.
Visualizing	Brown, Ruth. *Toad.* New York: Penguin, 1997. Yolen, Jane. *Color Me a Rhyme.* Honesdale, PA: Boyds Mills, 2003.
Questioning	Bunting, Eve. *How Many Days to America.* New York: Clarion, 1988. Gerstein, Mordicai. *Leaving the Nest.* New York: Farrar, Straus, & Giroux, 2007. Van Allsburg, Chris. *The Widow's Broom.* New York: Houghton Mifflin, 1992.
Retelling/Summarizing	Auch, Mary Jane & Herm. *The Plot Chickens.* New York: Holiday House, 2009. Martin, Jacqueline Briggs. *Snowflake Bentley.* New York: Houghton Mifflin, 1998. Swinburne, Stephen. *A Butterfly Grows.* Boston: Houghton Mifflin Harcourt, 2009.

Instructional Suggestions.   To teach students how to make connections, begin with an introduction in which you present a short selection to students and have them, in group discussion, say what they know about the topic, if the selection makes them think of other stories, and how they might respond to the selection. This models for students how they might make connections for other texts that they read.

Point out to students that these are different kinds of connections a reader can make to a selection, and explain that making connections helps readers understand stories better and enjoy them more. To assist in making these points and to keep them fresh in students' minds as you practice this strategy, post for students the three different kinds of connections a reader can make. Your visual should contain these three points:

- Connections to what a reader knows
- Connections to other stories
- Connections to story responses

Keeping these points visible for students to refer back to, you can then model how to make connections by using a selection from a read-aloud book, a magazine, or some other media. Read a part of the story and then think aloud as you make connections. Table 9.4 provides a list of specific questions that can be asked.

Guiding Students' Practice.   After you have modeled the process of reading a section of text and then asking specific questions in order to establish connections, have students practice making connections. Allow students time to read the next section of

Table 9.4 Questions for Making Connections

For making connections to . . .	You might ask . . .
What a reader knows	Can I say or write down those ideas? What do I know about this topic?
Other stories	Do I know other stories by this same author or illustrator? Does this story remind me of another story? How are they alike and different?
Story responses	Did I enjoy this story? Was it interesting or funny? What do I think about the characters or what happened?

Table 9.5 Making Connections Chart

Making connections to . . .	Before Reading	During Reading	After Reading
What I know			
Other stories			
Story responses			

the selection and ask themselves the connection questions. Provide support and extra modeling as necessary to guide students through the process of making connections.

Last, have students complete a connection chart as a group, with a partner, or individually, using Table 9.5 as an example. Have students discuss and write their connections in each of the three categories before, during, and after reading the selection.

Comprehension Strategy: Making Predictions

Making predictions is a reading comprehension strategy that requires students to do the following:

1. Use prior knowledge and information in a selection to make logical guesses or predictions about events in the selection
2. Read on to check (verify) their predictions
3. Change or make new predictions based on the new information in the selection

Instructional Suggestions. To introduce this strategy to students, present a picture or read a short selection to students and have them guess what is happening or what might happen next. Explain that these guesses are "predictions" and that making predictions helps readers think about the story and look for ideas the writer might tell them later. Describe how keeping these predictions in mind as they read and then checking predictions gives them another purpose for reading ("Did I predict correctly?") and helps them understand what they read.

With the basic understanding of predictions in students' minds, display the four steps, perhaps in a table like Table 9.6, for making predictions so that students may reference them throughout the instructional time.

Model these steps for students. First, read a selection from a book, magazine, or other media source. Second, think aloud as you make several predictions and write them down. Then, read more of the selection and think aloud as you check the predictions and write T (true), F (false), or CT (can't tell yet) after each. Last, change the predictions or make new ones from new ideas in the selection.

Guiding Students' Practice. After modeling this comprehension strategy, have students follow the four steps on the next portion of the selection or on a different selection. They should read, predict, check predictions, and change or make new predictions based on the results of their check. You may need to guide students through the prediction process by providing additional support and reteaching steps.

Table 9.6 Steps for Making Predictions

Step	Action
1.	Read a part of the story.
2.	Predict what will happen next.
3.	Read on and check predictions.
4.	Change or make new predictions.

When students are ready, have them complete a prediction equation as a group, with a partner, or individually. Ask students to write clues from the story and ideas they know that led them to a prediction. Then, have students check their predictions and either change them or make new ones.

Comprehension Strategy: Monitoring Understanding

The monitoring understanding strategy for comprehension has readers develop the ability to recognize comprehension breakdowns when they occur and then apply fix-up strategies to correct comprehension difficulties.

Instructional Suggestions.   A good way to introduce this strategy is to read a short selection to students, but insert several words or short sentences that do not make sense within the overall passage. Then, ask students "Did that story make sense? Why not?" They will likely point out the nonsense additions that you made. Explain that what they did, listening to what you read and then identifying the things that did not make sense, was to check or monitor their reading comprehension.

Make it clear to students that monitoring reading comprehension is an extremely important skill. It allows readers to tell when a selection is not making sense. When a reader knows that something is not making sense, they can then correct their understanding. Explain to students that whenever a passage does not make sense, they can employ a "fix-up" strategy to resolve the issue or bring clarity to the passage. Ways to better comprehend a passage include the following:

- Read the sentence or paragraph again.
- Retell the sentence or paragraph in your own words—crossing over into the "making connections" comprehension strategy.
- Ask a question or make a prediction—crossing over into the "making predictions" comprehension strategy.
- Read on and see if the selection makes sense.

After students have an understanding of the basic concept of this strategy, display the two steps for monitoring comprehension, as outlined in Table 9.7.

With the steps still visible to students, model how to monitor comprehension by selecting a challenging selection from a book or other media. Model monitoring by reading a paragraph, stopping, and then asking "Is this making sense?" If the answer to that question is "No," indicate what you find confusing. Is it the main idea that is not clear? Are you confused by a character's motive? Are you missing the cause–effect relationship? Or is there vocabulary you do not understand? Whenever a problem area is identified, select one or more of the fix-up strategies and model how to apply each by thinking aloud as you step through the process of clarification.

Guiding Students' Practice.   Invite students to read the next section and practice the monitoring strategy. Have them stop periodically and ask "Is this making sense?" Whenever they answer "No," encourage them to apply one or more of the fix-up strategies to aid their comprehension. If students are struggling, step through the modeling exercise again.

Table 9.7 Steps for Monitoring Understanding

Step	Action
1.	Read part of a selection, stop, and ask "Is this selection making sense?"
2.	If you answer "No," then try one or more of the fix-up strategies.

After you have guided students through a passage, it is time for them to practice on their own. A fun way for them to do this is to make comprehension monitoring "stop signs." Provide students with or have them make octagonal shapes. On one side, have them write the word "STOP" in large letters and the question "Is this making sense?" On the other side, have them write "To Fix Up" and then the list of choices "Reread, Retell, Question, Predict, or Read On." With this tool in hand, instruct students to use them as they read. Instruct them to stop at the end of each paragraph or page, put down the stop sign with the first side up, and ask themselves "Is this making sense?" If they answer "No," then have them turn the sign over and try one or more of the fix-up strategies.

Comprehension Strategy: Visualizing

Visualizing is a comprehension strategy in which readers create pictures in their minds to promote their understanding, recall, and appreciation of a selection.

Instructional Suggestions.   Introduce the concept of visualizing to students by asking them to close their eyes and listen carefully while you read aloud a short, descriptive selection. When you have finished, have students open their eyes, and ask the following:

- What was the selection about?
- Did anyone see a picture of what they heard?
- Can you tell us about the picture you drew in your mind?

Explain that making a mental picture, or visualizing, is a powerful way to help listeners and readers understand, remember, and enjoy a selection.

Next, display the steps shown in Table 9.8 to help students visualize as they are reading.

With these steps visible for students to refer to, model how to use the visualizing strategy. Read a selection from a book or other media. As you read part of the story, look for words to help you visualize, and pause to point these words out to students. Comment on words that tell about actions, colors, characters, sounds, or settings. Then, use the writer's words to paint a verbal picture of the scene or events in the selection.

Guiding Students' Practice.   Invite volunteers to read the next portion of the selection and talk about the words that help them draw pictures in their minds. Then have them describe their mental pictures as they read. Compare and contrast the visualizations that the students describe. Point out how different readers can get different pictures for the same selection. Discuss as a group how visualizing helps readers better understand, remember, or enjoy a selection.

To help students practice visualizing, have them read a selection while completing a visualizing chart in which they write the words that help them picture what the author is trying to convey. When they finish the passage, review the words listed and then ask them to draw pictures of what images came to their mind when they read or heard the passage.

Table 9.8 Steps for Visualizing

Step	Action
1.	Read a selection carefully.
2.	Look for words that tell about settings, actions, colors, characters, or sounds.
3.	Use the writer's words to visualize, or make a mental picture of, the selection.

Comprehension Strategy: Questioning

Through the questioning comprehension strategy, readers learn to generate questions as they read. This sort of self-questioning promotes active and engaged reading. It also enhances students' literal, inferential, and critical comprehension.

Instructional Suggestions. To introduce the questioning strategy to students, read a short selection that requires some interpretation. As you read, stop occasionally and ask questions like the following:

- Who is the main character?
- When does this story take place?
- What's the writer's main point here?
- What will happen next?

When you have finished reading the passage, ask the students if they know what you were doing. Explain to them that you were asking yourself questions about the selection as you read, and that this sort of questioning—readers asking themselves about the selection—is a useful way to better understand, remember, and enjoy what one reads.

Display categories and possible questions, like those shown in Table 9.9. Explain to students that these are the kinds of questions readers ask themselves as they try to understand a passage.

After you review these questions, model for students how to employ self-questioning while reading a selection from a book or other media. Think aloud by asking the appropriate setting, event, content, and response questions. Point out to students that there are no "right" questions and that the list shown is only of suggestions. Good questions are any that help them understand and appreciate what they are reading.

Guiding Students' Practice. As students read selections, encourage them to engage in self-questioning. Urge them to ask a variety of questions depending upon the content. It may help students to create a self-questioning chart like that shown in Table 9.10. To help students self-question as they read, have them write setting, event, content, and response questions on the chart.

Comprehension Strategy: Retelling/Summarizing

The retelling and summarizing strategies have readers identify and work with the main ideas and supporting details of a selection. Retelling requires students to restate the

Table 9.9 Questions for the Questioning Strategy

To understand, remember, and enjoy:	You might ask:
Setting	Who are the characters? When and where is this taking place?
Events	What happened? What caused it to happen? What did the author leave out and expect me to figure out? What was the result of these events?
Content	What do I know about this topic? What's the main idea here? How does one event lead to another? What conclusion can I draw?
Response	What would I do? Do I agree with the character's actions? What was funny, sad, or interesting? Does this remind me of something else I have read?

Table 9.10 Questioning Strategy Chart

Selection Title:		
	Questions	Answers
Setting		
Events		
Content		
Response		

major events and supporting details in a selection. Summarizing requires students to extract only the main ideas from a selection.

Instructional Suggestions.   As with all the comprehension strategies, the best way to introduce retelling is to read aloud a short selection and then demonstrate the use of the strategy. In this case, after you read a passage, retell it by restating the main events in order and summarize it by constructing a statement that tells the main ideas of the selection. Then, ask students whether they can describe the two things you just did as well as point out how these two things were alike and how they were different. To clarify their responses, explain that the first was a retelling (saying the events in a selection in the order in which they happened) and the second was a summarization (saying just the main ideas of a selection).

Display the information provided in Table 9.11 and Table 9.12. With the steps for retelling and summarizing visible to students, model how to perform these actions by selecting a short passage to read aloud. After you read the selection, retell it, including the main events and important details in the order in which they happened. Then, summarize the selection, thinking aloud to show how you figured out the main ideas. With the main ideas identified, construct a short statement to express these ideas. Ask students to differentiate between your retelling and your summary. Their answers should include pointing out that retelling is longer, and includes more detail or uses many words from the selection. They might also say that the summary is shorter and includes only the main ideas from the selection.

Guiding Students' Practice.   For students to begin practicing this strategy, select and read another short selection. Invite students, in the large group setting, to offer first a retelling of the passage and then a summary of it. Refer them to the displayed steps if necessary. As they perform the steps, write their retelling and their summary statements side-by-side so that everyone can see them. Then ask students to compare and contrast the retelling and the summary for similarities and differences.

Next, select a short passage for students to read on their own or in small groups, and have them generate both a retelling and a summary. Encourage them to write

Table 9.11 Steps for Retelling

Step	Action
1.	Say or write the main events and important details.
2.	Say or write them in the order in which they happened.

Table 9.12 Steps for Summarizing

Step	Action
1.	Figure out the most important ideas or events in the selection.
2.	Say or write them in a brief statement.

both on the same paper so that they can see them side-by-side, as you modeled in the large group practice. Then, have them consider how their retelling and summary are alike and how they are different. Guide students to thinking about how both practices are helpful for understanding and remembering important ideas in selections.

Enhanced eText Application Exercise 9.6: Ms. Maddox Teaches Specific Comprehension Strategies

---

Bridge: From Teaching Back to Understanding

When teachers find that _____,	then teachers can learn that _____.
What seems second-nature to many good readers may require explicit instruction and modeling for other readers,	Strategies and skills of good reading are often invisible, but teachable; the things strong readers do cannot remain hidden.
Readers' listening comprehension is stronger than their reading comprehension,	Discussions during read-alouds, and opportunities for students to retell and discuss what was read, are vital to both assessment and teaching of reading comprehension.
Students vary in when, where, and how they engage in higher-level thinking during reading,	Higher-level thinking involves an ongoing process of engagement and curiosity, prompting purposeful questions during reading that promote literal, interpretive, critical, and creative comprehension.

Revisiting the Opening Scenario

After reviewing and thinking about the teaching strategies presented in this chapter, provide Ms. Maddox with some specific suggestions on ways she can help Alan learn to use higher-order thinking skills during reading.

Authors' Summary

Before reading our summary statements for each outcome, we suggest you read each outcome and summarize it in your own words.

Once finished, cross-check your response with our brief summary to determine how well you recalled the major points.

9.1 *Discuss how listening comprehension relates to reading comprehension.*

- Both listening and reading comprehension are about ideas people construct from language. As students achieve skill at decoding words, differences in their reading abilities are often attributable to differences in listening vocabulary. Activity that encourages listening comprehension can give teachers valuable information about students' potential in reading comprehension.

9.2 *Discuss different ways to assess comprehension.*

- There are many different ways to assess comprehension, including observation, cloze procedure, maze procedure, oral and written retelling, questioning, and student self-assessment. Asking and

answering three questions will help to select the technique that will target specifically what it is you want to know about students' comprehension. These questions are: What do I want to know? Why do I want to know? How can I best discover this information?

9.3 *Explain one comprehension teaching strategy.*

- In the chapter, several strategies are discussed, including the DRTA, Think Aloud, Repeated Reading, Reciprocal Reading Instruction, Literature Webbing, Questioning, QARs, Re-Quest, and Questioning the Author. Each strategy works in a different way to help students think while they read and to help them get the message that reading is far more than "getting the words right."

9.4 *Explain what comprehension skills are, one way to assess them, and one way to teach them.*

- Comprehension skills fall under four categories in a taxonomy: Literal, Interpretation, Critical Reading, and Creative Reading. One way to assess comprehension skills is through questioning. Students may also demonstrate comprehension through performance, visualization, discussion, retelling, or summarizing.

9.5 *Define comprehension strategies, one way to assess them, and one way to teach them.*

- Strategies represent conscious techniques a student applies while reading to help focus on comprehension. Usually these strategies represent ways of thinking that people recognize among skilled readers but in which this student is not versed. For example, good readers usually recognize that they

should stop and repair when they do not understand. Listening to oral reading is a good way to assess this, because students who do not monitor understanding may continue to read words even after comprehension has broken down. The Think Aloud is a good teaching strategy for this situation, because narrating what the mind does while reading helps teachers (or other students) make the hidden aspects of good reading public for others to hear: "Hmm. I'm going to stop here and look back a few sentences, because I don't think I know what is going on anymore."

Think About It!

1. Generate reading comprehension questions for a selection that would elicit higher-level reading/thinking responses.

2. Present a reading comprehension lesson and record it. Note the kinds of questions you ask. Critique your lesson and state some ways in which you could improve it.

3. Use one of the strategies presented in this chapter to teach a reading lesson.

4. You have a student in your class who has difficulty answering comprehension questions. How would you go about assessing what his problems are? What could you do to help this student?

5. How would you develop a recreational reading program in your classroom? What techniques and procedures would you use? Suggest three ways to encourage students to read voluntarily.

Websites

- http://www.textmapping.org/

    This site provides lesson guides and opportunities to network with others, including teachers and education researchers. The site also contains links to research on reading comprehension skills instruction, and free resources for teacher-trainers, presenters, and university professors.

- https://teachersfirst.com/spectopics/readingstrategies.cfm

    This site provides strategies for before, during, and after reading for teachers to embed in their lesson plans. It contains a description of each strategy and its purpose(s), and then links to a full lesson containing the strategy, in which examples and differentiation possibilities are provided.

- http://www.world-english.org/listening_exercises.htm

    The World-English site provides a variety of listening comprehension exercises. Choose from a variety of topics and focus areas, including but not limited to family histories, news stories, and cars. The site also covers ESL listening comprehension.

Children's Literature Cited

Adler, David. *Don't Talk to Me About the War*. New York: Penguin, 2008.

Auch, Mary Jane, and Herm Auch. *The Plot Chickens*. New York: Holiday House, 2009.

Brown, Ruth. *Toad*. New York: Penguin, 1997.

Bunting, Eve. *How Many Days to America*. New York: Clarion, 1988.

Dewdney, Anna. *Llama Llama Mad at Mama*. New York: Penguin, 2007.

Doyle, A.C. (2009). The Adventures of Sherlock Holmes. Dover.

Doyle, A.C. (2012). A Study in Scarlet. Dover, p. 22.

Galdone, P. (1985). The Little Red Hen. HMH Books for Young Readers.

George, Lindsay Barrett. *In the Garden: Who's Been Here?* New York: HarperCollins, 2006.

Gerstein, Mordicai. *Leaving the Nest.* New York: Farrar, Straus, & Giroux, 2007.

Hall, Donald. *Ox-Cart Man.* New York: Puffin, 1983.

Lewis, J. Patrick. *Spot the Plot: A Riddle Book of Book Riddles.* San Francisco, CA: Chronicle, 2009.

Macdonald, Suse. *Shape by Shape.* New York: Simon & Schuster, 2009.

Martin, Jacqueline Briggs. *Snowflake Bentley.* New York: Houghton Mifflin, 1998.

Parish, Herman. *Amelia Bedelia's First Day of School.* New York: HarperCollins, 2009.

Parry, Florence. *The Day of Ahmed's Secret.* New York: HarperCollins, 2005.

Schaefer, Lola. *An Island Grows.* New York: HarperCollins, 2006.

Snicket, Lemony. *The Composer Is Dead.* New York: HarperCollins, 2009.

Sobol, D.J. (2007). Encyclopedia Brown: Box Set. Puffin.

Swinburne, Stephen. *A Butterfly Grows.* Boston: Houghton Mifflin Harcourt, 2009.

Van Allsburg, Chris. *The Widow's Broom.* New York: Houghton Mifflin, 1992.

Viorst, Judith. *Alexander and the Terrible, Horrible, No Good, Very Bad Day.* New York: Aladdin, 1987.

Yolen, Jane. *Color Me a Rhyme.* Honesdale, PA: Boyds Mills, 2003.

Endnotes

1. Kucer, S. (2009). *Dimensions of literacy* (2nd ed.). Mahwah, NJ: Erlbaum.

2. Ruddell, R. (1966, May). Oral language and the development of other language skills. *Elementary English*, 43, 489–498.

3. Jolly, T. (1980, February). Listen my children and you shall read. *Language Arts*, 57, 214–217.

4. Young, W. (1936, September). The relation of reading comprehension and retention to hearing comprehension and retention. *Journal of Experimental Education*, 5, 30–39.

5. Kelty, A. (1955). An experimental study to determine the effect of listening for certain purposes upon achievement in reading for those purposes. *Abstracts of Field Studies for the Degree of Doctor of Education, 15.* Greeley: Colorado State College of Education, 82–95.

6. Hoffman, S. (1978). *The effect of a listening skills program on the reading comprehension of fourth grade students* (Ph.D. dissertation). *Educational Research Quarterly*, 9, 40–46. Walden University; Dole, J., & Feldman, V. (1984–1985). The development and validation of a listening comprehension test as a predictor of reading comprehension: Preliminary results.

7. Sticht, T., et al. (1974). *Auding and reading: A developmental model.* Alexandria, VA: Human Resources Research Organization; Kintsch, W., & Kozminsky, E. (1977). Summarizing stories after reading and listening. *Journal of Educational Psychology*, 69, 491–499.

8. Dymock, S. (1993, October). Reading but not understanding. *Journal of Reading*, 37, 90.

9. Thorndike, E. (1917, June). Reading as reasoning: A study of mistakes in paragraph reading. *Journal of Educational Psychology* 8(6), 323.

10. Black, C., & Pressley, M. (Eds.). (2002). *Comprehension instruction: Research-based best practices.* New York: Guilford.

11. Taylor, B. (1980). Children's memory for expository text after reading. *Reading Research Quarterly*, 15(3), 399–411; Bartlett, B. (1978). *Top-level structure as an organizational strategy for recall of classroom text.* (unpublished doctoral dissertation). Arizona State University.

12. Richards, J., & Hatcher, C. (1977–1978). Interspersed meaningful learning questions as semantic cues for poor comprehenders. *Reading Research Quarterly*, 13(4), 551–552.

13. Richards and Hatcher, p. 552.

14. Stahl, S., Jacobson, M., Davis, C., & Davis, R. (1989, Winter). Prior knowledge and difficult vocabulary in the comprehension of unfamiliar text. *Reading Research Quarterly*, 24, 29.

15. Ibid., p. 30.

16. Bloom, B. (1956). *Taxonomy of educational objectives hand-book 1: The cognitive domain.* New York: David McKay Co.

17. Smith, N. (1969, December). The many faces of reading comprehension. *The Reading Teacher*, 23, 249–259, 291.

18. Ibid., pp. 255–256.

19. Although, as already stated, all the interpretive skills depend on the reader's ability to infer meanings, the specific skill of "reading between the lines" is the one to which teachers usually refer when they say they are teaching *inference.*

20. Bormuth, J. (1975). The cloze procedure: Literacy in the classroom. In W. Page (Ed.). *Help for the reading teacher: New directions in research* (p. 67). Urbana, IL: National Conference on Research in English.

21. Anderson, R., et al. (1985). *Becoming a nation of readers: The report of the commission on reading* (p. 72). Washington, DC: National Institute of Education.

22. Stauffer, R. (1975). *Directing the reading-thinking process* (p. 37). New York: Harper & Row.

23. Ibid.

24. Davey, B. (1983). Think aloud: Modeling the cognitive processes of reading comprehension. *Journal of Reading, 27*, 44–47.

25. Adapted from Dowhower, S. (1989, March). Repeated reading research into practice. *The Reading Teacher, 42*, 504–506.

26. See Brown, A., Palincsar, A., & Armbruster, B. (1984). Instructing comprehension-fostering activities in interactive learning situations. In H. Mandl, et al. (Eds.). *Learning and comprehension of text.* Hillsdale, NJ: Lawrence Erlbaum.

27. Reutzel, D., & Fawson, P. (1989, December). Using a literature webbing strategy lesson with predictable books. *The Reading Teacher, 43*, 208.

28. Ibid., p. 209.

29. Ibid.

30. Raphael, T. (1986, February). Teaching question-answer relationships, revisited. *The Reading Teacher, 39*, 517.

31. Ibid., p. 518.

32. Ibid.

33. Manzo, A. (1969). The re-quest procedure. *Journal of Reading, 13*, 123–126.

34. Beck, I., McKeown, M., Hamilton, R., & Kucan, L. (1977). *Questioning the author: An approach for enhancing student engagement with text.* Newark, DE: International Reading Association.

35. Afflerbach, P. (1990, Winter). The influence of prior knowledge on expert readers' main idea construction strategies. *Reading Research Quarterly, 25*, 44.

36. Ibid.

37. Cunningham, J., & Moore, D. (1986). The confused world of main idea. In J. Baumann (Ed.), *Teaching main idea comprehension* (p. 2). Newark, DE: International Reading Association.

38. Afflerbach, p. 45.

39. Hare, V., Rabinowitz, M., & Schieble, K. (1989, Winter). Text effects on main idea comprehension. *Reading Research Quarterly, 24*, 72.

40. Ibid.

41. Reed, R, & Lang, T. (1988). *Health behaviors* (p. 328). St. Paul, MN: West Publications.

42. Afflerbach, P., Pearson, P., & Paris, S. (2008). Clarifying differences between reading skills and reading strategies. *The Reading Teacher, 61*(5), 364–373.

Chapter 10
Vocabulary

Alexander Sviridov/Shutterstock

Chapter Outline

Scenario: Mr. Jackson and Vocabulary Expansion

Understanding Vocabulary Acquisition

Assessing Vocabulary

Teaching Vocabulary

Learning Outcomes

After reading this chapter, you should be able to . . .

10.1 Discuss what is involved in acquiring vocabulary.

10.2 Discuss different ways to assess vocabulary.

10.3 Explain guidelines for effective vocabulary instruction and one specific vocabulary teaching strategy.

Scenario

Mr. Jackson and Vocabulary Expansion

Mr. Jackson was feeling dismayed when one student in his sixth-grade reading class said to him, "Mr. Jackson, I have a great amount of animosity toward you."

Mr. Jackson was upset because he thought that he had very good rapport with the student, and thought the student enjoyed being in his class. Because the student's statement did not seem right, Mr. Jackson decided to question him.

"Craig," Mr. Jackson said, "is anything wrong? Have I done anything to offend you in any way?"

Craig appeared perplexed. He looked Mr. Jackson straight in the eye and said, "No, I like your class. I look forward to coming to it."

"If that is true," said Mr. Jackson, "then why did you say you disliked me?"

"I didn't," said Craig. "I said that I like you a lot. I said just the opposite."

What became clear to Mr. Jackson was that Craig did not know the meaning of *animosity*. When Mr. Jackson asked Craig why he used the word *animosity*, Craig replied, "I like the way it looks and sounds, so I use it a lot." This encounter reminded Mr. Jackson that many students use words they can pronounce yet may not fully understand.

Understanding Vocabulary Acquisition

As the opening scenario helps to illustrate, strong vocabulary and proficient reading go hand in hand. Readers must know the meanings words go with if they are to understand what they are reading. Readers need to know how word meanings function in sentences and paragraphs to comprehend texts.

As children advance in concept development, their vocabulary development also advances, because the two are interrelated. (See Chapter 8.) Years ago, MacGinitie noted that "vocabulary is a key variable in reading comprehension and is a major feature of most tests of academic aptitude."[1] Investigators continue to confirm this earlier finding.[2] For example, Daneman remarks: "Numerous researchers have noted that poor readers have smaller vocabularies than good readers. Indeed, vocabulary knowledge is one of the best single predictors of reading comprehension."[3] Current researchers point to the need for readers to have not only a wide reading vocabulary, but also depth in meaning for those words, and strengths in relatedness among meanings.[4] Wide, deep, and connected vocabulary is positively correlated to comprehension for a variety of texts.[5]

Just how is it that readers acquire a reading vocabulary? The easiest answer to this question is "through wide reading." Readers who already have a deep vocabulary are much less troubled by difficult text.[6] But this kind of research leaves teachers with a puzzle. How do we help people get this kind of rich background when they don't already have it, and may even become frustrated by failed attempts to succeed, or who do not read widely, because it is such hard labor? Foundational research in cognitive science suggests that there are two central facts about vocabulary that should shape assessment and teaching. The first is that meanings have words, and not the other way around. The second is that words are used in three main ways in life: for everyday social and personal use, for bookish academic use, and for specialist use.

Meanings have Words

Why insist that meanings have words, and not the other way around? Imagine a coat rack where kids hang things at the start of the day. Now imagine the coat rack without any hooks or hangers. What will happen when kids try to hang up hoodies, coats, and backpacks on a bare wall? Everything will fall to the ground. What will happen when kids go to collect their things at the end of the day? Chaos. Nothing will be where they thought they left it, and coats and backpacks will be mixed up and lost. Meanings are like hooks on a coat rack. Words are like jackets, backpacks, and hoodies. Without a hook, these items have nowhere to go and simply fall to the ground, and cannot be sorted or retrieved easily. All too frequently, young readers experience vocabulary instruction that works like a hookless coat rack. Teachers might teach words and give brief access to definitions (a suggestion that there should be a hook and maybe a glimpse of what a hook looks like). The old standby vocabulary list, copying the word, and copying its definition are familiar routines to most people who have gone through schools in the United States.

By contrast, effective vocabulary instruction involves far more focus on meaning than on lists of words. The teaching involves teachers either "installing the hooks" (teaching meaning) or finding hooks learners already have in place (building on prior knowledge). Paul Bloom's research suggests that when meanings are developed well first, words are merely information or labels that get associated with meaning. Meanings can gain deep and permanent places in long-term memory, and when words get associated with meanings, they not only last longer but they also function as a kind of index or mnemonic device to access meanings for use in the world. Words help learners call up memories. Knowing vocabulary words across time depends on their becoming associated with meaning. Without meanings, words have no place to go and will most likely be flushed out of short-term memory. During sleep, the brain organizes and consolidates short-term memories. Memories that cannot be organized and consolidated into existing long-term mental structures (like stories or useful categories) usually get wiped clean during sleep.

As an example of vocabulary learning, the history curriculum in the West has much vocabulary about gold mining. Two key vocabulary words show up in reading materials about gold mining: *placer* and *lode*. But most elementary students have not spent much time in and around gold mines. Saying these words and telling students the definitions is like trying to hang a coat on a wall with no hooks. Teachers must discover which learners already have hooks: basic images and ideas about what a gold mine is, how it works, what it looks like, and what people do there. Learning about existing hooks—background knowledge—is the starting point for learning and teaching vocabulary.[7] Those who recognize images of gold panning have a place where they can file the term "placer mining." Those who recognize a shaft mine or pit mine (even if only from a movie or game) have existing meaning for the term "lode mining." Showing students many pictures of gold mines and getting students talking about what they see can give teachers a sense for existing meanings, meanings to which words can be added. Even a student who has used a kitchen spoon to dig for pretend treasure in the yard has background knowledge to awaken when looking at pictures of miners and mining. For students new to these meanings, seeing pictures and videos, going on field trips, and handling mining equipment all would be important ways to build meaning to which words can attach. For students without much background knowledge, teaching a list of ten or twenty words without meanings would be pointless. Words are more likely to have hooks to hang on when teachers spend time assessing and teaching meaning.

Readers encounter unfamiliar words in all types of reading, and teachers certainly need to teach new vocabulary for reading in general and for content learning in specific. What is essential is that teachers not make the mistake of teaching words *instead of* meanings. Effective teachers must assess and teach with the understanding that meanings provide us with more hope of long-term memory for learned words. Building meaning is so much more than merely giving definitions.

Three Worlds of Words: Everyday, Academic, and Specialized

The way dictionaries are organized promotes the fallacy that words come first and meanings next. Dictionary definitions often depend on existing background knowledge. Good dictionary writers try to write definitions that connect to **everyday** language whenever possible. For example, the first definition for "difficult" at *Wiktionary. org* reads "Hard, not easy, requiring much effort." The writer of this dictionary entry worked to find common concepts a reader might already have available on which to hang the **bookish academic** word "difficult." By contrast, the mining definition for *placer* is third on its Wiktionary page: "occurring in a deposit of sand or earth on a riverbed or bank, particularly with reference to precious metals such as gold or silver." The reader who already has an image of gold panning in mind may be able to assimilate this **specialized** meaning and word. But to the reader without background knowledge in the very narrow field of gold mining, the definition for *placer* is just something vaguely involved with rivers and gold. Moreover, the definition depends on bookish academic words like *particularly, reference to* and *precious*. This writer assumed anyone looking up the specialized word *placer* must already have strengths in both gold mining and bookish academic words. Although dictionaries can be useful tools, teachers cannot rely on them to teach vocabulary, because access to meaning can be blocked by assumptions the writer makes about readers.

Enhanced eText **Application Exercise 10.1 (video):** Bookish and Specialized Words

Direct Vocabulary Instruction and Strategic Instruction

Certainly, explicit instruction is one way to develop vocabulary knowledge. In fact, the development of vocabulary is too important to readers' success to be left to chance. Teachers need to provide readers with a vocabulary growth program in all grades. "Direct vocabulary instruction is generally shown to result in an increase in both word knowledge and reading comprehension."[8] But remember that there are only about 175 days in a school year. Knowing that active readers may learn tens of thousands of meanings each year from free-choice reading alone reminds educators that only an extremely limited number of words and meanings can be taught directly by teachers. Because of these limits, selecting vocabulary meanings and words for direct teaching should reflect the content and thinking teachers and students agree they value the most.

For a vocabulary instruction program to be successful, teachers must recognize that individual differences exist between the amounts and kinds of words learners have in their listening vocabularies (i.e., the ability to understand a word when it is spoken). Some children come to school with a rich and varied set of meanings and words, whereas others have a more limited and narrow vocabulary.[9] How much the speaking and listening vocabulary expands for all readers in school depends on how much time is devoted to talking for a variety of purposes. In fact, recent researchers found that learners are better at inferring new word meanings in listening than in reading.[10] Unfortunately very few schools embrace and develop a curriculum for talk. So teachers should not be surprised when vocabulary gaps persist into intermediate grades and middle school, or when these affect overall reading achievement. Young children's listening vocabulary is usually larger than their speaking vocabulary, and both of these are usually much larger than reading and writing vocabularies.

Figure 10.1 Children's Vocabularies

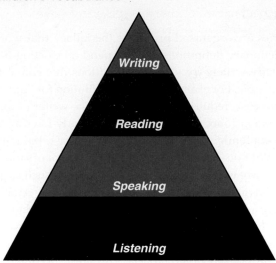

(See Figure 10.1.) Researchers suggest that people's reading vocabulary is mostly also found in their speaking and listening vocabularies.[11] All modes of language are strengthened by strengths in vocabulary. However, since children first learn language through listening and speaking, continuing to expand this oral-language vocabulary is necessary to build a foundation that can be used as a strength in learning to read and write.

There are three basic ways teachers can help children to acquire words: (1) create a meaning-rich environment; (2) facilitate independent word gathering; and (3) model the active search for words that go with meanings.[12] Taken together, all these routes to vocabulary acquisition help children to develop vocabulary consciousness, a principal objective of vocabulary instruction. Direct teaching of specific meanings and words is important and can be effective, yet vocabulary teaching *must also* include strategic thinking tools that help students gather and remember words on their own.[13] In assessment, teachers want to learn not only what kinds of meanings and words readers already know, but also about their strategies for noticing, gathering, and remembering new meanings and words. This will go far in helping students gain vocabulary knowledge from their free-choice and academic reading.

Gaps in vocabulary learning often form along the lines of academic and specialized language, so learners' awareness of these kinds of language is a fundamental area for assessment and teaching. For example, the synonyms *hard, difficult, complex, technical,* and *abstruse* are not experienced equally in life. People in general might have multiple daily encounters with the word "hard," fewer daily hits on "difficult," and still fewer for academic and specialized synonyms. English speakers and writers use academic and specialized words for two key reasons: First, these words connote nuances and precision that everyday social words do not; second, these forms of language are a way of assuming power or authority. Because teachers want young learners to gain access to the language of power and also to go beyond the limits of everyday social talk, teachers need to give them tools to help readers connect to academic and specialized meanings and the words that go with them.

In review, foundational research on vocabulary learning suggests that meanings have words, like hooks waiting for something to be hung on them. Time spent activating and building meaning is central to teaching and learning vocabulary words. Moreover, teachers and learners must understand and navigate three different worlds of vocabulary: the everyday social world, the bookish academic world, and the specialist world. Designing effective teaching and learning depends on these foundations.

Vocabulary Consciousness

In primary grades, children encounter words spelled the same but with different meanings, based on context in sentences. Students learn that the word *saw* in "I saw Jennifer" carries a different meaning than in "Andrew will help his uncle saw the wood." When children recognize that *saw, train, coat,* and many other words have multiple meanings that are discernable based on surrounding words, this is a sign they are building a reading **vocabulary consciousness.** Another sign is when they begin to ask about meanings of new words they come across. When teachers see these signs, they can be certain students are developing vocabulary consciousness—known by researchers to be a promising lead toward increasing comprehension.[14] Purposeful talking with children is one way to help them develop vocabulary consciousness.[15] Discussing word meanings every day is an important start to assessment, because through ongoing discussions, we as teachers will become aware that students develop word meanings through a developmental process.

Stages of Knowing a Word

Learners appear to go through several stages of knowing word meanings. We illustrate these levels as a ladder in Figure 10.2. The figure also shows that to move up the ladder, children need much meaningful practice and repeated exposure. The first level is where they display no awareness of the word, neither recognizing it visually nor understanding it. Assuming learners continue to work to acquire the word, they then move into the second level, which is where they begin to be somewhat acquainted with the word. Learners recognize it as familiar, but with difficulty recalling its meaning or pronunciation across contexts. This is similar to being introduced to a new person and then seeing the person in another situation and not recognizing them immediately. If we are fortunate to be with someone who can give us a hint, we might remember the person. We *recognize* the person because we were prompted. Likewise, familiar words can be remembered with prompts. The third level, the one learners strive to reach with words they feel are important, is the identification stage. At this level, they can identify a word instantaneously, have a working understanding of how and when to use it, and can develop deeper meanings along with the word. Once learners are at this third stage, they continue to deepen their mastery of meanings. Vocabulary acquisition is never truly "complete" for any word.[16] Take the word *catastrophe*, for example. While many are familiar with the word and can identify it without difficulty, 9/11 certainly helped many readers develop a deeper meaning of the word. Any life experience or new reading might lead to deeper meaning.

> **Enhanced eText**
> **Teacher Resource:**
> Vocabulary Knowledge Chart
> Vocabulary Bookish-Specialized Chart

Figure 10.2 Levels of Knowing a Word

Levels of Knowing a Word

- can identify
- attain deeper, richer knowledge of the word

- can recognize
- somewhat acquainted

- not known

Practice ~ Repeated exposure

Types of Words

When thinking of teaching reading vocabulary, teachers need to remember that not all words are created equal. Try this exercise and see if you can determine which word in each group is the easiest for a reader to learn:

Group 1	Group 2
ant	of
and	said
are	elephant

Did you select *ant* from the first group and *elephant* from the second group? If so, you are correct, because both are nouns. Nouns are easier to learn to read than other words because readers can associate a concrete image with them. Even though *elephant* is a much longer word, it is much easier to picture than *of*! Two reasons so many young children can identify the word for nearly any kind of a dinosaur are that they are interested in knowing about dinosaurs and that each name has a distinct image associated with it. Concrete words, such as action verbs, nouns, and adjectives, are easy for students to learn and do not make high demands for context. They can stand alone.

By contrast, grammatical function words (GFW) often are difficult to define and cannot be understood well without the other words they 'glue' together. Do you have a good definition for the word "the" that you could use to explain it to a person whose language does not have that meaning? Often grammatical function words contain fewer letters, but they also make high demands for context in order to be understood. For example, the preposition "to" is easy to demonstrate with the verb "give" and a noun: *Give the bag to Shawn*. Without this context, it is difficult to understand what "to" means. Linguistic terminology like "preposition" or "article" may not be helpful in early stages of vocabulary learning, because these labels assume learners have enough working knowledge of types of words to form a category.

Homophones and homographs—the two main kinds of homonyms—are other types of words common to English that may be more difficult to learn. The meaning of one word can get in the way of another word that sounds or looks the same.

Beyond these linguistic types of words, some of the most important categories for words are based on usage. Some words might be used in many general situations and others only in specific situations. For example, soap might be used in many different cleaning situations, but *detergent* is a word we tend to use for specific situations, like dishwashing or laundry. A specialized term like *amphiphilic surfactant* might be used only in a chemistry lab. Likewise, some words might be used more in everyday social language and others only in academic, bookish situations. Even when a word like *stay* might mean the same thing as *remain*, one is more likely to come up in everyday social conversation and the other more likely to appear in print. Both words can be used in both situations, but young learners need to develop awareness that there is another set of vocabulary and grammar words that follow printed language. This awareness will help learners to know how to pay attention to new words, connect them to known language, and predict situations where each kind of word is likely to show up.

In review, assessing and teaching vocabulary depends on teachers' knowledge about types of words. Teachers need to understand the difference between concrete words, with a clear sensory meaning, and grammatical function words, which are used to create relationships between other meanings. *Food* and *table* are concrete nouns. The word *on* in "The food is *on* the table" tells how the two nouns relate to each other. Try replacing the word *on* with *under, around, in,* or *by*. This makes it easy to visualize the way a grammatical function word changes the relationship between food and table. Other types of words are determined by situations. Teachers need to understand that some vocabulary learning depends on understanding general versus specialized meanings, and on understanding the difference between everyday social language and bookish academic language. Knowing these types of words will help teachers understand and use many of the assessment and teaching techniques researchers suggest are most important.

Sight Vocabulary

Sight words are those words that readers can identify without conscious decoding; they know them instantaneously. All readers have their own personalized sight vocabulary because they have varied interests, which lead them to read texts associated with those interests. For example, an individual who is interested in sports would have a different personalized sight vocabulary than a person interested in music. That said, when teachers talk of helping children to develop sight vocabulary, they are often really referring to **high-frequency** words. These are words that occur most often in children's books— hence the label *high-frequency*. Different researchers have compiled high-frequency lists. Two of the most common lists are the Dolch list and the Fry Instant Word List. Because the Fry Instant Word List is more current, we provide a copy of the first 100 words in Figure 10.3. Teachers need to recognize that children may come to school with a huge store of sight words because of interests and background knowledge, yet few of these sight words might come from the high-frequency lists.

Figure 10.3 The Instant Words* First Hundred

These are the most common words in English, ranked in frequency order. The first 25 make up about a third of all printed material. The first 100 make up about half of all written material. Is it any wonder that all students must learn to identify these words instantly?

Words 1–25	*Words 26–50*	*Words 51–75*	*Words 76–100*
the	or	will	number
of	one	up	no
and	had	other	way
a	by	about	could
to	word	out	people
in	but	many	my
is	not	then	than
you	what	them	first
that	all	these	water
it	were	so	been
he	we	some	call
was	when	her	who
for	your	would	oil
on	can	make	its
are	said	like	now
as	there	him	find
with	use	into	long
his	an	time	down
they	each	has	day
I	which	look	did
at	she	two	get
be	do	more	come
this	how	write	made
have	their	go	may
from	if	see	part

Common suffixes: *-s, -ing, -ed*

*Source: The Reading Teacher's Book of Lists by, 2000, Copyright [2000, E. Fry, D. Fountoukidis, and J. Polk.] "This material is reproduced with permission of John Wiley & Sons, Inc."

Defining Word Part Terms

Discussing vocabulary with readers depends on being able to describe and recognize different kinds of word parts. The subsections that follow define different word parts vital to assessment and teaching.

Affixes are word parts that can be added to **roots**. You can combine a root word with a meaning either at the beginning (**prefix**) or end (**suffix**) of the root word to form a new, related word—for example, *replay* or *played*. *Affix* is a term used to refer either to a prefix or a suffix. In the word *replayed, play* is a root or base, *re-* is a prefix, and *-ed* is a suffix. A **root** is the smallest part of a word that holds its basic meaning. It cannot be divided any further by removing affixes. *Replay* is simpler than *replayed*, but is not a root word, because it can still be subdivided into *re-* and *play. Play* is a root word, because it cannot be divided further and still retain a meaning related to the root word. When we divide *pl* and *ay*, we may find two useful phonics patterns, but not two meanings. Understanding *replayed* with its two affixes depends on understanding the root *play.* Many students experience confusion when they encounter words with multiple affixes in reading. It is vital that teachers encourage the use of academic–bookish language and specialized language in talking and listening throughout the school day.

Compound words are words made by combining roots, like *football, grandfather* or *boardwalk*. These words may be confusing to young learners who expect them to have a space between them. Teachers need to know and recognize compound words and how to help readers work with them in reading and writing. The word *understand* is a compound so old its history is not known, and breaking it into two parts does not automatically give away its meaning. But still, reading this word correctly depends on readers seeing the two parts of the compound. Some compounds that appear mostly in academic language are old compounds that are hard to understand merely by separating the roots, like *whatsoever,* or *inasmuch.*

Derivatives are usually discussed when a root changes because of its affixes For example, the word *arrive* loses its final *e* when it gets the suffix *-al* (as do all words with a silent final *e* in U.S. English), and the new words formed with suffixes are pronounced with a short vowel sound different from the root. The word *jumping* is not a derivative, because the root *jump* does not change in spelling or vowel sound due to the affix *-ing.* Much academic language will involve Latin, Greek, and English derivatives. For example, the word *imperative* (suggesting a command) derives from the same Latin root as *emperor* (someone who gives commands). Reading and spelling academic language depends less on full knowledge of Latin roots, and more on a working awareness of how Latin and Greek words are written and pronounced in today's English. How would you pronounce the made-up word *schimbational*? What working knowledge do you have of word parts that would help you make an educated guess rather than a random one?

Combining forms are usually roots borrowed from another language that join together with affixes or as compounds to form a new word. *Electro-* is a combining form, but cannot stand on its own as a word. We expect to see *electric* when this meaning is not combined, but in words like *electronic, electroshock,* or *electromagnetic,* we see the combining form. English uses a predictable set of combining forms from Greek and Latin.[17] Although we may understand the words *accelerate* and *decelerate,* the combining form is not used on its own in English—there is no word "celerate" or "celer" that stands on its own, even though English clearly has two words that use this Latin combining form.

Affixes, compounds, derivatives, and combining forms explain much of the diversity and variety in English vocabulary words. Language used in specialized situations or bookish academic situations often rely on the flexibility we have for inventing new words using Latin, Greek, and other roots. Before the 1800s, there was no such thing as a *refrigerator*. Before the 1990s, there was no widely used *Internet*. As teachers work with students beyond the primary grades, success in teaching reading and writing will depend on knowing when meanings of words depend on predictable parts.

Context Clues

Students need to learn that words have multiple meanings, and must understand how to determine the correct meanings from sentence context. Context clues are a vital aid in learning vocabulary and reading comprehension because there is such ambiguity in the English language. There are eight types of context clues. Each type needs to be taught to students so they have a variety of context-based strategies.[18]

1. **Definition, Explanation, and Description Context Clues.** There are times when you can get the meaning of a word from context clues. By *context*, we mean the words surrounding a word that can shed light on its meaning.

If the writer wants to make sure that you get the meaning of a word, she will define, explain, or describe the word in the sentence. The **context clue** in the form of definition, description, or explanation is the specific item of information that helps the reader to figure out the meaning of a particular word. For example, the word *context* has been defined because it is a key word in this section. The definition is the context clue. In the following examples, the writer actually gives the reader the definition of a word. (Authors of textbooks or technical journals are often coached by editors to provide this kind of definition context.)

Examples

1. An *axis* is a straight line, real or imaginary, that passes through the center of rotation of a revolving body at a right angle to the plane of rotation.
2. In geometry, a plane figure of six sides and six angles is called a *hexagon*.

In the next examples, notice how the writers *describe* the words they want readers to know.

1. Although my *diligent* friend works from morning to night, he never complains.
2. Interior paints no longer contain *toxic* materials that might endanger the health of infants and small children.
3. The *cryptic* message—which looks as mysterious and secretive as it is—is difficult to decode.

The word *or* may be used by the writer when he uses another word or words with a similar meaning. Example: John said that he felt ill after having eaten *rancid* or *spoiled* butter.

The words *that is* and its abbreviation *i.e.* usually signal that an explanation will follow. Example: "A human is a biped—that is, an animal with only two feet," or "A human is a biped (i.e., an animal with only two feet)."

2. **Example Context Clues.** Many times, an author helps readers get the meaning of a word by giving *examples* illustrating the use of the word. Notice how the example that the writer gives in the following sentence helps readers determine the meaning of the word *illuminated*.

   Example: The lantern *illuminated* the cave so well that we were able to see the crystal formations and even spiders crawling on the rocks.
   (From the sentence, you can determine that *illuminated* means "lit up.")

3. **Comparison Context Clues.** Another technique writers employ that can help readers gain the meaning of a word is *comparison*. Comparison usually shows the similarities between persons, ideas, and things. For example, in the following sentence, notice how readers can determine the meaning of *passive* through the writer's comparison of Paul to a bear in winter:

   Example: Paul is as *passive* as a bear sleeping away the winter.
   (From the sentence, you can determine that *passive* means "inactive.")

Enhanced eText
Video Example 10.1
In this **video clip**, a teacher works with students to determine meanings of unfamiliar words in a content-based text.

4. **Contrast Context Clues.** **Contrast** is another method writers use that can help readers figure out word meanings. Contrast is usually used to show differences between persons, ideas, and things. In the following sentence, readers can determine the meaning of *optimist* because they know that *optimist* is somehow the opposite of *"one who is gloomy or one who expects the worst."*

> *Example:* My sister Marie is an *optimist,* but her boyfriend is one who is always gloomy and expects the worst to happen.
> (From the sentence, you can determine that optimist means "one who expects the best" or "one who is cheerful.")

The writer may use the words *for example* or the abbreviation *e.g.* to signal that examples are to follow. Example: *Condiments*—for example, pepper, salt, and mustard—make food taste better. (From the examples of condiments, you can determine that condiments are seasonings.)

An example is something that is representative of a whole or a group. It can be a particular single item, incident, fact, or situation that typifies the whole.

Many times such words as *but, yet, although, however,* and *rather than* signal that a contrast is being illustrated. Example: My father thought he owned an *authentic* antique chest, but he was told recently that it was a fake. (From the sentence, you can tell that *authentic* is the opposite of *fake;* therefore, *authentic* means "not false but genuine or real.")

5. **Synonym and Antonym Context Clues.** Often a word can be defined by another, more familiar word having basically the same meaning. For example, *void* is defined as *empty* and *corpulent* is defined as *fat*. *Void* and *empty,* and *corpulent* and *fat,* are synonyms. **Synonyms** are different words that have the same or nearly the same meaning. Writers use synonyms to make their writing clearer and more expressive.

Examples

a. (1) The frightened child *looked* at the man.
   (2) The frightened child *peered* at the man.
b. (1) We *walked* through the park.
   (2) We *strolled* through the park.
c. (1) The *noise* brought the police to the scene.
   (2) The *uproar* brought the police to the scene.

Antonyms are words opposite in meaning to each other. Examples: tall–short; fat–thin; least–most; worst–best. Antonyms, which are used to show contrast, help to make sentences clearer and more informative.

Examples

1. My biology professor gives *succinct* lectures, but his assistant is *verbose*.

2. My math professor claims that all the problems she gives us are *simple* ones, but we feel that they are *intricate* and hard to solve.

6. **Homonym Context Clues.** Many words have multiple meanings, such as *will,* or *orange*. These words are called *homonyms*. The usage-specific meaning of a homonym is determined by the way it is used in a sentence. For example, see the multiple uses of the term *run* following. In the sentences here, notice how the word's placement in the sentence and the surrounding words help readers to figure out the appropriate meaning.

Examples

1. Walk, don't *run*.

2. I have a *run* in my stocking.

Enhanced eText
Video Example 10.2

In this **video clip**, a teacher works with a small group of students to demonstrate the strategy Word Snapshot.

3. Senator Jones said that he would not *run* for another term.

4. The trucker finished his *run* to Detroit.

5. She is going to *run* a ten-mile race.

6. The play had a *run* of two years.

In sentence 1, *run* means "go quickly by moving the legs more rapidly than at a walk."

In sentence 2, *run* means "a tear or an unraveling of stitches."

In sentence 3, *run* means "campaign as a candidate for election."

In sentence 4, *run* means "route."

In sentence 5, *run* means "take part in a race."

In sentence 6, *run* means "continuous course of performances."

7. **Homograph Context Clues.** Some pairs or groups of words are spelled the same but do not sound the same. For example, *refuse* means "trash"; *refuse* means "to decline to accept." In the sentences below, *refuse* meaning "trash" is pronounced differently from *refuse* meaning "to decline to accept." Readers can determine the meaning of *refuse* from the way it is used in the sentence—that is, from context clues.

   1. During the garbage strike, there were tons of uncollected *refuse* on the streets of the city.

   2. I *refuse* to go along with you on that project because it seems unethical to me.

8. **Homophone Context Clues.** *Homophones* are pairs or groups of words that sound alike but have different spellings and meanings. Here are some examples of homonyms or homophones. In the example sentences following, notice how the pronunciation of the words is the same, but the meanings and spellings are different.

   1. One *way* to stay healthy is to *weigh* oneself.

   2. I ate *plain* yogurt while flying on a *plane*.

Categorization

The ability to divide items into categories is an important thinking skill. As children advance as readers, they should be able to differentiate items and group them into increasingly more complex categories. Primary-grade children should be able to categorize a cat as distinct from a mouse or a rabbit. They should be able to group cat, dog, and cow together as animals. As these children develop their thinking skills, they should be able to proceed from more generalized classifications to more specialized ones. We provide assessment and teaching strategies for categorization later in this chapter.

Analogies

Analogies represent inferential thinking. They transfer relationships from one subject to another. Instead of comparing words directly, an analogy gets readers focused on the reasons for the connections between words. Analogies actually help students focus on the nature of the connection—why things compare, not just whether they do or do not compare. To make analogies, students must have a good stock of vocabulary and the ability to see relationships. Students who are able to classify often still need help understanding how analogies work.

Teachers can begin to expose children to simple analogies based on familiar relationships.[19] To be able to make the best use of analogies or to complete an analogy statement (sometimes called a *proportion*), children must (a) know the meanings of the words and (b) know the relationships between words. For example: *Sad is to happy as good is to _____*. Students who know the meanings of *sad* and *happy* may also know

Figure 10.4 The Analogy Compares the *Relationship* between Words

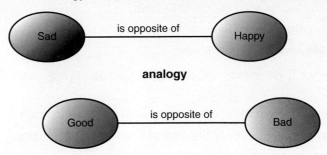

that *sad* is the opposite of *happy*; consequently, we can help them learn to complete the analogy with a word like *bad, evil, awful, naughty,* or *rotten.* (See Figure 10.4.)

Some of the relationships words may have to one another are similar meanings, opposite meanings, members of a class, going from particular to general, going from general to particular, degree of intensity, specialized labels, characteristics, cause and effect, function, whole to part, and ratio. There is almost no end to the ways we might characterize relationships, so the relationships mentioned above do not have to be memorized. Tell students they will gain clues from the pairs making up the analogies; that is, the words express the relationship. For example: with "*pretty* is to *beautiful*, "the relationship is degree of intensity (the state of being stronger, greater, or more than); for "*hot* is to *cold,*" the relationship is one of opposites; and with "*car* is to *vehicle,*" the relationship is classification.

To ensure students' success, review the word lists of the analogy exercises to determine whether students are familiar with the vocabulary. Encourage them to use dictionaries to look up any unfamiliar words. Analogy activities can be done in small groups or with the entire class as well as individually. If children work individually, review the answers together in a group so that interaction and discussion can further enhance vocabulary development. These activities can be done orally or with writing.

Enhanced eText Application Exercise 10.2: Mr. Jackson's Understanding of Vocabulary

---

Bridge: From Understanding to Assessment

When teachers understand that _____,	then teachers may want to assess _____.
Vocabulary depends on meanings and concepts,	Students' background knowledge in everyday synonyms for academic words and background knowledge in specialized topics before teaching and discussing these.
Speaking and listening vocabulary are related to reading vocabulary,	What kinds of words students know how to use in everyday social speech.
Academic and specialized words are less likely to already exist in many students' speaking and reading vocabularies,	Whether students are aware of differences between everyday social registers of language and the academic and specialized registers.
English words have many meaningful parts, including roots, affixes, and morphemes,	Whether specific affixes, roots, or morphemes are behind students' misunderstandings of word meanings.
Word identification in print is stronger for words students already know in their speaking and listening vocabularies,	Students' self-awareness of how familiar they are with words in a text.
Grammatical function words (GFWs) are less concrete than nouns, verbs, and adjectives,	Whether word miscues happen more frequently for abstract words than for concrete words.
There are many kinds of context clues readers use to understand new word uses,	Whether students use a breadth of context strategies to figure out meanings.

Assessing Vocabulary

As we mention throughout this text, assessment drives instruction. This is true for vocabulary instruction as for any other aspect of reading. Three questions continually surface: What do I want to know? Why do I want to know? How can I best discover it? In terms of vocabulary, we want to know about several dimensions. We can approach these questions in two main ways.

First, assessment techniques mentioned in earlier chapters such as observing reading and conferring with students are excellent tools for answering questions about word meanings. Teachers can use checklists such as those shown in Figure 10.5 and

Figure 10.5 Diagnostic Checklist for Vocabulary Development (Primary Grades)

	Yes	No
Student's Name: _____		
Grade: _____		
Teacher: _____		
1. The student shows that he or she is developing a vocabulary consciousness by recognizing that some words have more than one meaning.		
2. The student uses context clues to figure out word meanings.		
3. The student can state the opposite of words such as *stop, tall, fat, long, happy, big.*		
4. The student can state the synonym of words such as *big, heavy, thin, mean, fast, hit.*		
5. The student can state different meanings for homographs (words that are spelled the same but have different meanings) based on their use in a sentence. Examples: I did not *state* what *state* I live in. Do not *roll* the *roll* on the floor. *Train* your dog not to bark when he hears a *train.*		
6. The student is developing a vocabulary of the senses by being able to state words that describe various sounds, smells, sights, tastes, and touches.		
7. The student is expanding his or her vocabulary by combining two words to form compound words such as *grandfather, bedroom, cupcake, backyard, toothpick, buttercup, firefighter.*		
8. The student is expanding his or her vocabulary by combining roots of words with prefixes and suffixes. Examples: *return, friendly, unhappy, disagree, dirty, precook, unfriendly.*		
9. The student is able to give the answer to a number of word riddles.		
10. The student is able to make up a number of word riddles.		
11. The student is able to classify various objects such as fruits, animals, colors, pets, and so on.		
12. The student is able to give words that are associated with certain objects and ideas. Example: hospital—*nurse, doctor, beds, sick people, medicine,* and so on.		
13. The student is able to complete some analogy proportions such as *Happy is to sad as fat is to_____ .*		
14. The student shows that he or she is developing a vocabulary consciousness by using the dictionary to look up unknown words.		

Figure 10.6 Diagnostic Checklist for Vocabulary Development (Intermediate Grades)

Student's Name: _____

Grade: _____

Teacher: _____

	Yes	No
1. The student recognizes that many words have more than one meaning.		
2. The student uses context clues to figure out the meanings.		
3. The student can give synonyms for words such as *similar, secluded, passive, brief, old, cryptic, anxious.*		
4. The student can give antonyms for words such as *prior, most, less, best, optimist, rash, humble, content.*		
5. The student can state different meanings for homographs (words that are spelled the same but have different meanings) based on their use in a sentence, for example: It is against the law to *litter* the streets. The man was placed on the *litter* in the ambulance. My dog gave birth to a *litter* of puppies.		
6. The student is able to use word parts to figure out word meanings.		
7. The student is able to use word parts to build words.		
8. The student is able to complete analogy statements or proportions.		
9. The student is able to give the connotative meaning of a number of words.		
10. The student is able to work with word categories.		
11. The student is able to answer a number of word riddles.		
12. The student is able to make up a number of word riddles.		
13. The student uses the dictionary to find word meanings.		

Figure 10.6 to document observations for primary- and middle-grade readers' vocabulary development. Remember that these observations need to occur in a variety of contexts while students are reading a variety of texts.

Second, teachers can use teacher-created informal assessments such as the ones shown later in this chapter. These can be used to help shed light on which students might need additional help learning a given aspect of vocabulary.

Third, teachers can use a more formal tool such as the Peabody Picture Vocabulary Test (PPVT) or the Expressive Vocabulary Test (EVT) to get information about a reader's listening and speaking vocabulary. Although these tests cannot assess the number of words a reader knows, it can help teachers learn about specific categories of meaning and how strongly these categories are associated with words. These picture tests work on two principles teachers can adapt and use in the classroom for ongoing formative assessment: 1). Teachers can assess receptive vocabulary (words readers understand when they hear them) by bringing pictures to readers and asking them to point to specific things in the picture. By pointing, readers show they understand a word's meaning without needing to say it or read it; and 2). Teachers can assess expressive vocabulary (words readers know how to use in talking) by bringing pictures to readers and asking them to talk about what they see. In the EVT, a variety of prompts are designed to get readers thinking about synonyms, categories, and labels for meanings. These visual approaches do not guarantee children will have the same vocabulary for reading that they have for speaking and listening. But it is well understood that strengths found in the listening vocabulary are foundational for reading comprehension. Teachers can use pictures to learn which areas of spoken language are already strengths for each reader.

Clearly, purpose dictates the selection of the most appropriate assessment measure (Table 10.1). keep in mind that measuring the number of words in a person's vocabulary is nearly impossible. So what is essential is to know whether students have a store of words they can call on when reading, thereby enabling comprehension. Teachers must also find out about readers' vocabulary consciousness, which has to do with their desire to explore and add breadth (new words) and depth (added meanings) to their reading vocabulary.

Table 10.1 Three Important Questions for Assessing Vocabulary

What Do I Want to Know?	Why Do I Want to Know?	How Can I Best Discover It?
Do students have a store of sight words?	Having a sight vocabulary is essential for reading. If a student is limited in this area, I need to provide opportunities for the students to acquire and apply new words.	• Observation • Word test from IRI
Are students developing a vocabulary consciousness?	Having a desire to learn words is a sure way for students to continue to expand their vocabularies, making comprehension of increasingly more complex texts possible.	• Self-selection strategy • Talking with students • Students' contributions to Word Wall
Are students able to apply what they know about word parts as one way to learn about new words?	The purpose for learning word parts is to use them when reading. I want to know if students are applying what they are learning, and if not, why not.	• Talking with students • Observation
How much time do students spend reading?	Wide reading is one way for students to acquire a large vocabulary. I need to ensure the allocation of time in school for this reading, especially if students are not able to read after school for one reason or another.	• Independent Reading Record • Observation
How do students use context clues?	Good readers use a variety of context clues to figure out word meanings. Teachers need to know which clues students use, and which ones they need to learn.	• Observation
In what ways do students categorize words?	When students divide items into categories, it shows that they are organizing words into meaningful schemata, or mental maps.	• Chart for Categorizing Vocabulary Usage (Figure 10.7)
In what ways do students use relationships between and among words to better understand them?	Relationships are connections, and students who can see relationships between words and classifications of words show evidence of a meaningful schema, and also of higher-level thinking skills.	• Observation during oral analogies exercises

---

Enhanced eText Application Exercise 10.3: Mr. Jackson Assesses Vocabulary

---

Bridge: From Assessment to Teaching

If an assessment shows that ____,	then teachers may want to teach ____.
Readers understand and read concrete words correctly, but not grammatical function words (GFWs),	Students to be aware of how these words change the meanings of phrases and sentences (*what* instead of *where*, or *this* instead of *that*).
Readers miscue mostly on new specialized content words (such as science or social studies terms),	Readers to preview these words before beginning. Activating background knowledge that may include synonyms and meanings useful for this specialty area. Some words that will be most essential for many readers to succeed at reading about a specialized topic. Overall awareness of the specialized register (Tier 3) as compared with everyday social speech.
Readers miscue mostly on academic, bookish words,	Overall awareness of the academic register, compared with everyday social speech. A small number of academic words likely to show up in grade-level reading.
Unknown word meanings are leading to breakdowns in comprehension, A reader understands far more in listening than in speaking,	Readers to expand oral-language use through additional speech genres, such as storytelling, conversation, singing, jokes, and topical discussions.

Teaching Vocabulary

Learning vocabulary can be a fun and rewarding experience.[20] Remember that one goal of the vocabulary program is to help children develop a vocabulary consciousness. To do so, teachers need to integrate vocabulary instruction across all content areas so readers can see the meaningful use of words in different contexts. Teachers also need to provide readers with enough repetition so they can learn to identify many words. Finally, instruction should be designed to use what students know to teach them something they need to learn. For example, students might know *car*, and teachers can use that word to help them learn the word *vehicle*, a broader category to which a car belongs.

Drawing on the research of those who study vocabulary development, we provide some general guidelines for effective vocabulary instruction. Many of the teaching strategies that follow are ways to put these guidelines into action.[21]

Guidelines for Effective Vocabulary Instruction

1. Create a word-rich environment.
   √ Promote wide reading.
   √ Provide time for discussion of new words and ideas.
   √ Intentionally focus on word learning in all content areas.
   √ Use time-effective strategies such as "word of the day."
   √ Be enthusiastic about acquiring new words.
2. Create independent word learners.
   √ Select and teach words that are central to the understanding of a topic.
   √ Show students how to use context clues.
   √ Show students how to use word parts.
   √ Allow for some self-selection.
3. Model good word learning.
   √ Show active involvement.
   √ Use graphic displays with discussion.
   √ Personalize words.
   √ Gather information from different sources.
   √ Play and experiment with words.

Teaching Strategies

There are several ways to teach vocabulary. *Purpose* is what guides selection of any specific teaching strategy. Many of these strategies can be used when designing explicit vocabulary instruction focused on helping students understand key vocabulary. Remember, though, that we are teaching for independence; we want to equip students to employ several of these strategies when they are on their own and come to unknown words. And remember the value of providing time for children to read books and other print sources in class. Wide reading is one sure way to help children acquire a large store of words.[22] What follow are ten specific ways that teachers can help children toward this goal.

1. ***Use Explicit Teaching.***

   When designing explicit instruction, you might find STAR[23] helpful. Here are the steps:

   - **S** (Select). Determine which words students need to know to better understand the text at hand. Keep the number limited to no more than six words.

   - **T** (Teach). Teach an appropriate strategy to help students learn the words. Some strategies work best before students read, whereas others work best during or after reading. For example, the *Knowledge Rating* (see page 238) is excellent to use before students actually begin reading. *Word Chain* (see page 238) is a perfect fit for review that takes place after reading. The *Context-Use* lesson (see page 226) is a natural strategy to use both before and during reading.

   - **A** (Activate). Connect the words with students' writing. Think about creating a set of words that contain some of the words they are learning. In other words, give them many exposures to the words in different contexts to provide them with meaningful repetition that will better ensure their understanding of the word(s).

   - **R** (Revisit). Use review activities such as *Word Chain* to help students revisit words. You might also ask students to use their words to create games such as crossword puzzles.

2. ***Teach Students How to Use Context Clues.***

   Below are two specific lesson structures that can be used across grade levels to help students learn to use context clues. Following these lessons,[24] we provide an extensive list of stand-alone techniques you can use for vocabulary instruction at any time.

Three-Day Lesson for Teaching Students to Use Context Clues

Day 1:

- Read a riddle aloud and ask students to guess the answer: "I am a color which symbolizes wealth. I am often seen on the robes of queens and kings. I am also on petals of flowers. What am I?" (Answer: purple)

- Have students point out any clues or cues that gave away the answer.

- Have students create a riddle to share with others.

Day 2:

- Provide time for students to share their riddles. As each is solved, ask students how the clues in each helped them find the answer.

- Tell students that context clues, like clues in a riddle, are the clues in the text that can help them understand a word they might not know.

- Provide students with a short passage that contains an unknown word.

    Example: The *werbert* Sam brought for lunch looked delicious. It had layers of roast beef, cheese, lettuce, and tomato piled between two slices of bread.

- Ask students to read the passage and underline the unknown word.
- Ask students to look for clues in the text that help reveal the meaning of the word.
- Using these clues, have students predict the meaning of the word.
- Repeat the procedure with other passages.

Day 3:

- Review the steps that can be used to find context clues in a passage.
- Have students find an unknown word in the dictionary and write a short passage using it. Make sure they add clues as to the meaning.
- Have students exchange passages with others and use the process described on Day 2 to figure out unknown words.

Context-Use Lesson[25]

- Write a passage on a chart or on an overhead transparency, omitting a contextually explained word.
- Show students how they can use context using the following steps. Actually go through the process yourself and think aloud so that they can better understand how to use the process:

    o LOOK before, at, and after the word.

    o REASON. Connect what you know with what the author has written.

    o PREDICT a possible meaning.

    o RESOLVE OR REDO. Decide if you know enough or should keep going.

- Insert the omitted word.
- Display another passage, and have the students go through the process with your guidance.
- Allow for discussion.
- Reveal the author's word choice.

Additional Techniques for Teaching Context Clues

- Present to your students the following sentence, which should have an unfamiliar word in it:

    Mary is usually a prudent person. However, yesterday she was very foolish.

    Ask students how they can use the second sentence to figure out the meaning of *prudent.* Discuss how the second sentence gives a clue to the word *prudent.* From the second sentence, we want readers to realize that *prudent* means the opposite of *foolish.*

- Put the following sentences on the chalkboard, and have the students use the context clues to help them figure out the meanings of each underlined word. Tell them that sometimes the clue that will help them figure out the word meaning is in the next sentence. Review each sentence with the students.

    o My kitten is very <u>tame.</u> She will not hurt anyone.

    o Everyone seems to know her. She must be a <u>famous</u> writer.

    o That is such an <u>enormous</u> ice cream cone. You will have to get lots of people to help you eat some of it.

○ That street is so <u>broad</u> that we can all walk side by side.

○ The lion is a <u>fierce</u> animal that devours its prey.

- Hold up two pictures—one of a train, and another of a boy trying to train his dog. Ask what the two pictures have in common. Try to get students to make up sentences about what is taking place. Write the sentences about the two pictures on the board. Ask students to use the word *train* for both pictures.

- Ask students to construct sentences using a homograph, homophone, or homonym. Ask them to make an illustration to coincide with the sentence. Collected sentences can be made into a class book demonstrating how all three types of context clues are used by authors.

- Give students a sentence that uses comparison and ask them to see if they can figure out the meaning of an unfamiliar word:

  Fred is as *obstinate* as a mule.

  Ask the students to give you the meaning of *obstinate*. Since a mule is an animal that is considered stubborn, your students should get an idea of *obstinate* as meaning "stubborn."

- Present students with a number of phrases. Tell them that the same word can fit in each set of phrases. The meaning of the word changes based on the words surrounding it (context). For example: a *brush* with the law; *brush* your teeth; a *brush* for your hair.

- State a word such as *run*. Present sentences to your students and ask them to give the meaning of *run* in each sentence. Have them note that the meaning is different for each. Have them write four other sentences using *run* in different ways. Show them multiple definitions for *run* in the dictionary.

3. **Teach Students to Use Word Part Clues.**
   Vocabulary expansion depends on students' past reading, past experiences, and interests. If students are curious about sea life and you have an aquarium in the classroom, *combining forms* such as *aqua,* meaning "water," and *mare* (meaning "sea") could help them develop meaningful associations. A reader could combine the form *aqua* to generate such terms as *aquaplane, aqueduct,* and *aquanaut.* Since *mare* means "sea," students could be given the term *marine* for discussion. Students also need to be aware of how they can break words apart using affixes and root words. For example, when coming to the word *discontinued,* students can be taught how to break the prefix "dis" away from the word "continue," and to understand the meaning of the prefix.

   We might present combining forms in a chart or diagram. Following, the forms *cardio, tele, graph,* and *gram* are organized together:

   | cardiograph | telegraph |
   | cardiogram | telegram |

   After students know that *cardio* means "heart" and *tele* means "from a distance," ask them to try to determine the meaning of *graph,* as used in *cardiograph* and *telegraph.* Have them try to figure out the meaning of *gram,* as used in *telegram* and *cardiogram.*

   These types of word-combining activities are designed to help students increase their vocabulary consciousness. They come to realize that words are human-made, that language is living and changing, and that as people develop new concepts, they create new words to identify them. *Astronaut* and *aquanaut* are good examples of this last idea: words that came into being because of space and undersea exploration.

   Next we present information and sample lessons for combining forms and for breaking forms apart.

Combining Affixes and Roots Lesson

- State and write the combining form *bi* on the board.
- Challenge the students to generate any words that they can think of that have this combining form—for example, *bicycle, bimonthly,* and *biweekly.*
- Since the most common word is *bicycle,* ask the students if they can figure out the meaning of *bi* from *bicycle.* Someone will probably volunteer *two* because a bicycle is a *two*-wheeler.
- Ask for volunteers to state other *bi* words and write them on the board. For example, *biped;* say "We know that *bi* means *two;* let's see if we can figure out what *biped* means."
- State two sentences using *biped:* e.g., *All humans are bipeds. However, not all animals are bipeds.* Ask "Can anyone guess what *biped* means? Remember, you know what *bi* means."
- To encourage and help students more, say "Let me give you another word containing the combining form *ped.* Perhaps that will help you to get the meaning of *biped.*"
- State and write *pedestrian* on the board and write the following sentence on the board: *Motorists must look out for pedestrians.* If the students still need help with the analysis, ask the students to state what they do when they ride a bicycle. Ideally, someone will say "pedal." If not, suggest "pedal" and write the following sentence on the board: *People pedal hard when they want to go fast.* At this point, students should be able to give the meaning of *ped* as "foot." *Biped* should be defined as "two-footed," and *pedestrian* as someone "who is on foot or walking."
- Tell students about how useful combining forms can be in expanding vocabulary and in helping them figure out unknown words when reading.

Breaking Apart Affixes[26]

- Lay aside the prefix.
- Lay aside each suffix, one at a time.
- If the root is unfamiliar, decode it.
- Put back the suffix closest to the root.
- If there is a second suffix, add it next.
- Put back the prefix.
- Read the word in the sentence to check meaning.

Teaching Prefixes[27]

- Present a prefix in isolation and attached to four words.

    Example: *con-; construct, converge, conference, connect*

- Define the prefix.

    Example: *Con-* means "to put together."

- Use the whole words in sentences:

    Example: Builders *construct* houses.

- Define the whole words.

    Example: To *construct* means to put or fit together.

- After completing the above four steps with several prefixes, have students practice matching different prefixes to their meanings and root words to prefixes.
- Have students identify the meanings of new words with familiar prefixes.

Here is a list of some often-used word parts and vocabulary words derived from them:

Word Parts	Vocabulary Words
anthropo—man	anthropology
astro—star	astronomy, astrology
audio—hearing	audiology, auditory, audition, audible
auto—self	automatic, autocracy
bene—good	benefit, beneficiary
bio—life	biology, biography, autobiography
chrono—time	chronological, chronometer
cosmo—world	microcosm, cosmology, cosmopolitan
gamy—marriage	monogamy, bigamy, polygamy
geo—earth	geography, geology
gram—written or drawn	telegram, monogram
graph—written or drawn, instrument	telegraph, graphic

4. *Teach Students to Categorize Words*

When readers **categorize** words, they are working on incorporating the words into a larger structure of meaning. Categorized words have connections based on word meaning, usage, and the function of the words. We want to teach students to talk about the categories words fit into and do not fit into. This will help them make places for the words to "live" in their minds.

The difference between everyday social language and academic language is one key way to categorize vocabulary. The vocabulary students encounter in text and in the classroom is not the same as the vocabulary they learn with friends and family. For example, when children first encounter a word like *difficult,* they may not have much experience with this academic synonym for *hard.*

Another key schema for vocabulary is a continuum of general to specific usage. For example, the word *stop* is used fairly generally, and yet the word *freeze* means "to stop" in highly specific situations, such as for police, or with financial institutions. Figure 10.7 shows these categories in grid form.

Figure 10.7 Chart for Categorizing Vocabulary Usage

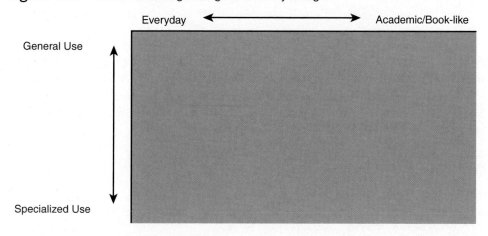

Try placing these words and phrases in the grid above:

- Stay, remain, linger
- In back, behind, posterior
- Soap, detergent, amphiphilic surfactant
- Church, religion, belief system, mysticism
- Act, behave, act out, behavior, drama, dramatize, histrionics
- Find, locate, pinpoint
- See, notice, perceive
- Good at, proficient
- Good for, healthy
- Snacks, hors d'oeuvres, nutrients
- Sick, under the weather, disease

By the time children begin school, they are able to make many discriminations and are beginning to classify. Here are some suggested activities appropriate for children in different grade levels.

- Five-year-olds can put things together that belong together—blocks of the same size in the same place; clothes for each doll in the right suitcase; parts of a puzzle in the right box; scissors, brushes, and paints in the spaces designated for these materials.

- First-graders may separate things that magnets can pick up from things they do not pick up by using two boxes—one marked "yes" and the other marked "no." They can think of two kinds of stories—true and make-believe stories. They can make booklets representing homes, dividing the pictures they have cut from magazines into several categories—living rooms, dining rooms, bedrooms, and so on. They can make two piles of magazines labeled "To Cut" and "To Read."[28]

- Second-grade readers continue to put things together that belong together—such as outdoor temperature readings and indoor temperature readings, valentines in individual mailboxes in the play post office, and flannel graph figures in the envelope they can use to retell a specific story. In addition, seven-year-olds begin to understand finer classifications under large headings; for example, in a study of the job of a florist, plants may be classified as "plants that grow indoors" and "plants that grow outdoors." Indoor plants may be further subdivided into "plants that grow from seeds," "plants that grow from cuttings," and "plants that grow from bulbs." After visiting the local bakery, second-graders who are writing stories and drawing pictures of their trip can list the details in two columns—in one, "things we saw in the store"; in the other, "things we saw in the kitchen."

- Third-grade students have many opportunities to classify their ideas and organize them. During a study of food in their community, one group put up a bulletin board to answer the question "What parts of plants do we eat?" The pictures and captions followed this tabulation formulated by the third-graders:

Leaves	Seeds	Fruits	Roots
cabbage	peas	apples	carrots
lettuce	beans	oranges	radishes
spinach	corn	plums	

The file of "Games We Know" in one third-grade class was divided into two parts by the students—"indoor games" and "outdoor games." Each of these categories was further subdivided into "games with equipment" and "games without equipment."

After a visit to the supermarket, a third-grade class made a book containing stories and pictures of the trip. The organization of the booklet with its numbered pages was shown in the Table of Contents:

Our Visit To The Grocery Store

Sample Exercises

- Group these words into categories: apples, peaches, potatoes, rice, oats, cucumbers, barley, peanuts, acorns, pecans, almonds, pears. (A possible outcome is given below.)

Nuts	Fruits	Vegetables	Grains
peanuts	apples	potatoes	rice
acorns	peaches	cucumbers	oats
pecans	pears		barley
almonds			

- Circle the word that does not belong.

  Airedale   Persian   Angora   Siamese

Discuss why you circled the word you did.

- Present students with the following list of words and have them group them in as many ways as they can think of:

chalk	book
checkers	library
pencil	auditorium
paper	science books
student	baseball
teacher	nurse
chalkboard	jump rope
desk	basketball
classroom	pen
principal	chess
history books	spelling books

- Present the following exercise to your students. Tell them, "Here is a group of words. Put the words into five groups according to a common feature for each group and state that feature." This activity is a more difficult one because students have to state the common feature. Partner or group discussion during an exercise like this is appropriate—it gives students a chance to see how others think and categorize, and gives them many opportunities to use target vocabulary words. After students have finished the exercise, lead some whole-class discussion about their decisions.

    Wood, brass, round, silk, oil, wheat, tin, wool, satin, coal, nylon, iron, barley, oats, oval, cylindrical

- _____
  _____
  _____ Common feature _____

- _____
  _____
  _____ Common feature _____

- _____
  _____
  _____ Common feature _____

- _____
  _____ Common feature _____

- _____
  _____
  _____ Common feature _____

Answers: 1. Wood, oil, coal—fuels. 2. Brass, tin, iron—metals. 3. Silk, wool, satin, nylon—fabrics. 4. Round, cylindrical, oval—shapes. 5. Wheat, barley, oats—grains.

The Frayer Model and List-Group-Label are two additional ways to teach categorizing.

Frayer Model[29]

Step	Example Using the Word "Treasurer"
Define the new concept, discriminating the attributes relevant to all instances of the concept.	The discriminating attributes of *treasurer* are membership in an organization and responsibility for the accounts.
Discriminate the relevant properties of the concept from the irrelevant ones.	The amount of money the treasurer is responsible for is an irrelevant attribute.
Provide an example of the concept.	The "treasurer of the school board" or the "treasurer of the school book club"
Provide a nonexample of the concept.	The "chairman or secretary of the board" or a "banker"
Relate the concept to a subordinate concept.	Generic instances of a treasurer, such as the treasurer of a country club or another club
Relate the concept to a superordinate concept.	People who deal with money
Relate the concept to a coordinate term.	Bookkeeper

List-Group-Label[30]

- Provide students with a list of words related to a given subject. Keep the list to no more than 25 words.
- Provide students with time to group them.
- Ask students to label each group of words.
- If you want, collect different categories of words and display them for the whole class. If some words do not fit, have a miscellaneous category, or ask students to brainstorm additional words to go with them to form another category.

5. *Teach Students to Make Analogies.*
   Here are some instructional procedures and materials that you can use to help students understand *analogies*:

   - Present students with the words *hot* and *cold*. Ask them what the relationship between the two words is. Help them to recognize that *hot* and *cold* are opposites. Present students with the words *tall* and *short*. Ask them what the relationship between the words is. Again, help them to recognize that they are opposites. Tell them that they are going to work with word relationships. The first relationship will be opposites. Put the following on the chalkboard:

     Thin is to *fat* as *little* is to _____.

     Ask them to give you a word that would fit the blank. Present a number of opposite relationships to your students.

   - Present students with the words *little* and *small*. Ask them what the relationship between the words is. Help them to recognize that these words have the same meaning; they are synonyms. Present students with the words *big* and *large.* Ask them what the relationship between the words is. Again, help them to recognize that the words are similar in meaning. Tell the students that they are going to work with word relationships. This time, the word relationship is synonyms. Put the following on the chalkboard:

     Sad is to *gloomy* as *happy* is to _____.

     Ask them to give you a word that would fit the blank. Present a number of such relationships to your students.

- Do the same as above for different kinds of relationships. Go over each analogy with the students. Have them explain why they chose the word that they did.

- Discuss the various relationships that words can have to one another and ask the students to give examples. Put the examples on large newsprint so that students can refer to them. As students learn new relationships, have them add to the list.

  For example:

  Opposites: *hot* is to *cold*

  Similarities: *thin* is to *lean*

  Degree of intensity: *pretty* is to *beautiful*

  Classification: *boat* is to *vehicle*

  Ratio: *5* is to *10*

  Part is to whole: *finger* is to *hand*

  Whole is to part: *foot* is to *toe*

  Parent is to child: *bear* is to *cub*

- Have students construct their own analogies.

Enhanced eText **Application Exercise 10.4:** Word Sorts.

---

6. ***Teach Vocabulary with Children's Literature.***

Reading literature aloud to children is a viable means of increasing vocabulary and reading achievement.[31] Be sure to choose books that appeal to children. The authors of these books must be aware of what is important to a child and what is likely to be confusing, so that they can build meaning out of words through the kind of imagery that makes sense to a child. For example, in *Mike Mulligan and His Steam Shovel*, the meaning of *steam shovel* is clarified by giving numerous examples in which a steam shovel is used. In Margaret Wise Brown's book *The Dead Bird*, the meaning of *dead* is given by a description of the bird's state.[32]

Here are some additional titles sure to assist vocabulary development:

Adler, David. *Millions, Billions, & Trillions: Understanding Big Numbers*. New York: Holiday House, 2013.

———. *How Tall, How Short, How Far Away?* New York: Holiday House, 1999.

———. *Perimeter, Area, and Volume: A Monster Book of Dimensions*. New York: Holiday House, 2012.

Adoff, Arnold. *Outside, Inside*. San Diego, CA: Harcourt, 1981.

Agee, Jon. *Palindromania*. New York: Farrar, Straus, & Giroux, 2002.

———. *Elvis Lives! And Other Anagrams*. New York: Farrar, Straus, & Giroux, 2000.

———. *Who Ordered the Jumbo Shrimp? And Other Oxymorons*. New York: Farrar, Straus, & Giroux, 1998.

Appelt, Kathi. *Piggies in a Polka*. San Diego, CA: Harcourt, 2003.

Arnold, Tedd. *More Parts*. New York: Dial, 2001.

Ballard, Robin. *Carnival*. New York; Greenwillow, 1995.

Bang, Molly, and Penny Chisolm. *Ocean Sunlight: How Tiny Plants Feed the Seas*. New York: The Blue Sky Press, 2012.

Barretta, Gene. *Zoola Palooza: A Book of Homographs*. New York: Henry Holt, 2011.

Bass, Hester. *The Secret World of Walter Anderson*. Somerville, MA: Candlewick, 2009.

Becker, Bonny. *The Sniffles for Bear*. Somerville, MA: Candlewick, 2011.

Bee, William. *Whatever*. Cambridge, MA: Candlewick, 1995.

Biggs, Brian. *Everything Goes in the Air*. New York: HarperCollins, 2012.

Blexbolex. *People*. New York: Enchanted Lion Books.

Boisrobert, Anouck. *Popville*. New York: Roaring Book Press, 2010.

Burns, Lori G. *Citizen Scientists: Be a Part of Scientific Discovery from Your Own Backyard*. New York: Henry Holt, 2012.

Chin, Jason. *Island: A Story of the Galapagos*. New York: Roaring Brook Press, 2012.

Close, Chuck, and Ascha Drake. *Chuck Close: Face Book*. New York: Harry N. Abrams, 2012.

Coffelt, Nancy. *Aunt Ant Leaves Through the Leaves: A Story of Homophones and Homonyms*. New York: Holiday House, 2012.

———. *Big, Bigger, Biggest*. New York: Holt, 2009.

Cohen, Peter. *Boris's Glasses*. New York: Farrar, Straus, & Giroux, 2003.

Crimi, Carolyn. *Outside, Inside*. New York: Simon & Schuster, 1995.

Crowther, Robert. *Colors*. Cambridge, MA: Candlewick, 2001.

DeCristafano, Carolyn C., and Michael W. Carroll. *A Black Hole Is Not a Hole*. New York: Charlesbridge, 2012.

Degman, Lori. *1 Zany Zoo*. New York: Simon & Schuster, 2010.

DeGross, Monalisa. *Donovan's Word Jar*. New York: HarperCollins, 1998.

Dunphy, Madeline. *Here Is the Southwestern Desert*. New York: Hyperion, 1995.

———. *Here Is the Tropical Rain Forest*. New York: Hyperion, 1994.

———. *Here Is the Arctic Winter*. New York: Hyperion, 1993.

Egielski, Richard. *Captain Sky Blue*. New York: Michael di Capua Books, 2010.

Elya, Susan. *Oh No, Gotta Go!* New York: Putnam, 2003.

Emberly, Ed. *Glad Monster, Sad Monster: A Book about Feelings*. New York: Little, Brown, 1997.

Fearnley, Jan. *Milo Armadillo*. Somerville, MA: Candlewick, 2009.

Frasier, Debra. *Miss Alaineus: A Vocabulary Disaster*. San Diego, CA: Harcourt, 2000.

Gibson, Amy. *Around the World on Eighty Legs*. New York: Scholastic, 2011.

Glassman, Peter. *My Dad's Job*. New York: Simon & Schuster, 2003.

Goldstone, Bruce. *That's a Possibility: A Book About What Might Happen*. New York: Holt, 2013.

Grover, Max. *Max's Wacky Taxi Day*. San Diego, CA: Harcourt, 1997.

Hale, Nathan. *Nathan Hale's Hazardous Tales: One Dead Spy*. New York: Harry N. Abrams, 2012.

Harley, Avis. *African Acrostics*. Somerville, MA: Candlewick, 2009.

Hirschi, Ron. *Faces in the Forest*. New York: Cobblehill/Dutton, 1997.

Hoban, Tana. *So Many Circles, So Many Squares*. New York: Greenwillow, 1998.

———. *All About Where*. New York: Greenwillow, 1991.

———. *Shapes, Shapes, Shapes*. New York; Greenwillow, 1986.

———. *Is it Larger? Is it Smaller?* New York: Greenwillow, 1985.

Jenkins, Steve. *Just a Second*. New York: Houghton Mifflin, 2011.

Jeppson, Ann-Sofie. *Here Comes Pontus!* New York: Farrar, Straus, & Giroux, 2000.

Juster, Norton. *The Odious Ogre.* New York: Michael di Capua Books, 2010.

Kalman, Maira. *What Pete Ate from A to Z.* New York: Putnam, 2001.

Khan, Hena. *Golden Domes and Silver Lanterns: A Muslim Book of Colors.* New York: Chronicle Books, 2012.

Kirk, Daniel. *Trash Trucks!* New York: Putnam, 1997.

Kiss, Andrew. *A Mountain Alphabet.* Toronto, Canada: Tundra, 1996.

Lasky, Kathryn. *Pond Year.* Cambridge, MA: Candlewick, 1995.

Leedy, Loreen. *Crazy Like a Fox—A Simile Story.* New York: Holiday House, 2008.

———. *Seeing Symmetry.* New York: Holiday House, 2012.

Levitt, Paul, Douglas Burger, and Elissa Guralnick. *The Weighty Word Book.* Boulder, CO: Manuscripts Ltd, 1985.

Levy, Joel. *Phobiapedia: All the Things We Fear the Most!* New York: Scholastic, 2011.

Lewin, Ted. *Fair!* New York: Lothrop, 1997.

Lichtenheld, Tom. *E-mergency!* San Francisco, CA: Chronicle, 2011

Maloney, Peter. *One Foot, Two Feet: An Exceptional Counting Book.* New York: Putnam, 2011.

McMullan, Kate and Jim. *I'm Fast!* New York: HarperCollins, 2012.

Messner, Kate. *Over and Under the Snow.* San Francisco, CA: Chronicle, 2011.

Mitchell, Joyce Slayton. *Tractor-Trailer Trucker: A Powerful Truck Book.* Berkeley, CA: Tricycle Press, 2000.

Morris, Ann. *Shoes, Shoes, Shoes.* New York: Lothrop, 1995.

Mortensen, Jesper. *I Scream Ice Cream.* San Francisco, CA: Chronicle, 2012.

Nivola, Claire A. *Life in the Ocean: The Story of Oceanographer Sylvia Earle.* New York: Farrar, Straus & Giroux, 2012.

Paleja, S. N. *Native Americans: A Visual Exploration.* New York: Annick Press, 2013.

Parish, Herman. *Go West, Amelia Bedelia!* New York: Greenwillow, 2011.

Preus, Margi. *Celebritrees: Historic & Famous Trees of the World.* New York: Henry Holt, 2010.

Reinhart, Matthew. *Animal Opposites: A Pop-Up Book of Opposites.* New York: Little Simon, 2002.

Rosenthal, Amy Krouse. *Wumbers.* San Francisco, CA: Chronicle, 2012.

———. *This Plus That: Life's Little Equations.* San Francisco, CA: HarperCollins 2011.

Rosenthal, Betsy. *Which Shoes Would You Choose?* New York: Putnam.

Rotner, Shelly, and Richard Olivo. *Close, Closer, Closest.* New York: Atheneum, 1997.

Rusch, Elizabeth. *The Mighty Mars Rovers.* New York: Houghton Mifflin, 2012.

Samoyault, Tiphanie. *Alphabetical Order: How the Alphabet Began.* New York: Viking, 1998.

Schaefer, Lola M. *Lifetime: The Amazing Numbers in Animals' Lives.* San Francisco, CA: Chronicle, 2013.

Shulman, Mark. *Ann and Nan Are Anagrams.* San Francisco, CA: Chronicle, 2013.

Siebert, Diane. *Truck Song.* New York: Harper Trophy, 1984.

Silverstein, Shel. *Runny Babbit: A Billy Sook.* New York: HarperCollins, 2005.

Smith, Charles R. Jr. *Short Takes.* New York: Dutton, 2001.

Snicket, Lemony. *13 Words.* New York: HarperCollins, 2010.

Sobel, June. *B Is for Bulldozer: A Construction ABC.* San Diego: Harcourt, 2003.

Spires, Elizabeth. *Riddle Road: Puzzles in Poems and Pictures.* New York: McElderry, 1999.

Stojic, Manya. *Hello World! Greetings in 42 Languages Around the Globe!* New York: Scholastic, 2002.

Studios, Woof. *A Zeal of Zebras: An Alphabet of Collective Nouns.* San Francisco, CA: Chronicle, 2011.

Sullivan, Sarah. *Passing the Music Down.* Somerville, MA: Candlewick, 2011.

Thong, Roseanne. *Round Is a Tortilla: A Book of Shapes.* San Francisco, CA: Chronicle, 2013.

Tobias, Tobi. *A World of Words: An ABC of Quotations.* New York: Lothrop, 1998.

Van Dusen, Chris. *King Hugo's Huge Ego.* Somerville, MA: Candlewick, 2011.

Van Lieshout, Maria. *Flight 1-2-3.* San Francisco, CA: Chronicle, 2013.

Yoe, Craig. *Mighty Book of Jokes.* New York: Price, Stern, Sloan, 2001.

———. *Mighty Book of Riddles.* New York: Price, Stern, Sloan, 2001.

7. *Teach Vocabulary Using Technology.*

   Websites provide a vehicle that can help students get excited about vocabulary study. Technology can be integrated into explicit teaching before, during, or after a reading experience. Likewise, students can use websites independently for meaningful vocabulary activities. Here are some they might want to visit:

   > vocabulary.com can be used by middle and high school students and teachers. It contains several kinds of puzzles written at different levels. Emphasis is placed on definitions and root words. This is also a good site for those trying to improve their vocabularies in preparation for the SAT.

   > rhymezone.com contains a rhyming dictionary and thesaurus. Visitors can type in a word and locate several words associated with it such as rhymes, synonyms, definitions, quotations, pictures, and words with similar spellings.

   > wordsmith.org/awad contains a word a day. Visitors can subscribe so that they receive a word each day through e-mail. They can find additional words by searching the archives. An explanation of origin, a definition, a pronunciation guide, and at least one quote using the word are provided.

   > englishclub.net provides grammar and vocabulary activities, word games, and other activities. It also offers free handouts for ESL teachers.

   > www.m-w.com is a site from Merriam-Webster that offers several resources, including an online dictionary and daily word games.

8. *Use a Word Wall.*

   Most teachers recognize that children need direct instruction in vocabulary and that students enjoy various fun word activities that help them to develop needed skills. A Word Wall is a display of words on cards. It is most meaningful when it is created by students and their teacher. It is versatile, and its use is limited only by the teacher's creativity. A Word Wall can be used for review, reinforcement, skill enhancement purposes, teaching a new skill, or as a writing reference.

   Teachers can work with one specific category, such as contractions, or with a number of categories. What the teacher does is based on his objectives. The teacher can have the whole class involved or children can work in groups or teams.

   Word Walls are most often seen in the primary grades, but they can be used at any grade level. In the upper grades, teachers generally use Word Walls to expand students' vocabulary.

   In preparing to use a Word Wall, teachers must be clear about their purposes. For example, a teacher who is reviewing homophones, homographs, word families, and contractions can have available a box of representative word cards of similar size. At the top of the Word Wall, the four categories being reviewed could be listed. In turn, children could draw two cards from the box and place the words under the correct category. If one word were a contraction, the other card would have to have the two words that made up the contraction. If the two words were *red* and *read*, the words would be placed under homophones. If the two words were *cake* and *bake*, the words would be listed under word families.

9. *Use a Variety of Other Vocabulary-Oriented Activities to Engage All Students*

Self-Selection Strategy[33]

- Invite students to bring two words to class that they have found in reading or listening.
- Allow students to present their words to the group.
- Ask the group to vote on 5–8 words to be learned for the week.
- Lead a class discussion to clarify, elaborate on, and extend word meanings.
- Have students enter their words into personal word logs, and ask them to create some sort of memory and meaning device (e.g., chart, diagram, picture, or word map).
- Ask students to use the words in various ways to provide practice with them.

Yea/Nay[34]

- Provide students with two different cards, one that says "Yea" and one that says "Nay."
- Read a question with one or two words that students might or might not understand. *Example:* Would a *corpse* be a good *conversationalist*?
- After reading the question, give students 5–10 seconds to think and then say, "Yea or nay? 1, 2, 3."
- On the count of 3, students hold up their choices while you call on individuals to explain their choices.

Create Word Riddles[35]

- Pick a subject (e.g., *pig*).
- Generate a list of related words (e.g., *ham, pen,* and *hog*).
- Pick a word (e.g., *ham*), drop the first letter(s) to get a shortened version (e.g., *am*), and find a list of words that begin the way the shortened version begins (e.g., *ambulance; amnesia*).
- Put back the missing letter to create a new word (e.g., *hambulance*).
- Make up a riddle to which this word is the answer (e.g., *What do you use to take a pig to the hospital?*).

Semantic Feature Analysis[36]

- Select a category.
- List words in the category on the left-hand column of a grid.
- List and add features across the top row of the grid.
- Determine feature possession. Which words have which features? Place an "X" in each corresponding cell.
- Add more words and features.
- Continue completing the grid.
- Examine and discuss the grid.

Word Map[37]

- Divide a piece of paper into four parts.
- Write a word in the center of the paper.
- Label each square with one of the following labels: synonym, antonym, example, or nonexample.
- Have students write the distinguishing features for the word in the center.

Synonym: Mad	**Antonym:** Happy

Angry

Example: My Dad when I do something wrong	**Nonexample:** When I *hit a home run*

Word Chain[38]

- Identify a word associated with what you have been studying.
- Write the word for all to see.
- Tell students that they need to think of a second word that begins with the last letter of the displayed word. The word also has to relate to the displayed word in some way.
- Continue building the chain until all possibilities have been exhausted.

  Note: I have been very successful using this as a small group activity in college classes.

Knowledge Rating[39]

- Present students with a list of words in grid form, as shown below.

Word	Know Well	Seen/Heard It	Don't Know It
Apartment	√		
Villa		√	
Geodesic dome		√	
Yurt			√

- Ask students to rate their understanding of each term by placing a √ in the appropriate column on the grid.
- After students have rated themselves, invite them to share their ideas about the words, and highlight the words that you feel need to be addressed.
- Have students make predictions about what they will be reading based on these words. For example, you might say something like "What do you think the topic of this chapter will be, based on our discussion of these words?"

Book Aids[40]

Experienced readers know that authors use aids to signal important words, which helps the reader to comprehend. Most often, these aids and their functions have to be taught to students. Here are some examples:

- *The use of boldface type and italics*
- *Glossaries*
- *Pronunciation guides*
- *Words defined contextually* (e.g., "Pollution, the soiling of the air and water, is an increasing threat to wildlife in the Gulf region.")
- *End-of-unit exercises* (Emphasize how important it is to look at these BEFORE reading, to see what will be highlighted.)

A-to-Z Chart[41]

This activity is especially good for the end of a unit of study as a review and informal assessment of words students acquired related to the topic. Here's how it works:

- Break students into small groups.
- Give each group an A-to-Z chart. (See sample following.)

A	B	C	D	E
F	G	H	I	J
K	L	M	N	O
P	Q	R	S	T
U	V	W	X	Y and Z

- Have each group brainstorm words related to the topic and write them in the corresponding boxes using the beginning letter to classify the words.
- After 15 minutes, reconvene the class. Using an interactive whiteboard, display a blank A-to-Z chart, and have volunteers from each group state words.
- Once a word has been offered, others can challenge it and ask that the group state its reasoning for including it as an important word for the topic.

Rivet[42]

- Select 5–10 words that students will need to learn to make sense of the reading in which they will encounter the words.
- Write numerals, and next to each, write the number of lines corresponding to the number of letters in the word (see sample below).

> 1. _ _ _ _ _ _ _ _
> 2. _ _ _ _ _ _ _ _ _ _

- For each word, fill in each letter in sequence, one at a time.
- Pause after you write each letter to provide students with time to make their best guesses about what the word might be (similar to the clues given in the popular game show *Wheel of Fortune*).
- Tell students that when they think they know the word, they can state it out loud.
- Once the word has been guessed, fill in the remaining letters of the word and ask for volunteers to state the meaning of the word. More than one association with the word is possible—and encouraged—because many words have multiple meanings, and the context in which the word is used will determine the pertinent meaning in a given story.
- Once all suggestions have been offered, proceed in like fashion with the remaining words.
- Once all words are displayed, and pronounced, ask students if they see any possible relationships among the words.
- Students then use the words by stating at least one prediction about the text they will be reading.
- After you have a few predictions, have students read the text to see if their predictions were accurate, and if the meanings of the words they stated were as well.
- Once the reading finishes, have students use the words by writing about events that happened, using the words.

    Cunningham notes, "Rivet is a very motivating way to introduce vocabulary when the words that need to be introduced are words most of your class has concepts for and some of your students have some meanings for."

10. *Use a Five-Day Plan to Organize Your Robust Vocabulary Program.*
Vocabulary instruction can occur within a readers' workshop approach, and Feezell[43] offers these suggestions:

Instructional Preparations

- Begin by creating a word box. (A shoebox with a slit in the lid works well.)
- Allow students to write words of interest that they want to learn more about on index cards (one word per card). The word, the text where the word occurs, and the student's name need to be on each card.
- Students place the words in the word box all week.
- On Friday, open the box and choose five words to teach the following week. These will be whole-class lessons. Words are selected based on their usefulness. Consider choosing words that students will encounter frequently.
- Write each word on an index card with a definition. Display the words on the chalk ledge with children's additional notes about the given words from the word box.
- Use the words throughout the following week following this plan. Each lesson is about 15 minutes.

Monday

- Display the words, read them and the sentences where they appeared, and read the child's name that submitted the word.
- Invite children to talk about what they think the word means based on the sentence.
- Once children have exhausted their ideas, share the definition. If possible, show a picture of the word.
- At some point in the day, put the words on the Word Wall.

Tuesday

- Using shared writing, have students write sentences for each word. First review the definition. Next, provide a prompt and ask students to complete the sentence. To engage all students in this collaborative activity, pair students and use think-pair-share, where students think about how they might finish the prompt, talk with their partner, and report to the whole class.
- Once volunteers have had time to share their ideas, combine students' suggestions to create a sentence, and write it on an interactive whiteboard or chart large enough for all to see.

Wednesday and Thursday

- Use a variety of vocabulary activities. You might select from the ten listed here or use some activities that you have acquired.
- Have students use the words to complete the activities.

Friday

- Prepare ten questions to read aloud for one student to respond to orally. The Word Wall can be used to answer all questions.
- The remaining students use their traffic light cards (red, green, and yellow), holding up the appropriate card after the oral response to show whether they agree (green), disagree (red), or are unsure (yellow).
- Review the answers at the end of the session to make sure that all students have accurate understandings.

○ Reflect on the experience and make decisions about what to do with the words that were used for the ten-question activity. You might remove those words from the wall and keep them for later review. You might also remove any words from the wall that you feel students have internalized, as evidenced by their using them in their speaking and writing.

Enhanced eText Application Exercise 10.5: Mr. Jackson Teaches Vocabulary

---

Bridge: From Teaching Back to Understanding

If students _____,	then teachers have learned _____.
Miscue on fewer words when they have time to preview and discuss what they are reading before they start,	That learners file their vocabulary knowledge in their brain within schemata; students need to learn to access the appropriate schema when reading.
Improve reading of long words based on instruction in word parts, such as affixes and morphemes,	That it is normal for longer words with multiple meaningful parts to take more effort to learn.
Still do not understand words even when taught to apply context clues,	That vocabulary growth cannot be solved with a simple lesson; applying strategies such as context clues may develop over weeks and months, not hours or days.
Recognize the difference between everyday social language and the bookish academic register,	Vocabulary usage is often about the need for precision and nuance in meaning, but it is also about the need to express power and authority.
Recognize specialized words in one area (such as science) but not another (such as geography),	That specialized meanings and their words depend on background knowledge. How to connect meanings from everyday experience and popular media to the specialized vocabulary.

Revisiting the Opening Scenario

Craig already has an "opening" in his mind for the word *animosity*. Craig's desire to use a new word shows vocabulary consciousness. So while his "incorrect" use of the words may seem like an error at first, it is actually a strength on which to build. Using context, categorization, analogies, literature, and other tools, how can Mr. Jackson use what Craig knows to help him learn what he does not yet know about the word?

Authors' Summary

Before reading our summary statements for each outcome, we suggest you read each outcome and summarize it in your own words.

Once finished, cross-check your response with our brief summary to determine how well you recalled the major points.

10.1 Discuss what is involved in acquiring vocabulary.

- All children have four vocabularies, and they are listed from largest to smallest: listening, speaking, reading, and writing. Enhancing each of these vocabularies is essential for reading growth. Reading a word that children have heard is much easier than reading one they have not.

- Children need to have a vocabulary consciousness and a thorough understanding of words of many different types, including content-specific words and sight words. They also need an understanding of word parts (i.e., root words, prefixes, and suffixes).

- Understanding how to use context clues to ascertain the meanings of words is one way for children to acquire new words. Wide reading and explicit instruction are also essential to their vocabulary growth.

10.2 Discuss different ways to assess vocabulary.

- There are many ways to assess vocabulary, including observation, the word test for the IRI, self-selection strategy, independent reading records, and the chart for categorizing vocabulary usage. Asking and answering three questions will help to select the technique that will target specifically what it is you want to know about students' comprehension. These questions are: What do I want to know? Why do I want to know it? How can I best discover this information?

10.3 Explain guidelines for effective vocabulary instruction and one specific vocabulary teaching strategy.

- There are three primary guidelines for effective vocabulary instruction:
  1. Create a word-rich environment.
  2. Create independent word learners.
  3. Model good word learning.
- Teaching strategies are plentiful, and range from using children's literature to specific vocabulary activities. A Word Wall is one specific teaching strategy. It entails having students generate words from many different content areas and placing them on a wall large enough for all to see. The wall is used as a reference when students are reading and spelling words. The wall constantly changes, and reflects students' ongoing learning of new words.

Think About It!

1. You are interested in developing a vocabulary expansion program using combining forms. How would you go about doing it? What kinds of activities would you develop for students who were weak in vocabulary?

2. Explain how you can assess students' vocabulary strengths and needs in content areas.

3. You have been asked to generate a number of diagnostic tests for intermediate-grade students in vocabulary development. What kind of diagnostic tests would you develop?

4. Develop a Word Wall activity to help your students learn to read and spell.

Websites

- http://www.vocabulary.com/

    This vocabulary website offers lessons and materials on root words, thematic puzzles, word lists, test preparation, and various topical vocabulary-related links.

- http://teachersfirst.com/vocabulary.cfm

    This site provides access to various websites and resources centered on the various issues associated with teaching vocabulary. With in-depth annotations on this main page, teachers can pick and choose relevant sites in a matter of minutes.

- http://www.superkids.com/aweb/tools/words/

    The SuperKids website provides a variety of word games, puzzles, scrambles, and more. The site is organized in such a way that teachers can project the activities on a screen for whole-class interaction or set up individual work.

- https://studyspanish.com/vocab?var_vocab=select

    Offering numerous opportunities and free memberships for teachers, the StudySpanish website provides vocabulary, pronunciation, and grammar-building in Spanish. Though no English connections are made, teachers could provide Spanish-speaking students with ways to connect the English words to Spanish words.

Children's Literature Cited

Adler, David. *How Tall, How Short, How Far Away?* New York: Holiday House, 1999.

Adoff, Arnold. *Outside, Inside.* San Diego, CA: Harcourt, 1981.

Agee, Jon. *Palindromania.* New York: Farrar, Straus, & Giroux, 2002.

———. *Elvis Lives! And Other Anagrams.* New York: Farrar, Straus, & Giroux, 2000.

———. *Who Ordered the Jumbo Shrimp? And Other Oxymorons*. New York: Farrar, Straus, & Giroux, 1998.

Appelt, Kathi. *Piggies in a Polka*. San Diego, CA: Harcourt, 2003.

Arnold, Tedd. *More Parts*. New York: Dial, 2001.

Ballard, Robin. *Carnival*. New York; Greenwillow, 1995.

Bass, Hester. *The Secret World of Walter Anderson*. Somerville, MA: Candlewick, 2009.

Bee, William. *Whatever*. Cambridge, MA: Candlewick, 2005.

Coffelt, Nancy. *Big, Bigger, Biggest*. New York: Holt, 2009.

Cohen, Peter. *Boris's Glasses*. New York: Farrar, Straus, & Giroux, 2003.

Crimi, Carolyn. *Outside, Inside*. New York: Simon & Schuster, 1995.

Crowther, Robert. *Colors*. Cambridge, MA: Candlewick, 2001.

DeGross, Monalisa. *Donovan's Word Jar*. New York: HarperCollins, 1998.

Dunphy, Madeline. *Here Is the Southwestern Desert*. New York: Hyperion, 1995.

———. *Here Is the Tropical Rain Forest*. New York: Hyperion, 1994.

———. *Here Is the Arctic Winter*. New York: Hyperion, 1993.

Elya, Susan. *Oh No, Gotta Go!* New York: Putnam, 2003.

Emberly, Ed. *Glad Monster, Sad Monster: A Book about Feelings*. New York: Little, Brown, 1997.

Frasier, Debra. *Miss Alaineus: A Vocabulary Disaster*. San Diego, CA: Harcourt, 2000.

Glassman, Peter. *My Dad's Job*. New York: Simon & Schuster, 2003.

Grover, Max. *Max's Wacky Taxi Day*. San Diego, CA: Harcourt, 1997.

Harley, Avis. *African Acrostics*. Somerville, MA: Candlewick, 2009.

Hirschi, Ron. *Faces in the Forest*. New York; Cobblehill/Dutton, 1997.

Hoban, Tana. *So Many Circles, So Many Squares*. New York: Greenwillow, 1998.

———. *All About Where*. New York: Greenwillow, 1991.

———. *Shapes, Shapes, Shapes*. New York; Greenwillow, 1986.

———. *Is It Larger? Is It Smaller?* New York: Greenwillow, 1985.

Jeppson, Ann-Sofie. *Here Comes Pontus!* New York: Farrar, Straus, & Giroux, 2000.

Kalman, Maira. *What Pete Ate from A to Z*. New York: Putnam, 2001.

Kirk, Daniel. *Trash Trucks!* New York: Putnam, 1997.

Kiss, Andrew. *A Mountain Alphabet*. Toronto, Canada: Tundra, 1996.

Lasky, Kathryn. *Pond Year*. Cambridge, MA: Candlewick, 1995.

Leedy, Loreen. *Crazy Like a Fox—A Simile Story*. New York: Holiday House, 2008.

Levitt, Paul, Douglas Burger, and Elissa Guralnick. *The Weighty Word Book*. Boulder, CO: Manuscripts Ltd., 1985.

Lewin, Ted. *Fair!* New York: Lothrop, 1997.

Mitchell, Joyce Slayton. *Tractor-Trailer Trucker: A Powerful Truck Book*. Berkeley, CA: Tricycle Press, 2000.

Morris, Ann. *Shoes, Shoes, Shoes*. New York: Lothrop, 1995.

Reinhart, Matthew. *Animal Opposites: A Pop-Up Book of Opposites*. New York: Little Simon, 2002.

Rotner, Shelly, and Richard Olivo. *Close, Closer, Closest*. New York: Atheneum, 1997.

Samoyault, Tiphanie. *Alphabetical Order: How the Alphabet Began*. New York: Viking, 1998.

Siebert, Diane. *Truck Song*. New York: Harper Trophy, 1984.

Silverstein, Shel. *Runny Babbit: A Billy Sook*. New York: HarperCollins, 2005.

Smith, Charles R., Jr. *Short Takes*. New York: Dutton, 2001.

Sobel, June. *B Is for Bulldozer: A Construction ABC*. San Diego: Harcourt, 2003.

Spires, Elizabeth. *Riddle Road: Puzzles in Poems and Pictures*. New York: McElderry, 1999.

Stojic, Manya. *Hello World! Greetings in 42 Languages Around the Globe!* New York: Scholastic, 2002.

Tobias, Tobi. *A World of Words: An ABC of Quotations*. New York: Lothrop, 1998.

Yoe, Craig. *Mighty Book of Jokes*. New York: Price, Stern, Sloan, 2001.

———. *Mighty Book of Riddles*. New York: Price, Stern, Sloan, 2001.

Endnotes

1. MacGinitie, W. (1969). Language development. *Encyclopedia of Educational Research*, (4th ed., p. 693). London: Collier-Macmillan.

2. Fitzgerald M., & Graves, M. (2004). *Scaffolding reading experiences for English-language learners*. Norwood, MA: Christopher Gordon.

3. Daneman, M. (1991). Individual differences in reading skills. In R. Barr, M. L. Kamil, P. Mosenthal & P. D. Pearson (Eds.), *Handbook of Reading Research* (Vol. II, p. 524). New York: Longman.

4. Daugaard, H., Trebbien H., Cain K., & Elbro, C. (2017). From words to text: Inference making mediates the role of vocabulary in children's reading comprehension. In *Reading and Writing* 30.8, 1773–1788.

5. Swart, N., et al. (2017). Differential lexical predictors of reading comprehension in fourth graders. In *Reading and Writing* 30.3, 489–507; Blachowicz C., & Fisher, P. (2001). *Teaching vocabulary in all classrooms* (2nd ed.). Columbus, OH: Merrill/Prentice-Hall; Beck, I., McKeown, M., & Kucan, L. (2002). *Bringing words to life: Robust vocabulary instruction.* New York: Guilford Press; Graves, M. (2006). *The vocabulary book: Learning and instruction* Newark, DE: International Reading Association; Hattie, J. (2012). *Visible learning for teacher* New York: Routledge; Cunningham, P. (2014) *What really matters in vocabulary instruction* (2nd ed.). New York: Pearson.

6. Taylor, J., Nelson, J. & Perfetti C. (2016). Eye movements reveal readers' lexical quality and reading experience. In *Reading and Writing* 29.6, 1069–1103.

7. Anderson, R. & Pearson P. (1984). A schematheoretic view of basic processes in reading comprehension. In *Handbook of Reading Research* 1, 255–291; McVee, M., Dunsmore, K. & Gavelek, J.(2005). Schema theory revisited. In *Review of Educational Research* 75.4, 531–566.

8. Lee, S. (2017). Learning vocabulary through e-book reading of young children with various reading abilities. In *Reading and Writing* 30.7, 1595–1616; Adams, M. (1990). *Beginning to read: thinking and learning about print* (p. 29). Cambridge, MA: MIT Press; Hickman, P., Pollard-Durodola, S., & Vaughn, S. (2004). Storybook reading: Improving vocabulary and comprehension for English language learners. In *The Reading Teacher* 57, 720–730; *National reading panel.* (2000), p. 464.; Lane H., & Allen S. (2010). The vocabulary-rich classroom: Modeling sophisticated word use to promote word consciousness and vocabulary growth. In *The Reading Teacher* 63, no. 5, 362–370; Bauman, J. (2009). Vocabulary and reading comprehension. In S. E. Israel & G. G. Duffy (Eds.), *Handbook of Research on Reading Comprehension* (pp. 323–346). New York: Routledge.

9. Hart, B., & Risley, T. (1995). *Meaningful differences in the everyday experience of young American children.* Baltimore: Brookes; Lee, U., & Burkam D. (2002). *Inequality at the starting gate: Social background differences in achievement as children begin school.* Washington, D.C.: Economic Policy Institute.

10. Geva, E., et al. (2017). Learning novel words by ear or by eye? An advantage for lexical inferencing in listening versus reading narratives in fourth grade. *Reading and Writing* 30.9, 1917–1944.

11. Braze, D., et al. (2016). Vocabulary does not complicate the simple view of reading. In *Reading and Writing* 29.3, 435–451.

12. Blachowicz, C., & Fisher, P. (2000). Vocabulary instruction. In M. L. Kamil, P. B. Mosenthal, P. D. Pearson, & R. Barr (Eds.), *Handbook of Reading Research* (Vol. III, pp. 503–523). Mahwah, NJ: Erlbaum.

13. Nelson, K., et al. (2015). Vocabulary instruction in K-3 low-income classrooms during a reading reform project. In *Reading Psychology* 36.2, 145–172.

14. Wright, T. & Cervetti, G. (2017). A systematic review of the research on vocabulary instruction that impacts text comprehension. In *Reading Research Quarterly* 52.2, 203–226.

15. Wasik, B. & Iannove-Campbell, C. (2012). Developing vocabulary through purposeful strategic conversations. In *The Reading Teacher* 66, no. 2, 321–332.

16. McVee, M., Gavelek, J. & Dunsmore, K. (2007). Considerations of the social, individual, and embodied: A response to comments on "Schema theory revisited". In *Review of Educational Research* 77, no. 2, 245–248.

17. Rubin, D. (2000). *Gaining word power*, (5th ed.). Boston: Allyn and Bacon; Cunningham, P. (2014). *What really matters in vocabulary.* Upper Saddle River, NJ: Pearson.

18. Allen, J. (1999). Words, words, words: Teaching vocabulary in grades 4–12. Portland, ME: Stenhouse; Greenwood, S. and Flanagan, K. (2007). Overlapping vocabulary and comprehension: Context clues complement semantic gradients. In *The Reading Teacher* 61, 249–254.

19. Sister Josephine. (1965). An analogy test for preschool children. In *Education*, 235–237.

20. Blachowicz, C., & Fisher, P. (2004). Keep the 'fun' in fundamental: Encouraging word awareness and incidental word learning in the classroom through word play. J. F. Bauman & E. J. Kame'enui (eds.), Vocabulary Instruction, (pp. 219–238). New York: Guilford.

21. Blachowicz, C., & Fisher, P. (2009). *Teaching vocabulary in all classrooms* (4th ed.). New York: Pearson.

22. Allington, R., & McGill-Franzen, A. (2012). Summer reading: Closing the rich/poor reading achievement gap. New York: Teachers College Press.

23. Blachowicz, C., & Fisher, P. (2004, March). Vocabulary lessons. In *Educational Leadership*, 66–69.

24. Nickerson, L. (1998). *Quick activities to build a very voluminous Vocabulary.* New York: Scholastic.

25. Blachowicz and Fisher (2009).

26. Durkin, D. (1989). *Teaching them to read.* Boston: Allyn and Bacon.

27. Graves, M. Hammond, H. (1980). A validated procedure for teaching prefixes and its effect on students' ability

to assign meanings to novel words. In M. Kamil & A. Moe (Eds.), *Perspectives on Reading Research & Instruction* 184–188. Washington, D.C.: National Reading Conference; Graves, M. (2004). Teaching prefixes: As good as it gets? In J. F. Baumann and E. J. Kame'enui (Eds.), *Vocabulary Instruction*, 81–99. New York: Guilford.

28. Although grade designations are given, teachers must take the individual differences of students into account. Some first-graders may be functioning at a developmental level typical of children in third grade, while others may be at a first-grade skill developmental level or lower.

29. Frayer, D., Frederick, W., & Klausmeier, H. (1969). A scheme for testing the level of concept mastery (Working Paper no. 16). Madison, WI: University of Wisconsin.

30. Readence. J. & Searfoss, L. (1980). Teaching strategies for vocabulary development. In *English Journal* 69, 43–46.

31. Cohen, D. (1968, February). The effect of literature on vocabulary and reading achievement. In *Elementary English* 45, 209–213, 217.

32. Cohen, D. (1969, November). Word meaning and the literary experience in early childhood. In *Elementary English* 46, 914–925.

33. Haggard, M. (1982). The vocabulary self-selection strategy: An active approach to word learning. In *Journal of Reading* 26, 203–207.

34. Beck, I., & McKeown, M. (1983). Learning words well: A program to enhance vocabulary and comprehension. In *The Reading Teacher* 36, 622–625.

35. Thaler, M. (1988). Reading, writing, and riddling. In *Learning*, 58–59.

36. Pittelman, S., Heimlich, J., Berglund, R., & French, M. (1991). Semantic feature analysis: classroom applications. Newark, DE: International Reading Association.

37. Schwartz, R., & Raphael, T. (1985). Concept of definition: A key to improving students' vocabulary. In *The Reading Teacher* 39, 198–205.

38. Trussell-Cullen, A. (1998). 50 wonderful word games. New York: Scholastic.

39. Blachowicz, C. (1994). Problem-solving strategies for academic success. In G. P. Wallach & K. G. Butter (Eds.), *Language Learning Disabilities in School-Aged Children and Adolescents: Some Principles and Applications* (pp. 304–322). Englewood Cliffs, NJ: Merrill/Prentice Hall.

40. Blachowicz, C. & Fisher, P. (2002). Teaching vocabulary in all classrooms, (2nd ed.). Upper Saddle River, NJ: Merrill/Prentice Hall.

41. Cunningham, P. What really matters in vocabulary: Research-based practices across the curriculum, (2nd ed.). New York: Pearson.

42. Ibid., p. 129.

43. Feezell, G. (2012). Robust vocabulary instruction in a readers' workshop. In *The Reading Teacher* 66, no. 3, 233–237.

Chapter 11
Phonics

Rawpixel.com /Shutterstock

 Chapter Outline

Scenario: Understanding Jorge

Understanding Phonics

Phonics Content Knowledge

Assessing Phonics Teaching Phonics

 Learning Outcomes

After reading this chapter, you should be able to . . .

11.1 Describe the position of phonics assessment and instruction in a diagnostic approach to teaching reading.

11.2 Correctly identify, sort, and label phonics facts—matches between sounds and letters in English words.

11.3 Apply five different techniques for assessing phonics knowledge.

11.4 Explain guidelines for effective phonics instruction, and apply both direct and inductive techniques for teaching phonics.

Scenario

Understanding Jorge

Jorge is a student in Ms. Mills's third-grade class. He scored at a 1.2 level on the reading comprehension subtest of the *California Achievement Tests.* Ms. Mills is confused about this score because Jorge is quite verbal; he always has a lot of information to contribute on many topics; and he is able to answer comprehension questions with ease. To better understand Jorge's reading ability, Ms. Mills decides to give him an Informal Reading Inventory.

To encourage feelings of success from the beginning of the assessment, Ms. Mills starts Jorge two grade levels below his current grade level. She discovers that Jorge is able to answer all the comprehension questions for the oral- and silent-reading passages through the third level, albeit with numerous word errors in the oral-reading passages. At the third-grade level, the number of word errors increases to a frustrational level. Consequently, she decides to continue the passages as a listening capacity test. She reads aloud one passage from each level and asks Jorge the questions. Jorge is able to answer all questions correctly up to the eighth level.

In talking to Jorge, Ms. Mills learns that Jorge's parents are both professionals and well known in their fields, that Jorge is an only child, that he goes everywhere with his parents, and that he is included in their interesting conversations. Jorge's background information certainly matches his propensity to engage in conversations and answer questions, but it tells Ms. Mills little about his word identification in reading. She suspects a mismatch between phonics skill and comprehension could explain his achievement test score. She wants to know how she can gain greater insight into Jorge's decoding abilities.

Understanding Phonics

Phonics is the study of sound–letter matches in printed words. It is one aspect of word identification. When readers identify words well during reading, they balance affective, cognitive, and behavioral skills and strategies. For example, oral-vocabulary knowledge, a cognitive aspect of reading, predicts strength in reading words. Also, affective aspects of reading, such as interest, are positively correlated to both comprehension and word identification. The cognitive and affective aspects of reading are often called "deep structure" because they are under the surface, in the student's mind and heart. By contrast, surface structures, such as phonics knowledge, are easily noticed in oral reading. Because of this, using **miscues** to diagnose needs in phonics knowledge can be tempting.[1] In one research study that followed teachers closely, it was found that even for teachers who conferred one-on-one with their students, it was easy to spend too much time on surface structure elements of reading such as phonics.[2]

But phonics knowledge is in a functional relationship with cognitive and affective aspects of reading. Surface-level phonics errors may be caused by needs in deep structure, such as comprehension, metacognition, purpose, or engagement. Conversely, strengths and needs in phonics knowledge can impact comprehension, attitude, and interest.

Within a diagnostic approach to assessing and teaching, it is important to examine phonics knowledge while students read high-interest texts and other texts where they are likely to know many words. This approach allows teachers to check phonics knowledge when both affective and cognitive knowledge are strong. When students miscue on words in texts that do not interest them, or for which they have little background knowledge, the potential for accurate assessment and effective teaching is weak.

Figure 11.1 Reader Profile Diagram

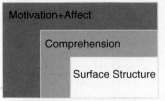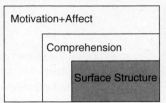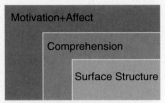

A reader profile is only partly complete until teachers learn about phonics and other surface structures of student' reading.

A Reader Profile is more obviously incomplete when teachers learn only about surface structures such as phonics.

A reader profile that is most complete organizes information about phonics in relation to information about deep structures.

Positioning phonics knowledge is important to the diagnostic approach we endorse in this book. In our diagnostic model, we position surface structure elements of reading such as phonics in a subordinate relationship to affective and cognitive aspects of reading. That is, phonics is a skill that is meant to serve comprehension and engagement, not to be an end unto itself with the hope that it will someday result in understanding and purposeful reading. To organize this relationship, teachers have used the Reader Profile diagram in Figure 11.1 to describe what they know and want to know about each aspect of reading for each student.[3]

Phonics Content Knowledge

Applying phonics is a comprehension strategy.[4] Readers apply phonics when they encounter unknown words in a text they want to understand. As diagrammed in Figure 11.2, using sound–letter matches to pronounce a printed word helps readers consider whether they already know the word from listening and speaking, and whether they know what it means. (See Figure 11.2.) When phonics is the only strategy for unknown words, however, reading can feel inefficient and frustrating. The path to meaning is indirect. But when applied well, phonics is a tool that helps readers comprehend what they read.

Think about your own reading. When you lose your purpose and motivation to understand what you read, decoding unknown words may feel like hard work with no payoff. However, as long as your purpose and motivation to understand stay strong, you may be patient with decoding unknown words. When phonics knowledge is applied with purpose and meaning, it can help readers experience success and feel competent.

Figure 11.2 World Analysis Across the Grades

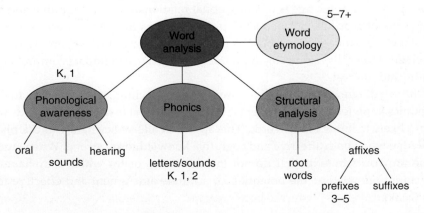

There is no evidence that memorizing rules beyond the basic phonics facts presented below has important effects in word identification. For example, rhymes such as "when two vowels go walking, the first one does the talking" are commonly heard in schools, but more than fifty years ago Clymer demonstrated this rule applies to real words only 45 percent of the time.[5] Abstract rules like this take more time to remember and apply than direct phonics facts as found in groups of similar words (*steak, break, great,* but *weak, leak, beat*), and rules often have so many confusing exceptions that they are difficult to justify as good teaching. To be plain, memorizing rules doesn't help children decode words quickly and efficiently in reading text. What does help decoding is encouraging readers to apply phonics in meaningful reading situations and with the most efficient and direct paths to comprehension possible.[6]

Factors That Affect Phonics Knowledge

As discussed in Chapter 2, ruling out nonreading factors that have an impact on reading success is important. Successful work with phonics depends on auditory discrimination and visual discrimination. These broad developmental skills can affect how parts of words are heard and how letters are perceived on the page. When teachers detect possible developmental difficulty in discriminating pieces and parts of spoken and printed words, they will want to seek additional testing and instructional ideas.

Auditory Discrimination. **Auditory discrimination** is the ability to detect differences and similarities in sounds. Auditory processing is totally dependent on hearing and auditory areas of the brain, not on letter identification. Children can have strong auditory awareness and yet still be unable to identify or use alphabet letters. Early in reading, these are separate skill sets.

SAMPLE EXERCISE

Directions: Partner up. Have one person take on the role of teacher, and the other the role of student. The teacher says: "Listen carefully. See if you can tell me which pairs of words are the same." Be careful not to show the student the printed words.

sat	set	ball	bell
cap	cap	sing	singe
hand	hand	pan	pan
sail	sell	burn	but

Directions: Listen carefully. Give me another word that rhymes with

can _____ fat _____

sail _____ day _____

Directions: Listen carefully. Give me another word that begins like

baby _____ can _____

door _____ fat _____

Visual Discrimination. **Visual discrimination** is the ability to detect similarities and differences among written symbols. As with auditory discrimination, children can know and recognize letters without visual discrimination. Remember, the two are separate skill sets, especially for early readers.

Phonics Content

Following is an outline of content addressed in phonics programs. In the text that follows the outline, for each element we provide a definition, examples, and exercises to help teachers better internalize phonics content that they need to help their students grow as readers. Recent research has suggested that many teachers do not yet know enough about English phonics to be of great help to readers who experience long-term failures with reading. This held true even for teachers in schools with well-structured phonics programs. Understanding phonics content is essential for teaching all readers, so knowing what to look for and what kinds of questions to ask is foundational to a diagnostic approach to teaching.[7] Having a great phonics program from which to teach is no substitute for diagnostic decision-making!

Consonants

Consonants are sounds that are obstructed in the mouth by positioning the tongue and shaping the mouth inside and out. There are only 21 consonant letters (graphemes) in English but 26 consonant sounds (phonemes). The match is imperfect because of the way English developed over centuries of history, with no consistent language authority designing the match of sounds to letters. This mismatch in the number of sounds and letters has resulted over time in thousands of word spellings that are unpredictable, including many consonants.

1. *Consonant onsets, or initial consonants.* At the beginning of a word, before the first vowel, onsets are highly predictable and regular.

a. Single consonant onsets: One letter matches one sound	b d f h j k l m n p r s t v w y z				
	c	/k/ as in *cat*, or /s/ as in *city*			
	g	/g/ as in *go*, or /dʒ/ as in *gem*.			
b. Consonant blend onsets: Two (or three) consonant sounds match two (or three) letters, with no vowel between them.	bl	fl	pr	sm	Tr
	br	fr	qu	sn	spl
	cl	gl	sc	sp	spr
	cr	gr	sk	st	squ
	dr	pl	sl	sw	str
c. Consonant digraph onsets: One sound matches two letters.	th	Voiced as in *this* Unvoiced as in *thin*	kn	/n/ as in *knife*	
	wh	/w/ as in *when* /h/ as in *who*	gh	/g/ as in *ghost*	
	wr	/r/ as in *write*	ch	/tʃ/ as in *chew* /k/ as in *choir*	
	sh	/ʃ/ as in *she*	ph	/f/ as in *phone*	
d. Blend + digraph onset: a combination of both	sch, as in *school* or *schedule* chr as in *chrome* or *Christ*				

2. *Consonant finals.* At the end of a word or syllable, consonants are often pronounced differently (allophones) than they are in the onset position. Many other patterns for the final position are best shown later in the *vowel phonograms* section. Unpredictable spellings for consonants (such as -ck) tend to be found more in word finals or medials (middle syllables) than as onsets.

a. Single-letter finals: One letter matches one sound.	-b, -c, -d, -f, -g, -m, -n, -p, -r, -s, -t, -z -s can have the /z/ sound as in *as, his, is, was*
b. Final consonant blends: Two letters match two sounds.	-ct, -ft, -lb, -ld, -lf, -lk, -lm, -lp, -lt, -mp, -nd, -nk, -nt, -pt, -sk, -sp, -st
c. Final consonant digraphs: Two letters match one sound.	-ng, -sh, -ch, -ck, -th, -gh
d. Final *x*: One letter matches two sounds.	-x as in *fox*, matches to the sounds /ks/
e. Double-letter finals: Two letters match one sound.	dd *add* ff *off* gg *egg* ll *hill*
	n *inn* ss *miss* rr *burr* zz *buzz*
f. Silent-letter finals: When there are two ways to pronounce a consonant letter, a silent *e* can mark the alternate pronunciation. Final *ve* is a historical anomaly—English words rarely end with a plain *v*.	-ce (ice), -ge (age), -que (unique), -the (breathe), -che (ache). -ve (have, give, live)

Vowels

Vowels are sounds made from the vocal chords, with no stopping effort from the tongue. Vowel sounds are formed by shaping the cheeks, lips, and tongue to shape the sound to be

- issued from the front or back of the mouth
- more open or more closed
- more round or flat

All English words have at least one vowel sound. The main vowel letters in English are A, E, I, O, U, and Y. W is a vowel when combined (ew, ow, aw). These letters have to be manipulated to cover 15–18 vowel sounds, and the first 5 letters do most of this work. The mismatch between letters and sounds again comes from centuries of historical change, with no people intelligently designing it. Because of the far-reaching change in vowel sounds over the centuries, vowel letters and sounds match with far more irregularity and unpredictability than do consonants.

3. *"Long" and "short" vowels.* Each of the five main vowel letters covers two sounds, one that matches the letter name and one that does not. They are called long and short for historical reasons, not because there is any significance to length of pronunciation today. Although these terms are convenient for sorting, there is no evidence to suggest the words *long* and *short* are helpful to learners.

a. Short vowels: When reading single-syllable words with a CVC spelling (consonant, vowel, consonant) or VC spelling, readers expect the short vowel sound. (*Many* words do not fit this pattern.)	A	hat, pan, dad, fad, cash, black, as, at
	E	bed, hen, bled, then, pet, neck, shed
	I	bit, it, in, pin, lid, snip, wind
	O	pop, on, hot, odd
	U	cut, bun, up, spud, shuck, hull
b. Long vowels: When reading single-syllable words with a CVCe or VCe spelling, readers expect the vowel to have the same pronunciation as the letter name. (*Many* words do not fit this pattern.)	A	cake, tame, scare, late, sale, mane
	E	these, here, complete
	I	kite, twine, wire, hike, pile, dine
	O	mole, phone, smoke, bore, home
	U	Cute, flume, tune, fluke, pure, mule
		(The long *u* is often pronounced as a blend with /y/—as in *use*.)

4. *The rest of the vowels.* The long–short pairs cover only 10 vowel sounds. There are 5–8 other important vowel sounds in English. Historical forces also explain the poor match in numbers for vowels. Many vowel letters are doubled up or put in combination with other letters to match sounds.

a. Y: Makes a vowel sound in the final or medial position.		try, fly, bye, by, dye, pyre, lyre, gym, rhythm baby, happy, windy
b. /ʊ/ The vowel in the word **book**. This vowel sound shares a double *o*, letter *u*, and *ou* spelling.		look, put, soot, push, good, sure, could
c. Vowel blends: Two vowel letters match two vowel sounds. Another term for these is *diphthong*.	oy	toy, boy, buoy, ploy
	oi	oil, coin, voice, soil
	ow	plow, brow, cow, down, crowd
	ou	foul, loud, out, house, our
d. Vowel digraphs: Two vowel letters match one vowel sound.		ay, ai, ee, oo, ue, au, aw
e. Schwa: This unstressed sound is very similar to the short *u* as in *cut*, but it is a sound we use in English to mark changes in rhythm. Any word in an unstressed position might be pronounced with a schwa sound.		Sof**a**, moth**e**r, fam**ou**s, **a**bove, qui**e**t, are**a**, th**e**, **a**, office It is common in phrases and sentences to unstress all but the most important words, so half or more words in authentic reading may be pronounced with this sound, no matter what the letters.

f. **R-control:** When readers might expect a vowel to be pronounced with the short vowel pattern, *r* provides the cue for a different pronunciation.	R-control vowel	Expected short vowel
	car	cat
	fur	fun
	stir	still
	her	hen
	corn	con

5. *Phonics effectiveness.* The National Reading Panel did a comparative analysis of many research studies on phonics teaching programs. The following conclusions[8] are based on the panel's report:

- Programs of phonics instruction are effective when they are
  - Systematic—the plan of instruction includes a carefully selected set of letter–sound relationships that are *organized into a logical sequence.*
  - Explicit—the *programs provide teachers with precise directions* for the teaching of these relationships.
- Effective phonics programs provide ample opportunities for children to *apply what they are learning* about letters and sounds to the reading of words, sentences, and stories.[9]
- Systematic and explicit phonics instruction is *most effective when it begins in kindergarten or first grade*, and becomes *progressively less effective in grades 2–12.*

Keep in mind that no specific system or sequence has been shown to be more effective than any other, so if a program is needed, one is as good as another. It is important for educators to beware of sales pitches that promote any one program's effectiveness over another, and of government policies that often grow to favor specific programs.[10]

Items 1–5 above represent the most basic phonics facts and research for many programs, and all children should get effective and complete teaching during grades K–1. In a diagnostic approach to assessing and teaching, discovering whether this has already occurred is important. If it has not, providing children with such instruction for the first time is necessary.

However, repeating this basic instruction during and after grade 2 is *not* supported by the research. For readers with phonics needs during and after grade 2, a diagnostic approach consists of asking focused questions about each reader's existing phonics knowledge to identify specific strengths and needs. In grades 2 and beyond, teachers need to expand their thinking about what word analysis entails. (See Figure 11.2.) For example, phonological awareness is primarily geared toward grades K–1, whereas word etymology toward grades 5–7. Although some children in grades K–2 find word etymology and structural analysis useful, rarely are these areas the primary instructional focus of these grades. The same is true for grades 3–7, where more time should be spent on structural analysis and word etymology than on phonics and phonological awareness. Although phonological awareness and phonics are two keys that open the door to word knowledge, structural analysis and word etymology enable readers to enter more complex text.

Items 6 and 8 below represent phonics content important for instruction beyond grade 2.[11]

6. *Phonograms.* Phonograms are spelling patterns for sounds. This term usually refers to "chunks" or groups of letters that match groups of sounds, such as those in Figure 11.3. The long and short patterns cover only some words, with many exceptions left to confuse readers. When words that make the same sound are placed next to each other, spelling can feel almost random: *do, shoe, through, glue, chew, fruit, you.* It is exactly this kind of variety that makes vowels difficult for young learners to read and write. But when each spelling for a vowel sound is treated as a category, groupings emerge.

Figure 11.3 Single-Syllable Phonograms

In linguistics, the term "rime" means the same thing as "rhyme"—a word ending that can take more than one beginning (or "onset"). Students who learn to see these endings as single chunks will not need to decode each letter–sound relationship. Teachers should demonstrate which words can be made by combining various onsets with just one rime phonogram, such as -oat: e.g., *float, boat, gloat, bloat, moat, coat,* and *goat*.

Rime Phonograms					Onset Phonograms
-ab	-eak	-igh	-oke	-uff	b
-able	-eal	-ight	-old	-ug	c
-ace	-eam	-ike	-ole	-ull	ch
-ack	-ean	-ild	-olt	-um	f
-add	-ear	-ile	-ome	-umble	ph
-ade	-east	-ilk	-ond	-ump	g
-ag	-eat	-ill	-ong	-un	gh
-age	-eck	-im	-ood	-unch	h
-aid	-ed	-ime	-ook	-ung	j
-ail	-ee	-imp	-ool	-unk	k
-ain	-eed	-in	-oom	-unt	l
-air	-eek	-ind	-oon	-up	m
-ake	-eel	-ine	-oop	-ur	n
-ale	-eem	-ing	-oot	-urn	kn
-alk	-een	-ink	-op	-ush	o
-all	-eep	-int	-ope	-usk	p
-am	-eer	-ip	-ore	-ust	qu
-ame	-eet	-ipe	-ork	-ut	r
-amp	-eeze	-ire	-orm		s
-an	-eg	-irl	-orn		sh
-and	-eld	-irt	-ort		t
-ane	-ell	-ish	-ose		tr
-ang	-elp	-isk	-oss		th
-ank	-elt	-iss	-ost		v
-ant	-em	-ist	-ot		w
-ap	-en	-it	-ote		wh
-ape	-ench	-ite	-ouch		wr
-ar	-end	-ive	-oud		y
-ard	-ent	-ix	-ought		z
-are	-ept	-oad	-ound		bl
-ark	-ess	-oal	-our		br
-arm	-est	-oam	-ouse		cl
-art	-et	-oast	-out		cr
-ash	-ew	-oat	-ove		d
-ast	-ib	-ob	-ove		dr
-aste	-ice	-obe	-ow		f
-at	-ick	-ock	-owl		fl
-ate	-id	ocket	-own		fr
-aw	-ide	-od	-ox		g
-awn	-ie	-ode	-oy		gl
-ay	-ief	-oe	-ub		gr
-ea	-ife	-oft	-uck		pl
-each	-ift	-og	-ud		pr
-ead	-ig	-oil	-udge		sch
					sk
					sl
					sp
					spl
					spr
					st
					str

Long *u* phonograms

who	do	to	two		you	group	soup	youth	through
glue	cue	true	blue		chew	few	new	dew	blew	threw
fruit	suit	juice	cruise		shoe

Of all the spellings for the long *u* sound, only *shoe* is alone. Categorizing separates what is truly irregular and strange from what belongs in a group. This kind of grouping and sorting is what adds predictability and a "system" to some of the strangest English vowel phonics. In a diagnostic approach, sorting and categorizing phonograms is the next level of phonics beyond the basics. Identifying phonograms as chunks of letters that go together based on spelling and sound helps learners "swim into the deep end of the pool" of English words.

7. *High-frequency words, or sight words.* Of the truly irregular words in English, unfortunately 94 percent happen to be the most common in-print, high-frequency words. (See the section on Sight Vocabulary in Chapter 10 and Figure 10.3.) Yet many of these irregular words also fit into groups or categories that can help learners discover phonogram patterns. For example, the long *u* sound made by the letter *o* in the words *do, who, to,* and *two* may seem strange until they are put into a category or pattern; the vowel in the word *of* might seem "irregular" until it is placed next to the dozens of other words in which the letter *o* makes the short *u* sound, such as *color, love, among, from,* and *son.*[12] Strange spellings for words seem less strange when they are part of a category or pattern. Categories are mnemonic devices—that is, they provide the structure needed for long-term memory.

8. *Multiple syllables.* A **syllable** is a vowel sound with the consonants that surround it. English has thousands of single-syllable words, and tens of thousands of multiple-syllable words. The phonics facts and principles described in items 1–6 above help readers mostly with single-syllable words. Multiple-syllable words represent the broader phonics challenge for readers in grades 4–12. Still, even for younger readers, multiple-syllable words appear in most books, magazines, and other materials written for them. In fact, the following 31 multiple-syllable words are in the top 200 high-frequency words:

other	into	people	only	water	little	very	after
any	also	around	another	because	different	away	again
number	every	between	under	never	along	below	something
always	often	together	going	important	until	children	

Enhanced eText
Video Example 11.1
In this **video clip**, a teacher works with a first-grade student on word recognition and chunking.

Equipping children with the basic tools for reading multiple-syllable words gives them a wider repertoire of strategies when reading for purpose and meaning. The list above embodies key facts about multiple-syllable words. Multiple-syllables can come from the following:

- Compound words: in-to, some-thing, al-ways, an-other, to-gether (gather)
- Grammatical endings: go-ing, tak-en, catch-er
- English affixes + roots: *be*cause, *be*tween, *be*low, *a*long, *a*gain, *a*way, child*ren*
- Latin and French affixes + roots: *im*port*ant*, differ*ent*

Multiple-syllable words also follow a phonogram principle, where grouping words into categories helps readers understand how they can derive the sound–letter match from known words. Examples of derivational phonogram categories are

little → battle, kettle, nettle, brittle, scuttle

Under → other, water, bitter, father, other

bucket → thicket, rocket, socket, locket, docket, thicket

Young readers are often intimidated by multiple-syllable words. To help alleviate this intimidation, teachers must assess how readers perceive the "chunks" that segment words into manageable parts, and teach the students how to chunk if necessary.

In English speech, many unstressed syllables are elided, or mashed with the consonants around them. In a word like *little*, speakers may say /litt·l/ and elide the final syllable /l/—not pronouncing a clear vowel before /l/. For a word like *different*, speakers may elide the middle syllable and say an unstressed schwa for the final syllable: /dif·rnt/. It is important for readers to know that they can match the words they know from speech to written words, so that they don't feel pressure to pronounce each chunk unnaturally.

Enhanced eText **Application Exercise 11.1:** Ms. Mills' Understanding of Phonics

Bridge: From Understanding to Assessment

When teachers understand that _____,	then teachers may want to assess _____.
English phonics do not have a one-sound-to-one-letter correspondence,	How students read word parts, including syllables, onset-rime, consonant blends and digraphs, and vowel diphthongs.
The highest-frequency words in English account for most of the irregularity in phonics,	Students' knowledge of opaque spellings, especially for vowels (such as *do* or *to,* as opposed to *no* or *go*).
All students need and deserve a systematic, sequential introduction to English phonics,	Whether this instruction has already happened.
The basic introduction to phonics is most effective in the first two years of instruction, and then less effective thereafter,	The specific phonics patterns that pose problems for each reader from grades 2–12.
Phonics instruction must be applied to authentic reading tasks to support comprehension,	How students use phonics knowledge when they read free-choice books and other authentic texts.

Assessing Phonics

As emphasized throughout this text, assessment leads to instruction. This is true for phonics as well as for any other aspect of reading. Teachers need to ask and answer three questions in order to conduct meaningful assessment: *What* do I want to know? *Why* do I want to know? *How* can I best discover this information?

Related to phonics, then, *what* we want to know is how students are using phonics skills in their everyday reading. *Why* we want to know centers on students' making the connection between instruction and their reading, seeing phonics as a tool to assist them as they construct meaning. Many phonics tests, such as the recently validated CORE Phonics Survey, can provide useful information on specific aspects of phonics.[13] But this test, like many others, has been criticized for its focus on word parts outside of meaningful contexts, including the use of nonsense words, phonics patterns not found in real English words, and the lack of coverage for phonics patterns applied widely for reading and spelling English words (*-ight, -ick, -all*). Fortunately, there are some practical, meaningful, and yes, even standardized ways *how* to discover students' facility with phonics.

Five Meaningful Ways to Assess Phonics

1. *Observation.* As noted in Chapter 3, observation can reveal much about students' reading behaviors. Using a checklist such as the one shown in Figure 11.4, teachers can watch and listen to children read, and learn what students do when they come to unknown words. They can then document what they see and hear on the checklist.

2. *Names Test.*[14] This test, developed by Cunningham and later validated by Dufflemeyer and colleagues, assesses students' ability to use what they know about phonics in a meaningful context. The test is most useful for assessing children in second through fifth grade. Directions for administering the test and the accompanying forms are as follows:

Administration Procedures:

1. Make enough copies of the Names Test Scoring Sheet and Scoring Matrix (see Figure 11.5) so that you have enough for each student who will be assessed.

Figure 11.4 Diagnostic Checklist for Word Recognition Skills

	Yes	No
1. The student uses		
a. context clues.		
b. picture clues (graphs, maps, charts).		
2. The student asks someone to state the word.		
3. The student uses the dictionary to try to unlock unknown words.		
4. The student uses phonic analysis by recognizing		
a. consonants.		
(1) single consonants: initial, final.		
(2) consonant blends (clusters) (*br, sl, cl, st,* and soon).		
(3) consonant digraphs (*th, sh, ph, ch,* and so on).		
(4) silent consonants (*kn, gn, pn*).		
b. vowels.		
(1) short vowels (*cot, can, get,* and so on).		
(2) long vowels (*go, we, no,* and so on).		
(3) final silent *e* (*bake, tale, role*).		
(4) vowel digraphs (*ea, oa, ee, ai,* and so on).		
(5) diphthongs (*oi, oy*).		
c. the effect of *r* on the preceding vowel.		
d. special letters and sounds (*y, c, g,* and *q*).		
e. known phonograms or graphemic bases (a succession of graphemes that occurs with the same phonetic value in a number of words [*ight, id, at, ad, ack*]).		

2. Write each name on a card or make a class roster that shows the names. Students will read the names from these cards or this class roster.

3. Individually administer the test. Hand the name cards or the class roster to the child and say something like "I want you to pretend that you are the classroom teacher and that you are calling out names to see who is in school today."

4. As the child reads the names, write exactly what the child says above each name on the Names Test Scoring Sheet.

5. Use the Scoring Matrix to analyze the child's performance:

   • Locate each name on the matrix.

   • Circle any phonic elements that were mispronounced.

   • Count the circled elements for each category.

   • Record the total number of errors next to the total possible on the Names Test Scoring sheet.

6. Make some decisions about which phonic elements the child needs to learn how to use.

7. Design instruction to address the needs.

Figure 11.5 Names Test Scoring Sheet and Scoring Matrix

Name _____ Grade _____ Teacher _____ Date _____

Jay Conway	Tim Cornell	Chuck Hoke	Yolanda Clark
Kimberly Blake	Roberta Slade	Homer Preston	Gus Quincy
Cindy Sampson	Chester Wright	Ginger Yale	Patrick Tweed
Stanley Shaw	Wendy Swain	Glen Spencer	Fred Sherwood
Flo Thornton	Dee Skidmore	Grace Brewster	Ned Westmoreland
Ron Smitherman	Troy Whitlock	Vance Middleton	Zane Anderson
Bernard Pendergraph	Shane Fletcher	Floyd Sheldon	Dean Bateman
Austin Shepherd	Bertha Dale	Neal Wade	Jake Murphy
Joan Brooks	Gene Loomis	Thelma Rinehart	

Phonics category	_Errors_
Initial consonants	___ /37
Initial consonant blends	___ /19
Consonant digraphs	___ /15
Short vowels	___ /36
Long vowel/VC-final _e_	___ /23
Vowel digraphs	___ /15
Controlled vowels	___ /25
Schwa	___ /15

(continued)

3. *Early Names Test*.[15] Based on the work of Cunningham and Dufflemeyer, Mather and colleagues adapted the Names Test so that it would be more appropriate to use with first-grade students as well as with older readers who may still have needs in basic phonics. Directions for administering the test and the accompanying forms are as follows:

Administration Procedures:

1. Make enough copies of the Early Names Test and Scoring Sheet (see Figure 11.6) so that you have enough for each student who will be assessed.

2. Write each name on a card or make a class roster that shows the names. Students will read the names from these cards or this class roster.

Figure 11.5 *(Continued)*

Table 4
Scoring Matrix for the Names Test

Name _____ Date _____

Name	InCon	InConBl	ConDgr	ShVow	LngVow/VC-e	VowDgr	CtrVow	Schwa
Anderson				A			er	o
Austin						Au		i
Bateman	B				ate			a
Bernard	B						er, ar	
Bertha	B		th				er	a
Blake		Bl			ake			
Brewster		Br					ew, er	
Brooks		Br				oo		
Chester			Ch	e			er	
Chuck			Ch	u				
Cindy	C			i	y			
Clark		Cl					ar	
Conway	C			o		ay		
Cornell	C			e			or	
Dale	D				ale			
Dean	D					ea		
Dee	D					ee		
Fletcher		Fl	ch	e			er	
Flo		Fl			o			
Floyd		Fl				oy		
Fred		Fr		e				
Gene	G				ene			
Ginger	G			i			er	
Glen		Gl		e				
Grace		Gr			ace			
Gus	G			u				
Hoke	H				oke			
Homer	H				o		er	
Jake	J				ake			
Jay	J					ay		
Joan	J					oa		
Kimberly	K			i	y		er	
Loomis	L					oo		i
Middleton	M			i				o
Murphy	M		ph		y		ur	

3. Individually administer the test. Hand the name cards or the class roster to the child and say "I want you to pretend that you are a teacher and you are calling out your students' names to take attendance. You are trying to figure out who is at school and who is not. Some of these names may be hard, but just do the best you can."

4. As the child reads the names, follow the scoring procedures on the form: Record a "1" for every correct response and a "0" for an incorrect response. Score both first and last names. Write incorrect responses directly above the name.

Figure 11.5 (Continued)

Table 4
Scoring Matrix for the Names Test (cont'd.)

Name _____ Date _____

Name	InCon	InConBl	ConDgr	ShVow	LngVow/VC-e	VowDgr	CtrVow	Schwa
Neal	N					ea		
Ned	N			e				
Patrick	P			a, i				
Pendergraph	P		ph	e, a			er	
Preston		Pr		e				o
Quincy				i	y			
Rinehart	R				ine		ar	
Roberta	R				o		er	a
Ron	R			o				
Sampson	S			a				o
Shane			Sh		ane			
Shaw			Sh				aw	
Sheldon			Sh	e				o
Shepherd			Sh	e			er	
Sherwood			Sh			oo	er	
Skidmore		Sk		i			or	
Slade		Sl			ade			
Smitherman		Sm	th	i			er	a
Spencer		Sp		e			er	
Stanley		St		a		ey		
Swain		Sw				ai		
Thelma			Th	e				a
Thornton			Th				or	o
Tim	T			i				
Troy		Tr				oy		
Tweed		Tw				ee		
Vance	V			a				
Wade	W				ade			
Wendy	W			e	y			
Westmoreland	W			e			or	a
Whitlock			Wh	i, o				
Wright					i			
Yale	Y				ale			
Yolanda	Y			a	o			a
Zane	Z				ane			

5. Use the Scoring Matrix to analyze the child's performance:

- Locate each name on the matrix.
- Circle any phonic elements that were mispronounced.
- Count the circled elements for each category.
- Record the total number of errors next to the total possible on the Early Names Test and Scoring Sheet.

6. Make some decisions about which phonic elements the child needs to learn how to use.

7. Design instruction to address the needs.

Figure 11.6 Early Names Test and Scoring Sheet

Administration Instructions and Scoring Sheet

Say: "I want you to pretend that you are a teacher and you are calling out your students' names to take attendance. You are trying to figure out who is at school and who is not. Some of these names may be hard, but just do the best you can."

Scoring: Record a 1 for a correct response and a 0 for an incorrect response. Score both first and last names. Write incorrect responses directly above the name.

Student's Name _____ Grade _____ Date _____

Rob___ Hap___	Jud___ Lem___	Ray___ San___	Pat___ Ling___
Tim___ Bop___	Brad___ Tash___	Pam___ Rack___	Trish___ Mot___
Fred___ Tig___	Bab___ Fum___	Kate___ Tide___	Brent___ Lake___
Flip___ Mar___	Jet___ Mit___	Rand___ Lun___	Jen___ Dut___
Jake___ Bin___	Sid___ Gold___	Frank___ Lug___	Grace___ Nup___
Beck___ Daw___	Dell___ Smush___	Gus___ Lang___	Lex___ Yub___
Ross___ Quest___	Dane___ Wong___	Tom___ Zall___	Gail___ Vog___
Rod___ Blade___	Tag___ Shick___		TOTAL_____

**Phonics category**	_**# missed/# possible**_
Initial consonants	____/48
Ending consonants	____/40
Consonant blend	____/11
Consonant digraph	____/10
Short vowel	____/46
Long vowel/VC-final _e_	____/7
Vowel digraph	____/2
Rime	____/58

Source: Based on N. Mather et al. (2009), Adaptations of the Names Test: Easy-to-use phonics assessments, John Wiley and Sons, 60(2), 114–122.

Enhanced eText Application Exercise (video) 11.2: Early Names Test

---

4. *Tile Test.*[16] This is a more comprehensive assessment of early readers' understanding of English orthography. Norman and Calfee explain that the test "provides a hands-on interactive experience with letters and sounds for teachers who want to delve more deeply into students' underlying thinking."[17] Using tiles and specific prompts, the teacher asks individual children to perform a variety of

Figure 11.6 *(Continued)*

Scoring Matrix for the Early Names Test

Name _____ Grade _____ Date _____

Name	Initial consonant	Ending consonant	Consonant blend	Consonant digraph	Short vowel	Long vowel/ Vowel-consonant-final *e*	Vowel digraph	Rime
Bab	B	-b			a			-ab
Beck	B			-ck	e			-eck
Bin	B	-n			i			-in
Blade		-d	Bl-			a-e		-ade
Bop	B	-p			o			-op
Brad		-d	Br-		a			-ad
Brent			Br- -nt		e			-ent
Dane	D	-n				a-e		-ane
Daw	D						-aw	-aw
Dell	D	-ll			e			-ell
Dut	D	-t			u			-ut
Flip		-p	Fl-		i			-ip
Frank			Fr- -nk		a			-ank
Fred		-d	Fr-		e			-ed
Gold	G		-ld					-old
Grace			Gr-			a-e		-ace
Gus	G	-s			u			-us
Hap	H	-p			a			-ap
Jake	J	-k				a-e		-ake
Jen	J	-n			e			-en
Jet	J	-t			e			-et
Jud	J	-d			u			-ud
Kate	K	-t				a-e		-ate
Lake	L	-k				a-e		-ake
Lang	L			-ng	a			-ang
Lem	L	-m			e			-em
Lex	L	-x			e			-ex
Ling	L			-ng	i			-ing
Lug	L	-g			u			-ug
Lun	L	-n			u			-un
Mar	M							-ar
Mit	M	-t			i			-it

(continued)

activities, each designed to reveal the child's understanding of phonics elements and metalinguistic awareness. Directions for administrating each section of the test are shown on the Tile Test Recording Sheet. (See Figure 11.7.) Make enough copies so that you have one for each student who will be assessed. And, as with other phonics assessments, use what you discover to design appropriate instruction. The Developmental Spelling Inventory in the *Words Their Way* program takes a similarly comprehensive review of phonics knowledge.

Figure 11.6 (*Continued*)

Scoring Matrix for the Early Names Test (cont'd.)								

Name _____ Grade _____ Date _____

Name	Initial consonant	Ending consonant	Consonant blend	Consonant digraph	Short vowel	Long vowel/ Vowel-consonant-final *e*	Vowel digraph	Rime
Mot	M	-t			o			-ot
Nup	N	-p			u			-up
Pam	P	-m			a			-am
Pat	P	-t			a			-at
Quest	(Qu)*		-st		e			-est
Rack	R			-ck	a			-ack
Rand	R		-nd		a			-and
Ray	R						-ay	-ay
Rob	R	-b			o			-ob
Rod	R	-d			o			-od
Ross	R	-ss			o			-oss
San	S	-n			a			-an
Shick				Sh- -ck	i			-ick
Sid	S	-d			i			-id
Smush			Sm-	-sh	u			-ush
Tag	T	-g			a			-ag
Tash	T			-sh	a			-ash
Tide	T	-d				i-e		-ide
Tig	T	-g			i			-ig
Tim	T	-m			i			-im
Tom	T	-m			o			-om
Trish	T		Tr-	-sh	i			-ish
Vog	V	-g			o			-og
Wong	W			-ng	o			-ong
Yub	Y	-b			u			-ub
Zall	Z	-ll						-all

Note: *Qu is sometimes referred to as a consonant oddity or a consonant blend.*

5. *Running Record.*[18] Perhaps one of the easiest ways for teachers to see how children apply phonics to decode unknown words is to watch students read an authentic text and make note of what they see (i.e., running record). All forms and administration procedures can be found in Chapter 4.

Enhanced eText Application Exercise 11.3: Ms. Mills Assesses Phonics

Bridge: From Assessment to Teaching

When teachers understand that _____,	then teachers may want to assess _____.
Phonics knowledge is most useful when applied to text,	Readers' phonics knowledge by observing them as they read authentic text.
Phonics knowledge should be applied simultaneously with meaning,	Using the Names Test or Early Names Test, where readers know the words have focused meanings.
Phonics knowledge includes many kinds of parts and structures important for reading words,	Using a comprehensive test of strategies and phonics content, such as the Tile Test or the Developmental Spelling Inventory.

FIGURE 11.7 Tile Test Recording Sheet

Name _____ Date _____

Letters and sounds: Display letter tiles m, a, p, i, s, t, d, n.

"Here are some letters. I'll say the name of a letter and ask you to point to the letter. Point to the tile that has the letter *m*." (Record. Continue procedure with each letter.)

"Now, I'll point to a tile and you'll tell me two things about the letter. First, the *name* of the letter and, second, the *sound* that it makes." (Record.)

Identification	Name	Sound	Identification	Name	Sound
m			s		
a			t		
p			d		
i			n		

Words: Add letter tiles f, b.

Decoding. "Now let's put some letters together to make words. I'll go first and make a word, then I'll ask you to read it for me." (Manipulate only necessary letters. Stop after *sat* and ask the first metalinguistic question.)

pat	_____	fin	_____
sat*	_____	pit	_____
sam	_____	tab	_____
fan	_____	mid	_____

*Metalinguistic question: "How did you know to say *sat* (or other pronunciation) that way?" _____
_____

Metalinguistic question: Rebuild the word that the student had the most difficulty with but decoded correctly. "How did you know to say_____that way?" _____

Spelling. "Now, I'll say a word, and you'll build it for me." (As you dictate, clearly articulate by "stretching and exaggerating." Example: tan = /ta:::n:::/. Stop after *tad* and ask the first metalinguistic question.)

tan	_____	sip	_____
tad*	_____	tin	_____
mad	_____	pad	_____
sap	_____	fit	_____

*Metalinguistic question: "How did you know to (spell) *tad* that way?"_____

Metalinguistic question: Rebuild the word that the student had the most difficulty with but built correctly. "How did you know to build_____that way?" _____
_____

Sight-word reading. Lay out the collection of word tiles. "I'll show you some words, and you read each one." (Record.)

I	_____	me	_____	the	_____	a	_____
is	_____	at	_____	look	_____	dog	_____
cat	_____	big	_____	map	_____	can	_____
sat	_____	fat	_____	sit	_____	on	_____
run	_____						

"I'll make a sentence with some words, and you read the sentence for me."

I can run. _____
Look at me. _____
I sat on the cat. _____
The map is big. _____
Sit the dog on the fat cat. _____

"Now I'll say a sentence, and you can make it for me." [Have the student read the sentence after building it. (*Record sentence made and the student's read of it.*)

I can sit. _____
The dog is fat. _____
Look at the map. _____
A dog can look at me. _____
The big cat sat on the dog. _____

"Now I want you to read one sentence for me." (*Give the student the sheet with the sentence printed on it. Record the student's reading.*)

Kim and Nate smiled as they hopped on the trip home at sunset. _____
_____

General Observations: _____
_____
_____
_____

Teaching Phonics
Guidelines for Exemplary Phonics Instruction

Phonics instruction needs to excite and stimulate language learning. Children need to understand the joy in being able to manipulate the sounds and letters of their language to create words. Phonics instruction that is going to be most useful to children requires careful thought and planning. The instruction need not use worksheets, nor should it be a chore or a bore. Authors of many different commercial programs aim to help teachers with this thoughtful planning by providing scripted teacher manuals with accompanying student materials. But how can we be sure that these materials are the best to use?

Fortunately, there are some research-based guidelines for exemplary phonics instruction. These guidelines can provide a framework for designing phonics programs. If teachers must use a commercial phonics program, these guidelines can be helpful when examining the materials that comprise the program.

Exemplary phonics instruction can be characterized as follows:

1. Builds on what children already know about reading, such as how print functions, what stories are and how they work, and the purpose for reading.

2. Builds on a foundation of phonological awareness. (See Chapter 8.)

3. Is clear and direct. That is, the explanations make sense, and the teacher uses demonstrations to help children better understand how to apply what they are learning.

4. Is integrated into a total reading program. In terms of explicit, formal instruction, this means that no more than 15–20 minutes per day is allotted to it. Children are provided with many reading and writing opportunities to apply their phonics knowledge—above and beyond the practice activities teachers assign.

5. Focuses on reading words rather than learning rules. To help children see that the purpose of phonics is to acquire words, children need to be taught how to look for patterns in words rather than how to memorize "rules."

6. Leads to automatic word identification. The purpose of phonics is to help children acquire a large store of words so that they can read with greater ease. They need much meaningful practice so that they can use these words instantaneously while reading.[19]

Eight Ways to Teach Phonics

There are two basic approaches to teaching phonics: implicit instruction and explicit instruction. Implicit instruction leads children to discover parts of words, whereas in explicit instruction, teachers tell students what the parts are. Regardless of whether teachers use one or both approaches, instruction needs to be coupled with demonstrations. Because teachers want children to actually transfer this knowledge to their reading, they need to model how students can use what they just learned.

As with any good instruction, purpose is what guides the selection of a specific way to teach. Below we provide eight methods for helping students gain and use phonics knowledge as a comprehension tool.

All phonics activities work on either breaking words apart (**analytic phonics**) or putting words together (**synthetic phonics**). Be mindful of giving children opportunities to both *analyze* and *synthesize* word parts. Some researchers promote the idea that only synthetic phonics aids in reading, whereas analytic phonics aids in spelling. But other researchers have found analytic phonics to also have important value for reading. No responsible reading of the research suggests any specific program or method should be promoted over others, as long as each reader gets a systematic and well-sequenced program of instruction during her earliest years learning to read.[20]

1. *Teach Word Identification Strategies.* Strategies are techniques learners use when they do not know what to do quickly and automatically. **Word identification** strategies

help learners problem-solve how to pronounce and understand words. Students may apply a pronunciation strategy in one reading situation, and on the very next page apply a meaning-based strategy. Both are used to help readers find the shortest path to comprehension.

Overemphasizing pronunciation strategies at the expense of meaning sends students a message about the purpose of reading—they may think reading is all about calling words. Overemphasizing meaning at the expense of pronunciation may send students a message that reading the printed words accurately does not matter. In truth, good readers use a variety of strategies to identify words that do not come to them quickly.

One of the best ways to teach these strategies is to ask a whole class of readers to come together just after reading. Ask them to tell what they do when they see a word that does not come to them quickly. Write their responses on charts labeled *Meaning Strategies* and *Pronunciation Strategies*.

A typical list of "word attack" strategies follows:

Meaning Strategies	*Pronouncing Strategies*
• Reread the sentence.	• Break the word into chunks.
• Skip the word and read to the end of the phrase.	• Try first sounds to see if the rest will come.
• Look at the pictures for a word clue.	• Try substituting a different vowel sound for those vowel letters.

2. *Teach from Whole to Part Using Rhymes from Children's Literature.* Getting a sense of the whole is often a sure way to help children understand the parts.[21] Meaningful associations are made when students see how the parts relate to the overall text. There are a couple of ways to implement whole-to-part instruction.

Whole-Part-Whole with Rhymes or Poems.   The inverted triangle shown in Figure 11.8 is one way to think about whole-to-part instruction. Using this diagram, then, a teacher might begin with a well-known rhyme, such as "Humpty Dumpty,"

Figure 11.8 Whole-to-Part Phonics Instruction

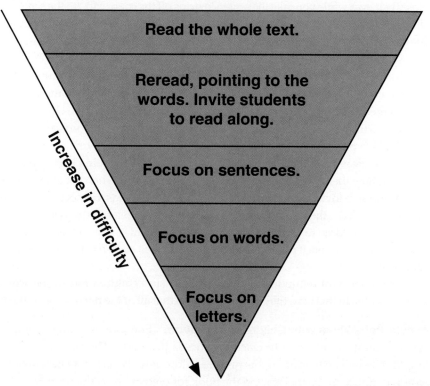

Figure 11.9 Whole-Part-Whole Phonics Instruction

Whole

- Read aloud.
- Model expressive reading.
- Promote enjoyment.
- Provide extension activities:
  - dramatization
  - compare/contrast

Part

- Focus on phonic element.
- Use portion from text.
- Children participate.
- Provide visual reminder.
- Word slotter: build words.

Whole

- Present new book, same phonic element.
- Children read the story:
  - choral reading
  - partner reading
  - individual reading

Source: Based on P. Trachtenburg, "Using Children's Literature to Enhance Phonics Instruction," *The Reading Teacher* 43 (1990): 648–654.

that is displayed on a chart large enough for all to see. After reading the entire text a few times, the teacher invites the children to read along.

The second step involves writing each line of the rhyme on a sentence strip. Read the sentence strips to the children, placing them in a pocket holder for all to see. Ideally, the chart containing the whole rhyme is next to the pocket chart. Point out (if no student tells you) that the two are the same. In turn, take each sentence strip out of the holder and place it on top of the sentence shown on the original chart. Reread the rhyme with the children, pointing to each word. Having modeled the process, ask the children to close their eyes while you take the sentence strips off the chart. Mix up the sentences and distribute them to some volunteers. In turn, each volunteer comes to the chart and places the sentence over the matching sentence on the chart. Reread the rhyme with the children.

The third step helps children to better understand "wordness" (i.e., word boundaries). Using a pair of scissors, cut each sentence strip apart and ask the children to count the number of words that fall on the floor. They can then reassemble the rhyme by placing the words over the matching words on the chart.

A fourth step involves helping children understand that words are made of letters. Make word cards for some of the words shown in the rhyme, or use the words from the cut-apart sentences. Tell the children that you are going to cut apart a given word to show them how many letters make up that word. Then cut apart each word.

A fifth step involves phonic elements. Choose the words that focus on the phonics element you want them to notice and use these words to teach the skill. For example, if you want children to learn about the initial consonant *h*, select those words and use either explicit or implicit phonics instruction (described above) to teach them this initial consonant.

One important reminder is in order: Make sure children reread the whole text every session. In this way, they will begin to see that all of the parts relate to the whole.

Whole-Part-Whole with Children's Literature. Sometimes, using an entire children's literature selection to teach phonics is desirable. The procedures listed in Figure 11.9 will be helpful in this process. Although phonics may be a major focus, you will notice that experiencing the book for enjoyment is the first step.

Of utmost importance is identifying the specific phonic element you want to teach and rounding up the children's books that contain enough examples so that children can apply what they have learned when reading a text. The following list identifies some books that can be used to teach both long and short vowels.

Children's Literature for Whole-Part-Whole Phonics Instruction

Long a: Cohen, C. L. *How Many Fish?* New York: HarperCollins, 1998.

Long e: Milgrim, D. *See Pip Point.* New York: Atheneum, 2003.

Long i: Ziefert, H. *A New House for Mole and Mouse.* New York: Puffin, 1987.

Long o: Bauer, M. D. *Rain.* New York: Aladdin, 2004.

Long u: Segal, L. *Tell Me a Trudy.* New York: Farrar, Straus, & Giroux, 1977.

Short a: Carle, E. *From Head to Toe.* New York: HarperCollins, 1997.

Short e: Ets, M. *Elephant in a Well.* New York: Viking, 1972.

Short i: Meister, C. *When Tiny Was Tiny.* New York: Puffin, 1999.

Short o: Foster, K., and G. Erickson, *A Mop for Pop.* New York: Barron's, 1991.

Short u: Lewison, W. C. *Buzz Said the Bee.* New York: Scholastic, 1992.

Additional Children's Literature to Enhance Phonics Knowledge

Baker, Keith. *Just How Long Can a Long String Be?!* New York: Scholastic, 2009.

———. *Cat Tricks.* San Diego, CA: Harcourt, 1997.

Ehlert, Lois. *Top Cat.* San Diego, CA: Harcourt, 1998.

Emberley, Rebecca, Adrian Emberley, and Ed Emberley. *There Was an Old Monster!* New York: Scholastic, 2009.

Enderle, Judith Ross, and Stephanie Gordon Tessler. *Six Creepy Sheep.* Honesdale, PA: Boyds Mills, 1992.

Hawkins, Colin, and Jacqui Hawkins. *Jen the Hen.* New York: G. P. Putnam's Sons, 2002.

Hepworth, Cathi. *Antics.* New York: G. P. Putnam's Sons, 1992.

———. *Bug Off!* New York: G. P. Putnam's Sons, 1998.

Johnston, Tony. *It's About Dogs.* San Diego, CA: Harcourt, 2000.

Le Guin, Ursula K. *Cat Dreams.* New York: Scholastic, 2009.

Mitton, Tony. *Farmer Joe and the Music Show.* New York: Scholastic, 2008.

Potter, Alicia. *Fritz Danced the Fandango.* New York: Scholastic, 2009.

Priceman, Marjorie. *Froggie Went A-Courting.* Boston: Little, Brown, and Company, 2000.

Pulver, Robin. *Silent Letters Loud and Clear.* New York: Holiday House, 2008.

Shaw, Nancy. *Sheep Take a Hike.* Boston: Houghton Mifflin, 1994.

Singer, Marilyn. *I'm Your Bus.* New York: Scholastic, 2009.

Wilbur, Richard. *The Pig in the Spigot.* San Diego, CA: Harcourt, 2000.

Wilhelm, Hans. *Come Rhyme with Me!* New York: Scholastic, 2008.

Yolen, Jane, and Mark Teague. *How Do Dinosaurs Say Good Night?* New York: Scholastic, 2000.

Zuckerman, Andrew. *Creature.* San Francisco, CA: Chronicle, 2009.

3. *Use Word Sorts.* Sorting is a way of categorizing pictures or words with similar sound features. Pictures or words can be sorted into several categories, such as those that rhyme, beginning sounds, phonograms, and vowel sounds. Sorting activities help children form schema for phonics elements.

There are two basic ways to have children sort. In a *closed sort*, you give students the categories and ask them to sort a given number of cards. This type of sort leads to convergent thinking. In an *open sort*, you invite students to create and name the categories. This type of sort encourages divergent thinking. Both types of sorts are valuable and will help you to see what students know about words. However, open sorts lend even more insight into what students are noticing on their own—what they have internalized.

Here are some suggested steps for using word sorts:

1. Model what you expect students to do.
2. Give children several cards to sort into contrasting categories.
3. Provide practice with your guidance.
4. Have students work with one another to sort.

Enhanced eText
Video Example 11.2

In this **video clip**, a group of children uses word cards, word family mats, and wipe-off boards to match and write words belonging to the word families /a/, /et/, /op/, and /ug/.

4. *Teach Students How to Decode by Analogy.* Teaching students how to decode by analogy involves having them use a word they know to identify a word they do not know. For example, a child might know the word *cat*, yet not know the word *bat*. Assuming that both words are in the child's listening vocabulary, the teacher asks if *bat* looks like any other word that the child knows. If not, the teacher writes the word the child does know, *cat*, right above *bat*. He then has the child read *cat*. Most often, the child will see how the two words are the same and will read *bat* without additional help. Sometimes a prompt is provided, such as "If this word is *cat*, then this one has to be ———," to get the child to decode the word.

5. *Use Writing.* Perhaps one of the best ways for children to apply what they know about phonics and to learn more about it is for them to write. Regardless of what we *think* children know about phonics or what we *think* we taught them, their writing will show us what they have actually internalized to the point of being able to apply it. For example, after learning about the *"ai"* spelling for long *a*, children may use it to spell all words having the long *a* sound. Just like when they are learning spoken language, they may overgeneralize. That is, you may see correct words like *rain* and *pain*, but also overgeneralizations such as *caik* and *maik*.

We suggest giving each student a blank book and using class time for writing at least once a day. Daily writing can serve as evidence of the children's performance and growth in phonics knowledge over time.

6. *Teach Students How to Make Words.* Making words is a manipulative word-building activity designed by Cunningham.[22] This activity involves having children put letter cards together to form words, and it can be used to either teach or reinforce building words with phonograms. Figure 11.10 provides an example.

7. *Glass Analysis.* To help students learn how sounds and letters match, ask them to analyze and synthesize words for which they already know the meaning. Decide in advance what kinds of parts to break the words into: onset-rime, syllables, or phonemes.

Make each word on a card. Show and say the word for students, then tell them the sound–letter matches. Then blend the sounds back into the whole word. Then ask students to tell you the chunks, either for sounds or letters.

> Teacher demonstrates: "The word is *chunk*. Letters *ch* say /tʃ/, letters *unk* say /uŋk/. The word is *chunk*."

> Students respond with letters: "Which letters say /tʃ/? (*ch*) Which letters say /uŋk/? (*unk*)" "What is the word? *Chunk*."

> Students respond with sounds: "What do letters *ch* c-h say? /tʃ/ What do letters u-n-k say? /uŋk/" "What is the word? *Chunk*."

This technique works well for individual students when paired with Elkonin boxes, where the teacher draws large boxes to match the number of chunks being

Figure 11.10 Make Words Lesson

Letters: a   d   n   s   t
Words: at   an   and   Dan   tan   ant   sat   sad   sand   stand

Name letters and their common sounds: Before beginning to make words, have the students hold up each letter, name it, and say its common sound. Have the students show both the lowercase and capital letters

Make words: Have the students make these words, then send one student to make each word using the big letters. DO NOT wait for everyone to make the word before sending someone up. Keep the lesson fast-paced and the students will pay better attention. When the word is made with the big letters, ask everyone to check their words and fix them if necessary.

1. Take 2 letters and make **at**. We are **at** school.
2. Take the **t** away and add a different letter to make **an**. I ate **an** apple.
3. Add a letter to **an** and you can spell **and**. I like apples **and** bananas.
4. Now we are going to do a trick with **and**. Move the letters in **and** around so that they spell **Dan**. Stretch out **Dan** and listen for where you hear the **D** and the **a** and the **n**. (Look for a student who has **Dan** spelled with a capital letter **D**, and send that student to make **Dan** with big letters.) My cousin's name is **Dan.**
5. Take the **D** away and add a letter to spell **tan**. I got a **tan** at the beach.
6. Now let's do the "move the letters around" trick with **tan** to spell **ant**. Stretch out **ant** with me and listen for where you hear the sounds. The **ant** is tiny.
7. Let's start over and make another 3-letter word, **sat**. The boy **sat** down.
8. Take the **t** away, add another letter, and you can spell **sad**. He was very **sad.**
9. Now we are going to spell a 4-letter word. Add 1 letter to **sad** and you can spell **sand**. Let's all say **sand** and listen for the letter we need to add. She digs in the **sand.**
10. The last word in every lesson is the secret word. Add 1 letter to **sand** and you can spell another word. I am going to look and see if anyone has figured out the secret word. (Give them no more than a minute to try to figure it out and then say a sentence with the secret word. Everyone **stand** up.) Have someone make **stand** with the big letters.

Sort: Collect the letters, then read with the students all the words in the pocket chart. Next, have them sort the words into columns according to their first letter.

at	sat	Dan	tan
an	sad		
and	sand		
ant	stand		

Transfer: Say some words in sentences and have the students repeat the words and decide what letter they begin with.

| dog | top | sun | add | apple | teacher | doctor | sister |

demonstrated. When it is the students' turn, let them either write the letters or place a cut-up word card inside the boxes.

| ch | unk |

8. *Use Prompts When Reading with Students.* As expert readers, we know that there are several strategies we can employ to figure out unknown words. We want to pass this expertise along to students so that they, too, can be independent readers. We want to help them develop what Clay calls a "self-extending system."[23] Prompting is one way to help them develop this system.

Knowing the type of prompt to provide depends on what we know about both the student and the word that is posing difficulty. Table 11.1 gives some guidance.

Table 11.1 Word Analysis Prompts

Strategy	Use When	Example Prompt
Word part a student can pronounce	The unknown word has a part you know the student can pronounce	"There's a part of that word you can say. Find it and say it."
Analogy	The unknown word is similar to a word you know the student knows	"This word is like another one you know."
Each sound	The student has difficulty with chunking words, yet can figure out the word using each sound	"Say each sound in this word."
Context	The student is weak in using phonics clues	"Read to the end of the sentence and ask yourself what would make sense."

Source: Based on T. Gunning, *Assessing and Correcting Reading and Writing Difficulties*, 3rd ed. (Boston: Allyn and Bacon, 2006).

Enhanced eText **Application Exercise 11.4:** Ms. Mills Teaches Phonics

---

Bridge: From Teaching Back to Understanding

When teachers understand that _____,	then teachers may want to assess _____.
Many children's authors write texts based on word play with phonics elements,	How children apply phonics knowledge in books with rhyming, alliteration, and other phonics-based poetic devices.
Synthesizing word parts into whole words is important for applying phonics,	How students make words with manipulatives materials made of word parts (as in the Glass Analysis technique).
Analyzing whole words into phonics elements is important for learning how English words work,	How students split words into parts (as in the Glass Analysis technique).

Revisiting the Opening Scenario

Ms. Mills was trying to decide how to best ascertain Jorge's decoding abilities and how to teach the phonics he needed to learn. Now that you have read the chapter, you have an understanding of phonics content, assessment strategies, and teaching strategies. How would you recommend Ms. Mills proceed?

Enhanced eText **Application Exercise: 11.5:** Ms. Mills Reflects on Assessing and Teaching Phonics

Authors' Summary

Before reading our summary statements for each outcome, we suggest you read each outcome and summarize it in your own words.

Once finished, cross-check your response with our brief summary to determine how well you recalled the major points.

11.1 Describe the position of phonics assessment and instruction in a diagnostic approach to teaching reading.

- Phonics assessment should answer specific questions teachers have about students' word identification. Meaning has an impact on word identification. So comprehension and vocabulary questions should be answered before assuming students have phonics needs. Also, phonics assessment should be used to seek out strengths first, needs second. Use strengths as the basis for teaching. For example, a reader knows words starting with *st* and *sp* blends, but is having difficulty reading words with *str* and *spl* blends. Use a review of the strength to set up teaching the need.

11.2 Correctly identify, sort, and label phonics facts— matches between sounds and letters in English words.

Word	Phonics Facts
chunk	Single syllable. Initial digraph *ch*. Short vowel *u*. Final blend *nk*.
brought	Single syllable. Initial blend *br*. Phonogram *–ought* (thought, ought, wrought, sought, bought).
father	Two syllables. Initial consonant *f*. Phonogram *a* (water, want, all). Digraph *th*. R-controlled *er*.
because	• Stressed first syllable, unstressed second syllable → BEE-cuz (U.S. Midwest regional pronunciation) • Unstressed first syllable, stressed second syllable clue. → buh-KOZ (U.S. Southern regional pronunciation)

11.3 Apply five different techniques for assessing phonics knowledge.

- Observation
- Names Test
- Early Names Test
- Tile Test
- Running Record

11.4 Explain guidelines for effective phonics instruction, and apply both direct and inductive techniques for teaching phonics.

- Only teach the phonics students need to gain comprehension. A complete sequence of phonics is recommended only in grades K–1, with effectiveness declining thereafter. Direct techniques: When listening to a child's reading, she pronounces the word *fight* correctly and later miscues the words *sight* and *light*, pronouncing the *g* and *h*. The teacher asks her to return to the sentence with *fight* to point out her strength, and then uses a word card to show her that *sight* and *light* have the same *–ight* phonogram. The teacher then asks her to reread passages with these words. This is an example of direct teaching of the analogy strategy. Indirect techniques: Ask students to skim their reading to predict words that might be difficult to read. Ask them to talk about which word attack strategies would help them identify the word and to practice these strategies on the selected words. Because the words are drawn from their free reading and because they select the strategies, this is all inductive teaching.

Think About It!

1. You have been appointed to a special primary-grade reading committee. Your task is to help teachers better understand the role that phonics plays in the word recognition process. How would you go about doing this?

2. Design a workshop on meaningful ways to teach phonics. What will you present?

3. Present a lesson that would help a primary-grade student learn about a phonic element of your choice.

4. Your state legislators are proposing a bill to mandate the teaching of phonics in all schools. How do you feel about this? Prepare a talk expressing your views.

Websites

- https://scholarworks.gvsu.edu/cgi/viewcontent.cgi?article=1435&context=lajm

    This link provides access to Constance Weaver's fact sheet on teaching phonics. In the article, Weaver explains the research behind integrating phonics instruction in a whole-language curriculum. In addition to providing general information, the fact sheet includes an extensive bibliography.

Endnotes

1. Cunningham, P. (2013). *Phonics they use*. New York: Pearson.
2. Pletcher, B., & Christensen, R. (2017). Conferring in the CAFÉ: One-to-one reading conferences in two first grade classrooms. *Reading Horizons* 56.3, 1.
3. Erekson, J., Adam, A., & McGoldrick, R. (2012, February). Counting what counts. Denver, CO: International Reading Association.
4. McKee, P. (1966). *The teaching of reading in the elementary school*. New York: Houghton Mifflin.
5. Clymer, T. (1963, January). The utility of phonic generalizations in the primary grades. *The Reading Teacher* 16, 252–258.
6. Cunningham, J., & Cunningham, P. (2000). What we know about how to teach phonics. In A. E. Farstrup & S. J. Samuels (Eds.), *What Research Has to Say About Reading Instruction* (3rd ed., pp. 87–109). Newark, DE: International Reading Association.
7. Cohen, R., et al. (2017). A comparison of schools: Teacher knowledge of explicit code-based reading instruction. *Reading and Writing* 30.4, 653–690.
8. CIERA & NIFL. (2003) *Put reading first*. Washington, DC: National Institute for Literacy.
9. Mesmer, H., & Williams, O. (2014). Modeling first grade reading development. *Reading Psychology* 35.5, 468–495.
10. Ellis, S. & Moss, G. (2014). Ethics, education policy and research: The phonics question reconsidered. *British Educational Research Journal* 40.2 (2014): 241–260; National Reading Panel (US), National Institute of Child Health, & Human Development (US). (2000). *Report of the national reading panel: Teaching children to read: An evidence-based assessment of the scientific research literature on reading and its implications for reading instruction: Reports of the subgroups*. National Institute of Child Health and Human Development, National Institutes of Health.
11. Cunningham and Cunningham (2000), pp. 87–109.
12. Erekson, J., & Olmsted, C. (2012, November). Irritable vowel syndrome: Primary grade students schematizing vowel orthography. San Diego, CA: Literacy Research Association.
13. Reutzel, D., et al. (2014). Exploration of the consortium on reading excellence phonics survey: An instrument for assessing primary-grade students' phonics knowledge. *The Elementary School Journal* 115.1, 49–72.
14. Cunningham, P. (1990). The names test: A quick assessment of decoding ability. *The Reading Teacher* 44, 124–129; Dufflemeyer, F., Kruse, A., Merkley, D., & Fyfe, S. (1994). Further validation and enhancement of the names test. *The Reading Teacher* 48, 118–128.
15. Mather, N., Sammons, J., & Schwartz, J. (2006) Adaptations of the names test: Easy-to-use phonics assessments. *The Reading Teacher* 60, 114–122.
16. Norman, K., & Calfee, R. (2004). Tile test: A hands-on approach for assessing phonics in the early grades. *The Reading Teacher* 58, 42–52.
17. Ibid., p. 42.
18. Clay, M. (1985). *The early detection of reading difficulties*. Portsmouth, NH: Heinemann.

19. Stahl, S. (1992). Saying the 'p' word: Nine guidelines for exemplary phonics instruction. *The Reading Teacher* 45, 618–625; Stahl, S., Duffy-Hester, A., & Stahl, K. (1998). Everything you wanted to know about phonics (but were afraid to ask). *Reading Research Quarterly* 33, 338–355.

20. Glazzard, J. (2017). Assessing reading development through systematic synthetic phonics. *English in Education* 51.1, 44–57.

21. Erekson, J. (2009). Putting Humpty Dumpty together again: When illustration shuts down interpretation. *Journal of Visual Literacy* 28, 145–162.

22. Cunningham, P. & Cunningham, J. (1992). Making words: enhancing the invented spelling-decoding connection. *The Reading Teacher* 46, 106–115.

23. Clay, M. (1979). *The early detection of reading difficulties.* Portsmouth, NH: Heinemann.

Chapter 12
Fluency

Perfect Lazybones/Shutterstock

∨ Chapter Outline

Scenario: Ms. Lewis Teaches Fluency

Understanding Reading Fluency

Assessing Fluency

Teaching Fluency

∨ Learning Outcomes

After reading this chapter, you should be able to . . .

12.1 Discuss what is involved in acquiring reading fluency.

12.2 Discuss different ways to assess fluency.

12.3 Explain guidelines for effective fluency instruction and one specific fluency teaching strategy.

Scenario

Ms. Lewis Teaches Fluency

Ms. Lewis is a fifth-grade teacher who wants her students to learn more about natural disasters during Social Studies. Taking a look at the texts with her students in mind, she knows that most will be able to read them without much difficulty. She also knows that she can help students make connections to natural disasters by reading them a recent newspaper article about hurricanes that hit the coast of the United States. She has two purposes in mind for this read-aloud. First, she wants students to comprehend the article. In particular, she wants to provide students with practice using the "determining importance" comprehension strategy. Second, she wants her students to learn more about the importance of phrasing, intonation, and expression when reading to others.

She opens the lesson by putting the article on the document camera and reading aloud. Once finished, she thinks aloud to model determining importance, saying, "The author of this article included a lot of information. But I notice she keeps returning to points about the hardships hurricanes cause for real people." She highlights these parts of the article as students watch.

Ms. Lewis then reminds students how important it is to read with expression and phrasing, so that the reading sounds more like talking. She returns to one highlighted sentence and rereads it with new expression. She asks students to talk about what the words mean when she reads them with meaningful expression as opposed to reading the sentence with proper phrasing alone. To end the lesson, she comments, "Reading aloud with expression helps readers and listeners think about what the words might mean." Finally, she reminds students that she applied her expression to a passage she already understood was important.

Ms. Lewis then tells students that hurricanes are only one type of natural disaster, and asks for volunteers to name other kinds of natural disasters (e.g., earthquakes), writing their ideas on the board using a semantic map. Next, she tells students that they will be reading about specific kinds of natural disasters from a variety of texts over the next few days. Today they will be reading about tornadoes and earthquakes. She helps students find a partner, then directs them to a table with many books and articles. She then explains procedures for reading.

"Today you are going to be reading to yourself and to a partner. You have been learning about how to determine importance when reading to best comprehend, and today you are going to get some practice." She continues by stating, "You have also been learning about the importance of fluency when reading. What you are going to practice today is phrasing, intonation, and expression. All three are important when reading to others, so that your partner can understand about tornadoes and earthquakes. Remember how I tried to read the article on hurricanes so you could learn and understand—not just hear the words? I want you to do the same." She then provides students with directions for practicing their reading and allots time for students to switch between reading to each other and responding to what they understand.

Enhanced eText
Video Example 12.1
In this **video**, watch the classroom fluency instruction and the discussion of research on oral reading fluency.

Understanding Reading Fluency

Prior to the National Reading Panel report[1] (2000), researchers saw reading fluency as a necessary yet neglected part of reading instruction.[2] No longer neglected, fluency is now a mainstay in reading programs. Teachers who subscribe to a diagnostic approach to assessing and teaching reading find that fluency is a necessary but not sufficient component of helping children to read proficiently.

According to the reported results of the 2002 National Assessment of Education Progress (NAEP), "Students who can read text passages aloud accurately and fluently at an appropriate pace are more likely to understand what they are reading, both silently and orally."[3] However, evidence from the same study indicated that many of those tested needed additional instruction to enhance their comprehension ability. Said another way, beautiful, word-perfect oral reading is not a guarantee of reading comprehension. So although reading fluency is something many proficient readers often display, we have to guard against thinking of it as the missing link that will help all students better comprehend. Instead, we need to keep comprehension front and center and look for fluency as one sign that comprehension is occurring.[4]

An important distinction we need to make clear is one between *proficient reader* and *fluent reader*. The two are not automatically synonymous. Children who are proficient readers do the following:[5]

- Attempt to make what they read sound like language and make sense
- Monitor what they read to make sure that it is making sense and that it is coherent
- Construct meaning using the text, their purpose for reading, and their background knowledge
- Flexibly use a variety of strategies—such as rereading, substituting words that make sense, decoding, and using text aids—when meaning is disrupted
- Sample print selectively, using both visual and nonvisual information
- Vary their rate of reading depending on the purpose for reading
- Correct miscues more often than not
- Correct miscues that disrupt the meaning of the text they are reading
- Approach unfamiliar words in chunks rather than letter by letter

Proficient readers who exhibit these behaviors will sometimes sound fluent but not always. Fluency will depend on the nature of the text and the tasks for which it is used.

Fluent readers, on the other hand, are those children who consistently sound fluent. These readers may sound strong, but fluency alone does not guarantee proficient reading. Two aspects of reading on which they might be focused at the expense of others: saying words accurately and saying them smoothly. Fluent readers most often read all text in a similar manner; they often read too quickly; and often their focus on accuracy and pace may make it difficult for them to comprehend. In other words, fluent readers can sound perfectly competent but may be missing many of the aspects of proficient reading.

The point of making this distinction is to remind teachers using a diagnostic approach to assessing and teaching reading that we want to help children become *proficient readers who at appropriate times sound fluent* rather than *fluent readers who are not proficient*.

Defining Fluency

Although definitions of fluency vary, there is common agreement in the professional literature that fluency is "an effortless, smooth, and coherent oral production of a given passage in terms of phrasing, adherence to the author's syntax, and expressiveness."[6] Our definition goes a bit further. We define it as the ability to silently or orally read a text with appropriate pace (adjusting it as needed within a sentence, paragraph, and/or text), with relative accuracy (depending on the purpose for reading, some miscues might be left alone when they do not affect meaning), and with prosody (phrasing, intonation, and expression), all for the purpose of *enhancing comprehension*, which is the essence of reading.

We see fluency as a dynamic rather than static process that fluctuates depending on factors such as interest, motivation, purpose for reading, text difficulty, and background knowledge for the topic being read. As one researcher commented, "Fluency is situational. This means that fluency is like happiness, in that we are not happy all the time, and neither are we fluent readers all the time."[7] Reading comprehension, rather than fluency, is the ultimate goal of teaching readers.

Fluency Development

Fluency is certainly one ingredient in comprehension, but how the recipe works is still unclear. Some have stated that fluency is the bridge to comprehension.[8] This view holds that readers begin to read by learning to decode words. Once they can do so automatically, then—and only then—can they cross the fluency bridge (i.e., using speed, accuracy, and expression), arriving at comprehension, their final destination. This is a bottom-up model (see Chapter 1) that does not include comprehension until after much work with decoding and fluency.

A top-down approach to fluency and comprehension asks teachers to think about the bridge in a slightly different way. Researchers have helped us to see[9] that readers can begin with background knowledge and understanding of how to navigate text to get an overall view of what they will be reading. In other words, they can begin with reader-based aspects of comprehension rather than text-based aspects. Consequently, readers approach the bridge of fluency with understanding and are therefore able to read more fluently because they are trying to comprehend. Their sense of purpose leads to better identification of words. In other words, it is understanding—not just skilled word decoding—that enables fluent reading. Seen as a top-down process, comprehension is a bridge to fluency rather than the other way around.

A third way researchers explain the relationship between fluency and comprehension emphasizes the interactive model (bottom-up and top-down) in which readers use visual features of words and their own background knowledge simultaneously to read with greater fluency.[10] For example, in the original repeated reading procedure,[11] the teacher first read the text aloud while students followed along. Doing so enabled students to listen to the entire text for understanding. They also got to hear a model of fluent reading—not too fast, too slow, or read in monotone. Instead, the teacher adjusted pace and expression as appropriate to help listeners comprehend. Students were then permitted to read the text silently as many times as needed so they could feel comfortable reading the text aloud. In other words, the students began with comprehension, then they had opportunities to look for unfamiliar or difficult words as they practiced silently, and only then did they read aloud. Understanding the text and practicing words helped them to be fluent.

An two-way interaction between meaning and word identification for readers is more likely than a one-directional process.[12] Although there is still no definitive research on how comprehension and fluency relate, assessing whether reading is purposeful and meaningful often provides information that teachers can use to impact readers' fluency. Likewise, assessing readers' confidence and competence with word identification often yields information teachers can use to help readers improve fluency. Finally, assessing whether readers understand how to control pace, phrasing, and expression can help teachers pinpoint what instruction is most appropriate to help readers read with meaning. Any readers whose reading suffers because of fluency deserve appropriate assessments to discover strengths they can use as a basis for fluent reading.

Enhanced eText **Application Exercise 12.1:** Ms. Lewis's Understanding of Fluency

Bridge: From Understanding to Assessment

When teachers understand that _____,	then teachers may want to assess _____.
Fluency is a combination of accuracy, pace, phrasing, and expression,	Fluency holistically, attending to all four aspects, instead of focusing on only one (such as pace).
Appropriate pace often has to do with student engagement in the text,	Authentic text reading to check whether interpretations of passage-based test scores change with more meaningful text.
Fluency and comprehension are related,	How students read when prepared with purposes and comprehension goals.
Fluency and word identification are related,	What kinds of texts or what wide range of levels pose the fewest challenging words for each student.
Reading out loud is a challenging kind of public performance,	Fluency with "warm" instead of "cold" readings Whether fluency changes in less challenging situations, such as small groups, pairs, solo reading, and silent reading.
Thinking and reading at the same time is challenging,	What kinds of texts or what range of levels of texts are easiest for readers to read aloud and also comprehend.
The demand for fluency changes with different sections within a single text, and across different texts,	Fluency with a variety of types of text, including books but also real-life texts.

Assessing Fluency

As with all other aspects of reading, assessment drives fluency instruction. The best fluency assessments help teachers to answer multiple questions about reading fluency. A strong fluency assessment provides information about phrasing and expression,[13] as well as pace and accuracy. Moreover, a strong fluency assessment should make connections to comprehension.[14] With this holistic definition of fluency in mind, three questions can be used to ensure proper fluency assessment: What do I want to know about a student's reading fluency? Why do I want to know that? How can I best discover this information? (See Table 12.1.)

We have provided here a Holistic Oral-Reading Fluency rubric (Figure 12.1) that includes four research-based elements of fluency. This rubric can be used by teachers

Table 12.1 Three Important Questions for Assessing Fluency

What Do I Want to Know?	Why Do I Want to Know?	How Can I Best Discover It?
Do students understand how to vary their reading rate within and across texts?	• Adjusting reading rate to purpose is one hallmark of a proficient reader. I want to know if students understand the importance of speeding up and slowing down in and across texts as a way of best understanding the text. • Some students may have the misperception that good reading means fast reading. I want to identify these students so that I can help them to better understand how to use rate of reading as a tool for understanding.	• Observation • Recorded readings • Student self-report
To what degree do students read with accuracy?	• Being able to identify words accurately and instantaneously can facilitate students' reading fluency. I need to discover if they are able to do both so that I can help those children in need. • Some students may have the misunderstanding that they must identify every word with 100 percent accuracy, and it could be retarding their reading growth. I need to help these students understand that readers rarely read with 100 percent accuracy but instead focus on the understanding of the text.	• Running Record • Modified Miscue
Do students understand how to use prosody when reading?	• Reading with expression, in meaningful phrases, and with attention to typographical cues facilitates comprehension. All three can help students better interpret the meaning of a text. • Proficient readers chunk what they read rather than process letter by letter. I want to make sure students understand how to chunk.	• Holistic Oral-Reading Fluency rubric • Observation
How much time are students reading?	• A high volume of engaged reading is one way for students to develop a large vocabulary and thus read with more fluency, both silently and orally. I want to make sure that all students are given ample time to read in school, especially if they are not able to read after school for one reason or another. I also want to provide easy access to all kinds of texts, attractive books included.	• Independent Reading Record • Observation

Figure 12.1 The Holistic Oral Reading Fluency Rubric

Name _____   Date _____

Holistic Oral Reading Fluency Rubric

Rate the student's reading fluency in each category by circling the rating in the Category Rating column. In the Additional Observations column, make a mark through any applicable items. Use the formula at the bottom of the form for an Overall Fluency Rating.

	1	2	3	4	Additional Observations	Category Rating
Expression	No evidence of meaningful expression or conversational tone	Few moments of meaningful expression, or little evidence of conversational tone	Some meaningful, expressive reading and some conversational tone	Consistent expressive reading and conversational tone	• Shows interpretation and comprehension • Matches character feelings • Changes voice to differentiate dialogue • Uses intonation to express emotion • Uses punctuation as expression cue (? ! …)	1 2 3 4
Phrasing	Word-by-word reading; no evidence of phrase boundaries	Mixed word-by-word reading with some two- to three-word phrases	Mostly well-phrased with some word-by-word reading or missed punctuation	Consistent phrasing and punctuation	• Sounds like real speech • Intonation varies from phrase to phrase • Uses commas for phrasing • Uses quotations to phrase dialogue • Shows comprehension	1 2 3 4
Accuracy	Frequent mispronunciations, repetitions, false starts, miscues	Mixed accuracy; many mispronunciations, repetitions, false starts, miscues	Mixed accuracy: Some mispronunciations, repetitions, false starts, miscues	Accurate and automatic word identification	• Reads without pausing on individual words • Pronounces difficult words accurately • Is accurate with 'glue' words (grammar words: *because, thus, again, instead, their*) • Is accurate with content words	1 2 3 4
Pace	Slow and laborious reading pace; difficult to listen and understand	Mostly slow with some appropriate increases in pace during reading	Mostly well-paced with some inappropriate slow-downs in pace during reading	Pace appropriate for the reader's purpose and/or the text	• Reading sounds confident • Pace approximates reader's speaking pace • Pace changes based on changes in the text • Pace changes based on shifts in reader's purpose	1 2 3 4

Total of Category Ratings:

_____ / 4 = [☐] [Total of Category Ratings / 4 = Average Fluency Rating]

Retelling Rating

1	2	3	4	Additional Observations	Retelling Rating
Cannot retell main idea/plot event or details	Retells either main idea/plot event or some details	Retells main idea/plot event with some details	Retells main idea/plot event, with numerous details	• Retells events in order • Creates an interpretation of the text • Makes inferences or clear connections	1 2 3 4

Source: "Holistic Oral Reading Fluency Rubric" from Accessible Assessment: How 9 Sensible Techniques Can Power DATADRIVEN Reading Instruction by Michael F. Optiz, Michael P. Ford, and James A. Erekson. Copyright © 2011 by Michael F. Optiz, Michael P. Ford, and James A. Erekson. Published by Heinemann, Portsmouth, NH. Reprinted by permission of the Publisher. All Rights Reserved.

Figure 12.1 (*Continued*)

Administration and Scoring Procedures

ESTIMATED TIME: *5 to 7 minutes per student*

Administering

1. Choose a passage or section of a text that a student has previously read. This should be a text that the student is familiar with and can come from one that has been read during independent reading.
2. Make a photocopy of the passage. This is the one you will make notations on as the student reads from the actual text.
3. Make a photocopy of the Holistic Oral Reading Fluency Rubric so that you have enough copies for each student you will assess. Carefully read it so that you understand what you will be rating.
4. Show the text and provide the student with time to practice reading it silently at least one time. Once finished, say something such as "I am going to listen to you read aloud and use this copy to remind me of how well you read. When you are finished, I am going to ask you to tell me about what you read."
5. As the student reads, make notations about how the student reads. For example, make slash marks between words to show how the student phrases. Also note other observations as noted on the Holistic Oral Reading Fluency Rubric.
6. Once the oral reading concludes, have the child do a retelling of the passage.

Scoring

1. Use the Holistic Oral Reading Fluency Rubric to rate the students' oral reading fluency and retelling. Indicate your rating following the directions as stated on the form.
2. Attach the passage you used to assess the student's fluency to the rubric.
3. Use the class matrix (see page 280) to record students' individual performances. List students' names down the left. Copy your ratings from the individual Holistic Oral Reading Fluency Rubric onto the appropriate sections on the class matrix.
4. Take a look at students' oral reading performances, both individually and as a class, to note areas of strengths and needs.
5. To help students understand that they are a part of the assessment cycle, provide them with the self-assessment form shown on page 287.

to rate fluency while observing reading, or by students in self-assessment. This rubric can also be used as a checklist to evaluate whether other assessments address enough of fluency to be valid. For example, in reviewing the administration guide for one Oral-Reading Fluency test, we found that only reading rate and word accuracy were tested. Because these are only two elements of fluency, this test provides only partial information about reading fluency, and is *insufficient for decision making* about instruction. Moreover, the rules for many oral-reading fluency tests require students to read "cold," without any preview or practice of the passages, decreasing the likelihood of activating comprehension or strategically identifying words. Thus the results of such tests can be used only as suggestions, after which fluency should be checked up on more closely with classroom assessments.

Figure 12.1 (*Continued*)

Class Matrix

Student Name	Expression	Phrasing	Accuracy	Pace	Overall Fluency Rating	Comprehension Rating

Fluency Ratings span the Expression, Phrasing, Accuracy, and Pace columns.

Enhanced eText Application Exercise (video) **12.2:** Holistic Fluency Rating

We wholeheartedly believe that to be successful in assessing all aspects of fluency, teachers need to allow students time to warm up before having them read aloud. This view is supported by scholars such as Karp, who wrote more than fifty years ago, "Basic to reading with expression is reading with comprehension, which comes as a result of having an overview of, and an insight into, a passage of prose or poetry."[15] Building on these thoughts, Erekson notes that specific passages of texts may demand specific emphasis or expression to show comprehension.[16] To that end, we offer these suggestions for valid fluency assessment:

- *Provide students with a warm-up before assessing.* We can see three possible options for providing this warm-up. First, teachers can tell students an overview of the passage they will be reading. Doing so enables students to call forth during reading what they expect from the passage, activating comprehension as a necessary fluency ingredient. Then, provide time for students to preview or practice the passage before rating their overall performance using the rubric shown in Figure 12.1. Second, teachers can read the passage to students while they follow along. After discussing what was read, provide students with time to practice reading. Finally, have students reread the passage, and assess this rereading while using the rubric shown in Figure 12.1. Third, teachers can provide students with background for the passage and time to read it silently or orally to themselves. Once the students feel they have a good understanding of the passage, have them read it to you out loud, and rate and score this performance using the rubric.

- *Assess with authentic children's literature and authentic real-world text.* Children are more likely to see the connection to what they are reading when they are engaged in information or in a story. Likewise, sitting next to children during independent reading time and asking them to reread a page from their text is an excellent way to check in on their fluency development in a naturalistic way. Passages constructed for required testing of fluency may suffer in validity because they lack authentic context, and scores should always be confirmed or disconfirmed with authentic text.

- *Remember that there are many factors that affect reading rate.* Although there continues to be a tremendous amount of interest in assessing how many words students can correctly read within one minute (WCPM—words correct per minute), researchers[17] remind us that there are ten factors that can affect reading rate, and that we need to be mindful of these factors to truly understand how to help children become fluent readers:

  - *Self-confidence*
  - *Purpose and desire*
  - *Individual style*
  - *Understanding that reading must make sense*
  - *Lack of background for the text*
  - *Text difficulty*
  - *Reading environment*
  - *Audience*
  - *Limited sight vocabulary*
  - *Inability to apply phonics skills to decode unknown words*

Enhanced eText
Teacher Resource:
Holistic Fluency Rubric

It is a nationwide epidemic that students are asked to set goals based on norms for words per minute. Remember that norms are normal. This means that it is normal for half of fifth-grade students to read below the 50th percentile. A reading rate below the average should only be cause for concern if it impacts comprehension and engagement, or if it is usually accompanied by low ratings in accuracy, phrasing, and expression.

- *Use assessment measures mentioned throughout this book to inform your thinking.* As we show in Table 12.1, assessment measures mentioned in other chapters of this book are related to reading fluency. These include observations, student self-reports, independent reading records, the running record, and modified miscue analysis.

- *Remember our cautions about standardized test scores.* Low test scores do not explain themselves. No test ever tells a teacher the reason a student missed an item. Only with consistently high scores can teachers assume that a score points to competence, and even this depends on what the test is supposed to be used for (and *not* used for). For example, the DIBELS test and others like it are frequently misused as diagnostic tests in schools when they were never designed for this use. But regardless of which test a score comes from, teachers need to know how to interpret low fluency test scores. Fluency test passages are often devoid of context that helps readers activate background knowledge or strategic thinking. Passages are often boring and so students can have difficulty finding a sense of purpose for reading—they complete passages because they were told to. Many passages have hidden cultural biases that can make them difficult to understand. Each of these reasons, and more, could explain missed items and a low test score. Teachers have to follow up on low scores by observing reading in more authentic situations in the classroom. Only by doing so can teachers interpret the outcomes of tests.

- *Use the Holistic Oral-Reading Fluency rubric to assess all aspects of fluency.* Using this rubric will provide insights into how children are using all three aspects of fluency. It also provides a brief comprehension measure as a means of helping children understand that fluency is used as a comprehension tool and that reading always has to make sense. The administration and scoring procedures follow the rubric. This rubric is designed to provide scores that fit with the four-point scale used nationwide in the NAEP test. Rubric scores not only yield an overall score but also provide teachers with specific scores and supporting information on each aspect of fluency. When used to rate students (or to self-assess) reading from a variety of authentic texts, the rubric can provide teachers with clear information related to their questions about each reader's fluency.

Enhanced eText **Application Exercise (video) 12.3:** Applying the Holistic Fluency Rubric

Enhanced eText **Application Exercise 12.4:** Ms. Lewis Assesses Reading Fluency

Bridge: From Assessment to Teaching

If an assessment shows that _____,	then teachers may want to teach _____.
Readers read storybooks with holistic fluency, but informational texts without expression,	By modeling reading informational text with meaningful prosody.
Students read test passages with little attention to phrasing,	That test passages should be read with attention to meaning, just like other texts.
Students are reading assignments just to finish them, as quickly as possible,	Students to set purposes before reading.
Word identification is impacting fluency,	Students to find, select, and read many free-choice books at a just-right level (95 percent to 98 percent accuracy).
Students read more fluently in small groups and pairs, and less fluently in large groups,	Previewing and warm-up strategies to help readers gain confidence before reading in front of larger groups.
Some readers have a hard time comprehending when they have to concentrate on reading out loud,	Repeated reading. Comprehension strategies such as reciprocal questioning. Silent reading.

Teaching Fluency

Helping children grasp how fluency can facilitate better understanding and expressing the author's intended meaning is a primary goal of fluency instruction. Although some students have little difficulty developing this understanding, others have more. We want to underscore that helping students develop a *fluency consciousness*—an ear for what fluent reading sounds like and a desire to be fluent to help themselves and others understand the author's intended meanings—is a necessary part of fluency instruction.

Fortunately, there are concrete suggestions for how to help children develop this fluency consciousness using authentic language activities. Here are seven:

1. *Set goals based on proficiency first and fluency second.* When students read for meaning and for authentic purposes, they are more likely to apply prosody that makes their reading sound like natural speaking. In school, it is well worth the time to use prereading discussions and questions to help students orient themselves to the reading, preparing to find out what happens next in a story or what they might learn from informational text.

2. *Encourage students to talk with one another for a variety of purposes.* As a result of talking, students' reading fluency is enhanced. Consider students who talk with one another about a topic of interest. They can't help but use all aspects of fluency (speed, accuracy, and prosody) as they speak. Using these elements of language is natural, even though students might not be conscious that they are using the elements of fluency when communicating. Oral language sets the stage for helping children make the connection to the written word. When teaching children about using appropriate speed in reading, for example, we can call on their experiences with how they talk with one another so that they can understand one another's messages. We can then explain how the same is true with reading.

3. *Provide time for independent silent reading.* Providing time for students to read silently enables them to develop the ability to have their eyes move ahead of the text, enabling them to read without hesitation. In Betts's words, "the individual develops a desirable eye-voice span."[18] In addition to fluency, another important reading skill that silent reading fosters is increased vocabulary growth.[19] There is ample evidence to support what seems like common sense: students who read more are better readers. Silent reading allows students to do just that—read more.[20] Given that the purpose of silent reading is to understand the text, it is a logical approach when we want students to express this meaning to others orally.

4. *Use graphic design cues in children's literature.* Authors use a variety of graphic cues (e.g., bold and italic print, punctuation marks, large print, and lines of varying lengths) to help convey meaning to readers. Knowing these cues helps readers

transact with authors and, when reading silently, better understand the intended meaning. When reading orally, they are able to use the same cues to convey the author's intended meaning to an interested audience. Likewise, matching up texts with what readers know and what they need to know about fluency is a way to teach from a strength to a need. For example, if some students read word by word, teachers can select a book in which the author has written one word per line and show it to the child, commenting, "The way you are reading is just how this author writes! Good for you!" Taking it a step further, though, to help students better understand how to use phrases, the teacher can show another book where the author has used two- and three-word phrases, commenting, "Take a look at what the author has done here!" and pointing out the two- and three-word phrases. "As readers, we have to use the author's secret code to know how to read the book. In this case, the author wants you to read in groups of two and three words." See Figure 12.2 for suggested titles that can be used for this type of instruction.

5. *Use a variety of assisted fluency activities.* Deliberate use of an activity specifically designed to heighten students' understanding of fluency is necessary in order to provide meaningful instruction and practice. And we are not at a loss for activities that can be used for this purpose. In fact, the problem is not having activities, but choosing the best from among them.

In searching out the fluency activities to include in this chapter, we took the advice of Kuhn and Stahl,[21] who note that assisted fluency activities model fluent reading behaviors to children, provide a wealth of print exposure, and emphasize practice to help enhance not only all areas of fluency but also comprehension. These kinds of meaningful activities are more effective in terms of advancing reading fluency than are unassisted activities (i.e., those that build on independent learning via independent practice).

A second reason for using assisted activities is that social interaction is a big part of any language-rich classroom. This interaction is what helps students better see the purpose of fluent oral and silent reading.

A third reason for using assisted reading activities is that some dysfluent behaviors may have been learned in school. In grades K–1, the practice and reinforcement given to phonics may result in students' believing that the main purpose of reading is to demonstrate knowledge of how to sound out words. The modeling in assisted reading activities gives teachers an opportunity to give students permission to read with meaning.

A fourth reason for using assisted reading activities is that the majority begin with comprehension and proceed to fluency. Students are given some kind of overview, such as the teacher's reading of the entire text while students listen and follow along. Discussion then follows this reading. Then, and only then, do students practice the text in whole or part with a focus on fluency. The purpose of all of these activities is to enhance comprehension of texts. They are not a prerequisite to comprehension. We reviewed numerous professional publications in our effort to provide you with the meaningful activities in Figure 12.3.

6. *Use a variety of grouping options.* Different grouping structures lend themselves well to the fluency activities shown above. In Figure 12.4, we show how the various activities apply with different grouping sizes.

7. *Use explicit integrated fluency lessons.* Putting all of the pieces together to design integrated fluency instruction is advantageous for students. When designing this instruction, consider using the following procedures, making note of each on the lesson plan form shown in Figure 12.5:

- *Decide on the purpose for the lesson.* According to your analysis of assessment results, what do students need to learn about fluency? Which students appear to need further help with this aspect of fluency?

Enhanced eText
Video Example 12.2

In this **video**, the strategy of repeated reading is demonstrated with a small group.

Enhanced eText
Teacher Resource:
The Big Bad Wolf

Figure 12.2　Bibliography of Children's Literature to Enhance Reading Fluency

Title	Author/Illustrator	Publisher/Year	Use for . . .
Ocean Sunlight: How Tiny Plants Feed the Seas	Molly Bang and Penny Chisholm	Scholastic/2012	Prosody: Phrasing, typographical cues
America the Beautiful: Together We Stand	Katherine Lee Bates and Bryan Collier	Scholastic/2013	All aspects of fluency
Squish Rabbit	Katherine Battersby	Viking/2011	Prosody: Phrasing (three- to four-word phrases)
Dinosaur Thunder	Marion Dane Bauer and Margaret Chodos-Irvine	Scholastic/2012	Prosody: Typographical cues, type size
Bailey at the Museum	Harry Bliss	Scholastic/2012	Phrasing with word bubbles
Five Little Monkeys	Eileen Christelow	Clarion/2011	Prosody: Expression
There Was an Old Lady Who Swallowed Some Books!	Lucille Colandro and Jared D. Lee	Scholastic/2012	Prosody: Phrasing and expression
Homer	Elisha Cooper	Greenwillow/2012	Prosody: Phrasing (three to four words); expression
Rock 'n' Roll Mole	Carolyn Crimi and Lynn Munsinger	Dial/2011	Prosody: Expression
A Place to Call Home	Alexis Deacon	Candlewick/2011	Prosody: Phrasing (one- to four-word phrases)
Here Comes Trouble!	Corinne Demas and Noah Z. Jones	Scholastic/2013	Prosody: Phrasing, typographical cues, expression
Foxy	Emma Dodd	Harper/2012	Prosody: Using typographical cues
Princess Zelda and the Frog	Carol Gardner and Shane Young	Feiwel and Friends/2011	Prosody: Expression (using typographic cues)
Dot	Patricia Intriago	Farrar/Straus/Giroux/2011	Prosody: Phrasing (two- to four-word phrases)
Hornbooks and Inkwells	Verla Kay and S.D. Schindler	Putnam/2011	Prosody: Phrasing (one- to four-word phrases)
Same, Same, but Different	Jenny Sue Kostecki-Shaw	Holt/2011	Prosody: Expression and phrasing (phrases begin with one word)
Otto: The Boy Who Loved Cars	Kara LaReau and Scott Magoon	Roaring Brook/2011	Prosody: Phrasing and expression
Wodney Wat's Wobot	Helen Lester and Lynn Munsinger	Houghton Mifflin/2011	Prosody: Expression

- *Integrate the instruction with other content areas.* To better help children understand that fluency fits into a larger reading scheme and is used as a comprehension tool, integrate the fluency instruction with a specific content area. For example, if students need to better understand reading with accuracy and at varying speeds, design your lesson using mathematics story problems. As we all know, story problems necessitate reading slowly with accuracy. Regardless of the speed or

Figure 12.2 (Continued)

Title	Author/Illustrator	Publisher/Year	Use for . . .
A Is for Autumn	Robert Maass	Holt/2011	Prosody: One-word lines
One Love	Bob Marley	Chronicle/2011	Prosody: Expression and phrasing
Miss Nelson Is Back (includes read-along CD)	Harry G. Allard Jr. and James Marshall	Houghton Mifflin/2011	All aspects of fluency
Polar Bear, Polar Bear, What Do You Hear? (includes CD read by Gwyneth Paltrow)	Bill Martin Jr. and Eric Carle	Holt/2011 20th Anniversary Edition	Prosody: Phrasing and expression
These Hands	Margaret Mason and Floyd Cooper	Houghton Mifflin/2011	Prosody: Expression and phrasing
The Jungle Run	Tony Mitton and Guy Parker-Rees	Orchard/2012	All aspects of fluency
Lucky Ducklings	Eva Moore and Nancy Carpenter	Orchard/2013	Phrasing, beginning with one word
Cindy Moo	Lori Mortensen and Jeff Mack	Harper/2012	Prosody: Phrasing, expression, typographical cues
Where's the Party?	Katharine Robey and Kate Endle	Charlesbridge/2011	Prosody: Expression using typographic cues
Exclamation Mark	Amy Krouse Rosenthal and Tom Lichtenheld	Scholastic/2013	Typographical cues
Oliver	Judith Rossell	HarperCollins/2012	Prosody: Expression using typographic cues; phrasing (two or more words)
Those Darn Squirrels	Adam Rubin and Daniel Salmieri	Clarion/2008	Prosody: Phrasing and connecting to lines with several phrases
Skippyjon Jones, Class Action (includes CD)	Judy Schachner	Dutton/2011	All aspects of fluency
Swirl by Swirl	Joyce Sidman and Beth Krommes	Houghton Mifflin/2011	Prosody: Phrasing beginning with one word
The Amazing Adventures of Bumblebee Boy	David Soman and Jacky Davis	Dial/2011	Prosody: Expression using typographic cues
Road Work Ahead	Anastasia Suen and Jannie Ho	Viking/2011	Prosody: Three-word phrases
Tumford the Terrible	Nancy Tillman	Feiwel and Friends/2011	Prosody: Phrasing
Little Man (includes CD narrated by Dionne Warwick)	Dionne Warwick and David Wooley	Charlesbridge/2011	All aspects of fluency
Can You See What I See? Out of this World	Walter Wick	Cartwheel/2013	Three- and four-word phrases in lists
What Time Is It? It's Duffy Time!	Audrey and Don Wood	Blue Sky/2012	Building phrases beginning with two words

accuracy, students will develop a better understanding that the whole purpose of reading story problems—or any text, for that matter—is comprehension.

- *Select texts that will best help you to accomplish your purpose.* As we show in Figure 12.2, there are many different kinds of texts that you can use to teach students about fluency. Also consider using the many different types of

Figure 12.3 Fluency Activities and Brief Descriptions

Name of Activity	Brief Description
Shared Book Experience (SBE)	Students are seated in front of a big book. After a focused introduction and a first read by the teacher, students chime in on a second reading.
Echo Reading	The teacher reads aloud a segment of text while students follow along. Then, in unison, students reread the same segment.
Choral Reading	Students read a text in unison.
Fluency-Oriented Reading Instruction (FORI)/Wide-Reading FORI	Students read a grade-level text after the teacher first reads the text aloud and leads a discussion of the text. Students then practice reading the text in and out of school and read their part of the text to a partner the following day.
Read-Aloud	Teacher selects and practices a book to read aloud with specific emphases in mind.
Partner Reading	In some manner, students are paired and they read a text together. There are many variations of this procedure, as noted in the Appendix.
Readers' Theater	Students read their part of a script and once the group feels prepared, present the play to the class by reading their script.
Cross-Age Reading	Students of different ages are paired for reading. They then read the same text.
Poetry Club	After hearing the teacher read some poetry and explain why a given poem was selected for reading aloud, students select their own poems and, after practicing, read them aloud to an interested audience.
Read Around	Students gather around a table with sharing in mind. In turn, they state the title of their book, provide a brief overview, and read a selected portion aloud to the group.
Cut-Apart	A story is cut up into sections, one section for each class member. After practice, students then read their section in sequence.
Say It Like the Character	Students read a section of narrative text to themselves and decide how the character would actually say the text if he/she were present. Students then read the part aloud trying to sound just like the character.
Close-Captioned Television	The sound is turned off and the captions are turned on. Students then watch and read a given television show.

Source: Based on M. Kuhn, The Hows and Whys of Fluency Instruction (New York: Allyn and Bacon, 2009).

texts shown and explained in Chapter 7. Remember that reading challenging text with support using a strategy such as Wide-Reading FORI[22] is an excellent way to boost children's reading comprehension and reading fluency simultaneously.

- *Think about how you need to group students to best accomplish your purpose.* There are different ways to group students, and there are advantages and disadvantages to each structure. If all students in your class need to learn a given fluency skill, you may decide to use the whole-class grouping structure to best utilize your time. At other times, you might decide to use different grouping structures within different phases of your lesson to best help you achieve your purpose. For instance, you might start with the whole class for the prereading activity, move to small groups during reading itself, and return to the large group after reading.

- *Select appropriate teaching strategies.* Perhaps the best way to select a strategy is to think about what you are trying to accomplish. Say, for example, you want students to learn how to read a grade-level textbook with fluency and

Figure 12.4 Fluency Activities and Group Sizes

Activity	Whole Class	Small Group	Partner	Individual	Combination
Shared Book Experience (SBE)	•				
Echo Reading	•	•			
Choral Reading	•	•			
Fluency-Oriented Reading Instruction (FORI)/Wide-Reading FORI	•				•
Read-Aloud	•				
Partner Reading			•		
Readers' Theater					•
Cross-Age Reading			•		
Poetry Club	•	•		•	
Read Around		•			
Cut-Apart	•	•			•
Say It Like the Character	•	•			
Close-Captioned Television	•	•			

Figure 12.5 Integrated Fluency Lesson Plan Form

Integrated Fluency Lesson

Content Area:

Comprehension Objective:

Fluency Objective:

Text(s):

Teaching Considerations	Teaching Notes
BEFORE READING *Grouping Technique* (Check all that apply): __ whole group __ small groups of _____ *Other teaching strategy:*	
DURING READING *Grouping Technique* (Check all that apply): __ whole group __ small groups of _____ __ individual *Fluency teaching strategy:* Materials:	
AFTER READING *Grouping Technique* (Check all that apply): __ whole group __ small groups of _____ __ individual *Other teaching strategy:*	

understanding. You know that the text will be difficult for some students and just right for others. You decide to use the Fluency-Oriented Reading Lesson because it will provide students with much support at the start of the lesson and with meaningful needed practice throughout the week.[23] Or use a variation of dyad reading to model and guide fluent reading practices.[24]

- *Gather all necessary materials.* Explicit teaching as described here requires preparation. Checking to make sure that all materials are at hand leads to greater success.

- *Use a three-phase instructional framework to ensure the success of all students.* The one shown here was originally developed by Herber[25] as a way for teachers of content areas to better plan for instruction. Since that time, the form has become commonplace in most elementary classrooms.

Enhanced eText Application Exercise 12.5: Ms. Lewis Teaches Fluency

---

Bridge: From Teaching Back to Understanding

If students _____,	then teachers have learned _____.
Continue to read without phrasing or expression after being taught,	To make plans that involve repeated opportunities to apply learning *over time.*
Read fluently when reading the captions in a magazine, but lose fluency when reading the full article,	That features and structures in text affect fluency. That caption reading is a strength on which to build.
Read texts more fluently when they have background knowledge or practice,	That purpose and comprehension can impact fluency.
Improve fluency when previewing difficult words before starting,	That oral reading is a public performance, and that readers need opportunities to gain confidence before reading aloud to others.
Read content text (such as Social Studies texts) more fluently after discussing the topic in class,	That unfamiliar vocabulary words are easy to get stuck on and need to be previewed and heard in talk before reading.

Revisiting the Opening Scenario

Now that you have had some time to read this chapter, take a look back at the Opening Scenario, the chapter Bridges, and the Application Exercises. Discuss the teaching strategies that Ms. Lewis used to help readers pay attention to fluency as part of their toolbox for proficiency in reading content area text.

Enhanced eText Application Exercise 12.6: Ms. Lewis Reflects on Assessment and Teaching of Fluency

---

Case Study: Etext Applications

Extend your understanding of writing, writing assessment, and writing instruction by visiting the Instructor's Manual (embed link in title) for this text. You will find an in-depth case study of Ms. Lewis and her students, including interactive applications that extend processes and tools employed by teachers with a diagnostic mindset.

Authors' Summary

Before reading our summary statements for each outcome, we suggest you read each outcome and summarize it in your own words.

Once finished, cross-check your response with our brief summary to determine how well you recalled the major points.

12.1 Discuss what is involved in acquiring reading fluency.

- Fluency is one ingredient in comprehension, but how the recipe works is still unclear. Some have stated that fluency is the bridge to comprehension. The basic idea with this view is that readers begin by learning to decode words. Once they can do so automatically, then, and only then, can they cross the fluency bridge (i.e., using speed, accuracy, and expression), arriving at comprehension, their final destination.

- Another way to explain the interplay between fluency and comprehension is to think about the bridge in a slightly different way. When readers approach a text by activating background knowledge and asking questions, they approach the bridge more likely to comprehend. Because they approach the text with meaning in mind, they are able to read more fluently. The 'flow' that fluency implies is connected directly to meaning. Reading for meaning leads to strength in identifying words. In other words, they can begin with reader-based rather than text-based processes. Consequently, readers approach the bridge with understanding and are therefore able to read more fluently, because they already have some understanding of the text, and want to read it with meaning. Their fluent reading leads to better identification of words. In other words, it is the understanding that is enabling the fluency to occur. Seen this way, then, comprehension is the bridge to fluency rather than the other way around.

- A third way to explain the relationship between fluency and comprehension emphasizes a nonlinear process in which readers use both visual features of words and background knowledge simultaneously to read with greater fluency. For example, in the original repeated reading procedure, the teacher first read the text aloud while the students followed along. Doing so enabled students to hear that fluent reading sounds like talking. It's not too fast, too slow, or read in monotone. Instead, the reader adjusts the speed as appropriate, and with prosody, to best help listeners comprehend. Students were then permitted to read the text silently as many times as they needed so that they could feel comfortable reading the text aloud. In other words, the students first used comprehension, but they also had to use words as they were practicing the text. Both understanding and the specific words helped them to be fluent.

12.2 Discuss different ways to assess fluency.

- There are many different ways to assess fluency, including observation, recorded readings, student self-reports, running records, modified miscue analysis, the Holistic Oral-Reading Fluency rubric, and independent reading records. Asking and answering three questions will help to select the technique that will target specifically what it is you want to know about students' comprehension. These questions are: What do I want to know? Why do I want to know it? How can I best discover this information?

12.3 Explain guidelines for effective fluency instruction and one specific fluency teaching strategy.

- Teaching strategies are plentiful, and range from using children's literature to specific fluency activities. Fluency-Oriented Reading Instruction is one specific teaching strategy. It entails having students read a grade-level text after the teacher first reads the text aloud and leads a discussion of the text. Students then practice reading the text in and out of school and read their part of the text to a partner the following day. In all, the procedure lasts an entire week.

Think About It!

Consider an authentic situation where reading for a comprehension purpose might lead to more fluent-sounding reading.

Consider a different authentic situation where reading fluently might lead to better comprehension.

What is the relationship between reading fluency and reading comprehension?

Try This!

1. Using the procedures described in this chapter, design an integrated fluency lesson in a content area of your choice.

2. Create a fluency activity bag in which you insert a specific text and directions for how to use it, including a specific fluency activity, for families to use.

3. Use the Holistic Oral-Reading Fluency rubric to zoom in on one student. Then try zooming out by administering it to all students in your class.

Websites

- http://www.aaronshep.com/rt/RTE.html
  This site offers a wealth of Reader's Theater scripts aimed at children ages 8–15. All can be downloaded and printed without any fee. Tips for using the scripts are provided.

- http://www.teachingheart.net/readerstheater.htm
  This site offers numerous Reader's Theater scripts for grades K–3. All are free of charge, and there are scripts representing several genres. Each script shows the suggested age range, number of readers needed to complete the reading, and approximate time allotment.

- http://www.poetry4kids.com/
  This site is filled with many different poems sure to delight children, teachers, and parents. Funny Poems, classic poems, and poems by topic are just three of the many poetry categories on this site.

Endnotes

1. National Institute of Child Health and Human Development (NICHD). (2000). Report of the national reading panel. *Teaching Children to Read: Reports of the Subgroups (NIH Publication no. 00–4754).* Washington, D.C.: U.S. Government Printing Office.

2. Allington, R. (1983). Fluency: The neglected goal. *The Reading Teacher 36,* 556–561.

3. Manzo, K. (2005). More focus on reading fluency needed, study suggests. *Education Week 25,* 11.

4. Erekson, J. (2003, May). *Prosody: The problem of expression in fluency.* Orlando, FL: International Reading Association.

5. Kucer, S. (2005). *The dimensions of literacy: A conceptual base for teaching reading and writing in school settings* (2nd ed.). Mahwah, NJ: Erlbaum.

6. Manzo (2005), p. 11.

7. Samuels, J. (2006). Toward a model of reading fluency. In S. J. Samuels & A. Farstrup (Eds.), *What Research Has to Say About Fluency Instruction* (p. 39). S. J. Samuels and A. Farstrup. Newark, DE: International Reading Association.

8. Rasinski, T. (2006). Keynote address. *Georgia Conference on Teaching Reading and Writing;* Perry, G., Johns, J., & Berglund, R. *Fluency strategies and assessments* (2nd ed.). Newark, DE: International Reading Association.

9. Brown, J., Goodman, K., & Mark, A. (1996). *Studies in miscue analysis: An annotated bibliography.* Newark, DE: International Reading Association; Schwanenflugel, P., Kuhn M., Strauss, G., and Morris, R. (2006). Becoming a fluent and automatic reader in the early elementary school years. *Reading Research Quarterly 41,* no. 4, 496–522; Walczyk, J., & Griffith-Ross, D. (2007). How important is reading skill fluency for comprehension? *The Reading Teacher 60,* no. 6, 560–569; Applegate, T., & Applegate, M. (2009). She's my best reader: She just can't comprehend. *The Reading Teacher 62,* no. 6, 512–521.

10. Kuhn, M. (2009). *The hows and whys of fluency instruction.* New York: Allyn and Bacon.

11. Samuels, J. (2006). Toward a model of reading fluency. In S. J. Samuels & A. Farstrup (Eds.) *What Research Has to Say About Fluency Instruction* (pp. 24–46). Newark, DE: International Reading Association.

12. Rumelhart, D. (YEAR). Toward an interactive model of reading. In H. Singer & R. B. Ruddell (Eds.), *Theoretical Models and Processes of Reading,* (3rd ed., pp. 722–750). Newark, DE: International Reading Association.

13. Moser, G., Sudweeks, R., Morrison, T., & Wilcox, B. (2014). Reliability of ratings of children's expressive reading. *Reading Psychology,* 35:1, 58–79, DOI: 10.1080/02702711.2012.675417.

14. Morris, D., Trathen, W., Gill, T., Schlagal, R., Ward, D., & Frye, E. (2017). Assessing reading rate in the primary grades (1–3). *Reading Psychology* 38:7, 653–672, DOI: 10.1080/02702711.2017.1323057.

15. Karp, M. (1943). Silent before oral reading. *Elementary School Journal* 44, no. 2, 103.

16. Erekson, J. (2010). Prosody and meaning. *Reading Horizons* 50, no. 2, 80–98.

17. Allington, R. (2006). *What really matters for struggling readers: Designing research-based programs* (2nd ed.). New York: Pearson Allyn and Bacon; Flurkey, A. (2006). What's 'normal' about real reading? In K. Goodman (Ed.), The Truth About DIBELS: What It Is and What It Does (pp. 40–49). Portsmouth, NH: Heinemann; Goodman, K. (2006). A critical review of DIBELS. In K. Goodman (Ed.), The Truth About DIBELS: What It Is and What It Does (pp. 1–39). Portsmouth, NH: Heinemann; Harris, A. & and Sipay, E. (1990). *How to increase reading ability: A guide to developmental and remedial methods.* New York: Longman; Heibert, E. (2006). Becoming fluent: Repeated reading with scaffolded texts. In S. J. Samuels & A. Farstrup (Eds.), *What Research Has to Say About Fluency Instruction* (pp. 204–226). Newark, DE: International Reading Association; Walczyk, J., & Griffith-Ross, D. (2007). How important Is reading skill fluency for comprehension? *The Reading Teacher* 60, no. 6, 560–569.

18. Betts, E. (1946). *Foundations of reading instruction* (p. 385). New York: American Book Company.

19. Anderson, R. (1996). Research foundations to support wide reading. In V. Greaney (Ed.), *Promoting Reading in Developing Countries* (pp. 55–77). Newark, DE: International Reading Association; Linehart, G., Zigmond, N., & Cooley, W. (1981). Reading instruction and its effects. *American Educational Research Journal* 18, 343–361; Reutzel, D., & Hollingsworth, P. (1991). Investigating topic-related attitude: Effect on reading and remembering text. *Journal of Educational Research* 84, no. 6, 334–344; Guthrie, J., Wigfield, A., Metsala, J., & Cox, K. (1999). Motivational and cognitive predictors of text comprehension and reading amount. *Scientific Studies of Reading* 3, 231–256.

20. Trainin, G., Hiebert, H. & Wilson, K. (2015). A comparison of reading rates, comprehension, and stamina in oral and silent reading of fourth-grade students. *Reading Psychology* 36:7, 595–626, DOI: 10.1080/02702711.2014.966183.

21. Kuhn, M., & Stahl, S. (2000). Fluency: A review of developmental and remedial practices. *CIERA Report #2-008*. Ann Arbor, MI: Center for the Improvement of Early Reading Achievement [CIERA], University of Michigan.

22. Kuhn, M. (2009). *The hows and whys of fluency instruction*. New York: Allyn and Bacon; Johns, J., & Berglund, R. *Fluency strategies and assessments* (2nd ed.). Newark, DE: International Reading Association; Allington, R. (2006). *What really matters for struggling readers: designing research-based programs* (2nd ed.). New York: Pearson Allyn and Bacon; Opitz, M. (1998). *Flexible Grouping in Reading.* New York: Scholastic; Opitz, M. and Rasinski, T. (2008). *Good-bye round robin: 25 effective oral reading strategies.* Portsmouth, NH: Heinemann.

23. Klvacek, M., Monroe, E., Wilcox, B., Hall-Kenyon, K. & Morrison, T. (2017). Follow the reader: An effective strategy to support students reading more complex text. *Reading Psychology* 38:5, 542–551, DOI: 10.1080/02702711.2017.1310159.

24. H. Herber, H. (1978). *Teaching reading in content areas* (2nd ed.). Englewood Cliffs, NJ: Prentice-Hall.

25. Kuhn (2009).

Chapter 13
Teaching Writing

Dean Drobot/Shutterstock

Chapter Outline

Scenario: Mr. Cowen Teaches Writing

Understanding Writing Acquisition

Assessing Writing

Teaching Writing

Learning Outcomes

After reading this chapter, you should be able to . . .

13.1 Explain developmental writing and spelling stages.

13.2 Describe ways to purposefully assess writers and use assessment data to plan subsequent instruction.

13.3 Identify instructional ideas used to meet the needs of individual writers.

Scenario

Mr. Cowen Teaches Writing

Mr. Cowen relishes teaching writing. As a writer himself, he knows the process can be messy, scary, and challenging, but also exhilarating, rewarding, and self-fulfilling. He knows that true writing growth comes from practice.

Fortunately, he also knows that students acquire their writing and spelling skills as they pass through a series of developmental stages. His knowledge of such stages associated with writing growth supports his understanding that each student may be at a different place in the process, with different skills, experiences, and perceptions. As a result, he approaches writing assessment and instruction with great openness. Writing is personal and each student is unique.

Mr. Cowen hopes to use a writer's workshop model to teach his third-graders about the writing process. He knows from past experiences teaching writing that students often rush the process and their products suffer as a result. This time through, he aims to slow them down, honor the process for drafting, and give them plenty of time to develop as writers. He plans to do so by incorporating many purposeful assessment and instruction strategies into his writer's workshop on a regular basis. But all of his plans will have to wait.

He launches the writer's workshop mini-lesson by referring to the interest inventory he gave yesterday and the interviews each student conducted with a classmate this morning. He reminds them of the purposes of the inventory and interviews. He tells them that they will get to write about any one of the interests or experiences that they revealed during the process, or any other topic of interest. He asks them to begin, and to raise their hand if they have a question.

Many of the students begin writing immediately. A few look confusedly around at others. Two take trips to the classroom library, and one takes a bathroom break. He takes note. That leaves three with hands raised. Chelsea wants to know if she can write poetry. Jasmine asks to use a dictionary, and Sirus asks if spelling is important because he "ain't that good at it." Mr. Cowen collects all of this information and continues to circulate to observe and collect notes on each student before sitting down to write a bit himself.

To bring the writer's workshop to a close, Mr. Cowen invites students to reflect on today's writing process. He asks students to write a challenge, a celebration, and a question about writing on their exit slip for him to analyze.

Mr. Cowen is delighted to have learned so much about his students during writer's workshop. He will use these insights, data from the exit slips, and samples of writing created to monitor the writing acquisition of each of his students and prepare meaningful instructional plans to support them along the way.

Enhanced eText
Video Example13.1
This video includes a discussion about finding writing ideas. Cue the video to 00:50 to learn about strategies for helping students find "seed" ideas for writing. https://www.youtube.com/watch?v=p8xYC-mWs_A

Understanding Writing Acquisition

What is writing acquisition? Why do teachers with a diagnostic mindset need to know about it? How do they best discover each student's acquisition? These questions guide educators' understanding, assessment, and instruction of writing as part of a meaning-based view of literacy education. Essentially, these questions challenge teachers to make decisions based on the real writing perceptions, goals, needs, strengths, behaviors, processes, and interests of students. Learning to write is complex. Fortunately, developmental and procedural guides help teachers make sense of writing acquisition.

What is a Developmental Writing Continuum?

Children exhibit a consistent series of behaviors while learning to write which are directly connected to reading development[1]. Knowing how readers and writers develop

Figure 13.1 Stages of Writing Development and Instructional Implications

Stages	Characteristics Learners . . .	Instruction Teacher can . . .
Emergent	• Begin to understand links between sounds and symbols • Realize the concept of writing as a written form of speaking • Acquire print concepts • Begin to collect a set of high-frequency words they can write • Approximate the spelling of words	• Teach letter sounds through the read-aloud of repetitive texts • Model writing aloud • Dictate students' spoken ideas in writing • Expose students to a print-rich environment • Facilitate the study of visual word features • Inspire and model punctuation examination and use
Early	• Gain control over letter combinations at the beginnings of words • Develop beginning, middle, and ending sounds and letters in words • Identify some misspellings and partial or missing ideas in writing • Use problem-solving strategies to identify words to use in writing	• Teach how to apply visual patterns of words to write new words • Teach editing and revising processes and tools • Challenge students to self-correct misspelled words • Teach students to edit by identifying confusing, limited, and erroneous words • Expand purposes and genres of writing
Transitional	• Use correct capitalization and punctuation • Strengthen spelling skills with growing repertoire of writing vocabulary • Use advanced print features like dialogue and graphics • Strengthen ideas in conclusions and use various genres • Use more purposeful word choices	• Offer rich mentor texts that include various genres, literary elements, strong word choices, and a variety of text features • Expand student vocabulary study and collection • Focus on ideas and strategies for strengthening leads and conclusions • Teach students to expand written texts through planning, drafting, and revision
Fluent	• Develop strategies for strengthening voice • Write for their audience • Write about experiences and topics of interest • Revise for clarity and enhanced description • Spell correctly and edit work with greater efficiency • Conform to expository text structures like procedural and cause and effect • Identify examples of the writing craft in mentor texts	• Lead the study of voice through reading and book studies • Explore an abundance of sentence structures and promote experimentation • Challenge student creation and use of checklists and tools to support planning, editing, and revision • Challenge writers to expand their topics • Regularly practice writing in various genres • Capitalize on authentic opportunities to write

makes the teaching of writing more logical and the learning of writing more explicit. Four general writing stages, or phases, serve to support writing teachers with a diagnostic mindset: emergent, early, transitional, and fluent. See Figure 13.1 for a display of developmental writing characteristics and purposeful instructional implications beyond providing the obvious supports: time to write and one-to-one conferencing.

Individual writers vary greatly regardless of age or grade level, depending on a number of factors, including amount of writing experience, levels of encouragement, and interest. Furthermore, individual writers exhibit characteristics across multiple stages in one writing sample. Understanding the characteristics that define these specific stages allows teachers who have a diagnostic mindset to do the following:

- Establish reasonable expectations for individual writers
- Identify writing strengths and needs of the individual
- Set goals for and with a writer
- Assess and monitor individual growth
- Determine activities and instruction to meet individual needs

What is Developmental Spelling

We teach phonics as a tool for reading comprehension. (See Chapter 11.) And so too, we teach spelling as a tool for conveying meaning. Let's take a look at the process for learning to spell in order to purposefully situate spelling assessment and instruction within a meaning-based system.

Learning to spell is a complex undertaking that involves more than simply memorizing words; it is developmental in nature and requires the acquisition and application of knowledge of spoken and written language.[2] By *developmental, we mean that learning to spell is ongoing and based on the cognitive development of the child*. Conventional spelling is learned gradually as a child writes over the years.

Why do teachers want to know about developmental spelling? Young children's spelling is based on their present knowledge of the language system, so when they spell, they may use *invented spelling*. When young children begin asking about adults' writing, it is often a signal that they want to write, too. They may begin by using invented spelling. The pattern of invented spelling will vary from one child to another. However, an analysis of children's invented spelling indicates that they progress through stages that make use of their years of experience with oral language. Some researchers claim that children's spelling development parallels earlier stages of oral-language development. This language-based hypothesis about how children learn to spell argues that children "internalize information about spoken and written words, organize that information, construct tentative rules based on that information, and apply these rules to the spelling of words."[3]

Gentry has developed a model to show four stages children often go through before they develop standard or correct spelling.[4] The first is called the *precommunicative stage* (formerly known as the deviant stage) because the appearance of the child's spelling attempts shows that the child has no knowledge of letter–sound correspondence. At the *semiphonetic stage,* the child demonstrates some letter–sound correspondences; that is, the child is beginning to gain the concept that letters represent sounds and that these are used to write words. Semiphonetic spelling is abbreviated spelling in which one, two, or three letters usually represent the word; for example, U = *you*, B = *Be*, and LEFT = *elephant* show that the "speller represents words, sounds, or syllables with letters that match their letter name."[5] At this stage, the child is also gaining the concept that letters are arranged in a left-to-right orientation, knows the alphabet, and can form the letters.

At the *phonetic stage,* a direct match between letters and sounds characterizes a child's spelling. The child's spelling includes all sound features as he hears and says them. As a result, the child's spelling at this stage does not resemble standard spelling—for example, "MONSTR" = *monster* and "DRAS" = *dress*. The *transitional stage,* which is the final stage in this model, precedes standard spelling. At this stage, the child is better acquainted with standard spelling, and words look like English, even though they are misspelled. The child includes vowels in every syllable, so phonetic "EGL" for *eagle* at this stage becomes "EGUL." It is at this stage that the child moves from phonological to morphological and visual spelling (e.g., EIGHTEE instead of the phonetic ATE [*eighty*])[6] and begins to use more conventionally spelled words in writing.

Eight specific writing stages and associated characteristics can be used to further understand this developmental process as it relates to spelling and word knowledge:

1. **Scribbling**
   - Seemingly random markings
   - May look like drawing.
   - Do not appear as print.
   - Used by child to show ideas

2. **Letter-Like Symbols**
   - Random symbols resembling letters appear.
   - May be mixed with numbers.
   - Child begins to explain what they have written.

3. **Strings of Letters**
   - Legible letters appear.
   - Mostly capital letters used
   - Reveal child's beginning of sound-to-symbol understanding.

4. **Beginning Sounds Emerge**
   - Child begins to show understanding of letters and words.
   - May begin to use spacing between words.
   - Messages match pictures and make sense.

5. **Consonants Represent Words**
   - Most words written mainly with consonants
   - Mix of capital and lowercase letters
   - Use of spacing between words
   - Punctuation explored

6. **Initial, Middle, and Final Sounds**
   - Familiar words spelled correctly (e.g., environmental print and sight words)
   - Unfamiliar words spelled phonetically, the way they sound
   - Writing is readable.

7. **Transitional Phase**
   - Greater conventional spelling used
   - Standard letter patterns used often

8. **Standard Spelling**
   - Spells most words correctly.
   - Use of compound words and contractions
   - Uses knowledge to spell new words.

Why do teachers with a diagnostic mindset want to know about developmental spelling, and what do they do to gauge student ability to spell developmentally? If children are given many opportunities to write for many different purposes, they will progress through these stages with teacher guidance. Forcing the child to move into the next stage without time to develop the concepts in the current stage can actually thwart progress rather than advance it. Correction of spelling during these early stages is ineffective. Children need long time periods to "live" and figure things out in each stage.[7]

What is Meant by Writing Process?

Strong writing products come from several kinds of effort—not just sitting down and banging out a finished product. The basic process of writing is a recursive set of steps (see Figure 13.2), meaning that each step of the process may be returned to or repeated multiple times before publishing a piece. These include prewriting, drafting, revising, editing, and publishing. The process is rarely linear and often visually represented using a circular chart with roughly equal parts. However, to represent the essence of its recurring nature, a web or mind map with arrows leading to and from each action of the process is ideal.

Figure 13.2 The Process of Writing

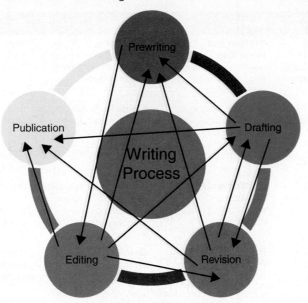

Prewriting

- Choosing a topic
- Organizing the text
- Creating purposes
- Research/gathering information

Drafting

- Writing a beginning draft
- Rewriting drafts
- Writing a final draft

Revising

- Reading
- Questioning whether purposes are met
- Obtaining feedback from others
- Negotiating changes
- Rewriting sentences and paragraphs

Editing

- Analyzing conventions
- Returning to purposes

Publishing

- Formatting
- Text features
- Visual elements

Enhanced eText
Video Example 13.2
Ann Wilson describes how to teach the process of writing. Cue to 5:12 where the video features an anchor chart and teaching suggestions.
https://www.youtube.com/watch?v=p8xYC-mWs_A

The writing process is unique to the individual writer and project. As seen below in Figure 13.3, the process can follow any path and require multiple visits by the writer to any one part. This is not unique to any field or subject of study. This phenomenon is what makes learning to write for many purposes so involved. Learning to write requires time and repeated practice. A one-week unit on writing is not sufficient for teachers to see improvement. Writing must be integrated into each week's and day's plans.

Figure 13.3 The Recursive Nature of the Writing Process

Day/Class	Math	Reading	Science	Writing	Social Studies
Monday	**Prewriting:** Choosing a math concept for review—writing a word problem	**Prewriting: "Read to Write"** Searching for writing ideas while reading independently	**Drafting and Prewriting:** Crafting a question to guide inquiry and researching to explore concept	**Prewriting:** Studying prewriting and organizing ideas identified during "Read to Write"	**Prewriting:** Researching a topic for National History Day (NHD)
Tuesday	**Prewriting and Drafting:** Writing a draft of the math problem and researching accuracy	**Prewriting: "Read to Write"** Researching for NHD resources	**Drafting:** Crafting a hypothesis and planning an experiment	**Revising:** Seeking feedback through peer-conference, return to reading for additional ideas	**Drafting, revising, and editing:** Organizing and crafting a draft of research paper, reading to revise and edit throughout
Wednesday	**Revising:** Adding extraneous details and clarifying main math question	**Revising:** Reading feedback from teacher on NHD project to plan changes	**Drafting and Revising:** Conducting experiments and recording results throughout	**Editing and Prewriting:** Returning to purposes for writing piece, mapping writing	**Prewriting and Editing:** Reviewing purposes and researching and gathering more information
Thursday	**Editing:** Using checklist for spelling and use of key math vocabulary and terms	**Publishing:** Reading mentor texts for text feature ideas for NHD final draft	**Revising and Editing:** Returning to hypothesis and analyzing data	**Drafting and Editing:** Editing while crafting draft	**Revising, Editing, and Prewriting:** Analyzing conventions and researching to add details
Friday	**Editing and Publishing:** Returning to purposes to check final product and presenting to peers to solve	**Prewriting:** Reading poetry for creative idea of conveying new math concept	**Publishing and Editing:** Crafting final write-up of results and performing final edit	**Publishing and Editing:** Creating final draft with final edit	**Publishing and Editing:** Crafting final product and using checklist to determine accuracy

> **Enhanced eText Application Exercise 13.1:** Writing Acquisition, Developmental Spelling, and the Writing Process

Bridge: From Understanding to Assessment

When teachers understand that _____,	then teachers may want to assess _____.
Writing acquisition follows a developmental series of stages,	Writing samples crafted by the student, and how elements of her writing reveal her current developmental stage(s).
Invented spelling occurs as writers explore a holistic perspective of encoding to convey a message,	Spelling miscue patterns evident in a child's writing, and how invented spelling allows the writer to focus on making meaning.
The writing process is a recursive one that can be used to guide writing practice,	A writer's use of each part of the writing process, and connections between individual writing needs and neglected part(s) of the process.

Assessing Writing

Teachers with a diagnostic mindset want to know what a student considers while attempting to generate an idea for his writing. They want to know how a student views herself as a writer. They want to know what writing goals a student chooses to set for himself and why. They want to know *how* a student might self-regulate her skills and strategies while crafting a polished draft. Beyond knowing 'what,' they want to know *how* they might best discover answers to these questions in order to inform instruction. There are many ways to assess writing (see Figure 13.4), and those that follow embrace the diagnostic mindset of this text.

Pre-Assessment

To find out whether primary students have a writing vocabulary, teachers can give them a blank sheet of paper and ask them to write all of the words they know. To get a view of the children's understandings about the alphabetic principle, teachers can give

Figure 13.4 The HOW of Assessing Writing

Grade Level	WHAT Do I Want to Know?	WHY Do I Want to Know? So that I Can . . .	HOW Can I Best Discover?
K–6	What are the student's writing strengths and needs?	Collect baseline data to monitor growth; group based on interests, strengths, and needs; and initiate the writing assessment and instruction process.	Pre-Assessment
K–6	What is the student's most immediate writing need?	Initiate a teachable moment during the conference.	Conferencing
2–6	How does the student feel and think about his own writing?	Celebrate areas of growth and encourage goal setting in one-to-one conferencing.	Reflecting
3–6	What is the student's ability to analyze her own writing based on writing concepts learned?	Determine revision and editing strategies that I need to model.	Student Self-Assessment
K–6	What is the student's ability to identify and use writing skills taught?	Promote self-regulatory writing behaviors by re-teaching one-to-one or in small groups.	Checklists

them a blank piece of paper and tell them to write a message. Then watch what they do and make note of their observations using a form such as the one shown in Figure 13.5.

To pre-assess writers in the older grades who are beyond the Standard Spelling stage or who have accelerated writing skills associated with formal writing processes, teachers can ask them to create a beginning draft of a specific type of writing, like Mr. Cowen did in the opening scenario. Then collect their drafts and review them to look for existing strengths and needs. The lenses teachers with a diagnostic mindset look through during this part of the assessment process depend on the writing element that they are planning on teaching next. Apparent strengths and needs allow them to sort students based on individual levels of writing skill or understanding. Assessing in this manner allows teachers to aggregate data and sort students into groups for guided writing instruction.

As pre-assessment is integral to the diagnostic mindset of teaching writing, so is conferencing. Teachers with a diagnostic mindset choose to perform one-to-one conferences to glean insights about student thinking while writing to make meaning.

Conferencing

Conferencing is one of the most useful ongoing assessment techniques for getting inside the head of the writer. Just like listening to a learner read orally can yield an understanding of the thought processes and rationale used to comprehend, a one-to-one writing conference allows a teacher to get as close to the thinking of an individual writer as possible. Good assessment takes time. That time is well spent on conferences by the teacher with a diagnostic mindset. Initially, until a teacher becomes accustomed to the conferencing process and the students become acclimated to the purposes and routine, a conference may take 10–15 minutes to purposefully conduct. In time, a conference that allows the teacher to capture data to guide a powerful teachable moment may only take a few minutes.

Ensuring that teachers conduct highly effective conferences requires persistence, purpose, and planning. Persistence makes conferencing possible. Teachers with a diagnostic mindset see where writing practice fits into plans for developing more effective writers and tenaciously allocate space for an abundance of student writing. Their purpose for each conference is to understand the writer's views, goals, and strategic plans for achieving those goals. They seek their own understanding in order to nurture student understanding. Following a four-step plan allows teachers to do so. In every conference, they set out to research, decide, teach, and link.[8]

Figure 13.5 Observing Student Writing

Directions: Ask the student to write. Observe and collect data below with a check (✓) for each element and create plans for future writing instruction.

Frequency of Behavior	NA	Never	Occasionally	Often	Always
Direction of Writing					
Writes from left to right					
Writes from top to bottom					
Letter Formation					
Scribbles					
Forms letters					
Creates repeated letters					
Creates repeated words					
Conventions					
Uses spaces to separate words					
Uses punctuation					
Explanation of Writing					
Student explains writing					
Student reads own writing					

Conclusions/Instructional Plans (Based on data above):

Source: Based on Jerry Johns, The Basic Reading Inventory, 8th edition, p. 425. Copyright © 2001 by Kendall/Hunt.

Research Each conference is led by a probing question, statement, or observation. Begin by stating, "Tell me what you have been working on." Listening critically to determine student efficacy, or listening strategically for student agency, allows us to purposefully ask follow-up questions and dig deeper into the views, goals, and strategies of the writer. Not only that, regular prompting builds a student's ability to explain who she is becoming as a writer. Seek evidence by prompting the student with "Please show me what you mean in your writing." This allows you to name what the child has done effectively, intentionally or not, in order to support understanding and encourage continued use. You might say, "As a reader, I found the details you include here to be very useful for helping me feel what the character is feeling. Your strategic use of details—specifically, vivid verbs—makes your writing powerful. I look forward to reading more of your detailed writing." Carefully crafted feedback showcases specific writing successes to encourage continued use and inspire opportunities for exploring new writing practices.

Decide A decision must be made to support and/or change a writer's practices during the conference. The research performed helps you decide what, why, and how you will teach the writer. Your decision focuses on immediate and long-term writing impact for the writer and relies on your knowledge of teaching writing.[9] Experience with the writing process and an insightful understanding of the writer's goals support your ability to identify what to teach the individual. Curriculum alignment and assessment data support your rationale for why your instructional decision makes sense. And finally, planning decisions lead to determining how to teach by considering your repertoire of effective teaching methods, including guided practice, demonstration, explaining and offering models, and inquiry.

Teach This step of the conference may be thought of as a mini-lesson. Begin by explaining what will be taught and why. Connect the lesson explicitly to the writer's work, if possible, and perform the lesson using one or more effective teaching methods. Examples of teaching ideas that might be used during the conference can be found in the Teaching Writing section found later in this chapter.

Link The writing conference is a powerful assessment. Teachers gain an understanding of a writer's views, goals, and strategic plans. Not only that, they identify effective behaviors. Evaluate this data to end each conference by naming an example of effective practice used by the writer and encouraging him to continue the practice in the future, and by linking it to other practices, like reading. Showcasing the practice supports the writer's efficacy and agency.

Enhanced eText
Video Example 13.3

This video shows how to conduct research during a conference to identify what to teach the writer.
https://www.youtube.com/watch?v=U8UXb-Nq4Gg&list=PLBp0rwdGswKb2zxCuK_t3PlqF9nbeWL0s

Conference Example: Fifth-Grade Student

Teacher: *Tell me what you are working on.*

Student: *I am working on word choice and things that are more dramatic. I am working on a plan that will allow me to be more dramatic. I think, write down an idea, and then write a draft.*

Teacher: *Do you use a particular method or organizer/tool to organize your thoughts and plans?*

Student: *I didn't before now. I just wrote. This time I started just with a list, but now I am putting those list ideas into categories as I go. I am working on organizing my writing better so that I can write more descriptively and play more with dialogue in my writing.*

Teacher: *How do you feel about your organization now?*

Student: *I feel great. It feels good to be organizing my writing ideas as I go so that I can write more.*

Teacher: *You are doing something that writers do all the time to make their writing more descriptive and more exciting to the reader. Keep practicing this writing behavior. I look forward to hearing and seeing how it is supporting you when we conference next time.*

Student Reflection and Self-Assessment

Writing away from the teacher is as important as writing with the teacher. Independent writing is essential for young writers to develop the skills that are necessary for strengthening their craft. Independent writing can be purposeful when built upon a foundation of explicit writing instruction in whole-class and small-group settings and one-to-one conferencing. The support of the teacher does not have to stop when a writer takes time to explore the craft on her own. Teaching students how to reflect and assess their own writing, while the teacher is working with others through small-group instruction or conferencing, arms them with valuable practices that make independent writing purposeful for achieving continued individual writing goals.

Figure 13.6 Questions to Inspire Student Self-Reflection

Self-Reflection Questions

- What is one specific writing goal you have achieved?
- What are a few examples in your writing that show that you have achieved this goal?
- What tool helps you plan your writing? Why is it helpful?
- Identify a section of your writing that you are proud of. Why did you choose to showcase this sample?
- Identify a section of your writing that showcases your learning as a writer. What skill does it showcase?

Enhanced eText Application Exercise 13.2: Conferencing and Student Reflection

Reflection Students are guided through a process of reflection by answering questions about their writing through writing and speaking. The questions can be posed by the teacher to scaffold young writers or more advanced writers who are being introduced to the practice of reflecting on their own writing. Student responses to questions about their own writing are used to identify and celebrate areas of growth, set individual goals, and offer insights to the teacher during conferencing. As student efficacy grows, students are encouraged to create their own questions to inspire self-reflection. These student-generated questions become powerful data during the research step of teacher and student conferencing. Figure 13.6. shows a list of possible questions to get started in the reflection process. Consider making these accessible to students by including them on an anchor chart for all to see.

Student Self-Assessment Assessing one's own writing can be a difficult task, because most writers have a habit of viewing their own writing based on what they were *intending* to do. Therefore, when looking at one's own draft, it may appear more as a final version with little room for revision, editing, organization, etc. This phenomenon reminds teachers with a diagnostic mindset to teach students *how* to self-assess. This certainly can be done through one-to-one conferencing later, but in the beginning, it is helpful to plan self-assessment into model lessons that regularly launch writer's workshop. Essentially, we teachers must use our own writing to help students navigate the challenging path of self-assessment.

Identify a piece of writing that may serve to support efforts to teach a currently taught process or writing skill. Identify a tool that may be used to make the self-assessment process more concrete and focused. Use think-aloud while answering a series of *questions* about your writing. Model the process for all to see using the document camera to make the process explicit. Show the piece of writing and list the questions on the board with space to write answers. For example, the questions may be focused on conventions to guide the students through the process of self-assessing their ability to properly use capitalization, grammar, punctuation, and spelling. The key is to share your own thinking while you answer each question. Figure 13.7 shows a list of possible questions that involve deep and surface-level analysis to use while thinking aloud as students observe and take notes.

Figure 13.7 Questions to Ask During a Write-Aloud

	Question
Meaning-Level Analysis	
	Do my sentences make sense?
	Does each sentence connect to the one before it?
Surface-Level Analysis	
	Is the beginning letter of each sentence capitalized?
	Does each of my sentences end with a period, question mark, or exclamation point?

Any questions that are answered with a "No" can be attended to during the model or used to guide revision and editing after guided practice.

Checklists

The process for student self-assessment can also be taught using a well-crafted checklist. The checklist can be used to parse out the finite elements of writing that have been taught. Each time an element is taught, add it to the checklist to ensure that students continue to attend to the element in order to make it a skill that they strive toward using regularly in their writing. Figure 13.8 provides a sample checklist for an advanced punctuation study.

Enhanced eText Application Exercise 13.3: Assessing Writing

Bridge: From Assessment to Instruction

If teachers learned _____ from assessment,	then during instruction, teachers might _____.
Self-regulation data: Jonas reactively uses writing checklists after writing that results in his being overwhelmed due to an abundance of revisions and edits,	Compliment Jonas for using the checklists after writing, reminding him that effective writers do so. Reflect, using a think aloud, on their own use of a checklist with their own writing. Launch writing practice during writer's workshop with a proactive reminder to use a checklist to plan (before), revise (during), and edit (after) their writing. Challenge Jonas to create or modify a checklist to achieve his writing goals and meet his needs.
Perceptions data: Sirus does not like to write, because he can't come up with good ideas and is not a very good writer,	Teach a multitude of strategies for generating writing ideas. Conduct an interest inventory to help Sirus identify a topic that he knows a lot about and would be interested in writing about. Remind him that effective writers write about what they know and are passionate about. Remind Sirus that he can locate great writing ideas by reading for enjoyment.
Goals data: Peter does not set specific goals to improve as a writer,	Keep it simple and guide Peter to set a small goal, like using the thesaurus to make three words in his writing more descriptive. Coach Peter to set a specific goal for his writing during the teach portion of a one-to-one conference. Model goal setting as writers themselves. Challenge Peter to make his writing goals known to others through writing or speaking.
Strategic plans data: Brianna sets goals that she does not achieve because she lacks a plan for overcoming her challenges as a writer,	Outline a plan based on one of Brianna's writing goals. Write the plan with her so that she can follow it during her writing practice time. Review her plan with her during one-to-one conferences and informal monitoring opportunities. Guide her to use strategies like the Cueing Questions to reflect on her goal.
Needs data: Sarah needs to be able to see examples of the Six Traits in order to understand them, then identify them, and finally practice applying them in her own writing,	Define a Six Trait for Sarah through writing and speaking. Locate several mentor texts that have distinct examples of the specific trait to share with Sarah. Have Sarah identify examples in other texts, even in the texts she chooses to read during independent reading time. Model the creation of examples of the trait using think aloud. Guide Sarah through the creation of viable examples of the trait.
Process data: Victor completes a final written draft with no planning, revision, or editing,	Structure a process of peer conferencing for the class. Assign a partner to Victor who can expose him to her process-oriented writing strengths, one who might benefit from one of Peter's strengths as well. Plan for writing partners to meet as a team before writing, during writing, after finishing a draft, and after revising, and use a checklist of goals during each peer conference.

Figure 13.8 Advanced Punctuation Study Checklist

Advanced Punctuation Study Checklist		
Name:	Writing Sample:	Date:
Directions: Check off the kinds of punctuation you use in your writing. Attach this checklist to your writing sample and add it to your writer's notebook.		
	Ellipses	
	Hyphen	
	Parentheses	
	Semi-colon	

Teaching Writing

As Donald Murray noted 50 years ago, there is no single way to teach writing.[10] Murray's years of writing practice as a published author and university writing instructor revealed the fact that writing becomes a personal endeavor unique to the practitioner. As a result, elementary teachers' views of the process vary.[11]

We believe in using a diagnostic mindset as we approach writing instruction. Doing so enables us to constantly look at what children are showing and need to know as writers. The following questions guide our diagnostic efforts:

- What do I want to know?
- Why do I want to know?
- How do I best discover?

These questions are a means to an end. They lead us to purposeful instruction that answers the practical question *What do I do with what I learn?* Not only that, they support a diagnostic mindset that embraces the deliberate and effective teaching of writing.

Practices of Good Writing Teachers

Research on writing instruction over the past four decades has identified practices that improve the quality of student writing. A dozen identified through a meta-analysis of research studies are showcased here to guide the efforts of elementary writing teachers with a diagnostic mindset as they strive to support student growth:

1. Teach writers the writing process (i.e., planning, drafting, and revising).
2. Teach writers how and when to apply writing strategies.
3. Teach writers imagery and other forms of creative writing.
4. Teach writers about and how to use text structure.
5. Teach writers how to spell and handwriting/keyboarding skills.
6. Teach writing through collaborative activities.
7. Teach writers how to set and work towards specific writing goals.
8. Teach writers how to generate and organize ideas before drafting.
9. Teach writers by assessing, monitoring progress, and offering meaningful feedback.
10. Teach writers to use word processing and software to support their efforts.
11. Teach writers by increasing writing opportunities.
12. Teach writers using a comprehensive writing program.[12]

Although each of these practices has been found to positively impact student writing success, a combination serves to embellish rewards for students.

In research among effective writing teachers in upper elementary and middle school classrooms, three dimensions of effective practice were found. Effective teachers did the following:

1. Created purposeful and personal writing tasks.

2. Explicitly demonstrated how to craft text with students while using higher-level questioning.

3. Promoted self-regulatory behaviors through an abundance of individual and collaborative student writing experiences.[13]

These two lists of effective practices have much in common. For one, effective teachers devote a specific amount of class time to writing throughout the day. Not only that, effective teachers also take part in the writing process as practitioners and use their experiences to explicitly teach and explore the craft with their students. They teach as Donald Murray has advocated for half a century—they teach writing as writers.[14]

Scenario

Mrs. Mills Reflects with Vincent

A writing reflection:

Mr. Cowen sidles up to Vincent's desk as he sits hunched over a word-filled sheet of lined paper. She relishes the opportunity to conference with him to find out how he is progressing towards his modest recent writing goals. He continues writing. Mrs. Mills waits, reading over his shoulder in the meantime.

Completing a thought, Vincent raises his head. His furrowed brow is typical. The reason for it is not. "I am having trouble explaining this part." Vincent laments.

"What are you trying to say?" Mrs. Mills inquires.

"Well, I want to explain that my main character is jealous of his friend and that is why he said such mean things to him. His behavior had nothing to do with disliking his friend. It was actually based on the value of their friendship."

"Why not begin by writing just what you told me?" asks Mrs. Mills. "One of my favorite strategies for adding detail and clarity to my writing is talking my ideas over with my friend Susi and then adding my insights to my writing."

Verbal rehearsal is a strategy that might come naturally to students. Many writers, like Mrs. Mills, use speaking to develop an idea for writing. Mrs. Mills's support of Vincent here relies on her personal experiences as a writer.

To bring the reading block to a close, Mrs. Mills invites students to rehearse what they plan on adding to their drafts with a peer. Mrs. Mills is delighted by her own efforts to grow as a writer and by her own insights on how her authentic experiences as a writer might be used to support her students. She continues to collect data as she circulates during peer rehearsal, taking advantage of several teachable moments that arise. Additionally, she will use the notes she has taken throughout the writing block to inform tomorrow's instruction.

Mrs. Mills, driven by a diagnostic mindset, models a one-to-one conference and showcases many of the practices definitive of good writing teachers. With a sound understanding of purposeful procedures for assessing student writing and the practices of effective writing teachers, let's take a look at six ideas for teaching writing and their purposes (see Figure 13.9) for nurturing student writing growth.

Teaching Writing Through Self-Reflection

Learning to write is an essential part of elementary education.[15] Considering its importance, elementary teachers benefit by being students of the craft as well.[16] Like Mrs. Mills shows, some of the best fuel for meeting the needs of students comes from

Figure 13.9 Ideas for Writing Instruction with Individuals, Partners, Guided Groups, and Whole Class and their Purposes

Teaching Idea / Grouping	Individual	Partners	Guided Group	Whole Class
Self-Reflection	• Low-stakes practice • Teacher monitor	• Set goals • Accountability	• Model • Guide practice	• Promote risk taking • Define • Model
Six Traits	• One-to-one conference • Review written drafts	• Trait exploration • Peer support	• Trait focus • Meet needs of several • Share strengths with peers	• Create knowledge base • Read aloud from mentor texts
Thesaurus and Dictionary	• Examples of personal use • Exploration	• Self-regulation	• Model • Guide practice	• Provide access • Shared experience
Cueing Questions	• Practice • Peer conference	• Peer feedback • Accountability	• Model • Guide practice	• Model • Review and link to reading
Offering Feedback	• Written • Peer conference	• Observe • Verbal feedback	• Showcasing writing behaviors and effort	• Define types and purposes • Showcase examples
Peer Conferencing	• Set goals • Define role	• Authentic practice • Feedback • Set goals	• Guide practice • Social learning	• Model with peer • Fishbowl

personal writing experiences. Essentially, to teach writing effectively, writing teachers must be students of the craft. This does not mean teachers need to have a published piece in order to effectively teach writing. It does, however, mean they need to be writing for a variety of purposes that can be directly connected to the processes and forms of writing taught to students.

Returning to the major tenets of Chapter 6 reminds us that great teaching is made possible through an understanding of ourselves. I (RS) recently heard a speaker at a National History Day conference. He made a powerful statement that has helped me become a more thoughtful teacher of diverse students. He exclaimed that a teacher needs "to understand her own culture before she can begin to understand the varied cultures of her students." It is a matter of self-awareness.

The process of self-reflection must be taught. Through effective practices useful for revealing the thinking associated with reading, like think aloud, teachers may make the role and potential of self-reflection explicit to students. Repeated modeling makes self-reflection accessible to students. An abundance of guided practice makes self-reflection useful. Not only will this practice support individual student writing growth, it will also serve to scaffold a community of writers who become aware of the qualities of good writing.

Teaching the Six Traits of Writing

Just like learning to read, learning to write is based on meaning. But in the case of writing, the practice involves the initiation of meaning as opposed to responding with meaning to a written text as a reader. So yes, effective writing instruction is grounded in and directly linked to learning to read.

Additionally, writing can be taught effectively and made accessible to all students by creating a community of writing practitioners built on a foundation of common *writing language*.[17] Common writing language can be drawn from qualities that writers and teachers of writing view as significant. In fact, decades ago, teachers of writing were brought together to determine elements of writing they deemed most important. That is where the major elements, or six traits, became illuminated. As a result, we can help students make sense of the writing process by learning about the traits that are a part of the process to make it more transparent, explicit, and accessible to students. Teaching students how writers think about *ideas, organization, voice, word choice, sentence fluency,* and *conventions* throughout the writing process enhances their ability to take control of the writing process, compare and contrast writing quality, and use the understanding of quality writing to read and revise their own drafts.

Teaching Ideas. "You can write about anything, anything you want." This statement, although it might seem optimistic to many a writing teacher, can be downright daunting to student writers. Comparable to the stagnation in reading momentum that can come from not having a "book on deck" after finishing a cherished read, choosing a topic from thin air can be difficult. Although there are many suggestions for generating ideas for engaged writing,[17] we seem to fall back on *Read to Write*. Here is a sample procedure to teach young writers when they need an idea.

1. Tell students that writing ideas often come from reading.

2. Inform them that all kinds of reading can generate ideas, like reading book titles, reading a text for fun, reading environmental print, reading a newspaper or magazine, or reading their favorite website.

3. Model the process for reading titles in the classroom library using think aloud.

4. While looking through an interesting section of the classroom library, read aloud the titles you see. Make comments as you explore those titles, such as "Oh, *Snakeopedia*[20] is a book that I have not seen before. Snakes are interesting and I know a lot about their scales, eating habits, and species. I think that reading this book will help me decide on a topic to write about."

5. Move to the whiteboard with book in hand. While perusing and reading the table of contents aloud, jot down a few snake topics that interest you.

6. Stand back, study the list for a moment, and circle one before heading back to an appropriate space to begin writing, all the while thinking aloud for students to explicitly understand your process for landing on a topic.

7. Reinforce the idea that writers are readers. Reading as a writer can help them not only generate topics for writing, but help them structure their writing as well by using a text as a mentor.

8. Encourage writers who do not have a topic for writing to use the *Read to Write* strategy to identify topics of interest to write about.

Each of the Six Traits can be taught in the above manner. Actually, each can be taught by attending to the key ingredients of any quality lesson. Figure 13.10 showcases these elements and offers ideas for teaching each trait.

Thesaurus and Dictionary

Creating "wordologists" is made possible through resources like the thesaurus and dictionary. These resources come alive and become priceless tools for learning to write when we explicitly unpack processes for using them and what they have to offer. Refrain from simply offering them to students. Guide and explore their many uses through constructive learning experiences. The teaching ideas to use with the thesaurus that follow may be altered to use with the dictionary, or other compiled resources as well.

Thesaurus. Guiding student use of the thesaurus may begin with a definition. Begin by posting the following riddle:

> *I save, store, and stockpile,*
> *Amass, assemble, and accrue.*
> *Creative, imaginative, and artistic words I file,*
> *Such as cerulean, cobalt, or azure for blue.*
> *What am I?*

Figure 13.10 Teaching the Six Traits

Trait	Grade Level Focus	Purpose	Reading Connection	Sample Lesson Plan	Sample Mentor Text
Ideas	K–6	Generate interesting writing ideas	Read to identify ideas to write about	Writing Workshop: Helping Writers Choose and Focus on a Topic	*Snakeopedia*
Organization	3–5	Use text features to guide the reader	Mentor texts—table of contents and chapter titles	Traveling Terrain: Comprehending Nonfiction Text on the Web	*Who Was Jules Verne?*
Voice	K–2	Explore voice with a wordless picture book	Using picture cues to create a story	This is My Story: Encouraging Students to Use a Unique Voice	*The Marvelous Misadventures of Fun Boy*
Word Choice	2–5	Understand idioms to make writing descriptive	Mentor texts—reading definitions of common idioms	Figurative Language: Teaching Idioms	*In a Pickle: And Other Funny Idioms*
Sentence Fluency	3–5	Write to convey deeper meaning through comparisons	Reading examples and definitions of similes	As Slippery as an Eel: An Ocean Unit Exploring Simile and Metaphor	*Stubborn as a Mule: And Other Silly Similes*
Conventions	K–2	Promote accessibility to the reader	Conventions used in mentor texts to support reading comprehension	Inside or Outside? A Minilesson on Quotation Marks and More	*Punctuation Takes a Vacation*

Developing an enticing introduction to the thesaurus, no matter students' prior exposure, can enlighten them to the hidden beauty of words and the value of the tool. I (RS) used this riddle process for building anticipation for introducing the thesaurus to my third graders. Each day a new riddle, espousing a plethora of purposefully chosen synonyms, was displayed in writing before the school day adjacent to our living word wall that showcased key science and math vocabulary. Seven days of these riddles, written only and otherwise ignored by me, proved to entice student interest and showcase thinking through their informal comments, questions, and predictions as our daily experiences as writers revealed the need to a focus on word choice. Each day they entered the classroom with anticipation, looking forward to a new riddle and an unwritten invitation to think about its meaning.

On the eighth day, students arrived to find a thesaurus on each desk. Written instructions on the board challenged them to "Define the thesaurus using examples **from** the thesaurus in writing with a peer or on your own." Student interest in using this tool proved mighty as they engaged in excited page flipping, text exploration, peer discussion, and writing. Pencil and paper in hand, I circulated to capitalize on the learning activity, collect data to assess individual student familiarity with the resource, and plan any subsequent whole-group, small-group, and individual instruction. My data collection proved useful for identifying student strengths and needs. (See Figure 13.11.)

Evaluation of the data helped me to plan a small-group lesson focused on using guidewords to navigate the thesaurus, since only six students needed the support. I planned a guided writing lesson that would be taught to two groups of three students during the independent writing portion of writer's workshop over the next few days. My evaluation also revealed student challenges for choosing grammatically correct words from the thesaurus. I chose to attend to this student need by returning to the use of cueing questions, a skill that they had recently learned to monitor reading comprehension.

Figure 13.11 Thesaurus Data

Lesson: Thesaurus Riddles Student		KEY: Guide Words, Cueing Questions (parts of speech) *Label shows need for continued instruction.*			
Sara	G C	Jasmine	C	Joshua	G C
Jerome	G C	Ryan	C	Hannah	C
Clifford	C	Arturo	C	Jessica	C
Klara	C	Naro	C	Morgan	C
Trevor		Katie	G C	Maggie	C
Bruce	C	Lisa	C	Peter	C
Rylan	C	Julieann	C	Aaron	G C
Baseley	C	Shailyn	C	Lindrey	G

Using the Cueing Questions to Teach Writing

Student skills for examining reading miscues can be used to evaluate the appropriateness of words they choose to use from the thesaurus in their writing. All but two students proved a need for this lesson. (See Figure 13.11.) I decided to give Lindrey and Trevor the opportunity to participate in teaching the whole group mini-lesson, or to continue working independently on their own writing. Both agreed to help teach the rest of the class.

I chose to modify the strategy "Verbs That Match the Meaning" by Jennifer Seravallo[18] to teach my students. After constructing my plans, I met with Lindrey and Trevor to coach them on their roles as models. Here is the procedure that we followed:

1. Tell students that the purpose of this activity is to help them choose verbs from the thesaurus that make sense and make their writing more descriptive.

2. Remind them that they have been learning about using the cueing questions to monitor their thinking while reading when they make a miscue.

3. Ask them if they remember the three questions we ask ourselves while doing so.

4. Instruct them to write down those three questions in their journal and to be sure to include an icon or picture that is associated with each if that will help them recall each.

5. Circulate and monitor individual student ability to list and visually represent the three questions.

6. Clarify by referring to the anchor chart posted for all to see and reading aloud the cueing questions.

7. Instruct students to read the list of procedures showcased for all to see as you orally read through them one by one. Have the steps displayed on an anchor chart or use the document camera.

   - *Find a current sample of writing you have been working on.*
   - *Locate and highlight several verbs in your sample.*
   - *Use the thesaurus to find alternatives to one of the verbs you used.*
   - *List those alternative verbs on your paper.*
   - *Evaluate each alternative using the cueing questions "Does that make sense?" and "Does that sound right?"*
   - *If the answer to both of these questions is "Yes" then consider using that verb in your writing. If the answer is "No," draw a line through the word.*
   - *Continue identifying the verbs in your sample and evaluating alternatives using your thesaurus.*

8. Explain to the students that the process for choosing and evaluating verbs to replace meek verbs in their writing will be available.

9. Ask the students to raise their hands if they need more instruction on this process.

10. If only part of the class proves to need more support, instruct them to move to one of the two small-group areas, where Lindrey and Trevor will model the process using think aloud for them to follow.

11. If most of the class needs further support, have Lindrey and Trevor model the process using the fishbowl modeling technique in turn while peers observe and listen strategically.

12. Instruct students who are ready to "peel off" and begin following the steps of the process to evaluate their own writing.

13. Circulate to listen-in on the models and prompts offered by student helpers like Lindrey and Trevor. Offer support if necessary.

14. Circulate to attend to teachable moments and collect data on individual student skills during independent practice.

15. Use prompts if necessary to explore use of the cueing questions. Example: "Show me a word that you used the cuing questions to analyze. Share your thinking using a think aloud."

16. Encourage students to share verbs that proved to "fit" with a peer or small group after an abundance of practice time.

17. Tell students to continue using the cueing questions as they revise their own writing during independent writing.

Extend the learning experience by offering text sets that encourage student exploration of using the thesaurus to locate more descriptive words.

- Thesaurus Rex (Steinburg, 2003)[19]
- Flip's Fantastic Journal (DeCesare, 1999)[20]
- Max's Words (Blank, 2006)[21]
- The Boy Who Loved Words (Schotter, 2006)[22]
- The Word Collector (Wimmer, 2012)[23]

Offering Feedback

Offering feedback to developing writers is essential. Feedback can come from the teacher or other students.[24] The key is to develop a writing community that looks forward to and relishes opportunities to offer and gather feedback.

Feedback is useful when based on specific assessment criteria that serve to ground writing practice.[25] In other words, the expectations for writing need to be clear. Students must be immersed in processes that are directly linked to an abundance of quality writing samples, explanations of what makes those samples high-quality, and tools to match their own writing to exemplar models. Using feedback to scaffold, challenge, and celebrate student writing practice can only be done when the process, purposes, and procedures for writing have been established.

There certainly are guidelines to effectively offering feedback to students. Such feedback invigorates writers, challenges their levels of thinking, and honors their efforts. Feedback teaches. The ten guidelines in Figure 13.12 showcase a synthesis of the literature in relation to offering feedback.

Figure 13.12 Ten Guidelines for Offering Oral and Written Writing Feedback

Guideline	Sample Statement
Be Concise	"I want to address a few ideas we have studied."
Ask a Research Question	"What have you been focused on in your writing?"
Reference a Writing Guide	"I can see that you have been using our punctuation checklist to edit your writing."
Ask for Permission	"May I write on your draft?"
Offer an Example	"Let me show you what I mean in this mentor text."
Celebrate Growth	"You are doing what effective writers do."
Challenge Further Efforts	"What is your next writing goal and plan for achieving it?"
Wrap-Up with a Link	"Be sure to use this writing skill when you write your thank-you letter today."
Offer Feedback Often	"I aim to review and offer written feedback to those of you who request it today."
Follow Up with a Conference	"I will be conferencing with the following six students today."

Peer Conferencing

Peer conferences are an essential element of the writer's workshop. Incorporating all 12 of the research-based practices that improve the quality of student writing showcased at the beginning of this chapter can be a challenging task. We cannot do it on our own, nor should we. Luckily, we have our students to lean on for support. There are key reasons for developing a community of writers grounded in the practice of peer conferencing. Peer conferencing promotes

- Accountability and responsibility by building a pattern of consistent writing practice driven by the expectation of meeting regularly with peers

- Experiences with others who face similar challenges and those whose strengths may inspire our own writing

- Knowledge sharing between writers to promote the realization that we are all experts on particular topics and those topics may serve to build our own writing efficacy and agency

- Problem-solving strategies through interdependence with peers as they strive for solutions to writing challenges[26]

We must teach our students *how* to support the writing community through peer conferencing as we lead them to realize the incredible value of their fellow writers. Teacher–student conferences can lead to student–student conferences when we showcase our own conferences with students as a model for them to use with one another. The procedure of conferencing can be passed on to our students through consistent practice, by naming each part of the process, and making the purposes for the conference explicit. Helping students create a personal anchor chart for their writer's notebooks can help.

Enhanced eText Application Exercise: **13.4:** Teaching Writing

---

Bridge: From Teaching Back to Understanding

If writers respond to _____,	then teachers might learn to _____.
Feedback by stating that they still don't understand, or are failing to demonstrate the use of the behavior taught,	Visually represent their idea by displaying their text with the document camera for students to see and hear. Guide students through role playing with one another using the practice of think aloud to show their understanding of the skill modeled. Explicitly reveal the purposes for using the skill in relation to actions that effective writers perform.
The teaching of a specific Trait by stating that they don't understand the trait or showing inability to use it in their writing,	Define the trait orally, in writing, and visually for persistent reference. Offer various examples of the trait, especially non-examples and exemplars. Include more examples of the trait with mentor texts. Employ practices like write-aloud during small-group and individual instruction.
Challenges to use the thesaurus (or dictionary) to support their writing by not using it throughout the writing process or using it ineffectively,	Lay thesauruses out for easy access. Create engaging activities for using the thesaurus. Model personal use of the tool, often. Unpack all parts and elements of the tool. Enhance the study of words, 'wordology'.
Teaching regarding the cueing questions to enhance writing skills by neglecting to understand their value or not using them during any part of the writing process,	Model think alouds using the questions to teach transitions, weak word replacement, or determining a title, for example. Practice guiding cueing questions during reading conferences with links to continued writing practice. Display the cueing questions with examples on anchor charts for all to see. Expect students to incorporate the use of the cueing questions into their writing checklist practices.
Feedback offered by ignoring it or misunderstanding the intended message(s),	Express the importance of focusing on the audience while writing. Remind students that effective writers grow from feedback from their readers. Make feedback clear. Honor writing effort through celebratory feedback. Challenge writers to grow by addressing a specific need.
Peer conferencing by ineffectively communicating or showing confusion about the purposes, procedures, or roles associated,	Define and model the process for an effective peer conference using a series of fishbowl models. Model a peer conference with another teacher. Guide students to set goals for their conference before, monitor their role during, and reflect on the value of the conference after. Teach students the five listening levels and set clear expectations for listening to one another.

Revisiting the Scenarios

Now that you have had some time to learn about writing acquisition, assessing writing, and teaching writing, take another look at what Mrs. Mills and Mr. Cowen were doing in their classrooms. Which practices of effective writing teachers do they seem to exemplify? What assessment and instruction strategies did they employ?

Authors' Summary

Before reading our summary statements for each outcome, we suggest you read each outcome and summarize it in your own words.

Once finished, cross-check your response with our brief summary to determine how well you recalled the major points.

13.1 Explain developmental writing and spelling stages.

- Developmental writing stages and procedural guides help teachers make sense of writing acquisition.

- Understanding the characteristics that define these specific stages allows teachers who have a diagnostic mindset to establish reasonable expectations for individual writers, identify writing strengths and needs of the individual, set goals for and with a writer, assess and monitor individual growth, and determine activities and instruction to meet individual needs.

13.2 Describe ways to purposefully assess writers and use assessment data to plan subsequent instruction.

- There are many ways to assess writing. Writing teachers with a diagnostic mindset choose to use assessments that lead to the most valuable

instructional actions based on insights gained. Such insights are sought regarding student writing self-regulation behaviors, perceptions, goals, strategies, needs, and processes.

- Pre-assessment, conferencing, self-reflection, student self-assessment, and checklists can be used to acquire meaningful data for guiding effective writing instruction.

13.3 Identify instructional ideas used to meet the needs of individual writers.

- There are practices exhibited by writing teachers that have proven to effectively impact student writing growth. Effective teachers devote a sufficient amount of class time to writing throughout the day. Not only that, effective teachers take part in the writing process as practitioners and use their experiences to explicitly teach and explore the craft with their students.

- Six ideas for writing instruction are showcased to enhance teaching practice, including self-reflection, the Six Traits, thesaurus and dictionary, cueing questions, offering feedback, and peer conferencing.

Think About It!

1. When reflecting on your own personal history with writing, how did your own attitudes, identity, and interests form?

2. When did educators take an active role in assessing you and teaching you to grow in positive attitudes and identity, or to develop your writing to your benefit? If you do not have a positive outlook on writing, how might you change that? Is it necessary for you to have a positive outlook to effectively teach your writers?

3. How do students respond to your instruction? By applying assessment and instruction techniques with

professional writers, what have you learned about the practical relationship between student perceptions of themselves as writers and their growth?

4. How might your personal history and your experience with students shape the way you approach teaching writing for diverse learners? What if you were a classroom teacher with 20–30 students each day? What if you were a middle school teacher with 150 students, and only saw each student in one 50-minute or 85-minute class? What if you were an intervention teacher and saw each student only for a half-hour each day or three times per week?

Websites

- https://www.nwp.org/cs/public/print/resource/922
    The National Writing Project resource site includes a multitude of guides and strategies for teaching writing. In particular, the "30 Ideas for Teaching Writing" include topics from generating writing ideas to using writing to develop classroom community.

- https://www.time4learning.com/teaching-writing.shtml
    Time 4 Learning offers a wealth of ideas to support the teaching of writing to students specifically in elementary and middle school. The site includes, but is not limited to, definitions and suggestions for teaching writing skills and the writing process.

- http://teacher.scholastic.com/professional/teachwriting/
    This Scholastic site focuses on inspiring writers by challenging them to think critically about important topics. A wide variety of focused writing activities, articles, resources, and lesson plans are offered to encourage writing in various subject areas.

YouTube Videos

- Lucy Calkins on Mini-lessons
    In this YouTube video, Lucy Calkins explains the rationale for teaching writing with mini-lessons.

- Execute Mini-Lessons in 4 Steps
    This video presents four steps to teaching a mini-lesson.

Endnotes

1. R. Gentry Interview, https://www.scholastic.com/teachers/videos/teaching-content/teacher-talk-richard-gentry-phases-development-reading-and-writing/.

2. Hodges, R. (1981). The language base of spelling. In V. Froese & S. B. Straw (Eds.), *Research in the Language Arts: Language and Schooling*, (p. 218). Baltimore, MD: University Park Press.

3. Beers, J. (1980). Developmental strategies of spelling competence in primary-school children. In E. H. Henderson & J. W. Beers (Eds.), *Developmental and Cognitive Aspects of Learning to Spell*, (p. 36). Newark, DE: IRA.

4. Gentry, R. (1982, November). An analysis of developmental spelling in GYNS at WRK. *The Reading Teacher* 36, 192–200.

5. Ibid., p. 194.

6. Ibid., p. 197.

7. Kucer, S. (2009). *Dimensions of literacy*, (3rd ed.). Mahwah, NJ: Lawrence Erlbaum.

8. Calkins, L., Hartman, A., & White, Z. (2005). *One to one: The art of conferring with young writers*. Portsmouth, NH: Heinemann.

9. Ritchey, K., Coker, D. Jr., & Jackson, A. (2017). The relationship between early elementary teachers' instructional practices and theoretical orientations and students' growth in writing. *Reading and Writing* 28, 1333–1354.

10. D. Murray. (1968). A Writer Teaches Writing: A Practical Method of Teaching Composition. Houghton Mifflin, NY.

11. Elementary Teachers' Perceptions of Process Writing ARTICLE

12. Graham, S., et. al. (2012). A meta-analysis of writing instruction for students in the elementary grades. *Journal of Educational Psychology*. Vol. 104, No. 4, 879–896. American Psychological Association.

13. Gadd, M. & Parr, J. (2017). Practices of effective writing teachers. *Reading and Writing* 30, 1551–1574.

14. Murray, D. (1968). A writer teaches writing: A practical method of teaching composition. New York, NY: Houghton Mifflin.

15. Mo, Y., Kopke, R. A., Hawkins, L. K., Troia, G. A., & Olinghouse, N. G. (2014). The neglected "R" in a time of Common Core. The Reading Teacher, 67(6), 445–453.

16. Murray, D. (YEAR?). A writer teaches writing: A practical method of teaching composition. New York, NY: Houghton Mifflin.

17. Spandel, V. (2001). Creating writers: Through 6-trait writing assessment and instruction (3rd Ed.). New York, NY: Addison, Wesley, Longman.

18. Serravallo, J. (2017). *The writing strategies book:* Your everything guide to developing skilled writers. Portsmouth, NH: Heinemann.

19. Thesaurus Rex (Steinburg, 2003).

20. Flip's Fantastic Journal (DeCesare, 1999).
21. Max's Words (Blank, 2006).
22. The Boy Who Loved Words (Schotter, 2006).
23. The Word Collector (Wimmer, 2012).
24. Zoi A. Philippakos, "Giving feedback: Preparing students for peer review and self-evaluation." *The Reading Teacher* 71.1 (2017): 13–22.
25. Wang, E., Matsumura, L., & Correnti, R. (2017). Written feedback to support students' higher level thinking about texts in writing. *The Reading Teacher*, 71.1, 101–107. DOI: 10.1002/trtr.1584.
26. Philippakos (2017).

Chapter 14
Partnering with Families, Teachers, and Community

Nong Mars/Shutterstock

Chapter Outline

Scenario: David's Father Talks with Mr. Gonzalez

Partnering with Families

Partnering with Teachers

Partnering with the Community

Learning Outcomes

After reading this chapter, you should be able to . . .

14.1 Explain how partnering with families can support literacy learning.

14.2 Explain how participating in professional learning communities can support literacy assessment and instruction.

14.3 Explain how partnering with the community can support literacy learning.

Scenario

David's Father Talks with Mr. Gonzalez

"He seems so unmotivated to read these days," David's father comments to Mr. Gonzalez, David's third-grade teacher. "I mean," he continues, "I used to be able to get David to read just about anything I told him to read but now he has lost interest. He seems more interested in sports or goofing around with his friends."

Curious, Mr. Gonzalez asks questions to see how he might be able to help the situation. He comments, "I have noticed David likes to read riddle books, comics, and stories about sports figures." David's father looks a little surprised. He asks, "Are these okay for David to read? Will they really help him to be a better reader?"

Mr. Gonzalez uses this question as an opener to talk with David's father about how having David read these and other types of self-selected books will increase his reading skills. He explains that David's vocabulary only stands to increase as a result of doing much independent reading on topics of his choice. He also explains that David might need to understand that even though he likes to play sports and play games with friends, he can still make time for reading. He might need to be taught how to balance his time. Mr. Gonzalez ends his discussion by sifting through a collection of magazines that have been added to the classroom library by the teacher candidates that train in his classroom.

"Yes, here they are," says Mr. Gonzales, handing two sports magazines to David's father. Additionally, he hands him a couple of riddle books donated by the local bookstore, informing him that they can be traded for credit towards new books at that store. He also reminds David's father to let David choose what to read and to set a time for David to read independently.

"I'll give it a try, Mr. Gonzalez. Thanks for taking some time to help us out." With that, David's father leaves. A firm believer in parental involvement, Mr. Gonzalez reflects on the exchange and plans to share it with his professional learning community. He feels pleased that he has such a close relationship with his students' caregivers that they feel comfortable talking to him whenever the need arises. Mr. Gonzalez shows he understands what many researchers report about parental involvement: It is essential in order for their children to maximize their reading potential.

Understanding Family Involvement

Family involvement in schools is ever present. Caregivers sit on boards of education; they are involved in parent–teacher associations, family councils, and caregiver clubs. Caregivers help formulate school policy, have a say in curriculum, and even help to choose textbooks. Families definitely have a voice in school matters. In many school districts across the country, families are seen as partners and resources.

Although most agree that family involvement helps students to achieve better, just how to best involve them is another question. For example, if teachers invite caregivers to come to evening meetings, many may not be able to attend for legitimate reasons. After working all day, getting dinner prepared and served, tidying the kitchen, and making sure children are doing their chores and homework, some families may be too exhausted to go to an evening meeting. Finding a sitter may also be difficult, which is another reason families may stay home.

Figure 14.1 A Parent Checklist

	Often	Seldom
I listen to my child.		
I read aloud to my child every day.		
I discuss ideas with my child.		
I explain concepts to my child.		
I spend time with my child.		
I ask my child good questions.		
I ask my child to read picture books to me.		
I watch special TV shows with my child.		
I encourage my child.		
I am patient with my child.		
I take my child to interesting places.		
I do not pressure my child.		
I read and write in the presence of my child.		
I am a good role model for my child.		

There are numerous other issues, including working with caregivers who are challenged readers and writers themselves and with those whose first language is not English. The good news is that recognizing the issues puts teachers in a better position to work through them. If they sense that they are working with caregivers who have negative histories with school and literacy, for example, they can use telephone calls rather than a printed newsletter to communicate. If they are working with those whose first language is not English, teachers can seek out people in the community to help them communicate with these families in their first languages. If they are working with families unlikely to leave home for an evening school meeting primarily because they cannot afford to hire a babysitter, teachers can structure the meetings so children can accompany caregivers.

The checklist shown in Figure 14.1 can be a valuable aid for caregivers interested in helping their young children. It provides a list of family behaviors that lead to increased student learning. Caregivers can use the list as a way of remembering what they can be doing with their children. The International Literacy Association publishes several pamphlets related to many of the attributes shown on the checklist. Teachers and families can access them online by visiting the ILA's website, www.literacyworldwide.org. All can be downloaded for free.

Research on Family Involvement in Education

Home support is a major factor in fostering higher achievement; in fact, "one of the clearest predictors of early reading ability is the amount of time spent reading with [caregivers]."[1] Researchers also consistently suggest that caregivers who expect their children to do well and encourage them enhance their young children's literacy development.[2] The authors of the National Assessment of Educational Progress (NAEP) reports confirm the importance of family involvement in children's education. They consistently report that students who have home support for literacy usually have higher average reading achievement than students without home support.[3]

In *The Basic School: A Community for Learning*, the late Ernest Boyer, former president of the Carnegie Foundation for the Advancement of Teaching, stresses that what elementary schools need most is a greater bond between families and teachers.[4] When interviewed, he stated: "School is a partnership. If education is in trouble, it's not the school that has failed. It's the partnership that has failed." He also stated that "at many schools, parents still feel that they are on the edges. If parents are going to be made partners, schools are going to have to be the ones to reach out. They control the gates."

Boyer then presented examples of schools that give families realistic ways to become involved. He also showed how employers were getting into the act by giving employees paid time off to volunteer in schools. Patricia Edwards mentions several other ways that a community can help families make time to be in school.[5] For example, she found that in many working-class neighborhoods, caregivers were working either multiple shifts or shifts that conflicted with school programs. Also, there were many single-caregiver homes. So to get families involved in school activities, she had to have the buy-in of many community leaders and proprietors. Among those she found useful were church leaders, bar and restaurant owners, store proprietors, and employers. These people were interested in children's reading success because they could see the direct impact of it when employing and involving people from the community. This made it easier for them to change schedules around important school events—without penalizing families. Church leaders agreed to avoid conflicting with school meetings and to promote attendance of the school meetings as a benefit to the congregation. When community leaders and business owners agree on the value of a more literate community, it is easier for families to do the same.

Enhanced eText **Application Exercise 14.1:** Understanding Family Partnerships

---

Bridge: From Understanding to Self-Assessment

When teachers understand that _____,	then they will self-assess _____.
School success equals success in creating partnerships with all families,	The success of partnership invitations for all families.
Invitations to partnership often fail for legitimate family reasons,	The variety of ways they have of communicating invitations, and the variety of ways people can become involved.
Reading in the home is a powerful predictor of reading success in school,	How much they know about kinds of texts most likely available at home.

Family Involvement in Schoolwide Reading Programs

Caregivers sometimes become more involved in school programs when their children have a specific reading need; however, the trend appears to be one of increasing family involvement even for those without reading needs.

The participation of families in many school districts is often dependent on how aggressive the educators and caregivers are in demanding such involvement. The presence of the families in the reading program varies from district to district, and even from school to school in some school districts. In one school system, you will find an organized program, and in another, you will find that the program is up to the individual teacher in each individual class. The programs that do exist usually are similar in format; they generally include workshops, instructional materials, and text suggestions. What is presented, however, will vary from district to district. Here are some examples:

Example 1: New Jersey   The following is an example of a program that was developed by employees in a New Jersey school system to incorporate family involvement in its regular reading program for all children in grades 1–5. The program consists of instructional packets, book suggestions, and three workshops. At the first workshop, a reading specialist explains the reading program in use in the school system. The caregivers are acquainted with the reading program and its corresponding terminology. At the second workshop, caregivers watch a reading lesson, which shows a teacher and children engaged in a Directed Reading Lesson. The third session, "A Book Talk," provides caregivers with appropriate children's books at different readability and interest levels. They are also given several suggestions for how to involve their children in reading them.

Another part of the program concerns instructional materials. For those children who have reading needs, teachers construct family packets that consist of activities based on the skills and strategies that children are learning. Different parent packets are available for different grade levels. For those children who have few reading problems, the packets contain suggestions for ways to extend learning. Yet another packet, which emphasizes more complex books, such as several Newbery Award winners, is available for caregivers of children who want to read such material.

Example 2: Junior Great Books   **Junior Great Books** is a program aimed at readers in grades 2–6, their teachers, and their caregivers. It involves 12 volunteer caregivers and 12 teachers. A caregiver and a teacher are paired up to work together as a team to plan and lead reading discussion sessions for students. The caregivers who volunteer participate in a two-day training session, which is conducted by a specialist from the Great Books Foundation, located in Chicago. The training consists primarily of helping caregivers learn about the kinds of questions they should ask their students, as well as how to conduct the discussions. The caregiver–teacher team meets every week to plan for the reading discussion, which takes place in the regular classroom during the regularly scheduled 45-minute reading period. Both the caregiver and the teacher lead the discussion with a particular group of children.

Example 3: Reading Olympics   The structure of **Reading Olympics** programs varies from school system to school system, from school to school, and even from one class to another; however, all include reading books and sharing them in some way with families. Here is how one such program works in the middle part of the year in a first-grade class.

Children are challenged to read as many books as they can. They must read these books aloud to one of their caregivers, and after they finish reading the book aloud, the caregiver asks them questions about the story or has them retell it. Completed books are recorded on a reading record form similar to the one shown in Figure 14.2.

Example 4: Paired Reading   Another helpful practice for families is **paired reading**. This is a method where caregivers and children read aloud simultaneously. This technique is generally used with children who need additional support when reading, but it can be used with any child to provide structure for reading together. At any time during the simultaneous reading, the child can signal that she wishes to read alone. The caregiver praises the child's desire to do so and allows the child to read alone. As Johnston notes, "The child is encouraged to read alone by lack of criticism and by frequent praise for any independent reading."[6] This technique is powerful because it keeps the focus on reading for enjoyment. Families need not be concerned with helping their children learn specific reading strategies when doing paired reading. They focus instead on the moments of competence that happen in the flow of the activity.

Figure 14.2 Reading Record

Day	Title of reading material	Amount of time spent reading / Number of pages read	Comments
Sunday			
Monday			
Tuesday			
Wednesday			
Thursday			
Friday			
Saturday			

Paired reading was originally designed for families to use with their children,[7] and the growth that children showed in both reading vocabulary and reading comprehension was so startling that it is now used by reading tutors in more structured situations.

Here are some suggested procedures:[8]

1. Agree on a time at which the reading will regularly occur.

2. Provide time for the reader to select the material to be read. This material can be changed from one session to another. That is, if a child selects reading material and decides at the end of the session not to continue with it at the next session, they can bring another text to the next session.

3. Sit side by side, because you will both want to see the text with ease. Make sure that you select a place that is free of all distractions.

4. Agree on a starting signal, such as "1, 2, 3." Begin reading together. Also establish a signal for when the reader wants to read solo; a tap on the shoulder is often used. When the reader chooses to read solo, reinforce the reader for taking this risk by saying something such as "Good!"

5. Stop at logical points to talk about the meaning of what is being read.

6. If the reader makes a miscue, wait to see if they self-correct. If not, and if the miscue alters the author's intended meaning, point to the word, say it for the child, and have the child repeat it. Continue reading aloud with the child until the solo signal is again given.

Example 5: Family Literacy Project Many school district personnel are so interested in family involvement that they design specific programs for families. The Family Literacy Project is one such program. Developed by Irvine Unified School District educators, the project aims to provide families with both encouragement and support in their efforts to instill lifelong reading habits in their children. To accomplish this, they provide numerous tips such as "Tips for Reading to Your Child," "Ten Tips: Helping Your Child Read Effectively," and "Helping Children Develop Oral-Language Skills." All of this information is easily accessible in hard copy. These resources are available for order to any educators who wish to distribute or display them.

All of these examples show that there are many ways to involve families. They also show that caregivers can do much at home to assist their children. We have featured ways they can volunteer right from home! Viewing caregivers as partner educators "acknowledges the home–school relationship as a rich potential shared among equals, equals who bring important and divergent experiences to bear upon individual and often limited perspectives."[9]

Regardless of which ways teachers choose to involve families, we offer the following reminders:

- Rather than overwhelming families by providing them with many activities all at one time, provide them with one idea and include all the reading materials they will need to complete the reading activity with their children. Consider putting both the explanation and the text in a large envelope or backpack.

- Keep communication as jargon-free as possible. Focus on exactly what caregivers need to do with their children in plain everyday language.

- Remember that many caregivers are at a loss when it comes to knowing which text or texts their children should be reading. They need help. One way to help them is to provide them with specific titles that are sure to entice their children to practice reading. Many of these titles are listed in this book, as are suitable online resources.

- All families need direct and welcoming invitations. There are many cultures where caregiver–teacher interactions are very different from what we expect in the United States. Caregivers from other cultural backgrounds need to know it is okay to be involved. Also, many caregivers did not have positive interactions with school as children, and they need to feel a strong motivation for coming to school and getting involved.

Bridge: From Assessment to Teaching

When teachers have learned that _____,	then they might invite families to _____.
Families want to know what to do and want a structure for participating in regular instruction,	Participate directly in the reading program with parent workshops, packets, and book suggestions.
Caregivers are often very good at and interested in discussing books with young readers,	Participate in discussion-based programs such as Junior Great Books.
Caregivers and families work well with the motivation of a competitive timeline,	Participate in programs like Reading Olympics.
Reading with students is difficult for many caregivers,	Learn the routines of paired reading, which can defuse much of the tension and demand in reading with students.
Families have limits to what they can do along with all their other demands,	Adopt doable activities from a menu of options, like those in the Family Literacy Project.

Television, Computers, and Reading

Television

We would be remiss if we did not discuss the impact of technology on children's reading. The question of the influence of screen time on children's reading skills has been debated since television was first introduced. The findings have not been definitive. Authors of some studies suggest that "television viewing has a considerable negative impact on reading achievement only for children who watch for relatively many hours—more than 4 to 6 hours a day."[10] Television also seems to affect different groups of children in different ways. The reading achievement of children of high socioeconomic status decreased when they watched greater amounts of television, whereas the converse appeared to be true for low-socioeconomic-status children; that is, heavier viewing for these children increased their reading achievement.[11]

Although we want children to be engaged with a variety of texts and to develop a habit of reading for a variety of purposes, we need to remember that we live in an information age, and as such, there are many ways to obtain information. Families can use television to stimulate children's reading habits by developing their interests and reinforcing these interests with a variety of texts. Using television to its best advantage can help children to see that there is room for a variety of activities in their lives and that just because they read does not mean that they cannot watch television. The reverse is also true.

Fortunately for caregivers and teachers alike, there is quite a bit of information about the wise use of technology. One source of information is a brochure published by the International Literacy Association entitled "You Can Use Television to Stimulate Your Child's Reading Habits." Along with several practical suggestions, the authors of the brochure provide a simple checklist that caregivers can use to determine whether they are teaching their children how to be wise television watchers. Our version of this checklist is shown in Table 14.1. In addition, NAEYC (National Association for the Education of Young Children) and the Fred Rogers Institute have published a list of recommendations for encouraging active and interactive use of technology to counter the effects of passive media consumption.[12]

Captioned Television. The captions used on television appear to affect students' learning.[13] Watching television shows with accompanying captions appears to improve students' reading. Listening to the script for a show while simultaneously reading it reinforces students' word recognition and reading fluency. Teachers can encourage caregivers to turn on the captioning feature when their children watch television. They can lower the volume several decibels so that children have to look at the text to better

---

Table 14.1 Using Television to Spur Reading

Statement	Rating (1 = low degree, 5 = high degree)
1. My child uses good judgment when selecting programs to watch.	1 2 3 4 5
2. My child talks to me about some of the ideas gained from television shows.	1 2 3 4 5
3. Television is one of several of my child's free-time activities.	1 2 3 4 5
4. My child appears to be motivated to read about some of the ideas presented on the viewed television shows.	1 2 3 4 5
5. My child sees me both reading and watching television.	1 2 3 4 5
6. Many different kinds of reading materials are available in my home, and they are easy for my child to access.	1 2 3 4 5
7. Reading gets as much time as television watching.	1 2 3 4 5

understand what is happening on the show. Keep in mind, however, that the match between captions and audio is rarely perfect. Despite this shortcoming, captioned television is still a valuable learning tool.

Computers

Many online resources are available for families to use at home. Some of these are created by educators, whereas others are created by professional organizations and publishers. Several of these are listed here.

Online Books and Literacy Activities for Families

- Hoopla provides digital books, comics, and audiobooks as well as movies and other media through libraries that subscribe to its service. Check your local library to see if you can access digital material for free, or visit https://www.hoopladigital.com.

- Unite for Literacy provides free online books for Pre-K–1 readers. All the informational books are written by the company to address known interests of early childhood readers. The key strength of the collection, which may make it interesting for older readers too, is that each book is available in many languages. When clicking into an individual title, readers can find a "Narration" button that enables online audio to hear the book in Arabic, Spanish, Somali, and many other languages. Many of the books are also printed in Spanish. http://www.uniteforliteracy.com/

- Epic! is a company that provides a deep catalog of engaging online books for kids. It is free for educators and by subscription for families. Its strength is that the books can be sorted by age of the reader and include a wide variety of well-known children's literature titles as well as many topic-based collections to match student interests. https://www.getepic.com/

- ReadWriteThink provides a strong bank of enrichment activities designed for families to use during the school year and the summer. This kind of activity bank is useful because many parents can get access to books and writing materials but want help with what to do or how to organize an activity. http://www.readwritethink.org/

- Reading Rockets has a strong online presence for parents as well as educators. It provides a deep bank of ideas for activities that engage readers in summer reading, discussing books, choosing books to match their interests, and many activities using writing to extend reading. But sections of its site also relay ideas on how families can connect with their children's schools, and it also partners with PBS television. http://www.readingrockets.org/audience/parents

Professional organizations

- The National Center for Families Learning has been focused on family partnerships in children's reading and writing for decades. Parents and educators can sign up for a monthly newsletter and also get access to a bank of ideas for family activities at home, as well as ideas on partnerships with schools. http://www.familieslearning.org/

- The National Education Association provides resource pages on how parents can engage with schools as partners. http://parents.nea.org

---

Bridge: From Understanding to Assessment

When teachers understand that _____,	then they will assess _____.
Readers' use of media can provide them with rich sources of language use,	Students' actual interests and engagement in television, movies, and video games to learn what kinds of language and literacy they can build on.
Active and interactive media have more positive impacts on students' growth than passive consumption of media,	Their classroom resources to learn whether most of the available technology encourages active and interactive use.

Partnering with Other Teachers

Teachers with a diagnostic mindset seek answers, insights, new ideas, additional perspectives, and a greater repertoire of assessment and instructional methods in order to help students thrive. They know that what they seek can be found through partnerships with other teachers, their peers. A partnership can take many forms: data teams, grade-level teams, Response to Intervention groups, peer mentorship, or faculty book clubs, for instance. Professional Learning Communities (PLCs) serve as a viable way to structure and guide teacher partnerships, no matter the form.

PLCs have transformed collaborative partnerships over the past two decades, allowing teachers to support one another for the benefit of their students. Adherence to the strategies and structures of PLCs is requisite for turning teachers' literacy knowledge inquiry and sharing into effective action. The foundation of PLCs involves six principles that guide teacher teams to do the following:

1. Target learning.
2. Work collaboratively.
3. Study effective practices.
4. Learn through experience.
5. Commit to growth.
6. Diagnose impact.[14]

Target Learning

This principle serves as the cornerstone of the PLC. It involves a commitment to the literacy learning of each student. That commitment is proven by the actions of the members. Members develop clearly defined roles that focus on the diagnosis of each student. Members determine what they want to know about each student, why they want to know, what they might do to discover it, and what will be done with the data they discover. Essentially, all members of the PLC adopt a diagnostic mindset.

The purpose of the PLC goes beyond the learning of the student. It extends to the learning of the teachers/members as well.[15] In order for students to reach their literacy learning potential, their teachers must desire to learn how to get them there. Therefore, professional development opportunities are embedded through a strong PLC model to meet the learning needs of its members and extend assessment and instructional skills.

Work Collaboratively

PLCs only work if members work together. Working together does not ensure success. Success is made possible with shared goals. Collaboration serves as a tool for meeting the needs of an individual learner.[16] A teacher with a diagnostic mindset seeks to improve her practice for the benefit of each student. She does so by partnering with others in the PLC.

Study Effective Practices

This principle involves a collective determination to understand the school, the teachers, the students, and effective literacy practices. It involves a paradigm shift of its members. Partnering in this capacity allows a cultural shift in teaching and learning. The PLC becomes open to understanding what is best for learners as it critically examines present practices, knowledge, and achievement of students. A teacher with a diagnostic mindset can admit to his current instructional needs and any lacking knowledge. This ability allows collective inquiry to be used effectively and members to learn and work together.

Learn Through Experience

PLCs are grounded in taking risks. A teacher with a diagnostic mindset welcomes stepping away from her comfort zone and trying something new, something different. This principle rides on the need to take action and put ideas to work in the classroom. This expectation is essential for changing results. It is learning through experience in meaningful and purposeful ways.[17]

Commit to Growth

Teachers in effective PLCs have a passion for improvement. They seek new and better ideas that may serve to meet the literacy needs of each student, not only those striving to catch up. The commitment is systemic. Although shown to improve the identification and frequency of strategies used,[18] the ultimate goal is to create an environment where innovative and experimental practices become ancillary to strategic literacy teaching.

Diagnose Impact

A focus on proving the effectiveness of the PLC is essential. The truth is, it doesn't matter how hard the team worked, or the amount of time it put into the collaborative process of learning and working together, if students didn't gain from it. Proving effectiveness requires the use of purposeful and formative literacy assessments like those showcased in this text. Returning to the why, how, and what of assessment is necessary to ensure that valid and reliable student data are collected as proof. Also, the data collected becomes an integral part of the PLC process.

Enhanced eText **Application Exercise 14.2:** Understanding Teacher Partnerships

---

Bridge: From Understanding to Self-Assessment

When teachers understand that _____,	then they will self-assess _____.
Teacher partnerships thrive when they are given time and structure,	The quality of their opportunities for collaborating with other teachers.
Their own investment in partnerships with other teachers is a key form of leadership,	Their willingness to engage with other teachers within and across grades, and their ability to work with teachers whose approaches and opinions differ from their own.

Partnering with the Community

Teachers with a diagnostic mindset know that their ability, passion, knowledge, experience, resources, and effort alone cannot adequately meet the needs of each learner. They realize they are not alone, and seek the support of families and other teachers. They also know that the community—the environments that anxiously anticipate the arrival of our students in their businesses, associations, and companies—can serve as a powerful resource for meeting the literacy needs of those students.[19]

Of the many ways to partner with the community and possible models, service learning serves as an exemplar to examine in support of teachers with a diagnostic mindset. Service learning is a purposeful way of using learning to positively impact the community through a service.

Service learning is intended to take students beyond knowing and being able to do.[20] It is an ardent effort to develop a sense of community, moral responsibility, and

Figure 14.3 Types of Service Projects

Type	Direct	Indirect	Advocacy	Research
Definition	Perform a service that is in direct contact with the community based on a need they have.	Perform a service that supports the community without contact or meeting.	Write or speak in favor of supporting a community effort or group.	Conduct research on a topic that is intended to impact the community.
Example	Buddy reading with younger students	Collecting books for a neighborhood literacy program	Writing persuasive letters to the city council to renovate a park in a local neighborhood	Interviewing new members of the school, and creating a podcast explaining their roles in the school community

cultural awareness in students. To do so, many service learning programs follow a variation of these principles:

1. Promote actions that positively impact the world.
2. Inspire critical reflection of service.
3. Showcase clear goals for learning and service.
4. Base service on the needs defined by community partners.
5. Define responsibilities of all involved.
6. Expect continuous and righteous involvement.
7. Include rigorous management of learning and service goals.
8. Ensure realistic attention to time.
9. Commit to diverse populations.[21]

These principles serve as a starting point of the conversation for literacy teachers with a diagnostic mindset. Upon initiating a partnership opportunity with the community, these principles serve as a guide to planning, decision making, role definitions, and goal setting.

Literacy learning should be authentic and experiential, and should apply to the lives of students. However, students' lives are different from one another, and so are their mannerisms, personalities, and interests. Fortunately, we don't have to interact directly with the community in order to create service learning experiences. This fact allows us to connect learning and service to far-off locations, minimize expense, and use safety precautions. According to Learning to Give,[22] a website focused on supporting philanthropy education, there are four types of service projects: direct service, indirect service, advocacy, and research. (See Figure 14.3.)

Enhanced eText **Application Exercise 14.3:** Understanding Community Partnerships

---

Bridge: From Understanding to Assessment

When teachers understand that _____,	then they will assess _____.
Service learning and community engagement provide many opportunities for authentic reading and writing,	The availability of opportunities to partner with community members on projects with immediate benefits to students and impact on the community.

Revisiting the Opening Scenario

Mr. Gonzalez was able to get David's father involved by listening to his concerns and giving him some specific ideas about ways to help David at home. Now that you have read the chapter, what are some additional suggestions you might give to David's father?

Authors' Summary

Before reading our summary statements for each outcome, we suggest you read each outcome and summarize it in your own words.

Once finished, cross-check your response with our brief summary to determine how well you recalled the major points.

14.1 Discuss issues that might need to be thought through when partnering with families.

- Many issues can surface when working with families. These include working with low-literate caregivers, working with caregivers who have difficulty speaking English because it is not their first language, and economic variables, which might prevent families from attending school events. Thinking through each variable leads to ways to work through them. For example, communicating with families by calling them rather than sending home printed announcements can better ensure that they understand the purpose and content of the message.

- Ways to involve families in schoolwide reading programs vary. Regardless, all generally include workshops, instructional materials, and text suggestions. Junior Great Books is one type of program that calls on caregiver-and-teacher teams to work together to plan reading discussion sessions for students. Sessions most often take place during the school day as a part of the reading instruction provided to students. Both caregivers and teachers lead the sessions.

- Television is a reality in this millennium, so families are advised to learn how to use it to their best advantage. There are many suggestions for how to do that. They include parents' watching some programs with their children and talking with them about what they are viewing; helping children develop a balance between viewing television and reading texts, and modeling this behavior themselves; and providing children with a wealth of reading materials that capitalize on their interests. Using websites that specifically focus on reading is an excellent way to help children learn how to read electronic texts. One helpful website is www.magickeys.com/books/, which offers children's storybooks online.

14.2 Explain how participating in professional learning communities can support literacy assessment and instruction.

- Partnering with other teachers through PLCs can serve to change the culture of a school and direct much-needed attention to the literacy needs of learners. Adhering to the principles of PLCs creates opportunities for teachers to evaluate the current situation, set goals, determine roles, delve into effective practice together, learn by doing, and monitor growth based on student success.

14.3 Explain how partnering with the community can support literacy learning.

- One way to make learning authentic and purposeful is through service learning. Service learning extends student literacy learning in meaningful ways that promote a sense of community, moral responsibility, and cultural awareness.

Think About It!

1. You have been put on a committee in your school district that is looking for ways to involve families. Using information you gained from this chapter, construct a list of suggestions.

2. You know that your students are involved in a variety of extracurricular activities that could involve reading but do not. How can you help families get involved with reading that matches well with what children do outside of school?

3. Choose a school in your area. Schedule an appointment with an administrator to learn how that school involves families in its reading programs.

4. Examine the processes of your PLC in relation to the literature cited and the principles showcased.

5. Check with your district or school about beginning a PLC.

6. Check with your district about getting involved with the service learning efforts. Create a service learning literacy project for your students with a community agency.

Websites

- http://www.colorincolorado.org/

    Colorín Colorado is a bilingual site geared toward Spanish-speaking families and teachers of English language learners (ELL). The site contains both Spanish and English pages with book lists, activities, downloadable guides and projects, and much more.Education World provides a great article on families and teachers working together. The links provided offer additional resources and avenues of support. In this **video clip**, the principal and teachers demonstrate and discuss how schools communicate about mission and programs with families.

- http://www.education-world.com/a_curr/profdev/profdev124.shtml

    Educational Leadership presents an overview of the Big Ideas of PLCs, with links to prominent resources for understanding their purpose, structure, potential, and processes.

- http://www.ascd.org/publications/educational-leadership/may04/vol61/num08/What-Is-a-Professional-Learning-Community%C2%A2.aspx

    Learning to Give offers a Literacy Service Learning Tool-Kit filled with service learning project ideas. It includes lesson plans, literature guides, and examples.

- https://www.learningtogive.org/resources/literacy-service-learning-toolkit

    The Library of Congress provides free professional development to teachers across the country. At this site, teachers can explore the professional development content from the Library of Congress's professional development institutes and workshops.

- http://www.loc.gov/teachers/tps/

    The Library of Congress awards grants to a diverse array of educational organizations, including school districts, universities, historical societies, foundations, and companies, to assist in design and delivery of the Teaching with Primary Sources (TPS) program. These grantees, who comprise the TPS Consortium, deliver TPS professional development and academic courses, design curriculum and apps/online interactives using primary sources from the Library's collections, and conduct research on the classroom use of primary sources.

Endnotes

1. Paris, S., Wasik, B., & Turner, J. (1991). The development of strategic readers. In R. Barr, M. L. Kamil, P. Mosenthal, & P. D. Pearson (Eds.), *Handbook of Reading Research*, (Vol. II, p. 628). New York, NY: Longman.
2. Ibid.
3. Donahue, P., et al. (1999). *NAEP 1998 reading report card for the nation and the states* (p. 101). Washington, D.C.: United States Department of Education.
4. Boyer, E. (1995). *The basic school: A community for learning*. Princeton, N.J.: Carnegie Foundation for the Advancement of Learning.
5. Edwards, P. (2004). *Children's literacy development: Making it happen through school, family, and community involvement*. Boston, MA: Allyn and Bacon.
6. Johnston, K. (1989, February). Parents and reading: A U.K. perspective. *The Reading Teacher* 42, 355.
7. Topping, K. (1987). Paired reading: A powerful technique for parent use. *The Reading Teacher* 40, 604–614.
8. Ibid.
9. Goodman, G. (1989, January). Worlds within worlds: Reflections on an encounter with parents. *Language Arts* 66, 20.
10. Beentjes, J., & Van Der Voort, T. (1988, Fall). Television's impact on children's reading skills: A review of research. *Reading Research Quarterly* 23, 401.
11. Ibid.
12. National Association for the Education of Young Children and the Fred Rogers Center for Early Learning and Children's Media. (2012). *Technology and interactive media as tools in Early Childhood Programs Serving children from birth through age 8: A position statement*. https://www.naeyc.org/sites/default/files/globally-shared/downloads/PDFs/resources/topics/PS_technology_WEB.pdf
13. Koskinen, P., Wilson, R., Gambrell, L., & Neuman, S. (1993). Captioned video and vocabulary learning: An innovative practice in literacy instruction. *The Reading Teacher* 47, 36–43.

14. DuFour, R., DuFour, R., Eaker, R., & Many, T. (2006). *Learning by doing: A handbook for professional learning communities at work.* Bloomington, IN: Solution Tree.

15. D'Ardenne, C., Barnes, D., Hightower, E., Lamason, P., Mason, M., Patterson, P., Stephens, N., Wilson, C., Smith, V., & Erickson, K. (2013). PLCs in action: Innovative teaching for struggling 3–5 graders. *The Reading Teacher* 67, 143–151.

16. Christ, T., Arya, P. & Ming Chiu, M. (2017). Relations among resources in professional learning communities and learning outcomes. *Teaching Education* 28, 94–114.

17. Dewey, J. (1938). *Experience and Education.* New York, NY: Collier Books.

18. Mundy, M., Howe, M., & Kupczynski, L. (2015). Teachers' perceived values on the effect of literacy strategy professional development. *Teacher Development* 19, 116–131.

19. G. Johnson, Dempster, N., & McKenzie L. (2013). The principals as literacy leaders with indigenous communities: Professional learning and research. *Journal of Education for Teaching* 39. 457–458.

20. Dooley, C., & Mays, L. (2014). Literacy teachers engage in service-learning via community organization involvement. *The Teacher Educator* 49, 44–60.

21. endall, J. & Associates. (1990). *Combining service and learning: A resource book for community and public service* I. Raleigh, NC: National Society for Internships and Experiential Education.

22. https://www.learningtogive.org/about

Appendix A
Informal Reading Inventory Administration and Scoring Procedures

- You will need to make a copy of the *examiner booklet* for each student, as this is the copy you will use to make notes about each student's reading performance.

- You will need to make only one copy of the student booklet. You might want to assemble the word lists in one binder and the graded passages in another.

- Make sure that you have carefully read all passages before you begin so that you are very familiar with them and the comprehension questions for each.

Step 1: Establish Rapport

Establishing rapport with the reader who is to be assessed is an important first step. If you are the reader's teacher, you will have already established a level of trust and will be able to put the reader at ease about reading to you. If the reader is new to you, we always suggest administering an interest inventory and student interview to better know the reader before administering the IRI (see page 334).

Make sure that the reader understands that the purpose of reading and answering questions is to help you learn more about how well she or he reads and thinks about text. Say something such as, "I would like to hear how well you read. While you are reading, I am going to take some notes to help me remember."

Step 2: Word Recognition Inventory (WRI)

The WRI is used only to determine at what level to begin the oral reading passages of the IRI. If you feel that you already know where to begin with passages the student will read with ease and success, skip this step. If you do use the WRI make sure that you begin by having the reader read the list that is one or two grade levels below the student's estimated grade-level placement.

1. Determine which word list to use as a starting point.

2. Determine how you will show the words to the student. Here are two options:

   Option 1: Cut out a rectangle no more than ⅜ inch × 1½ inches in the center of an index card. Expose the words one at a time through the rectangular opening.
   Option 2: Use an index card and move it down the list, uncovering one word at a time.

   Regardless of the option, remember to show only one list at a time. Doing so might mean that you decide to fold the paper into three columns so that only one list can be seen at a time. You might also decide to cut the lists into word strips and show one strip at a time.

3. Show the reader the list and say something such as, "I would like you to read these words aloud. If you come to a word you do not recognize, skip it and read the next word."

4. Use the word list in the examiner's booklet to make notes about those words the reader reads using this marking procedure:

Reader's response	Marking
Correct	Check next to the word
Initial response incorrect but student makes a correction	Check next to the word (write what the reader said if at all possible)
Incorrect response	Place a minus next to the word
Sounding out the word	Check next to the word (write that the reader decoded the word, if decoded correctly or self-corrected)

5. After the student has responded to all words on the list, record the total number correct (all those that have a check mark by them) and write that number in the appropriate space on the form.

6. Continue having the student read the lists until the student misses four or more words at any level.

7. Start the oral reading passages of the IRI at the highest level where the reader scored 90 to 100 percent on the word lists.

8. Do not use the WRI for any other assessment or evaluation. It is designed only to help teachers find the appropriate starting level for the passages.

Step 3: Oral and Silent Reading of Passages

1. Begin by having the student read the passage that corresponds to the highest level where the student scored 90 to 100 percent on the WRI.

2. Explain the reading procedure: "I would like to listen to how well you read. I am going to take some notes to help me remember. When you are finished, I am going to ask you some questions about what you read."

3. Introduce the story to the student by reading the statement shown on the passage in the examiner's booklet. Hand the reader the *student booklet.*

4. While the student reads from the *student booklet,* use the notations shown in the upper right-hand corner of the scoring guide of the passage in the examiner's booklet to note what the reader does when reading.

5. Once the reader finishes reading the passage, count the number of miscues the reader made and subtract this number from the total number of words to determine the number of words the student read correctly and the word recognition reading level. Substituted words and omitted words are counted as miscues, but self-corrections and repetitions are not counted as miscues.

Also note the strategies you saw the reader using and place a check next to each in the Reading Strategies section at the bottom of the form.

6. There are a few options to assess comprehension of the passage. The most important point to keep in mind is that once selected, the same procedure needs to be used for all students. The scoring procedure explained in option 1 applies to all options.

Option 1: Have the reader turn over the booklet and say, "Now that you have read this passage, I have some questions about it for you." Ask each question shown on the examiner passage form. Place a + next to each question the reader answers correctly and a − next to it if incorrect. Sometimes students will offer a response that is partially correct. In instances such as these, indicate as a fraction (½).

When making a decision about scoring, refer to the type of question being asked. If it is a literal question and the reader offers an answer that makes sense, yet is not literally stated, mark the answer as incorrect, but note what the reader said as the response might be an indication that the reader is using background knowledge. If on the other hand the reader offers a logical response for an inferential type of question, count the response as correct.

Option 2: Allow the reader to look back at the passage as needed when answering questions. The advantage to this option is that it lessens emphasis on short-term memory, and thus might be a better indication of the reader's ability to process information and to make connections to existing knowledge and experience.

Option 3: Have the reader do a retelling. Say something such as, "Now I would like you to tell me this story as if I have never heard it before." As the reader retells the story, place a check next to each question the reader addresses. Once finished, ask any questions that were not addressed in the retell.

7. Determine the comprehension reading level by tallying correct responses, and circling the appropriate comprehension reading level on the examiner form.

8. Direct the reader to read the silent reading passage for the same level, and once finished reading, assess comprehension using one of the three options noted above for oral reading.

9. Determine the silent comprehension reading level by tallying the correct and incorrect responses, and circle the appropriate reading comprehension level on the examiner form.

10. Repeat steps 3 through 9 until the reader reaches frustrational level in word recognition, comprehension, or both.

Step 4: The Listening Capacity Test

The purpose of administering the listening capacity test is to determine how well readers comprehend when the text is being read to them. Only administer this test when you have specific questions about comprehension that are not answered well by the oral and silent passage reading. Administering this test can help to determine if word recognition and navigating through text is taking away from the reader's ability to devote necessary energy to comprehension. In other words, freed of reading words, does the comprehension remain? Using the same IRI, continue with these procedures:

1. Once the reader has reached frustrational level on the last passage he or she has read, begin the listening capacity test with the next silent reading passage.

2. Read the passage aloud to the reader, and assess comprehension by asking the questions for that passage using one of these two options:

Option 1: Say, "Now that you have heard this passage, I have some questions about it for you." Ask each question shown on the examiner passage form. Place a + next to each question the reader answers correctly and a – next to it if incorrect. Sometimes students will offer a response that is partially correct. In instances such as these, indicate as a fraction (½).

When making a decision about scoring, refer to the type of question that is being asked. If it is a literal question and the reader offers an answer that makes sense, yet is not literally stated, mark the answer as incorrect, *but* note what the reader said as the response might be an indication that the reader is relying heavily on background knowledge. If on the other hand the reader offers a logical response for an inferential type of question, count the response as correct. This scoring procedure also applies to option 2.

Option 2: Have the reader do a retelling. Say something such as, "Now that you have listened to this story, I would like you to tell it to me like I have never heard it before." As the reader retells the story, place a check next to each question the reader addresses. Once finished, ask any questions that were not addressed in the retell and score accordingly.

3. Repeat steps 1 and 2, reading the succeeding oral and silent reading passages to the reader until she or he reaches frustration.

Step 5: Assmimilating the Results

Record all information on the IRI Summary Form. Use the scoring scales along with your notes in each reader's *Examiner Booklet* to gain an overall view of the reader's performance on the IRI. Use this combination of information to interpret the IRI results. Use your interpretation of IRI results primarily to create a range for authentic text selections that will include mostly independent and instructional level text. Use your interpretation of IRI results in concert with and in comparison to other assessment results.

Appendix B
Examiner Booklet

Informal Reading Inventory
Summary Sheet

Name _____   Age _____

Grade _____   Teacher _____

Reader Level* (Circle the level the WRI indicates to start with)	Oral Reading			
	W.R.			
	# Miscues/ Total Words	# Correct/ # Possible	# Correct/ # Possible	# Correct/ # Possible
Preprimer				
Primer (A)				
First (B)				
2^1 (C)				
2^2 (D)				
3^1 (E)				
3^2 (F)				
4 (G)				
5 (H)				
6 (I)				
7 (J)				
8 (K)				
Overall levels	Ind _____ Inst _____ Frust _____	Ind _____ Inst _____ Frust _____	Ind _____ Inst _____ Frust _____	Ind _____ Inst _____ Frust _____

*The superscript after each grade level indicates a beginning of year level (1) or end of year level (2).

Word Recognition Inventory (WRI)

Primer (A)		First (B)	
1. blow	_____	1. soup	_____
2. little	_____	2. tents	_____
3. many	_____	3. afternoon	_____
4. bright	_____	4. baked	_____
5. old	_____	5. family	_____
6. won	_____	6. alone	_____
7. things	_____	7. great	_____
8. yellow	_____	8. white	_____
9. farm	_____	9. soft	_____
10. friend	_____	10. boy	_____
11. more	_____	11. dinner	_____
12. thanks	_____	12. does	_____
13. snow	_____	13. wife	_____
14. some	_____	14. horse	_____
15. cows	_____	15. head	_____
16. game	_____	16. sorry	_____
17. please	_____	17. summer	_____
18. leaves	_____	18. hungry	_____
19. draw	_____	19. drank	_____
20. work	_____	20. enough	_____
No. Correct	_____	**No. Correct**	_____
TOTAL	_____	**TOTAL**	_____

Word Recognition Inventory (WRI)

2¹ (C)		2² (D)	
1. brave	_____	1. office	_____
2. noon	_____	2. perfect	_____
3. park	_____	3. patient	_____
4. strange	_____	4. enemy	_____
5. November	_____	5. donkey	_____
6. money	_____	6. dirt	_____
7. library	_____	7. clever	_____
8. join	_____	8. company	_____
9. angry	_____	9. candle	_____
10. apple	_____	10. beard	_____
11. carrots	_____	11. bundle	_____
12. class	_____	12. address	_____
13. answer	_____	13. snowflake	_____
14. loud	_____	14. sailors	_____
15. mouth	_____	15. score	_____
16. matter	_____	16. tune	_____
17. hurry	_____	17. thirsty	_____
18. idea	_____	18. unload	_____
19. carve	_____	19. view	_____
20. clothes	_____	20. trouble	_____
21. delicious	_____	21. south	_____
22. below	_____	22. shy	_____
23. boil	_____	23. ambulance	_____
24. built	_____	24. tiny	_____
25. dragons	_____	25. hobby	_____
No. Correct	_____	No. Correct	_____
TOTAL	_____	TOTAL	_____

Word Recognition Inventory (WRI)

3¹ (E)		3² (F)	
1. plow	_____	1. petal	_____
2. horn	_____	2. rein	_____
3. hesitate	_____	3. furious	_____
4. neglect	_____	4. popular	_____
5. deaf	_____	5. identify	_____
6. language	_____	6. forecast	_____
7. attention	_____	7. attach	_____
8. drawn	_____	8. bought	_____
9. complain	_____	9. admire	_____
10. fame	_____	10. noble	_____
11. goal	_____	11. migrate	_____
12. familiar	_____	12. patient	_____
13. elevator	_____	13. novel	_____
14. plunge	_____	14. ruin	_____
15. nature	_____	15. rescue	_____
16. poem	_____	16. unusual	_____
17. stall	_____	17. x-ray	_____
18. talent	_____	18. wisdom	_____
19. worthy	_____	19. rough	_____
20. lung	_____	20. protest	_____
21. medal	_____	21. persuade	_____
22. mistake	_____	22. influence	_____
23. customer	_____	23. prince	_____
24. courage	_____	24. bandage	_____
25. announce	_____	25. bridge	_____
No. Correct	_____	No. Correct	_____
TOTAL	_____	TOTAL	_____

Word Recognition Inventory (WRI)

4 (G)		**5 (H)**	
1. gracious	_____	1. tragedy	_____
2. imitate	_____	2. applause	_____
3. defense	_____	3. amazement	_____
4. declare	_____	4. harvest	_____
5. electronics	_____	5. thaw	_____
6. punishment	_____	6. original	_____
7. robot	_____	7. balcony	_____
8. uniform	_____	8. marvel	_____
9. twilight	_____	9. mileage	_____
10. tragedy	_____	10. cluster	_____
11. stranger	_____	11. architect	_____
12. tame	_____	12. heroine	_____
13. technique	_____	13. audition	_____
14. suspect	_____	14. interrupt	_____
15. ordinary	_____	15. landscape	_____
16. native	_____	16. petition	_____
17. haughty	_____	17. permission	_____
18. hostile	_____	18. vessel	_____
19. entire	_____	19. promotion	_____
20. errand	_____	20. violence	_____
21. average	_____	21. voyage	_____
22. appetite	_____	22. vast	_____
23. radiant	_____	23. nuisance	_____
24. prowl	_____	24. luxury	_____
25. caution	_____	25. lonely	_____
No. Correct	_____	No. Correct	_____
TOTAL	_____	TOTAL	_____

Word Recognition Inventory (WRI)

6 (I)		7 (J)	
1. tenement	_____	1. sham	_____
2. rebel	_____	2. scrutiny	_____
3. ease	_____	3. refuge	_____
4. exhibit	_____	4. prestigious	_____
5. appoint	_____	5. quarrel	_____
6. shuttle	_____	6. nomad	_____
7. unwilling	_____	7. fault	_____
8. recede	_____	8. flattery	_____
9. wizard	_____	9. hindrance	_____
10. wrench	_____	10. imperative	_____
11. revenge	_____	11. colleague	_____
12. tiresome	_____	12. trifle	_____
13. spout	_____	13. souvenir	_____
14. strategy	_____	14. chore	_____
15. pamphlet	_____	15. aggressive	_____
16. persist	_____	16. barometer	_____
17. heritage	_____	17. emigrate	_____
18. conquer	_____	18. verdict	_____
19. humble	_____	19. zodiac	_____
20. arrogant	_____	20. wrench	_____
21. astronomy	_____	21. probe	_____
22. distinguish	_____	22. momentum	_____
23. gratitude	_____	23. mortal	_____
24. guarantee	_____	24. exile	_____
25. legacy	_____	25. limitation	_____
No. Correct	_____	No. Correct	_____
TOTAL	_____	TOTAL	_____

Word Recognition Inventory (WRI)

8 (K)

1. prospect   _____
2. quest   _____
3. scoop   _____
4. journalism   _____
5. invincible   _____
6. listless   _____
7. mirror   _____
8. circuit   _____
9. defy   _____
10. anguish   _____
11. augment   _____
12. aristocratic   _____
13. formidable   _____
14. faculty   _____
15. seizure   _____
16. terrace   _____
17. scrabble   _____
18. undermine   _____
19. sphere   _____
20. naïve   _____
21. plateau   _____
22. recitation   _____
23. jaunt   _____
24. frugal   _____
25. hysteria   _____

No. Correct   _____

TOTAL   _____

Primer (A)

ORAL READING

> **Introduction: Read this story aloud to find out what Sara wants.**

Sara sat and sat, looking out at the
big tree. She looked at her mother and asked,
"Mom, do you have some string?"
"Yes, here is some red string,"
said Sara's mother. "Is it for your hair?"
"No," said Sara, "It's not for my hair."
"I know," said Mother. "You are going to
fix something with it."
"No," said Sara. "You'll see."
Sara saw that her father had
some string, too. She asked him for it.*

Coding Guide

- (Circle) any omitted word.
- Write ~~substituted~~ words above the text. *(substitution)*
- Write word and use a caret. *(inserted)* ^
- Write a P above any prompted word.
- Note word reversals
- Write SC above self-corrected word.
- Underline repetitions.

Comprehension Questions

*√ if correct, ½ if partly correct,
blank if incorrect or unanswered*

(Literal)	1. What was Sara looking at? (The big tree)
(Literal)	2. What did Sara want from her mother? (String)
(Literal)	3. What color string did her mother have? (Red)
(Literal)	4. What did Sara's mother first think the string was for? (Sara's hair)
(Inference)	5. Who thought something was broken? (Sara's mother)
(Inference)	6. How do we know Sara's mother thought something was broken? (She thought the string was to fix something.)
(Literal)	7. Who else had string? (Her father)
(Literal)	8. What did Sara do when she saw her father had some string? (She asked him for it.)

Passage A, Primer Level

Reading Accuracy: 76 - _____ = _____

          (Total words)   (Words missed)   (Total words correct)

Word Accuracy Reading Level: (Circle the one that indicates the total words correct.)

Independent	Instruction	Buffer	Frustration
75–76	72–74	69–71	68 or less
(99%–100%)	(95%–98%)	(91%–94%)	(90% or less)

Comprehension Level: (Circle the one that indicates total number of correct responses.)

Independent	Instruction	Buffer	Frustration
7–8	6–7	5–6	4 or less
(95%–100%)	(75%–94%)	(51%–74%)	(50% or less)

Reading Strategies When Encountering Unknown Words: (Check all that apply.)

__made no attempt   __self-corrected   __repeated   __asked for help

__used sentence sense   __used word meaning   __used word parts

__used letters/sounds   __skipped and read on   __other: _____

*Jane Mechling, "A Rainbow for Sara," Level 4, *Make a Wish* (Needham, MA: Silver Burdett & Ginn, 1989), pp. 32–34.

Primer (A)

SILENT READING

Introduction: **Read this story to find out more about Sara and her string.**

Sara ran outside to play with Peter
and Anna.
"I am keeping string in a box,"
said Sara.
"I have some green string in my
pocket. You may have it," said Peter.
"You are keeping string?"
said Anna. "What are you going
to do with all that string? Will
you and your cat play with it?"
"No," said Sara. "You'll see."
Soon Sara had all the string she needed.
She had red string, orange string,
green string, and yellow string.*

Comprehension Questions

*√ if correct, ½ if partly correct,
blank if incorrect or unanswered*

(Literal)	1. Where did Sara go? (Outside)
(Literal)	2. Why did Sara go outside? (To play with Peter and Anna)
(Literal)	3. Where was Sara keeping her string? (In a box)
(Inference)	4. Who else was saving string (Peter)
(Literal)	5. What color string did Peter have? (Green)
(Literal)	6. Where did Peter keep his string? (In his pocket)
(Inference)	7. Does Sara have a pet? If she does, what is it? (Yes; a cat)
(Literal)	8. What were the colors of the string Sara had? (Red, orange, green, and yellow)

Passage A, Primer Level

Comprehension Level: (Circle the one that indicates total number of correct responses.)

Independent	Instruction	Buffer	Frustration
7–8	6–7	5–6	4 or less
(95%–100%)	(75%–94%)	(51%–74%)	(50% or less)

*Jane Mechling, "A Rainbow for Sara," Level 4, *Make a Wish* (Needham, MA: Silver Burdett & Ginn, 1989), pp. 35–36.

First (B)

ORAL READING

> **Introduction: Read this story aloud to find out about Fred and Anna.**
>
> Fred and Anna lived on a farm. It was a small farm. It was also very dry, and things did not grow well. So Fred and his wife, Anna, were poor.
> One day there was a tap, tap, tap on the door. A woman had come to the farm. She had been walking most of the day, and she was hungry. She asked Fred and Anna to give her something to eat. Fred and Anna had a pot of soup. They let the woman come in to eat.*

Coding Guide

- Circle any omitted word.
- Write ~~substituted~~ words above the text. *(substitution)*
- Write ∧word and use a caret. *(inserted)*
- Write a P above any prompted word.
- Note |word| |reversals|
- Write SC above self-corrected word.
- Underline repetitions.

Comprehension Questions

✓ if correct, ½ if partly correct, blank if incorrect or unanswered

(Literal)	1. Where did Fred and Anna live? (On a farm)
(Literal)	2. What kind of farm was it? (Small, dry)
(Inference)	3. Why were Fred arid Anna poor? (Things didn't grow well on their farm.)
(Inference)	4. Why didn't things grow well? (It was too dry.)
(Word meaning)	5. What does *poor* mean? (Not having money; not having much food to eat)
(Inference)	6. Who knocked on Fred and Anna's door? (A woman)
(Literal)	7. What had the woman been doing? (Walking all day)
(Literal)	8. How did the woman feel? (Hungry)
(Literal)	9. What did Fred and Anna have? (A pot of soup)
(Inference)	10. How do we know Fred and Anna are kind people? (Even though they are poor, they share their soup with the woman.)

Passage B, First Level

Reading Accuracy: 88 - _____ = _____

           (Total words)   (Words missed)   (Total words correct)

Word Accuracy Reading Level: (Circle the one that indicates the total words correct.)

Independent	Instruction	Buffer	Frustration
87–88	83–86	80–82	79
(99%–100%)	(95%–98%)	(91%–94%)	(90% or less)

Comprehension Level: (Circle the one that indicates total number of correct responses.)

Independent	Instruction	Buffer	Frustration
9–10	7.5–8.5	5–7	4 or less
(95%–100%)	(75%–94%)	(51%–74%)	(50% or less)

Reading Strategies When Encountering Unknown Words: (Check all that apply.)

__made no attempt   __self-corrected   __repeated   __asked for help

__used sentence sense   __used word meaning   __used word parts

__used letters/sounds   __skipped and read on   __other: _____

---

*Verna Aardema, "The Three Wishes," Level 5, *A New Day* (Needham, MA: Silver Burdett & Ginn, 1989), p. 160.

First (B)

SILENT READING

Introduction: Fred and Anna are given some wishes by the woman. Read to find out what Fred and Anna do with one of the wishes.

For most of the day, Fred and Anna talked about the three wishes they would make. They talked long after it was time to eat again, and they forgot to cook. They began to get hungry.

By the time Anna and Fred made soup, they were both very, very hungry. As they sat down to eat, Fred said, "I wish we had a sausage to go with this soup."

And there on the table was a great big brown sausage!*

Comprehension Questions

√ if correct, ½ if partly correct, blank if incorrect or unanswered

(Literal)	1. How many wishes were Fred and Anna given? (Three)
(Literal)	2. How long did they talk about the wishes? (For most of the day)
(Literal)	3. What did they forget to do? (Cook)
(Inference)	4. Why did they forget to cook? (They were excited about the three wishes; they were busy talking about them.)
(Inference)	5. How did they know they hadn't eaten? (They became hungry.)
(Literal)	6. What did they make to eat? (Soup)
(Literal)	7. How did they feel when the soup was ready? (Very, very hungry)
(Literal)	8. Who wished for something? (Fred)
(Literal)	9. What did Fred wish for? (A sausage to go with the soup)
(Literal)	10. What did the wish bring? (A great big brown sausage)

Passage B, First Level

Comprehension Level: (Circle the one that indicates total number of correct responses.)

Independent	Instruction	Buffer	Frustration
9–10	7.5–9.5	5–7	4 or less
(95%–100%)	(75%–94%)	(51%–74%)	(50% or less)

*Verna Aardema, "The Three Wishes," Level 5, *A New Day* (Needham, MA: Silver Burdett & Ginn, 1989), p. 163.

Level 2¹ (C)

ORAL READING

> **Introduction: Read this story aloud to find out why a farmer needs help.**

Once there was a farmer who went to the town wise man because he had a problem, and he did not know what to do. "How can I help you?" the wise man asked.

"I have a house with one small room," sighed the farmer.

"That is not a problem," the wise man said.

"It is a problem," the farmer sighed. "I live in this one small room with my wife and my seven children. We are always in one another's way, and we are always talking at the same time. It is so loud that I can hardly hear myself think. I cannot stand it any longer. Can you help me?"*

Comprehension Questions

√ if correct, ½ if partly correct, blank if incorrect or unanswered

(Literal)	1. To whom did the farmer go? (To the town wise man)
(Word meaning)	2. What is a *town wise man*? (A person who can help other; a man who knows lots of things; he can answer many questions.)
(Literal)	3. Why did the farmer go to the town wise man? (He had a problem.)
	4. Where does the farmer live? (In a house with one small room)
(Literal)	5. How many people live in the house? (Nine: seven children, the
(Inference)	farmer, and his wife)
	6. Explain whether you think the farmer is rich or poor. (Poor,
(Inference)	because he lives in one room with such a large family.)
	7. What is the farmer's problems? (It is too noisy in his house.)
(Inference)	8. What does everyone in the house do at the same time? (Talk)
(Literal)	9. What is the noise stopping the farmer from doing? (Thinking)
(Literal)	10. What does the farmer want the town wise man to do?
(Inference)	(Help the farmer solve his problem)

Passage C, Level 2-1

Reading Accuracy: 112 - _____ = _____
　　　　　　　　　(Total words)　　(Words missed)　　(Total words correct)

Word Accuracy Reading Level: (Circle the one that indicates the total words correct.)

Independent	Instruction	Buffer	Frustration
111–112	106–110	102–105	101 or less
(99%–100%)	(95%–98%)	(91%–94%)	(90% or less)

---

*Michael Patrick Hearn, "Not So Wise as You Suppose," Level 6, *Garden Gates* (Needham, MA: Silver Burdett & Ginn, 1989), pp. 94–95.

Comprehension Level: (Circle the one that indicates total number of correct responses.)

Independent	Instruction	Buffer	Frustration
9–10	7.5–8.5	5–7	4 or less
(95%–100%)	(75%–94%)	(51%–74%)	(50% or less)

Reading Strategies When Encountering Unknown Words: (Check all that apply.)

__made no attempt   __self-corrected   __repeated   __asked for help

__used sentence sense   __used word meaning   __used word parts

__used letters/sounds   __skipped and read on   __other: _____

Level 2¹ (C)

SILENT READING

Introduction: Read this story to find out what the farmer does to solve his problem.

The wise man stroked his chin and thought.
"Do you have a horse?" the wise man asked.
"Yes, I have a horse," the farmer said.
"Then the answer is simple," the wise man
said, "but you must do as I tell you. Tonight you
must bring the horse into your house to stay with
you, your wife, and your seven children."
The farmer was surprised to hear such a plan,
but he did as he was told.
The next morning he returned to the wise man.
He was quite upset.
"You are not so wise as you suppose!" the farmer said.
"Now my house is even louder. The horse just kicks and
neighs morning, noon, and night! I cannot stand it any longer."*

Comprehension Questions

*√ if correct, ½ if partly correct,
blank if incorrect or unanswered*

(Literal)	1. What did the wise man stroke? (His chin)
(Literal)	2. What was the wise man doing when he stroked his chin? (Thinking)
(Literal)	3. What did the wise man ask the farmer? (If he had a horse)
(Word meaning)	4. What does *simple* mean? (Easy)
(Literal)	5. What did the wise man say was simple? (The answer to the farmer's problem)
(Literal)	6. What did the wise man want the farmer to do? (To bring the horse into the house to stay with the farmer and his family)
(Literal)	7. When was the farmer supposed to bring the horse into the house? (That night)
(Inference)	8. Explain how you know whether the wise man's plan worked. (It didn't work because the farmer came in very upset.)
(Literal)	9. What did the horse do in the house? (Kicked and neighed)
(Literal)	10. What did the farmer think about the wise man now? (That the wise man was not as wise as he thought he was)

Passage C, Level 2-1

Comprehension Level: (Circle the one that indicates total number of correct responses.)

Independent	Instruction	Buffer	Frustration
9–10	7.5–8.5	5–7	4 or less
(95%–100%)	(75%–94%)	(51%–74%)	(50% or less)

*Michael Patrick Hearn, "Not So Wise as You Suppose," Level 6, *Garden Gates* (Needham, MA: Silver Burdett & Ginn, 1989), p. 96.

Level 2² (D)

ORAL READING

Introduction: Read this story aloud to find out about the children's surprise.

The children sat down in a big circle on the ground. Everyone was excited. Mr. Ortero (or-té-rō) had promised them a surprise.

Mr. Ortero walked into the middle of the circle. He ran the after-school program in the park.

"I have a mystery today," Mr. Ortero said. "A treasure is hidden somewhere in the park. Your job is to solve the mystery and find the treasure."

Marita (mä-rō -ta) raised her hand. "What is the treasure?" she asked.

"That's part of the mystery," Mr. Ortero answered.

Marita laughed with everyone else. Mr. Ortero liked to tease them.

"Each of you gets one clue," Mr. Ortero said. He started around the circle, handing out the clues. Marita was sitting between Jenny and Mike.

"I'm really a good detective," Mike said. "I bet I'll find the treasure."*

Coding Guide
• ⬭Circle any omitted word.
• Write ~~substituted~~ ^substitution^ words above the text.
• Write ^inserted^ word and use a caret. ∧
• Write a P above any prompted word.
• Note |word| |reversals|
• Write SC above self-corrected word.
• <u>Underline</u> repetitions.

Comprehension Questions

√ if correct, ½ if partly correct, blank if incorrect or unanswered

(Literal)   1. How were the children sitting? (In a big circle on the ground)

(Literal)   2. Why were they excited? (Mr. Ortero had promised them a surprise.)

(Literal)   3. Who was Mr. Ortero? (The person who ran the after-school program in the park)

(Literal)   4. What did Mr. Ortero have for the children? (A mystery)

(Word meaning)   5. What is a *mystery*? (Something that is not known; a secret; a puzzle that has to be solved or figured out)

(Literal)   6. What is the mystery Mr. Ortero has for the children? (He has hidden a treasure in the park and wants the children to find it.)

(Literal)   7. What did Marita want to know? (What the treasure is)

(Inference)   8. Why didn't Mr. Ortero tell the children what the treasure is? (The treasure is part of the mystery and therefore might give the mystery away; it might make it too easy to solve the mystery.)

(Literal)   9. What did Mr. Ortero do to help the children find the treasure? (He gave each child a clue.)

(Inference)   10. Why does Mike think he will find the treasure? (Because he thinks he's a good detective)

---

*Judith Stamper, "The Treasure Hunt," Level 7, *Going Places* (Needham, MA: Silver Burdett & Ginn, 1989), p. 197.

Passage D, Level 2-2

Reading Accuracy: 131 - _____ = _____

               (Total words)   (Words missed)   (Total words correct)

Word Accuracy Reading Level: (Circle the one that indicates the total words correct.)

Independent	Instruction	Buffer	Frustration
130–131	124–129	119–123	118 or less
(99%–100%)	(95%–98%)	(91%–94%)	(90% or less)

Comprehension Level: (Circle the one that indicates total number of correct responses.)

Independent	Instruction	Buffer	Frustration
9–10	7.5–8.5	5–7	4 or less
(95%–100%)	(75%–94%)	(51%–74%)	(50% or less)

Reading Strategies When Encountering Unknown Words: (Check all that apply.)

__made no attempt   __self-corrected   __repeated   __asked for help

__used sentence sense   __used word meaning   __used word parts

__used letters/sounds   __skipped and read on   __other: _____

Level 2² (D)

SILENT READING

Introduction: Read this story to find out more about the treasure hunt.

Jenny looked at Marita and smiled. They both liked Mike, but he bragged a lot.

Mr. Ortero gave Jenny her clue. Marita was next, and then Mike. Soon, each child had a clue to open and read. Mr. Ortero stepped back into the middle of the circle.

"Listen to the rules," he said. "First, stay inside the park. The treasure is hidden here. Second, don't harm any plants or trees. Third, you must find the treasure in twenty minutes. Meet me back here in twenty minutes. Good luck!"

The children jumped to their feet and ran in different directions.

Marita read her clue over and over. It said:

Thirsty, tired, and very hot?

I'm near what's cool and hits the spot.

"Near something to drink," Marita thought. She ran to find the nearest water fountain. She looked all around the fountain, but there was no treasure.*

Comprehension Questions

√ if correct, ½ if partly correct, blank if incorrect or unanswered

(Literal)	1. How did Jenny and Marita feel toward Mike? (They liked him.)
(Word meaning)	2. What does *brag* mean? (To boast)
(Inference)	3. Why did Jenny smile at Marita? (Because Mike is probably always bragging; they were used to his bragging.)
(Literal)	4. What did Mr. Ortero do after he gave each child a clue? (He gave them rules.)
(Word meaning)	5. What is a *rule*? (Something you have to follow)
(Literal)	6. What were the three rules he gave the children? (Stay inside the park; don't harm any plants or trees; they must find the treasure in twenty minutes.)
(Inference)	7. How do we know Mr. Ortero is concerned about the park? (He tells children not to harm the plants or trees.)
(Literal)	8. What did Marita run to find? (The water fountain)
(Inference)	9. Why did Marita run to the water fountain? (Because of her clue)
(Inference)	10. What did Marita expect to find at the water fountain? (The treasure)

*Judith Stamper, "The Treasure Hunt," Level 7, *Going Places* (Needham, MA: Silver Burdett & Ginn, 1989), p. 198.

Passage D, Level 2-2

Comprehension Level: (Circle the one that indicates total number of correct responses.)

Independent	Instruction	Buffer	Frustration
9–10	7.5–8.5	5–7	4 or less
(95%–100%)	(75%–94%)	(51%–74%)	(50% or less)

Level 3¹ (E)

ORAL READING

Introduction: Read this story aloud to find out what Jason wants.

Coding Guide

- Circle any omitted word.
- Write ~~substituted~~ words above the text. *(substitution)*
- Write ₍inserted₎ word and use a caret.
- Write a P above any prompted word.
- Note word reversals
- Write SC above self-corrected word.
- Underline repetitions.

Every time ten-year-old Jason Hardman wanted a book from a library, he borrowed his sister's bike and pedaled six miles to the next town, Monroe. Since Jason's favorite thing to do was to read books, he spent hours pedaling.

Jason's town of Elsinore, Utah, had only 650 people, too tiny for a library of its own. Elsinore was so small that the children even went to school in Monroe.

One night, Jason said to his parents, "I want to start a library in Elsinore." They were pleased but told him that he would have to talk with the town council.

"What is a town council?" Jason asked.

"It's a group of about eight elected members and the mayor. They run all the town's business," his mom said. "Elsinore, like all towns, collects taxes from its citizens and uses the money for public services, such as fire and police protection," she explained.*

Comprehension Questions

√ if correct, ½ if partly correct, blank if incorrect or unanswered

(Literal)	1. How old is Jason Hardman? (Ten years old)
(Word meaning)	2. What does *borrow* mean? (To use something that belongs to someone else after agreeing to return it)
(Literal)	3. What did Jason borrow? (His sister's bike)
(Inference)	4. Where did Jason spend a lot of time? (In the Monroe library)
(Literal)	5. What was Jason's favorite thing? (Reading)
(Literal)	6. Why didn't Jason's town have a library? (It was too small.)
(Literal)	7. What did Jason want to do? (Start a library)
(Inference)	8. Why did Jason want to start a library? (Because he loved to read and didn't want to keep pedaling to Monroe to get library books)
(Literal)	9. What is a town council? (A group of about eight elected members and a mayor, who run the town's business)
(Main idea)	10. What is the main idea of the story? (Jason Hardman wants to start a library.)

*Margaret Tuley Patton, "Jason Wants a Library," Level 8, *Castles of Sand* (Needham, MA: Silver Burdett & Ginn, 1989), pp. 184–185.

Passage E Level 3-1

Reading Accuracy: 151 _____ = _____

            (Total words)   (Words missed)   (Total words correct)

Word Accuracy Reading Level: (Circle the one that indicates the total words correct.)

Independent	Instruction	Buffer	Frustration
149–151	143–148	137–142	136 or less
(99%–100%)	(95%–98%)	(91%–94%)	(90% or less)

Comprehension Level: (Circle the one that indicates total number of correct responses.)

Independent	Instruction	Buffer	Frustration
9–10	7.5–8.5	5–7	4 or less
(95%–100%)	(75%–94%)	(51%–74%)	(50% or less)

Reading Strategies When Encountering Unknown Words: (Check all that apply.)

__made no attempt   __self-corrected   __repeated   __asked for help

__used sentence sense   __used word meaning   __used word parts

__used letters/sounds   __skipped and read on   __other: _____

Level 3¹ (E)

SILENT READING

> **Introduction: Jason meets with the town council and tells them he wants to start a library. Read the story to find out more about Jason and his library.**

Another week passed. Every day when Jason came off the school bus, he'd ask his mother: "Did the mayor phone?" Each day, the answer was, "No." Jason phoned the mayor every night for two weeks. Each night, the same answer was given: "The council is still thinking about it." Jason grew tired of waiting. "Why can't I use the town hall basement for my library?" he thought to himself.

During those weeks, Jason pedaled often to Monroe for library books. "I wonder if I will be biking these six miles forever for a book?" he asked himself sadly. He began to doubt that he would ever get a library for Elsinore.

At last it happened. When he phoned the mayor, Jason was invited to the council's next meeting. The mayor told him they might find space in the town hall basement. It was just too good to be true.*

Comprehension Questions

√ if correct, ½ if partly correct, blank if incorrect or unanswered

(Literal)	1. What did Jason ask his mother when he came home from school? (Did the mayor phone?)
(Inference)	2. Explain how you know whether Jason lived close or far from his school. (He didn't live close because he rode a bus to school.)
(Literal)	3. What did Jason do every night? (He phoned the mayor every night.)
(Literal)	4. What answer was he always given? (The council is still thinking about it.)
(Literal)	5. Where did Jason want to have his library? (In the town hall basement)
(Literal)	6. What did Jason do while he was waiting? (Pedaled often to the library in Monroe)
(Word meaning)	7. What does *forever* mean? (Always)
(Literal)	8. What finally happened? (Jason was invited to the council's next meeting. They told him they might find space in the town hall basement for his library.)
(Inference)	9. How do we know Jason could hardly believe his ears. (In the story it says, "It was too good to be true.")
(Main idea)	10. What is the main idea of the story? (After Jason waits a few weeks, the mayor finally tells Jason that he might be able to use the town hall basement for his library.)

---

*Margaret Tuley Patton, "Jason Wants a Library," Level 8, *Castles of Sand* (Needham, MA: Silver Burdett & Ginn, 1989), p. 187.

Passage E, Level 3-1

Comprehension Level: (Circle the one that indicates total number of correct responses.)

Independent	Instruction	Buffer	Frustration
9–10	7.5–8.5	5–7	4 or less
(95%–100%)	(75%–94%)	(51%–74%)	(50% or less)

Level 3² (F)

ORAL READING

Introduction: Read this story aloud to find out what King Midas loves.

Once upon a time there was a very rich king named Midas. He lived in a fine castle with his daughter, Marygold. The two things he loved best in life were gold and Marygold. He loved to go into his treasure room and count his coins. No one, not even Marygold, was allowed into the king's treasure room.

One day Midas was sitting in the treasure room dreaming about his gold. In his dream, he saw a shadow fall across the piles of valuable gold coins. He looked up and saw a stranger standing near him. Since no one was allowed into his treasure room, Midas was surprised. The stranger looked kind, however, so Midas wasn't afraid. He greeted the man, and they began to talk of gold.

"You certainly have a lot of gold," said the stranger.

"It's not so much," said Midas.

The stranger smiled. "Do you want even more gold than this?" he asked.

"If I had my way, everything I touched would turn into gold," Midas replied.*

Comprehension Questions

√ if correct, ½ if partly correct, blank if incorrect or unanswered

(Literal)	1. What were the two things that Midas loved best in the world? (Gold and his daughter, Marygold)
(Word meaning)	2. What is the meaning of *valuable*? (Worth a lot such as gold, money, or jewelry)
(Literal)	3. Where was no one allowed to go? (In the King's treasure room)
(Literal)	4. What did King Midas love to do in his treasure room? (Count his coins)
(Inference)	5. How do we know Midas loves gold very much? (He spends a lot of times sitting in the treasure room counting the coins. He also dreams about the gold.)
(Word meaning)	6. What is a *stranger*? (A person who is unknown to you; someone you don't know)
(Literal)	7. Where did Midas see a stranger? (In his dream while sitting in the treasure room)
(Literal)	8. Why was Midas surprised when he saw a stranger in his treasure room? (Because no one was allowed in the room)
(Inference)	9. How do we know Midas is not satisfied with what he has? (Even though he is very rich and has so much gold, he says that it's not so much. He also says he'd like everything he touched to turn into gold.)
(Main idea)	10. What is the main idea of the story? (Even though King Midas is very rich and has lots of gold, he thinks it's not so much.)

*"King Midas and the Golden Touch," retold by Judy Rosenbaum, Level 9, *On the Horizon* (Needham, MA: Silver Burdett & Ginn, 1989), pp. 130–131.

Passage F, Level 3-2

Reading Accuracy: 171 - _____ = _____

(Total words)   (Words missed)   (Total words correct)

Word Accuracy Reading Level: (Circle the one that indicates the total words correct.)

Independent	Instruction	Buffer	Frustration
169–171	162–168	155–161	154 or less
(99%–100%)	(95%–98%)	(91%–94%)	(90% or less)

Comprehension Level: (Circle the one that indicates total number of correct responses.)

Independent	Instruction	Buffer	Frustration
9–10	7.5–8.5	5–7	4 or less
(95%–100%)	(75%–94%)	(51%–74%)	(50% or less)

Reading Strategies When Encountering Unknown Words: (Check all that apply.)

__made no attempt   __self-corrected   __repeated   __asked for help

__used sentence sense   __used word meaning   __used word parts

__used letters/sounds   __skipped and read on   __other: _____

Level 3² (F)

SILENT READING

Introduction: The stranger tells King Midas that he will give him the Golden Touch. Everything he touches will turn to gold. Read the story to find out what happens.

Midas was so excited that he could hardly wait until morning. At last the sun rose. Still dreaming, Midas sat up and reached for the water jug by his bed. At once it became gold. Midas was so overjoyed, he got up and danced around the room, touching everything within his reach. Soon he had a room full of gleaming gold objects. When he reached for his clothes, they turned into heavy golden cloth. "Now I shall really look like a king," he said. He got dressed and admired himself in the mirror. Midas was impressed by his golden clothes, though they were so heavy he could hardly move.

His looking glass was more of a problem. He tried to use it to see his new treasures better. To his surprise, he could not see anything through it. He put it on the table and found that it was now gold, but Midas was too excited to worry. He said, "I can see well enough without it. Besides, it is much more valuable now."*

Comprehension Questions

✓ if correct, ½ if partly correct, blank if incorrect or unanswered

(Literal)	1. What did Midas first do after the sun rose? (He reached for the water jug.)
(Literal)	2. What happened to the water jug after he touched it? (It turned to gold.)
(Literal)	3. What did Midas do after the water jug turned to gold? (He got up and danced around the room, touching everything within his reach.)
(Literal)	4. What happened to everything he touched? (It turned to gold.)
(Inference)	5. Why were his clothes so heavy? (They too had turned to gold because he had to touch them to put them on.)
(Inference)	6. Why had his looking glass become gold? (He had touched it.)
(Inference)	7. Were all these things really happening to Midas? Explain. (No. Midas was dreaming it all.)
(Word meaning)	8. What does *admire* mean? (To think of someone with approval and respect)
(Literal)	9. What did Midas say when his looking glass turned to gold? (I can see well enough without it. Besides, it is much more valuable now.)
(Main idea)	10. What is the main idea of the story? (In his dream, King Midas is very excited because everything he touches turns to gold.)

*"King Midas and the Golden Touch," retold by Judy Rosenbaum, Level 9, *On the Horizon* (Needham, MA: Silver Burdett & Ginn, 1989), p. 132.

Passage F, Level 3-2

Comprehension Level: (Circle the one that indicates total number of correct responses.)

Independent	Instruction	Buffer	Frustration
9–10	7.5–8.5	5–7	4 or less
(95%–100%)	(75%–94%)	(51%–74%)	(50% or less)

Level 4 (G)

ORAL READING

Introduction: Read the story to find out how a writer begins a book for young people.

How does a writer such as Mr. Pinkwater begin a novel for young readers? How does he work? "When I'm beginning a new book," he states, "I am almost like an actor getting into character. I listen to music. I watch television. I talk to people. I turn up at a K-Mart store and go through all the motions of being an ordinary citizen."

"When I start a novel, all I'm really doing is waiting for the characters to show up. It's like the movie *Close Encounters of the Third Kind*. The people who have been 'selected' to be in this story show up. It is a very interesting experience."

He does not sit down and write every day. "It would be terrible if I had to work that way. I show up at my office every day in the event that something may want to happen, but if nothing happens, I don't feel that I have failed to perform. If something gets started, fair enough. If it doesn't, and I feel I've given it enough time, I go to K-Mart. I showed up, the story didn't!"*

Comprehension Questions

√ if correct, ½ if partly correct, blank if incorrect or unanswered

(Literal)	1. To whom does Mr. Pinkwater compare himself when he first begins to write? (An actor)
(Literal)	2. State three things Mr. Pinkwater does when he begins to write. (Listen to music, watch television, talk to people)
(Inference)	3. What does listening to music, watching television, and talking to people help him do? (Get into character for his book)
(Literal)	4. When he first starts writing what is he waiting for? (For his characters to show up)
(Literal)	5. What place does Mr. Pinkwater visit? (K-Mart)
(Word meaning)	6. What does *ordinary* mean? (Not special; usual; normal)
(Inference)	7. What does Mr. Pinkwater mean when he says he goes through the motions of the being an ordinary person? (He is acting; he is trying to act like the people who go shopping at K-Mart, so he can learn what it feels like.)
(Literal)	8. What movie does Mr. Pinkwater refer to? (*Close Encounters of the Third Kind*)
(Inference)	9. What are Mr. Pinkwater's feeling about writing every day? (He doesn't feel he has to. He doesn't feel he is a failure if he doesn't perform every day.)
(Main idea)	10. What is the main idea of the story? (Mr. Pinkwater describes what he does in beginning to write a book)

*Lee Bennett Hopkins, "Daniel Manus Pinkwater," Level 10, *Silver Secrets* (Needham, MA: Silver Burdett & Ginn, 1989), p. 56.

Passage G, Level 4

Reading Accuracy: 187 - _____ = _____

(Total words) (Words missed) (Total words correct)

Word Accuracy Reading Level: (Circle the one that indicates the total words correct.)

Independent	Instruction	Buffer	Frustration
185–187	177–184	170–176	169 or less
(99%–100%)	(95%–98%)	(91%–94%)	(90% or less)

Comprehension Level: (Circle the one that indicates total number of correct responses.)

Independent	Instruction	Buffer	Frustration
9–10	7.5–8.5	5–7	4 or less
(95%–100%)	(75%–94%)	(51%–74%)	(50% or less)

Reading Strategies When Encountering Unknown Words: (Check all that apply.)

__made no attempt   __self-corrected   __repeated   __asked for help

__used sentence sense   __used word meaning   __used word parts

__used letters/sounds   __skipped and read on   __other: _____

Level 4 (G)

SILENT READING

Introduction: Read this story to find out how Daniel Pinkwater feels while he is writing his books.

"I love the story as it is being written. Sometimes it's as though it were happening without my doing it. I'll go to bed, excited about what's going to happen tomorrow. I know something's got to happen because I've only got 175 pages done and I've got to do more.

"To me, the beauty in writing is making the words come out as clear as a pane of glass. That I can do, and I'm rather pleased because it took me years to learn how.

"Writing for girls and boys has helped me to remember my own childhood. And since I'm writing books for a specific reader, namely, myself at different ages, I've gotten more and more expert at revisiting that person within me at different ages."

He sometimes uses a computer. "The computer allows me to think in a different way. It helps me to be a better, more daring writer. Using a computer was a breakthrough for me."*

Comprehension Questions

√ *if correct, ½ if partly correct,*
blank if incorrect or unanswered

(Literal) 1. What does Mr. Pinkwater love? (The story as it is being written)

(Literal) 2. How does Mr. Pinkwater feel when he goes to bed after working on a story? (Excited)

(Inference) 3. Why is Mr. Pinkwater excited when he goes to bed after working on his story? (He can't wait to see what will happen or how his story will turn out.)

(Literal) 4. How does Mr. Pinkwater know something has to happen? (Because he only has 175 pages done and he has to do more.)

(Inference) 5. What is the beauty in writing for Mr. Pinkwater? (His being able to make words come out as clear as a pane of glass)

(Inference) 6. What does it mean when he says that his words are as clear as a pane of glass? (That it is easy to understand what he is saying; he gets his ideas across; his words help bring pictures to your mind.)

(Inference) 7. How do we know it wasn't always easy for him to make his words as clear as a pane of glass? (He said it took him years to learn how.)

(Literal) 8. What has writing for children helped him to do? (Remember his own childhood)

(Literal) 9. How does the computer help Mr. Pinkwater? (It allows him to think in a different way; it helps him to be a better, more daring writer.)

(Main idea) 10. What is the main idea of the story? (Mr. Pinkwater describes what he does and how he feels while writing a story.)

*Lee Bennett Hopkins, "Daniel Manus Pinkwater," Level 10, *Silver Secrets* (Needham, MA: Silver Burdett & Ginn, 1989), pp. 56–57.

Passage G, Level 4

Comprehension Level: (Circle the one that indicates total number of correct responses.)

Independent	Instruction	Buffer	Frustration
9–10	7.5–8.5	5–7	4 or less
(95%–100%)	(75%–94%)	(51%–74%)	(50% or less)

Level 5 (H)

ORAL READING

Introduction: Read this story aloud to find out about how the Davidsons lived years ago.

Early in April of 1872, the Davidsons's covered wagon rolled onto their 160-acre land claim in eastern Nebraska. There was no shelter waiting for them. Like most settlers in the Great Plains, the Davidsons had to build their own shelter. At first, the family lived in the covered wagon. That was all right for a while. But by fall, they needed more protection from Nebraska's cold and windy climate.

Back east, the Davidsons had lived in a wooden farmhouse. They would have liked to build a wooden house on the Plains, too. But there wasn't a tree in sight. Lumber for building wasn't available in Nebraska, even if the family had been able to afford it.

There wasn't time for building, anyway. As farmers, the Davidsons knew they had to get on with the all-important work of plowing and planting. Only then would their new land provide enough harvest to see them through the winter.

Rabbits and foxes dig their burrows and dens in hillsides, and that's what the Davidsons did too. The settlers chose the streambank location because it was conveniently close to water. There were no building materials to buy or skilled workers to hire. After two days of digging, the Davidsons's new home was ready.*

Comprehension Questions

√ if correct, ½ if partly correct, blank if incorrect or unanswered

(Literal)   1. When did the Davidsons arrive at their destination? (In April of 1872)

(Literal)   2. What was their destination? (A 160-acre land claim in eastern Nebraska)

(Literal)   3. Where did they live when they first arrived? (In their covered wagon)

(Literal)   4. Why did they live in a covered wagon? (There was no shelter waiting for them.)

(Inference)   5. How do we know that the Davidsons weren't wealthy? (The story said that lumber wasn't available, even if the Davidsons could afford it. Also, they needed the harvest to see them through the winter.)

(Inference)   6. During what season or seasons of the year did the Davidsons live in their covered wagon? (During the spring and summer; a student may include the beginning of fall as part of the answer. Accept this also.)

(Inference)   7. What was the Davidsons's highest priority? (Plowing and planting)

*Duncan Searl, "A Sea of Grass," Level 11, *Dream Chasers* (Needham, MA: Silver Burdett & Ginn, 1989), pp. 423–424.

(Inference)
8. The Davidson's home was compared to homes built by what two animals? (Rabbits and foxes)

(Word meaning)
9. What is a *burrow*? (A hole that an animal digs in the ground)

(Main idea)
10. What is the main idea of the story? (The Davidsons's only choice to survive the cold and windy climate was for them, themselves, to dig a home in the hillside like the rabbits and foxes.)

Passage H, Level 5

Reading Accuracy: 208 - _____ = _____

            (Total words)   (Words missed)   (Total words correct)

Word Accuracy Reading Level: (Circle the one that indicates the total words correct.)

Independent	Instruction	Buffer	Frustration
205–208	197–204	188–196	187 or less
(99%–100%)	(95%–98%)	(91%–94%)	(90% or less)

Comprehension Level: (Circle the one that indicates total number of correct responses.)

Independent	Instruction	Buffer	Frustration
9–10	7.5–8.5	5–7	4 or less
(95%–100%)	(75%–94%)	(51%–74%)	(50% or less)

Reading Strategies When Encountering Unknown Words: (Check all that apply.)

__made no attempt   __self-corrected   __repeated   __asked for help

__used sentence sense   __used word meaning   __used word parts

__used letters/sounds   __skipped and read on   __other: _____

Level 5 (H)

SILENT READING

Introduction: Read this story to find out more about how the Davidsons lived years ago.

Most people believe in the old saying, "There's no place like home." The Davidsons, however, might not have felt that way about their dugout. The cramped dwelling was damp and dark, even on sunny days. Dirt from the roof sifted down into bedding and food. Insects and snakes were constant house guests.

Hoping their new shelter would be a temporary one, the Davidsons began to plow and plant. But this wasn't as easy as they had expected. In the early 1870s, more than a foot of thick sod covered almost every inch of the territory. Held together by a mass of tangled roots, this sod was almost impossible to cut through. It could take weeks to plow a single acre. Settlers like the Davidsons became known as "sodbusters."

The sod's toughness gave the settlers an idea. Why not build with it? The new fields were covered with long ribbons of sod that had been plowed up. It would be a simple matter to cut these into smaller pieces and use them as building blocks. The settlers even had a nickname for this unusual building material—"Nebraska marble."*

Comprehension Questions

√ if correct, ½ if partly correct, blank if incorrect or unanswered

(Literal)	1. What is the saying that most people believe in? (There's no place like home.)
(Inference)	2. How would the Davidsons feel about the saying "There's no place like home"? (They would not agree because they lived in a dugout that was not very comfortable.)
(Literal)	3. State three problems with their dugout. (It was cramped, damp and dark, dirt from the roof sifted down into bedding and food; and so on.)
(Literal)	4. Who were the Davidsons's constant, guests? (Insects and snakes)
(Inference)	5. How long had the Davidsons planned on staying in their dugout? (Not long; they hoped their new shelter would be a temporary one.)
(Word meaning)	6. What is the meaning of *temporary*? (Lasting for a short time; not permanent)
(Literal)	7. What covered almost every inch of the Davidsons's territory? (More than a foot of thick sod)
(Inference)	8. Why were the settlers known as "sodbusters"? (Because it was very hard to cut the sod; however, they did, even though, it could take weeks to plow one acre.)
(Literal)	9. What idea did the sod's toughness give the settlers? (To build with it)
(Main idea)	10. What is the main idea of the story? (The Davidsons, unhappy with their dugout, come up with the idea to use the tough sod for building material.)

*Duncan Searl, "A Sea of Grass," Level 11, *Dream Chasers* (Needham, MA: Silver Burdett & Ginn, 1989),p. 423–425.

Passage H, Level 5

Comprehension Level: (Circle the one that indicates total number of correct responses.)

Independent	Instruction	Buffer	Frustration
9–10	7.5–8.5	5–7	4 or less
(95%–100%)	(75%–94%)	(51%–74%)	(50% or less)

Level 6 (I)

ORAL READING

> Introduction: Read this story aloud to find out what is special about the Monterey Bay Aquarium.

You walk through the door—and immediately freeze. Overhead, to your left, a thresher shark whips its tail. To your right are three huge killer whales. Have you wandered into a nightmare? Hardly. You've just entered the Monterey Bay Aquarium.

The shark and whales, life-size and hanging from the ceiling, are fiberglass. The other 6,000 creatures you'll meet are not. On a visit to the aquarium, on the shores of California's Monterey Bay, you'll have a chance not only to see them swim, scurry, hunt, and court, but to pick up and handle a few as well.

One of the aquarium's most spectacular exhibits is the three-story-high kelp forest—the world's only kelp forest growing indoors. Clinging to the bottom with a rootlike "holdfast," the yellow-brown kelp reaches up through 28 feet of water, spreading out on the tank's sunlit surface. With "stipes" instead of trunks, and "blades" in place of leaves, the kelp forest resembles an underwater redwood grove. Sunbeams slant down from above, while the kelp sways gently back and forth. With a patient eye, you will begin to spot some of the many creatures that call the kelp forest home.

Long-legged brittle stars and crabs can be seen within the tangled holdfast. Watch for turban snails higher up. The fish of the kelp forest aren't as fast as those of the open ocean, but they're better at playing hide-and-seek. Special air sacs allow some of them to hover in hiding within the maze of blades. Many are completely camouflaged.*

Comprehension Questions

√ if correct, ½ if partly correct, blank if incorrect or unanswered

(Literal)	1. What do you first see when you walk through the door of the Monterey Bay Aquarium? (Overhead to your left a thresher shark and to your right three huge killer whales)
(Inference)	2. Why would you immediately freeze when you first walk through the door? (Because the thresher shark and three killer whales must look very real, but they aren't.)
(Literal)	3. How many real creatures are there in the aquarium? (6,000)
(Word meaning)	4. What does *spectacular* mean? (Of or like a remarkable sight; showy; striking)
(Literal)	5. What is one of the aquarium's most remarkable exhibits? (The three-story-high kelp forest)
(Inference)	6. Why is the kelp forest so remarkable? (It's the world's only indoor kelp forest.)

*Paul Fleischman, "The Monterey Bay Aquarium," Level 12, *Wind by the Sea* (Needham, MA: Silver Burdett & Ginn, 1989), pp. 395–396.

(Literal)   7. What does the kelp forest resemble? (An underwater redwood grove)

(Inference)   8. Why are the fish in the kelp forest better at playing hide-and-seek? (They can hover in hiding within the maze of blades so that they blend in with the blades; they are completely camouflaged.)

(Literal)   9. What allows some of the fish to hover in hiding? (Special air sacs)

(Main idea)   10. What is the main idea of the story? (The Monterey Sea Aquarium is a very unusual aquarium that houses the world's only kelp forest growing indoors.)

Passage I, Level 6

Reading Accuracy: 252 - _____ = _____

          (Total words)   (Words missed)   (Total words correct)

Word Accuracy Reading Level: (Circle the one that indicates the total words correct.)

Independent	Instruction	Buffer	Frustration
249–252	238–248	228–237	227 or less
(99%–100%)	(95%–98%)	(91%–94%)	(90% or less)

Comprehension Level: (Circle the one that indicates total number of correct responses.)

Independent	Instruction	Buffer	Frustration
9–10	7.5–8.5	5–7	4 or less
(95%–100%)	(75%–94%)	(51%–74%)	(50% or less)

Reading Strategies When Encountering Unknown Words: (Check all that apply.)

__made no attempt   __self-corrected   __repeated   __asked for help

__used sentence sense   __used word meaning   __used word parts

__used letters/sounds   __skipped and read on   __other _____

Level 6 (I)

SILENT READING

Introduction: Read this story to find out about one of the Monterey Bay Aquarium's residents.

Among the animals who depend on the kelp are the aquarium's most playful residents, the sea otters. Floating on their backs, doing somersaults in the water, taking part in high-speed games of tag, these smallest of the marine mammals charm every audience.

Their two-story tank lets you view them from above as well as from below the water's surface. In the wild, though, their home is the kelp beds. They live on creatures who live on the kelp. They depend on it for shelter during storms. Before sleeping, they wrap themselves in it to keep from drifting out to sea.

Why are otters so playful? No one knows, though part of the answer might lie in the fact that their constant motion helps to keep them warm. Unlike the whales and other marine mammals, otters have no layer of blubber between their warm-blooded insides and the cold water outside. So they move around a lot, which requires a lot of energy, which in turn requires a lot of eating. Could you eat 25 hamburgers a day? That's the equivalent of what an otter swallows, eating up to one-quarter of its body weight daily. If you're present at feeding time, you'll be amazed at how much fish, squid, and abalone an otter can eat. Wild otters eat so many purple sea urchins that their bones eventually turn purplish as well.

Otters have another defense against the cold—their coats. When you touch the soft sample of fur on the wall by their tank, you'll understand why they were hunted until they were nearly extinct.*

Comprehension Questions

*√ if correct, ½ if partly correct,
blank if incorrect or unanswered*

(Literal) 1. What animals are the aquarium's most playful residents?
(The sea otters)

(Literal) 2. How do the sea otters charm audiences? (They float on their backs, do somersaults, and play high-speed games of tag.)

(Literal) 3. Where do the otters live in the aquarium? (In a two-story tank)

(Literal) 4. Where do the otters live in the wild? (In the kelp beds)

(Literal) 5. What is the reason given for the otter's playfulness? (Their constant motion keeps them warm.)

(Inference) 6. Why do the otters have to move around a lot to keep warm? (The otters have no layer of blubber between their warm-blooded insides and the cold water outside.)

(Inference) 7. What is the effect of the great amount of movement? (The otters have to eat a lot because they use up a lot of energy; they eat one-quarter of their body weight daily.)

*Paul Fleischman, "The Monterey Bay Aquarium," Level 12, *Wind by the Sea* (Needham, MA: Silver Burdett & Ginn, 1989), p. 397.

(Word meaning)	8. What does *extinct* mean? (No longer existing; no longer living; having died out)
(Inference)	9. Why were otters hunted until they almost didn't exist anymore? (For their fur; it is very soft.)
(Main idea)	10. What is the main idea of the story? (The sea otters are the most playful aquarium residents because they need to move around a lot to keep warm.)

Passage I, Level 6

Comprehension Level: (Circle the one that indicates total number of correct responses.)

Independent	Instruction	Buffer	Frustration
9–10	7.5–8.5	5–7	4 or less
(95%–100%)	(75%–94%)	(51%–74%)	(50% or less)

Level 7 (J)

ORAL READING

> Introduction: Read this story aloud to find out what some courageous children do. (Etienne is pronounced ā-tyen'.)

The voice came from out of the sky, "Hey fellows, quick, grab those ropes and pull me into the wind as if I were a kite. Hurry!"

Looking up, the young people were startled to see a man waving wildly at them from a strange banana-shaped flying balloon—a balloon that was about to crash!

Sara reacted quickly and grabbed one of the ropes that dangled near her. But Sara could not even stop the flying contraption, let alone pull it in the other direction. As she attempted to dig her heels into the ground, the balloon nearly toppled her.

"Boys, don't just stand there. Help her," the man in the balloon shouted at Etienne and Louis.

Rushing to help their sister, the boys grabbed other ropes trailing from the balloon and frantically tugged at the runaway flying machine. Finally, the three of them were able to change the direction of the balloon, carrying it into the wind as the aeronaut had requested. The flying machine bobbed up like a kite.

As the young people pulled the balloon down, following the aeronaut's instructions, a crowd began to gather. The moment the flier was safe on the ground, he was surrounded by a large crowd of curious people, all talking at once.

Sara realized that the man she had rescued was the famous Monsieur Santos-Dumont, the wealthy Brazilian inventor and daredevil who predicted people would someday fly like birds.

"Where are the young people? They are the real heroes of this escape from the jaws of death," she heard him shout over the crowd.*

Coding Guide

- (Circle) any omitted word.
- Write ~~substituted~~ words above the text. (substitution)
- Write inserted word and use a caret. ^
- Write a P above any prompted word.
- Note |word| reversals|
- Write SC above self-corrected word.
- <u>Underline</u> repetitions.

Comprehension Questions

√ if correct, ½ if partly correct, blank if incorrect or unanswered

(Literal)	1. Describe what the children saw when they looked up in the sky. (A strange banana-shaped balloon that was about to crash)
(Inference)	2. How do we know the person in the balloon didn't expect the girl to help him? (He called out to the fellows)
(Literal)	3. What did he want the fellows to do? (To grab the ropes and pull him into the wind as if he were a kite)
(Literal)	4. What happened when Sara tried to help? (She couldn't stop the balloon, let alone pull it in the other direction.)

*David Fulton, "Through Skies Never Sailed," Level 13, *Star Walk* (Needham, MA: Silver Burdett & Ginn, 1989), pp. 353–354.

(Word meaning)	5. What is an *aeronaut*? (Someone who navigates in the air, especially a balloon)
(Inference)	6. What was needed to keep the balloon afloat? (The force of the wind)
(Inference)	7. What did the young people have to be able to do to pull down the balloon? (Follow the aeronaut's directions)
(Inference)	8. What kind of person was Monsieur Santos-Dumont? State four characteristics. Give proof for your answer. (Creative—the story said he was an inventor, reckless, adventurous—it said he was a daredevil: well-known—it said he was famous; rich—it said he was wealthy.)
(Literal)	9. What did Monsieur Santos-Dumont predict people would someday be able to do? (Fly like birds)
(Main idea)	10. What is the main idea of the story? (A courageous girl and her brothers rescue an aeronaut by helping to bring his flying balloon safely to the ground.)

Passage J, Level 7

Reading Accuracy: 263 - _____ = _____

          (Total words)   (Words missed)   (Total words correct)

Word Accuracy Reading Level: (Circle the one that indicates the total words correct.)

Independent	Instruction	Buffer	Frustration
259–263	248–258	238–247	237 or less
(99%–100%)	(95%–98%)	(91%–94%)	(90% or less)

Comprehension Level: (Circle the one that indicates total number of correct responses.)

Independent	Instruction	Buffer	Frustration
9–10	7.5–8.5	5–7	4 or less
(95%–100%)	(75%–94%)	(51%–74%)	(50% or less)

Reading Strategies When Encountering Unknown Words: (Check all that apply.)

__made no attempt   __self-corrected   __repeated   __asked for help

__used sentence sense   __used word meaning   __used word parts

__used letters/sounds   __skipped and read on   __other: _____

Level 7 (J)

SILENT READING

> **Introduction: Monsieur Santos-Dumont is very grateful to the children for saving his life. Read the story to see why he comes to the children's home.**

"The purpose of my visit, in fact, is related to the events of this afternoon. I came to invite your family for an excursion in one of my balloons."

Silence filled the Cote parlor as all eyes turned to Sara's father, awaiting his reply. "I don't wish to seem overly conservative or closed minded, Monsieur Santos-Dumont, but I wouldn't consider air travel sufficiently safe to risk my whole family. This afternoon's events are evidence of that."

"I certainly wouldn't ask you to endanger your family, but flying in a balloon, which is merely a big bag filled with hydrogen, has long been demonstrated to be a safe sport.

"I wouldn't suggest taking you in a craft such as the one I was flying this afternoon. That was a 'dirigible.' Its design is the latest breakthrough in the attempt to control the direction of flight. It's a balloon that has a gasoline engine suspended beneath it to direct its movement. Unfortunately, my colleagues and I have yet to work out all the problems. But we will. In any case, the dirigible may soon be obsolete. I recently heard a report at a meeting of the Aero Club, and I understand that some Americans have actually built a glider of some sort that is heavier than the air, and it is said they use a gasoline engine to power it. Now, that is really incredible."*

Comprehension Questions

√ *if correct, ½ if partly correct, blank if incorrect or unanswered*

(Literal)	1. What was the purpose of Monsieur Santos-Dumont's visit to the children's family? (To invite them on an excursion in one of his balloons)
(Word meaning)	2. What is an *excursion*? (A short pleasure trip)
(Literal)	3. How does the children's father feel about air travel? (He feels it is not safe.)
(Inference)	4. What evidence does the children's father give to back up his feelings? (The afternoon's events)
(Literal)	5. What does Monsieur Santos-Dumont claim is safe? (Flying in a balloon filled with hydrogen)
(Literal)	6. What kind of machine was Monsieur Santos-Dumont flying in the afternoon? (A dirigible, which has a gasoline engine: it's a gasoline engine suspended beneath it to direct its movement)
(Inference)	7. How do we know Monsieur Santos-Dumont is not working alone on developing the dirigible? (The story says that he and his colleagues have yet to work out the details.)
(Literal)	8. What does Monsieur Santos-Dumont feel is incredible? (The glider that the Americans have built, which is heavier than air and uses a gasoline engine to power it)

*David Fulton, "Through Skies Never Sailed," Level 13, *Star Walk* (Needham, MA: Silver Burdett & Ginn, 1989), p. 356.

(Inference)

9. What does Monsieur Santos-Dumont feel the Americans' flying machine will do to the dirigible? (Make the dirigible obsolete, that is, no longer useful or in use)

(Main idea)

10. What is the main idea of the story? (Monsieur Santos-Dumont tries to persuade the children's father to allow his family to go on a short trip in a balloon Monsieur Santos-Dumont insists is safe.)

Passage J, Level 7

Comprehension Level: (Circle the one that indicates total number of correct responses.)

Independent	Instruction	Buffer	Frustration
9–10	7.5–8.5	5–7	4 or less
(95%–100%)	(75%–94%)	(51%–74%)	(50% or less)

Level 8 (K)

ORAL READING

Introduction: **Read this story aloud to find out why Lo Tung came to America.**

Lo Tung leaned against the rattling wall of the freight car. Beneath him the floor moved as the wheels cracked over the rails. It was a long time since he'd sat or walked on anything steady. First there had been the long days and nights on the Pacific Mail Steamship that had brought him from China, then the riverboat from San Francisco to Sacramento, then the train, waiting on the levee.

He hadn't had time for more than a glimpse of the strange iron monster belching smoke before the boss man had hustled them aboard. It was hard to believe that he was here now, in this freight car along with other Chinese workers, rolling eastward across America.

Lo Tung looked sideways at his friend, Wei. Wei was fifteen years old, too, and as small and thin as Lo Tung.

"Not more than a hundred pounds, either of you," the agent had said in disgust. "You two will not be able to do the heavy railroad work."

"Don't worry. We are strong," Lo Tung had said. He had not added, "Ho Sen was strong, the strongest man in our village. And he was killed building the American railway." Now Ho Sen's bones lay somewhere in this strange country. And Chen Chi Yuen. He had gone and never been heard from again.

Sitting now in the freight car, thinking about the work, Lo Tung flexed his muscles. Strong for the work. Of course, strong and fearless.

It was growing dark. They had been closed in here together for hours, so many of them from the ship. The air was used up and the smells were bad.*

Comprehension Questions

√ if correct, ½ if partly correct, blank if incorrect or unanswered

(Literal)	1. What kind of car was Lo Tung in? (A Freight car)
(Inference)	2. How do we know Lo Tung has never seen a train before? (Lo Tung thought the locomotive was a strange iron monster. It wouldn't have been strange if he had seen it before.)
(Inference)	3. How do we know it has been a long time since Lo Tung was on land? (The story states that it was a long time since he was on anything steady.)
(Literal)	4. What means of transportation was used to get Lo Tung to his destination? (Steamship, riverboat, and train)

*Eve Bunting, "It's Not the Great Wall, But It Will Last Forever," Level 14, *Worlds Beyond* (Needham, MA: Silver Burdett & Ginn, 1989), pp. 238–239.

(Inference)   5. How long did Lo Tung have between getting off the riverboat and boarding the train? (Not long; he only had time to catch a glimpse of the train before he was hustled aboard.)

(Literal)   6. What was the agent concerned about? (That Lo Tung and his friend were too thin to work on the railroad)

(Literal)   7. What had happened to Ho Sen? (He had been killed working on the American railroad.)

(Inference)   8. Why were the smells on the freight bad? (There was not much air, and there were many people crowded together.)

(Literal)   9. In what direction was the train rolling across America? (Eastward)

(Main idea)   10. What is the main idea of the story? (Lo Tung's journey from China to America to work on the American railroad has been long and hard)

Passage K, Level 8

Reading Accuracy: 275 - _____ = _____

  (Total words)   (Words missed)   (Total words correct)

Word Accuracy Reading Level: (Circle the one that indicates the total words correct.)

Independent	Instruction	Buffer	Frustration
271–275	260–270	249–259	248 or less
(99%–100%)	(95%–98%)	(91%–94%)	(90% or less)

Comprehension Level: (Circle the one that indicates total number of correct responses.)

Independent	Instruction	Buffer	Frustration
9–10	7.5–8.5	5–7	4 or less
(95%–100%)	(75%–94%)	(51%–74%)	(50% or less)

Reading Strategies When Encountering Unknown Words: (Check all that apply.)

__made no attempt   __self-corrected   __repeated   __asked for help

__used sentence sense   __used word meaning   __used word parts

__used letters/sounds   __skipped and read on   __other: _____

Level 8 (K)

SILENT READING

> Introduction: Agents had advertised in Lo Tung's village for laborers to help build the railroad in California. They offered houses to live in, plenty of food, and thirty dollars a month. The passage to go was fifty-four dollars. Read the story to find out why Lo Tung signed on.

Fifty-four dollars was a fortune, and impossible for his mother! The agent had allowed them to borrow from him. That was when he'd complained of Lo Tung's size.

"Not a penny of your wages will be yours till you pay me back," he had warned.

Lo Tung had agreed. He would have agreed to almost anything. Not that he wanted to go to America. The thought of leaving his home brought tears to his eyes. But it was clearly his duty. He was, after all, the eldest son. Since his father's death the family responsibility had been his. If he went, his debt to the agent would be cleared in two months. Then he could begin sending money home for his mother and his sisters, and his little brother. He had to believe that he could save enough to go home himself some day.

Thinking of home here in the heat of the freight car made loneliness rise in him like water in a swamp. Fear was bad, but loneliness was worse. He would not allow himself to remember.

"We are slowing," Wei said. "I can see through a crack."

Someone else announced, "We are here." Tired men and boys staggered up, swaying, hoisting their bedrolls. As the train chugged to a stop they waited quietly for what was to come.

When the doors opened, Lo Tung saw that it was night outside, the sky filled with a million crystal stars.

"American stars," he whispered to Wei, pointing upward.

"Are they the same that shine over China or . . . "

"Out! Everyone out!" Men waited beside the train, big, bulky men who cast massive shadows.

"Hurry! Get a move on!" The words were not in Lo Tung's language but he understood the tone.*

Comprehension Questions

√ if correct, ½ if partly correct, blank if incorrect or unanswered

(Literal)   1. How were Lo Tung and his mother able to get enough money to go to America? (The agent had allowed them to borrow from him.)

(Inference)   2. Why was Lo Tung going to America? (Because his family needed the money; he couldn't earn the money they needed in his village.)

*Eve Bunting, "It's Not the Great Wall, But It Will Last Forever," Level 14, *Worlds Beyond* (Needham, MA: Silver Burdett & Ginn, 1989), p. 240.

(Inference)	3. Why did he feel he had to support his family? (Because his father was dead and he was the eldest son)
(Literal)	4. How long would it take to clear his debt to the agent? (Two months)
(Inference)	5. Does Lo Tung expect to stay in America? Explain. (No, the story states that he had to believe that he could save enough to go home himself some day)
(Literal)	6. What does Lo Tung feel is worse than fear? (Loneliness)
(Inference)	7. What simile is used to describe Lo Tung's loneliness. (Loneliness rose in him like water in a swamp; when it rains, water in a swamp rises very quickly, and that's how fast his loneliness rose.)
(Inference)	8. How do we know it was a clear night when they arrived at their destination? (The sky was filled with a million crystal stars.)
(Literal)	9. What kind of men were waiting beside the train? (Big, bulky men who cast massive shadows)
(Main idea)	10. What is the main idea of the story? (Even though Lo Tung does not want to leave his family, he goes to America so he can earn money for his family in China.)

Passage K, Level 8

Comprehension Level: (Circle the one that indicates total number of correct responses.)

Independent	Instruction	Buffer	Frustration
9–10	7.5–8.5	5–7	4 or less
(95%–100%)	(75%–94%)	(51%–74%)	(50% or less)

Appendix C
Informal Reading Inventory Student Booklet

Word Recognition Inventory (WRI)

A	B	C
1. blow	1. soup	1. brave
2. little	2. tents	2. noon
3. many	3. afternoon	3. park
4. bright	4. baked	4. strange
5. old	5. family	5. November
6. won	6. alone	6. money
7. things	7. great	7. library
8. yellow	8. white	8. join
9. farm	9. soft	9. angry
10. friend	10. boy	10. apple
11. more	11. dinner	11. carrots
12. thanks	12. does	12. class
13. snow	13. wife	13. answer
14. some	14. horse	14. loud
15. cows	15. head	15. mouth
16. game	16. sorry	16. matter
17. please	17. summer	17. hurry
18. leaves	18. hungry	18. idea
19. draw	19. drank	19. carve
20. work	20. enough	20. clothes
		21. delicious
		22. below
		23. boil
		24. built
		25. dragons

Word Recognition Inventory (WRI)

D	E	F
1. office	1. plow	1. petal
2. perfect	2. horn	2. rein
3. patient	3. hesitate	3. furious
4. enemy	4. neglect	4. popular
5. donkey	5. deaf	5. identify
6. dirt	6. language	6. forecast
7. clever	7. attention	7. attach
8. company	8. drawn	8. bought
9. candle	9. complain	9. admire
10. beard	10. fame	10. noble
11. bundle	11. goal	11. migrate
12. address	12. familiar	12. patient
13. snowflake	13. elevator	13. novel
14. sailors	14. plunge	14. ruin
15. score	15. nature	15. rescue
16. tune	16. poem	16. unusual
17. thirsty	17. stall	17. x-ray
18. unload	18. talent	18. wisdom
19. view	19. worthy	19. rough
20. trouble	20. lung	20. protest
21. south	21. medal	21. persuade
22. shy	22. mistake	22. influence
23. ambulance	23. customer	23. prince
24. tiny	24. courage	24. bandage
25. hobby	25. announce	25. bridge

Word Recognition Inventory (WRI)

G	H	I
1. gracious	1. tragedy	1. tenement
2. imitate	2. applause	2. rebel
3. defense	3. amazement	3. ease
4. declare	4. harvest	4. exhibit
5. electronics	5. thaw	5. appoint
6. punishment	6. original	6. shuttle
7. robot	7. balcony	7. unwilling
8. uniform	8. marvel	8. recede
9. twilight	9. mileage	9. wizard
10. tragedy	10. cluster	10. wrench
11. stranger	11. architect	11. revenge
12. tame	12. heroine	12. tiresome
13. technique	13. audition	13. spout
14. suspect	14. interrupt	14. strategy
15. ordinary	15. landscape	15. pamphlet
16. native	16. petition	16. persist
17. haughty	17. permission	17. heritage
18. hostile	18. vessel	18. conquer
19. entire	19. promotion	19. humble
20. errand	20. violence	20. arrogant
21. average	21. voyage	21. astronomy
22. appetite	22. vast	22. distinguish
23. radiant	23. nuisance	23. gratitude
24. prowl	24. luxury	24. guarantee
25. caution	25. lonely	25. legacy

Word Recognition Inventory (WRI)

J	K
1. sham	1. prospect
2. scrutiny	2. quest
3. refuge	3. scoop
4. prestigious	4. journalism
5. quarrel	5. invincible
6. nomad	6. listless
7. fault	7. mirror
8. flattery	8. circuit
9. hindrance	9. defy
10. imperative	10. anguish
11. colleague	11. augment
12. trifle	12. aristocratic
13. souvenir	13. formidable
14. chore	14. faculty
15. aggressive	15. seizure
16. barometer	16. terrace
17. emigrate	17. scrabble
18. verdict	18. undermine
19. zodiac	19. sphere
20. wrench	20. naïve
21. probe	21. plateau
22. momentum	22. recitation
23. mortal	23. jaunt
24. exile	24. frugal
25. limitation	25. hysteria

Level A

Sara sat and sat, looking out at the big tree. She looked at her mother and asked, "Mom, do you have some string?"

"Yes, here is some red string," said Sara's mother. "Is it for your hair?"

"No," said Sara, "It's not for my hair."

"I know," said Mother. "You are going to fix something with it."

"No," said Sara. "You'll see."

Sara saw that her father had some string, too. She asked him for it.

From: Jane Mechling, "A Rainbow for Sara," Level 4, *Make a Wish* (Needham, MA: Silver Burdett & Ginn, 1989), pp. 32–34.

Level A

Sara ran outside to play
with Peter and Anna.
"I am keeping string in
a box," said Sara.
"I have some green string
in my pocket. You may have
it," said Peter.
"You are keeping string?"
said Anna. "What are you going
to do with all that string? Will you
and your cat play with it?"
"No," said Sara. "You'll see." Soon
Sara had all the string she needed.
She had red string, orange string,
green string, and yellow string.

From: Jane Mechling, "A Rainbow for Sara," Level 4, *Make a Wish* (Needham, MA: Silver Burdett & Ginn, 1989), pp. 32–34.

Level B

ORAL READING

Fred and Anna lived on a farm.
It was a small farm. It was also very
dry, and things did not grow well.
So Fred and his wife, Anna, were poor.

One day there was a tap, tap, tap
on the door. A woman had come to the
farm. She had been walking most of
the day, and she was hungry. She asked
Fred and Anna to give her something
to eat. Fred and Anna had a pot of soup.
They let the woman come in to eat.

From: Verna Aardema, "The Three Wishes," Level 5, *A New Day* (Needham, MA: Silver Burdett & Ginn, 1989), p. 160.

Level B

For most of the day, Fred and Anna talked about the three wishes they would make. They talked long after it was time to eat again, and they forgot to cook. They began to get hungry.

By the time Anna and Fred made soup, they were both very, very hungry. As they sat down to eat, Fred said, "I wish we had a sausage to go with this soup."

And there on the table was a great big brown sausage!

From: Verna Aardema, "The Three Wishes," Level 5, *A New Day* (Needham, MA: Silver Burdett & Ginn, 1989), p. 160.

Level C

ORAL READING

Once there was a farmer who went to the town wise man because he had a problem, and he did not know what to do. "How can I help you?" the wise man asked.

"I have a house with one small room," sighed the farmer.

"That is not a problem," the wise man said.

"It is a problem," the farmer sighed. "I live in this one small room with my wife and my seven children. We are always in one another's way, and we are always talking at the same time. It is so loud that I can hardly hear myself think. I cannot stand it any longer. Can you help me?"

From: Michael Patrick Hearn, "Not So Wise as You Suppose," Level 6, *Garden Gates* (Needham, MA: Silver Burdett & Ginn, 1989), pp. 94–95.

Level C

The wise man stroked his chin and thought. "Do you have a horse?" the wise man asked.

"Yes, I have a horse," the farmer said.

"Then the answer is simple," the wise man said, "but you must do as I tell you. Tonight you must bring the horse into your house to stay with you, your wife, and your seven children." The farmer was surprised to hear such a plan, but he did as he was told.

The next morning he returned to the wise man. He was quite upset.

"You are not so wise as you suppose!" the farmer said. "Now my house is even louder. The horse just kicks and neighs morning, noon, and night! I cannot stand it any longer."

From: Michael Patrick Hearn, "Not So Wise as You Suppose," Level 6, *Garden Gates* (Needham, MA: Silver Burdett & Ginn, 1989), pp. 94–95.

Level D

ORAL READING

The children sat down in a big circle on the ground. Everyone was excited. Mr. Ortero (or-té-rō.) had promised them a surprise.

Mr. Ortero walked into the middle of the circle. He ran the after-school program in the park.

"I have a mystery today," Mr. Ortero said. "A treasure is hidden somewhere in the park. Your job is to solve the mystery and find the treasure."

Marita (mä-rḗ -ta) raised her hand. "What is the treasure?" she asked.

"That's part of the mystery," Mr. Ortero answered.

Marita laughed with everyone else. Mr. Ortero liked to tease them.

"Each of you gets one clue," Mr. Ortero said. He started around the circle, handing out the clues. Marita was sitting between Jenny and Mike.

"I'm really a good detective," Mike said. "I bet I'll find the treasure."

From: Judith Stamper, "The Treasure Hunt," Level 7, *Going Places* (Needham, MA: Silver Burdett & Ginn, 1989), p. 197.

Level D

Jenny looked at Marita and smiled. They both liked Mike, but he bragged a lot.

Mr. Ortero gave Jenny her clue. Marita was next, and then Mike. Soon, each child had a clue to open and read. Mr. Ortero stepped back into the middle of the circle.

"Listen to the rules," he said. "First, stay inside the park. The treasure is hidden here. Second, don't harm any plants or trees. Third, you must find the treasure in twenty minutes. Meet me back here in twenty minutes. Good luck!"

The children jumped to their feet and ran in different directions. Marita read her clue over and over. It said:

Thirsty, tired, and very hot?

I'm near what's cool and hits the spot.

"Near something to drink," Marita thought. She ran to find the nearest water fountain. She looked all around the fountain, but there was no treasure.

From: Judith Stamper, "The Treasure Hunt," Level 7, *Going Places* (Needham, MA: Silver Burdett & Ginn, 1989), p. 198.

Level E

Every time ten-year-old Jason Hardman wanted a book from a library, he borrowed his sister's bike and pedaled six miles to the next town, Monroe. Since Jason's favorite thing to do was to read books, he spent hours pedaling.

Jason's town of Elsinore, Utah, had only 650 people, too tiny for a library of its own. Elsinore was so small that the children even went to school in Monroe.

One night, Jason said to his parents, "I want to start a library in Elsinore." They were pleased but told him that he would have to talk with the town council.

"What is a town council?" Jason asked.

"It's a group of about eight elected members and the mayor. They run all the town's business," his mom said. "Elsinore, like all towns, collects taxes from its citizens and uses the money for public services, such as fire and police protection," she explained.

From: Margaret Tuley Patton, "Jason Wants a Library," Level 8, *Castles of Sand* (Needham, MA: Silver Burdett & Ginn, 1989), pp. 184–185.

Level E

Another week passed. Every day when Jason came off the school bus, he'd ask his mother: "Did the mayor phone?" Each day, the answer was, "No." Jason phoned the mayor every night for two weeks. Each night, the same answer was given: "The council is still thinking about it." Jason grew tired of waiting. "Why can't I use the town hall basement for my library?" he thought to himself.

During those weeks, Jason pedaled often to Monroe for library books. "I wonder if I will be biking these six miles forever for a book?" he asked himself sadly. He began to doubt that he would ever get a library for Elsinore.

At last it happened. When he phoned the mayor, Jason was invited to the council's next meeting. The mayor told him they might find space in the town hall basement. It was just too good to be true.

From: Margaret Tuley Patton, "Jason Wants a Library," Level 8, *Castles of Sand* (Needham, MA: Silver Burdett & Ginn, 1989), p. 187.

Level F

ORAL READING

Once upon a time there was a very rich king named Midas. He lived in a fine castle with his daughter, Marygold. The two things he loved best in life were gold and Marygold. He loved to go into his treasure room and count his coins. No one, not even Marygold, was allowed into the king's treasure room.

One day Midas was sitting in the treasure room dreaming about his gold. In his dream, he saw a shadow fall across the piles of valuable gold coins. He looked up and saw a stranger standing near him. Since no one was allowed into his treasure room, Midas was surprised. The stranger looked kind, however, so Midas wasn't afraid. He greeted the man, and they began to talk of gold.

"You certainly have a lot of gold," said the stranger.

"It's not so much," said Midas.

The stranger smiled. "Do you want even more gold than this?" he asked.

"If I had my way, everything I touched would turn into gold," Midas replied.

From: "King Midas and the Golden Touch," retold by Judy Rosenbaum, Level 9, *On the Horizon* (Needham, MA: Silver Burdett & Ginn, 1989), pp. 130–131.

Level F

Midas was so excited that he could hardly wait until morning. At last the sun rose. Still dreaming, Midas sat up and reached for the water jug by his bed. At once it became gold. Midas was so overjoyed, he got up and danced around the room, touching everything within his reach. Soon he had a room full of gleaming gold objects. When he reached for his clothes, they turned into heavy golden cloth. "Now I shall really look like a king," he said. He got dressed and admired himself in the mirror. Midas was impressed by his golden clothes, though they were so heavy he could hardly move.

His looking glass was more of a problem. He tried to use it to see his new treasures better. To his surprise, he could not see anything through it. He put it on the table and found that it was now gold, but Midas was too excited to worry. He said, "I can see well enough without it. Besides, it is much more valuable now."

From: "King Midas and the Golden Touch," retold by Judy Rosenbaum, Level 9, *On the Horizon* (Needham, MA: Silver Burdett & Ginn, 1989), p. 132.

Level G

How does a writer such as Mr. Pinkwater begin a novel for young readers? How does he work? "When I'm beginning a new book," he states, "I am almost like an actor getting into character. I listen to music. I watch television. I talk to people. I turn up at a K-Mart store and go through all the motions of being an ordinary citizen."

"When I start a novel, all I'm really doing is waiting for the characters to show up. It's like the movie *Close Encounters of the Third Kind*. The people who have been 'selected' to be in this story show up. It is a very interesting experience."

He does not sit down and write every day. "It would be terrible if I had to work that way. I show up at my office every day in the event that something may want to happen, but if nothing happens, I don't feel that I have failed to perform. If something gets started, fair enough. If it doesn't, and I feel I've given it enough time, I go to K-Mart. I showed up, the story didn't!"

From: Lee Bennett Hopkins, "Daniel Manus Pinkwater," Level 10, *Silver Secrets* (Needham, MA: Silver Burdett & Ginn, 1989), p. 56.

Level G

"I love the story as it is being written. Sometimes it's as though it were happening without my doing it. I'll go to bed, excited about what's going to happen tomorrow. I know something's got to happen because I've only got 175 pages done and I've got to do more.

"To me, the beauty in writing is making the words come out as clear as a pane of glass. That I can do, and I'm rather pleased because it took me years to learn how.

"Writing for girls and boys has helped me to remember my own childhood. And since I'm writing books for a specific reader, namely, myself at different ages, I've gotten more and more expert at revisiting that person within me at different ages."

He sometimes uses a computer. "The computer allows me to think in a different way. It helps me to be a better, more daring writer. Using a computer was a breakthrough for me."

From: Lee Bennett Hopkins, "Daniel Manus Pinkwater," Level 10, *Silver Secrets* (Needham, MA: Silver Burdett & Ginn, 1989), pp. 56–57.

Level H

ORAL READING

Early in April of 1872, the Davidsons's covered wagon rolled onto their 160-acre land claim in eastern Nebraska. There was no shelter waiting for them. Like most settlers in the Great Plains, the Davidsons had to build their own shelter. At first, the family lived in the covered wagon. That was all right for a while. But by fall, they needed more protection from Nebraska's cold and windy climate.

Back east, the Davidsons had lived in a wooden farmhouse. They would have liked to build a wooden house on the Plains, too. But there wasn't a tree in sight. Lumber for building wasn't available in Nebraska, even if the family had been able to afford it.

There wasn't time for building, anyway. As farmers, the Davidsons knew they had to get on with the all-important work of plowing and planting. Only then would their new land provide enough harvest to see them through the winter.

Rabbits and foxes dig their burrows and dens in hillsides, and that's what the Davidsons did too. The settlers chose the streambank location because it was conveniently close to water. There were no building materials to buy or skilled workers to hire. After two days of digging, the Davidsons's new home was ready.

From: Duncan Searl, "A Sea of Grass," Level 11, *Dream Chasers* (Needham, MA: Silver Burdett & Ginn, 1989), pp. 423–424.

Level H

Most people believe in the old saying, "There's no place like home." The Davidsons, however, might not have felt that way about their dugout. The cramped dwelling was damp and dark, even on sunny days. Dirt from the roof sifted down into bedding and food. Insects and snakes were constant house guests.

Hoping their new shelter would be a temporary one, the Davidsons began to plow and plant. But this wasn't as easy as they had expected. In the early 1870s, more than a foot of thick sod covered almost every inch of the territory. Held together by a mass of tangled roots, this sod was almost impossible to cut through. It could take weeks to plow a single acre. Settlers like the Davidsons became known as "sodbusters."

The sod's toughness gave the settlers an idea. Why not build with it? The new fields were covered with long ribbons of sod that had been plowed up. It would be a simple matter to cut these into smaller pieces and use them as building blocks. The settlers even had a nickname for this unusual building material—"Nebraska marble."

From: Duncan Searl, "A Sea of Grass," Level 11, *Dream Chasers* (Needham, MA: Silver Burdett & Ginn, 1989), p. 425.

Level I

ORAL READING

You walk through the door—and immediately freeze. Overhead, to your left, a thresher shark whips its tail. To your right are three huge killer whales. Have you wandered into a nightmare? Hardly. You've just entered the Monterey Bay Aquarium.

The shark and whales, life-size and hanging from the ceiling, are fiberglass. The other 6,000 creatures you'll meet are not. On a visit to the aquarium, on the shores of California's Monterey Bay, you'll have a chance not only to see them swim, scurry, hunt, and court, but to pick up and handle a few as well.

One of the aquarium's most spectacular exhibits is the three-story-high kelp forest— the world's only kelp forest growing indoors. Clinging to the bottom with a rootlike "holdfast," the yellow-brown kelp reaches up through 28 feet of water, spreading out on the tank's sunlit surface. With "stipes" instead of trunks, and "blades" in place of leaves, the kelp forest resembles an underwater redwood grove. Sunbeams slant down from above, while the kelp sways gently back and forth. With a patient eye, you will begin to spot some of the many creatures that call the kelp forest home.

Long-legged brittle stars and crabs can be seen within the tangled holdfast. Watch for turban snails higher up. The fish of the kelp forest aren't as fast as those of the open ocean, but they're better at playing hide-and-seek. Special air sacs allow some of them to hover in hiding within the maze of blades. Many are completely camouflaged.

From: Paul Fleischman, "The Monterey Bay Aquarium," Level 12, *Wind by the Sea* (Needham, MA: Silver Burdett & Ginn, 1989), pp. 395–396.

Level I

Among the animals who depend on the kelp are the aquarium's most playful residents, the sea otters. Floating on their backs, doing somersaults in the water, taking part in high-speed games of tag, these smallest of the marine mammals charm every audience.

Their two-story tank lets you view them from above as well as from below the water's surface. In the wild, though, their home is the kelp beds. They live on creatures who live on the kelp. They depend on it for shelter during storms. Before sleeping, they wrap themselves in it to keep from drifting out to sea.

Why are otters so playful? No one knows, though part of the answer might lie in the fact that their constant motion helps to keep them warm. Unlike the whales and other marine mammals, otters have no layer of blubber between their warm-blooded insides and the cold water outside. So they move around a lot, which requires a lot of energy, which in turn requires a lot of eating. Could you eat 25 hamburgers a day? That's the equivalent of what an otter swallows, eating up to one-quarter of its body weight daily. If you're present at feeding time, you'll be amazed at how much fish, squid, and abalone an otter can eat. Wild otters eat so many purple sea urchins that their bones eventually turn purplish as well.

Otters have another defense against the cold—their coats. When you touch the soft sample of fur on the wall by their tank, you'll understand why they were hunted until they were nearly extinct.

From: Paul Fleischman, "The Monterey Bay Aquarium," Level 12, *Wind by the Sea* (Needham, MA: Silver Burdett & Ginn, 1989), p. 397.

Level J

ORAL READING

The voice came from out of the sky, "Hey fellows, quick, grab those ropes and pull me into the wind as if I were a kite. Hurry!"

Looking up, the young people were startled to see a man waving wildly at them from a strange banana—shaped flying balloon—a balloon that was about to crash!

Sara reacted quickly and grabbed one of the ropes that dangled near her. But Sara could not even stop the flying contraption, let alone pull it in the other direction. As she attempted to dig her heels into the ground, the balloon nearly toppled her.

"Boys, don't just stand there. Help her," the man in the balloon shouted at Etienne and Louis.

Rushing to help their sister, the boys grabbed other ropes trailing from the balloon and frantically tugged at the runaway flying machine. Finally, the three of them were able to change the direction of the balloon, carrying it into the wind as the aeronaut had requested. The flying machine bobbed up like a kite.

As the young people pulled the balloon down, following the aeronaut's instructions, a crowd began to gather. The moment the flier was safe on the ground, he was surrounded by a large crowd of curious people, all talking at once.

Sara realized that the man she had rescued was the famous Monsieur Santos-Dumont, the wealthy Brazilian inventor and daredevil who predicted people would someday fly like birds.

"Where are the young people? They are the real heroes of this escape from the jaws of death," she heard him shout over the crowd.

From: David Fulton, "Through Skies Never Sailed," Level 13, *Star Walk* (Needham, MA: Silver Burdett & Ginn, 1989), pp. 353–354.

Level J

SILENT READING

"The purpose of my visit, in fact, is related to the events of this afternoon. I came to invite your family for an excursion in one of my balloons."

Silence filled the Cote parlor as all eyes turned to Sara's father, awaiting his reply. "I don't wish to seem overly conservative or closed minded, Monsieur Santos-Dumont, but I wouldn't consider air travel sufficiently safe to risk my whole family. This afternoon's events are evidence of that."

"I certainly wouldn't ask you to endanger your family, but flying in a balloon, which is merely a big bag filled with hydrogen, has long been demonstrated to be a safe sport.

"I wouldn't suggest taking you in a craft such as the one I was flying this afternoon. That was a 'dirigible.' Its design is the latest breakthrough in the attempt to control the direction of flight. It's a balloon that has a gasoline engine suspended beneath it to direct its movement. Unfortunately, my colleagues and I have yet to work out all the problems. But we will. In any case, the dirigible may soon be obsolete. I recently heard a report at a meeting of the Aero Club, and I understand that some Americans have actually built a glider of some sort that is heavier than the air, and it is said they use a gasoline engine to power it. Now, that is really incredible."

From: David Fulton, "Through Skies Never Sailed," Level 13, *Star Walk* (Needham, MA: Silver Burdett & Ginn, 1989), pp. 356.

Level K

Lo Tung leaned against the rattling wall of the freight car. Beneath him the floor moved as the wheels cracked over the rails. It was a long time since he'd sat or walked on anything steady. First there had been the long days and nights on the Pacific Mail Steamship that had brought him from China, then the riverboat from San Francisco to Sacramento, then the train, waiting on the levee.

He hadn't had time for more than a glimpse of the strange iron monster belching smoke before the boss man had hustled them aboard. It was hard to believe that he was here now, in this freight car along with other Chinese workers, rolling eastward across America.

Lo Tung looked sideways at his friend, Wei. Wei was fifteen years old, too, and as small and thin as Lo Tung.

"Not more than a hundred pounds, either of you," the agent had said in disgust. "You two will not be able to do the heavy railroad work."

"Don't worry. We are strong," Lo Tung had said. He had not added, "Ho Sen was strong, the strongest man in our village. And he was killed building the American railway." Now Ho Sen's bones lay somewhere in this strange country. And Chen Chi Yuen. He had gone and never been heard from again.

Sitting now in the freight car, thinking about the work, Lo Tung flexed his muscles. Strong for the work. Of course, strong and fearless.

It was growing dark. They had been closed in here together for hours, so many of them from the ship. The air was used up and the smells were bad.

From: Eve Bunting, "It's Not the Great Wall, But It Will Last Forever," Level 14, *Worlds Beyond* (Needham, MA: Silver Burdett & Ginn, 1989), pp. 238–239.

Level K

Fifty-four dollars was a fortune, and impossible for his mother! The agent had allowed them to borrow from him. That was when he'd complained of Lo Tung's size.

"Not a penny of your wages will be yours till you pay me back," he had warned.

Lo Tung had agreed. He would have agreed to almost anything. Not that he wanted to go to America. The thought of leaving his home brought tears to his eyes. But it was clearly his duty. He was, after all, the eldest son. Since his father's death the family responsibility had been his. If he went, his debt to the agent would be cleared in two months. Then he could begin sending money home for his mother and his sisters, and his little brother. He had to believe that he could save enough to go home himself some day.

Thinking of home here in the heat of the freight car made loneliness rise in him like water in a swamp. Fear was bad, but loneliness was worse. He would not allow himself to remember.

"We are slowing," Wei said. "I can see through a crack."

Someone else announced, "We are here." Tired men and boys staggered up, swaying, hoisting their bedrolls. As the train chugged to a stop they waited quietly for what was to come.

When the doors opened, Lo Tung saw that it was night outside, the sky filled with a million crystal stars.

"American stars," he whispered to Wei, pointing upward. "Are they the same that shine over China or . . . "

"Out! Everyone out!" Men waited beside the train, big, bulky men who cast massive shadows.

"Hurry! Get a move on!" The words were not in Lo Tung's language but he understood the tone.

From: Eve Bunting, "It's Not the Great Wall, But It Will Last Forever," Level 14, *Worlds Beyond* (Needham, MA: Silver Burdett & Ginn, 1989), pp. 240.

Glossary

Accommodation. Developing new categories for stimuli that do not fit into existing ones—another aspect of what Piaget refers to as cognitive development.

Affixes. Prefixes and suffixes.

Analogy. A comparison of relationships between words or ideas.

Analytic phonics instruction. The teacher presents students with a whole word and asks them to break it into its sounds and letters.

Anecdotal record. A record of observed behavior over a period of time.

Antonyms. Words opposite in meaning.

Assessment. Asking questions about students' knowledge and skills, and the process of getting answers.

Assimilation. A continuous process that helps the individual to integrate new incoming stimuli into existing concepts—one aspect of what Piaget refers to as cognitive development.

Astigmatism. A defect of vision that causes blurred vision.

Auditory discrimination. Ability to detect differences and similarities in sounds.

Authentic assessment. Using authentic, "real-life" materials to assess students' reading.

Bottom-up reading models. Models that consider the reading process as one of grapheme-phoneme correspondences; code emphasis or subskill models.

Buffer zone. The area that falls between the instructional and frustration levels.

Categorizing. A thinking skill involving the ability to classify items into general and specific categories.

Central idea. The main idea of a larger chunk of text.

Checklist. A means for systematically and quickly recording behavior; the observer checks items as present or absent.

Cloze procedure. A technique that helps teachers gain information about a variety of language facility and comprehension ability skills.

Cloze test. Reader must supply words that have been systematically deleted from a passage.

Combining forms. Roots borrowed from another language combine with each other or with affixes to form a word.

Comparison. A demonstration of the similarities between persons, ideas, things, and so on.

Comprehension. Understanding; the effort and process used to get the meaning of something.

Concept. A group of stimuli with common characteristics.

Concept development. Refers to development of thinking.

Content domain. Term that refers to subject matter covered.

Context clue. An item of information from the words surrounding a particular word in the form of a synonym, antonym, example, definition, description, explanation, and so on, that helps shed light on the meaning of that particular word.

Contrast. A demonstration of the differences between persons, ideas, things, and so on.

Creative reading. Uses divergent thinking skills to go beyond the literal comprehension, interpretation, and critical reading levels.

Criterion-referenced tests. Based on an extensive inventory of objectives in a specific curriculum area; they are used to help assess an individual student's performance with respect to his or her mastery of specified objectives in a given curriculum area.

Critical reading. A high-level reading skill that involves evaluation—making a personal judgment on the accuracy, value, and truthfulness of what is read.

Derivatives. Combinations of root words with prefixes or suffixes, or both.

Developmental spelling. Learning to spell is ongoing and based on the cognitive development of the child.

Diagnostic teaching. The practice of continuously trying a variety of instructional strategies and materials based on the current needs of students.

Directed listening/thinking approach. Requires teachers to ask questions before, during, and after a talk; consists of a number of steps; requires students to be active participants.

Directed Reading–Thinking Activity (DRTA). Requires teachers to nurture the inquiry process and students to be active participants and questioners; includes prediction and verification.

Divergent thinking. The many different ways to solve problems or to look at things.

In-school factors. Those factors that come under the domain or control of the educational system and influence learning.

Emergent literacy. The development of the association of print with meaning that begins early in a child's life and continues until the child reaches the stage of conventional reading and writing.

Emergent writing. Nonconventional writing that includes scribbling and nonphonetic letterings.

Equilibrium. According to Piaget, a balance between assimilation and accommodation in cognitive development.

Evaluation. Evaluation is interpreting evidence.

Example. Something representative of a whole or a group.

Explicit instruction. Instruction guided by a teacher, who uses various strategies to help students understand what they are reading.

Frustrational reading level. The child reads with many word recognition and comprehension errors. It is the lowest reading level and one to be avoided.

Grade equivalents. Description of year and month of school for which a given student's level of performance is typical.

High-frequency words. Words that appear most often in texts.

Home environment. Socioeconomic class, parents' education, and the neighborhood in which children live are some factors that shape children's home environments.

Homonyms. Words that are spelled and sound the same but have different meanings.

Hypermetropia. Farsightedness; difficulty with close-up vision.

Independent reading level. Level at which child reads words without any assistance and comprehends the text.

Inference. Understanding that is not derived from a direct statement but from an indirect suggestion in what is stated; understanding of what is implied.

Informal interviews. Teachers converse with students to learn about their interests and feelings.

Informal Reading Inventory (IRI). A valuable aid in helping teachers determine a student's reading levels and his or her strengths and needs. It usually consists of oral and silent reading passages and comprehension questions.

Instructional reading level. The teaching level.

Interactive reading models. Models that consider the top-down processing of information as dependent on the bottom-up processing, and vice versa.

Interest inventory. A statement or questionnaire method that helps teachers learn about students' likes and dislikes.

Interpretation. A reading level that demands a higher level of thinking ability because the material it involves is not directly stated in the text but only suggested or implied.

Junior Great Books Program. Program in which parent–teacher teams work together to plan reading discussion sessions for students; sessions take place during the school day and are led by both parent and teacher.

Listening capacity level. The highest level at which a learner can understand material when it is read aloud to him or her.

Listening vocabulary. The words one knows the meaning of when they are said aloud.

Literal comprehension. The ability to obtain a low-level type of understanding by using only information that is explicitly stated.

Literature webbing. A story map technique to help guide children in using predictable trade books.

Locator test. Used to determine at what level a student should begin testing.

Main idea. The central thought of a paragraph. All the sentences in the paragraph develop the main idea.

Maze procedure. Reader must choose the correct word from three choices for words that have been systematically selected from a passage.

Mean. Arithmetical average.

Measurement. Ways of gathering evidence for evaluation.

Miscue. Unexpected response to print.

Miscue analysis. A process that helps teachers learn how readers use language cues to construct meaning.

Myopia. Nearsightedness; difficulty with distance vision.

Newbery award books. Books that have received the Newbery Medal, which is given annually to the book in the United States that has been voted "the most distinguished literature" for children.

Out-of-school factors. Those factors that do not come under the domain or control of the educational system and that supposedly cannot be influenced by it.

Normal curve. Scores are symmetrically distributed around the mean.

Norms. Average scores for a given group of students, which allow comparisons to be made among different students or groups of students.

Norm-referenced tests. Standardized tests with norms so that comparisons can be made to a sample population.

Objective. Desired educational outcome.

Objectivity. The same score must result regardless of who grades the test.

Observation. A technique that helps teachers collect data about students' behavior.

Paired reading. The child reads aloud simultaneously with another person, usually the parent.

Percentile. A point on the distribution below which a certain percentage of the scores fall.

Performance assessment. Using a situation or project where learners can demonstrate knowledge.

Phonemic awareness. Awareness that words are made up of individual sounds.

Phonics. The study of the relationships between sounds and letters in a language.

Phonogram. Sets of letters with the same phonetic value in a number of words, that is, word families.

Phonological awareness. Awareness of spoken words, syllables, and phonemes.

Portfolio. A storage system that represents samples of students' reading and writing over a period of time.

Portfolio assessment. Material in a portfolio is evaluated in some way.

Practice test. Ensures that the actual test measures what students know rather than their test-taking ability; it familiarizes students with the test.

Prefix. A letter or a sequence of letters added to the beginning of a root word.

Pre-reading. Precursor to reading; before formal reading begins.

Projective technique. A method in which the individual puts himself or herself into a situation and reveals how he or she feels.

Questions. A good way for students to gain better insight into a subject; questioning also gives the teacher feedback.

Question–Answer Relationships (QARs). Helps students distinguish between "what they have in their heads" and information that is in the text.

Rating scale. An evaluative instrument used to record estimates of particular aspects of a student's behavior.

Raw score. The number of items that a student answers correctly on a test.

Reading. A dynamic, complex act that involves bringing meaning to and getting meaning from the printed page.

Reading autobiography. Students write or tell about their feelings and attempt to analyze their reading problems.

Reading comprehension. A complex intellectual process involving a number of abilities. The two major abilities involve knowing word meanings and reasoning with verbal concepts.

Reading comprehension taxonomy. A hierarchy of reading comprehension skills ranging from the more simplistic to the more complex ones; a classification of these skills.

Reading Olympics programs. Programs vary; however, most challenge students to read as many books as they can and to share them in some way with parents.

Reading readiness. Children demonstrate behaviors that show they are ready for reading instruction.

Reciprocal reading instruction. A teacher-directed technique consisting of four steps: summarizing, questioning, clarifying, and predicting.

Reliability. The extent to which a test instrument consistently produces similar results.

Repeated reading. Similar to paired reading; child reads along (assisted reading with model or tape) until he or she gains confidence to read alone.

Root. Smallest unit of a word that can exist and retain its basic meaning.

Running record. Documentation of a child's reading.

Schema theory. Deals with relations between prior knowledge and comprehension.

Schemata. These structured designs are the cognitive arrangements by which the mind is able to categorize incoming stimuli.

Self-fulfilling prophecy. Teacher assumptions about children become true, at least in part, because of the attitude of the teachers, which in turn becomes part of the children's self-concept.

Sight words. Words readers can identify instantaneously.

Standard Deviation. Deals with how widely scores vary from the mean.

Standard Scores. Used to compare test takers' assessment scores. Presented in terms of standard deviations.

Standardized tests. Tests that have been published by experts in the field and have precise instructions for administration and scoring.

Story sense. The understanding that there is a structure used to tell stories and that stories are written to be understood.

Suffix. A letter or a sequence of letters added to the end of a root word.

Suitability. The appropriateness of a test for a specific population of students.

Syllable. A vowel and the consonants around it.

Synonyms. Words similar in meaning.

Synthetic phonics instruction. Each sound associated with letters in a word is pronounced in isolation, and then the sounds are blended together.

Test. An assigned set of tasks to be performed.

Top-down reading models. Models that depend on reader's background of experiences and language ability in constructing meaning from the text.

Validity. The degree to which a test instrument leads to valid inferences—that is, the degree to which it really measures what it claims to measure.

Visual discrimination. Ability to detect similarities and differences among written symbols.

Vocabulary consciousness. An awareness that words may have different meanings based on their context and a desire to increase one's vocabulary.

Word identification. A twofold process that includes both pronunciation and knowledge of word meaning.

Index